Mobil
Travel Guide®

MID-ATLANTIC

ACKNOWLEDGEMENTS

We gratefully acknowledge the help of our representatives for their efficient and perceptive inspections of the lodging and dining establishments listed, the establishments' proprietors for their cooperation in showing their facilities and providing information about them, and the many users of previous editions who have taken the time to share their experiences. Mobil Travel Guide is also grateful to all the talented writers who contributed entries to this book.

ISBN: 0-8416-0311-1 or 978-0-8416-0311-0
Manufactured in Canada.

10 9 8 7 6 5 4 3 2 1

CONTENTS

MAPS

MID-ATLANTIC

CELEBRATING 50 YEARS

Because time is precious and the travel industry is ever-changing, having accurate, reliable travel information at your has fingertips is essential. Mobil Travel Guide provided invaluable insight to travelers for 50 years, and we are committed to continuing this service into the future.

The Mobil Corporation (known as Exxon Mobil Corporation since a 1999 merger) began producing the Mobil Travel Guide books in 1958 following the introduction of the U.S.-interstate highway system in 1956. The first edition covered only five Southwestern states. Since then, our books have become the premier travel guides in North America, covering all 50 states and Canada.

Since its founding, Mobil Travel Guide has served as an advocate for travelers seeking knowledge about hotels, restaurants and places to visit. Based on an objective process, we make recommendations to our customers that we believe will enhance the quality and value of their travel experiences. Our trusted Mobil One- to Five-Star rating system is the oldest and most respected lodging and restaurant inspection and rating program in North America. Most hoteliers, restaurateurs and industry observers favorably regard the rigor of our inspection program and understand the prestige and benefits that come with receiving a Mobil Star rating.

The Mobil Travel Guide process of rating each establishment includes:
★ Unannouced facility inspections
★ Incognito service evaluations for
★ A review of unsolicited comments from the general public
★ Senior management oversight

For each property, more than 450 attributes, including cleanliness, physical facilities and employee attitude and courtesy, are measured and evaluated to produce a mathematically derived score, which is then blended with the other elements to form an overall score. These scores form the basis that we use to assign our Mobil One- to Five-Star ratings.

This process focuses on guest expectations, guest experience and consistency of service, not just physical facilities and amenities. It's fundamentally a rating system that rewards those properties that continually strive for and achieve excellence each year. The very best properties are consistently raising the bar for those that wish to compete with them.

Only facilities that meet Mobil Travel Guide's standards earn the privilege of being listed in the guide. Deteriorating, poorly managed establishments are deleted. A Mobil Travel Guide listing constitutes a positive quality recommendation. Every listing is an accolade, a recognition of achievement.

★★★★★The Mobil Five-Star Award indicates that a property is one of the very best in the country and consistently provides gracious and courteous service, superlative quality in its facility and a unique ambience. The lodgings and restaurants at the Mobil Five-Star level consistently continues their commitment to excellence, doing so with grace and perseverance.

★★★★The Mobil Four-Star Award honors properties for outstanding achievement in overall facility and for providing very strong service levels in all areas. These award winners provide a distinctive experience for the ever-demanding and sophisticated consumer.

★★★The Mobil Three-Star Award recognizes an excellent property that provides full services and amenities. This category ranges from exceptional hotels with limited services to elegant restaurants with a less-formal atmosphere.

★★The Mobil Two-Star property is a clean and comfortable establishment that has expanded amenities or a distinctive environment. These properties are an excellent place to stay or dine.

★The Mobil One-Star property is limited in its amenities and services but provides a value experience while meeting travelers' expectations. Expect the properties to be clean, comfortable and convenient.

We do not charge establishments for inclusion in our guides. We have no relationship with any of the businesses and attractions we list and act only as a consumer advocate. We do the investigative legwork so that you won't have to.

Restaurants and hotels—particularly small chains and stand-alone establishments—change management or even go out of business with surprising quickness. Although we make every effort to update continuously information, we recommend that you call ahead to make sure the place you've selected is still open.

We hope that your travels are enjoyable and relaxing and that our books help you get the most out of every trip you take. If any aspect of your accommodation, dining, spa or sightseeing experience motivates you to comment, please contact us. Mobil Travel Guide, 200 W. Madison St., Suite 3950, Chicago, IL 60611, or send an e-mail to info@mobiltravelguide.com.
Happy travels.

HOW TO USE THIS BOOK

The Mobil Travel Guide Regional Travel Planners are designed for convenience. Each state has its own chapter, beginning with a general introduction that provides a geographical and historical orientation to the state and gives basic statewide tourist information. The remainder of each chapter is devoted to travel destinations within the state—mainly cities and towns, but also national parks and tourist areas—which, like the states, are arranged in alphabetical order.

MAPS

We have provided state maps as well as maps of selected larger cities to help you find your way.

DESTINATION INFORMATION

We list addresses, phone number and web sites for travel information resources—usually the local chamber of commerce or office of tourism—and a brief introduction to the area. Information about airports, ground transportation and suburbs is included for large cities.

DRIVING TOURS AND WALKING TOURS

The driving tours that we include for many states are usually day trips that make for interesting side excursions. They offer you a way to get off the beaten path. These trips frequently cover areas of natural beauty or historical significance.

WHAT TO SEE AND DO

Mobil Travel Guide offers information about thousands of museums, art galleries, amusement parks, historic sites, national and state parks, ski areas and many other attractions.

Following an attraction's description, you'll find the months, days and, in some cases, hours of operation, address, telephone number and web site (if there is one).

SPECIAL EVENTS

Special events are either annual events that last only a short time, such as festivals and fairs or longer, seasonal events such as horse racing, theater and summer concerts. Our Special Events listings also include infrequently occurring occasions that mark certain dates or events, such as a centennial or other commemorative celebration.

LISTINGS

Hotels, restaurants and spas are usually listed under the city or town in which they're located. Make sure to check the nearby cities and towns for additional options, especially if you're traveling to a major metropolitan area that includes many suburbs. If a property is located in a town that doesn't have its own heading, the listing appears under the town nearest it. In large cities, hotels located within 5 miles of major commercial airports may be listed under a separate Airport Area heading that follows the city section.

THE STAR RATINGS
MOBIL RATED HOTELS

Travelers have different needs when it comes to accommodations. To help you pinpoint properties that meet your particular needs, Mobil Travel Guide classifies each lodging by type according to the following characteristics.

★★★★★The Mobil Five-Star hotel provides consistently superlative service in an exceptionally distinctive luxury environment, with expanded services. Attention to detail is evident throughout the hotel, resort or inn, from bed linens to staff uniforms.

★★★★The Mobil Four-Star hotel provides a luxury experience with expanded amenities in a distinctive environment. Services may include automatic turndown service, 24-hour room service and valet parking.

★★★The Mobil Three-Star hotel is well appointed, with a full-service restaurant and expanded amenities, such as a fitness center, golf course, tennis courts, 24-hour room service and optional turndown service.

★★The Mobil Two-Star hotel is considered a clean, comfortable and reliable establishment that has expanded amenities, such as a full-service restaurant on the premises.

★The Mobil One-Star lodging is a limited-service hotel, motel or inn that is considered a clean, comfortable and reliable establishment For every property, we also provide pricing information. The pricing categories break down as follows:

★ **$** = Up to $150
★ **$$** = $151-$250
★ **$$$** = $251-$350
★ **$$$$** = $351 and up

All prices quoted are accurate at the time of publication, however prices cannot be guaranteed. In some locations, special events, holidays or seasons can affect prices. Some resorts have complicated rate structures that vary with the time of year, so confirm rates when making your plans.

SPECIALITY LODGINGS

A Speciality Lodging is a unique inn, bed and breakfast or guest ranch with limited service, but appealing, attractive facilities that make the property worth a visit.

MOBIL RATED RESTAURANTS

All Mobil Star-rated dining establishments listed in this book have a full kitchen and most offer table service.

★★★★★The Mobil Five-Star restaurant offers one of few flawless dining experiences in the country. These establishments consistently provide their guests with exceptional food, superlative service, elegant décor and exquisite presentations of each detail surrounding a meal.

★★★★The Mobil Four-Star restaurant provides professional service, distinctive presentations and wonderful food.

★★★The Mobil Three-Star restaurant has good food, warm and skillful service and enjoyable décor.

★★The Mobil Two-Star restaurant serves fresh food in a clean setting with efficient service. Value is considered in this category, as is family friendliness.

★The Mobil One-Star restaurant provides a distinctive experience through culinary specialty, local flair or individual atmosphere.

Each restaurant listing gives the cuisine type, street address, phone and website, meals served, days of operation (if not open daily year-round) and pricing category. Information about appropriate attire is provided, although it's always a good idea to call ahead and ask if you're unsure; the meaning of "casual" or "business casual" varies widely in different parts of the country. We also indicate whether the restaurant has a bar, whether a children's menu is offered and whether outdoor seating is available. If reservations are recommended, we note that fact in the listing. When valet parking is available, it is noted in the description. Because menu prices can fluctuate, we list a pricing category rather than specific prices. The pricing categories are defined as follows, per diner, and assume that you order an appetizer or dessert, an entrée and one drink:

★ **$** = $15 and under
★ **$$** = $16-$35
★ **$$$** = $36-$85
★ **$$$$** = $86 and up

All prices quoted are accurate at the time of publication, but prices cannot be guaranteed.

MOBIL RATED SPAS

Mobil Travel Guide is pleased to announce its newest category, hotel and resort spas. Until now, hotel and resort spas have not been formally rated or inspected by any organization. Every spa selected for inclusion in this book underwent a rigorous inspection process similar to the one Mobil Travel Guide has been applying to lodgings and restaurants

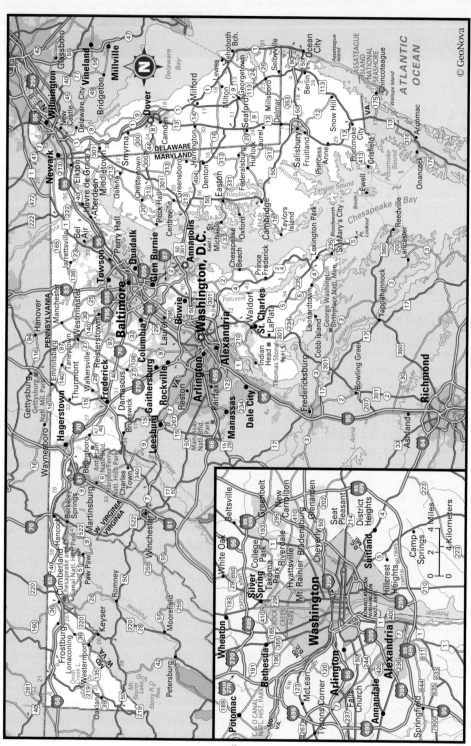

© GeoNova

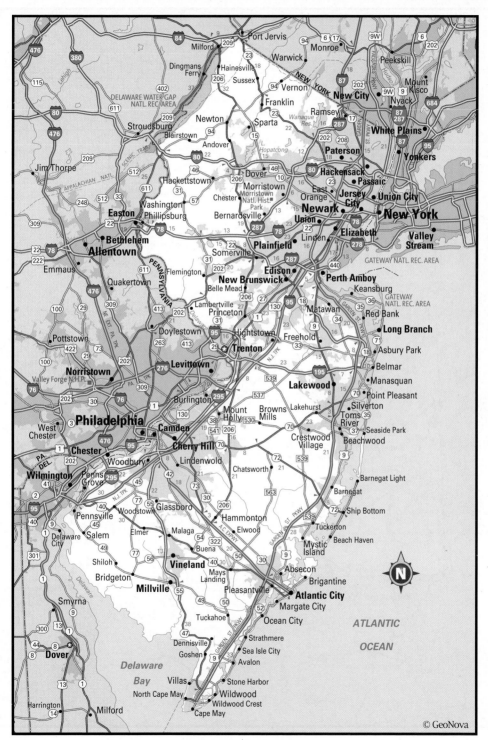

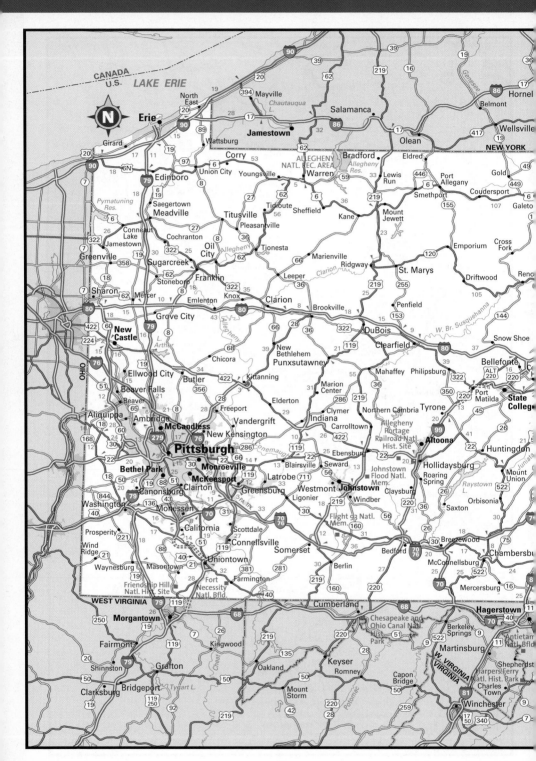

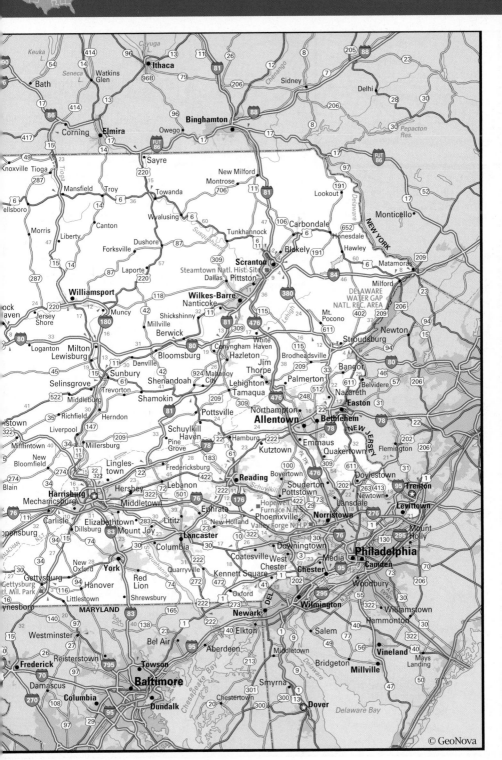

© GeoNova

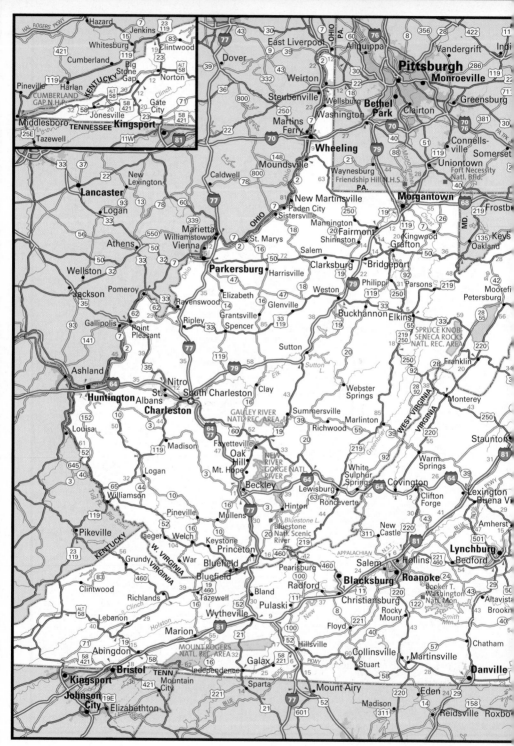

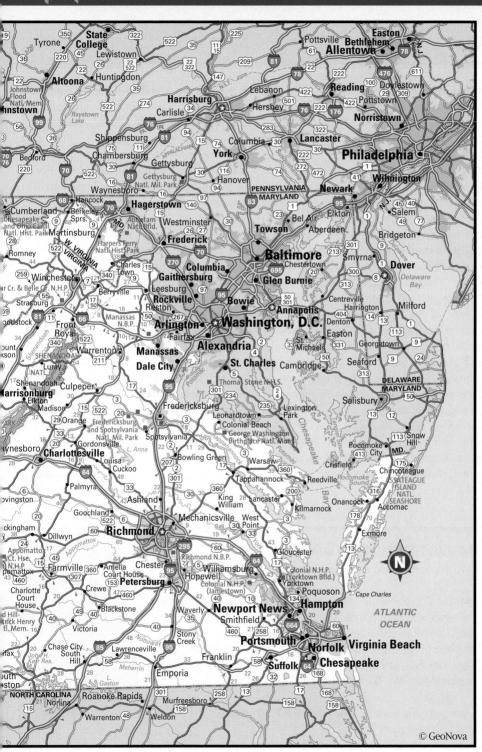

for five decades. After researching more than 300 spas and performing exhaustive incognito inspections of more than 200 properties, we narrowed our list to the best spas in the United States and Canada.

Mobil Travel Guide's spa ratings are based on objective evaluations of more than 450 attributes. Approximately half of these criteria assess basic expectations, such as staff courtesy, the technical proficiency and skill of the employees and whether the facility is maintained properly and hygienically. Several standards address issues that impact a guest's physical comfort and convenience, as well as the staff's ability to impart a sense of personalized service and anticipate clients' needs. Additional criteria measure the spa's ability to create a completely calming ambience. The Mobil Star ratings focus on much more than the facilities available at a spa and the treatments it offers. Each Mobil Star rating is a cumulative score achieved from multiple inspections that reflects the spa management's attention to detail and commitment to consumers' needs.

★★★★★The Mobil Five-Star spa provides consistently superlative service in an exceptionally distinctive luxury environment with extensive amenities. The staff at a Mobil Five-Star spa provides extraordinary service beyond the traditional spa experience, allowing guests to achieve the highest level of relaxation and pampering. A Mobil Five-Star spa offers an extensive array of treatments, often incorporating international themes and products. Attention to detail is evident throughout the spa, from arrival to departure.

★★★★The Mobil Four-Star spa provides a luxurious experience with expanded amenities in an elegant and serene environment. Throughout the spa facility, guests experience personalized service. Amenities might include, but are not limited to, single-sex relaxation rooms where guests wait for their treatments, plunge pools and whirlpools in both men's and women's locker rooms, and an array of treatments, including a selection of massages, body therapies, facials and a variety of salon services.

★★★The Mobil Three-Star spa is physically well appointed and has a full complement of staff

★ CELEBRATING ★
50 YEARS OF MOBIL TRAVEL GUIDE

1962 — **1964** — **1968** — **1971** — **1973**

1976 — **1978** — **1979** — **1986** — **1988**

1989 — **1992** — **1994** — **1997** — **2003**

DELAWARE

DELAWARE "IS LIKE A DIAMOND, DIMINUTIVE, BUT HAVING WITHIN IT INHERENT VALUE," John Lofland, the eccentric "Bard of Milford," wrote in 1847. Only 96 miles long and from nine to 35 miles wide, the state is a corporate and agricultural superpower. Soybeans, corn, tomatoes, strawberries, asparagus, fruit and other crops bring in about $170 million each year. And consistent state corporate policies have persuaded more than 183,000 corporations to make their headquarters in the "corporate capital of the world."

Within just 2,489 square miles, Delaware boasts rolling, forested hills in the north, stretches of bare sand dunes in the south and miles of marshland along the coast. Visitors can tour a modern agricultural or chemical research center in the morning and search for buried pirate treasures in the afternoon. In fact, Coin Beach in Rehoboth bears its name for the mysterious coins that frequently wash ashore, most likely pulled from the *Faithful Steward,* a passenger vessel lost in 1785. The *deBraak,* another doomed ship that foundered off Lewes in 1798, was raised in 1986 because of the belief that it may have had a fortune in captured Spanish coin or bullion aboard.

Despite Delaware's current riches, the state's history started on a grim note. The first 28 colonists landed in the spring of 1631, and following an argument with a Lenni-Lenape chief, their bones were found mingled with those of their cattle and strewn over their burned fields. In 1638, a group of Swedes established the first permanent settlement in the state—and the first permanent settlement of Swedes in North America—at Fort Christina, a spot now in Wilmington.

Henry Hudson, in Dutch service, first discovered Delaware Bay in 1609. A year later, Thomas Argall reported it to English navigators, naming it for his superior, Lord de la Warr, governor of Virginia. Ownership changed rapidly from Swedish to Dutch to English hands. The Maryland-Delaware boundary was set by British court order in 1750 and surveyed as part of the Mason-Dixon Line in 1763-1767. The boundary with New Jersey, also long disputed, was confirmed by the Supreme Court in 1935.

The "First State" (first to adopt the Constitution, on December 7, 1787) is proud of its history of sturdy independence, both military and political. During the Revolution, the "Delaware line" was a crack regiment of the Continental Army. The men would "fight all day and dance all night," according to a dispatch by General Greene. How well they danced is open to question, but they fought with such gallantry that they received regular praise in the general's dispatches.

Delaware statesman John Dickinson, "penman of the Revolution" and one of the state's five delegates to the Constitutional Convention, was instrumental in the decision to write a new federal constitution rather than to simply patch up the Articles of Confederation.

 SPOTLIGHT

★ Horseshoe crabs may be viewed in large numbers up and down the Delaware shore in May. The crabs, which have remained basically the same since the days of the dinosaur, endure extremes of temperature and salinity and can go a year without eating.

Along with Lofland and Dickinson, Delaware has produced many literary figures, including the 19th-century playwright and novelist Robert Montgomery Bird, writer and illustrator Howard Pyle, Henry Seidel Canby, founder of the *Saturday Review,* and novelist John P. Marquand.
Information: www.state.de.us

BETHANY BEACH

Originally a site for revival camp meetings, Bethany Beach is a quiet beach town on the Atlantic Ocean that offers excellent surf fishing and swimming.
Information: Bethany-Fenwick Area Chamber of Commerce,
36913 Coastal Hwy./DE 1,
Fenwick Island,
302-539-2100, 800-962-7873; www.bethany-fenwick.org

WHAT TO SEE AND DO

Holts Landing State Park
Bethany Beach,
302-539-9060 season, 302-227-2800 off-season;
www.destateparks.com/holts/hlsp.htm
A 203-acre park located along the Indian River Bay offering fishing, crabbing, clamming, sailing, boating (launch ramp providing access to bay) and picnicking, as well as playground and ball fields.

SPECIAL EVENTS

Boardwalk Arts Festival
The Boardwalk, Garfield Parkway,
Bethany Beach,
800-962-7873;
www.bethanybeachartsfestival
Juried, original handmade works; woodcarving, photography, jewelry, batik, watercolor paintings. Early September.

HOTELS

★Holiday Inn Express Bethany Beach
39642 Jefferson Bridge Road,
Bethany Beach,
302-541-9200, 888-465-4329;
www.holiday-inn.com
100 rooms. $

RESTAURANTS

★Mango's
97 Garfield Pkwy., Bethany Beach,
302-537-6621;
www.mangomikes.com
Caribbean menu. Lunch, dinner. Closed December-February, except December 31; also Monday-Thursday late March-May and late September-November. Bar. Children's menu. Casual attire. Outdoor seating. $$

CLAYMONT

HOTELS

★★Holiday Inn
630 Naamans Rd.,
Claymont,
302-792-2700, 888-465-4329;
www.holiday-inn.com
192 rooms. Airport transportation available.
$

DOVER

Dover, Delaware's capital since 1777, was designed by William Penn around the city's lovely green. Fine 18th- and 19th-century houses still line State Street.

Because of Delaware's favorable corporation laws, more than 60,000 U.S. firms pay taxes in Dover. At Dover Air Force Base, the Military Airlift Command operates one of the biggest air cargo terminals in the world. The city is also home to Delaware State College, Wesley College and the Terry campus of Delaware Technical and Community College.

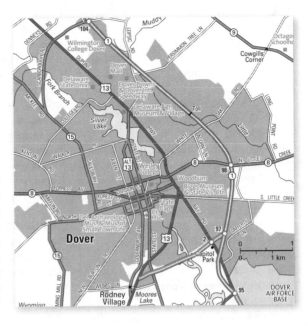

Information: Central Delaware Chamber of Commerce, 435 North DuPont Highway, Dover, 302-978-0892; www.cdcc.net

WHAT TO SEE AND DO

Air Mobility Command Museum

1301 Heritage Rd.,
Dover,
302-677-5938;
www.amcmuseum.org

Located in a historic hangar on Dover Air Force Base, the museum houses a collection of more than two dozen aircraft and historical artifacts dating back to World War II. Tuesday-Saturday 9 a.m.-4 p.m.

Delaware Agricultural Museum and Village

8866 N. DuPont Hwy. (Rte. 13), Dover,
302-734-1618;
www.agriculturalmuseum.org

Museum of farm life from early settlement to 1960. Main exhibition hall and historic structures representing a late-19th-century farming community; includes gristmill, blacksmith-wheelwright shop, farmhouse, outbuildings, one-room schoolhouse, store and train station. Gift shop. Tuesday-Saturday 10 a.m.-4 p.m.; Sunday 1-4 p.m.; closed Sunday in winter.

Delaware Public Archives

121 Duke Of York St.,
Dover,
302-744-5000;
www.archives.delaware.gov

Delaware's historical public records. Monday-Tuesday, Friday-Saturday 8 a.m.-4:30 p.m.; Wednesday-Thursday 8 a.m.-8 p.m.; closed Sunday.

Delaware State Museums

316 S. Governors Ave., Dover,
www.destatemuseums.org

Complex of three buildings:

Delaware Archeology Museum

316 S. Governors Ave., Dover,
302-739-4266

(1790) Housed in an old church, exhibits devoted to archaeology. Monday-Saturday 9 a.m.-4:30 p.m., Sunday 1:30-4:30 p.m.

Johnson Victrola Museum

Museum Square, 375 S. New St., Dover,
302-739-4266

Tribute to Eldridge Reeves Johnson, founder of the Victor Talking Machine Company. Collection of talking machines, Victrolas, early recordings and equipment. Monday-Saturday 9 a.m.-4:30 p.m., Sunday 1:30-4:30 p.m.

Museum of Small Town Life

316 S. Governors Ave., Dover,
302-739-4266
Turn-of-the-century drugstore, printing press, pharmacy, carpenter shop, general store, post office, shoemaker's shop and printer's shop; Johnson building. Tuesday-Saturday 9 a.m.-4:30 p.m., Sunday 1:30-4:30 p.m.

Delaware State Visitor Center

The Green, 406 Federal St., Dover,
302-739-4266;
www.destatemuseums.org/museums/vc/visitors.shtml
Administered by the Delaware State Museums, the center offers information on attractions throughout the state. Exhibit galleries. Monday-Saturday 9 a.m.-4:30 p.m., Sunday 1:30-4:30 p.m.

Dover Heritage Park

152 S. State St., Dover,
302-739-9194;
www.destateparks.com/heritagepark/index.asp
Guided walking tour of historic areas, buildings and other attractions. Monday-Saturday 9 a.m.-3 p.m., Sunday 1:30-3 p.m.

John Dickinson Plantation

340 Kitts Hummrock Rd., Dover,
302-739-3277;
www.history.delaware.gov/museums/jdp/jdp_main.shtml
(1740) Restored boyhood residence of Dickinson, the "penman of the Revolution." Reconstructed farm complex. Tuesday-Saturday 10 a.m.-3:30 p.m., Sunday 1:30-4:30 p.m., except closed Sundays in January and February.

The Old State House

The Green, 406 Federal St., Dover,
302-739-4266;
www.history.delaware.gov

(1792) Delaware's seat of government since 1787, the State House, restored in 1976, contains a courtroom, ceremonial governor's office, legislative chambers and county offices. A portrait of George Washington in the Senate Chamber was commissioned in 1802 by the legislature as a memorial to the nation's first president. Although Delaware's General Assembly moved to nearby Legislative Hall in 1933, the State House remains the state's symbolic capitol. Tuesday-Saturday 9 a.m.-4:30 p.m., Sunday 1:30-4:30 p.m.

SPECIAL EVENTS

Dover Downs Hotel, Casino, & International Speedway

1131 N. DuPont Hwy., Dover,
302-674-4600, 800-711-5882;
www.doverdowns.com
Racing events include NASCAR Winston Cup auto racing (June, September); harness racing (mid-November-April). Call for fees and schedule.

Old Dover Days

Dover,
800-233-5368
Tours of historic houses and gardens not usually open to the public. Crafts exhibits, many other activities. Contact Kent County Tourism. First weekend in May.

HOTELS

★Comfort Inn

222 S. DuPont Hwy.,
Dover,
302-674-3300, 877-424-6423;
www.choicehotels.com
89 rooms. Complimentary continental breakfast. $

★★★Sheraton Dover Hotel

1570 N. DuPont Highway,
Dover,
302-678-8500, 888-625-5144;
www.sheratondover.com
This hotel is conveniently located just minutes from shopping and local attractions in historic Dover.
152 rooms. $

4

DELAWARE

RESTAURANTS

★★★Atwoods
800 N. State St., Dover,
302-674-1776

Seafood, steak menu. Lunch, dinner. Closed Sunday. Bar. Children's menu. Casual attire. **$$$**

FENWICK ISLAND

Fenwick Island, at the southeast corner of Delaware, was named for Thomas Fenwick, a wealthy Virginia landowner who purchased the land in 1686. Once known for its "salt making"—after residents James and Jacob Brasure began extracting salt from the ocean in 1775—the island has become a popular summer resort.

Information: Bethany-Fenwick Area Chamber of Commerce, 36913 Coastal Hwy./DE 1, Fenwick Island,
302-539-2100, 800-962-7873; www.bethany-fenwick.org

WHAT TO SEE AND DO

DiscoverSea Shipwreck Museum
708 Ocean Hwy., Fenwick Island,
302-539-9366, 888-743-5524;
www.discoversea.com
Contains changing exhibits of shipwreck artifacts recovered on the Delmarva Peninsula. June-August: daily 11 a.m.-8 p.m.; September-May: Saturday-Sunday 11 a.m.-3:30 p.m.

Fenwick Island Lighthouse
146th St., and Lighthouse Lane,
Fenwick Island,
302-539-4115
Built in 1858, this popular attraction is 89 feet tall and houses a mini-museum in its base. A gift shop is nearby. Open most summer days, weather permitting.

Fenwick Island State Park
Fenwick Island,
302-539-9060;
www.destateparks.com/fenwick/fisp.asp

This 208-acre seashore park is located between the Atlantic Ocean and Little Assawoman Bay. Surfing, bathhouse, surf fishing, sailing (rentals). Standard hours, fees.

SPECIAL EVENTS

Delaware Seashore Fall Surf Fishing Classic
Hwy. 1 N,
Fenwick Island,
302-539-6243;
www.brtackles.com/tournaments/fallclassic.html
Fishing areas for this competition are located within Delaware Seashore State Park and Fenwick Island State Park. Late September.

HOTELS

★Atlantic Coast Inn
37558 Lighthouse Rd.,
Fenwick Island,
302-539-7673, 800-432-8038;
www.atlanticcoastinn.com
48 rooms. Closed October-mid-April. **$**

FORT DELAWARE STATE PARK

This grim, gray fort was built as a coastal defense in 1860. The fort was used as a prisoner of war depot for three years, housing up to 12,500 Confederate prisoners at a time. Its damp, low-lying terrain and poor conditions encouraged epidemics, leading to some 2,400 deaths. The fort was modernized in 1896 and remained in commission until 1943.

The site's restoration continues. Available are overlooks of heronry, picnicking and living history programs. The museum has a scale model of the fort, a model Civil War relics and an orientation video. There are special events throughout the summer, and a boat trip to the island from Delaware City (mid-June-Labor Day: Wednesday-Sunday; last weekend April–mid-June and September: Saturday, Sunday and holidays).

Information: Park Superintendent, 45 Clinton St., Delaware City,
302-834-7941; www.destateparks.com/fdsp/index.asp

LEWES

Lewes has been home base to Delaware Bay pilots for 300 years. Weather-beaten, cypress-shingled houses still line the streets where pirates plundered and Captain Kidd bargained away his loot. The treacherous sandbars outside the harbor have claimed their share of ships, and stories of sunken treasures have circulated for centuries. Some buildings show scars from cannonballs that hit their mark when the British bombarded Lewes in the War of 1812. Traces of the original stockade were discovered in 1964.

Information: Chamber of Commerce, Fisher-Martin House, 120 Kings Hwy., Lewes, 302-645-8073; www.leweschamber.com

ATLANTIC BEACHES

Graced with a beautiful 25-mile stretch of Atlantic beach, Delaware has done more than many eastern states to save much of the land from excessive development. From north to south, three state parks maintain the coast's natural look and several small resort towns retain an old-fashioned, early 20th-century flavor.

This one-day drive is rewarding any time of the year. Begin in Lewes, originally a Dutch whaling colony founded in 1631. Stroll along tree-shaded second Street, the main street, to browse the town's shops and view its rich architectural heritage and then drive east about a mile on Savannah Road, following the signs to 3,785-acre Cape Henlopen State Park. The park juts between the bay and the ocean, offering hiking and bicycling trails in pine forests, salt marshes and grass-topped dunes. Just inside the park, the Seaside Nature Center features a small aquarium displaying examples of local sea life, including the region's famed blue crabs. In mid-May, the park is a resting stop for shorebirds migrating north from South America to their summer breeding grounds in the Arctic.

From Lewes, take Highway 9 west briefly to State Route 1 south, which runs parallel to the coast for the length of this drive, to Rehoboth Beach. One of the mid-Atlantic's most popular beach resorts, Rehoboth hasn't lost its small-town appeal. At sunset, many people stroll along the boardwalk that links one end of the community to the other. In recent years, Rehoboth has grown into a sophisticated destination, with numerous bed-and-breakfasts, upscale restaurants and quality shops selling designer beach attire, expensive antiques and contemporary home furnishings. But the town remains true to its roots, with vendors selling burgers and hot dogs on the boardwalk and children enjoying a small amusement arcade called Funland.

South of Rehoboth on Route 1 is Dewey Beach, a much smaller resort town with a cluster of lively pubs that attract a young singles crowd. To the south is 2,656-acre Delaware Seashore State Park, another natural preserve offering swimming, surfing, fishing, picnicking, hiking and boating on Indian River Bay. Farther south is the little resort town of Bethany Beach, favored by families renting vacation homes or condominiums and beyond that is 442-acre Fenwick Island State Park, another natural area. End the tour just across the state line in sprawling Ocean City, Maryland, a bustling beach town that stands in sharp contrast to Delaware's quieter beach experience. Approximately 25 miles.

6

DELAWARE

★
★
★
★
★

DUTCH HERITAGE IN LEWES

As an Atlantic beach destination, historic Lewes is an offbeat choice. Lewes is Delaware's oldest community, which began as a Dutch attempt at establishing a whaling station in 1631. The neighborhood adjacent to the pleasure boat harbor on the Lewes & Rehoboth Canal is dotted with beautifully restored cottages and mansions from the 18th and 19th centuries that once housed ship pilots working Delaware Bay.

For a one-mile stroll through the Historic District, begin at the Zwaanendael Museum. Built in 1931, it was adapted from the 17th-century town hall of Hoorn in the Netherlands, from which Lewes's first colonists arrived. The museum details the town's history and explains that all 28 (some sources say 32) original colonists were killed in a dispute with local Native Americans. Behind the museum, the gambrel-roofed Fisher-Martin House (1730) houses the Visitor Information Center.

From the museum, head up 2nd Street in the shade of a canopy of giant, old trees. At 218 2nd Street, Lewes's oldest home, the little red- and yellow-shingled Ryves Holt House, is believed to have been built in about 1665. Once a colonial inn, it also housed the Officer of the Port. A few steps to the right at 118 Front Street, which parallels the canal, a cannonball fired by a British vessel in the War of 1812 still juts from the brick foundation of the Cannonball House Marine Museum (1797). Inside are nautical exhibits. Many of the town's Victorian homes are richly adorned with gingerbread trim, and several are brightly painted. Just off 2nd Street, the Ann Eliza Baker House is a dazzler in yellow, gold, purple and orange. Head north up 3rd Street to Shipcarpenter Street, where the Lewes Historical Society maintains an outdoor museum of early Delaware architecture. Several are scooter houses—homes relocated following local custom. Conclude this tour just up Shipcarpenter to the west at Shipcarpenter Square, an attractive development of restored 18th- and 19th-century scooter homes, all private residences, set around a nicely landscaped mall.

WHAT TO SEE AND DO

Cape Henlopen State Park
42 Cape Henlopen Dr., Lewes,
302-645-8983;
www.destateparks.com/chsp/chsp.htm
More than 3,000 acres at the confluence of Delaware Bay and the Atlantic Ocean; site of decommissioned Fort Miles, part of the U.S. coastal defense system during World War II. Supervised swimming, fishing; nature center, programs, trails, picnicking, concession, camping. Skiing Standard hours, fees.

Lewes Historical Society Complex
110 Shipcarpenter St.,
Lewes,
302-564-7670;
www.historiclewes.org

The restored buildings were moved here to create a feel for Lewes' early days. (June-Labor Day, Tuesday-Saturday) Tickets at Rabbit's Ferry House. Walking tours and events take place during summer season.

Buildings include:

Burton-Ingram House
Second St.,
Lewes,
302-564-7670
(Circa 1800) Log home made from hand-hewn timbers with cypress shingles. Holds beautiful antiques.

Cannonball House & Marine Museum
118 Front St., Lewes,
302-645-7670

Built in late 18th century. Originally called the David Rowland Home, it was hit by a cannonball during the War of 1812 and was renamed.

Early Plank House
Lewes,
302-564-7670
Swedish log cabin restored to reflect the home of an early settler.

Hiram R. Burton House
Second and Shipcarpenter streets,
Lewes,
302-564-7670
(Circa 1740) Houses antique furnishings and an 18th-century kitchen. Also includes a reading room with materials dedicated to Delaware history.

Old Doctor's Office
Third St., Lewes,
302-564-7670
(Circa 1836) Medical and dental museum.

Rabbit's Ferry House
Third St., Lewes,
302-564-7670
(Circa 1789) An 18th-century farmhouse with original paneling and period pieces.

Thompson Country Store
Third St., Lewes,
302-564-7670
(1800) Moved from original location in Thompsonville. The Thompson family ran it as a store until 1962.

Lewes-Cape May, NJ, Ferry
43 Henlopen Dr.,
Lewes,
302-644-6030, 800-643-3779;
www.capemaylewesferry.com
Sole connection between Highway 13 (Ocean Hwy.) on the Delmarva Peninsula and southern terminus of Garden State Parkway (NJ). Trip across Delaware Bay (16 miles) takes 70 minutes. Daily; 22 crossings in summer, 10 in winter, 14-18 in spring and fall.

Zwaanendael Museum
102 Kings Hwy., Lewes,
302-645-1148;
http://history.delaware.gov/museums/zm/zm_main.shtml
This adaptation of the Hoorn, Holland, town hall was built in 1931 as a memorial to the original Dutch founders of Lewes (1631). It highlights the town's maritime heritage with colonial, Native American and Dutch exhibits. Tuesday-Saturday 10 a.m.-4:30 p.m., Sunday 1:30-4:30 p.m.; closed Monday.

SPECIAL EVENTS
Coast Day
University of Delaware Marine Studies Complex, 700 Pilottown Rd.,
Lewes,
302-831-8083;
www.ocean.udel.edu/coastday
Facilities and research vessel open to the public; marine exhibits, research demonstrations, nautical films. First Sunday in October.

Great Delaware Kite Festival
Cape Henlopen State Park,
42 Henlopen Dr., Lewes,
302-645-8983;
www.destateparks.com/chsp/chsp.htm
Festival heralds the beginning of spring on the Friday before Easter.

Lewes Garden Tour
Zwaanendael Park, 120 Kings Hwy.,
Lewes,
302-645-8073
Visit the hidden gardens of Lewes. Vendors. Third Saturday in June.

HOTELS
★★★Inn at Canal Square
122 Market St., Lewes,
302-644-3377, 888-644-1911;
www.theinnatcanalsquare.com
Adjacent to the beautiful historic district, this charming, "Nantucket-style" bed-and-breakfast offers private waterfront porches. 24 rooms. Complimentary continental breakfast. $$

★

★

★

★

★

★★★Hotel Rodney
142 Second St., Lewes,
302-645-6466, 800-824-8754;
www.hotelrodneydelaware.com
Built in 1926, this sleek and stylish boutique hotel is located in historic downtown Lewes, minutes from the beach as well as shopping and dining options.
18 rooms, 5 suites. **$$**

RESTAURANTS
★★★The Buttery
102 Second St., Lewes,
302-645-7755;
www.butteryrestaurant.com

This charming restaurant, located in the restored Trader Mansion, offers a variety of entrees from Maryland crab cakes to Asian pad thai. Try the English bangers at Sunday brunch.
French menu. Lunch, dinner, brunch. **$$$**

★Lighthouse
Savannah and Anglers roads,
Lewes,
302-645-6271;
www.lighthouselewes.com
Seafood menu. Breakfast, lunch, dinner. Bar. Children's menu. Outdoor seating. **$$**

LITTLE CREEK

RESTAURANTS
★★Village Inn
Hwy. 9, Little Creek,
302-734-3245

Seafood menu. Lunch, dinner. Bar. **$$**

MILLSBORO

RESTAURANTS
★★Georgia House
119 Main St., Millsboro,
302-934-6737

American menu. Lunch, dinner. Closed Sunday, Monday. Children's menu. Casual attire. **$$**

MONTCHANIN

HOTELS
★★★Inn at Montchanin Village
Rte. 100 and Kirk Rd.,
Montchanin,
302-888-2133, 800-269-2473;
www.montchanin.com
Once part of the Winterthur Estate and listed on the National Register of Historic Places, this inn's white picket fence, winding walkways and country sensibilities create a relaxing retreat. Guests can stay in one of several carefully restored houses with four-poster beds and modern marble bathrooms. Nearby pastimes include antique stores, scenic country drives and the Longwood Gardens.
28 rooms. **$$**

RESTAURANTS
★★★Krazy Kat's
Rte. 100 and Kirk Rd., Montchanin,
302-888-2133, 800-269-2473;
www.montchanin.com
Krazy Kat's is set in a 19th-century blacksmith's shop neighboring the charming and historic Inn at Montchanin Village. Seats covered in plush zebra and leopard prints and animal portraits adorning the walls set the stage for a menu of signatures like grilled wild boar tenderloin satay with ginger jus, sesame-roasted fingerling potatoes and red cabbage daikon slaw. The wine list is extensive and international.
French menu. Breakfast, lunch, dinner. Business casual attire. Reservations recommended. Outdoor seating. **$$$**

NEW CASTLE

One of Delaware's first settlements, New Castle once served as a meeting place of the Colonial assemblies, the first capital of the state and an early center of culture and communication. Its fine harbor made it a busy port in the 18th century until Wilmington, a closer neighbor to Philadelphia, took over its commerce. Today, New Castle attracts historians and architects alike. New Castle lies at the foot of the Delaware Memorial Bridge, which connects with the southern end of the New Jersey Turnpike.

Information: Mayor and Council of New Castle, 220 Delaware St., New Castle, 302-322-9801; www.newcastlecity.net

WHAT TO SEE AND DO

Amstel House Museum
2 E. Fourth St., New Castle, 302-322-2794; www.newcastlehistory.org
(1730) Restored brick mansion of the seventh governor of Delaware; an earlier structure was incorporated into the service wing. Houses colonial furnishings and arts; complete colonial kitchen. Tuesday-Saturday 11 a.m.-4 p.m., Sunday 1-4 p.m. Combination ticket available with Old Dutch House.

George Read II House
42 The Strand, New Castle, 302-322-8411
(1804) A Federal-style house with elegant interiors: gilded fanlights, silver door hardware, carved woodwork and relief plasterwork. It's furnished with period antiques and the garden design dates from 1847. March-December: Tuesday-Saturday 10 a.m.-4 p.m., Sunday noon-4 p.m.; January-February: Saturday 10 a.m.-4 p.m., Sunday noon-4 p.m., weekdays by appointment.

The Green
Delaware and Third Streets, New Castle
Laid out under the direction of Peter Stuyvesant, this public square is surrounded by dozens of historically important buildings.

Old New Castle Court House Museum
211 Delaware St., New Castle, 302-323-4453
(1732) Original colonial capitol and oldest surviving courthouse in the state; furnishings and exhibits on display; cupola

is the center of a 12-mile circle that delineates the Delaware-Pennsylvania border. Tuesday-Saturday 10 a.m.-3:30 p.m., Sunday 1:30-4:30 p.m.; closed Monday.

Old Dutch House
32 E. Third St., New Castle, 302-322-2794; www.newcastlehistory.org
(Late 17th century) Thought to be Delaware's oldest dwelling in its original form; Dutch colonial furnishings; decorative arts. March-December: Tuesday-Saturday 11 a.m.-4 p.m., Sunday 1-4 p.m.; rest of year by appointment. Combination ticket available with Amstel House Museum.

Old Library Museum
40 E. Third St., New Castle, 302-322-2794; www.newcastlehistory.org
(1892) Unusual semi-octagonal Victorian building houses temporary exhibits relating to the area. March-December: Saturday-Sunday 1-4 p.m.

SPECIAL EVENTS

Band Concerts
Battery Park, Third and Delaware streets, New Castle, 302-328-4188
Wednesday evenings, June-early August.

Separation Day
Battery Park, New Castle, 302-322-9802
Observance of Delaware's declaration of independence from Great Britain. Regatta, shows, bands, concerts, fireworks. June.

★
★
★
★
★

HOTELS

★**Bridgeview Inn - New Castle**
1612 N. DuPont Hwy., New Castle,
302-658-8511
120 rooms. Complimentary continental
breakfast. **$**

RESTAURANTS

★★**Air Transport Command**
143 N. DuPont Hwy.,
New Castle,
302-328-3527

Lunch, dinner, Sunday brunch. Bar. Children's
menu. Reservations recommended. Outdoor
seating. Replica of World War II-era Scottish
farmhouse; war memorabilia. **$$**

★★**The Arsenal at Old New Castle**
30 Market St.,
New Castle,
302-323-1812;
www.arsena1812.net
American menu. Lunch, dinner. Closed
Monday. **$$$**

NEWARK

Newark was established at the crossroads of two well-traveled Native American trails.
Nearby, Cooch's bridge was the site of the only Revolutionary War battle on Delaware
soil. And according to tradition, Betsy Ross's flag was first raised in battle at the bridge on
September 3, 1777.
Information: Greater Wilmington Convention & Visitors Bureau-Visitors Center,
100 W. 10th St., Wilmington, 302-737-4059; www.wilmcvb.org

WHAT TO SEE AND DO

University of Delaware
196 S. College Ave.,
Newark,
302-831-2792;
www.udel.edu
(1743) 18,000 students. Founded as a small
private academy; stately elm trees, fine
lawns and Georgian-style brick buildings
adorn the central campus. Tours from Visitors Center (Monday-Friday, Saturday). On
campus is:

University of Delaware Mineral Collection
Mineralogical Museum in Penny Hall,
Academy St.,
Newark,
302-831-8242
Includes fossil exhibit. Tuesday-Thursday
noon-4 p.m.

White Clay Creek State Park
425 Wedgewood Rd.,
Newark,
302-368-6900;
www.destateparks.com/wccsp
A 1,483-acre day park with farmlands, forest and streams. Fishing; nature and fitness
trails, picnicking.

HOTELS

★★**Delaware Inn & Conference Center**
260 Chapman Rd., Newark,
302-738-3400, 800-633-3203
99 rooms. Complimentary continental breakfast. Restaurant, bar. **$**

★★★**Hilton Wilmington/Christiana**
100 Continental Dr.,
Newark,
302-454-1500, 800-445-8667;
www.hilton.com
This family- and business-friendly hotel is
situated on a sprawling country estate. For
an afternoon respite, take advantage of the
hotel's high tea. Enjoy a meal in one of
two restaurants—one casual and one more
upscale—or explore shopping and dining in
the surrounding area.
266 rooms. **$**

RESTAURANTS

★**Klondike Kate's**
158 E. Main St.,
Newark,
302-737-6100;
www.klondikekates.com
American, Southwestern menu. Lunch, dinner.
Bar. Children's menu. Outdoor seating. **$$**

11

DELAWARE

★
★
★
★
★

REHOBOTH BEACH

The "nation's summer capital" got its nickname because it was a favorite with Washington diplomats and legislators. A 2 1/2-hour drive from Washington, D.C., the largest summer resort in Delaware began as a spot for camp meetings amid sweet-smelling pine groves. In the 1920s, real estate boomed, triggering Rehoboth Beach's rebirth as a resort town with a variety of accommodations, shopping areas and eateries. The town's deep sea and fresh-water fishing, sailing, swimming and biking and strolling along cherry tree-lined Rehoboth Avenue make it a preferred retreat from Washington's summer heat.

Information: Rehoboth Beach-Dewey Beach Chamber of Commerce, 501 Rehoboth Ave., Rehoboth Beach, 302-227-2233, 800-441-1329; www.beach-fun.com

WHAT TO SEE AND DO

Delaware Seashore State Park
850 Inlet Rd.,
Rehoboth Beach,
302-227-2800;
www.destateparks.com/dssp/dssp.asp
This 7-mile strip of land separates Rehoboth and Indian River bays from the Atlantic. Bay and ocean swimming, Fishing, surfing, boating (marina, launch, rentals); picnicking, concession, primitive and improved campsites.

Jungle Jim's
8 Country Club Rd.,
Rehoboth Beach,
302-227-8444;
www.funatjunglejims.com
Fifteen acres of family fun include go-karts, batting cages, two miniature golf courses, bumper boats, rock climbing and a water park. Mid-June-Labor Day: daily; late May, early June, late September: limited hours.

Midway Speedway
Midway Shopping Center, Hwy. 1 N.,
Rehoboth Beach,
302-644-2042
This recreational racing park features four tracks including a Super 8 Track and Family Track, eight different styles of go-karts, and a kiddie raceway and bumper boats. Daily.

SPECIAL EVENTS

Bandstand Concerts
501 Rehoboth Ave.,
Rehoboth Beach,
302-227-6181

Open-air concerts. Memorial Day-Labor Day: Saturday and Sunday evenings.

Sea Witch Halloween and Fiddlers' Festival
501 Rehoboth Ave.,
Rehoboth Beach,
302-227-2233, 800-441-1329
This annual festival features contests, a parade, music and food. Late October.

HOTELS

★★★Boardwalk Plaza Hotel
Olive Ave. and the Boardwalk,
Rehoboth Beach,
302-227-7169, 800-332-3224;
www.boardwalkplaza.com
This Victorian-style hotel on Rehoboth Beach offers state-of-the-art comfort, with high-speed Internet access and whirlpool tubs. Enjoy the scenic ocean views at Victoria's restaurant.
84 rooms. $$$

★Brighton Suites Hotel
34 Wilmington Ave.,
Rehoboth Beach,
302-227-5780, 800-227-5788;
www.brightonsuites.com
66 rooms, all suites. $

★Comfort Inn
19210 Coastal Hwy.,
Rehoboth Beach,
302-226-1515, 877-424-6423;
www.comfortinn.com
97 rooms. Complimentary continental breakfast. $

★
★
★
★
★

SPECIALTY LODGINGS

The Bellmoor Inn

6 Christian St., Rehoboth Beach,
302-227-5800, 800-425-2355;
www.thebellmoor.com

The Bellmoor Inn is an elegant seaside retreat with Brazilian cherry floors, libraries, game rooms, gardens and a full-service day spa.

78 rooms. Complimentary full breakfast. $$$

RESTAURANTS

★★Blue Moon

35 Baltimore Ave., Rehoboth Beach,
302-227-6515;
www.bluemoonrehoboth.com

American menu. Dinner, Sunday brunch. Closed January. Bar. $$$

★★★Chez La Mer

210 Second St., Rehoboth Beach,
302-227-6494;
www.chezlamer.com

With an enticing gourmet menu featuring entrees such as crab imperial and country-style homemade pate, Chez La Mer has received an Award of Excellence from *Wine Spectator* magazine every year since 1993. French menu. Dinner. Closed November-March. Bar. Outdoor seating. Sun porch. $$$

★Iguana Grill

52 Baltimore Ave.,
Rehoboth Beach,
302-227-0948;
www.iguanagrill.com

American, Southwestern menu. Lunch, dinner. Closed November-first weekend of March. Bar. Casual attire. Outdoor seating. $

★★La La Land

22 Wilmington Ave.,
Rehoboth Beach,
302-227-3887;
www.lalalandrestaurant.com

American menu. Dinner. Closed December 31-Easter; also Monday-Wednesday from Easter-Memorial Day and October-December 31. Bar. Casual attire. Reservations recommended. Outdoor seating. $$

★★Sydney's Blues and Jazz Restaurant

25 Christian St., Rehoboth Beach,
302-227-1339, 800-808-1924;
www.rehoboth.com/sydneys

Creole menu. Dinner. Bar. Reservations recommended. Outdoor seating. $$

★Tijuana Taxi

207 Rehoboth Ave., Rehoboth Beach,
302-227-1986

Mexican menu. Dinner. Bar. Children's menu. Casual attire. $$

SMYRNA

In the 1850s, Smyrna—named for the chief seaport of Turkish Asia Minor—was an active shipping center for produce grown in central Delaware. Today, migratory birds, more so than produce, pass through this small port town.

Information: Chamber of Commerce, Dover, 302-653-9291, or visit the Smyrna Visitors Center, 5500 DuPont Hwy., Smyrna, 302-653-8910; www.smyrnadelaware.com

WHAT TO SEE AND DO

Bombay Hook National Wildlife Refuge

2591 Whitehall Neck Rd., Smyrna,
302-653-6872;
bombayhook.fws.gov

This annual fall and spring resting and feeding spot for migratory waterfowl, including a variety of ducks and tens of thousands of snow geese and Canada geese, is also home to bald eagles, shorebirds, deer, fox and muskrat. It includes an auto tour route (12 miles), wildlife foot trails, observation towers and visitor center offering interpretive and environmental education programs. Visitor center (spring and fall: daily; summer and winter: Monday-Friday). Golden Eagle, Golden Age and Golden Access passports accepted. Daily.

13

DELAWARE

Smyrna Museum
11 S. Main St., Smyrna,
302-653-1320
Tuesday, Thursdays and Saturday 10 a.m.-
1 p.m.
   Furnishings and memorabilia from early
Federal to late Victorian periods; changing
exhibits. Saturday 1-4 p.m.

RESTAURANTS
★★Thomas England House
1165 S. DuPont Boulevard (Highway 13),
Smyrna,
302-653-1420

American menu. Dinner. Bar. Children's
menu. Reservations recommended. $$$

★Wayside Inn
103 N. DuPont Hwy.,
Smyrna,
302-653-8047
Seafood, steak menu. Lunch, dinner. Chil-
dren's menu. $$

WILMINGTON

Wilmington, the "chemical capital of the world" and an international hub of industry and shipping, is the largest city in Delaware. The Swedish, Dutch and British have all left their marks on the city. The Swedes settled first, seeking their fortunes and founding the colony of New Sweden. In 1655, Dutch soldiers under Peter Stuyvesant, governor of New Amsterdam, took the little colony without bloodshed. Nine years later, the English arrived, and the town grew into a market and shipping center aided by wealthy Quakers. Wilmington has flourished as an industrial port because of its abundant water power and proximity to other eastern ports. From here come vulcanized fiber, glazed leathers, dyed cotton, rubber hose, autos and many other products.

Information: Greater Wilmington Convention & Visitors Bureau, 100 W. 10th St., Wilmington, 302-652-4088, 800-489-6664; www.wilmcvb.org

WHAT TO SEE AND DO
Amtrak Station
Martin Luther King Blvd. and French St.,
Wilmington,
302-429-6530
Restored Victorian railroad station, still
in use, designed by master architect Frank
Furness. Daily.

Banning Park
22 S. Heald St.,
Wilmington,
302-323-6422
Fishing; tennis, playing fields, picnicking
and pavilions. Daily.

BRANDYWINE VALLEY

The Brandywine Valley, just north of Wilmington, is a serene canvas of rolling hills, broad fields of corn and yellow sunflowers, rambling split-rail fences, horse pastures, ancient stone barns and narrow country roads lined by towering old trees. Tucked into this landscape is a diverse collection of fine arts, history and house museums, most of which were bequeathed by the du Pont family, the wealthy industrialists whose forebear, Pierre Samuel du Pont, arrived from France in 1800. Pierre's son, Eleuthere Irenee (E.I.) du Pont, established a black powder factory, harnessing Brandywine Creek for power and creating the du Pont fortune.

Nicknamed "Chateau Country," the valley contains many grand homes, typically set far back from the road. For more than 30 years, an environmental organization called the Brandywine Conservancy has worked to protect the valley's open pastoral look from threatening suburban sprawl.

Begin this one-day 50-mile tour into the scenic and artistic riches of the region in Wilmington. Your first stop is the Delaware Art Museum at 2301 Kentmere Parkway, which features a strong collection of American sculpture and painting, including works by Brandywine resident Andrew Wyeth.

From the museum, return to Route 52 north. Turn right at Route 141 to the Hagley Museum, which sits on the site of the first du Pont powder works, amid 230 acres of gardens and exhibits. The museum recalls industrial life in mid-19th-century America. A bit farther upstream along Brandywine Creek is Eleutherian Mills, the lovely Georgian-style house E.I. du Pont built in 1803. Double back on Route 141 to Route 100 north (Montchanin Rd.) to the village of Montchanin. Here, 11 varied structures that served as homes for workers at the du Pont mills have been converted into a luxury retreat, the 37-rooms Inn at Montchanin Village. Stroll the block-long cobblestone main street, which is named Privy Lane for the row of gray concrete privies standing behind the dwellings in military precision. (Today the privies store garden equipment.) Consider lunch at the inn's restaurant, Krazy Kats, one of Brandywine's best.

Continue north on Route 100 to Brandywine State Park for a chance to hike along Brandywine Creek. Stay on Route 100 north to Smith's Bridge Road, then make a left. Continue west via Centerville Road to Route 52, and turn south (left). At the sign, turn left into Winterthur, a nine-story museum of American decorative arts surrounded by 985 acres of gardens. This was the estate of Henry Francis du Pont, who collected antique furniture, porcelain, silver, rugs and draperies crafted from 1640 to 1860. These items are organized in period rooms, including a 17th-century Lancaster, Pa., bedroom and an 18th-century Tidewater, Va., plantation sitting room. The gardens reflect du Pont's goal of creating a masterpiece of 20th-century American naturalism. Return to Wilmington on Route 52 south. Approximately 50 miles.

Bellevue State Park
800 Carr Rd., Wilmington,
302-761-6963;
www.destateparks.com/bvsp/bvsp.htm

Fishing; nature, fitness and horseback riding trails; bicycling, tennis, game courts, picnicking (pavilions).

WILMINGTON'S PUBLIC ART

While the Brandywine Valley is known for its museums and gardens, Wilmington itself is no artistic slouch. The historic heart of the old city boasts a wealth of outdoor statuary in public squares and office courtyards. Much of it is representational, but there are also abstract and whimsical pieces. For the past several years, a picture book describing the collection has been published.

A one-mile walk through the city's commercial center is like a stroll through an urban sculpture garden. Begin at Rodney Square outside the elegant Hotel du Pont at 11th and Market streets. Dominating the view is the famous 1923 statue of Caesar Rodney astride his horse, galloping toward Philadelphia to cast the deciding vote for the Declaration of Independence in 1776. A city hallmark, the Rodney statue is a rare example of an equestrian sculpture in which the horse is in full gallop, its two front legs in the air and the weight of the statue resting on the two rear hooves.

Head north on Market Street to 13th Street and two blocks west (left) to Orange Street to the Brandywine Gateway, where you'll see the kinetic fountain at the foot of the Hercules Building (facing 13th Street) in Hercules Plaza. Three solid granite balls rest on three marble pillars in the middle of a large pool. The spheres are arranged so that water flowing over them suggests that they are rotating.

Retrace your path to 8th and Market and then turn east (left) to Spencer and Freedom plazas between French and Market streets. In Spencer Plaza stands "Father and Son," a larger-than-life bronze statue of a man with a child in his arms by Charles Park, a local artist. A plaque notes that this was the one-time site of the Mother African Union Methodist Protestant Church, the first black church in America wholly controlled by descendants of Africans.

Just across French Street in Freedom Plaza, in the shadow of a cluster of modern municipal buildings, is "The Holocaust." Both abstract and realistic, it shows the victims pressed against three unyielding pillars. End your tour at the plaque honoring abolitionists Harriet Tubman and Thomas Garrett and the Underground Railroad.

16

DELAWARE

Brandywine Creek State Park
Routes 92 and 100, Wilmington,
302-577-3534;
www.destateparks.com/bcsp/bcsp.asp
A 1,000-acre day-use park. Fishing; nature and fitness trails; cross-country skiing. Picnicking. Nature center.

Brandywine Springs Park
3300 Faulkland Rd.,
Wilmington,
302-395-5652
Site of a once-famous resort hotel (1827-1845) for Southern planters and politicos. Here, Lafayette met Washington under the Council Oak before the Battle of Brandywine in 1777. Picnicking, fireplaces, pavilions, baseball fields. Pets on leash only. Daily.

Brandywine Zoo and Park
1001 N. Park Dr.,
Wilmington,
302-571-7788;
www.destateparks.com/wilmsp/zoo
Designed by Frederick Law Olmsted, the park includes the Josephine Garden with a fountain and roses; stands of Japanese cherry trees. The zoo, along North Park Drive, features animals from North and South America. Picnicking, playgrounds. Daily 10 a.m.-4 p.m.

Delaware Art Museum

2301 Kentmere Pkwy., Wilmington,
302-571-9590;
www.delart.org

This museum features the Howard Pyle Collection of American Illustrations with works by Pyle, N. C. Wyeth and Maxfield Parrish; American painting collection, with works by West, Homer, Church, Glackens and Hopper; Bancroft Collection of English Pre-Raphaelite art, with works by Rossetti and Burne-Jones; and Phelps Collection of Andrew Wyeth works; also changing exhibits, children's participatory gallery; store. Guided tours by appointment. Closed Monday, Tuesday-Saturday 10:00 a.m.-4:00 p.m., Sunday noon-4 p.m.

Delaware History Museum

504 Market St., Wilmington,
302-656-0637;
www.hsd.org/dhm.htm

Changing exhibits on history and decorative arts. Closed Sunday and Monday, Tuesday-Friday 11:00 a.m.-4:00 p.m., Saturday 10:00 a.m.-4:00 p.m.

Delaware Museum of Natural History

4840 Kennett Pike, Wilmington,
302-658-9111;
www.delmnh.org

Exhibits of shells, birds, mammals; also the largest bird egg and a 500-pound clam. Monday-Saturday 9:30 a.m.-4:30 p.m., Sunday noon-4:30 p.m.

Fort Christina Monument

Foot of E. Seventh St., Wilmington,
302-652-5629

Monument marks the location where Swedes settled in 1638. The monument was presented in 1938 to Wilmington by the people of Sweden. Sculpted by Carl Milles. Complex includes nearby log cabin, moved to this location as a reminder of Finnish and Swedish contributions to the United States.

Grand Opera House

818 Market St., Mall, Wilmington,
302-658-7898;
www.grandopera.org

(1871) Historic landmark built by Masons, this restored Victorian theater now serves as Delaware's Center for the Performing Arts, home of Opera Delaware (November-May) and the Delaware Symphony (September-May). Facade is fine example of Second Empire style interpreted in cast iron.

Hagley Museum and Library

298 Buck Rd., Wilmington,
302-658-2400;
www.hagley.lib.de.us

Old riverside stone mill buildings, a one-room schoolhouse and a millwright shop highlight 19th-century explosive manufacturing and community life; 240-acre historic site of E.I. du Pont's original black powder mills includes an exhibit building, an operating waterwheel, a stationary steam engine and a fully operable 1875 machine shop. Admission includes a bus ride along the river for a tour of 1803 Eleutherian Mills, a residence with antiques reflecting five generations of du Ponts, a 19th-century garden and a barn with a collection of antique wagons. Museum store. January-mid-March: weekdays one tour 1:30 p.m., weekends 9:30 a.m.-4:30 p.m.; mid-March-January: daily 9:30 a.m.-4:30 p.m.

Holy Trinity (Old Swedes) Church and Hendrickson House

606 Church St., Wilmington,
302-652-5629;
www.oldswedes.org

Founded by Swedish settlers in 1698, the church stands as originally built and still holds regular services. The house, a Swedish farmhouse built in 1690, is now a museum containing 17th- and 18th-century artifacts. Monday-Saturday.

Nemours Mansion and Gardens

1600 Rockland Rd., Wilmington,
302-651-6912, 800-651-6912;
www.nemours.org/mansion.html

Country estate (300 acres) of Alfred I. du Pont. Mansion (1910) is modified Louis XVI, by Carre and Hastings, with 102 rooms of rare antique furniture, Asian rugs, tapestries and paintings dating from the 12th century. Formal French gardens with

17

DELAWARE

★
★
★
★
★

terraces, statuary and pools. Tours. May-October: Tuesday-Saturday 9 a.m., 11 a. m., 1 p.m., 3 p.m.; Sunday 11 a.m., 1 p.m., 3 p.m.; November-December limited basis; reservations required. Over 12 years only.

Rockwood Museum
610 Shipley Rd., Wilmington,
302-761-4340;
www.rockwood.org
A 19th-century Gothic Revival estate with gardens in English Romantic style. On grounds are manor house, conservatory, porter's lodge and other outbuildings. Museum furnished with English, European and American decorative arts of the 17th to 19th centuries. Guided tours. Tuesday-Sunday 10:00 a.m.-3:00 p.m.

Willingtown Square
505 N. Market St., Mall, Wilmington,
302-655-7161
Historic square surrounded by four 18th-century houses moved to this location between 1973 and 1976. Serves as office and conference space.

Wilmington & Western Railroad
Greenbank Station,
2201 Newport Gap Pike, Wilmington,
302-998-1930;
www.wwrr.com
Round-trip steam-train ride (nine miles) to and from Mount Cuba picnic grove. May-October: Sunday; rest of year, schedule varies.

SPECIAL EVENTS
Horse Racing, Delaware Park
777 Delaware Park Blvd.,
Wilmington,
302-994-2521, 800-417-5687;
www.delpark.com
Thoroughbred racing. Slots facility. Restaurants. Late April-mid-November.

Victorian Ice Cream Festival
Rockwood Museum, 610 Shipley Rd.,
Wilmington, 302-761-4340
Victorian festival featuring high-wheeled bicycles, hot-air balloons, marionettes, old-fashioned medicine show, baby parade and crafts; homemade ice cream. Mid-July.

Wilmington Garden Day
Wilmington,
302-428-6172;
www.gardenday.org
Tour of famous gardens and houses. First Saturday in May.

Winterthur Point-to-Point Races
Hwy. 52, Wilmington,
302-888-4600, 888-448-3883;
www.thebrandywine.com/special
An old-fashioned country horse race that features five races. May.

HOTELS
★Best Western Brandywine Valley Inn
1807 Concord Pike, Wilmington,
302-656-9436, 800-537-7772;
www.brandywineinn.com
95 rooms. Complimentary continental breakfast. **$**

★★Clarion Collection Brandywine Suites
707 N. King St., Wilmington,
302-656-9300, 800-756-0070;
www.brandywinesuites.com
49 rooms, all suites. Complimentary continental breakfast. Airport transportation available. **$**

★★Courtyard by Marriott
1102 West St., Wilmington,
302-429-7600, 800-321-2211;
www.courtyard.com
123 rooms. Airport transportation available. **$$**

★★Doubletree Hotel Wilmington
4727 Concord Pike, Wilmington,
302-478-6000, 800-222-8733;
wilmington.doubletree.com
244 rooms. **$$**

★★★Hotel du Pont
11th and Market Streets, Wilmington,
302-594-3100, 800-441-9019;
www.hoteldupont.com
The Hotel du Pont has been a Delaware institution since 1913. Constructed to rival the grand hotels of Europe with ornate plasterwork and gleaming brass, this palatial hotel

18

DELAWARE

enjoys proximity to the city's attractions while remaining in the heart of the scenic Brandywine Valley with its championship golf and estate tours. The guest rooms are classically decorated with mahogany furnishings, cream tones and imported linens. Patrons dine on French cuisine while listening to the gentle strains of a harp at the Green Room. 217 rooms. **$$$**

★★★Sheraton Suites Wilmington
422 Delaware Ave., Wilmington,
302-654-8300, 800-325-3535;
www.sheraton.com
Located in the heart of downtown Wilmington, this all-suite hotel offers spacious rooms and conference facilities just a short drive from a number of museums, within walking distance from the headquarters of several Fortune 500 companies and a few miles from major shopping malls. The contemporary guest rooms are decorated in navy and taupe and feature Sweet Sleeper mattresses. 223 rooms, all suites. **$$**

RESTAURANTS
★★821 Market Street Bistro
821 N. Market St., Wilmington,
302-652-8821;
www.restaurant821.com
American menu. Lunch, dinner. Closed Sunday; also one week in early January. Bar. Business casual attire. Reservations recommended. Valet parking. Credit cards accepted. **$$$**

★★Columbus Inn
2216 Pennsylvania Ave., Wilmington,
302-571-1492;
www.columbusinn.com
American menu. Lunch, dinner, brunch. Bar. Children's menu. Business casual attire. Reservations recommended. Valet parking. Outdoor seating. **$$**

★★Costas
1000 N. West St., Wilmington,
302-777-2268;
www.costasgrillandwinebar.com
Greek menu, Mediterranean menu. Lunch, dinner. Closed last week in August. Bar.

Children's menu. Business casual attire. Reservations recommended. Credit cards accepted. **$$$**

★★★The Green Room
11th and Market Streets,
Wilmington,
302-594-3155, 800-441-9019;
www.dupont.com/hotel/dining_green.htm
Located inside the historic Hotel DuPont, this restaurant's sophisticated dècor of carved oak paneling and a coffered ceiling is perfect for romantic or special-occasion celebrations. Live music enhances the dining experience Tuesday through Saturday evenings and during Sunday brunch.
French menu. Breakfast, lunch, dinner, Sunday brunch. Bar. Children's menu. Jacket required (dinner). Valet parking. **$$$**

★★★Harry's Savoy Grill
2020 Naaman's Rd.,
Wilmington,
302-475-3000;
www.harrys-savoy.com
A Brandywine Valley staple since 1988, Harry's Savoy Grill serves up the classics in an upscale English pub atmosphere. The bar and grill is known for its prime rib, its wine list and its "famous, eight-shake martinis."
American, seafood, steak menu. Lunch, dinner, late-night, Sunday brunch. Bar. Children's menu. Outdoor seating. **$$$**

★Kid Shelleens Charcoal House & Saloon
1801 W. 14th St., Wilmington,
302-658-4600;
www.kidshelleens.com
American menu. Lunch, dinner, late-night, Sunday brunch. Bar. Children's menu. Casual attire. Outdoor seating. **$$**

★★Toscana Kitchen + Bar
1412 N. DuPont St., Wilmington,
302-654-8001;
www.toscanakitchen.com
Northern Italian menu. Lunch, dinner. Bar. Business casual attire. Reservations recommended. Outdoor seating. Credit cards accepted. **$$**

MARYLAND

IN MARYLAND, THE BALTIMORE ORIOLE IS MORE THAN JUST THE STATE BIRD, TURTLES ARE sports heroes and crabs are regular fixtures at the dinner table. The seventh state owns a celebrated sports history, producing superstars such as Babe Ruth and Cal Ripken, Jr., and building the Orioles' Camden Yards, lauded for its classic design. Several noteworthy colleges and universities call Maryland home, including Johns Hopkins University and the University of Maryland, home of the Terrapins. And Maryland's Chesapeake Bay keeps restaurants across the nation well stocked, producing more than 50 percent of the United States' harvest of hard-shell crabs.

Maryland prides itself on its varied terrain and diverse economy. Metropolitan life around Baltimore and Washington, D.C. contrasts with life in the rural areas in central and southern Maryland and on the Eastern Shore, across the Chesapeake Bay. Green mountains in the western counties offset the east's white Atlantic beaches. State's prosperity stems from a flourishing travel industry, central Maryland's agricultural and dairy wealth, the seafood industry, manufacturing and commerce, and federal government and defense contracts.

Named in honor of Henrietta Maria, wife of Charles I, King of England, Maryland was first established in 1634 by Lord Baltimore's brother, Leonard Calvert. Calvert and 222 passengers aboard his ships purchased a Native American village and named it "Saint Maries Citty" (now St. Mary's City). The land was cleared, tobacco was planted, and over the years, profits built elegant mansions, many of which still stand.

Maryland has played a pivotal role in every war waged on U.S. soil. In 1755, British General Edward Braddock, assisted by Lieutenant Colonel George Washington, trained his army at Cumberland for the fight against the French and Indians. In the War of 1812, Fort McHenry at Baltimore withstood attacks by land and sea. The action was later immortalized in the national anthem by Francis Scott Key, a Frederick lawyer. And in the Civil War, Maryland was a major battleground at Antietam.
Information: www.mdisfun.org

ABERDEEN

Aberdeen is home to the 75,000-acre Aberdeen Proving Grounds, a federal reservation along Chesapeake Bay, where army materials, ranging from gun sights to tanks, are tested under simulated combat conditions.
Information: Aberdeen Chamber of Commerce, 115 N. Parke St., Aberdeen, 410-272-2580; www.aberdeencc.com

WHAT TO SEE AND DO
Recreation Area
Aberdeen, 410-457-5011
Fourteen-mile-long man-made lake; swimming pool (fee), boating (ramps, marinas), fishing; fishermen's gallery (over 12 years only); picnicking, hiking.

U.S. Army Ordnance Museum
2601 Maryland Blvd.,
Aberdeen,
410-278-3602;
www.goordnance.apg.army.mil/sitefiles/ordnancemuseum.htm

DEEP CREEK LAKE, MARYLAND'S WESTERN PLAYGROUND

In western Maryland's Garrett County, Deep Creek Lake is known as the state's hidden secret. But the secret is getting out. The massive lake now hosts waterskiing, whitewater rafting, hiking, back-road bicycling, kayaking, fly-fishing, canoeing, sailing and swimming. On a drive around the lake, you can partake in as many activities as you choose—outfitters are on hand to rent all the necessary equipment—or simply enjoy the sublime mountain views.

Deep Creek, Maryland's largest freshwater lake, is 12 miles long, but so etched with fingerlike coves that the shoreline stretches for 65 miles. Surrounded by the forested ridges and splashing streams of mountain wilderness, the lake, at an altitude of 2,300 feet, treats summer visitors to a cool respite from the city. Begin this two-day, 400-mile drive in Baltimore and head west on I-70 and I-68 to exit 14 at Keysers Ridge. Take Highway 219 south to the visitor center just outside the village of McHenry. Plan to spend the night in one of McHenry's inns, hotels or motels.

The trip from Baltimore to McHenry is about 180 miles, a scenic ride that carries you across a series of green mountain ridges. To break up the trip, pull off I-68 at Cumberland. George Washington is said to have assumed his first military command at Fort Cumberland, and his one-room log cabin and remnants of the fort can still be seen here. Cumberland is the terminus of the Chesapeake and Ohio Canal, which originates in Washington, D.C. You can rent a bicycle and ride along the towpath for miles.

At Deep Creek Lake, follow the signs to Deep Creek Lake State Park, which maintains a 700-foot-long sandy swimming beach. The Discovery Center, an attractive structure of stone, wood and soaring windows, features displays about the region's natural history and mining heritage. Ranger talks, walks and canoe trips are offered.

On the second day of your trip, take Highway 219 south from McHenry to the turn-off to Swallow Falls State Park. For an easy hike, follow the 1 1/2-mile path that scrambles in a loop past four waterfalls. At the trail head, the park has preserved a 37-acre stand of virgin hemlock and white pine estimated to be 300 years old. After 1/4 mile, Muddy Creek Falls—the state's highest at 52 feet—cascades down a staircase of rocks into a large pool. Next, follow signs south to the town of Oakland and then begin your scenic return to Baltimore via Route 135 northeast to Highway 220 north to I-68 east about 10 miles east of Cumberland. Take a break at Rocky Gap State Park, two minutes off the interstate, which tempts with a couple of fine sandy beaches in a forested mountain setting. Approximately 400 miles.

MARYLAND

Tanks, artillery, self-propelled artillery, extensive small arms, and an ammunition collection. Obtain a day pass at the Maryland Boulevard gate. Daily 9 a.m.-4:45 p.m.

HOTELS

★★**Holiday Inn**
1007 Beards Hill Rd., Aberdeen, 410-272-8100, 800-315-2621; www.holiday-inn.com/aberdeenmd
122 rooms. **$**

ANNAPOLIS

The capital of Maryland, Annapolis was the first peacetime capital of the United States. Congress met here from November 26, 1783, to August 13, 1784. In 1845, the U.S. Naval Academy was established here at the Army's Fort Severn. Every May, at commencement time, thousands of visitors throng the narrow, brick streets. **Information: Annapolis and Anne Arundel County Conference and Visitors Bureau, 26 West St., Annapolis, 888-302-2852; www.visit-annapolis.org Information is also available at the Visitor Information Booth located at the city dock.**

WHAT TO SEE AND DO

Boat Trips
980 Awald Rd., #202, at the City Dock
Annapolis,
410-268-7600
Forty-minute narrated tours of city harbor, USNA, and Severn River aboard "Harbor Queen" (Memorial Day-Labor Day: daily); 90-minute cruises to locations aboard *Annapolitan* and *Rebecca,* cruises to St. Michael's aboard the *Annapolitan II* (Memorial Day-Labor Day); 40-minute cruises up Spa Creek, residential areas, city harbor, and USNA aboard the *Miss Anne* and *Miss Anne II* (Memorial Day-Labor Day). Some cruises early spring and late fall, weather permitting. Fees vary.

Chesapeake Bay Bridge
357 Pier 1 Rd.,
Annapolis
The 7 1/4-mile link of Highway 50 across the Bay. Toll (charged eastbound only).

Chesapeake Sailing School
7080 Bembe Beach Rd.,
Annapolis,
410-269-1594, 800-966-0032;
www.sailingclasses.com

This school offers everything from weekend sailing classes for beginners (no experience necessary) to live-aboard, five-day cruises on gorgeous Chesapeake Bay, with basic and advanced instruction for individuals, families and corporate groups. You can also rent sailboats and go out on your own. April-October.

Government House
State Cir., Annapolis,
410-260-3930;
www.mdarchives.state.md.us/msa/
homepage/html/govhouse.html
(1868) This Victorian structure was remodeled in 1935 into a Georgian country house; furnishings reflect Maryland's history and culture. Tours by appointment. Monday, Wednesday, Friday 10:30 a.m.-2:30 p.m.

Hammond-Harwood House
19 Maryland Ave.,
Annapolis,
410-263-4683;
www.hammondharwoodhouse.org
(1774) Georgian house designed by William Buckland; antique furnishings; garden. Matthias Hammond, a Revolutionary patriot, was its first owner. Guided tours. Daily.

EASTERN SHORE OF THE CHESAPEAKE BAY

The Chesapeake Bay, North America's largest estuary, commands more than 4,500 miles of shoreline, much of it in Maryland. It is one of the Mid-Atlantic's most popular destinations, known for its rich history and savory shellfish.

A two-day driving tour covering about 250 miles makes a fine introduction to the bay. Begin your drive in Annapolis, Maryland's beautiful, old capital, which doubles as the bay's sailing headquarters. In summer, catch the regular Wednesday evening races, when as many as 100 boats may compete. The finish is easily visible from City Dock at the foot of the city's colonial-era streets.

From Annapolis, take Highway 50 east across the soaring Chesapeake Bay Bridge. Just before you reach the bridge, a five-minute detour leads to Sandy Point State Park, the only stop on this drive where you can take a dip in the bay. At the eastern end of the bridge, turn north onto Highway 301 to Route 213 north to Chestertown. Founded in 1706, Chestertown is a pretty village with a collection of 18th- and 19th-century homes, several of them situated along the scenic Chester River.

After browsing in the shops of High and Cross streets, take Route 213 south to Highway 50 south. In Easton, take Route 33 west to the historic sailing port of St. Michaels, an inviting place to spend the night. St. Michaels is one of the Mid-Atlantic's prettiest little towns, with lovely inns, fine restaurants, offbeat shops, expansive bay views and charming little back streets lined with homes dating to the 18th and 19th centuries. Your first stop should be the Chesapeake Bay Maritime Museum. The museum's 18-acre harbor site features more than a dozen historic structures, including a fully restored 1879 lighthouse. Stop by Waterman's Wharf, where you can try your skill at crab fishing. Boat builders are often at work restoring historic bay work boats for the museum's large collection. The "Patriot," a cruise ship departing from the museum's dock, takes visitors on a 60-minute tour up the Miles River, a bay tributary.

From St. Michaels, follow Route 33 to its end at Tilghman Island, a charter fishing port. Plan on having lunch at one of its waterside seafood houses. On the return trip to St. Michaels, stop about three miles east of the city and take the road south (right) to Bellevue. There you can catch the little Bellevue-Oxford Ferry for a 10-minute ride across the Tred Avon River to Oxford, a sleepy pleasure boat port dating back to 1694. To stretch your legs, walk along the Strand, a lovely river promenade, or rent a bicycle and ride along the quiet streets. From Oxford, return to Annapolis via Route 333 and Highway 50, stopping briefly in Easton to admire its attractive town center and to investigate its shops and galleries. Approximately 250 miles.

MARYLAND

HISTORY AND GOVERNMENT IN ANNAPOLIS

In the years just prior to the American Revolution, the colonial elite flocked to Annapolis, Maryland's capital on the Chesapeake Bay. This was the city's golden age, and many visitors were drawn by its spirited social life and elegant mansions built by wealthy tobacco planters. You can see some of the same sights on a one-mile stroll through the city's well-preserved historic district.

Begin at the visitor center, 26 West Street, where tourist parking is available. From the center, head east (left) on West Street; detour around St. Anne's Church (1859), noting its Tiffany windows. Pause on School Street to view Government House, the Georgian-style Maryland Governor's residence (remodeled 1936); and then climb the stairs to the Maryland State House on State Circle (1772), the oldest state capitol in continuous legislative use. Perched atop the city's highest hill, the State House provides a panoramic view of the bay. Inside, the Old Senate Chamber appears as it did on December 23, 1783, when George Washington resigned his commission as the victorious commander of the Continental Army.

Continue east from State Circle on Maryland Avenue, lined with antique shops, to the Hammond-Harwood Home (1774) at No. 19. A house museum, this Georgian structure features what is considered by many to be the most beautiful doorway in America. Double back one block on Maryland Avenue, pausing briefly at the Chase-Lloyd House (1769), another elegant Georgian mansion where Francis Scott Key, author of "The Star-Spangled Banner," was married in 1802. Turn toward the harbor (left) onto Prince George Street. The William Paca House (1765) at No. 186 and its two-acre colonial garden, carefully restored for authenticity, are national treasures. Now a house museum, the Paca house was the home of Maryland's Revolutionary War governor and a signer of the Declaration of Independence. Built in a symmetrical five-part format, it is considered one of the best examples of a Georgian home in America. Neighboring Brice House (1767) at 42 East Street is another magnificent Georgian mansion built by a wealthy merchant. To conclude this tour, continue downhill on Prince George Street, and turn west (right) one block onto Randall Street to City Dark for refreshments at Middleton Tavern. Once an "Inn for Seafaring Men," it has been serving Annapolis visitors since 1754.

MARYLAND

Historic Annapolis Foundation
18 Pinkney St., Annapolis,
410-267-7619, 800-603-4020;
www.annapolis.org
Self-guided audiocassette walking tours. Includes Historic District, State House, Old Treasury, U.S. Naval Academy and William Paca House. March-November: daily.

William Paca Garden
186 Prince George St., Annapolis,
410-990-4538, 800-603-4020
Restored two-acre pleasure garden originally developed in 1765 by William Paca, a signer of the Declaration of Independence and governor of Maryland during the Revolutionary War. Includes waterways, formal parterres and a garden wilderness. Monday-Saturday, also Sunday afternoons.

William Paca House
186 Prince George St.,
Annapolis,
410-990-4538, 800-603-4020
Paca built this five-part Georgian mansion in 1765. Monday-Saturday, also Sunday afternoons.

Historic Annapolis Foundation Welcome Center and Museum Store

77 Main St., Annapolis,
410-268-5576, 800-639-9153;
www.hafmuseumstore.com

This 1815 building stands on the site of a storehouse for Revolutionary War troops that burned in 1790. Audiocassette walking tours. Products reflecting Annapolis history. Monday-Thursday 10 a.m.-6 p.m., Friday-Saturday 10 a.m.-9 p.m., Sunday 10 a.m.-6 p.m.

Sailing Tours

80 Compromise St., Annapolis,
410-263-7837;
www.schooner-woodwind.com

Two-hour narrated trips through Chesapeake Bay aboard 74-foot sailing yacht "Woodwind." Departs from Pusser's Landing Restaurant at the Annapolis Marriott Waterfront Hotel. May-September: Tuesday-Sunday four trips daily, Monday Sunset Sail only; April, October, November: schedule varies.

Sandy Point State Park

1100 E. College Pkwy., Annapolis,
410-974-2149, 888-432-2267;
www.dnr.state.md.us/publiclands/
southern/sandypoint.html

On 786 acres. The park's location on the Atlantic Flyway makes it a fine area for bird-watching; view of Bay Bridge and oceangoing vessels. Swimming in the bay at two guarded beaches, two bathhouses, surf fishing, crabbing, boating (rentals, launches); concession. Daily, hours vary; call for schedule.

St. John's College

60 College Ave., Annapolis,
410-263-2371, 800-727-9238;
www.sjca.edu/main.html

(1784) 475 students. Nonsectarian liberal arts college. This 36-acre campus, one of the oldest in the country, is a National Historic Landmark. The college succeeded King William's School, founded in 1696. George Washington's two nephews and step-grandson studied here; Francis Scott Key was an alumnus. On campus is:

Elizabeth Myers Mitchell Art Gallery

Mellon Hall, 60 College Ave.,
Annapolis,
410-626-2556

Displays museum-quality traveling exhibitions. Academic year: Tuesday-Sunday noon-5 p.m., Friday 7-8 p.m.

State House

350 Rowe Blvd., State Circle,
Annapolis, 21401,
410-974-3400, 800-235-4045

(1772-1779) Oldest state house in continuous legislative use in United States, this was the first peacetime capitol of the nation. Here in 1784, a few weeks after receiving George Washington's resignation as commander-in-chief, Congress ratified the Treaty of Paris, which officially ended the Revolutionary War. Visitors Information Center. Guide service. Daily.

United States Naval Academy

121 Blake Rd., Annapolis,
410-263-6933;
www.usna.edu

Opened in 1845, the Naval Academy sits at the edge of the Chesapeake Bay and Severn River, occupying 338 acres. Tours of the campus are available through the academy's Armel-Leftwich Visitor Center. You will see the tomb of John Paul Jones, the chapel, the midshipmen's living quarters and the naval museum. The center also exhibits the original wooden figurehead of the Tecumseh and displays the *Freedom 7* space capsule. If you time your visit right, you can witness the Noon Formation, during which all present midshipmen line up and march in for the noon meal with military precision.

Note: Access to the Academy grounds is limited. Please check the current security restrictions before planning a visit. All visitors over the age of 16 must have a valid picture ID.

Watermark Tours

26 West St., Annapolis,
410-268-7601, 800-569-9622;
www.annapolis-tours.com

25

Walking tours of U.S. Naval Academy and Historic District conducted by guides in colonial attire. Tour includes historic Maryland State House, St. John's College, Naval Academy Chapel, crypt of John Paul Jones, Bancroft Hall dormitory and Armel-Leftwich Visitor Center. April-October: daily.

SPECIAL EVENTS

Annapolis by Candlelight

18 Pinkney St., Annapolis,
410-267-7619, 800-603-4020;
www.annapolis.org
This self-guided, candlelight walking tour leads visitors through private homes in the historic district. Curator-led tours are also available. For information and reservations contact Historic Annapolis Foundation. Early November.

Chesapeake Appreciation Days

Sandy Point State Park,
1100 E. College Pkwy., Annapolis,
410-974-2149
Skipjack sailing festival honors state's oystermen. Last weekend in October.

Christmas in Annapolis

Annapolis,
410-268-8687
Features decorated 18th-century mansions, parade of yachts, private home tours, pub crawls, concerts, holiday meals, First Night celebration, caroling by candlelight at the State House and other events. Call Visitors Bureau for free events calendar. Thanksgiving-January 1.

Maryland Renaissance Festival

1821 Crownsville Rd., Annapolis,
410-266-7304, 800-296-7304;
www.rennfest.com
Food, crafters, minstrels, dramatic productions. Usually last week in August-third weekend in October.

Maryland Seafood Festival

Sandy Point State Park,
1100 E. College Pkwy., Annapolis,
410-266-3113;
www.mdseafoodfestival.com

This family-friendly event offers up hearty portions of Maryland's favorite seafood dishes, including crab cakes, flounder, oysters, clams, trout and shrimp salad. Visitors will enjoy the beauty of the Chesapeake Bay, more than 50 quality arts and crafts exhibitors, and live musical entertainment. Weekend after Labor Day.

U.S. Powerboat Show

100 Severn Ave., Annapolis,
410-268-8828;
www.usboat.com
Extensive in-water display of powerboats; exhibits of related marine products. Mid-October.

U.S. Sailboat Show

100 Severn Ave., Annapolis,
410-268-8828;
www.usboat.com
Features world's largest in-water display of sailboats; exhibits of related marine products. Early-mid-October.

HOTELS

★Best Western Annapolis

2520 Riva Rd., Annapolis,
410-224-2800, 800-780-7234;
www.bestwesternannapolis.com
151 rooms. $

★Gibson's Lodgings

110 Prince George St., Annapolis,
410-268-5555, 877-330-0057;
www.gibsonslodgings.com
21 rooms. Children over 5 years only. Complimentary continental breakfast. $$

★★★Loews Annapolis Hotel

126 West St.,
Annapolis,
410-263-7777, 800-235-6397;
www.loewshotels.com
The Loews Annapolis Hotel offers 217 newly renovated rooms—18 of which are suites—within walking distance of the city's historic sites, with on-site laundry service, a beauty salon and a spa.
217 rooms. Airport transportation available. $$

26

MARYLAND

m o b i l t r a v e l g u i d e . c o m

★★★Marriott Annapolis Waterfront

80 Compromise St., Annapolis,
410-268-7555, 888-773-0786;
www.annapolismarriott.com

Many of the rooms in the Marriott Annapolis Waterfront offer views of the Chesapeake Bay or Annapolis Harbor.
150 rooms. **$$$**

★★★O'Callaghan Hotels

174 West St., Annapolis,
410-263-7700, 800-569-9983;
www.ocallaghanhotels.com

This small, intimate hotel welcomes guests with Irish hospitality and comfortable elegance. Black leather sofas, pale yellow walls and large brass chandeliers give the space a cozy, European touch, making it perfect for couples looking for a weekend getaway.
119 rooms. **$$**

★★★Sheraton Barcelo Annapolis

173 Jennifer Rd., Annapolis,
410-266-3131, 800-325-3535;
www.sheraton.com/annapolis

This warm, contemporary and newly renovated Sheraton hotel is located just outside the downtown area of Annapolis. Guests can take advantage of the hotel's transportation to get to downtown shops and restaurants.
196 rooms. **$**

SPECIALTY LODGINGS

Governor Calvert House

58 State Cir., Annapolis,
410-263-2641, 800-847-8882;
www.annapolisinns.com

Formerly inhabited by two Maryland governors, the Calverts, this tastefully restored colonial and Victorian residence also has a contemporary conference center.
51 rooms. **$$**

Robert Johnson House

23 State Cir., Annapolis,
410-263-2641, 800-847-8882;
www.annapolisinns.com

29 rooms. Consists of 18th-century mansion plus two connecting townhouses of the same period. **$$**

William Page Inn

8 Martin St., Annapolis,
410-626-1506, 800-364-4160;
www.williampageinn.com

Located in the Annapolis historic district, the William Page Inn puts guests within walking distance of shops, restaurants, the U.S. Naval Academy Visitors Center and the waterfront area. Built in 1908, the inn once served as the Democratic Club. It was carefully renovated in 1987.
5 rooms. Closed January. Children over 12 years only. Complimentary full breakfast. **$$**

RESTAURANTS

★★Breeze

126 West St., Annapolis,
410-295-3232;
www.loewsannapolis.com

Seafood, steak menu. Breakfast, lunch, dinner, Sunday brunch. Bar. Children's menu. Valet parking. **$$$**

★★Cafe Normandie

185 Main St., Annapolis,
410-263-3382

French menu. Breakfast, lunch, dinner. Bar. Children's menu. Outdoor seating. **$$$**

★Chick & Ruth's Delly

165 Main St., Annapolis,
410-269-6737;
www.chickandruths.com

American menu. Breakfast, lunch, dinner. Children's menu. Casual attire. **$**

★★Federal House Bar and Grille

22 Market Space, Annapolis,
410-268-2576;
www.federalhouserestaurant.com

Seafood, steak menu. Lunch, dinner, Sunday brunch. Bar. Children's menu. **$$**

★★Harry Browne's

66 State Cir., Annapolis,
410-263-4332;
www.harrybrownes.com

American menu. Lunch, dinner, Sunday brunch. Bar. Business casual attire. Valet parking. Outdoor seating. **$$$**

★Jimmy Cantler's Riverside Inn
458 Forest Beach Rd., Annapolis,
410-757-1311;
www.cantlers.com
Seafood menu. Lunch, dinner. Bar. Children's menu. Casual attire. Outdoor seating. **$$**

★★Lewnes' Steakhouse
401 Fourth St., Annapolis,
410-263-1617;
www.lewessteakhouse.com
Seafood, steak menu. Dinner. Bar. Casual attire. Reservations recommended. **$$$**

★★Middleton Tavern
2 Market Space,
Annapolis,
410-263-3323;
www.middletontavern.com
Seafood menu. Lunch, dinner. Bar. Outdoor seating. **$$$**

★★★Northwoods
609 Melvin Ave., Annapolis,
410-268-2609;
www.northwoodsrestaurant.com

Since 1985, Northwoods has served Italian, Mediterranean and American fare, including beef Wellington, shrimp sorrentina and zuppa de pesce angelico.
Continental menu. Dinner. Closed Monday. Bar. Business casual attire. Outdoor seating. **$$$**

★★O'Leary's Seafood
310 Third St., Annapolis,
410-263-0884;
www.olearysseafood.com
Seafood menu. Dinner. Bar. Children's menu. **$$$**

★★Treaty of Paris
58 State Cir.,
Annapolis,
410-263-2641
French, American menu. Lunch, dinner, Sunday brunch. Bar. Reservations recommended. Valet parking. **$$**

28

ANTIETAM NATIONAL BATTLEFIELD

On September 17, 1862, the bloodiest day in Civil War annals, more than 23,000 men were killed or wounded as Union forces blocked the first Confederate invasion of the North. The Union gained an advantage beforehand, when a soldier accidentally found Lee's orders wrapped around some cigars. Although he knew Lee's tactical game plan, General McClellan moved cautiously. The battle—critical because British aid to the Confederacy depended on the outcome—was a tactical draw but a strategic victory for the North. This victory allowed Lincoln to issue the Emancipation Proclamation, which expanded the war from simply reuniting the country to a crusade to end slavery. The rebels withdrew across the Potomac on the night of September 18, but for some reason McClellan, with twice the manpower, delayed his pursuit. Lincoln relieved him of command of the Army of the Potomac seven weeks later. Clara Barton, who founded the Red Cross 19 years later, tended the wounded at a field hospital on the battlefield.

Approximately 350 iron tablets, monuments and battlefield maps, located on eight miles of paved avenues, describe the events of the battle. The visitor center houses a museum and offers information, literature and a 26-minute orientation movie (shown on the hour). Visitor Center (daily); battlefield (daily); ranger-conducted walks, talks and demonstrations (Memorial Day-Labor Day: daily). For information, 301-432-5124.

BALTIMORE

Baltimore, a city of neighborhoods built on strong ethnic foundations, has achieved an incredible downtown renaissance in the past 20 years. New and renovated sports and entertainment venues have reinvigorated the city. Baseball fans flock to red brick Camden Yards, while football fans come out in force to support the Baltimore Ravens at M&T Bank Stadium. And residents and visitors alike crowd Baltimore's historic Inner Harbor to enjoy its museums, restaurants and nightlife.

Lying midway between the North and South—and enjoying a rich cultural mixture of both—Baltimore is one of the nation's oldest cities. When British troops threatened Philadelphia during the Revolutionary War, the Continental Congress fled to Baltimore, which served as the nation's capital for a little more than two months.

In October 1814, a British fleet attacked the city by land and sea. The defenders of Fort McHenry withstood the naval bombardment for 25 hours until the British gave up. Francis Scott Key saw the huge American flag still flying above the fort and was inspired to pen "The Star-Spangled Banner."

Politics was a preoccupation in the early 19th century, and the city hosted many national party conventions. At least seven presidents and three losing candidates were nominated here. Edgar Allan Poe's mysterious death in the city may have been at the hands of shady electioneers.

A disastrous fire in 1904 destroyed 140 acres of the business district but the city recovered rapidly and during the two World Wars, was a major shipbuilding and naval repair center.

In the 1950s and early 1960s, Baltimore was a victim of the apathy and general urban decay that struck the industrial Northeast. But the city fought back, replacing hundreds of acres of slums, rotting wharves and warehouses with gleaming new office plazas, parks and public buildings. The Inner Harbor was transformed into a huge public area with shops, museums, restaurants and frequent concerts and festivals. Millions of tourists and proud Baltimoreans flock downtown to enjoy the sights and activities.

Famous residents and native sons and daughters include Babe Ruth, Edgar Allan Poe, H. L. Mencken, St. Elizabeth Ann Seton, Ogden Nash, Thurgood Marshall, and sports legends Brooks Robinson, Johnny Unitas, Jim Palmer and Cal Ripken, Jr.

Information: Baltimore Area Convention & Visitors Association,
100 Light St., 12th floor, Baltimore, 410-659-7300, 877-225-8466;
www.baltimore.org

WHAT TO SEE AND DO

American Visionary Art Museum

800 Key Hwy., Baltimore,
410-244-1900;
www.avam.org

This museum defines visionary art as works produced by untrained individuals whose art stems from an inner vision. Opened in 1995, the museum displays more than 4,000 pieces. The main building holds seven indoor galleries. There's also a wildflower garden, a wedding chapel and altar built out of tree limbs and flowers, and a tall sculpture barn, which once showcased psychic Uri Geller's art, including a car he covered with 5,000 forks and spoon allegedly bent psychically. The museum also plans to add a Thou Art Creative Center, an interactive area for visitors. Tuesday-Sunday 10 a.m.-6 p.m.

Antique Row

N. Howard and W. Read Streets,
Baltimore

Antique Row, a Baltimore fixture for over a century, hosts more than 20 dealers and shops, along with restoration services. Shops specialize in items such as European furniture, Tiffany lamps, china and rare books.

The Avenue in Hampden

36th St., Baltimore,
www.hampdenmainstreet.org

Novelty shops, vintage clothing stores, casual restaurants and art galleries line Hampden's main drag, with treasures both kitschy and sublime.

Babe Ruth Birthplace and Museum

301 W. Camden St., Baltimore,
410-727-1539;
www.baberuthmuseum.com

Although Babe Ruth played for the New York Yankees, Baltimore calls him one of its native sons. The house where this legend was born has been transformed into a museum that showcases his life and career. Visitors can see rare family photographs as well as a complete record of his home runs. The museum also features exhibits about the Baltimore Colts and Orioles. Every February 6, the museum commemorates Babe Ruth's birthday by offering free admission to all visitors. April-October: daily 10 a.m.-6 p.m.; to 7:30 p.m. during all Orioles home games; November-March: daily 10 a.m.-5 p.m.

Baltimore & Ohio Railroad Museum

901 W. Pratt St., Baltimore,
410-752-2490;
www.borail.org

This museum, affiliated with the Smithsonian, celebrates the birthplace of railroading in America and depicts the industry's economic and cultural influences. Encompassing 40 acres, the museum's collection of locomotives is the oldest and most comprehensive in the country. In the Roundhouse, visitors can board and explore more than a dozen of the iron horses, which include a rail post office car and the Tom Thumb train. The second floor of the Annex building has an impressive display of working miniature-scale trains. The Mount Clair Station, exhibiting the story of the B & O Railroad, was built in 1851 to replace the 1829 original, which was the first rail depot in the country. Outside, the museum features more trains, such as the "Chessie," the largest steam locomotive. On certain weekends, visitors can take a train ride. Visitor access by appointment only due to renovations. Daily.

Baltimore Maritime Museum

Pier 3 and 5, Pratt St., and Market Place,
Baltimore,
410-396-3453;
www.baltomaritimemuseum.org

This museum's featured ships include the U.S.S. *Torsk,* a World War II submarine; the Coast Guard cutter *Taney;* and the lightship *Chesapeake.* All the ships have been designated National Historic Landmarks. Daily.

Baltimore Museum of Art

10 Art Museum Dr., Baltimore,
410-573-1700;
www.artbma.org

Located near Johns Hopkins University, this museum opened in 1923 and was designed by John Russell Pope, the architect of the National Gallery in Washington, D.C. The museum has eight permanent exhibits featuring works from the periods of Impressionism to modern art. It boasts the second largest collection of works by Andy Warhol. However, its jewel is the Cone collection, which includes more than 3,000 pieces by artists such as Picasso, Van Gogh, Renoir, Czanne and Matisse. The Matisse collection is the largest in the Western Hemisphere. Visitors will also want to see the three-acre sculpture garden, which contains art by Alexander Calder and Henry Moore. Wednesday-Friday 11 a.m.-5 p.m., Saturday-Sunday 11 a.m.-6 p.m. Free admission the first Thursday of each month.

Baltimore Museum of Industry
Inner Harbor South, 1415 Key Hwy.,
Baltimore,
410-727-4808;
www.thebmi.org
This museum educates visitors about the vital role that industry and manufacturing played in Baltimore's economic and cultural development. Located in a renovated oyster cannery on the west side of the Inner Harbor, the museum opened in 1977. Its exhibits showcase trades such as printing, garment making, canning and metalworking. Guests will learn about the invention of Noxema, the disposable bottle cap and even the first umbrella. Monday-Saturday 10 a.m.-4 p.m., Sunday 11 a.m.-4 p.m.; Memorial Day-Labor Day: Monday-Saturday 10 a.m.-4 p.m.

Baltimore Orioles (MLB)
Oriole Park at Camden Yards,
333 W. Camden St.,
Baltimore,
410-685-9800, 888-848-2479;
www.orioles.mlb.com
Professional baseball team.

Baltimore Ravens (NFL)
M&T Bank Stadium, 1101 Russell St.,
Baltimore,
410-261-7283;
www.baltimoreravens.com
Professional football team.

Baltimore Streetcar Museum
1901 Falls Rd., Baltimore,
410-547-0264;
www.baltimoremd.com/streetcar
Eleven electric streetcars and two horse cars used in the city between 1859 and 1963; 1 1/4-mile rides (fee). Sunday noon-5 p.m.; June-October, Saturday noon-5 p.m.

Battle Monument
Calvert and Fayette Streets,
Baltimore
(1815) Memorial to those who fell defending the city in the War of 1812. Climb the 228 steps to the top of the monument for a breathtaking view. Wednesday-Sunday 10 a.m.-4 p.m., first Thursday of every month until 8 p.m.

Charles Center
36 S. Charles St., Baltimore
Bounded by Charles, Liberty, Saratoga and Lombard streets, downtown.
Business area with European-style plazas, part of an overhead walkway system, shops, restaurants and outdoor activities. Prize-winning office building by Mies van der Rohe borders center plaza.

Church Home and Hospital
Broadway and Fairmount Avenues,
East Baltimore
Edgar Allan Poe died here in 1849.

City Court House
100 N. Calvert St., Baltimore
(1900) On the steps is a statue of Cecil Calvert, brother of Leonard and founder of Maryland as the second Lord Baltimore.

City Hall
100 N. Holiday St.,
Baltimore,
410-396-3100
Post-Civil War architecture, restored to original detail. Tours by appointment.

City of Baltimore Conservatory
Druid Hill Park, 2600 Madison Ave.,
Baltimore,
410-396-0180

This graceful building (circa 1885) houses a variety of tropical plants. Special shows during Easter, November and the Christmas season. Thursday-Sunday 10 a.m.-3 p.m.

Clyburn Arboretum
4915 Greenspring Ave., Baltimore,
410-367-2217;
www.cylburnassociation.org
Marked nature trails. Nature museum, ornithological room, horticultural library in a restored mansion; shade and formal gardens, All-American Selection Garden, Garden of the Senses. Grounds are open from dawn to dusk; Mansion Monday-Friday 7:30 a.m.-3:30 p.m.; Museums Tuesday, Thursday 1-3 p.m.

Duckpin Bowling
Throughout the city.
No ducks on the lanes, just smaller pins and balls in this game designed in Baltimore back in 1900. Alleys are open throughout Baltimore, including at Taylor's Stoneleigh Duckpin Bowling Center, 6703 York Rd., 410-377-8115.

Edgar Allan Poe Grave
Westminster Hall and Burial Grounds,
519 W. Fayette St., Baltimore,
410-706-2072
Baltimore's oldest cemeteries also contain the graves of many prominent early Marylanders. Westminster Burying Ground and Catacomb tours by appointment. April-November: first and third Friday and Saturday.

Edgar Allan Poe House and Museum
203 N. Amity St., Baltimore,
410-396-7932;
www.ci.baltimore.md.us/government/historic/poehouse.html
The famed author and father of the macabre lived in this house from 1832 to 1835. Haunted or not, the house and museum scare up many Poe artifacts, such as period furniture, a desk and telescope owned by Poe, and Gustave Dore's illustrations of "The Raven." Around January 19, the museum hosts a birthday celebration that includes readings and theatrical performances

of Poe's work. April-early December: Wednesday-Saturday noon-3:45 p.m.

Enoch Pratt Free Library
400 Cathedral St., Baltimore,
410-396-5430;
www.pratt.lib.md.us
City's public library. Includes H.L. Mencken and Edgar Allan Poe collections. Monday-Wednesday 11 a.m.-7 p.m., Thursday 10 a.m.-5:30 p.m., Friday-Saturday to 5 p.m.; also Sunday 1-5 p.m. from October-May.

Federal Hill
Charles and Cross Streets,
Baltimore
Bordered by Hughes St., Key Highway, Hanover St. and Cross St. Inner Harbor area. View of the city harbor and skyline. Named after a celebration that occurred here in 1788 to mark Maryland's ratification of the Constitution.

Fell's Point
Visitor's Center, 808 S. Ann St.,
Baltimore,
410-675-6750;
www.fellspoint.us
Shipbuilding and maritime center, this neighborhood dates back to 1730; approximately 350 original residential structures. Working tugboats and tankers can be observed from the docks.

First Unitarian Church
Charles and Franklin Streets,
Baltimore,
410-685-2330;
www.firstunitarian.net
(1817) William Ellery Channing preached a sermon here that hastened the establishment of the Unitarian denomination. Example of Classic Revival architecture.

Flag House & Star-Spangled Banner Museum
844 E. Pratt St., Baltimore,
410-837-1793;
www.flaghouse.org
Open to the public for over 75 years, this museum was the home of Mary Pickersgill,

★
★
★
★
★

who sewed the flag that Francis Scott Key eternalized in America's national anthem. Although the flag now hangs in the Smithsonian's National Museum of American History, visitors can tour the house to learn about its origins and Pickersgill's life. The house has an adjoining War of 1812 museum, which exhibits military and domestic artifacts and presents an award-winning video. Tuesday-Saturday 10 a.m.-4 p.m.

Fort McHenry National Monument and Historic Shrine

End of E. Fort Ave., Baltimore,
410-962-4290;
www.nps.gov/fomc

Fort McHenry boasts a stunning view of the harbor, authentic re-created structures and a wealth of living history. Not only was it the site of the battle that inspired Francis Scott Key to pen the national anthem in 1814, but the fort was also a defensive position during the Revolutionary War, a P.O.W. camp for Confederate prisoners during the Civil War and an army hospital during World War I. Summer weekends feature precision drill and music performed by volunteers in Revolutionary War uniforms. Labor Day-Memorial Day: daily 8 a.m.-4:45 p.m.; Memorial Day-Labor Day: daily 8 a.m.-7:45 p.m.

Harbor Cruises

301 Light St., Baltimore
Depart from Inner Harbor.

Minnie V Harbor Tours

Baltimore,
410-685-9062

Docks near Pier 1, Pratt St., Inner Harbor area. A 45-foot Chesapeake Bay skipjack sloop built in 1906. Ninety-minute harbor tours give 24 passengers the opportunity to help crew the boat (open summer weekends).

MV Lady Baltimore

561 Light St., Baltimore,
410-727-3113, 800-695-5239;
www.harborcruises.com

West Bulkhead. Round-trip cruises to Annapolis (June-August: Wednesday); also

cruises to the Chesapeake & Delaware Canal (three selected Sundays in October). *Bay Lady* has lunch and dinner cruises. April-October: daily; limited schedule rest of year.

Harborplace

200 E. Pratt St., Baltimore,
410-332-4191;
www.harborplace.com

This shopping mecca boasts more than 130 stores and restaurants. Visitors who want to take a break can go outside and walk on the brick-paved promenade that runs along the water's edge. Harborplace also has a small outdoor amphitheater, where in good weather, guests are treated to free performances by jugglers, musicians, singers and military and concert bands. Daily.

Holocaust Memorial

Water, Gay and Lombard Streets,
Baltimore

A simple marble slab memorial to the victims of the Holocaust.

Jewish Museum of Maryland

15 Lloyd St., Baltimore,
410-732-6400;
www.jhsm.org

Buildings include Lloyd St. Synagogue (1845), the oldest in Maryland; B'nai Israel Synagogue (1876); and the Jewish Museum of Maryland. Tuesday-Thursday, Sunday noon-4 p.m. or by appointment; closed Jewish holidays. Research archives. Monday-Friday, by appointment.

Johns Hopkins Medical Institutions

600 N. Wolf St., Baltimore,
410-955-5000;
www.hopkinsmedicine.org

(1889) Widely known as a leading medical school, research center and teaching hospital. Victorian buildings.

Peabody Institute of the Johns Hopkins University

1 E. Mount Vernon Place,
Baltimore

33

MARYLAND

★
★
★
★
★

(1857) 550 students. Music conservatory founded by philanthropist George Peabody; now affiliated with Johns Hopkins. Research and reference collection in library accessible to the public (Monday-Friday). The Miriam A. Friedberg Concert Hall seats 800. Orchestral, recital and opera performances.

Johns Hopkins University
3400 N. Charles St., Baltimore,
410-516-8000;
www.jhu.edu
Founded in 1876 and located in northern Baltimore, Johns Hopkins enrolls 18,000 students and is renowned for the Bloomberg School of Public Health, the Peabody Institute (a music conservatory) and its Applied Physics Laboratory, located 30 minutes outside of Baltimore. *US News & World Report* continuously ranks its affiliated hospital, which has its own separate campus in eastern Baltimore, as one of the top medical facilities in the country.
On grounds are:

Bufano Sculpture Garden
3400 N. Charles St., Baltimore
A wooded retreat with animals sculpted by artist Beniamino Bufano.

Evergreen House
4545 N. Charles St., Baltimore,
410-516-0341
On 26 wooded acres; features Classical Revival architecture and a formal garden. Library (35,000 volumes). Post-impressionist paintings, Japanese and Chinese collections and Tiffany glass. Tours (Tuesday-Sunday).

Homewood House Museum
3400 N. Charles St.,
Baltimore,
410-516-5589
(1801) Former country home of Charles Carroll, Jr., whose father was a signer of the Declaration of Independence; period furnishings. Guided tours every half hour. Tuesday-Friday 11 a.m.-4 p.m., Saturday-Sunday noon-4 p.m.

Joseph Meyerhoff Symphony Hall
1212 Cathedral St., Baltimore,
410-783-8000, 877-276-1444;
www.baltimoresymphony.org
Permanent residence of the Baltimore Symphony Orchestra.

Lacrosse Hall of Fame Museum
113 W. University Parkway,
Baltimore,
410-235-6882;
www.lacrosse.org/museum
Team trophies, lacrosse artifacts and memorabilia, including rare photographs and art, vintage equipment and uniforms. Also historical video documentary. February-May: Tuesday-Saturday 10 a.m.-3 p.m.; June-January: Monday-Friday 10 a.m.-3 p.m.

Lexington Market
400 W. Lexington St.,
Baltimore,
410-685-6169;
www.lexingtonmarket.com
This under-roof market is more than two centuries old. Covering two blocks, it has more than 130 stalls offering fresh vegetables, seafood, meats, baked goods and prepared foods. Vendors outside the market sell clothing, jewelry, T-shirts and other items. Throughout the year, the market hosts several events, such as the Chocolate Festival in October, which boasts free samples and a chocolate-eating contest. But the most anticipated event at the market is Lunch with the Elephants. Every March, Ringling Brothers and Barnum & Bailey Circus elephants parade up Eutaw Street accompanied by fanfare, live music and clowns. When they finally reach the market, they are served lunch, which consists of 1,100 oranges, 1,000 apples, 500 heads of lettuce, 700 bananas, 400 pears and 500 carrots. Monday-Saturday 8:30 a.m.-6 p.m.

Lovely Lane Museum
The Lovely Lane United Methodist Church,
2200 St. Paul St., Baltimore,
410-889-4458;
www.lovelylanemuseum.com

Permanent and changing exhibits of items of Methodist church history since 1760. Guided tours. Thursday-Friday.

Maryland Historical Society
201 W. Monument St.,
Baltimore,
410-685-3750;
www.mdhs.org
The state's oldest cultural institution includes a library, a museum and even a small press that promotes scholarship about Maryland's history and material culture. The library has more than 5.4 million works and is a valuable resource for genealogists. The society's collection of historical artifacts includes the original draft of "The Star Spangled Banner." Museum: Wednesday-Sunday 10 a.m.-5 p.m.; to 8 p.m. the first Thursday of every month. History and Genealogy Reading Room: Wednesday-Saturday 10 a.m.-4:30 p.m. Special Collections Reading Room: Wednesday-Friday 10 a.m.-4:30 p.m.; also open to the public on the third Saturday of every month.

Maryland Institute, College of Art
1300 Mount Royal Ave.,
Baltimore,
410-669-9200;
www.mica.edu
(1826) (880 students) Institute hosts frequent contemporary art exhibitions. Campus distinguished by recycled buildings and white marble Italianate main building. Daily.

Maryland Science Center & Davis Planetarium
601 Light St.,
Baltimore,
410-685-5225;
www.mdsci.org
Located in the Inner Harbor, the three-story building contains hundreds of exhibits guaranteed to spark young (and old) minds. In the Chesapeake Bay exhibit, you can learn about the bay's delicate ecosystem. Or you can explore the mysteries of the human body in BodyLink. The Kids Room, for guests eight and younger, gives children the chance to operate a fish camera or dress up like turtles. Don't miss the Hubble Space Telescope National Visitor Center, a 4,000-square-foot interactive space gallery with 120 high-resolution images that allow guests to see space through the Hubble's eye. Labor Day-Memorial Day: Tuesday-Friday 10 a.m.-5 p.m., Saturday 10 a.m.-6 p.m., Sunday noon-5 p.m.; rest of year: Sunday-Wednesday 10 a.m.-6 p.m., Thursday-Saturday until 8 p.m. IMAX theater is open later.

Maryland Zoo
1 Druid Hill Park Lake Dr.,
Baltimore,
410-366-5466;
www.marylandzoo.org
Located in Druid Hill Park, the third-oldest zoo in the United States covers 180 acres and features more than 2,250 animals. Children can visit the giraffes and elephants in the African Safari exhibit, as well as ride the carousel or try out the climbing wall. The zoo also hosts special events during Halloween and Christmas. March-December daily 10 a.m.-4 p.m.

Morgan State University
1700 E. Cold Spring Lane,
Baltimore,
443-885-3333;
www.morgan.edu
(1867) (5,100 students) The James E. Lewis Museum of Art has changing exhibits. Monday-Friday; weekends by appointment.

Mother Seton House
600 N. Paca St.,
Baltimore,
410-523-3443;
www.nps.gov/history/nr/travel/baltimore/b13.htm
Home of St. Elizabeth Ann Bayley Seton from 1808 to 1809. Here she established the forerunner of the parochial school system, as well as an order of nuns that eventually became the Daughters & Sisters of Charity in the U.S. and Canada. Saturday-Sunday 1-3 p.m., also by appointment.

★
★
★
★
★

Mount Clare Museum House
1500 Washington Blvd.,
Baltimore,
410-837-3262;
www.cr.nps.gov/nr/travel/baltimore/b2.htm
(1760) Oldest mansion in Baltimore, former
home of Charles Carroll, barrister. Eighteenth-
and 19th-century furnishings. Guided tours on
the hour. Tuesday-Saturday 10 a.m.-4 p.m.;
closed January.

Mount Vernon Place United Methodist Church
10 E. Mount Vernon Place, Baltimore,
410-685-5290
(Circa 1850) Brownstone with balcony and
grillwork extending the entire width of the
house; spiral staircase suspended from three
floors; library with century-old painting on
the ceiling; drawing room. Daily; closed the
Monday after Easter.

National Aquarium
501 E. Pratt St., Baltimore,
410-576-3800;
www.aqua.org
The National Aquarium introduces guests
to stingrays, sharks, puffins, seals and a
giant Pacific octopus. Visitors can explore
the danger and mystery of a living South
American tropical rain forest complete
with poisonous frogs, exotic birds, piranha
and swinging tamarin monkeys, or delight
in the underwater beauty of the replicated
Atlantic coral reef. The Children's Cove, a
touch pool, provides an interactive experience for kids. Feeding schedules are posted
in the lobby. Daily.
    Visitors cross an enclosed skywalk to
reach the adjacent wing, which houses:

Marine Mammal Pavilion
501 E. Pratt St., Baltimore,
410-576-3800
This unique structure features a 1,300-seat
amphitheater surrounding a 1.2-million-
gallon pool that houses Atlantic bottlenose
dolphins; underwater viewing areas enable
visitors to observe the mammals from
below the surface. The Discovery Room
houses a collection of marine artifacts,

the Resource Center is an aquatic learning
center for school visitors and the library
boasts an extensive collection of marine
science material. Daily.

Old Otterbein United Methodist Church
112 W. Conway St., Baltimore,
410-685-4703;
www.oldotterbein.com
(1785-1786) Fine Georgian architecture;
mother church of United Brethren. Tours of
historic building (Saturday-Sunday).

Old Town Mall
414 N. Gay St., Baltimore
This 150-year-old, brick-lined commercial
area has been beautifully refurbished; it's
closed to vehicular traffic.
Nearby is:

Stirling Street
1000 block of Monument Street
First community urban "homesteading"
venture in the U.S. Renovated homes date
to the 1830s. Original facades have been
maintained; interior rehabilitation ranges in
style from the antique to the avant garde.

Otterbein "Homesteading"
Area around S. Sharp St., Inner Harbor area
The original neighborhood dates back to
1785. Houses have been restored.

Patterson Park
200 S. Linwood Ave., Baltimore,
410-396-3932;
www.pattersonpark.com
Defenses here helped stop the British attack
in 1814. Breastworks and artillery pieces
are displayed.

Port Discovery
35 Market Place, Baltimore,
410-727-8120;
www.portdiscovery.org
Opened in 1998 in collaboration with Walt
Disney Imagineering, Port Discovery has
been ranked the fourth best children's
museum in the country by *Child* magazine. Kids will have a blast exploring the
three-story urban tree house. In MPT

36

MARYLAND

★
★
★
★
★

Studioworks, they can become producers of their own television broadcasts. The museum also operates the HiFlyer, a giant helium balloon anchored 450 feet above the Inner Harbor. The enclosed gondola holds 20 to 25 passengers and offers a spectacular view of the city. October-May: Tuesday-Friday 9:30 a.m.-4:30 p.m., Saturday 10 a.m.-5 p.m., Sunday noon-5 p.m.; Memorial Day-Labor Day: Monday-Saturday 10 a.m.-5 p.m., Sunday noon-5 p.m.

Power Plant
601 E. Pratt St., Baltimore,
410-752-5444
This commercial complex was once a power plant owned by Baltimore Gas & Electric. The renovated plant now houses a two-story Barnes & Noble bookstore, a Hard Rock Café and the original ESPN Zone, a 35,000-square-foot sports-themed restaurant and arcade.

Public Works Museum & Streetscape
Pier 7, 751 Eastern Ave., Baltimore,
410-396-5565
Museum exhibits the history and artifacts of public works. Located in a historic sewage pumping station. Streetscape sculpture outside depicts the various utility lines and ducts under a typical city street, in a walk-through model. Tuesday-Sunday 10 a.m.-4 p.m.

Sail Baltimore
1809 Thames St., Baltimore,
410-522-7300;
www.sailbaltimore.org
Sail Baltimore, a nonprofit organization, informs the public about a variety of citywide boating events that take place throughout the year. Its Web site provides an updated schedule of the different boats and ships that will be visiting the Inner Harbor. It also hosts the Great Chesapeake Bay Schooner Race in October, among other seasonal events.

Senator Theatre
5904 York Rd., North Baltimore,
410-435-8338;
www.senator.com
Movie buffs will appreciate the charm and history of the Senator, which *USA Today* rated as one of the top theaters in the country. Showing first-run, independent and classic films, the theater seats 900 and has a 40-foot-wide screen. Listed on the National Register of Historic Places, its architecture is elegant Art Deco. The theater recently added its own mini Walk of Fame outside its entrance.

Sherwood Gardens
Stratford Rd., and Greenway,
Baltimore,
410-785-0444
More than six acres in size, the gardens reach their peak of splendor in late April and early May, when thousands of tulips, azaleas and flowering shrubs bloom. Daily dawn-dusk.

Top of the World
World Trade Center, 401 E. Pratt St.,
Baltimore,
410-837-8439
Observation deck and museum on the 27th floor of the World Trade Center, which was designed by I. M. Pei. Exhibits describe the city's history, famous residents and the activities of the port. September-Memorial Day: Wednesday-Sunday; Memorial Day-Labor Day: daily.

University of Maryland at Baltimore
520 W. Lombard St., Baltimore,
410-706-3100;
www.umaryland.edu
5,476 students. The 32-acre downtown campus includes six professional schools; the University of Maryland Medical System and the Graduate School. Davidge Hall (1812) is the oldest medical teaching building in continuous use in the western hemisphere.

USS *Constellation*
301 E. Pratt St., Pier 1, Baltimore,
410-539-1797;
www.constellation.org
This retired sloop, anchored at Pier 1 in the Inner Harbor, has a proud naval history that spans from the Civil War to World War II.

37

MARYLAND

★
★
★
★
★

Visitors can board the ship for a self-guided audio tour. Kids can participate in the Powder Monkey program, in which they learn what it was like to serve in President Lincoln's navy. June-mid-August: daily 10 a.m.-6 p.m.; mid-September-April: daily 10 a.m.-4:30 p.m. Extended hours may be available June-August.

Vagabond Players
806 S. Broadway, Baltimore,
410-563-9135;
www.vagabondplayers.com
Oldest continuously operating "little theater" in the U.S. Recent Broadway shows, revivals and original scripts are performed. Early June-early July Friday-Sunday.

Walters Art Museum
600 N. Charles St., Baltimore,
410-547-9000;
www.thewalters.org
This museum's collection traces the history of the world from ancient times to the present day. Father and son William and Henry Walters gave the museum and its numerous holdings to Baltimore, though the New York Metropolitan Museum of Art also coveted it. With more than 30,000 pieces of art, the collection is renowned for its French paintings and Renaissance and Asian art. The museum also exhibits Faberge eggs, paintings by Raphael and El Greco, and an impressive assortment of ivories and Art Deco jewelry. Visitors will also want to check out the unique Roman sarcophagus. Wednesday-Sunday 10 a.m.-5 p.m.

Washington Monument
600 Charles St., Baltimore,
410-396-1049
(1815-1842) The first major monument to honor George Washington. There's a museum in the base; view the city from the top. Other monuments nearby honor Lafayette, Chief Justice Roger Brooke Taney, philanthropist George Peabody, lawyer Severn Teackle Wallis and Revolutionary War hero John Eager Howard.

SPECIAL EVENTS
American Craft Council Baltimore-Winter Show
Convention Center, 1 W. Pratt St.,
Baltimore,
410-649-7000, 800-836-3470;
www.craftcouncil.org
Craft festival features the works of nearly 800 artisans, with crafts ranging from clay and glass to furniture and toys. Three-day weekend in late February.

Artscape
1200 block of Mount Royal Ave.,
Baltimore,
877-225-8466;
www.artscape.org
This festival celebrates the area's abundance of visual, literary and performing arts. The three-day event takes place in the cultural corridor of the city's Bolton Hill neighborhood. It features live music performances, poetry and fiction readings by regional writers, and even a one-act opera. The Artists' Market exhibits and sells the work of more than 140 artists. The festival includes a wide variety of activities for children, which in the past have included a youth Shakespearean performance and an interactive art tent. Mid-July. Friday-Saturday noon-10 p.m., Sunday noon-8 p.m.

Cockpit in Court Summer Theatre
Essex Community College,
7201 Rossville Blvd., Baltimore,
410-780-6369
Theater in residence at Essex Community College. Four separate theaters offer a diverse collection of plays, including Broadway productions, contemporary drama, revues and Shakespeare. Mid-June-mid-August.

Maryland Film Festival
107 E. Read St., Baltimore,
410-752-8083;
www.mdfilmfest.com
Since 1999, this four-day festival has become a premier cinema event for Baltimore, presenting more than 120 foreign,

domestic and short films throughout the city's movie houses, including the famous Senator Theatre. Most screenings are followed by a discussion with the film's director or producer. The festival has also hosted films for children, such as a silent version of "Peter Pan" accompanied by an orchestra. Late April or early May.

Pier 6 Concert Pavilion
731 Eastern Ave., Pier 6, Baltimore,
www.piersixpavilion.com
Summertime outdoor concerts and plays at the water's edge. Some covered seating. June-September. Evenings.

Pimlico Race Course
5201 Park Heights Ave., Baltimore,
410-542-9400;
www.marylandracing.com
Home to the world-famous Preakness Stakes, this track features a 70-foot-wide and one-mile-long track, more than 750 betting windows, and a clubhouse and two grandstands that can accommodate more than 13,000 people. August.

Preakness Stakes and Celebration Week
Pimlico Race Course,
5201 Park Heights Ave.,
Baltimore,
410-542-9400, 877-206-8042;
www.preaknesscelebration.org
The Preakness Stakes, the second jewel in horse racing's Triple Crown, is a time-honored tradition in Baltimore. On the third Saturday in May, nearly 100,000 people from Maryland and around the world gather at the Pimlico Race Course. Celebration festivities begin one week before the race, with activities that include a parade, a hot-air balloon festival, outdoor concerts, boat races and 5K and 10K runs. On race day, the Preakness is the second-to-last race and begins at around 5:30 p.m. Visitors looking for a good value and an eye-level view of the horses should reserve seats in the infield. Those willing to spend more money—and dress more formally—should choose seats in the clubhouse or grandstand.

Showcase of Nations Ethnic Festivals
7 E. Redwood St., Suite 500,
Baltimore,
877-225-8466
Presenting the food, music and crafts of a different culture each weekend. June-October.

Taste of Baltimore
Camden Yards, 333 W. Camden St.,
Baltimore,
888-848-2473;
www.tasteofbaltimore.com
Dozens of restaurants set up shop in the ballpark to offer hungry attendees samples of their finest dishes, from Polish sausage and cheesesteak to pizza and Italian ice. Part of the proceeds from the event go to the Children's Cancer Foundation. Live music and family activities provide entertainment between bites. Mid-September.

HOTELS
★★Admiral Fell Inn
888 S. Broadway,
Baltimore,
410-522-7380, 866-583-4162;
www.harbormagic.com
80 rooms. Check-in 4 p.m. $$

★Celie's Waterfront Inn
1714 Thames St.,
Baltimore,
410-522-2323, 800-432-0184;
www.celieswaterfront.com
9 rooms. Complimentary continental breakfast. $$

★★Clarion Hotel Peabody Court
612 Cathedral St.,
Baltimore,
410-727-7101, 800-292-5500;
www.peabodycourthotel.com
104 rooms. $$

★★Days Inn Inner Harbor Hotel
100 Hopkins Place, Baltimore,
410-576-1000, 800-329-7466;
www.daysinnerharbor.com
250 rooms. $$

★★★Hyatt Regency Baltimore on the Inner Harbor

300 Light St., Baltimore,
410-528-1234, 800-233-1234;
www.baltimore.hyatt.com

Conveniently located across the street from Baltimore's Inner Harbor, this hotel is linked by a skywalk to the convention center and shopping at Harborplace. It is also situated within minutes of the National Aquarium, Maryland Science Center and Oriole Park. Guest rooms are decorated with off-white wall coverings resembling white leather, white bedding with gold accents and marble bathrooms. In addition to a rooftop pool and a huge fitness center, amenities include a basketball half-court, putting green and jogging track, along with 29,000 square feet of meeting space.
488 rooms. $$$

★Inn at Henderson's Wharf

1000 Fell St., Baltimore,
410-522-7777, 800-522-2088;
www.hendersonswharf.com
37 rooms. Complimentary full breakfast. $$

★★Inn at the Colonnade

4 W. University Pkwy., Baltimore,
410-235-5400, 800-222-8733;
www.colonnadebaltimore.com
125 rooms. $$

★★★InterContinental Harbor Court Hotel

550 Light St., Baltimore,
410-234-0550, 800-496-7621;
www.intercontinental.com/baltimore

The InterContinental Harbor Court Hotel, located across the street from the Inner Harbor and Harborplace, re-creates the spirit of a grand English manor home. Guest rooms offer views of the harbor or the garden on the courtside. The professional staff attends to every need, even offering hot, buttery popcorn for guests enjoying in-room movies. The hotel has a fitness center and yoga studio for athletic-minded guests.
195 rooms. $$

★★★Marriott Baltimore Waterfront

700 Aliceanna St.,
Baltimore,
410-385-3000, 800-228-9290;
www.baltimoremarriottwaterfront.com

With large rooms offering stunning views of the harbor to amenities, this hotel puts you in the center of Baltimore's Inner Harbor. Walk (or take a water taxi) to some of the city's premier tourist destinations: Little Italy, Pier 6 Concert Pavilion or Harborplace.
751 rooms. $$$

★★★Renaissance Harborplace Hotel

202 E. Pratt St.,
Baltimore,
410-547-1200, 800-535-1201;
www.renaissancehotels.com/bwish

This hotel adjoins the upscale Gallery mall, with four floors of shopping and dining. Nearby attractions include the National Aquarium, the Baltimore Convention Center and Ride the Ducks of Baltimore. Many guest rooms offer views of the harbor.
622 rooms. $$$

★★Tremont Park Hotel

8 E. Pleasant St.,
Baltimore,
410-576-1200, 800-873-6668;
www.1800tremont.com
58 rooms, all suites. Complimentary continental breakfast. $$

RESTAURANTS

★The Bayou Cafe

8133-A Honeygo Blvd.,
Baltimore,
410-931-2583;
www.thebayoucafe.com
American, Cajun menu. Lunch, dinner, Sunday brunch. Bar. Children's menu. Casual attire. Outdoor seating. $$

MARYLAND

★Bertha's
734 S. Broadway, Baltimore,
410-327-5795;
www.berthas.com
Seafood menu. Lunch, dinner. Bar. Children's menu. Casual attire. **$$**

★★★Black Olive
814 S. Bond St., Baltimore,
410-276-7141;
www.theblackolive.com
This Mediterranean restaurant (formerly Fells Point's General Store) has retained the building's original hardwood floors and brick archways. The restaurant also offers outdoor dining under a grape arbor. The food here is organic, and fresh fish is displayed in front of the open kitchen. Each fish entree is filleted tableside. The carrot cake is a perfect finale. Mediterranean, seafood menu. Lunch, dinner. Bar. Children's menu. Business casual attire. Reservations recommended. Valet parking. Outdoor seating. **$$$**

★★★Boccaccio
925 Eastern Ave., Baltimore,
410-234-1322;
www.boccaccio-restaurant.com
This Little Italy restaurant's specialty is classic Northern Italian fare. Specials change on a seasonal basis to reflect the chef's fresh, locally obtained ingredients. Italian menu. Lunch, dinner. Bar. Business casual attire. Reservations recommended. Valet parking. **$$$**

★★Brasserie Tatin
105 W. 39th St., Baltimore,
443-278-9110;
www.brasserietatin.com
French menu. Lunch, dinner. Bar. Business casual attire. Reservations recommended. Outdoor seating. **$$**

★Cafe Hon
1002 W. 36th St., Baltimore,
410-243-1230;
www.cafehon.com
American menu. Breakfast, lunch, dinner, brunch. Bar. Children's menu. Casual attire. **$$**

★★★★Charleston
1000 Lancaster St., Baltimore,
410-332-7373;
www.charlestonrestaurant.com
Chef/owner Cindy Wolf's regional American/French restaurant serves up dishes such as sauteed heads-on Gulf shrimp with andouille sausage and Tasso ham with creamy stone-milled grits. The restaurant also has an impressive wine program that includes several dozen sparkling wines and a selection of about 600 well-chosen whites and reds from the New World (Australia, South Africa, New Zealand and Chile) and the Old (France, Italy and Spain). Charleston also offers more than a dozen microbrews and imported beers.
American, French menu. Dinner. Closed Sunday. Bar. Business casual attire. Reservations recommended. Valet parking. Outdoor seating. **$$$**

★★★Della Notte
801 Eastern Ave., Baltimore,
410-837-5500;
www.dellanotte.com
A popular spot, Della Notte's interior is replete with faux white brick walls covered with murals and busts of Roman emperors. The menu offers a selection of antipasti, fish, meats and daily specials, along with a vast wine list of more than 1,400 selections. After dinner, settle into the Emperor's Lounge with an after-dinner drink and enjoy the live entertainment offered seven days a week.
Italian menu. Lunch, dinner. Bar. Business casual attire. Reservations recommended. Valet parking. **$$$**

★★Germano's Trattoria
300 S. High St., Baltimore,
410-752-4515;
www.germanostrattoria.com
Italian menu. Lunch, dinner. Bar. Casual attire. Reservations recommended. Valet parking. **$$**

★★The Helmand
806 N. Charles St., Baltimore,
410-752-0311;
www.helmand.com

MARYLAND

Middle Eastern menu. Dinner. Bar. Business casual attire. Reservations recommended. **$$**

★★★Ixia
518 N. Charles St., Baltimore,
410-727-1800;
www.ixia-online.com
This eclectic, international restaurant serves entrees such as rockfish and lump crabcake or French "moulard" confit. The lounge offers jazz on Friday nights.
International menu. Dinner. Closed Sunday-Monday. Bar. Business casual attire. Reservations recommended. **$$$**

★★John Steven, Ltd.
1800 Thames St., Baltimore,
410-327-0489;
www.johnstevenltd.com
Seafood menu. Lunch, dinner. Bar. Children's menu. Casual attire. Reservations recommended. Outdoor seating. **$$$**

★★La Scala
1012 Eastern Ave., Baltimore,
410-783-9209;
www.lascaladining.com
Italian menu. Dinner. Bar. Business casual attire. Reservations recommended. Valet parking. **$$**

★★Mt. Washington Tavern
5700 Newbury St., Baltimore,
410-367-6903;
www.mtwashingtontavern.com
American menu. Lunch, dinner, Sunday brunch. Four bars. **$$$**

★★Obrycki's Crab House
1727 E. Pratt St., Baltimore,
410-732-6399;
www.obryckis.com
Seafood menu. Lunch, dinner. Closed mid-November-mid-March. Bar. Children's menu. Casual attire. Reservations recommended. **$$**

★★★The Oceanaire Seafood Room
801 Aliceanna St.,
Baltimore,
443-872-0000;
www.theoceanaire.com
The restaurant's upscale decor features hardwood floors, rich cherry wood accents, wood blinds and leather. The menu changes daily, since seafood is the specialty and the restaurant has it flown and trucked in daily. Diners can choose how they would like their fish prepared—grilled, broiled, sauteed, steamed or fried.
Seafood menu. Dinner. Bar. Business casual attire. Reservations recommended. Valet parking. **$$$**

★★★Pazo
1425 Aliceanna, Baltimore,
410-534-7296;
www.pazorestaurant.com
Group dining is popular, with diners ordering multiple tapas entrees to share. The restaurant's soft lighting, wood tables, soaring high ceilings and wrought-iron accents make it a romantic spot.
Mediterranean, tapas menu. Dinner. Bar. Casual attire. Valet parking. **$$$**

★★Pierpoint
1822 Aliceanna St., Baltimore,
410-675-2080;
www.pierpointrestaurant.com
American menu. Lunch, dinner, brunch. Closed Monday. Bar. Business casual attire. Reservations recommended. **$$**

★★★The Prime Rib
1101 N. Calvert St., Baltimore,
410-539-1804;
www.theprimerib.com
The Prime Rib has been serving consistently good steaks, chops and seafood since 1965. With black walls, candlelit tables and tuxedoed wait staff, it's known as "the civilized steakhouse."
America, steak menu. Dinner. Bar. Jacket required. Reservations recommended. Valet parking. **$$$**

★★★Ruth's Chris Steak House
600 Water St., Baltimore,
410-783-0033;
www.ruthschris.com
Born from a single New Orleans restaurant that Ruth Fertel bought in 1965 for

42

MARYLAND

$22,000, the Ruth's Chris Steak House chain has made it to the top of every steak lover's list. Aged prime Midwestern beef is broiled to your liking and served on a heated plate, sizzling in butter. Sides such as creamed spinach and fresh asparagus with hollandaise are not to be missed. Choose from seven different potato preparations, from a one-pound baked potato with everything to au gratin potatoes with cream sauce and topped with cheese.

Steak menu. Dinner. Bar. Business casual attire. Reservations recommended. Valet parking. **$$$**

★★Sotto Sopra
405 N. Charles St., Baltimore,
410-625-0534;
www.sottosoprainc.com
Italian menu. Lunch, dinner. Bar. Business casual attire. Reservations recommended. Valet parking. Outdoor seating. **$$**

★★Tapas Teatro
1711 N. Charles St., Baltimore,
410-332-0110;
www.tapasteatro.net
Mediterranean, Spanish, Tapas menu. Dinner. Closed Monday Bar. Casual attire. Outdoor seating. **$$**

BALTIMORE/WASHINGTON INTERNATIONAL (BWI) AIRPORT AREA

HOTELS
★★Embassy Suites
1300 Concourse Dr., Linthicum,
410-850-0747, 800-362-2779;
www.embassy-suites.com
251 rooms, all suites. Complimentary full breakfast. Airport transportation available. **$$**

★★★Four Points By Sheraton BWI Airport
7032 Elm Rd., Baltimore,
410-859-3300, 800-368-7764;
www.fourpoints.com
Whether you are homeward bound or heading out for business or pleasure, this hotel at Baltimore's major airport can be your stepping stone to your final destination. City attractions, such as the Inner Harbor, Camden Yards and Laurel Racecourse, are less than 20 minutes away.
201 rooms. Airport transportation available. **$$**

★Hampton Inn
829 Elkridge Landing Rd., Linthicum,
410-850-0600, 800-426-7866;
www.hamptoninnbwiairport.com
182 rooms. Complimentary continental breakfast. Airport transportation available. **$**

★★★Marriott Baltimore Washington International Airport
1743 W. Nursery Rd., Linthicum,
410-859-8300, 800-228-9290;
www.marriott.com
310 rooms. Airport transportation available. **$$**

BELTSVILLE

HOTELS
★★★Sheraton College Park
4095 Powder Mill Rd., Beltsville,
301-937-4422, 800-325-3535;
www.sheraton.com
205 rooms. **$**

BERLIN

WHAT TO SEE AND DO

Assateague Island National Seashore
7206 National Seashore Lane, Berlin,
410-641-1441, 800-365-2267;
www.nps.gov/asis
Visitors interested in sandy beaches and wildlife should visit Assateague Island, which is about a four-hour drive from Baltimore. Straddling Maryland and Virginia, it contains a state park and a wildlife refuge, with swimming, hiking, canoeing, sea kayaking, biking and camping on the beach, and some of the best surf-fishing on the Atlantic Coast. Guests also come to see the wild horses. According to legend, the horses, which are only the size of ponies, swam to the island from a shipwrecked Spanish galleon. On every last Wednesday and Thursday in July, the world-famous Pony Penning event occurs. During this event, the horses swim from the Maryland side of the island to the Virginia side with a crowd of spectators cheering them on. The visitor center offers more information about the horses as well as the seashores many activities. Daily.
Also on the island is:

Assateague State Park
7307 Stephen Decatur Hwy., Berlin,
410-641-2120, 888-432-2267
Has 755 acres with two miles of ocean frontage and gentle, sloping beaches. Swimming, fishing, boat launch; picnicking, concession (summer), bicycle and hiking trails, camping. April-October.

SPECIAL EVENTS

Harness Racing
Ocean Downs, 10218 Racetrack Rd.,
Berlin,
410-641-0600;
www.oceandowns.com
Nightly Tuesday-Sunday. Children with adult only. Late July-Labor Day.

HOTELS

★★★Atlantic Hotel
2 N. Main St., Berlin,
410-641-9460, 800-814-7672;
www.atlantichotel.com
The Atlantic Hotel offers Victorian-decorated rooms centrally located in Berlin's historic district.
17 rooms. Complimentary full breakfast. Restaurant, bar. $

SPECIALTY LODGINGS

Merry Sherwood Plantation
8909 Worcester Hwy., Berlin,
410-641-2112, 800-660-0358;
www.merrysherwood.com
8 rooms. Children over Eight years only. Complimentary full breakfast. Built in 1859; on grounds of former plantation. $$

BETHESDA

A suburb of Washington, D.C., Bethesda is home to both the National Institutes of Health, and Bethesda Naval Hospital.
Information: The Greater Bethesda-Chevy Chase Chamber of Commerce, Landow Building, 7910 Woodmont Ave., Suite 1204, 301-652-4900; www.bccchamber.org

WHAT TO SEE AND DO

National Library of Medicine
8600 Rockville Pike, Bethesda,
301-594-5983, 888-346-3656;
www.nlm.nih.gov
World's largest biomedical library; rare books, manuscripts, prints; medical art displays. Monday-Saturday; closed Saturday before Monday holidays. Visitors center and guided tour. Monday-Friday, one departure each day.

HOTELS

★★★Hyatt Regency Bethesda
1 Bethesda Metro Center,
Bethesda,
301-657-1234;
www.bethesda.hyatt.com

Located at Metro Center and within steps to restaurants, theaters and shopping, this hotel is perfect for both the business and leisure traveler.
390 rooms. Children's activity center. **$$**

★★Marriott Suites Bethesda
6711 Democracy Blvd.,
Bethesda,
301-897-5600, 800-228-9290;
www.marriotthotels.com
274 rooms, all suites. **$$**

RESTAURANTS

★★Austin Grill
7278 Woodmont Ave., Bethesda,
301-656-1366;
www.austingrill.com
Tex-Mex menu. Lunch, dinner, late-night, brunch. Bar. Children's menu. Casual attire. Outdoor seating. **$$**

★★Bacchus Bethesda
7945 Norfolk Ave., Bethesda,
301-657-1722
Middle Eastern menu. Lunch, dinner. Casual attire. Valet parking. Outdoor seating. **$$**

★Bethesda Crab House
4958 Bethesda Ave., Bethesda,
301-652-3382
Seafood menu. Lunch, dinner, late-night. Casual attire. Outdoor seating. **$$**

★★Buon Giorno
8003 Norfolk Ave., Bethesda,
301-652-1400
Italian menu. Dinner. Closed Monday; also mid-August-mid-September. Bar. Valet parking (dinner). **$$**

★★★Cesco Trattoria
4871 Cordell Ave., Bethesda,
301-654-8333
Features breads that are baked fresh daily in a wood-burning oven, which is visible to diners.
Italian menu. Lunch, dinner. Bar. Casual attire. Valet parking (dinner). Outdoor seating. **$$$**

★★Foong Lin
7710 Norfolk Ave., Bethesda,
301-656-3427;
www.foonglin.com
Chinese menu. Lunch, dinner. Bar. Casual attire. **$$**

★★Frascati
4806 Rugby Ave., Bethesda,
301-652-9514
Italian menu. Lunch, dinner. Closed Monday. Reservations recommended. Outdoor seating. **$$**

★★Jean-Michel
10223 Old Georgetown Rd.,
Bethesda,
301-564-4910
French menu. Lunch, dinner. Closed Sunday in July-August. Casual attire. **$$$**

★★★Le Vieux Logis
7925 Old Georgetown Rd.,
301-652-6816
French menu. Dinner. Closed Sunday. Casual attire. Free valet parking. Outdoor seating. **$$$**

★Raku
7240 Woodmont Ave.,
Bethesda,
301-718-8680
Pan-Asian menu. Lunch, dinner. Children's menu. Outdoor seating. **$$**

★★★Ruth's Chris Steak House
7315 Wisconsin Ave., Bethesda,
301-652-7877;
www.ruthschris.com
Born out of a single New Orleans restaurant Ruth Fertel bought in 1965 by mortgaging her house. Thick, juicy USDA Prime steaks slathered with butter as well as market fresh seafood are the hallmarks of Ruth's Chris. Found on the ground floor of the Air Rights building, the dining room features a relaxed, informal atmosphere with dark wood accents, a large lobster tank and a cigar lounge.
Steak menu. Dinner. Bar. Business casual attire. Valet parking. **$$$**

45

MARYLAND

★★Thyme Square
4735 Bethesda Ave., Bethesda,
301-657-9077
American menu. Lunch, dinner. Bar. Children's menu. Casual attire. Outdoor seating. **$$**

★★★Tragara
4935 Cordell Ave., Bethesda,
301-951-4935;
www.tragara.com

Bathed in soft light with fresh roses on every linen-topped table, Tragara offers satisfying Italian cuisine and impeccable service. Tables fill up quickly at lunch and dinner. The impressive Italian kitchen offers a tempting menu of pastas, fish, meat and antipasti, but be sure to save room to indulge in the house-made gelato.
Italian menu. Lunch, dinner. Casual attire. Valet parking. **$$$**

BOONSBORO
Information: Hagerstown/Washington County Chamber of Commerce, 28 W. Washington St., Hagerstown, 301-739-2015; www.hagerstown.org

WHAT TO SEE AND DO
Crystal Grottoes Caverns
19821 Shepherdstown Pike,
Boonsboro (Washington County),
301-432-6336;
www.goodearthgraphics.com/showcave/md/crystal.html
Limestone caverns may be viewed from walkways. Picnicking. Guided tours. April-October: daily 9 a.m.-6 p.m.; November-March: Saturday-Sunday 11 a.m.-4 p.m.

Gathland State Park
Boonsboro,
301-791-4767, 888-432-2267;
www.dnr.state.md.us/publiclands/western/gathland.html
On 140 acres. A site once owned by George Townsend, Civil War reporter. A monument was built in 1896 to honor Civil War correspondents. The visitor center contains original papers. Picnicking, walking tour, winter sports.

Greenbrier State Park
21843 National Pike, Boonsboro,
301-791-4767, 888-432-2267;
www.dnr.state.md.us/publiclands/western/greenbrier.html
The Appalachian Trail passes near this 1,275-acre park and its 42-acre man-made lake. Swimming (Memorial Day-Labor Day: daily), fishing, boating (rentals; no gas motors); nature and hiking trails, picnicking.

Washington Monument State Park
21843 National Pike Rd., Boonsboro,
301-791-4767, 888-432-2267;
www.dnr.state.md.us/publiclands/western/washington.html
On 147 acres. A 34-foot tower of native stone (1827) was the first completed monument to honor George Washington. Views of nearby battlefields, two states (Pennsylvania and West Virginia). History Center displays firearms and Civil War mementos (by appointment). The Appalachian Trail leads through the park; hiking and picnicking.

BOWIE
Information: Greater Bowie Chamber of Commerce, 6911 Laurel Bowie Rd., Bowie, 301-262-0920; www.bowiechamber.org
Information is also available from Prince George's Conference & Visitors Bureau, 9475 Lottsford Road #130, Landover, 301-925-8300

46

MARYLAND

WHAT TO SEE AND DO

Belair Mansion

12207 Tulip Grove Dr., Bowie,
301-809-3089;
www.cityofbowie.org/comserv/museum
Georgian-style home (circa 1745) was home
of Governor Samuel Ogle in the 1700s; later
owned by the Woodward family, prominent
racehorse breeders in the first half of the
20th century. Tours. Wednesday-Sunday
noon-4 p.m., groups by appointment.

Belair Stable Museum

2835 Belair Dr., Bowie,
301-809-3089;
www.cityofbowie.org/comserv/museum
Part of famed Belair Stud, one of the premier thoroughbred racing stables of the
'30s, '40s and '50s. Was home to two
Triple Crown winners—Gallant Fox and
Omaha—and the 1955 Horse of the Year,
Nashua. Wednesday-Sunday noon-4 p.m.,
groups by appointment.

SPECIAL EVENTS

Heritage Day

Belair Mansion and Stable,
2835 Belair Dr., Bowie,
301-809-3089
Belair Mansion and Stable. Performance by
Congress' Own Regiment; tour of stables and
grounds; battle reenactments; demonstrations
of colonial crafts. Third Sunday in May.

HOTELS

★Hampton Inn Bowie

15202 Major Lansdale Blvd., Bowie,
301-809-1800;
www.hamptoninn.com
301 rooms. $

BUCKEYSTOWN

HOTELS

Catoctin Inn

3619 Buckeystown Pike, Buckeystown,
301-874-5555, 800-730-5550
20 rooms. Complimentary full breakfast.
Built in the 1780s; parlor with antique
sofas. $

Inn at Buckeystown

3521 Buckeystown Pike,
Buckeystown,
301-874-5755, 800-272-1190;
www.innatbuckeystown.com

This stately and elegant mansion opened
its doors in 1981, and today continues to
enchant guests with touches of luxury and
the charm of another era. Located in a
National Registered Historic Village, this
mansion delights with its warm hospitality, Victorian-style decor, and wonderful appointment of collectibles and period
pieces.
    9 rooms. $$

CAMBRIDGE

On the Eastern Shore, Cambridge is Maryland's second-largest deep-water port. Boating
and fishing opportunities are found in the Choptank and Honga rivers and Chesapeake, Tar
and Fishing bays.
Information: Dorchester County Visitors Center, 2 Rose Hill Place,
410-228-1000, 800-522-8687; www.tourdorchester.org

WHAT TO SEE AND DO

Blackwater National Wildlife Refuge

2145 Key Wallace Dr., Cambridge,
410-228-2677;
www.fws.gov/blackwater
Over 20,000 acres of rich tidal marsh,
freshwater ponds and woodlands. One of
the chief wintering areas for Canada geese
and ducks using the Atlantic Flyway; in fall,
as many as 33,000 geese and 17,000 ducks
swell the bird population. Also a haven for
the bald eagle, the Delmarva fox squirrel and the peregrine falcon. Scenic drive,
woodland trails, photo blind. Visitor center

(daily). Golden Age, Golden Eagle and Golden Access passports.

SPECIAL EVENTS

Antique Aircraft Fly-In

Dorchester Heritage Museum,
1904 Horn Point Rd., Cambridge,
410-228-5530, 800-522-8687
Old and new planes on display. Third weekend in May.

National Outdoor Show

Cambridge,
800-522-8687
Goose and duck calling, log sawing, crab picking, trap setting contests; entertainment. Last weekend in February.

CHESAPEAKE AND OHIO CANAL NATIONAL HISTORICAL PARK

As early as 1754, the enterprising George Washington, only in his twenties, proposed a system of navigation along the Potomac River valley. His Potowmack Canal Company, organized in 1785, cleared obstructions and built skirting canals to facilitate the transportation of goods from settlements beyond the Allegheny Mountains to the lower Potomac River towns.

These improvements eventually were renedered inadequate, and with Erie Canal's renowned, the Chesapeake and Ohio Canal Company was formed in 1828 to connect Georgetown with the Ohio Valley by river and canal. On July 4, 1828, President John Quincy Adams led the groundbreaking ceremony, declaring, "To subdue the earth is preeminently the purpose of this undertaking." Unfortunately, the earth was not easily subdued. President Adams bent his shovel with several attempts, before breaking into an energetic frenzy and successfully getting a shovelful of dirt.

The groundbreaking ceremony's difficulty foreshadowed the canal's short-lived future as a major transportation artery. Completed in 1850 as far as Cumberland, Md. (184 1/2 miles from Georgetown), the waterway was used extensively for the transportation of coal, flour, grain and lumber. Financial and legal difficulties, the decline of commerce after the Civil War, the Baltimore & Ohio Railroad and the advent of improved roads cut deeply into the commerce of the waterway, and it gradually faded into obsolescence. The canal still had limited commercial use as late as 1924, when a flood destroyed many of the canal locks and nothing was restored.

The C & O Canal's unfortunate demise is now a blessing for hikers, canoeists and bikers, who can find access to the towpath along the banks of the waterway. One of the least altered of old American canals, the Chesapeake and Ohio is flanked by ample foliage throughout most of its 20,239 acres.

Many points of interest include exhibits in Cumberland, Georgetown, Hancock and Williamsport, and at a museum near the Great Falls of the Potomac. Mule-drawn canal boat rides are offered April-October at Georgetown and Great Falls. Camping for hikers and bikers is available throughout the park.

For information about the canal contact the C & O Canal National Historical Park, Sharpsburg, 21782, 301-739-4200. Visitor centers are located in Cumberland, Georgetown, Great Falls, Hancock and Williamsport.

CHESAPEAKE BAY BRIDGE AREA

The majestic twin spans of the Chesapeake Bay Bridge carry visitors to the Eastern Shore, a patchwork of small picturesque towns, lighthouses and fishing villages tucked away from the city. Scenic rivers and bays, wildlife, gardens and wildflowers fill the countryside. The main attractions of any visit, however, are the many fine inns and the restaurants specializing in local seafood.

WHAT TO SEE AND DO

Wye Oak State Park
Hwy. 662, Wye Mills,
410-820-1668;
www.dnr.state.md.us/publiclands/
eastern/wyeoak.html
On the Eastern Shore in Talbot County, approximately one mile from the junction of Routes 50 and 404. The official state tree of Maryland is in this 29-acre park; it is the largest white oak in the United States (108 feet high, 28 feet around) and is believed to be over 460 years old; a new tree has been started from an acorn. A restored 18th-century one-room schoolhouse and the Old Wye Mill (late 1600s) are nearby.

HOTELS

★Comfort Suites
160 Scheeler Rd., Chestertown,
410-810-0555, 877-424-6423;
www.comfortinn.com
53 rooms. Complimentary continental breakfast. $

★★★Kent Manor Inn
500 Kent Manor Dr., Stevensville,
410-643-7716, 800-820-4511;
www.kentmanor.com
This historic 1820 inn sits among 220 wooded acres on picturesque Thompson Creek, a tributary to the Chesapeake Bay. Just 12 miles from Annapolis, the hotel is a convenient spot for both business and leisure travelers. The guest rooms feature poster beds, Italian marble fireplaces and stunning views of the grounds. Several rooms also have window seats and porches—perfect spots to curl up with a good book. There are many outdoor activities for guests to enjoy, including bike and paddleboat rentals.
24 rooms. Complimentary continental breakfast. $$

SPECIALTY LODGINGS

Huntingfield Manor
4928 Eastern Neck Rd., Rock Hall,
410-639-7779, 800-720-8788;
www.huntingfield.com
6 rooms. Complimentary continental breakfast. Telescope-type house on a working farm that dates to the middle 1600s. $

Inn at Mitchell House
8796 Maryland Pkwy.,
Chestertown,
410-778-6500;
www.innatmitchellhouse.com
Built in 1743, this historic manor house welcomes guests with friendly service, set amidst lush woods and 10 beautiful acres. 5 rooms. Complimentary full breakfast. $$

White Swan Tavern
231 High St., Chestertown,
410-778-2300;
www.whiteswantavern.com
6 rooms. Complimentary continental breakfast. Former house and tavern built in 1733 and 1793, respectively; restored with antique furnishings; museum. $

RESTAURANTS

★★Fisherman's Inn and Crab Deck
3116 Main St., Kent Narrows,
410-827-8807;
www.fishermansinn.com
Seafood, steak menu. Lunch, dinner. Bar. Children's menu. Casual attire. $$

★Harris Crab House
433 Kent Narrows Way N.,
Grasonville,
410-827-9500;
www.harriscrabhouse.com
American, seafood menu. Lunch, dinner. Bar. Children's menu. Casual attire. Outdoor seating. $$

★★★Narrows
3023 Kent Narrows Way S., Grasonville,
410-827-8113;
www.thenarrowsrestaurant.com
This restaurant offers waterfront dining
with a spectacular view of the narrows.
Regional eastern shore menu. Lunch, dinner, brunch. Bar. Children's menu. **$$**

★Waterman's Crab House
21055 Sharp St., Rick Hall,
410-639-2261;
www.watermanscrabhouse.com
On Rock Hall Harbor. Seafood menu.
Breakfast, lunch, dinner. Bar. Children's
menu. Casual attire. Reservations recommended. Outdoor seating. **$$**

CHEVY CHASE

RESTAURANTS
★★★La Ferme
7101 Brookville Rd., Chevy Chase,
301-986-5255;
www.lafermerestaurant.com
In a French country house setting, La Ferme
serves entrees such as a hickory-smoked
and grilled double-cut pork chop with
potato gratin, grilled vegetables and Meaux
mustard sauce.

French menu. Lunch, dinner. Closed
Monday. Reservations recommended. Outdoor seating. **$$**

HOTELS
★★Holiday Inn
5520 Wisconsin Ave., Chevy Chase,
301-656-1500, 800-315-2621;
www.holiday-inn.com
215 rooms. **$**

COCKEYSVILLE

Information: Baltimore County Chamber of Commerce, 102 W. Pennsylvania Ave.,
Towson, 410-825-6200

SPECIAL EVENTS
Point-to-Point Steeplechase
Cockeysville,
410-825-6200
Three well-known meets on consecutive
weekends: My Lady's Manor, in Monkton.
Mid-April. Grand National, in Butler. Mid-
April. Maryland Hunt Cup, in Glyndon.
Late April.

RESTAURANTS
★★The New York Inn
10010 York Rd.,
Cockeysville,
410-666-0006
American, vegetarian menu. Dinner, Sunday
brunch. Closed Monday. Bar. Business casual
attire. Reservations recommended. **$$**

COLLEGE PARK
Information: Prince George's County Conference & Visitors Bureau,
9200 Basil Court, Largo, 301-925-8300, 888-925-8300;
www.goprincegeorgescounty.com

WHAT TO SEE AND DO
College Park Aviation Museum
1985 Corporal Frank Scott Dr.,
College Park,
301-864-6029;
www.collegeparkaviationmuseum.com

World's oldest operating airport, started by
Wilbur Wright in 1909 to train two military
officers in the operation of aircraft. First
airplane machine gun and radio-navigational
aids tested here; first air mail and controlled
helicopter flights. Museum (daily 10 a.m.-
5 p.m.).

Greenbelt Park
**6565 Greenbelt Rd., College Park,
301-344-3948**
A 1,100-acre wooded park operated by the National Park Service that includes 174 sites. Nature trails, picnicking, camping. Skiing. Self-registration; first-come, first-served. Standard fees.

University of Maryland
**Hwy. 1, College Park,
301-405-1000;
www.umd.edu**
(1865) (35,000 students) Tawes Fine Arts Theater has plays, musicals, concerts, dance, opera and music festivals. Tours.

HOTELS
★★Holiday Inn
**10000 Baltimore Ave., College Park,
301-345-6700, 800-315-2621;
www.holiday-inn.com**
222 rooms. **$**

COLUMBIA
A planned city built on a tract of land larger than Manhattan Island, Columbia comprises 11 villages surrounding a central downtown service area. Construction of the city began in 1966.
Information: Howard County Tourism Council, 8267 Main St., Ellicott City, 410-313-1900, 800-288-8747; www.visithowardcounty.com

WHAT TO SEE AND DO
African Art Museum of Maryland
**5430 Vantage Point Rd., Columbia,
410-730-7106;
www.africanartmuseum.org**
Masks, sculptured figures, textiles, basketry, household items and musical instruments displayed in a 19th-century manor. Tuesday-Friday 10 a.m.-4 p.m., Sunday noon-4 p.m.

Howard County Center of African-American Culture
**5434 Vantage Point Rd., Columbia,
410-715-1921**
Contains artifacts and memorabilia depicting images of African-Americans over the last 200 years. Extensive collection of spiritual, jazz and rap music; more than 2,000 books and periodicals; hands-on exhibit for children. Tuesday-Friday noon-5 p.m., Saturday noon-4 p.m., Sunday by appointment.

SPECIAL EVENTS
Columbia Festival of the Arts
**5575 Sterrett Place, Columbia,
410-715-3044;
www.columbiafestival.com**
Music, dance, theater, lakeside entertainment. Ten days in mid-June.

Symphony of Lights
Columbia, 410-313-1900
Animated lighting displays along a 1 1/2-mile park route. Late November-early January.

Wine in the Woods
**Symphony Woods,
10475 Little Patuxent Pkwy., Columbia,
410-313-4700;
www.wineinthewoods.com**
Symphony Woods at Merriweather Post Pavilion. Two-day celebration featuring Maryland wines, gourmet food, entertainment, arts and crafts. Third weekend in May.

HOTELS
★★★Hilton Columbia
**5485 Twin Knolls Rd., Columbia,
410-997-1060, 800-445-8667;
www.columbia.hilton.com**
Located in the heart of Columbia and set amidst a park-like setting, this hotel offers a very relaxing stay, with a glassed atrium and well-appointed guest rooms.
152 rooms. **$$**

51

MARYLAND

★
★
★
★
★

★★★Sheraton Columbia Hotel
10207 Wincopin Cir., Columbia,
410-730-3900, 800-638-2817;
www.sheratoncolumbia.com
Recognized for its gracious accommodations, superb service and handsomely appointed guestrooms, this hotel is a welcome retreat for both business and leisure travelers. 288 rooms. **$$**

RESTAURANTS
★★★King's Contrivance
10150 Shaker Dr., Columbia,
410-995-0500;
www.thekingscontrivance.com
Guests can enjoy fine country dining in this 1900 mansion with Early American decor. The menu offers selections such as crab cakes, venison and rack of lamb, as well as an extensive wine list.
American menu. Lunch, dinner. Bar. Children's menu. Reservations recommended. Valet parking (weekends). **$$$**

CRESAPTOWN

RESTAURANTS
★★Warner's German Restaurant
Route US 220 S. McMullen Highway,
Cresaptown,
301-729-2361

German menu. Lunch, dinner. Closed Monday. Bar. Children's menu. Casual attire. Outdoor seating. **$$**

CRISFIELD

52

Information: Crisfield Area Chamber of Commerce, 906 W. Main St., Crisfield, 410-968-2500, 800-782-3913; www.crisfieldchamber.org

WHAT TO SEE AND DO
Janes Island State Park
26280 Alfred J. Lawson Dr., Crisfield,
410-968-1565, 800-521-9189;
www.dnr.state.md.us/publiclands/eastern/
janesisland.html
These 3,147 acres are nearly surrounded by Chesapeake Bay and its inlets. Swimming, fishing, boat ramp (rentals); cabins, camping. Standard fees.

Smith Island Cruises
Somers Cove Marina, Seventh St., Crisfield,
410-425-2771;
www.smithislandcruises.com
The *Chelsea's Lane Tyler* and the *Captain Tyler* make approximately one-hour cruises to Smith Island. Bus tour of the two villages on the island, with spare time to visit the rest of the island; lunch available (fee). Tour length approximately 4 1/2 hours. Memorial Day: weekend-mid-October.

Tangier Island Cruises
1001 W. Main St., Crisfield,
410-968-2338;
www.tangierislandcruises.com
Trips to the fishing village of Tangier Island, VA. Mid-May-October.

SPECIAL EVENTS
National Hard Crab Derby & Fair
Somers Cove Marina, Seventh St., Crisfield,
410-968-2500, 800-782-3913;
www.crisfieldchamber.com/crabderby.htm
Cooking, crab picking, boat docking contests; crab racing; fireworks and parade. Friday-Sunday, Labor Day weekend.

HOTELS
★Pines Motel
127 N. Somerset Ave., Crisfield,
410-968-0900;
www.crisfield.com/pines
40 rooms. **$**

CUMBERLAND

Cumberland is nestled between Pennsylvania and West Virginia in western Maryland. George Washington, who once defended the town, thought the nation's primary east-west route would eventually pass through Cumberland. In 1833, the National Road (Hwy. 40 Alternate) made the town a supply terminus for overland commerce. Today's economy includes services and recreational facilities.

Information: Allegany County Convention & Visitors Bureau, 13 Canal St., Cumberland, 301-777-5132, 800-425-2067; www.mdmountainside.com

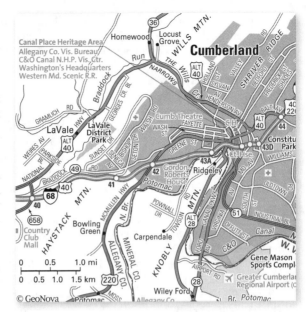

WHAT TO SEE AND DO

Fort Cumberland Trail
Cumberland
Walking trail covers several city blocks downtown around the site of Fort Cumberland. Includes boundary markers, narrative plaques.

George Washington's Headquarters
Greene St.,
Cumberland,
310-777-8214
(Circa 1755) His first military headquarters. Taped narration.

Gordon-Roberts House
218 Washington St.,
Cumberland,
301-777-8678;
www.historyhouse.allconet.org/house
(Circa 1867) Restored 18-room Victorian house with nine period rooms; costumes; research room. Tuesday-Saturday 10 a.m.-5 p.m.

The Narrows
Rte. 40, Cumberland
Picturesque 1,000-foot gap through Alleghenies (Highway 40A) used by pioneers on their way to the West.

Rocky Gap State Park
12500 Pleasant Valley Rd. NE, Cumberland, 301-722-1480, 888-432-2267;
www.dnr.state.md.us/publiclands/western/rockygap.html
Mountain scenery around 243-acre lake with three swimming beaches. Swimming, fishing, boating (electric motors only; rentals); nature and hiking trails, picnicking, cafe, improved camping (reservations accepted one year in advance), winter activities. Resort; 18-hole golf course. Standard fees.

Western Maryland Station Center
13 Canal St., Cumberland,
301-724-3655;
www.cr.nps.gov/nr/travel/cumberland/wmd.htm
This 1913 railroad station houses Canal Place Authority, Industrial and Transportation Museum; C & O Canal National Historical Park Visitors Center and Allegany County Visitors Center. Daily.

This is also the departure point for:

Western Maryland Scenic Railroad
13 Canal St., Cumberland,
301-759-4400, 800-872-4650

Excursion train makes scenic trip 17 miles to Frostburg and back. May-October, Tuesday-Sunday; November-mid-December, weekends.

SPECIAL EVENTS
Agricultural Expo and Fair
Allegany County Fairgrounds,
11490 Moss Ave., Exit, Cumberland,
301-729-1200;
www.alleganycofair.org
Poultry, livestock, carnival, entertainment. Late July.

Drumfest
Greenway Ave. Stadium, Greenway Ave., Cumberland, 301-777-8325
Drum and bugle corps championship. Last Saturday in July.

Rocky Gap Music Festival
Allegany Colle,
12401 Willow Brook Rd. SE, Cumberland,
888-762-5942
Features bluegrass and country music; children's activities, crafts, workshops. Friday-Sunday. First weekend August.

Street Rod Roundup
Cumberland,
301-729-5555
At fairgrounds. Hundreds of pre-1950 hot rods on display and in competitions. Labor Day weekend.

HOTELS
★★Holiday Inn
100 S. George St., Cumberland,
301-724-8800, 800-315-2621;
www.holiday-inn.com
130 rooms. Airport transportation available. $

Inn at Walnut Bottom
120 Greene St., Cumberland,
301-777-0003, 800-286-9718;
www.iwbinfo.com
At this elegant retreat, guests are offered their choice of two accommodations. The Georgian-style architecture of the Cowden House welcomes guests with a formal doorway and chimneys at each end, while the Queen Anne-style Dent House features a round turret on the corner.
12 rooms. Complimentary full breakfast. $

54

EASTON
Information: Talbot County Chamber of Commerce, 11 S. Harrison St., Easton, 410-770-8000; www.talbotchamber.org

WHAT TO SEE AND DO
Academy Art Museum
106 South St., Easton,
410-822-2787;
www.art-academy.org
Housed in a renovated 1820s schoolhouse, the Academy exhibits works of local and national artists in its permanent collection. Also hosts over 250 visual and performing arts programs annually. Monday-Saturday 10 a.m.-4 p.m., Wednesday 10 a.m.-9 p.m.

Historical Society of Talbot County
25 S. Washington St., Easton,
410-822-0773;
www.hstc.org
A three-gallery museum in a renovated early commercial building; changing exhibits, museum shop. Historic houses: 1810 Federal town house, 1700s Quaker cabinetmaker's

cottage, period gardens; tours. Monday-Saturday 10 a.m.-4 p.m., by advance appointment.

Third Haven Friends Meeting House
405 S. Washington St., Easton,
410-822-0293;
www.thirdhaven.org
(1682-1684) One of the oldest frame-construction houses of worship in U.S. Daily.

SPECIAL EVENTS
Eastern Shore Chamber Music Festival
21 S. Harrison St., Easton,
410-819-0380;
www.musicontheshore.org
Various locations. World-class chamber music; young people's concert. Two weeks in June.

Tuckahoe Steam and Gas Show and Reunion
210 Marlboro Ave.,
Easton,
410-643-6123;
www.tuckahoesteam.org
Old steam and gas engines; antique tractors and cars. Demonstrations in soap and broom making; flour milling. Gas and steam wheat threshing, sawmill working, flea market, crafts, parade, entertainment. Usually the weekend after July 4.

Waterfowl Festival
40 S. Harrison St.,
Easton,
410-822-4606;
www.waterfowlfestival.org
Downtown and various locations in and around town. Exhibits on waterfowl, pictures, carvings, food. First or second weekend in November.

HOTELS
Bishop's House
214 Goldsborough St.,
Easton,
410-820-7290, 800-223-7290;
www.bishopshouse.com
This Victorian house, circa 1880s, was built for Philip Frances Thomas, governor of Maryland from 1848 to 1851, and Clintonia Wright May Thomas. Although the house is decorated with antiques throughout, it also features modern amenities.
5 rooms. Closed January-February. Children over 12 years only. Complimentary full breakfast. Built in 1880; antiques, toys, porcelains. **$**

★Holiday Inn Express
8561 Ocean Gateway,
Easton,
410-819-6500, 877-327-8661;
www.hotel-easex.com
73 rooms. Complimentary continental breakfast. **$**

★★★Robert Morris Inn
314 N. Morris St., Oxford,
410-226-5111, 888-823-4012;
www.robertmorrisinn.com
Rooms at the Robert Morris Inn include private porches with views of the Chesapeake Bay. Relax in an Adirondack chair on the inn's property, which rolls down to the water's edge.
35 rooms. Closed December-March. Children over 10 years only. Restaurant. **$$**

RESTAURANTS
★★★★The Inn at Easton
28 S. Harrison St.
Easton,
410-822-4910
Housed in a Federal-style mansion, the dining room at the Inn at Easton delivers the unexpected. The room is fresh and contemporary, not stuffy, and the food is modern Australian, not classic American. Chef Andrew Evans puts his knowledge of clean, unfussy, fresh Down Under cuisine (he spent a year cooking in Brisbane and married an Aussie) to work in recipes like barramundi en papillote with red Thai curry and jasmine rice, or coffee-crusted rack of lamb with potato purée and wilted spinach. The wine list draws heavily from Australian produces, whose bold shirazes and chardonnays pair well with Andrews' inventive food.
Australian menu. Dinner. Closed Monday-Tuesday. Business casual attire. Reservations recommended. Outdoor seating. **$$**

★★★Restaurant Local
101 E. Dover St.,
Easton,
410-822-1300;
www.tidewaterinn.com
Opened in 2006 as part of the Historic Tidewater Inn's renovations, Restaurant Local serves contemporary American cuisine in a modern but casual setting. Entrees include a local rockfish filet with shrimp and basil risotto, mushrooms and saffron butter, and filet mignon with roasted garlic potatoes, grilled asparagus and wild mushroom bordelaise.
American menu. Breakfast, lunch, dinner, Sunday brunch. Bar. Valet parking. Outdoor seating. **$$**

55

MARYLAND

★
★
★
★

ELLICOTT CITY

Originally named Ellicott Mills, this town was founded by three Quaker brothers as the site of their gristmill. Charles Carroll of Carrollton, whose Doughoregan Manor can still be seen nearby, lent financial help to the Ellicotts, and the town eventually became the site of ironworks, rolling mills and the first railroad terminus in the United States. The famous Tom Thumb locomotive race with a horse took place near here. Many of the town's original stone houses and log cabins, on hills above the Patapsco River, have been preserved.
Information: Howard County Tourism Council, 8267 Main St., Ellicott City, 410-313-1900, 800-288-8747; www.visithowardcounty.com

WHAT TO SEE AND DO

Ellicott City B & O Railroad Station Museum
2711 Maryland Ave.,
Ellicott City,
410-461-1945;
www.ecborail.org
Completed by the Baltimore and Ohio Railroad in 1830, the Ellicott City Station is the oldest surviving railroad station in America and the site of the original terminus of the first 13 miles of commercial track constructed in the United States In the 1970s the station was restored as a museum, and a second restoration in 1999 returned the building to its 1857 appearance. Today, the site interprets the story of transportation and travel in early America through seasonal exhibits, education programs and living history programs. Wednesday-Sunday 11 a.m.-4 p.m.; last admission is one half-hour before closing.

Patapsco Valley State Park
8020 Baltimore National Pike,
Ellicott City,
410-461-5005, 888-432-2267;
www.dnr.state.md.us/publiclands/central/patapscovalley.html
Spread across three counties, this great nature and recreational area runs along a 32-mile stretch of the scenic Patapsco River, spans 14,000 acres and contains five sites. Guests can hike, bike, ride horses, fish, camp, canoe, tube or picnic. The park also includes the world's largest multiple-arched stone railroad bridge, a 300-foot suspension bridge, and a paved hiking trail for the disabled. Park: daily dawn-dusk. Information desk: daily 8 a.m.-4:30 p.m.

HOTELS

★★★Turf Valley Resort and Conference Center
2700 Turf Valley Rd., Ellicott City,
410-465-1500, 888-833-8873;
www.turfvalley.com
This full-service resort (formerly a thoroughbred farm and country club) is convenient to Baltimore and offers well-appointed guest rooms. The resort also features a full-service European spa, two golf courses, tennis courts and a nightly hors d'oeuvres and cocktail reception.
234 rooms. $$

RESTAURANTS

★★Crab Shanty
3410 Plumtree Dr.,
Ellicott City,
410-465-9660;
www.crabshanty.com
Seafood menu. Lunch, dinner, brunch. Bar. Children's menu. Business casual attire. $$

★★★Tersiguel's
8293 Main St.,
Ellicott City,
410-465-4004;
www.tersiguels.com
Tersiguel's offers fine dining in a 19th-century home with six individual dining rooms. Chefs prepare seasonal cuisine with fresh vegetables and herbs from their garden, and chevre cheese is made daily.
French menu. Lunch, dinner. Bar. Business casual attire. Reservations recommended. $$$

56

MARYLAND

★
★
★
★
★

FLINTSTONE

WHAT TO SEE AND DO

Green Ridge State Forest
28700 Headquarters Dr. N.E., Flintstone,
301-478-3124;
www.dnr.state.md.us/publiclands/
western/greenridge.html
These 44,000 acres of forest land stretch
across mountains of western Maryland and
occupy portions of Town Hill, Polish Mountain and Green Ridge Mountain. Abundant
wildlife. Fishing, boat launch, canoeing; hiking trails, camping, winter sports. C & O
Canal runs through here into 3,118-foot
Paw-Paw Tunnel.

HOTELS

★★Rocky Gap Lodge & Golf Resort
16701 Lakeview Rd. N.E., Flintstone,
301-784-8400, 800-724-0828;
www.rockygapresort.com
217 rooms. Children's activity center.
Beach. Airport transportation available. **$$**

FREDERICK

Home of dauntless Barbara
Frietschie, who reportedly
spoke her mind to Stonewall Jackson and his "rebel
hordes," Frederick is a town
filled with history. Named
for Frederick Calvert, sixth
Lord Baltimore, it is the seat
of one of America's richest
agricultural counties. Francis
Scott Key and Chief Justice
Roger Brooke Taney made
their homes here. Court
House Square was the scene
of several important events
during the Revolutionary
War, including the famed protest against the Stamp Act, in
which an effigy of the stamp
distributor was burned.

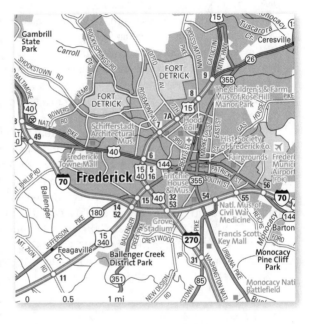

MARYLAND

During the Civil War, Frederick was a focal point for strategic operations by both sides.
In the campaign of 1862, the Confederacy's first invasions of the North were made at nearby
South Mountain and Sharpsburg, at Antietam Creek. Thousands of wounded men were cared
for here. In July 1864, the town was forced to pay a $200,000 ransom to Confederate General
Jubal Early before he fought the Battle of Monocacy a few miles south. Frederick today is an
educational center, tourist attraction, the location of Fort Detrick army installation, and home
to diversified small industry. A 33-block area has been designated a Historic District.
Information: Tourism Council of Frederick County, 19 E. Church St., Frederick,
301-663-8687, 800-999-3613; www.visitfrederick.org

WHAT TO SEE AND DO

Barbara Frietschie House and Museum
154 W. Patrick St.,
Frederick,
301-698-0630
Exhibits include quilts, clothing made by
Frietschie, her rocker and Bible, the bed in
which she died, and other items; 10 minute film;
garden. April-September: Monday, Thursday-
Sunday; October-November: Saturday-Sunday.

CIVIL WAR SITES OF FREDERICK

A well-preserved city of elegant 18th- and 19th-century structures, Frederick is a necessary stop on any tour of Civil War landmarks. It is an especially appropriate sequel to a visit to nearby Antietam National Battlefield, the site of the single bloodiest day of the Civil War—September 17, 1862. At the end of the battle, thousands of Union wounded were transported to Frederick, where 29 buildings were turned into makeshift hospitals. President Lincoln later praised townsfolk for their humanity. This heritage led to Frederick's selection as the site of the National Museum of Civil War Medicine.

Begin an hour-long, one-mile walking tour of the city's historic district at the museum at 48 East Patrick Street. The museum tells the story of radical improvements in medical treatment during the four years of the war, as the divided nation coped with the flood of ill or wounded soldiers on both sides of the Mason-Dixon line. From the museum, walk three blocks west (left) to the reconstructed Barbara Frietschie House & Museum at 154 West Patrick. Frietschie was immortalized in John Greenleaf Whittier's Civil War poem, "Shoot if you must, this old gray head, but spare your country's flag." According to legend, she waved a Union flag defiantly at Stonewall Jackson, who was leading a Confederate army through the city. In truth, she may have waved a flag, but to honor Union troops passing by later.

Double back on Patrick Street to Court Street and walk north (left) one block to tour Courthouse Square. On Court Street, opposite City Hall, is the small office where Francis Scott Key, author of "The Star-Spangled Banner," practiced law. Revolutionary War General Lafayette was a guest at 103 Council Street during his ceremonial U.S. tour in 1824. At 119 Record Street, Lincoln visited a wounded general and addressed a crowd from its steps after the Antietam battle. Head east (left) on West Church Street. Conclude your tour two blocks east at the Historical Society of Fredericksburg at 24 East Church. A large 1820 home, it is maintained as a house museum furnished with local antiques—appropriately so, because nearby East Patrick Street has been dubbed "Antique Row" for its many antique shops.

★
★
★
★
★

Children's Museum of Rose Hill Manor
1611 N. Market St., Frederick,
301-694-1646, 800-999-3613
Hands-on exhibits of 19th-century family life; carriage museum, colonial herb and fragrant gardens, farm museum, blacksmith shop, log cabin. April-October: daily; November: Saturday-Sunday.

Gambrill State Park
8602 Gambrill Park Rd., Frederick,
301-271-7574, 888-432-2267;
www.dnr.state.md.us/publiclands/western/
gambrill.html

Park has 1,136 acres with two developed areas. Fishing; nature and hiking trails, picnicking, tent and trailer sites (standard fees). Tea room. Two overlooks.

Historical Society of Frederick County Museum
24 E. Church St., Frederick,
301-663-1188
House, built in early 1800s, shows both Georgian and Federal details. Portraits of early Frederick residents. Genealogy library (Tuesday-Saturday). Monday-Saturday; also Sunday afternoons.

Monocacy National Battlefield
4801 Urbana Pike, Frederick,
301-662-3515;
www.nps.gov/mono/home.htm
On July 9, 1864, Union General Lew Wallace and 5,000 men delayed General Jubal Early and his 23,000 Confederate soldiers for 24 hours, during which Grant was able to reinforce, and save Washington, D.C., New Jersey, Vermont and Pennsylvania. Confederate monuments mark the area. Labor Day-Memorial Day 8 a.m.-4:30 p.m., Memorial Day-Labor Day 8:30 a.m.-5 p.m.

Mount Olivet Cemetery
515 S. Market St., Frederick,
301-662-1164, 888-662-1164;
www.mountolivetcemeteryinc.com
(1852) Monuments mark graves of Francis Scott Key and Barbara Frietschie. Flag flies over Key's grave.

Roger Brooke Taney Home
121 S. Bentz St., Frederick,
301-663-8687
Chief Justice of the United States from 1835-1864, Taney was chosen by Andrew Jackson to succeed John Marshall. He swore in seven presidents, including Abraham Lincoln, and issued the famous Dred Scott Decision. He is buried in the cemetery of St. John's Catholic Church at E. Third and East streets. April-October: weekends.

Schifferstadt Architectural Museum
1110 Rosemont Ave., Frederick,
301-663-3885;
www.smallmuseum.org/schifferstadt.htm
(1756) Fine example of German Colonial farmhouse architecture. Tours of architectural museum Gift shop. April-mid December: Wednesday-Friday 10 a.m.-4 p.m.; Saturday-Sunday noon-4 p.m.

Trinity Chapel
W. Church St., Frederick,
301-694-2489
(1763) Graceful colonial church; Francis Scott Key was baptized here. Steeple houses town clock and 10-bell chimes; chimes play every Saturday evening.

The chapel is now used as Sunday School for:

Evangelical Reformed Church
15 W. Church St., Frederick,
301-662-2762;
www.erucc.org
United Church of Christ (1848). A Grecian-style building modeled after the Erechtheum, with two towers resembling Lanterns of Demosthenes. Here Stonewall Jackson slept through a pro-Union sermon before the Battle of Antietam; Barbara Frietschie was a member.

SPECIAL EVENTS
Beyond the Garden Gates Tour
19 E. Church St., Frederick,
301-394-2489
Downtown. Tour historic and contemporary gardens. Early May.

Fall Festival
Rose Hill Manor,
1611 N. Market St., Frederick,
301-600-1650;
www.co.frederick.md.us/Parks/rosehill.html
Apple butter making, music, crafts demonstrations, tractor pull, hay rides, country cooking. Early October.

Great Frederick Fair
797 E. Patrick St., Frederick,
301-663-5895;
www.thegreatfrederickfair.com
Frederick county fair. Mid-late September.

Lotus Blossom Festival
Lilypons Water Garden,
6800 Lilypons Rd., Buckeystown,
301-874-5133, 800-723-7667
Endless blooms of water lilies and lotus, water garden; arts and crafts, food, entertainment, lectures. First double-digit weekend in July.

HOTELS
★Fairfield Inn
5220 Westview Dr., Frederick,
301-631-2000, 800-228-2800;
www.marriott.com

59

MARYLAND

★
★
★
★

105 rooms. Complimentary continental breakfast. **$**

★★Hampton Inn
5311 Buckeystown Pike, Frederick,
301-698-2500, 800-426-7866;
www.hamptoninnfrederick.com
161 rooms. Complimentary continental breakfast. **$**

RESTAURANTS
★★Red Horse Steak House
996 W. Patrick St.,
Frederick,
301-663-3030;
www.redhorseusa.com
Steak menu. Dinner. Bar. Children's menu. Casual attire. Reservations recommended. **$$**

FROSTBURG

RESTAURANTS
★★★Au Petit Paris
86 E. Main St., Frostburg,
301-689-8946;
www.aupetitparis.com

The a la carte menu at Au Petit Paris will satisfy the most discriminating gourmet. The wine cellar boasts the most extensive collection in western Maryland.
French menu. Dinner. Closed Sunday-Monday. Bar. Children's menu. **$$$**

GAITHERSBURG
Information: Chamber of Commerce, 9 Park Ave., Gaithersburg,
301-840-1400; www.ggchamber.org

★

★

★

★

★

WHAT TO SEE AND DO
Seneca Creek State Park
11950 Clopper Rd., Gaithersburg,
301-924-2127, 888-432-2267;
www.dnr.state.md.us/publiclands/central/seneca.html
Stream valley park of 6,109 acres with 90-acre lake. Historic sites with old mills, an old schoolhouse, stone quarries. Fishing, boating (rentals); picnicking, disc golf, hiking, bicycle and bridle trails, winter sports. Standard fees.

SPECIAL EVENTS
Montgomery County Agricultural Fair
16 Chestnut St., Gaithersburg,
301-926-3100;
www.mcagfair.com
One of the East Coast's leading county fairs. Mid-late August.

HOTELS
★Comfort Inn
16216 Frederick Rd., Gaithersburg,
301-330-0023, 877-424-6423;
www.choicehotels.com
126 rooms. Complimentary full breakfast. **$**

★★Courtyard by Marriott
805 Russell Ave., Gaithersburg,
301-670-0008, 800-336-6880;
www.courtyard.com
203 rooms. **$**

★★★Hilton Gaithersburg
620 Perry Pkwy., Gaithersburg,
301-977-8900, 800-445-8667;
www.hilton.com
301 rooms. **$$**

★★Holiday Inn
2 Montgomery Village Ave., Gaithersburg,
301-948-8900, 800-465-4329;
www.higaithersburg.com
300 rooms. **$**

★★★Residence Inn By Marriott Gaithersburg Washingtonian Center
9751 Washingtonian Blvd., Gaithersburg,
301-590-0044;
www.marriott.com
This hotel offers suites with full kitchens and a social hour Mondays through Thursdays. 284 rooms. **$$**

RESTAURANTS

★Chris' Steak House
201 E. Diamond Ave., Gaithersburg,
301-869-6116
Steak menu. Lunch, dinner. Closed Sunday.
Bar. Children's menu. **$$**

★★Golden Bull Grand Cafe
7 Dalamar St., Gaithersburg,
301-948-3666;
www.golden-bull.com
American menu. Lunch, dinner. Bar. Children's menu. Casual attire. Reservations
recommended. **$$**

★★Old Siam
108 E. Diamond Ave., Gaithersburg,
301-926-9199

Thai menu. Lunch, dinner. Casual attire.
$

★★Peking Cheers
519 Quince Orchard Rd.,
Gaithersburg,
301-216-2090
Chinese menu. Lunch, dinner. Casual attire.
Reservations recommended. **$**

★Roy's Place
2 E. Diamond Ave.,
Gaithersburg,
301-948-5548;
www.roysplacerestaurant.com
American menu. Lunch, dinner. Bar. Casual
attire. Outdoor seating. **$$**

GRANTSVILLE

Information: Garrett County Chamber of Commerce,
15 Visitors Center Dr., McHenry, 301-387-4386; www.garrettchamber.com

WHAT TO SEE AND DO

Casselman River Bridge State Park
Rte. 40, Grantsville,
301-895-5453;
www.dnr.state.md.us/publiclands/western/
casselman.html
This single-span stone arch bridge over the
Casselman River was built in 1813.

New Germany State Park
349 Headquarters Lane, Grantsville,
301-895-5453, 888-432-2267;
www.dnr.state.md.us/publiclands/western/
newgermany.html
A 13-acre lake built on site of a once prosperous milling center. Swimming, fishing,
boating; nature, hiking trails, winter sports,
picnicking, playground, concession, improved
campsites, cabins (fee).

Savage River State Forest
349 Headquarters Lane, Grantsville,
301-895-5759;
www.dnr.state.md.us/publiclands/
western/savageriver.html
Largest of Maryland's state forests comprises about 52,800 acres of near wilderness.

A strategic watershed area, the northern
hardwood forest surrounds the Savage River
Dam. Fishing, hunting, hiking trails, winter
sports, primitive camping (permit required).

Spruce Forest Artisan Village
177 Casselman Rd., Grantsville,
301-895-3332;
www.spruceforest.org
Original log cabins and other historic buildings serve as studios for a potter, internationally recognized bird carver, weaver, spinner
stained-glass maker and other artisans. Village. Monday-Saturday 10 a.m.- 5 p.m. Special events (summer; fee). Restaurant.

SPECIAL EVENTS

Spruce Forest Summerfest and Quilt Show
Spruce Forest Artisan Village,
177 Casselman Rd., Grantsville,
301-895-3332;
www.spruceforest.org
More than 200 quilts on display. Second full
Thursday, Friday and Saturday weekend in
July.

RESTAURANTS

★★Penn Alps
125 Casselman Rd., Grantsville,
301-895-5985;
www.pennalps.com

Dutch menu. Breakfast, lunch, dinner, Sunday brunch. Children's menu. **$$**

GREENBELT

WHAT TO SEE AND DO

NASA/Goddard Visitor Center
Greenbelt,
301-286-9041;
www.gsfc.nasa.gov/vc
Satellites, rockets, capsules and exhibits in all phases of space research. Monday-Friday 9 a.m.-4 p.m.

HOTELS

★★Courtyard by Marriott
6301 Golden Triangle Dr., Greenbelt,
301-441-3311, 800-321-2211;
www.marriott.com
152 rooms. **$**

★★★Marriott Greenbelt
6400 Ivy Lane, Greenbelt,
301-441-3700, 800-228-9290;
www.marriott.com
287 rooms. Children's activity center. **$$**

RESTAURANTS

★★Siri's Chef's Secret
5810 Greenbelt Rd.,
Greenbelt,
301-345-6101
Thai menu. Lunch, dinner. Closed Labor Day. Business casual attire. **$$**

★
★
★
★
★

HAGERSTOWN

Visitors to Hagerstown might appear lost in thought, alternately staring at their shoes and turning their gaze to the heavens as they walk. But they're actually soaking in some history on the town's walking tour—points of interest are marked on downtown sidewalks and walking paths in city parks. South Prospect Street is one of the city's oldest neighborhoods, listed on the National Register of Historic Places. The tree-lined street is graced by homes dating back to the early 1800s.
Information: Hagerstown/
Washington County Tourism
Office, 16 Public Square, Hagerstown,
301-791-3246, 888-257-2600;
www.marylandmemories.org

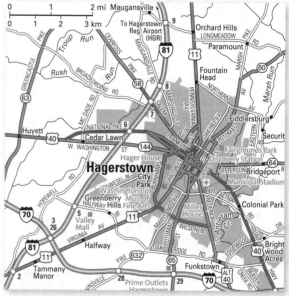

WHAT TO SEE AND DO

Hagerstown Roundhouse Museum
300 S. Burhans Blvd.,
Hagerstown,
301-739-4665;
www.roundhouse.org
Museum houses photographic exhibits of the seven railroads of Hagerstown; historic railroad memorabilia, tools and equipment; archives of maps, books, papers and related items. Gift shop. Friday-Sunday 1-5 p.m.

Jonathan Hager House and Museum
110 Key St.,
Hagerstown,
301-739-8393;
www.fortedwards.org/cwffa/hager.htm
(1739) Stone house in park setting; authentic 18th-century furnishings. April-December: Tuesday-Saturday 10 a.m.-4 p.m., Sunday 2-5 p.m.

Miller House
135 W. Washington St.,
Hagerstown,
301-797-8782
Washington County Historical Society Headquarters. Federal townhouse (circa 1820); three-story spiral staircase, period furnishings, garden, clock, doll and Bell pottery collections; Chesapeake and Ohio Canal and Civil War exhibits; 19th-century country store display. April-December: Wednesday-Saturday 1-4 p.m., Sunday afternoons; closed first two weeks in December.

Washington County Museum of Fine Arts
91 Key St.,
Hagerstown,
301-739-5727;
www.wcmfa.org
Paintings, sculpture, changing exhibits; concerts, lectures. Tuesday-Friday 9 a.m.-5 p.m., Saturday 9 a.m.-4 p.m., Sunday 1-5 p.m.; closed Monday.

SPECIAL EVENTS

Alsatia Mummers Halloween Parade Festival
Hagerstown,
301-739-2044

Ten thousand participants enter this downtown Hagerstown parade, which includes floats, bands, organizations and mummers. Saturday, weekend closest to Halloween.

Hagerstown Railroad Heritage Days
Hagerstown Roundhouse Museum,
300 S. Burhans Blvd., Hagerstown,
301-739-4665;
www.roundhouse.org
Special events centered on the Roundhouse Museum. Mid-June.

Jonathan Hager Frontier Craft Day
Jonathan Hager House and Museum,
110 Key St., Hagerstown,
301-739-8393;
www.fortedwards.org/cwffa/hager.htm
Colonial crafts demonstrated and exhibited. Bluegrass music; food. First weekend in August.

Leitersburg Peach Festival
21378 Leiters Mill Rd.,
Hagerstown
Peach-related edibles, farmers market, bluegrass music. Second weekend in August.

Williamsport C & O Canal Days
30 W. Potomac St.,
Hagerstown,
301-767-3714
Arts and crafts, Indian Village, National Park Service activities; food. Late August.

HOTELS

★★Clarion Hotel
901 Dual Hwy.,
Hagerstown,
301-733-5100, 877-424-6423;
www.clarionhotels.com
210 rooms. Airport transportation available. $

★★Plaza Hotel
1718 Underpass Way,
Hagerstown,
301-797-2500, 800-732-0906;
www.plazahotelhagerstown.com
153 rooms. Airport transportation available. $

63

MARYLAND

HAVRE DE GRACE

Information: Chamber of Commerce, 450 Pennington Ave., Havre de Grace, 410-939-3303, 800-851-7756; www.hdgchamber.com

WHAT TO SEE AND DO

Concord Point Lighthouse
At foot of Lafayette St., Havre de Grace; www.nps.gov/history/maritime/light/concord.htm
(1827) Built of granite, considered the oldest continuously used lighthouse on the East Coast. It was automated in 1928. May-October: weekends and holidays only.

Decoy Museum
215 Giles St., Havre de Grace,
410-939-3739;
www.decoymuseum.com
Adjacent to the blue waters of Chesapeake Bay is a museum dedicated to a sport the locals call waterfowling. The museum houses a large collection of working and decorative decoys used in the Chesapeake Bay area. It also offers workshops on creating effective decoys, honors some of the great decoy makers and hunters of the area and even hosts talks from those currently in the practice of decoy making. Daily 11 a.m.-4 p.m.

Susquehanna State Park
Rock Run Rd., Havre de Grace,
410-734-9035, 888-432-2267;
www.dnr.state.md.us/publiclands/central/susquehanna.html
A 2,639-acre park. Fishing, boat launch; nature, riding and hiking trails; cross-country skiing, picnicking, camping. May-September; fee. In the park is:

Steppingstone Museum
461 Quaker Bottom Rd., Havre de Grace,
410-939-2299, 888-419-1762;
www.steppingstonemuseum.org
Self-guided tour of museum grounds includes sites of a once working Harford County farm; farmhouse is furnished as a turn-of-the-century country home; nearby shops and barn hold many displays and exhibits of the 1880-1920 period; demonstrations of rural arts and crafts of the period. Also here are blacksmith, woodworking, cooper and dairy shops.

May-September, Saturday-Sunday 1-5 p.m. Special events held throughout the year.

SPECIAL EVENTS

Decoy & Wildlife Art Festival
Decoy Museum, 215 Giles St., Havre de Grace,
410-939-3739;
www.decoymuseum.com
Decoys on display, auction. Carving, gunning and calling contests. Refreshments. Early May.

Fall Harvest Festival and Craft Show
Steppingstone Museum,
461 Quaker Bottom Rd.,
Havre de Grace,
410-939-2299, 888-419-1762;
www.steppingstonemuseum.org
Features activities related to the harvest and preparation for winter: apple pressing, scarecrow stuffing and other events. Entertainment. Last full weekend in September.

HOTELS

Vandiver Inn
301 S. Union Ave., Havre de Grace,
410-939-5200, 800-245-1655;
www.vandiverinn.com
This elegant Victorian mansion was built in 1886 and is listed on the National Historic Register. Located just blocks from the Chesapeake Bay, charming antique stores and numerous water activities, this inn offers a relaxing veranda and elegantly appointed guest rooms.
17 rooms. Complimentary full breakfast. Check-in 3-9 p.m. $

RESTAURANTS

★★Bayou
927 Pulaski Hwy. (Rte. 40),
Havre de Grace,
410-939-3565
Seafood menu. Lunch, dinner. Closed Monday; also week of July 4. Children's menu. Casual attire. $$

MARYLAND

HUNT VALLEY

HOTELS

★★★Marriott Hunt Valley Inn
245 Shawan Rd., Hunt Valley,
410-785-7000;
www.marriott.com

Located on 18 acres of land 20 minutes north of Baltimore's Inner Harbor, this hotel offers comfortable guest rooms with the amenities that business and leisure travelers expect. Play a round of golf at one of the six nearby golf courses. For your business needs, take advantage of Marriott's Wired for Business program that offers high-speed Internet access and unlimited local and long distance calls for a low daily fee. 390 rooms. **$$**

RESTAURANTS

★★★The Oregon Grille
1201 Shawan Rd., Hunt Valley,
410-771-0505;
www.theoregongrille.com

The Oregon Grille succeeds in differentiating itself from the fray by offering not only a terrific selection of impeccably prepared steaks (all beef is dry-aged USDA Prime), but also a creative selection of classic American cuisine, including free-range poultry, fresh seafood and vibrant first courses with regional ingredients. The restaurant, set in a renovated 19th-century stone farmhouse, has four fireplaces and is filled with deep, luxurious banquettes.
American menu. Lunch, dinner, Sunday brunch. Bar. Jacket required. Reservations recommended. Outdoor seating. **$$$**

LA PLATA

Information: Charles County Chamber of Commerce, 6360 Crain Hwy., La Plata, 301-932-6500, or the Department of Tourism 301-645-0558; www.charlescountychamber.org

HOTELS

★Best Western La Plata Inn
6900 Crain Hwy.,
Rte. 301, La Plata,
301-934-4900, 877-356-4900;
www.bestwestern.com
73 rooms. Complimentary continental breakfast. **$**

RESTAURANTS

★★★Gustavo Ristorante Italiano
6810 Crain Hwy., La Plata,
301-934-6200

This Tuscan-inspired restaurant offers a menu of hearty Italian favorites including fettuccine Bolognese and penne alla vodka, along with an award-winning wine list.
Italian menu. Lunch, dinner, brunch. Business casual attire. Outdoor seating. **$$**

MARYLAND

LAUREL

Information: Baltimore/Washington Corridor Chamber of Commerce, 312 Marshall Ave., Laurel, 301-725-4000; www.laurel.md.us

WHAT TO SEE AND DO

Montpelier Mansion
9650 Muirkirk Dr., Laurel,
301-953-1376;
www.pgparks.com/places/eleganthistoric/montpelier_visitor.html

(Circa 1780) Built and owned for generations by Maryland's Snowden family; Georgian architecture. George Washington and Abigail Adams were among its early visitors. On the grounds are boxwood gardens, an 18th-century herb garden, and a small summer house. Tours; purchase ticket in gift shop. March-November: Sunday-Thursday noon-3, p.m.; December-February: Sunday 1 p.m., 2 p.m.; weekday groups by appointment. Candlelight tours held in early December.

National Wildlife Visitor Center
10901 Scarlet Tanager Loop, Laurel,
301-497-5760;
www.fws.gov/northeast/paxtuxent/
vcdefault.html
A 12,750-acre national wildlife refuge and research area. Interactive exhibits focus on global environmental issues, migratory birds, wildlife habitats and endangered species. Tram tours available of surrounding forests and lakes (weather permitting; fee). Trails. Gift shop. Daily 9 a.m.-4:30 p.m.

SPECIAL EVENTS
Thoroughbred Racing
Laurel Race Course, Racetrack Rd. and Rte. 198, Laurel,
301-725-0400, 800-638-1859;
www.laurelpark.com

HOTELS
★★Ramada Inn Laurel
3400 Fort Meade Rd., Laurel,
301-498-0900;
www.ramadalaurel.com
166 rooms. $

LA VALE

WHAT TO SEE AND DO
Toll Gate House
Hwy. 40, LaVale,
301-777-5132
(1836) Built to collect tolls from users of Cumberland Road (National Rd.,); only remaining toll house in state; restored. Late May-late October: Saturday-Sunday 1:30-4:30 p.m.

HOTELS
★★Best Western Braddock Motor Inn
1268 National Hwy., La Vale,
301-729-3300, 800-296-6006;
www.bestwesternbraddock.com
105 rooms. Complimentary continental breakfast. Airport transportation available. $

★Super 8
1301 National Hwy., La Vale,
301-729-6265, 800-800-8000;
www.super8.com
63 rooms. Complimentary continental breakfast.$

LEONARDTOWN
Information: St. Mary's County Division of Tourism,
23115 Leonard Hall Dr., Leonardtown,
301-475-4411, 800-327-9023; www.co.saint-marys.md.us

WHAT TO SEE AND DO
Calvert Marine Museum
14150 Solomons Island Rd., Leonardtown,
410-326-2042;
www.calvertmarinemuseum.com
Museum complex with exhibits relating to the culture and marine environment of Chesapeake Bay and Patuxent River estuary; fossils of marine life; estuarine biology displays, aquariums, touch-tank; maritime history exhibits, includes boat-building gallery. Also here is the restored Drum Point Lighthouse, built in 1883. Daily 10 a.m.-5 p.m.

Old Jail Museum
11 Court House Dr.,
Leonardtown,
301-475-2467

Local historical exhibits housed in an old jail; also a genealogy library for researchers. A cannon from Leonard Calvert's ship, the "Ark," is mounted in front. Tuesday-Saturday 10 a.m.- 4 p.m.; closed last week in December.

SPECIAL EVENTS
St. Mary's County Fair
County Fairgrounds, Rte. 5, Leonardtown, 301-475-2256

MCHENRY

SPECIAL EVENTS
Garrett County Agricutural Fair
Garrett County Fairgrounds, Rte. 219, McHenry,
301-533-1010;
www.garrettcountyfair.org
Agricultural exhibits, animals, a 4-H sale and carnival are among the attractions at this county fair. Early August.

McHenry Highland Festival
Rte. 219, McHenry,
www.highlandfest.info

Midway, seafood, horse shows. Late September.

St. Mary's County Oyster Festival
County Fairgrounds, Rte. 5,
Leonardtown,
301-863-5015;
www.usoysterfest.com
National oyster shucking contest; oyster cook-off, seafood and crafts. Third weekend in October.

Deep Creek Lake in McHenry. Traditional Scottish and Celtic festival. First Saturday in June.

RESTAURANTS
★★Point View Inn
609 Deep Creek Dr.,
Mc Henry,
301-387-5555;
www.pointviewinn.com
American menu. Breakfast, lunch, dinner. Closed November-April. Bar. Casual attire. Outdoor seating. $$

OAKLAND
Information: Garrett County Chamber of Commerce, 200 S. Third St., Oakland, 301-387-4386; www.garrettchamber.com

WHAT TO SEE AND DO
Backbone Mountain
Highest point in the state (3,360 feet).

Garrett State Forest
222 Herrington Lane, Oakland,
301-334-2038;
www.dnr.state.md.us/publiclands/western/garrett.html
Approximately 6,800 acres. The forest contains much wildlife. Fishing; hunting, hiking and riding trails, winter activities, primitive camping. Forestry demonstration area.
   Within the forest are:

Herrington Manor State Park
222 Herrington Manor Rd., Oakland,
301-334-9180, 888-432-2267;
www.dnr.state.md.us/publiclands/western/herringtonmanor.html
Well-developed 365-acre park with housekeeping cabins, 53-acre lake. Swimming, fishing, boating (launch, rentals); hiking trails, concession, picnicking, cross-country skiing (rentals). Interpretive programs (summer). Standard fees.

Swallow Falls State Park
222 Herrington Lane, Oakland,
301-387-6938, 888-432-2267;
www.dnr.state.md.us/publiclands/western/swallowfalls.html

67

Surrounding 257 acres, the Youghiogheny River tumbles along the park's boundaries, passing through shaded rocky gorges and over sunny rapids. Muddy Creek produces a 52-foot waterfall. The last remaining stand of virgin hemlock dwarfs visitors. Fishing; nature trails, hiking, picnicking, improved campsites. Pets atregistered campsites only. Standard fees.

Potomac State Forest
1431 Potomac Camp Rd., Oakland, 301-334-2038;
www.dnr.state.md.us/publiclands/western/potomacforest.html
More than 10,685 acres for hiking, riding and hunting. Primitive camping. Timber is harvested regularly here. The area is important in the management of watershed and wildlife programs.

SPECIAL EVENTS
Autumn Glory Festival
Countywide, Oakland,
301-387-4386;
www.garrettchamber.com

Celebrates fall foliage. Features arts and crafts, five-string banjo contest, state fiddle contest, western Maryland tournament of bands, parades, antique show. Mid-October.

Winterfest
15 Visitors Center Dr., Oakland
Deep Creek Lake in McHenry. Ski races, parade, fireworks. Late February or early March.

SPECIALTY LODGINGS
Haley Farm Bed and Breakfast Spa & Retreat Center
16766 Garrett Hwy., Oakland, 301-387-9050, 888-231-3276;
www.haleyfarm.com
Built in 1923; formerly a working farm; near Deep Creek Lake, Swallow Falls and five state parks.
10 rooms. Children over 12 years only. Complimentary full breakfast. $

OCEAN CITY
Deep-sea fishing is highly regarded in Maryland's only Atlantic Ocean resort. The white sand beach, three-mile boardwalk, amusements, golf courses and boating draw thousands of visitors every summer.
Information: Chamber of Commerce, 12320 Ocean Gateway, Ocean City, 410-213-0552; www.oceancity.org

SPECIAL EVENTS
Fishing Contests and Tournaments
Ocean City,
410-213-0552
Many held throughout the year. For exact dates contact the Chamber of Commerce.

HOTELS
★Best Western Ocean City Hotel & Suites
5501 Coastal Hwy., Ocean City,
443-664-4001;
www.bestwestern.com
72 rooms. Complimentary breakfast. $$

★★Clarion Resort Fountainebleau Hotel
10100 Coastal Hwy., Ocean City,
410-524-3535, 877-424-6423;
www.clarioninn.com
250 rooms. Airport transportation available. $$

★Comfort Inn
507 Atlantic Ave., Ocean City,
410-289-5155, 800-228-5150;
www.comfortinnboardwalk.com
84 rooms. Closed December-February. Complimentary continental breakfast. On ocean. $$

★★Holiday Inn
6600 Coastal Hwy., Ocean City,
410-524-1600, 800-315-2621;
www.holiday-inn.com
216 rooms. Children's activity center. Beach.
$$

The Lighthouse Club Hotel
56th St., in the Bay, Ocean City,
410-524-5400, 888-371-5400;
www.fagers.com
Located on the Isle of Wight Bay at Fager's Island, this three-story octagonal hotel offers elegant, beachy accommodations with spectacular views of waterfowl in flight and sunsets over the natural wetlands.
23 rooms. Complimentary continental breakfast. **$$**

★★Princess Royale Ocean Front Resort
9100 Coastal Hwy., Ocean City,
410-524-7777, 800-476-9253;
www.princessroyale.com
310 rooms. Swimming beach, ocean deck, private boardwalk. **$**

★★Quality Inn
5400 Coastal Hwy., Ocean City,
410-524-7200, 877-424-6423;
www.choicehotels.com
126 rooms. On ocean, swimming beach. **$**

RESTAURANTS

★★Bonfire
71st St., Ocean City,
410-524-7171;
www.thebonfirerestaurant.com
American menu. Dinner. Closed Monday-Thursday in winter. Bar. Children's menu. **$$**

★★Embers
2305 Philadelphia Ave., Ocean City,
410-289-3322;
www.embers.com
American menu. Dinner. Closed December-February. Bar. Children's menu. **$$**

★★★Fager's Island
201 60th St., Ocean City,
410-524-5500;
www.fagers.com
The outdoor deck overlooking the bay is the perfect spot to take in a glorious summer sunset. The menu does well with standard and creative seafood preparations as well as classics like prime rib. Choose from a wine list that features over 500 bottles to accompany your meal.
Pacific-Rim/Pan-Asian, seafood menu. Lunch, dinner, brunch. Bar. **$$**

★★Harrison's Harbor Watch
806 S. Boardwalk, Ocean City,
410-289-5121
Seafood menu. Dinner. Closed Monday-Thursday December-March. Bar. Children's menu. **$$**

★★★Hobbit
101 81st St., Ocean City,
410-524-8100
This restaurant serves many of your old favorites, as well as creative new items. After dinner, browse through the unique gift shop for Hobbit memorabilia.
American, seafood menu. Lunch, dinner. Bar. Children's menu. **$$**

★Marina Deck Restaurant
306 Dorchester St., Ocean City,
410-289-4411;
www.marinadeckrestaurant.com
Seafood, steak menu. Breakfast, lunch, dinner. Closed mid-November-mid-March. Bar. Children's menu. Casual attire. Outdoor seating. **$**

★★Ocean Club
49th St., Ocean City,
410-524-7500
Seafood menu. Breakfast, lunch, dinner. Closed Monday-Tuesday off-season; mid January-February. Bar. Children's menu. **$$**

★★Phillips Crab House
2004 Philadelphia Ave., Ocean City,
410-289-6821;
www.phillipsoc.com
Seafood menu. Lunch, dinner. Closed November-March. Bar. Children's menu. **$$**

MARYLAND

★★Phillips Seafood House
14101 Coastal Hwy., Ocean City,
410-250-1200, 800-799-2788;
www.phillipsseafoodhouse.com

OWINGS MILLS

WHAT TO SEE AND DO

MPT (Maryland Public Television)
11767 Owings Mills Blvd.,
Owings Mills,
410-356-5600, 800-223-3678;
www.mpt.org
Tours of the state's television network studios. By appointment.

Soldiers Delight Natural Environment Area
5100 Deer Park Rd., Owings Mills,
410-461-5005;
www.dnr.state.md.us/publiclands/central/
soldiers.html
This 1,725-acre park has 19th-century chrome mines; restored log cabin, scenic overlook, hiking and nature trails, picnicking (at visitor center only). It is the only undisturbed serpentine barren in the state. Pets must be on leash. Visitor center: Wednesday-Sunday 9 a.m.-4 p.m.

RESTAURANTS

★★★Linwood's
25 Crossroads Dr., Owings Mills,
410-356-3030;
www.linwoods.com
Dishes have included honey-lavender grouper with porcini and leek risotto and grilled asparagus; grilled black Angus steak with truffle-infused pommes frites, jumbo asparagus and black pepper steak sauce; and grilled veal chop with caramelized peaches, buttered spinach and potato Ann.
American menu. Lunch, dinner. Bar. Business casual attire. Reservations recommended. Outdoor seating. **$$$**

Seafood menu. Lunch, dinner. Closed late November-late February. Bar. Children's menu. **$$**

PHOENIX

RESTAURANTS

★★Peerce's Plantation
12460 Dulaney Valley Rd., Phoenix,
410-252-3100

American menu. Lunch, dinner, brunch. Bar. Children's menu. Jacket required. Valet parking. Outdoor seating. **$$$**

PIKESVILLE

HOTELS

★★Hilton Pikesville
1726 Reisterstown Rd., Pikesville,
410-653-1100, 800-283-0333;

www.pikesville.hilton.com
171 rooms. **$$**

POTOMAC

RESTAURANTS

★★★Normandie Farm
10710 Falls Rd., Potomac,
301-983-8838;
www.popovers.com
Normandie Farm is reminiscent of a country home, serving entrees such as fresh soft-

shell crab with bacon, scallions, pine nuts and citrus beurre blanc or tenderloin tips with mushrooms, sun-dried tomatoes and cabernet sauce.
French, seafood menu. Lunch, dinner, brunch. Closed Monday. Bar. **$$**

★★★Old Angler's Inn
10801 MacArthur Blvd., Potomac,
301-299-9097;
www.oldanglersinn.com
Located in a Tudor-style house built in 1860, the rustic dining room is a perfect spot for a cozy evening. In winter get a table near the fireplace. In summer the terrace provides a lovely setting.
Seafood menu. Lunch, dinner. Closed Monday. Bar. Outdoor seating. **$$**

ROCKVILLE
Located at the northern edge of D.C., Rockville is the second-largest city in Maryland. The Great Falls of the Potomac are nine miles south off Highway 189. Stone locks and levels are still visible from the Chesapeake & Ohio Canal, which was built to circumvent the falls. St. Mary's Cemetery holds the graves of F. Scott and Zelda Fitzgerald.
Information: Chamber of Commerce, 250 Hungerford Dr., Rockville, 301-424-9300; www.rockvillechamber.org

WHAT TO SEE AND DO
Beall-Dawson House
103 W. Montgomery Ave.,
Rockville,
301-762-1492
(1815) Federal architecture; period furnishings, library; museum shop, 19th-century doctor's office. Tours guided by docents. Tuesday-Saturday noon-4 p.m.

Cabin John Regional Park
7700 Tuckerman Lane,
Rockville,
301-299-0024
This 551-acre park has playgrounds, miniature train ride, nature center; concerts (summer evenings; free); tennis courts, game fields, ice rink, nature trails and picnicking. Fee for some activities. Daily.

SPECIAL EVENTS
Hometown Holidays
Rockville,
301-424-9300
Family entertainment; carnival rides and games, arts and crafts, music, food, skate park. Memorial Day weekend.

HOTELS
★★Courtyard by Marriott
2500 Research Blvd.,
Rockville,
301-670-6700;
www.courtyard.com
147 rooms. **$**

★Crowne Plaza
3 Research Court, Rockville,
301-840-0200, 800-496-7621;
www.crowneplaza.com
124 rooms. Complimentary full breakfast. **$**

★★Hilton Executive Meeting Center
1750 Rockville Pike, Rockville,
301-468-1100, 800-445-8661;
www.hilton.com
315 rooms. **$$**

RESTAURANTS
★A and J
1319-C Rockville Pike, Rockville,
301-251-7878
Chinese menu. Lunch, dinner. Casual attire. **$**

★★Addie's
11120 Rockville Pike, Rockville,
301-881-0081;
www.addiesrestaurant.com
American menu. Lunch, dinner, brunch. Closed Sunday. Bar. Children's menu. Outdoor seating. **$$**

★★Andalucia
12300 Wilkens Ave.,
Rockville,
301-770-1880
Spanish menu. Lunch, dinner. Closed Monday. Bar. Reservations recommended. **$$**

★★Bombay Bistro
98 W. Montgomery Ave., Rockville,
301-762-8798;
www.bombaybistro.com
Indian, vegetarian menu. Lunch, dinner. Closed
Labor Day. **$$**

★★Copeland's of New Orleans
1584 Rockville Pike, Rockville,
301-230-0968;
www.copelandsofneworleans.com
Cajun/Creole, seafood menu. Lunch, dinner.
Bar. Children's menu. **$**

★Hard Times Cafe
1117 Nelson St., Rockville,
301-294-9720;
www.hardtimes.com
American menu. Lunch, dinner. Bar. Children's menu. **$**

★★Il Pizzico
15209 Frederick Rd., Rockville,
301-309-0610;
www.ilpizzico.com
Italian menu. Lunch, dinner. Closed Sunday.
Bar. **$**

★Red Hot & Blue
16811 Crabbs Branch Way,
Rockville,
301-948-7333;
www.redhotandblue.com
American menu. Lunch, dinner. Bar. Children's
menu. Outdoor seating. Blues memorabilia. **$$**

★Seven Seas
1776 E. Jefferson St., Rockville,
301-770-5020;
www.sevenseasrestaurant.com
Chinese, Japanese menu. Lunch, dinner. Bar.
$$

★Silver Diner
11806 Rockville Pike, Rockville,
301-770-1444;
www.silverdiner.com
American menu. Breakfast, lunch, dinner.
Children's menu. **$**

★★Tara Asia
199D E. Montgomery Ave., Rockville,
301-315-8008
Pan-Asian menu. Lunch, dinner. Bar. Casual
attire. Outdoor seating. **$$**

★★Taste of Saigon
410 Hungerford Dr., Rockville,
301-424-7222
Vietnamese menu. Lunch, dinner. Bar. Outdoor seating. **$$**

★★That's Amore
15201 Shady Grove Rd., Rockville,
301-268-0682;
www.thatsamore.com
Italian menu. Lunch, dinner. Bar. **$$**

SALISBURY
"Central City of the Eastern Shore" and of the Delmarva Peninsula, Salisbury has a marina
on the Wicomico River providing access to Chesapeake Bay. It lies within 30 miles of duck
hunting and deep-sea fishing.

Information: Wicomico County Convention & Visitors Bureau, 8480 Ocean Hwy.,
Delmar, 410-548-4914; 800-332-TOUR.

Information is also available from the Chamber of Commerce, 144 E. Main St.,
410-749-0144; www.salisburyarea.com

WHAT TO SEE AND DO
Poplar Hill Mansion
117 Elizabeth St., Salisbury,
410-749-1776;
www.poplarhillmansion.org
(Circa 1805) Example of Georgian- and
Federal-style architecture; Palladian and
bull's-eye windows, large brass box locks
on doors, woodwork, mantels and fireplaces. Period furniture; country garden.

First & third Sundays of the month 1-4 p.m.; Tuesday-Saturday by appointment. Admission is free on Sunday.

Salisbury Zoological Park
755 S. Park Dr., Salisbury,
410-548-3188;
www.salisburyzoo.org
Natural habitats for almost 400 mammals, birds and reptiles. Major exhibits include bears, monkeys, jaguars, bison, waterfowl. Also exotic plants. Memorial Day-Labor Day: daily 8 a.m.-7:30 p.m.; rest of year: daily 8 a.m.-4:30 p.m.

Ward Museum of Wildfowl Art
909 S. Schumaker Dr.,
Salisbury,
410-742-4988;
www.wardmuseum.org

Displays include the history of decoy and wildfowl carving in North America; wildfowl habitats; contemporary wildfowl art. Changing exhibits. Gift shop. Monday-Saturday 10 a.m.-5 p.m., Sunday noon-5 p.m.

HOTELS
★**Comfort Inn**
2701 N. Salisbury Blvd., Salisbury,
410-543-4666, 800-638-7949;
www.choicehotels.com
96 rooms. Complimentary continental breakfast. **$**

★★**Ramada Inn**
300 S. Salisbury Blvd., Salisbury,
410-546-4400;
www.ramada.com
156 rooms. Airport transportation available. **$**

SEVERNA PARK

RESTAURANTS
★★★**Cafe Bretton**
849 Baltimore-Annapolis Blvd.,
Severna Park,
410-647-8222

French menu. Dinner. Closed Sunday-Monday. Bar. Reservations recommended. **$$$**

SILVER SPRING
Information: Chamber of Commerce, 8601 Georgia Ave., Silver Spring, 301-565-3777; www.gsscc.org

RESTAURANTS
★★**Blair Mansion Inn**
7711 Eastern Ave., Silver Spring,
301-588-6646;
www.blairmansion.com
American menu. Lunch, dinner. Closed Monday. Bar. 1890s Victorian mansion; gaslight chandelier, 7 fireplaces. Murder mystery dinners. Thursday-Sunday. **$$**

★★**Mrs. K's Toll House**
9201 Colesville Rd., Silver Spring,
301-589-3500;
www.mrsks.com

American menu. Lunch, dinner, Sunday brunch. Closed Monday. Children's menu. Business casual attire. Reservations recommended. Outdoor seating. **$$**

★**Vicino**
959 Sligo Ave., Silver Spring,
301-588-3372
Italian menu. Lunch, dinner. Children's menu. Outdoor seating. **$$**

★
★
★
★

SNOW HILL

WHAT TO SEE AND DO

Nassawango Iron Furnace

Pocomoke Forest, Old Furnace Rd.,
Snow Hill,
410-632-2032

One of the oldest industrial sites in Maryland and one of the earliest hot blast mechanisms still intact. The stack was restored in 1966; archaeological excavations were made and a canal, dike and portion of the old waterwheel used in the manufacturing process were found. The remains of the area are undergoing restoration. April-October: daily 11 a.m.-5 p.m. Surrounding the iron furnace is:

Furnace Town

Pocomoke Forest
3816 Old Furnace Rd., Snow Hill,
410-632-3732;
www.dnr.state.md.us/publiclands/eastern/
pocomokeforest.html

This 1840s industrial village occupies 22 acres and includes six historic structures, a working 19th-century blacksmith shop, a museum and company store and archaeological excavations. Nature trail and picnic area. Special events take place throughout the season. Same hours and fees as Nassawango Iron Furnace.

SPECIALTY LODGINGS

River House Inn

201 E. Market St., Snow Hill,
410-632-2722;
www.riverhouseinn.com
8 rooms. This inn was built in 1860. **$**

SPARKS

RESTAURANTS

★★★The Milton Inn

14833 York Rd., Sparks,
410-771-4366;
www.miltoninn.com
This old stone house has been restored for use as a country inn that serves exceptional food in an authentic colonial atmosphere.
American menu. Lunch, dinner. Closed Saturday. Bar. Children's menu. Business casual attire. Reservations recommended. Outdoor seating. **$$$**

ST. MARY'S CITY

Under the leadership of Leonard Calvert, Maryland's first colonists bought a Native American village on this site upon their arrival in the New World. The settlement was the capital and hub of the area until 1694, when the colonial capital was moved to Annapolis, and the town gradually disappeared. The city and county are still rich in historical attractions.
Information: St. Mary's County Division of Tourism, 23115 Leonard Hall Dr.,
Leonardtown, 301-475-4411, 800-327-9023;
www.co.saint-marys.md.us

WHAT TO SEE AND DO

Historic St. Mary's City

Rte. 5 and Rosecroft Rd., St. Mary's City,
240-895-4990, 800-762-1634;
www.stmaryscity.org

Outdoor museum at site of Maryland's first capital (1634) includes reconstructed State House (1676), replica of the original capitol building; other exhibits include the "Maryland Dove," replica of a 17th-century ship, and archaeological exhibits. Also a 17th-century tobacco plantation, reconstructed 17th-century inn; visitor center, outdoor cafe. Call or visit the Web site for hours.

Also here is:

Margaret Brent Memorial
Trinity Churchyard, 18751 Hogaboom Lane, St. Mary's City
Gazebo overlooking the river; memorial to the woman who being a wealthy landowner, requested the right to vote in the Maryland Assembly in 1648 to settle Leonard Calvert's affairs after his death.

Leonard Calvert Monument
Trinity Churchyard, 18751 Hogaboom Lane, St. Mary's City
Monument to Maryland's first colonial governor.

Point Lookout State Park
St. Mary's City,
301-872-5688, 888-432-2267;
www.dnr.state.md.gov/publiclands/ southern/pointlookout.html

Site of Confederate Monument, the only memorial erected by U.S. government to honor P.O.W.s who died in Point Lookout Prison Camp during Civil War (3,384 died here). Swimming, fishing, boating; hiking, picnicking, improved camping. April-October; self-contained camping units year-round. Nature center. Civil War museum. Standard fees. May-September: weekends.

SPECIAL EVENTS
Crab Festival
41348 Medley's Neck Rd., St. Mary's City
Steamed crabs, and other dishes. Arts and crafts, antique and classic car show. First Sunday in June.

Maryland Days
38370 Point Breeze Rd., St. Mary's City
Boat rides, seafood, 17th-century militia musters. Third weekend in March.

ST. MICHAELS
Chartered in 1804, Saint Michaels now offers visitors an abundance of shops, marinas, restaurants, bed-and-breakfasts and country inns, as well as many Federal- and Victorian-period buildings.
Information: Talbot County Chamber of Commerce, Easton Plaza Suite 53, Easton, 410-822-4653; www.talbotchamber.org

WHAT TO SEE AND DO
Chesapeake Bay Maritime Museum
Mill St. and Navy Point, St. Michaels,
410-745-2916;
www.cbmm.org
This waterside museum consists of nine buildings and includes a historic lighthouse, floating exhibits, boat-building shop with working exhibit, ship models, small boats and more. Special events are held throughout the year. Daily 9 a.m.-5 p.m.; summer to 6 p.m.; winter to 4 p.m.

The Footbridge
109 S. Talbot St., St. Michaels
Joins Navy Point to Cherry St. Only remaining bridge of three that once connected the town with areas across the harbor.

The Patriot
Chesapeake Bay Museum Dock, St. Michaels,
410-745-3100;
www.patriotcruises.com
A one-hour narrated cruise on Miles River. Four trips daily at 11 a.m., 12:30 p.m., 2:30 p.m., 4 p.m. April-October.

St. Mary's Square

This public square was laid out in 1770 by Englishman James Braddock. Several buildings date to the early 1800s, including the Cannonball House and Dr. Miller's Farmhouse. The Ship's Carpenter Bell was cast in 1842; across from the bell stand two cannons, one dating from the Revolution, the other from the War of 1812.

Also here is:

St. Mary's Square Museum

409 St. Mary's Square, St. Michaels, 410-745-9561
Mid-19th-century home of "half-timber" construction; one of the earliest buildings in St. Michaels. Exhibits of historical and local interest. Early May-late October: Saturday-Sunday 10 a.m.-4 p.m.; also by appointment. Inquire about the town walking tour brochures. Contact the Town Office.

SPECIAL EVENTS

Mid-Atlantic Maritime Festival

Chesapeake Bay Maritime Museum, Mill St. at Navy Point, St. Michaels, 410-745-2916
Nautical celebration with fly-fishing demonstration, skipjack races, boat building contest, boat parade, seafood festival cooking contest. Three days in mid-May.

HOTELS

★★Harbourtowne Golf Resort & Conference Center

Rte. 33 and Martingham Dr., St. Michaels, 410-745-9066, 800-446-9066;
www.harbourtowne.com
111 rooms. Complimentary full breakfast. Golf. $$

★★★Inn At Perry Cabin

308 Watkins Lane, St. Michaels, 410-745-2200, 866-278-9601;
www.perrycabin.com
Built just after the War of 1812, the Inn at Perry Cabin looks and feels like a gracious manor house, with mahogany sleigh beds, antiques and views of the Miles River. Cycling, golfing and sailing are popular pastimes. The inn offers high tea and scones with Devonshire cream and shortbread served at evening turndown. Also offers a spa.
81 rooms. Children over 10 years only. $$$

★★★St. Michaels Harbour Inn, Marina, & Spa

101 N. Harbor Rd., St. Michaels, 410-745-9001, 800-955-9001;
www.harbourinn.com
From this waterfront resort, visitors can take a short stroll down the main road to shops, museums and historical sites.
46 rooms. $$$

SPECIALTY LODGINGS

Parsonage Inn

210 N. Talbot, St. Michaels, 410-745-5519, 800-394-5519;
www.parsonage-inn.com
Restored in 1985, this inn is located just steps from the Maritime Museum, restaurants and shops. Guests are welcome to borrow the inn's bicycles to explore the historic area.
8 rooms. Complimentary full breakfast. Check-in 2-7 p.m. $$

Wade's Point Inn

Wades Point Rd., St. Michaels, 410-745-2500, 888-923-3466;
www.wadespoint.com
This bed-and-breakfast is located just outside historic St. Michaels. It is situated on 120 acres of fields, woodlands and 1/2 mile of coastline overlooking Chesapeake Bay.
24 rooms. Closed mid-December-mid-March. Complimentary continental breakfast. $$

RESTAURANTS

★★★208 Talbot

208 N. Talbot St., St. Michaels, 410-745-3838;
www.208talbot.com
Chef Brendan Keegan puts a sophisticated, soulful twist on local ingredients, serving entrees including corn flake-crusted fried mahi mahi with basil potato salad, sweet corn cream and grape tomato relish; and braised pork shoulder with peach chutney, a corn tamale and salsa roja.

MARYLAND

★
★
★
★
★

★★Bistro St. Michaels

403 S. Talbot St., St. Michaels,
410-745-9111;
www.bistrostmichaels.com
French bistro menu. Dinner. Closed
Tuesday-Wednesday; February. Bar. Casual
attire. Outdoor seating. **$$$**

★★Chesapeake Landing Seafood

23713 St. Michael's Rd., St. Michaels,
410-745-9600
Seafood menu. Lunch, dinner. Children's
menu. Casual attire. **$$**

★★★Sherwood's Landing

308 Watkin Lane, St. Michaels,
410-745-2200, 866-278-9601;
www.perrycabin.com
Located in the Inn at Perry Cabin, Sherwood
Landing serves continental selections
made with regional ingredients such as
crab spring rolls with pink grapefruit, avocado and toasted almonds; and honey- and
tarragon-glazed lamb shank with sun-dried
tomato sauce.
American menu. Breakfast, lunch, dinner.
Bar. Children's menu. Valet parking. Out-
door seating. **$$$**

★★Shore Restaurant & Lounge

101 N. Harbor Rd., St. Michaels,
410-924-4769;
www.shorerestaurant.net
American, International menu. Breakfast,
lunch, dinner, Sunday brunch. Bar. Busi-
ness casual attire. Outdoor seating. **$$$**

★St. Michaels Crab House

305 Mulberry St.,
St. Michaels,
410-745-3737;
www.stmichaelscrabhouse.com
Seafood menu. Lunch, dinner. Closed
Wednesday; mid-December-March. Bar.
Children's menu. Casual attire. Outdoor
seating. **$$**

SWANTON

WHAT TO SEE AND DO

Deep Creek Lake State Park

898 State Park Rd., Swanton,
301-387-4111, 888-432-2267;
www.dnr.state.md.gov/publiclands/
western/deepcreeklake.html
Approximately 1,800 acres with 3,900-acre
man-made lake. Swimming, bathhouse,
fishing, boating (rowboat rentals); nature
and hiking trails, picnicking (shelters),
playground, concession, improved camp-
sites (fee).

SPECIALTY LODGINGS

Carmel Cove Bed and Breakfast

105 Monastery Way, Oakland,
301-387-0067;
www.carmelcoveinn.com
This bed-and-breakfast was once a monas-
tery and now offers fine accommodations
surrounded by beautiful mountains and the
clear lake.
10 rooms. Children over 12 years only.
Complimentary full breakfast. Whirlpool.
Built in 1945. **$$**

TANEYTOWN

SPECIALTY LODGINGS

Antrim 1844

30 Trevanion Rd.,
Taneytown,
410-756-6812, 800-858-1844;
www.antrim1844.com
This country inn is located on 23 acres
of property in the Catoctin Mountains.
Guest rooms and suites are decorated with
antiques.
27 rooms. Complimentary full breakfast.
Spa. **$$**

RESTAURANTS

★★★Antrim 1844
30 Trevanion Rd., Taneytown,
410-756-6812, 800-858-1844;
www.antrim1844.com

The Paris-trained chef at Antrim 1844 serves a unique menu each night, with entrees such as filet mignon with bacon and walnut, braised lamb volcano or porcupine shrimp.

American, French menu. Breakfast, dinner. Bar. Business casual attire. Reservations recommended. Outdoor seating. $$$$

THURMONT

Information: Tourism Council of Frederick County, 19 E. Church St., Frederick, 301-228-2888, 800-999-3613; www.visitfrrederick.org

WHAT TO SEE AND DO

Catoctin Mountain National Park
Park Central Rd.,
Thurmont,
301-663-9388;
www.nps.gov/cato

Located one hour outside Baltimore, this 5,810-acre forest is an easily accessible nature retreat. The park is adjacent to two state parks and Camp David, the weekend mountain home of the U.S. president. The park offers camping, picnicking areas, fishing and playgrounds. Park: Open year-round during daylight hours. Visitor Center: Monday-Thursday 10 a.m.-4:30 p.m., Friday 10 a.m.-5 p.m., Saturday-Sunday 8:30 a.m.-5 p.m.

Cunningham Falls State Park
14039 Catoctin Hollow Rd.,
Thurmont,
301-271-7574, 888-432-2267;
www.dnr.state.md.gov/publiclands/
western/cunninghamfalls.html

This state park encompasses 4,950 acres in the Catoctin Mountains. Two recreation areas: Houck, five miles west of town, has swimming, fishing, boating (rentals); picnicking, camping, hiking trails that lead to 78-foot falls and scenic overlooks. Manor Area, three miles south of town on Route 15, has picnicking, camping, playground. Trout fishing in Big Hunting Creek. Ruins of Iron Masters Mansion and the industrial village that surrounded it are also here.

SPECIAL EVENTS

Catoctin Colorfest
6602 Foxville Rd.,
Thurmont,
301-271-4432;
www.colorfest.org

Fall foliage; arts and crafts show. Second weekend in October.

Maple Syrup Demonstration
Cunningham Falls State Park,
14039 Catoctin Hollow Rd.,
Thurmont,
301-271-7574;
www.dnr.state.md.us/publiclands/western/
cunninghamfalls.html

Tree tapping, sap boiling; carriage rides; food; children's storytelling corner. Usually second and third weekends in March.

HOTELS

★★Cozy Country Inn Thurmont
103 Frederick Rd., Thurmont,
301-271-4301;
www.cozyvillage.com

21 rooms. Complimentary continental breakfast. Restaurant, bar. Children's activity center. $

★
★
★
★
★

TILGHMAN ISLAND

SPECIALTY LODGINGS

Chesapeake Wood Duck Inn
21490 Gibsontown Rd. at Dogwood
Harbor, Tilghman Island,
410-886-2070, 800-956-2070;
www.woodduckinn.com

This waterfront, Victorian-style bed-and-breakfast was first used as a boarding house, but has since been remodeled to provide comfortable and intimate lodging for guests.

7 rooms. Children over 14 permitted. Complimentary full breakfast. **$$**

Lazyjack Inn
5907 Tilghman Island Rd.,
Tilghman Island,
410-886-2215, 800-690-5080;
www.lazyjackinn.com

4 rooms. Children over 12 years only. Complimentary full breakfast. **$$**

RESTAURANTS

★★Bay Hundred Restaurant
6178 Tilghman Island Rd., Tilghman,
410-886-2126;
www.bayhundredrestaurant.net

Seafood menu. Lunch, dinner, brunch. Children's menu. Outdoor seating.

★★The Bridge
6136 Tilghman Island Rd.,
Tilghman Island,
410-886-2330;
www.bridge-restaurant.com

American menu. Lunch, dinner. Bar. Children's menu. Casual attire. Reservations recommended. Outdoor seating. **$$**

TIMONIUM

SPECIAL EVENTS

Maryland State Fair
Maryland Fairgrounds, 2100 York Rd.,
Timonium,
410-252-0200;
www.marylandstatefair.com

Ten-day festival of home arts; entertainment, midway; agricultural demonstrations, Thoroughbred horse racing, livestock presentations. Late August-early September.

RESTAURANTS

★★Liberatore's
9515 Derreco Rd., Timonium,
410-561-3300;
www.liberatores.com

Italian menu. Dinner. Bar. Business casual attire. Reservations recommended. Outdoor seating. **$$**

TOWSON

Information: Baltimore County Chamber of Commerce, 102 W. Pennsylvania Ave., Towson, 410-825-6200

WHAT TO SEE AND DO

Hampton National Historic Site
535 Hampton Lane,
Towson,
410-823-1309;
www.nps.gov/hamp

Includes ornate Georgian mansion (circa 1790) (tours), formal gardens and plantation outbuildings. Gift shop. Grounds: daily 9 a.m.-5 p.m.; Mansion tours: daily on the hour, 9 a.m.-4 p.m. Tea room open for luncheon. Daily; closed six weeks mid-January-early March.

Towson State University
8000 York Rd., Towson,
410-704-2000;
www.towson.edu

(1866) 15,000 students. On campus are three art galleries, including Holtzman Art Gallery, with an extensive collection of art media. September-May, Tuesday-Saturday. Concerts and sporting events are held in the Towson Center.

SPECIAL EVENTS
Maryland House and Garden Pilgrimage
1105-A Providence Rd.,
Towson,
410-821-6933;
www.mhgp.org
More than 100 homes and gardens throughout the state are open. Late April-early May.

HOTELS
★★★**Sheraton Baltimore North**
903 Dulaney Valley Rd., Towson,
410-321-7400, 800-423-7619;
www.sheratonbaltimore.com
283 rooms. **$$**

RESTAURANTS
★★**Cafe Troia**
28 W. Allegheny Ave., Towson,
410-337-0133;
www.cafetroia.com
Italian menu. Lunch, dinner. Closed Sunday. Bar. Casual attire. Reservations recommended. Outdoor seating. **$$**

UPPER MARLBORO

WHAT TO SEE AND DO
Marlton Golf Club
9413 Midland Turn, Upper Marlboro,
301-856-7566;
www.marltongolf.com
Marlton is a very narrow course that like many others in the area, requires the ability to play a number of different types of shots.

Some holes require arrow-straight drives, some fly over large expanses of water to medium-sized greens and some make approaching the green impossible from one side of the fairway. However, for the challenge, the price is cheap: just $24 for 18 holes on weekdays.

WALDORF
Information: Tourism Director, La Plata,
301-645-0558, 800-766-3386; www.explorecharlescomd.com

WHAT TO SEE AND DO
Dr. Samuel A. Mudd House Museum
3725 Dr. Samuel Mudd Rd.,
Waldorf,
301-645-6870
(Circa 1830) Where Dr. Mudd set John Wilkes Booth's broken leg, unaware that Booth had just shot the president. Mudd was convicted and imprisoned for life, but pardoned four years later by President Andrew Johnson. Tours conducted by costumed docents, some of whom are Dr. Mudd's descendants. April-November: Saturday-Sunday, Wednesday 11 a.m.-4 p.m.; last tour at 3:30 p.m.

Farmer's Market and Auction
29890 Three Notch Rd., Waldorf,
301-884-3108
Nearby Amish farms offer fresh baked goods and produce (auction Wednesday) for sale; more than 90 shops. Antique dealers. Wednesday and Saturday.

Maryland Indian Cultural Center
16816 Country Lane,
Waldorf,
301-372-1932;
www.somd.com/Detailed/1482.php
Exhibits reflect diverse tribal structures, art, lodging construction and cultures of Native

Americans. Tuesday, Thursday, Sunday afternoons.

SPECIAL EVENTS

John Wilkes Booth Escape Route Tour

Surrat House and Tavern,
9118 Brandywine Rd., Waldorf,
301-868-1121;
www.surratt.org/su_bert.html
Day-long bus tour of Booth's route from Ford's Theatre, Washington, through southern Maryland to site of Garrett's farm, Virginia, with expert commentary. Select dates in April, May, September and October.

HOTELS

★★Holiday Inn

45 St. Patrick's Dr., Waldorf,
301-645-8200, 800-645-8277;
waldorfmd.holiday-inn.com
191 rooms. **$**

WESTMINSTER

Westminster, a Union supply depot at the Battle of Gettysburg, saw scattered action before the battle. It was the first town in the United States to offer complete rural free delivery mail service (started in 1899 with four two-horse wagons).

HOTELS

★Best Western Westminster Catering & Conference Center

451 WMC Dr., Westminster,
410-857-1900, 800-780-7234;
www.bestwesternwestminster.com
102 rooms. Complimentary continental breakfast. **$**

RESTAURANTS

★★Johansson's Dining House

4 W. Main St., Westminster,
410-876-0101
American menu. Lunch, dinner. Bar. Children's menu. Business casual attire. **$$**

81

MARYLAND

NEW JERSEY

FROM INDUSTRIAL CITIES TO LUSH, TREE-SHADED, 18TH-CENTURY TOWNS TO SMALL SEASIDE communities, New Jersey is a state of contrasts. Hard-working areas such as Newark and Elizabeth might lead the unacquainted visitor to believe that the Garden State is a misnomer, but traveling deeper into New Jersey—out of the cities and off the highways—will reveal the flourishing greenery that earned the state its nickname.

The swampy meadows west of the New Jersey Turnpike have been reclaimed and transformed into commercial and industrial areas. The Meadowlands, a multimillion-dollar sports complex, offers horse racing, the New York Giants and the New York Jets NFL football teams, the New Jersey Devils NHL hockey team and the New Jersey Nets NBA basketball team. But commercial and industrial interests have reached only so far into the state's natural resources. More than 800 lakes and ponds, 100 rivers and streams and 1,400 miles of freshly stocked trout streams are scattered throughout the state's wooded, scenic northwest corner. The coastline, stretching 127 miles from Sandy Hook to Cape May, offers excellent swimming and ocean fishing.

New Jersey is also rich in history. George Washington spent a quarter of his time here as commander-in-chief of the Revolutionary Army. On Christmas night in 1776, he crossed the Delaware and surprised the Hessians at Trenton. A few days later, he marched to Princeton and defeated three British regiments. He then spent the winter in Morristown, where the memories of his campaign are preserved in a national historical park.

Information: www.state.nj.us/travel

ALLAIRE STATE PARK

Allaire State Park has more than 3,000 acres and offers a fishing pond for children under 14; multiuse trails, picnic facilities, playground, camping (summer) and the opportunity to visit a historic 19th-century village. Park (daily).

Information: 732-938-2371;
www.state.nj.us/dep/parksandforests/parks/allaire.html

WHAT TO SEE AND DO

Historic Allaire Village

524 Allaire Rd., Farmingdale,
732-915-3500;
www.allairevillage.org

In 1822, James Allaire bought this site as a source of bog ore for his ironworks. The furnace also produced items such as hollowware pots and kettles, stoves, sadirons and pipes for New York City's waterworks. Today, visitors can explore the bakery, general store, blacksmith and carpentry shops, worker's houses, the community church and other buildings still much as they were in 1836. Village grounds and center (daily 10 a.m.-4 p.m.); village buildings (Memorial Day-Labor Day: Wednesday-Sunday noon-4 p.m.; Labor Day-November: Saturday-Sunday noon-4 p.m.); special events (February-December).

Train Rides

Historic Allaire Village,
Allaire State Road,
Farmingdale,
732-915-3500

Narrow-gauge steam and diesel locomotive rides. April-mid-October: daily.

ASBURY PARK

This popular shore resort was bought in 1871 by New York brush manufacturer James A. Bradley and named for Francis Asbury, first American Bishop of the Methodist Episcopal Church. Bradley established a town for temperance advocates and good neighbors. The beach and the three lakes proved so attractive that by 1874, Asbury Park had grown into a borough, and by 1897, a city. It is the home of the famous boardwalk, Convention Hall and the Paramount Theatre. In September 1934, the SS *Morro Castle* was grounded off this beach and burned with a loss of 122 lives. Asbury Park became the birthplace of a favorite sweet when a local confectioner introduced saltwater taffy. Today, this is a popular resort area for swimming and fishing.

Information: Greater Asbury Park Chamber of Commerce, 308 Main St., Asbury Park, 732-775-7676; www.asburyparkchamber.com

WHAT TO SEE AND DO

Stephen Crane House
508 Fourth Ave.,
Asbury Park,
732-775-5682
Early home of the author of *The Red Badge of Courage* contains photos, drawings and other artifacts. Tours by appointment.

The Stone Pony
913 Ocean Ave.,
Asbury Park,
732-502-0600;
www.stoneponyonline.com
This legendary nightclub is known for unexpected visits from Bruce Springsteen and others. Includes the Asbury Park Gallery, with a collection of photographs and other memorabilia. Daily.

SPECIAL EVENTS

Horse Racing
Monmouth Park, 175 Oceanport Ave.,
Oceanport,
732-222-5100;
www.monmouthpark.com
Thoroughbred racing. Memorial Day-Labor Day: Wednesday-Sunday.

Jazz Fest
1 Municipal Plaza,
Asbury Park,
732-775-7676
Late June.

Metro Lyric Opera Series
Paramount Theatre, Asbury Park,
732-720-9200
At the Paramount Theatre on the Boardwalk. Saturday evenings, July-August.

Ocean Grove House Tour
50 Pitman Ave.,
Ocean Grove,
732-774-1869;
www.oceangrove.org
Tour of Victorian cottages. July.

RESTAURANTS

★★Moonstruck
517 Lake Ave.,
Asbury Park,
732-988-0123;
www.moonstrucknj.com
Italian, Mediterranean menu. Dinner. Closed Monday-Tuesday; also January-mid-February. Outdoor seating. $$

ATLANTIC CITY

Honeymooners, conventioneers, Miss America and some 37 million annual visitors have made Atlantic City the best-known New Jersey beach resort. Built on Absecon Island, the curve of the coast shields it from battering northeastern storms while the nearby Gulf Stream warms its waters, helping to make it a year-round resort. A 60-foot-wide boardwalk extends along five miles of beaches. Hand-pushed wicker rolling chairs take visitors up and down the Boardwalk. Absecon Lighthouse ("Old Ab"), a well-known landmark, was first lit in 1857 and now stands in an uptown city park.

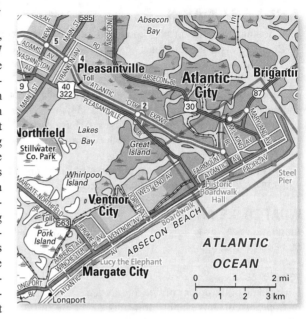

Information: Atlantic City Convention & Visitors Authority, 2314 Pacific Ave., Atlantic City, 609-449-7147, 888-262-7892, 800-228-4748; www.atlanticcitynj.com

NEW JERSEY

★
★
★
★
★

THE AMUSEMENTS OF THE JERSEY SHORE

Pennsylvania Route 40 leads to the Jersey Shore, Atlantic City, Ocean City and historic Cape May. Atlantic City offers fun activities for everyone. Children love Lucy the Margate Elephant, a six-story, elephant-shaped building with an observation deck on her back, and Storybook Land, with its rides, animals, a playground and more than 50 storybook buildings. Older children will enjoy the Ripley's Believe It or Not Museum. And adults will have a great time exploring the Renault Winery, Noyes Museum and Smithville's specialty shops and restaurants. Travelers can also visit one of the many recreation areas or amusement piers along the coast, as well as the Marine Mammal Stranding Center and Museum, the Edwin B. Forsythe National Wildlife Refuge and the casinos.

Head south from Atlantic City to Ocean City, a popular family resort with eight miles of beaches. Walk along the boardwalk. Take a ride to the top of the 140-foot Ferris wheel, or take a turn at the video arcades, roller coasters and water slides. Stop for a snack at one of the outdoor cafes or fill up on ice cream and cotton candy.

Cape May, the nation's oldest seaside resort, is at New Jersey's southernmost tip. Explore historic Cold Spring Village, a restored 1870 farm village with craft shops and demonstrations. Take the ferry across Delaware Bay, or take a guided walking tour of the historic district or a one-hour Ocean Walk tour of the area's beaches and marine life. Approximately 125 miles.

WHAT TO SEE AND DO

Absecon Lighthouse

31 S. Rhode Island Ave.,
Atlantic City,
609-449-1360;
www.abseconlighthouse.org

Climb the 228 steps to the top of this 1857 lighthouse, designed by Civil War general George Gordon Meade. Tallest lighthouse in New Jersey, third-tallest in the United States. July-August: daily 10 a.m.-5 p.m.; September-June: Thursday-Monday 11 a.m.-4 p.m.

Atlantic City Boardwalk Hall

2301 Boardwalk, Atlantic City,
609-348-7000, 800-736-1420;
www.boardwalkhall.com

Seats 13,800; special events, concerts, boxing, ice shows, sports events; site of the annual Miss America Pageant.

Edwin B. Forsythe National Wildlife Refuge, Brigantine Division

Box 72, Great Creek Rd.,
Oceanville,
609-652-1665;
forsythe.fws.gov

Wildlife drive; interpretive nature trails (daily). Over the years, more than 200 species of birds have been observed at this 45,000-acre refuge. Public-use area has an eight-mile wildlife drive through diversified wetlands and uplands habitat; most popular in the spring and fall, during the course of the waterbird migration and at sunset, when the birds roost for the evening. Refuge headquarters. Monday-Friday 8 a.m.-4 p.m.

Fishing

Surf and deep-sea fishing. License may be required, check locally. Charter boats (March-November). Many tournaments are scheduled. Contact Atlantic City Party and Charter Boat Association.

Garden Pier

Boardwalk and New Jersey Ave.,
Atlantic City,
609-347-5837;
www.acmuseum.org

The Atlantic City Art Center and Atlantic City Historical Museum are located here. Daily 10 a.m.-4 p.m.

Historic Gardner's Basin

800 New Hampshire Ave., Atlantic City,
609-348-2880

An eight-acre, sea-oriented park featuring working lobstermen; Ocean Life Center, eight tanks totalling 29,800 gallons of aquariums, exhibiting more than 100 varieties of fish and marine animals, 10 exhibits featuring themes on the marine and maritime environment. Picnicking. Daily.

The Shops on Ocean One

1 Atlantic Ocean, Atlantic City,
609-347-8082

A 900-foot, three-deck shopping pier houses shops, food court and restaurants. January-May: daily 10 a.m.-7 p.m.; June-August: daily 10 a.m.-9 p.m.; September-December: daily 10 a.m.-8 p.m.

SPECIAL EVENTS

Atlantic City Marathon

Atlantic City,
609-822-6911;
www.atlanticcitymarathon.org
Mid-October.

Miss America Pageant

Atlantic City Boardwalk Hall,
2301 Boardwalk, Atlantic City,
609-449-2064;
www.missamerica.com

Usually first or second weekend after Labor Day.

ShopRite LPGA Atlantic City Classic

Seaview Marriott Resort & Spa, 401 S. New York Rd., Galloway Township,
609-927-7888;
www.seaviewmarriott.com
Late June.

HOTELS

★★★Bally's Park Place Casino Resort

Park Place and Boardwalk, Atlantic City,
609-340-2000, 800-225-5977;
www.ballysac.com

NEW JERSEY

A geometric glass chandelier twinkles overhead at the entrance to this large, classic Boardwalk casino. There are several dining options to choose from, including some that fit into the Wild West theme of the hotel's annex casino. 1,246 rooms. Spa. Casino. **$$**

★★★Borgata Casino Hotel And Spa
One Borgata Way, Atlantic City,
609-317-1000, 866-638-6748;
www.theborgata.com

The Borgata Hotel Casino & Spa is a stylish resort, where the rooms and suites are luxurious havens from the traditional casino style, with cool earth tones, contemporary furnishings and advanced in-room technology. The hotel's five restaurants include Wolfgang Puck's American Grille and Bobby Flay Steak. Those who may have not succeeded at the blackjack tables find themselves lucky to be ensconced in the confines of Spa Toccare, where a wide variety of relaxing treatments melt tension away, or in the hotel's several high-end boutiques. 2,002 rooms. Spa. Casino. **$$$**

★★★Caesars Atlantic City Hotel Casino
2100 Pacific and Arkansas Avenues,
Atlantic City,
609-348-4411, 800-223-7277;
www.caesarsac.com

This oceanfront hotel, dubbed "Rome on the Jersey shore," houses 26,000 square feet of meeting space and a nicely appointed business center. Enjoy an international dish at the hotel's Chinese, Japanese and American restaurants, Roman-themed eateries, casual restaurants and lounges. 1,144 rooms. Spa. Beach. Casino. **$$**

★Hampton Inn
7079 Black Horse Pike, West Atlantic City,
609-484-1900, 800-426-7866;
www.hamptoninn.com

143 rooms. Complimentary continental breakfast. **$**

★★★Hilton Casino Resort
Boston and the Boardwalk, Atlantic City,
609-340-7235, 800-257-8677;
www.hiltonac.com

The Hilton Casino Resort offers convenient access to everything in the area, though the luxurious hotel might lure guests inside. On-site offerings include a 9,000-square-foot pool, full-service health spa, 60,000-square-foot casino with a poker room and Asian gaming room, an assortment of fine dining restaurants and an entertainment venue. 804 rooms. Spa. Beach. Casino. **$$**

★★★Resorts Atlantic City
1133 Boardwalk, Atlantic City,
609-344-6000, 800-336-6378;
www.resortsac.com

Opened in 1978, Resorts Atlantic City offered the first casino in the area. The hotel's charmingly beachy 480-room Ocean Tower offers views of and convenient access to the boardwalk, and the newly renovated Rendezvous Tower boasts the largest guest rooms in Atlantic City. 412 rooms. Whirlpool. Airport transportation available. Casino. **$$**

★★★Sheraton Atlantic City Convention Center Hotel
2 Miss America Way, Atlantic City,
609-344-3535, 800-325-3535;
www.sheraton.com

This tower hotel with Art Deco accents is near Atlantic City's boardwalk as well as designer outlet shops. All guests will appreciate the Sheraton's signature "Sweet Sleeper Bed" (also available for man's best friend) and in-room movies and games, while business travelers will be able to work in comfort with oversized desks, ergonomic chairs and an in-room fax/copier/printer. During the summer season, in-room massages and poolside massages are available. Dogs up to 80 pounds are welcome and receive doggie treats and bowls. 502 rooms. **$$**

★★★Trump Plaza Hotel & Casino
The Boardwalk and Mississippi Ave.,
Atlantic City,
609-441-6000, 800-677-7378;
www.trumpplaza.com

When you've had enough casino excitement and want to unwind, head to the

hotel's health spa, where you can relax in the sauna or Jacuzzi, indulge in a massage, body scrub or wrap, or take in a workout in the well-equipped fitness center.
904 rooms. Spa. Casino. **$$**

★★★Trump Taj Mahal Casino Resort

1000 Boardwalk, Atlantic City,
609-449-1000, 800-825-8888;
www.trumptaj.com

This opulent property boasts a 4,500-square-foot suite named for Alexander the Great that features its own steam room, sauna, weight room, lounge and pantry. And rooms for those guests who aren't rolling in riches are impressive enough to make them feel like millionaires.
1,250 rooms. Spa. Casino. **$$**

SPAS

★★★Spa Toccare

1 Borgata Way, Atlantic City,
609-317-7555, 866-692-6742;
www.theborgata.com

Facials use bilberry for sensitive skin and rainforest propolis for hydration. A special treatment menu for men offers unique baths, massages therapies and facials created for their needs.

RESTAURANTS

★★★Brighton Steakhouse

Indiana Ave. at Brighton Park,
Atlantic City,
609-441-4259

This classic steak house in the Sands Casino Hotel offers thick cuts of steak, veal and lamb as well as fresh seafood and poultry dishes. Escape into the warm, rose-colored décor to unwind from the casino's hectic pace.
Steak menu. Dinner. Closed Tuesday-Wednesday. Bar. Business casual attire. Reservations recommended. Valet parking. **$$$**

★★Chef Vola's

111 S. Albion Place, Atlantic City,
609-345-2022

Italian, American menu. Dinner. Closed Monday. Casual attire. Reservations recommended. **$$$**

★★Dock's Oyster House

2405 Atlantic Ave., Atlantic City,
609-345-0092;
www.docksoysterhouse.com

Seafood menu. Dinner. Bar. Business casual attire. Reservations recommended. **$$$**

★Irish Pub and Inn

St. James Place and Boardwalk,
Atlantic City,
609-344-9063;
www.theirishpub.com

American, Irish menu. Lunch, dinner, late-night. Bar. Casual attire. Outdoor seating. **$**

★★Old Waterway Inn

1660 W. Riverside Dr., Atlantic City,
609-347-1793

Seafood menu. Dinner. Closed Monday-Tuesday; open only on weekends January-February. Bar. Children's menu. Casual attire. Reservations recommended. Outdoor seating. **$$**

★Scannicchio's

119 S. California Ave.,
Atlantic City,
609-348-6378

American, Italian menu. Dinner. Bar. Casual attire. Reservations recommended. **$$**

★★★Seablue by Michael Mina

One Borgata Way, Atlantic City,
609-317-1000, 866-692-6742;
www.theborgata.com

Fresh fish options are grilled over mesquite wood in a tandoori oven. The eight-page menu includes a page for guests to design their own salad—crayons are placed on the table for filling in the blanks—and dessert consists of three different items, always with one ice cream or sherbet.
Seafood menu. Dinner. Bar. Business casual attire. Reservations recommended. Valet parking. **$$$**

★★★Specchio

One Borgata Way, Atlantic City,
609-317-1000, 866-692-6742;
www.theborgata.com

Specchio, at the Borgata Casino Hotel and Spa, features contemporary design with an eye-catching Dale Chihuly glass sculpture suspended from the ceiling. The menu offers Italian cooking with a modern twist. Fish and meat figure largely in the offerings, while pasta and risotto dishes are always crowd-pleasers. Many antipasti and entree selections have a suggested wine pairing. Italian menu. Dinner, late-night. Closed Wednesday in July-September, Sunday-Monday in October-June. Business casual attire. Reservations recommended. Valet parking. $$$

AVALON

HOTELS

★★Avalon Golden Inn Hotel & Conference Center
7849 Dune Dr., Avalon,
609-368-5155;
www.goldeninn.com
54 rooms. Children's activity center. Beach. $

★★Desert Sand Resort Complex
7888 Dune Dr.,
Avalon,
609-368-5133, 800-458-6008;
www.desertsand.com
90 rooms. Closed November-mid-April. $

RESTAURANTS

★Antonio's Pizzeria & the Catalina Cabaret
230 Crescent Ave., Avalon,
310-510-0008
Italian menu. Breakfast, lunch, dinner. Bar. Casual attire. Outdoor seating. $$

★★Mirage
7888 Dune Dr., Avalon,
609-368-1919;
www.desertsand.com
Continental menu. Breakfast, dinner. Closed November-March. Bar. Children's menu. Casual attire. Reservations recommended. $$

BATSTO

The Batsto Iron Works, established in 1766, made munitions for the Revolutionary Army from the bog iron ore found nearby. Its furnaces shut down for the last time in 1848. Eighteen years later, Joseph Wharton, whose immense estate totaled nearly 100,000 acres, bought the land. In 1954, the state of New Jersey bought nearly 150 square miles of land in this area, including the entire Wharton tract, for a state forest.

WHAT TO SEE AND DO

Wharton State Forest
4110 Nesco Rd., Hammonton,
609-561-0024;
www.state.nj.us/dep/parksandforests/parks/wharton.html
Streams wind through 110,000 acres of wilderness. Swimming, fishing, canoeing; limited picnicking, tent and trailer sites, cabins. Standard fees. Also here is:

Atsion Recreation Area
744 Hwy. 206,
Batsto,
609-268-0444
Swimming, canoeing; picnicking, camping.

BEACH HAVEN

SPECIAL EVENTS

Surflight Theatre
Beach and Engleside Avenues, Beach Haven,
609-492-9477;
www.surflight.org
Broadway musicals nightly. Children's theater, Wednesday-Saturday. May-mid-October.

HOTELS

★★The Engleside Inn
30 E. Engleside Ave., Beach Haven,
609-492-1251, 800-762-2214;
www.engleside.com
72 rooms. Beach. **$$**

BEAR MOUNTAIN

WHAT TO SEE AND DO
Palisades Interstate Parks
Bear Mountain,
845-786-2701
This 81,008-acre system of conservation and recreation areas extends along the west side of the Hudson River from the George Washington Bridge at Fort Lee, N.J., to Saugerties, N.Y. The main unit is the 51,680-acre tract of Bear Mountain and Harriman state parks. Included in the system are 17 parks and six historic sites.

Bear Mountain (5,067 acres) extends westward from the Hudson River opposite Peekskill. Only 45 miles from New York City via the Palisades Interstate Parkway, this is a popular recreation area, with all-year facilities, mainly for one-day visits. Bear Mountain has picnic areas, hiking

RESTAURANTS

★Roberto's Dolce Vita
12907 Long Beach Blvd.,
Beach Haven Terrace,
609-492-1001
Italian menu. Dinner. Casual attire. Reservations recommended. **$$**

trails, a swimming pool with bathhouse, boating on Hessian Lake, fishing and an artificial ice rink. Perkins Memorial Drive goes to the top of Bear Mountain, where there is a picnic area and a sightseeing tower. Near the site of Fort Clinton, just west of Bear Mountain Bridge, is Trailside Museums and Wildlife Center, with native animals and exhibit buildings (daily; 845-786-2701).

Harriman (46,613 acres), southwest of Bear Mountain, consists of wilder country. Fishing, boating, scenic drives, lakes, bathing beaches at Lakes Tiorati, Welch and Sebago; tent camping at Lake Welch and cabins (primarily for family groups) at Lake Sebago. The Silver Mine Area, four miles west of Bear Mountain, has fishing, boating and picnicking. Charges for parking and for most activities vary.

BERNARDSVILLE

HOTELS

★★★Bernards Inn
27 Mine Brook Rd.,
Bernardsville,
908-766-0002, 888-766-0002;
www.bernardsinn.com
This historic property is a favored retreat for locals looking for a night out. Guest rooms are individually decorated with antiques and reproductions. The restaurant serves sophisticated American food in an upscale, clubby setting.
20 rooms. Complimentary full breakfast. **$$**

RESTAURANTS

★★★The Bernards Inn
27 Mine Brook Rd., Bernardsville,
908-766-0002, 888-766-0002;
www.bernardsinn.com
This traditional dining room features chef Edward Stone's creative contemporary American menu—along with an 8,000-bottle wine cellar—in a rustic, intimate setting that's just a short drive from New York City.
American menu. Lunch, dinner. Closed Sunday. Bar. Business casual attire. Reservations recommended. Valet parking. Outdoor seating. **$$$**

★
★
★
★
★

BORDENTOWN

Bordentown was once a busy shipping center and a key stop on the Delaware and Raritan Canal. In January 1778, Bordentown citizens filled numerous kegs with gunpowder and sent them down the Delaware River to Philadelphia hoping to blow up the British fleet stationed there. But the plan was discovered, and British troops intercepted the kegs and discharged them. In 1816, Joseph Bonaparte, exiled king of Spain and brother of Napoleon, bought 1,500 acres and settled here.

Information: Historical Society Visitors Center, Old City Hall, 13 Crosswicks St., Bordentown, 609-298-1740

WHAT TO SEE AND DO
Clara Barton Schoolhouse
142 Crosswicks St., Bordentown, 609-298-0676
This building was in use as a school in Revolutionary days. In 1851, Clara Barton, founder of the American Red Cross, established one of the first free public schools in the country in this building. By appointment.

BRIDGETON

Bridgeton has been recognized as New Jersey's largest historic district, with more than 2,200 registered historical landmarks. There are many styles of architecture here, some of which date back nearly 300 years.

Information: Bridgeton-Cumberland Tourist Association, 50 E. Broad St., Bridgeton, 856-451-4802, 800-319-3379

WHAT TO SEE AND DO
City Park
Mayor Aitken Dr., Bridgeton, 856-455-3230
A 1,100-acre wooded area with swimming (protected beaches, Memorial Day-Labor Day), fishing, boating (floating dock), canoeing. Picnic grounds, recreation center; zoo. Daily.

Also here is:

New Sweden Farmstead Museum
City Park, Mayor Aitken Dr., Bridgeton, 856-455-3230
Reconstruction of the first permanent European settlement in Delaware Valley. Seven log buildings including smokehouse/sauna, horse barn, cow and goat barn, threshing barn; blacksmith shop; family residence with period furnishings. Costumed guides. May-Labor Day: Saturday 11 a.m.-5 p.m., Sunday noon-5 p.m.; rest of year: by appointment.

George J. Woodruff Museum of Indian Artifacts
Bridgeton Public Library, 150 E. Commerce St., Bridgeton, 856-451-2620
Approximately 20,000 local Native American artifacts, some up to 10,000 years old; clay pots, pipes, implements. September-May: Monday-Saturday 1-4 p.m.; June-August: Saturday 11 a.m.-2 p.m.; rest of year: by appointment.

Old Broad Street Church
W. Broad St. and West Ave., Bridgeton
(1792) Outstanding example of Georgian architecture, with Palladian window, high-backed wooden pews, wine glass pulpit, brick-paved aisles and brass lamps that once held whale oil.

SPECIAL EVENTS
Concerts
856-451-9208
Riverfront. Performances by ragtime, military, country and western bands and others. Sunday nights. Nine weeks in July-August.

BURLINGTON

In 1774, like New York, Philadelphia and Boston, Burlington was a thriving port. A Quaker settlement, it was one of the first to provide public education. A 1682 Act of Assembly gave Matinicunk (now Burlington) Island in the Delaware River to the town with the stipulation that the revenue it generated would be used for public schools; that act is still upheld. Burlington was the capital of West Jersey; the legislature met here, and in the East Jersey capital of Perth Amboy, from 1681 until after the Revolution. In 1776, the Provincial Congress adopted the state constitution here.

Information: Burlington County Chamber of Commerce, 900 Briggs Road, Mount Laurel, 856-439-2520; www.bccoc.com

WHAT TO SEE AND DO

Burlington County Historical Society
451 High St., Burlington,
609-386-4773;
www.tourburlington.org
The society maintains D. B. Pugh Library. Also includes Revolutionary War exhibit; James Fenimore Cooper House (circa 1780), birthplace of the famous author; Bard-How House (circa 1740) with period furnishings; Captain James Lawrence House, birthplace of the commander of the *Chesapeake* during the War of 1812 and speaker of the immortal words "Don't give up the ship." Tours: Tuesday-Saturday 1-5 p.m.; tours leave every 50 minutes.

Friends Meeting House
340 High St., Burlington,
609-387-3875
(1784) The house is now a regional conference center for Southeastern Pennsylvania/New Jersey Quakers operated by the Philadelphia Yearly Meeting. By appointment.

Historic Tours
Foot of High St., Burlington,
609-386-3993
Guided walking tours of 33 historic sites (1685-1829), eight of which are open to the public. Daily.

Old St. Mary's Church
145 W. Broad St., Burlington,
609-386-0902;
www.stmarysburlington.org
(1703) The oldest Episcopal Church building in the state. By appointment.

Thomas Revell House
213 Wood St., Burlington,
609-386-3993
(1685) The oldest building in Burlington County. Included in Burlington County Historical Society home tour. By appointment and during Wood Street Fair.

SPECIAL EVENTS

Wood Street Fair
609-386-0200;
www.woodstreetfair.com
Re-creation of colonial fair; crafts, antique exhibits; food, entertainment. First Saturday after Labor Day.

RESTAURANTS

★★★Cafe Gallery
219 High St.,
Burlington,
609-386-6150;
www.cafegalleryburlington.com
Local artwork adorns the walls, and large windows offer views of the Delaware River and the brick terrace. The well-landscaped outdoor terrace is set with umbrella-topped tables and a large fountain. The creative menu includes options such as roast Long Island duckling with orange and cognac sauce, braised pork loin in champagne with baked apples and pineapple, and sauteed rainbow trout on crust with almond butter sauce.
Continental, French menu. Lunch, dinner, Sunday brunch. Bar. Children's menu. Business casual attire. Reservations recommended. Outdoor seating. $$

NEW JERSEY

★
★
★
★
★

PHILADELPHIA AND WESTERN NEW JERSEY

This drive meanders up New Jersey's western border, following the scenic Delaware River from the greater Philadelphia area through the timberlands of Delaware Water Gap National Recreation Area.

From Philadelphia, follow Route 130 to Route 73 North. Turn left and then right onto County Route 543. The drive becomes leisurely, following local roads through the small towns of Palmyra, Riverton and Riverside. It merges with Route 130, a major thoroughfare just south of Burlington. In Burlington, go south onto High Street and into the historic district, which dates back to 1677. (Ben Franklin learned the printing trade here.) The Burlington Center offers walking tours (609-298-1740), and the Burlington County Historical Society is at 457 High Street. Tours are also offered of the James Fenimore Cooper House. The town offers several fine restaurants.

Leave Burlington northbound on County Route 656, bringing you back to Route 130. Take 130 North into Trenton, the state capital and home of the Old Barracks Museum, the State House, the Contemporary Victorian Museum, the War Memorial Theater and the New Jersey State Museum and Planetarium. Leave Trenton on NJ 29 North. Near the junction of I-95 stands the New Jersey State Police Museum and soon after Titusville, Washington Crossing State Park. Washington's crossing of the Delaware is reenacted here every Christmas Day. The park also offers walking paths, river views, picnic areas and historical information. Also in Titusville is the Howell Living History Farm at 101 Hunter Road, a circa 1900 horse-powered farm where visitors join in field, barn and craft programs on weekends.

Continue on NJ 29 northbound into Lambertville, a well-maintained town with many Federal and Victorian buildings, antiques shops, bed-and-breakfasts and access to the Delaware & Raritan Canal State Park. NJ 29 continues

CALDWELL

WHAT TO SEE AND DO

Grover Cleveland Birthplace State Historic Site
207 Bloomfield Ave., Caldwell, 973-226-0001;
www.westessexguide.com/gcb

Built in 1832, this building served as the parsonage of the First Presbyte-rian Church. It is the birthplace of Grover Cleveland, the only president born in New Jersey. He lived here from 1837 to 1841. The house is listed on the New Jersey and National Registers of Historic Places. Self-guided and guided tours are available, and reservations are recommended. Wednesday-Sunday afternoons, call for hours.

CAMDEN

Camden's growth as the leading industrial, marketing and transportation center of southern New Jersey dates from post-Civil War days. Its location across the Delaware River from Philadelphia prompted large companies such as Campbell's Soup (national headquarters) to establish plants here. Walt Whitman spent the last 20 years of his life in Camden.

north along the river. The Stockton Inn on Main Street in Stockton offers nice accommodations. The Prallsville Mills at Delaware & Raritan Canal State Park consists of nine structures from 1796. The Bull's Island Recreation Area offers 30 miles of hiking trails and great bird watching. In Frenchtown, Hunterdon House and the Guesthouse at Frenchtown Brown's Old Homestead are two fine bed-and-breakfasts, and Poor Richard's Winery offers tours and tastings.

In Frenchtown, go left on Ridge Street, then right on Harrison Street, which becomes Millford-Frenchtown Road and eventually Frenchtown Road, leading into Milford, home to the Ship Inn, New Jersey's first brewpub. Follow County Route 627 out of Milford. In Holland Township, the Vollendam Windmill Museum shows its operational gristmill and replica windmills on summer weekends. In Mount Joy, Route 627 veers inland. Follow it to a merge with Route 173, bearing right, then to the junction of I-78 (exit 6). Take I-78 westbound to exit 4, and follow County Route 687 towards Lower Harmony, switching to County Route 519 northbound in Harmony. Follow Route 519 to Belvidere and visit Four Sisters Winery at Matarazzo Farms, which not only produces nice wines, but also has an excellent bakery and stages special events. The Pequest River Book Company, which stocks local, historical books and has an art gallery and café, is also in town.

Continue on Route 519 north until it meets US 46/I-80 at Columbia. Follow I-80 westbound to exit 1 and stop to visit the Delaware Water Gap National Recreation Area, with its swimming, fishing, camping, cross-country skiing and other outdoor activities. The Kittatinny Ranger Station offers an audio-visual program and displays, and rangers present impromptu "Terrace Talks" on weekends. Make the trip to Millbrook Village, located about 12 miles north of I-80 along Old Mine Road, a 19th-century settlement in an ongoing process of restoration. Approximately 115 miles.

★
★
★
★

WHAT TO SEE AND DO

USS *New Jersey*

Camden Waterfront,
Camden,
856-966-1652, 866-877-6262;
www.battleshipnewjersey.org

The United States Navy permanently berthed the USS *New Jersey* (or Big J), one of the nation's largest and most decorated battleships, at the Camden Waterfront in 2000 and has transformed it into a floating museum. First launched in 1942, the ship was commissioned for operations during World War II at Iwo Jima and Okinawa. The ship conducted its last mission, to provide fire support to Marines in embattled Beirut, Lebanon, in 1983. Military history buffs will be awed by the guided two-hour tour through this 887-foot, 11-story, 212,000-horsepower, Iowa-class ship. Big J is available for special events, retreats and overnight encampments. April-September: daily 9 a.m.-5 p.m.; October-March: daily 9 a.m.-3 p.m.

Camden County Historical Society-Pomona Hall

1900 Park Blvd., Camden,
856-964-3333;
www.cchsnj.com

(1726/1788) Brick Georgian house that belonged to descendants of William Cooper, an early Camden settler; period furnishings. Museum exhibits focus on regional history and include antique glass, lamps, toys and early hand tools; fire-fighting equipment; Victor Talking Machines. Library (fee) has more than 20,000 books, as well as maps (17th century-present), newspapers (18th-20th century), oral history tapes, photographs and genealogical material. Tuesday-Thursday, Sunday; closed August.

New Jersey State Aquarium
1 Riverside Dr.,
Camden,
856-365-3300;
www.njaquarium.org
This home to more than 4,000 fish of some 500 species is just minutes across the Ben Franklin Bridge in Camden, on the Delaware River waterfront. Curious kids can find out how fish sleep and which fish can change from male to female and back again. You will also find exhibits of seals, penguins, sharks, turtles and tropical fish, as well as elaborate rain forest, water filtration and conservation awareness displays. January-February: 10 a.m.-3 p.m., March-April and September-December: 9:30 a.m.-3 p.m., May-August 9:30 a.m.-5 p.m.

Tomb of Walt Whitman
Harleigh Cemetery, 1640 Haddon Ave.,
Camden,
856-963-0122
The vault of the "good gray poet," designed by the poet himself, is of rough-cut stone with a grillwork door.

Walt Whitman Arts Center
Second and Cooper Streets, Camden,
856-964-8300;
www.waltwhitmancenter.org
Poetry readings, concerts and gallery exhibits (October-May). Children's theater (late June-August, Friday). Art gallery; statuary. Center (Monday-Friday).

Walt Whitman House State Historic Site
328 Mickle Blvd.,
Camden,
856-964-5383
The last residence of the poet and the only house he ever owned; he lived here from 1884 until his death on March 26, 1892. Contains original furnishings, books and mementos. Wednesday-Saturday, also Sunday afternoons.

★
★
★
★
★

CAPE MAY

Cape May, the nation's oldest seashore resort, is located on the southernmost tip of the state. Popular with Philadelphia and New York society since 1766, Cape May has been host to presidents Lincoln, Grant, Pierce, Buchanan and Harrison, as well as notables such as John Wanamaker and Horace Greeley. The entire town has been proclaimed a National Historic Landmark because it has more than 600 Victorian homes and buildings, many of which have been restored. The downtown Washington Street Victorian Mall features three blocks of shops and restaurants. Four miles of beaches and a 1 1/4-mile paved promenade offer vacationers varied entertainment. "Cape May diamonds," often found on the shores of Delaware Bay by visitors, are actually pure quartz, rounded by the waves.
Information: Chamber of Commerce, 609-884-5508 or
Welcome Center, 405 Lafayette St., Cape May,
609-884-9562;
www.capemaychamber.com

CAPE MAY: AN ARCHITECTURAL BOUNTY

The Center for the Arts, located at the historic Emlen Physick Estate at 1048 Washington Street (609-884-5404), is a good place to begin a walking tour that explores some of the more than 600 Victorian-era buildings in Cape May. Take the 45-minute house tour. Leaving the estate, turn left, go right onto Madison, and having arrived at the corner of Virginia Street, turn left and walk amid the grid created by Madison, Philadelphia and Reading streets as they intersect Virginia, Ohio, Cape May, Idaho, Maryland, New York and New Jersey streets. The entire neighborhood is rich in antique homes.

Return to Madison. Turn left onto Sewell, then right onto Franklin. At the corner of Columbia Avenue, note the Clivedon Inn (709 Columbia) on the right. Turn left on Columbia. Here stand the Henry Sawyer Inn (722 Columbia) with its magnificent garden; the Dormer House (800 Columbia), a Colonial Revivalist home; the Inn at Journeys End (710 Columbia); and the Mainstay Inn (635 Columbia), once a gentlemen's gambling house.

Walk toward the ocean on Howard Street. At Beach Drive is the Hotel Macomber (727 Beach Drive), built in the Shingle style. Turn right, walk three blocks to Ocean Street, turn right and look for the Queen Anne-style Columbia House (26 Ocean St.) and Twin Gables (731 Ocean St.). Go left on Hughes to Decatur, turn right and in three short blocks enter the downtown shopping district. Here, along the Washington Street Mall, Lyle Lane, Jackson Street and Perry Street are dozens of shops, restaurants and inns. Stop at the corner of the Washington Street Mall and Perry to look at Congress Hall, a gargantuan hotel. At 9 Perry, near Beach Drive, stands the Kings Cottage, built in the Mansard style with Stick-style detailing. Another excellent Queen Anne-style building, the Inn at 22 Jackson, is found on Jackson Street parallel to Perry. Nearby, the Virginia Hotel (25 Jackson) serves elegant meals in its upscale dining room. You could also enjoy a meal at the Mad Batter (19 Jackson), a Victorian bed-and-breakfast inn, where breakfast on the veranda is a long-standing Cape May tradition.

For a classic Jersey shore finish, return to the beach (at Jackson and Beach Dr.) and stroll along the water's edge, or shop and snack along the Promenade. On a summer's eve, another option is to take in a play performed by the professional Cape May Stage. To reach them, stroll back up Jackson (away from the ocean), past the Washington Street Mall to Lafayette Street. Turn right—the theater is in the Visitor Center.

★
★
★
★
★

WHAT TO SEE AND DO

Cape May-Lewes (Del.) Ferry
Sandman Blvd. and Lincoln Dr.,
North Cape May,
609-889-7200, 800-643-3779;
www.capemaylewesferry.com
Sole connection between southern terminus of Garden State Parkway and Highway 13 (Ocean Highhway) on the Delmarva Peninsula. 17-mile, 80-minute trip across Delaware Bay. Daily.

Emlen Physick Estate
1048 Washington St., Cape May,
609-884-5404
(1879) Authentically restored 18-room Victorian mansion designed by Frank Furness. Mansion is also headquarters for the Mid-Atlantic Center for the Arts. Daily.

Historic Cold Spring Village
720 Rte. 9, Cape May,
609-898-2300;
www.hcsv.org
Restored early 1800s South Jersey farm village; 25 restored historic buildings on 22 acres. Craft shops, spinning, blacksmithing, weaving, pottery, broom making, ship modeling demonstrations, folk art; bakery and food shops, restaurant. Memorial Day-June and Labor Day-mid-September: weekends 10 a.m.-4:30 p.m., July-Labor Day Saturday-Tuesday 10 a.m.-4:30 p.m.

Tours
1048 Washington St., Cape May,
609-884-5404, 800-275-4278;
www.capemaymac.org
The Mid-Atlantic Center for the Arts offers the following tours:

Cape May INNteriors Tour & Tea
202 Ocean St., Cape May,
809-884-5404
Features a different group of houses each week, visiting five or more bed-and-breakfast inns and guesthouses. Innkeepers greet guests and describe experiences. Summer: Monday; rest of year: Saturday; no tours December-January.

Combination Tours
Cape May,
609-884-5404
Begin at Emlen Physick Estate.

Mansions by Gaslight
Cape May,
609-884-5404
Three-hour tour begins at Emlen Physick Estate. Visits four Victorian landmarks: Emlen Physick House, the Abbey (1869), Mainstay Inn (1872) and Humphrey Hughes House (1903); shuttle bus between houses. Mid-June-September: Wednesday evenings; rest of year: holiday and special tours.

Ocean Walk Tours
Promenade and Beach drives,
Cape May,
609-884-5404
A 1 1/2-hour guided tour of Cape May's beaches. Guide discusses marine life and history of the beaches, including legends of buried treasure. May-September: Tuesday-Saturday.

Trolleys
Cape May,
609-884-5404
Half-hour tours on enclosed trolley bus or open-air carriage; three routes beginning at Ocean St. opposite the Washington St. Mall. June-October, daily; reduced schedule rest of year.

Walking Tours of the Historic District
Washington St. Mall and Ocean St.,
Cape May,
609-884-5404
Begin at Information Booth on Washington St. Mall at Ocean St. Three 90-minute guided tours give historical insight into the customs and traditions of the Victorians and their ornate architecture. June-September: daily; reduced schedule rest of year.

SPECIAL EVENTS
Tulip Festival
513 Washington, Cape May,
609-884-5508
Celebrate Dutch heritage with ethnic foods and dancing, craft show, street fair, garden and house tours. April.

Victorian Week
Tours, antiques, crafts, period fashion shows. Mid-October.

HOTELS
★Avondale By The Sea
Beach and Gurney Avenues, Cape May,
609-884-2332, 800-676-7030;
www.avondalebythesea.com
46 rooms. Complimentary continental breakfast. $$

★★Carroll Villa Hotel
19 Jackson St., Cape May,
609-884-5970, 877-275-8452;
www.carrollvilla.com
46 rooms. Complimentary continental breakfast. $$

★
★
★
★
★

★★★Congress Hall
251 Beach Ave., Cape May,
609-884-8421, 888-944-1816;
www.congresshall.com

Guests feel like royalty when they step beneath the 32-foot tall roofed colonnade and into Congress Hall's beautiful lobby, complete with the hotel's original black-and-white marble floor, 12-foot tall doors and black wicker furniture The guest rooms feature views of the Atlantic, antiques, custom furnishings and large bathrooms with 1920s-style tubs and pedestal sinks. The Blue Pig Tavern is a great place to stop for a bite to eat or meet up with new friends, and the Grand Ballroom is not to be missed.
108 rooms. Closed mid-week January and February. Children's activity center. Beach. $$$

★★★Mainstay Inn
635 Columbia Ave., Cape May,
609-884-8690;
www.mainstayinn.com

This Victorian-style inn near the water offers breakfast by the fireplace or on the private porch.
16 rooms. Children over 12 years only. Complimentary full breakfast. $$$

★★Montreal Inn
1019 Beach Dr., Cape May,
609-884-7011, 800-525-7011;
www.montreal-inn.com

70 rooms. Closed December-mid-March. Children's activity center. Airport transportation available. $

★★★The Southern Mansion
720 Washington St., Cape May,
609-884-7171, 800-381-3888;
www.southernmansion.com

Originally built as a country estate in 1863 by Philadelphia industrialist George Allen, the Victorian decor of this painstakingly restored home has graced the covers of several magazines. Each room is meticulously decorated with antiques and vibrant colors, and feature private bathrooms. The hotel's location puts guest within walking distance of beaches, shops and restaurants.

24 rooms. Children over 10 years only. Complimentary full breakfast. $$$

★★★Virginia Hotel
25 Jackson St.,
Cape May,
609-884-5700, 800-732-4236;
www.virginiahotel.com

This hotel, built in 1879, has been recently remodeled and no detail was overlooked. Bright and airy rooms feature flat-screen televisions, Italian duvet covers, Belgian linens and Bulgari bath products.
24 rooms. Closed January-February. Complimentary continental breakfast. $$$

SPECIALTY LODGINGS
Angel of the Sea
5 Trenton Ave.,
Cape May,
609-884-3369, 800-848-3369;
www.angelofthesea.com

Just steps from the beach, this Victorian inn offers wrap-around porches and balconies from which to take in the ocean view.
27 rooms. Children over eight years only. Complimentary full breakfast. $$

Queen's Hotel
601 Columbia Ave., Cape May,
609-884-1613

11 rooms. Complimentary continental breakfast. $$

The Queen Victoria B & B Inn
102 Ocean St., Cape May,
609-884-8702;
www.queenvictoria.com

Guests at this historic inn can enjoy British high tea just steps from the ocean.
21 rooms. Complimentary full breakfast. $$

Victorian Lace Inn
901 Stockton Ave., Cape May,
609-884-1772;
www.victorianlaceinn.com

Spacious suites feature kitchenettes as well as fireplaces to curl up to on cool nights, while a barbecue grill and picnic table

97

NEW JERSEY

are found outside on the well-manicured lawns.

7 rooms, all suites. Closed January-mid-February. Children over 5 years only. Complimentary full breakfast. Built in 1869. **$$**

RESTAURANTS
★★410 Bank Street
410 Bank St., Cape May,
609-884-2127;
www.410bankstreet.com
Cajun, Caribbean menu. Dinner. Closed October-May. Outdoor seating. Restored 1840 Cape May residence. Casual attire. Reservations recommended. **$$$**

★★Aleathea's
7 Ocean St., Cape May,
609-884-5555, 800-582-5933;
www.aleatheas.com
American menu. Breakfast, lunch, dinner, brunch. Closed various days in October-March. Bar. Children's menu. Casual attire. Reservations recommended. **$$**

★★Alexander's Inn
653 Washington St., Cape May,
609-884-2555, 877-484-2555;
www.alexandersinn.com
French menu. Dinner, Sunday brunch. Closed early January-mid-February. Casual attire. Reservations recommended. Outdoor seating. **$$$**

★★Blue Pig Tavern
251 Beach Ave., Cape May,
609-884-8422;
www.congresshall.com
American menu. Breakfast, lunch, dinner. Closed mid-week January and mid-week February. Bar. Children's menu. Casual attire. Reservations recommended. Valet parking. Outdoor seating. **$$**

★★★Ebbitt Room
25 Jackson St., Cape May,
609-884-5700, 800-732-4236;
www.virginiahotel.com
Nestled in an 1870s Victorian in the charming Virginia Hotel, the equally charming Ebbitt Room reflects the quaint Cape May atmosphere while serving plates of contemporary American fare.
American menu. Dinner. Closed mid-January-February. Bar. Valet Parking. Casual attire. Reservations recommended. Outdoor seating. Intimate Victorian dining room. **$$$**

★★Mad Batter
19 Jackson St.,
Cape May,
609-884-5970;
www.madbatter.com
American menu. Breakfast, lunch, dinner. Bar. Children's menu. Outdoor seating. Casual attire. Reservations recommended. **$$**

★★Merion Inn
106 Decatur St.,
Cape May,
609-884-8363;
www.merioninn.com
Seafood, steak menu. Dinner, late-night. Closed weekdays in January-February; also Memorial Day. Bar. Children's menu. Outdoor seating. Casual attire. Reservations recommended. Valet parking. **$$$**

★★★Washington Inn
801 Washington St.,
Cape May,
609-884-5697;
www.washingtoninn.com
The Washington Inn is located in a former plantation house in the heart of the Cape May Historic District. An impressive wine list beautifully complements the seasonal American menu, which may include appetizers like a warm goat cheese tart and entrees such as pan-seared filet mignon and fig-and hazelnut-crusted rack of lamb.
American menu. Dinner. Closed January-mid-February. Bar. Business casual attire. Reservations recommended. Valet parking. Fireside seating. **$$$**

98

NEW JERSEY

CAPE MAY COURT HOUSE

To be accurately named, this county seat would have to be called Cape May Court Houses, since there are two of them—one of which is a white, 19th-century building now used as a meeting hall.

Information: Cape May County Chamber of Commerce, Cape May Court House, 609-465-7181; www.cmccofc.com

WHAT TO SEE AND DO

Cape May County Historical Museum
504 N. Hwy. 9,
Cape May Court House,
609-465-3535;
www.cmcmuseum.org

Period dining room (predating 1820), 18th-century kitchen, doctor's room, military room with Merrimac flag, Cape May diamonds. Barn exhibits, whaling implements, Indian artifacts, pioneer tools, lens from Cape May Point Lighthouse. Genealogical library. October-May Saturday 10 a.m.-2 p.m., June-September Friday and Saturday 10 a.m.-2 p.m.

Cape May County Park
707 N. Hwy. 9,
Cape May Court House,
609-465-5271

Zoo has over 100 types of animals. Jogging path, bike trail, tennis courts, picnicking, playground. Daily.

Victorian Houses
Over 600 fine examples of 19th-century architecture located in the area. Information can be obtained at the Chamber of Commerce Information Center, Crest Haven Road and Garden State Parkway, milepost 11. Easter-mid-October: daily; rest of year: Monday-Friday.

CHATHAM

Information: Township of Chatham, 58 Meyersville Road, Chatham, 973-635-4600; www.chathamtownship.org

RESTAURANTS

★★★Restaurant Serenade
6 Roosevelt Ave., Chatham,
973-701-0303;
www.restaurantserenade.com

Owned by husband and wife James and Nancy Sheridan Laird, Restaurant Serenade opened in 1996. The kitchen uses seasonal, local ingredients to create innovative, contemporary French cuisine with Asian flair, such as seared sea bass with cantaloupe risotto, opal basil, purslane and Romano beans, or roasted rack of lamb with grilled corn, escarole, feta cheese and spicy tomato coulis. Lunch, dinner. Closed Sunday. Bar. Jacket required. Reservations recommended. **$$$**

NEW JERSEY

CHERRY HILL

Information: Chamber of Commerce, 1060 Kings Highway N., Cherry Hill, 856-667-1600; www.cherryhillregional.com

WHAT TO SEE AND DO

Barclay Farmstead
209 Barclay Lane, Cherry Hill,
856-795-6225;
www.barclayfarmstead.org

One of the earliest properties settled in what is now Cherry Hill; origins traced to 1684. The township-owned site consists of 32 acres of open space; restored Federal-style farmhouse; Victorian spring house. Grounds (all year); house tours. Tuesday-Friday, first Sunday each month; and by appointment.

HOTELS

★★Clarion Hotel
1450 Rte. 70 E., Cherry Hill,
856-428-2300, 877-424-6423;
www.choicehotels.com
213 rooms. Airport transportation available.
$

★★★Crowne Plaza Hotel
2349 W. Marlton Pike, Cherry Hill,
856-665-6666, 800-496-7621;
www.crowneplaza.com
This suburban hotel is located only 10 minutes from Philadelphia's historic and business districts, and just a few miles from the Aquarium and the Cherry Hill Mall.
408 rooms. $

★★Holiday Inn
2175 Marlton Pike, Cherry Hill,
856-663-5300, 800-315-2621;
www.holiday-inn.com
186 rooms. $

RESTAURANTS

★★★La Campagne
312 Kresson Rd., Cherry Hill,
856-429-7647;
www.lacampagne.com
This 150-year-old restaurant and farmhouse serves country French cuisine with an emphasis on the Provencal region of southeast France.

French menu. Lunch, dinner, Sunday brunch. Closed Monday; also one week in July. Children's menu. Business casual attire. Reservations recommended. Outdoor seating. $$$

★★Melange Cafe
1601 Chapel Ave.,
Cherry Hill,
856-663-7339;
www.melangecafe.com
Cajun/Creole, Italian menu. Lunch, dinner. Closed Monday. Children's menu. Business casual attire. Reservations recommended. Outdoor seating. $$

★Red Hot & Blue
Rte. 70 and Sayer Ave.,
Cherry Hill,
856-665-7427;
www.redhotandblue.com
American menu. Breakfast, lunch, dinner, late-night. Bar. Children's menu. Casual attire. Outdoor seating. Blues Friday-Saturday. $

★★Siri's Thai French Cuisine
2117 Rte. 70 W,
Cherry Hill,
856-663-6781;
www.siris-nj.com
Thai, French menu. Lunch, dinner. Casual attire. Reservations recommended. $$

CLIFTON

Information: North Jersey Regional Chamber of Commerce, 1033 Rte. 46 E, Clifton, 973-470-9300; www.njrcc.org

WHAT TO SEE AND DO

Hamilton House Museum
971 Valley Rd., Clifton,
973-744-5707
Early 19th-century sandstone farmhouse with period furniture; country store, exhibits. Open-hearth cooking demonstrations by costumed guides. March-December: First Sunday each month, Tuesday-Thursday afternoons; closed holiday weekends.

HOTELS

★Wellesley Inn
265 Rte. 3 E,
Clifton,
973-778-6500, 800-444-8888;
www.wellesleyonline.com
225 rooms. Complimentary continental breakfast. $

CLINTON

WHAT TO SEE AND DO

Red Mill Museum Village
56 Main St., Clinton,
908-735-4101;
www.theredmill.org

Four-story gristmill (circa 1810). Ten-acre park houses education center, quarry and lime kilns, blacksmith shop, general store, one-room schoolhouse, log cabin, machinery sheds, herb garden. Also home of Clinton's landmark red mill. April-October: Tuesday-Sunday. Outdoor concerts some Saturday evenings in summer (fee).

Round Valley State Park
1220 Lebanon Stanton Rd., Clinton,
908-236-6355;
www.state.nj.us/dep/parksandforests/
parks/round.html

A 4,003-acre park. Swimming, fishing, boating; picnicking, concession (Memorial Day-Labor Day), wilderness camping (access to campsites via hiking or boating only). Standard fees.

Spruce Run State Recreation Area
1 Van Syckles Rd., Clinton,
908-638-8572;
www.state.nj.us/dep/parksandforests/
parks/spruce.html

Swimming, fishing, boating (launch, rentals); picnicking, concession, camping. April-October. Standard fees.

HOTELS

★★Holiday Inn
111 Rte. 173,
Clinton,
908-735-5111, 800-315-2621;
www.holiday-inn.com
142 rooms. $

RESTAURANTS

★★Clinton House
2 W. Main St.,
Clinton,
908-730-9300;
www.theclintonhouse.com

American menu. Lunch, dinner. Bar. Business casual attire. Reservations recommended. $$

EDISON

Although Thomas A. Edison's house has been destroyed, Menlo Park and the Edison Memorial Tower stand in tribute to the great American inventor. It was here, on December 6, 1877, that Edison invented the phonograph. Two years later, he perfected the first practical incandescent light, designing and constructing electrical equipment we now take for granted. (His workshop has been moved to the Ford Museum in Dearborn, Mich.) Edison also built the first electric railway locomotive here in 1880; it ran 1 1/2 miles over the fields of Pumptown.
Information: Chamber of Commerce, 336 Raritan Center Parkway, Campus Plaza 6, Edison, 732-738-9482; www.edisonchamber.com

WHAT TO SEE AND DO

Edison Memorial Tower and Menlo Park Museum
37 Christie St., Edison,
732-248-7298;
www.edisonnj.org/history/tower.asp

A 131-foot tower topped by a 13 1/2-foot-high electric light bulb stands at the birthplace of recorded sound. Museum contains some of Edison's inventions. Wednesday-Saturday 10 a.m.-4 p.m.

HOTELS

★★Clarion Hotel
2055 Lincoln Hwy., Edison,
732-287-3500, 877-424-6423;
www.choicehotels.com
169 rooms. Complimentary full breakfast.
Airport transportation available. **$**

★★★Sheraton Edison Hotel Raritan Center
125 Raritan Center Pkwy., Edison,
732-225-8300, 800-325-3535;
www.sheraton.com/edison
The Sheraton Edison Hotel Raritan Center
is just a half-hour from New York City.
A large indoor pool, well-equipped fitness
facility and sauna offer on-site recreation,
while Lily's Restaurant is the hotel's casual
bistro.
275 rooms. **$$**

RESTAURANTS

★★Charlie Brown's
222 Plainfield Rd.,
Edison,
732-494-6135;
www.charliebrowns.com
American menu. Lunch, dinner, late-night.
Bar. Children's menu. Casual attire. Out-
door seating. **$$**

★★Moghul
1665-195 Oaktree Center,
Edison,
732-549-5050;
www.moghul.com
Indian menu. Lunch, dinner, brunch. Closed
Monday. Business casual attire. Reserva-
tions recommended. **$$$**

EGG HARBOR CITY

WHAT TO SEE AND DO

Renault Winery
72 N. Bremen Ave.,
Egg Harbor City,
609-965-2111;
www.renaultwinery.com
Guided tour (approximately 45 minutes)
includes wine-aging cellars; free wine tasting.
Restaurants. Guided tours and wine tasting:
Monday-Friday 11 a.m.-4 p.m., Saturday
11 a.m.-8 p.m., Sunday noon-4 p.m. Free tour
with dinner on Saturday night.

Storybook Land
6415 Black Horse Pike,
Egg Harbor Township,
609-641-7847;
www.storybookland.com
More than 50 storybook buildings and
displays depicting children's stories; live
animals, rides, picnic area, concession.
Christmas Fantasy with Lights and visiting
with Mr. and Mrs. Santa (Thanksgiving-
December 30, nightly). Admission includes
attractions and unlimited rides. Schedule
varies, call for hours.

HOTELS

★Days Inn
6708 Tilton Rd.,
Egg Harbor City,
609-641-4500, 800-329-7466;
www.daysinn.com
117 rooms. Complimentary continental
breakfast. **$**

RESTAURANTS

★★★Renault Winery
72 N. Bremen Ave.,
Egg Harbor City,
609-965-2111;
www.renaultwinery.com
This gourmet restaurant offers three differ-
ent dining experiences: guests may enjoy a
six-course dinner with two wine samplings
(reservations are required), relax at the gar-
den cafe for an afternoon meal or try the
Sunday country brunch.
Dinner, Sunday brunch. Closed Monday-
Thursday. Reservations recommended. **$$$**

★
★
★
★

ELIZABETH

More than 1,200 manufacturing industries are located in Elizabeth and Union County. Long before the Revolution, Elizabeth was not only the capital of New Jersey, but also a thriving industrial town. The first Colonial Assembly met here from 1669-1692. Princeton University began in Elizabeth in 1746 as the College of New Jersey. More than 20 pre-Revolutionary buildings still stand. Noteworthy citizens include: William Livingston, first governor of New Jersey; Elias Boudinot, first president of the Continental Congress; Alexander Hamilton; Aaron Burr; General Winfield Scott; John Philip Holland, builder of the first successful submarine; and Admiral William J. Halsey. The Elizabeth-Port Authority Marine Terminal is the largest container port in the United States.

Information: Union County Chamber of Commerce, 135 Jefferson Ave., Elizabeth, 908-352-0900; www.gatewaychamber.com

WHAT TO SEE AND DO

Boxwood Hall State Historic Site
1073 E. Jersey St., Elizabeth,
973-648-4540
Home of Elias Boudinot, president of the Continental Congress (1783) and director of the U.S. Mint. Boudinot entertained George Washington here on April 23, 1789, when Washington was on his way to his inauguration. Monday-Saturday.

First Presbyterian Church and Graveyard
42 Broad St., Elizabeth,
908-353-1518
The first General Assembly of New Jersey convened in an earlier building in 1668. The burned-out church was rebuilt in 1785-1787, and again in 1949. The Reverend James Caldwell was an early pastor. Alexander Hamilton and Aaron Burr attended an academy where the parish house now stands.

Trailside Nature and Science Center
452 New Providence Rd., Mountainside,
908-789-3670
Nature exhibits, special programs, planetarium shows (Sunday; fee). Museum (late March-mid-November: daily; rest of year, weekends only). Visitor Center with live reptile exhibit (daily, afternoons).

Warinanco Park
Elizabethtown Town Plaza, Elizabeth,
908-527-4900
One of the largest Union County parks. Fishing, boating (rentals June-September, daily); running track, parcourse fitness circuit, tennis (late April-early October), handball, horseshoes, indoor iceskating (early October-early April: daily). Henry S. Chatfield Memorial Garden features tulip blooms each spring; azaleas and Japanese cherry trees; summer and fall flower displays. Some fees.

Watchung Reservation
Between Routes 22 and 78,
Elizabeth,
908-527-4900
A 2,000-wooded-acre reservation in the Watchung Mountains includes the 25-acre Surprise Lake. Nature and bridle trails, ice skating, picnic areas, playground. Ten-acre nursery and rhododendron display garden.

HOTELS

★★★Hilton Newark Airport
1170 Spring St.,
Elizabeth,
908-351-3900, 800-445-8667;
www.hilton.com
With the airport at its doorstep and a fully equipped business center, the Hilton Newark Airport is an ideal choice for business travelers. But with kids' movies and games available in rooms and dining menus just for the little ones, the hotel is also great for families.
374 rooms. Airport transportation available. **$$**

★
★
★
★
★

FLEMINGTON

Originally a farming community, Flemington became a center for the production of pottery and cut glass at the turn of the century.

Information: Hunterdon County Chamber of Commerce, 2200 Rte. 31, Lebanon, 908-735-5955; www.hunterdon-chamber.org

WHAT TO SEE AND DO

Black River & Western Railroad

Rte. 12, Flemington, 908-782-9600

Excursion ride on old steam train, 11-mile round trip to Ringoes; museum; Picnic area. July-August: Thursday-Sunday; April-June and September-December: Saturday-Sunday and holidays.

County Courthouse

Main St., Flemington

(1828) For 46 days in 1935, world attention was focused on this Greek Revival building where Bruno Hauptmann was tried for the kidnapping and murder of the Lindbergh baby.

Fleming Castle

5 Bonnell St., Flemington, 908-782-4607; www.flemingcastle.com

(1756) Typical two-story colonial house built as a residence and inn by Samuel Fleming, for whom the town is named. By appointment.

RESTAURANTS

★★Union Hotel

76 Main St., Flemington, 908-788-7474; www.unionhotelrestaurant.com

American menu. Lunch, dinner. Bar. Casual attire. Reservations recommended. Outdoor seating. $$

104

FORKED RIVER

RESTAURANTS

★★Captain's Inn

304 E. Lacey Rd., Forked River, 609-693-3351; www.captainsinnnj.com

American menu. Breakfast, lunch, dinner. Bar. Children's menu. Docking. $$

★

★

★

★

★

FORT LEE

North and south of the George Washington Bridge, Fort Lee is named for General Charles Lee, who served in the Revolutionary Army under George Washington. Its rocky bluff achieved fame as the cliff from which Pearl White hung in the early movie serial "The Adventures of Pearl White." From 1907-1916, 21 companies and seven studios produced motion pictures in Fort Lee. Stars such as Mary Pickford, Mabel Normand, Theda Bara and Clara Kimball Young made movies here.

Information: Greater Fort Lee Chamber of Commerce, 2357 Lemoine Ave., Fort Lee, 201-944-7575; www.greaterfortleechamber.com

WHAT TO SEE AND DO
Fort Lee Historic Park
Hudson Terrace and Palisades Interstate, Fort Lee,
201-461-3956

HOTELS
★★Crowne Plaza Hotel Englewood
401 S. Van Brunt St., Englewood,
201-871-2020, 800-496-7621;
www.crowneplaza.com
194 rooms. $$

★★★Hilton Fort Lee George Washington Bridge
2117 Rte. 4, Fort Lee,
201-461-9000, 800-445-8667;
www.hilton.com

This hotel sits near the George Washington Bridge. Along with its convenient location, this Hilton offers its guests two restaurants, a lounge, a karaoke night club, an indoor pool and a modern fitness center.
236 rooms. $$

★★Holiday Inn
2339 Rte. 4 E, Fort Lee,
201-944-5000, 800-315-2621;
www.holiday-inn.com
184 rooms. $

FREEHOLD
George Washington and the Revolutionary Army defeated the British under General Sir Henry Clinton at the Battle of Monmouth near here on June 28, 1778. Molly Hays carried water to artillerymen in a pitcher, and from that day on she has been known as "Molly Pitcher." Formerly known as Monmouth Courthouse, Freehold is the seat of Monmouth County.
Information: Western Monmouth Chamber of Commerce, 17 Broad St., Freehold, 732-462-3030; www.wmchamber.com

★
★
★
★
★

WHAT TO SEE AND DO
Covenhoven House
150 W. Main St., Freehold,
732-462-1466
(1756) House with period furnishings; once occupied by General Sir Henry Clinton prior to the Battle of Monmouth in 1778. May-September: Tuesday, Thursday, Saturday and Sunday afternoons.

Monmouth County Historical Museum and Library
70 Court St., Freehold,
732-462-1466
Headquarters of the Monmouth County Historical Association. Changing exhibits center on aspects of life in Monmouth county and include collections of silver, ceramics and paintings, exhibits on the Battle of Monmouth. Museum (Tuesday-Saturday, 10 a.m.-4 p.m.); library (Wednesday-Saturday).

Turkey Swamp Park
200 Georgia Rd.,
Freehold,
732-462-7286;
www.monmouthcountyparks.com/parks/turket.asp
An 1,004-acre park with fishing, boating (rentals); hiking trails, ice skating, picnicking (shelter), playfields, camping. (March-November; fee). Special events.

SPECIAL EVENTS
Harness Racing
Freehold Raceway,
Routes 9 and 33, Freehold,
732-462-3800;
www.freeholdraceway.com
The nation's oldest and fastest daytime half-mile harness racing track features Standard-bred harness races for trotters and pacers. Mid-August-May: Tuesday-Saturday.

RESTAURANTS
★Golden Bell Diner
3320 Rte. 9, Freehold,
908-462-7259

GALLOWAY

HOTELS
★★★Marriott Seaview Resort and Spa
401 S. New York Rd., Galloway,
609-652-1800, 800-205-6518;
www.seaviewgolf.com
A golfer's dream, this hotel is located on 670 secluded acres near Reeds Bay and offers two 18-hole championship golf courses. It is also only 15 minutes from the bright lights of Atlantic City. The hotel's lobby has a traditional 1912 elegance and features black-and-white antique golf pictures, mahogany furniture and bar, overstuffed brown leather chairs and large windows with views of the grounds. Guests can enjoy a well-equipped recreation room with pool tables and PlayStations, volleyball and basketball courts, a kids' playground, the Faldo Golf School and the Elizabeth Arden Red Door Spa.
297 rooms. $$$

Italian, American menu. Lunch, dinner. Children's menu. Greenhouse atrium. $$

RESTAURANTS
★★★Ram's Head Inn
9 W. White Horse Pike,
Galloway City,
609-652-1700;
www.ramsheadinn.com
This continental restaurant is also a busy banquet facility that can accommodate up to 350 people. Dine in a glass-enclosed veranda, ballroom or brick courtyard.
Continental menu. Lunch, dinner. Closed Monday. Bar. Children's menu. Jacket required. Reservations recommended. Valet parking. Outdoor seating. $$$

106

GATEWAY NATIONAL RECREATION AREA (SANDY HOOK UNIT)

Sandy Hook is a barrier peninsula that was first sighted by the crew of Henry Hudson's *Half Moon* (1609). It once was owned (1692) by Richard Hartshorne, an English Quaker, but has been government property since the 18th century. Fort Hancock (1895) was an important harbor defense from the Spanish-American War through the Cold War era. Among Sandy Hook's most significant features are the Sandy Hook Lighthouse (1764), the oldest operating lighthouse in the United States, and the U.S. Army Proving Ground (1874-1919), the army's first new-weapons testing site.

The park offers swimming (lifeguards in summer), fishing; guided and self-guided walks, picnicking and a concession. Visitors are advised to obtain literature at the Visitor Center (daily). There is no charge for entrance and activities scheduled by the National Park Service. Parking fee, Memorial Day weekend-Labor Day. Daily, sunrise-sunset; some facilities closed in winter.
Information: 732-872-5970

WHAT TO SEE AND DO
Twin Lights State Historic Site
Rte. 36 and Light House Rd.,
Highlands,
732-872-1814

(1862) A lighthouse built to guide ships into New York harbor; now a marine museum operated by the State Park Service. May-October: daily 10 a.m.-4:30 p.m.; rest of year: Wednesday-Sunday 10 a.m.-4:30 p.m.

RESTAURANTS

★★Bahr's Restaurant & Marina
2 Bay Ave., Highlands,
732-872-1245;
www.bahrs.com
Seafood menu. Lunch, dinner. Bar. Children's menu. **$$**

★★Doris & Ed's
348 Shore Dr., Highlands,
732-872-1565;
www.doris-and-eds.com
Dinner. Closed Monday-Tuesday, also January-February. Children's menu. **$$$**

HACKENSACK

Hackensack was officially known as New Barbados until 1921 when it received its charter under its present name, thought to be derived from the Native American word "Hacquinsacq." The influence of the original Dutch settlers who established a trading post here remained strong even after British conquest. A strategic point during the Revolutionary War, the city contains a number of historical sites from that era. Hackensack is the hub for industry, business and government in Bergen County. Edward Williams College is located here.
Information: Chamber of Commerce, 190 Main St., Hackensack, 201-489-3700

WHAT TO SEE AND DO

Church on the Green
42 Court St., Hackensack,
201-342-7050
Organized in 1686, the original building was built in 1696 (13 monogrammed stones preserved in east wall) and rebuilt in 1791 in Stone Dutch architectural style. It is the oldest church building in Bergen County. Museum contains pictures, books and colonial items. Enoch Poor, a Revolutionary War general, is buried in the cemetery. Tours. Weekdays on request.

USS *Ling* Submarine
Court and River Streets, Hackensack,
201-342-3268;
www.njnm.com
Restored World War II fleet submarine; New Jersey Naval Museum. Saturday-Sunday afternoons.

RESTAURANTS

★★★Stony Hill Inn
231 Polifly Rd., Hackensack,
201-342-4085;
www.stonyhillinn.com
Housed in a historic Dutch colonial house (1818), this restaurant offers seven dining rooms, all decorated in 18th-century style. Some rooms are themed, such as the Pipe Room or Herb Room, while other rooms, such as the Green Room and Apricot Room, are more sophisticated. Menu specialties include chateaubriand bouquetiere for two and grilled double cut loin veal chop. The cigar-friendly bar is decorated in deep, rich tones, with lots of mahogany woodwork. On Friday and Saturday evenings, guests can enjoy live entertainment performed in the Garden Room. American menu. Lunch, dinner. Bar. Business casual attire. Reservations recommended. Valet parking. **$$$**

NEW JERSEY

HACKETTSTOWN

First called Helm's Mills and then Musconetcong, citizens renamed this town in honor of Samuel Hackett, the largest local landowner. His popularity increased when he treated the town to unlimited free drinks at the christening of a new hotel. Hackettstown is located in the Musconetcong Valley between the Schooleys and Upper Pohatcong mountains.
Information: Town Hall, 215 Stiger St., Hackettstown, 908-852-3130

WHAT TO SEE AND DO
Allamuchy Mountain State Park, Stephens Section
800 Willow Grove St., Hackettstown, 908-852-3790;
www.state.nj.us/dep/parksandforests/parks/allamuch.html

Allamuchy Mountain State Park (7,263 acres) is divided into three sections. The Stephens Section (482 acres) is developed; the rest (Allamuchy) is natural. Fishing in Musconetcong River; hunting, hiking, picnicking, playground, camping.

HADDONFIELD

Haddonfield is named for Elizabeth Haddon, a 20-year-old Quaker girl whose father sent her here from England in 1701 to develop 400 acres of land. This assertive young woman built a house, started a colony and proposed to a Quaker missionary who promptly married her. The "Theologian's Tale" in Longfellow's "Tales of a Wayside Inn" celebrates Elizabeth Haddon's romance with the missionary.
Information: Visitor/Information Center, 114 Kings Hwy. E, Haddonfield, 856-216-7253; www.haddonfieldnj.org

WHAT TO SEE AND DO
Greenfield Hall
343 Kings Hwy. E (Rte. 41), Haddonfield,
856-429-7375

Haddonfield's Historical Society headquarters in old Gill House (1747-1841) contains personal items of Elizabeth Haddon; furniture, costumes, doll collection. Boxwood garden; library on local history. On grounds is a house (circa 1735) once owned by Elizabeth Haddon. Library: Tuesday, Thursday mornings. Museum: Wednesday-Friday afternoons, other days by appointment; closed August.

Indian King Tavern Museum State Historic Site
233 Kings Hwy. E, Haddonfield,
856-429-6792

Built as an inn; state legislatures met here frequently, passing a bill (1777) substituting "State" for "Colony" in all state papers. Colonial furnishings. Guided tours. Wednesday-Sunday; closed Wednesday if following a Monday or Tuesday holiday.

The Site of the Elizabeth Haddon House
Wood Lane and Merion Ave., Haddonfield
Isaac Wood built this house in 1842, on the foundation of Elizabeth Haddon's 1713 brick mansion, immediately after it was destroyed by fire. The original brew house Elizabeth built (1713) and the English yew trees she brought over in 1712 are in the yard. Private residence; not open to the public.

HOTELS
★★★Haddonfield Inn
44 West End Ave., Haddonfield,
856-428-2195, 800-269-0014;
www.haddonfieldinn.com

Located in a Victorian home, the Haddonfield Inn offers well-appointed rooms and suites with varying styles and themes, including the Dolly Madison Room, with an antique desk, Franklin stove and pewter light fixtures, and the DubLynn Room, with antiques and a lace-canopied, four-poster King bed. All rooms feature fireplaces and high-speed Internet access. Each morning, a gourmet breakfast is served in the dining room or on the wrap-around porch and complimentary beverages, coffee, tea and snacks are available throughout the day. 9 rooms. Complimentary full breakfast. Airport transportation available. $$

★
★
★
★
★

HASBROUCK HEIGHTS

HOTELS

★★★Hilton Hasbrouck Heights
650 Terrace Ave., Hasbrouck Heights,
201-288-6100, 800-445-8667;
www.hilton.com
The Hilton Hasbrouck Heights is conveniently located near New York City and the Meadowlands. The on-site restaurant, Bistro 650, offers casual American fare for breakfast, lunch and dinner.
355 rooms. Airport transportation available.
$$

HIGH POINT STATE PARK

High Point's elevation (1,803 feet), the highest point in New Jersey, gave this 15,000-acre park its name. Marked by a 220-foot stone war memorial, the spot offers a magnificent view overlooking Tri-State—the point where New Jersey, New York and Pennsylvania meet—with the Catskill Mountains to the north, the Pocono Mountains to the west and hills, valleys and lakes all around. Elsewhere in the forests of this Kittatinny Mountain park are facilities for swimming, fishing, boating; nature center, picnicking, tent camping. Standard fees.
Information: 973-875-4800; www.state.nj.us/dep/parksandforests/parks/highpoint.html

HO-HO-KUS

In colonial times, Ho-Ho-Kus was known as Hoppertown. Its present name is derived from the Chihohokies, who also had a settlement on this spot.
Information: Borough of Ho-Ho-Kus, 333 Warren Ave.,
201-652-4400

WHAT TO SEE AND DO

The Hermitage
335 N. Franklin Turnpike, Ho-Ho-Kus,
201-445-8311;
www.thehermitage.org
Stone Victorian house of Gothic Revival architecture superimposed on original 18th-century house. Grounds consist of five wooded acres, including a second stone Victorian house. Docents conduct tours of site and the Hermitage. Changing exhibits. Special events held throughout the year. Tours.

★
★
★
★
★

HOBOKEN

In the early 19th century, beer gardens and other amusement centers dotted the Hoboken shore, enticing New Yorkers across the Hudson. John Jacob Astor, Washington Irving, William Cullen Bryant and Martin Van Buren were among the fashionable visitors. By the second half of the century, industries and shipping began to encroach on the fun. Today, Hoboken is returning to its roots, as bars, restaurants and shops do steady business there, and young commuters flock to the birthplace of Frank Sinatra for more affordable housing than New York can provide. Hoboken is connected to Manhattan by the PATH rapid-transit system and New Jersey Transit buses.
Information: Hoboken Community Development,
94 Washington St., Hoboken, 201-420-2013; www.hobokennj.org

WHAT TO SEE AND DO

Stevens Institute of Technology
Hudson and Eighth Streets, Hoboken,
201-216-5105;
www.stevens.edu
(1870) (3,600 students.) A leading college of engineering, science, computer science management and the humanities; also a center for research. Campus tours.

On campus:

Davidson Laboratory
Hudson and Seventh Streets, Hoboken,
201-216-5290
One of the largest privately owned hydrodynamic labs of its kind in the world. Testing site for models of ships, hydrofoils, America's Cup participants and the Apollo command capsule. Limited public access.

Samuel C. Williams Library
Stevens University, Hoboken,
201-216-5421
(1969) Special collections include a set of facsimiles of every drawing by Leonardo da Vinci; library of 3,000 volumes by and about da Vinci; Alexander Calder mobile; the Frederick Winslow Taylor Collection of Scientific Management. Academic year.

Stevens Center
(1962) The 14-story hub of campus. Excellent view of Manhattan from George Washington Bridge to the Verrazano Bridge.

HOPE

WHAT TO SEE AND DO

Land of Make Believe
354 Great Meadows Rd., Hope,
908-459-9000;
www.thelandofmakebelieve.com
Amusement park at foot of Jenny Jump Mountain includes the Old McDonald's Farm, the Red Baron airplane, Santa Claus at the North Pole, a Civil War train, a maze, water park, hayrides, picnic grove, fudge factory. Mid-June-Labor Day: daily; Memorial Day weekend-mid-June, weekends; September, weekend after Labor Day.

RESTAURANTS

★★Baja Mexican Cuisine
104 14th St.,
Hoboken,
201-653-0610;
www.bajamexicancuisine.com
Mexican menu. Lunch, dinner, brunch. Bar. Casual attire. Reservations recommended. $$

★Cafe Michelina
423 Bloomfield St.,
Hoboken,
201-659-3663;
www.cafemichelina.com
Italian menu. Dinner. Closed Monday. Casual attire. Reservations recommended. Outdoor seating. $

★Grimaldi's
133 Clinton St.,
Hoboken,
201-792-0800;
www.grimaldis.com
Italian menu. Lunch, dinner. Closed Monday. Outdoor seating. $$

★Odd Fellows
80 River St., Hoboken,
201-656-9009;
www.oddfellowsrest.com
Creole/Cajun menu. Lunch, dinner. Bar. Casual attire. Outdoor seating. Blues Thursday, Sunday. $$

HOTELS

★★★The Inn at Millrace Pond
313 Johnsonberg Rd., Rte. 519 N, Hope,
908-459-4884, 800-746-6467;
www.innatmillracepond.com
This colonial-style bed-and-breakfast features guest rooms in three historic buildings: the Grist Mill, built in 1769 by Moravian settlers; the Miracle House, built in the early 19th century; and the Stone Cottage, the home of the mill's caretaker. Some accommodations feature fireplaces, televisions and whirlpool tubs. The on-site

restaurant offers a freshly prepared, contemporary American menu for dinner, while the Colonial Tavern features casual pub fare in 18th-century surroundings.

18 rooms. Complimentary full breakfast. Restaurant. Airport transportation available. **$**

JERSEY CITY

Located on the Hudson River, due west of the southern end of Manhattan Island, Jersey City is now the second-largest city in New Jersey. New Yorkers across the bay tell time by the Colgate-Palmolive Clock at 105 Hudson Street; the dial is 50 feet across, and the minute hand, weighing 2,200 pounds, moves 23 inches each minute. Linking Jersey City with New York are the 8,557-foot Holland Tunnel, which is 72 feet below water level; the Port Authority Trans-Hudson (PATH) rapid-transit system; and New York Waterways Ferries, which run between Exchange Place, the city's Financial District and the World Financial Center in lower Manhattan.
Information: Jersey City Cultural Affairs, 1 Chapel Ave., Jersey City, 201-547-5522

WHAT TO SEE AND DO

Liberty State Park
Morris Pesin Dr., Jersey City,
201-915-3400;
www.libertystatepark.com
Off NJ Turnpike, exit 14B; on the New York Harbor, less than 2,000 feet from the Statue of Liberty. Offers breathtaking view of New York City skyline; flag display includes state, historic and U.S. flags; boat launch; fitness course, picnic area. Historic railroad terminal has been partially restored. The Interpretive Center houses an exhibit area; adjacent to the Center is a 60-acre natural area consisting mostly of salt marsh. Nature trails and observation points complement this wildlife habitat. Boat tours and ferry service to Ellis Island and Statue of Liberty are available. Daily.
  Also in park:

Liberty Science Center
251 Phillip St., Jersey City,
201-200-1000
Four-story structure encompasses Environment, Health and Invention exhibit areas that feature more than 250 hands-on exhibits. Geodesic dome houses IMAX Theater with a six-story screen. Daily.

LAKE HOPATCONG

WHAT TO SEE AND DO

Hopatcong State Park
Lakeside Blvd., Landing,
973-398-7010;
www.state.nj.us/dep/parksandforests/
parks/hopatcong.html
SW shore of lake. A 113-acre park with swimming, bathhouse, fishing; picnicking, playground, concession. Historic museum (Sunday afternoons). Standard fees.

Lake Hopatcong
NJ 15, Rockaway
The largest lake in New Jersey, Hopatcong's popularity as a resort is second only to the seacoast spots. It covers 2,443 acres and has a hilly shoreline of approximately 40 miles. The area offers swimming, stocked fishing and boating.

HOTELS

★★**Courtyard by Marriott**
15 Howard Blvd., Mount Arlington,
973-770-2000, 800-321-3211;
www.marriot.com/ewrma
125 rooms. **$**

★
★
★
★

LAKEWOOD

A well-known winter resort in the 1890s, many socially prominent New Yorkers such as the Astors, Goulds, Rhinelanders, Rockefellers and Vanderbilts maintained large homes on the shores of Lake Carasaljo.

Information: Chamber of Commerce, 395 Rte. 70 W, Lakewood, 732-363-0012; www.mylakewoodchamber.com

WHAT TO SEE AND DO

Ocean County Park #1
659 Ocean Ave., Lakewood,
732-506-9090
The 325-acre former Rockefeller estate. Lake swimming, children's fishing lake; tennis, platform tennis, picnicking (grills), playground, athletic fields. Daily. Entrance fee. July-August: weekends.

HOTELS

★★Best Western Leisure Inn
1600 Rte. 70, Lakewood,
732-367-0900;
www.bestwestern.com
105 rooms. Restaurant, bar. **$**

LAMBERTVILLE

Information: Lambertville Area Chamber of Commerce, 60 Wilson St., Lambertville, 609-397-0055; www.lambertville.org

WHAT TO SEE AND DO

John Holcombe House
260 N. Main St., Lambertville,
609-397-2752
Washington stayed here just before crossing the Delaware. Privately owned residence.

Marshall House
62 Bridge St., Lambertville,
609-397-0770
(1816) James Marshall, who first discovered gold at Sutter's Mill in California in 1848, lived here until 1834. Period furnishings; memorabilia of Lambertville; small museum collection. May-mid-October: weekends or by appointment.

HOTELS

Chimney Hill Farm Estate
207 Goat Hill Rd., Lambertville,
609-397-1516, 800-211-4667;
www.chimneyhillinn.com
12 rooms. Children over 12 years only. Complimentary full breakfast. Elegant stone and frame manor house built in 1820; furnishings are antiques and period reproductions. **$$**

★★★Inn At Lambertville Station
11 Bridge St.,
Lambertville,
609-397-4400, 800-524-1091;
www.lambertvillestation.com
On the banks of the Delaware River, the Inn at Lambertville Station offers beautiful views and accommodations inspired by different time periods and international locations. A complimentary continental breakfast is served each morning, and the Lambertville Station restaurant serves a menu of creative American cuisine for brunch, lunch and dinner.
45 rooms. Complimentary continental breakfast. Restaurant. **$**

RESTAURANTS

★★Anton's at the Swan
43 S. Main St.,
Lambertville,
609-397-1960;
www.antons-at-the-swan.com
American menu. Dinner. Closed Monday. Bar. **$$$**

★★Lambertville Station
11 Bridge St., Lambertville,
609-397-8300, 800-524-1091;
www.lambertvillestation.com
American menu. Lunch, dinner, Sunday brunch. Bar. Children's menu. Casual attire. Reservations recommended. **$$**

LAMBERTVILLE'S UNIQUE SHOPPING

Once the country's hairpin-making capital, Lambertville is now a fine antiques and art center, rich in history, antique shops, fine restaurants and historic Federalist and Victorian homes. The town's streets are set out in a grid, with Union and Main streets running north and south, parallel to the river and a series of short cross-streets passing between them. Lambertville has long been the state's shad-fishing center, and still celebrates the annual Shad Festival.

This tour can cover anywhere from 1.5 to many miles, depending on your chosen route. Start at the historic Marshall House at 62 Bridge Street. A classic Federalist building, this is the home of the Lambertville Historical Society, which leads one-hour guided walking tours from late June through September, presents a 30-minute film on Lambertville's history and can supply you with a guide to the town's historic buildings. After visiting the Marshall House, proceed west to Union Street and head north into the heart of the shopping district, where you'll find: Phoenix Books (49 N. Union), a treasure trove of rare and out-of-print volumes; the Five and Dime (40 N. Union), which houses an equally fascinating collection of antique toys; and all along the street, a number of high-quality antique shops and galleries.

At the north end of Union (10 blocks north), turn right onto Cherry Street. Follow Cherry to North Main, turn right and begin weaving among the cross streets between North Union and North Main back to Bridge Street. Along North Main, A Mano Gallery specializes in American crafts, jewelry and glass, while Almirah focuses on colonial-era Indian antique furniture and gifts. Shopping, window-shopping and gallery hopping are best done on Perry, York, Coryell, Church Bridge and Ferry streets. More shops can be found on Kline's Court (one block on the left from Bridge St.) and Lambert Lane (just across the canal on the right). From Lambert Lane, cross the footbridge onto Lewis Island, home of Fred Lewis, the state's only commercially licensed freshwater shad fisherman.

Back on Bridge Street, take a break at Lambertville Station, which serves New American cuisine, or return to town for other dining options, including the Fish House (2 Canal St.) for local catches of the day, Anton's at the Swan (43 South Main St.) for upscale dining in an historical building, or the Church Street Bistro (11 Church St.) for intimate dining.

For those with stamina, add one of the two extended walk options. Follow the walking/biking path along the Delaware & Raritan Canal, which travels south for many miles, presenting a bucolic view of the canal and the Delaware River. Another option is to cross the Delaware on the Bridge Street bridge and enter New Hope, Pennsylvania, a treasure trove of antique shops and restaurants.

LIVINGSTON

This suburban community in southwestern Essex County is named for William Livingston, the first governor of New Jersey.

HOTELS

★★★Hotel Westminster

550 W. Mount Pleasant Ave., Livingston,
973-533-0600;
www.westminsterhotel.net
The Hotel Westminster provides classic, sophisticated accommodations in the heart of Livingston. Guest rooms feature Egyptian cotton sheets and marble baths. The hotel also offers a well-equipped business center, state-of-the-art fitness facility and spa.
187 rooms. Complimentary continental breakfast. $$

LONG BEACH ISLAND

Six miles out to sea, this island is separated from the New Jersey mainland by Barnegat and Little Egg Harbor bays. Route 72, going east from Manahawkin on the mainland, enters the island at Ship Bottom. The island is no more than three blocks wide in some places and extends 18 miles from historic Barnegat Lighthouse to the north. It includes towns such as Loveladies, Harvey Cedars, Surf City, Ship Bottom, Brant Beach and the Beach Havens at the southern tip. A popular family resort, the island offers fishing, boating, swimming in the bay and in the ocean's surf.

Tales are told of pirate coins buried on the island and over the years, silver and gold pieces have occasionally turned up. Whether they are part of pirate treasure or the refuse of shipwrecks remains a mystery.
Information: www.longbeachisland.com

WHAT TO SEE AND DO

Barnegat Lighthouse State Park
Long Beach Island,
609-494-2016;
www.state.nj.us/dep/parksandforests/
parks/barnlig.html
Barnegat Lighthouse, a 167-foot red and white tower, was engineered by General George G. Meade and completed in 1858; a 217-step spiral staircase leading to the lookout offers a spectacular view. Fishing; picnicking. Park (daily); lighthouse (Memorial Day-Labor Day: daily; May and Labor Day-October: weekends only).

Fantasy Island Amusement Park
320 W. Seventh St., Beach Haven,
609-492-4000;
www.fantasyislandpark.com
Family-oriented amusement park featuring rides and games; family casino arcade. June-August: daily; May and September: weekends; schedule varies.

SPECIAL EVENTS

Surflight Theatre
Beach and Engleside avenues, Beach Haven,
609-492-9477;
www.surflight.org
Broadway musicals nightly. Children's theater, Wednesday-Saturday. May-mid-October.

HOTELS

★★The Engleside Inn
30 E. Engleside Ave.,
Beach Haven,
609-492-1251, 800-762-2214;
www.engleside.com
72 rooms. $$

★★★Sand Castle Bed and Breakfast
710 Bayview Ave.,
Barnegat Light,
609-494-6555, 800-253-0353;
www.sandcastlelbi.com
This intimate bayfront bed-and-breakfast features five uniquely appointed guest rooms and two spacious, luxurious suites. Each morning, guests will awaken to find a full breakfast served in the dining room, while complimentary tea, coffee and soft drinks are available throughout the day. The outdoor pool is a popular spot.
7 rooms. Closed December-January. No children allowed. Complimentary full breakfast. $$

SPECIALTY LODGING

Amber Street Inn Bed & Breakfast

118 Amber St., Beach Haven,
609-492-1611;
http://amberstreetinn.com

This 1885 building has been lovingly restored. Each guest room is unique, with king- or queen-sized beds, ceiling fans, private verandas and sitting rooms.

6 rooms. Closed November-January. Children over 14 years only. Complimentary full breakfast. Built in 1885; antiques. $$

RESTAURANTS

★★Buckalew's

101 N. Bay Ave.,
Beach Haven,
609-492-1065;
www.buckalews.com

American menu. Breakfast, lunch, dinner. Bar. Children's menu. Casual attire. Reservations recommended. $$

★★Leeward Room

30 E. Engleside Ave.,
Beach Haven,
609-492-5116, 800-762-2214;
www.engleside.com

American, sushi menu. Lunch, dinner. Children's menu. Casual attire. Outdoor seating. $$

★★Tucker's

Engleside Ave. and West St.,
Beach Haven,
609-492-2300

American, seafood menu. Lunch, dinner. Bar. Children's menu. Casual attire. Outdoor seating. $$

MADISON

For many years, the quiet suburban town of Madison was called the "Rose City" because of the thousands of bouquets produced in its many greenhouses.

Information: Chamber of Commerce, 155 Main St., Madison, 973-377-7830;
www.madisonnjchamber.org

★
★
★
★
★

WHAT TO SEE AND DO

Drew University

36 Madison Ave., Madison,
973-408-3000;
www.drew.edu

(1867) (2,100 students) A 186-acre wooded campus west of town. College of Liberal Arts, Theological School and Graduate School. On campus are a Neoclassical administration building (1833), the United Methodist Archives and History Center, and the Rose Memorial Library containing Nestorian Cross collection, government and UN documents, and manuscripts and memorabilia of early Methodism. Tours.

Fairleigh Dickinson University-Florham-Madison Campus

285 Madison Ave., Madison,
973-443-8661;
www.fdu.edu

(1958) (3,889 students) (One of three campuses.) On site of Twombly Estate (1895); many original buildings still in use. Friendship Library houses numerous special collections including Harry A. Chesler collection of comic art, and collections devoted to printing and the graphic arts. Academic year: Monday-Friday; closed school holidays. Tours of campus by appointment.

Museum of Early Trades and Crafts

9 Main St., Madison,
973-377-2982;
www.metc.org

Hands-on look at 18th- and 19th-century artisans. Special events include Bottle Hill Craft Festival (October). Tours. Tuesday-Saturday, also Sunday afternoons.

SPECIAL EVENTS
New Jersey Shakespeare Festival
36 Madison Ave., Madison,
973-408-5600;
www.njshakespeare.org

In residence at Drew University. Professional theater company. Includes Shakespearean, classic and modern plays; special guest attractions and classic films. Mid-May-December.

MAHWAH

WHAT TO SEE AND DO
Campgaw Mountain Ski Area
200 Campgaw Rd., Mahwah,
201-327-7800;
www.skicampgaw.com
Two double chairlifts, T-bar, two rope tows; patrol, school, rentals, snowmaking; cafeteria. Eight runs, longest run 600 feet; vertical drop 275 feet. Early December-mid-March, daily. Lighted cross-country trails; half-pipe, cross-country and snowboard rentals, night skiing (Monday-Saturday), snow tubing.

HOTELS
★★★Sheraton Crossroads Hotel
1 International Blvd., Mahwah,
201-529-1660, 800-325-3535;
www.sheraton.com/crossroads
This hotel offers rooms with a garden or a fountain view as well as an indoor heated pool, tennis courts, two restaurants and two lounges. Golfers will enjoy the nearby courses.
225 rooms. **$$**

MARGATE

WHAT TO SEE AND DO
Lucy, the Margate Elephant
9200 Atlantic Ave.,
Margate City,
609-823-6473;
www.lucytheelephant.org
Guided tour and exhibit inside this six-story elephant-shaped building. Built in 1881; spiral stairs in Lucy's legs lead to main hall and observation area on her back. Gift shop.

Mid-June-Labor Day: daily; September-December: Saturday-Sunday 10 a.m.-5 p.m.

RESTAURANTS
★★Steve and Cookie's by the Bay
9700 Amherst Ave., Margate,
609-823-1163;
www.steveandcookies.com
American menu. Dinner, brunch. Bar. Children's menu. Casual attire. **$$**

MATAWAN
Information: Matawan-Aberdeen Chamber of Commerce, Matawan, 732-290-1125; www.matabchamber.org

WHAT TO SEE AND DO
Cheesequake State Park
300 Gordon Rd., Matawan,
732-566-2161;
www.state.nj.us/dep/parksandforests/
parks/cheesequake.html
This 1,300-acre park offers swimming, bathhouse, fishing; nature tours, picnicking, playground, concession, camping (fee; dump station).

SPECIAL EVENTS
Concerts
PNC Bank Arts Center, 3215 Rte. 35,
Matawan,
732-442-9200;
www.gsafoundation.org
A 5,302-seat amphitheater; lawn area seats 4,500-5,500. Contemporary, classical, pop and rock concerts. Mid-June-September.

RESTAURANTS

★★Buttonwood Manor
845 Rte. 34, Matawan,
732-566-6220;
www.buttonwoodmanor.com

Seafood, steak menu. Lunch, dinner. Bar. Children's menu. Lakeside dining. **$$**

MEDFORD

RESTAURANTS

★★★Beau Rivage
128 Taunton Blvd., Medford,
856-983-1999;
www.beaurivage-restaurant.com
Beau Rivage offers a casual but classic dining atmosphere. Menu selections include jumbo lump crab cakes with plum tomato salsa, and roast half duck with blueberry and lemon compote.
French menu. Lunch, dinner. Closed Monday. Bar. Business casual attire. Reservations recommended. Two dining areas, one upstairs. **$$$**

★★★Braddock's Tavern
39 S. Main St., Medford Village,
609-654-1604;
www.braddocks.com
This casual restaurant features traditional American cuisine with European influences. Don't miss the cooking classes held throughout the year.
American menu. Lunch, dinner, Sunday brunch. Bar. Business casual attire. Reservations recommended. **$$**

MILLVILLE
Information: Chamber of Commerce, 4 City Park Drive, Millville, 856-825-2600; www.millville-nj.com

WHAT TO SEE AND DO
Wheaton Village
1501 Glasstown Rd., Millville,
856-825-6800, 800-998-4552
Buildings include the Museum of American Glass, which houses an extensive glass collection; working factory where demonstrations of glassmaking are given; general store; restored train station; 1876 one-room schoolhouse. Crafts demonstrations, arcade, shops.

Restaurant, hotel. Self-guided tours. January-February: Friday-Sunday: March: Wednesday-Sunday: April-December: daily.

HOTELS
★★Country Inns & Suites
1125 Village Dr. at Wade Blvd., Millville,
856-825-3100, 888-201-1746;
www.countryinns.com
100 rooms. **$**

MONTCLAIR
Originally a part of Newark, the area that includes Montclair was purchased from Native Americans in 1678 for "two guns, three coats and 13 cans of rum." The first settlers were English farmers from Connecticut who came here to form a Puritan church of their own. Shortly after, Dutch from Hackensack arrived and two communities were created: Cranetown and Speertown. The two communities later were absorbed into West Bloomfield.

In the early 1800s, manufacturing began, new roads opened and the area grew. In 1856-57, a rail controversy arose: West Bloomfield citizens wanted a rail connection with New York City; Bloomfield residents saw no need for it. In 1868, the two towns separated and West Bloomfield became Montclair. One of the town's schools is named for painter George Inness, who once lived here.
Information: North Essex Chamber of Commerce, 3 Fairfield Ave., W. Caldwell, 973-226-5500; www.northessexchamber.com

WHAT TO SEE AND DO

Israel Crane House
110 Orange Rd.,
Montclair,
973-744-1796
(1796) Federal mansion with period rooms; working 18th-century kitchen, school room; special exhibits during the year. Country Store and Post Office have authentic items; old-time crafts demonstrations. Research library. June-August: Thursday-Saturday; September-May: Sunday afternoons; other times by appointment.

The Montclair Art Museum
3 S. Mountain Ave., Montclair,
973-746-5555;
www.montclairartmuseum.org
American art, Native American gallery, changing exhibits. (Tuesday-Sunday.) Gallery lectures (Sunday). Concerts; film series.

Presby Iris Gardens
Mountainside Park, 474 Upper Mountain Ave., Montclair,
973-783-5974;
www.presbyirisgardens.org
Height of bloom in mid-May or early June.

MORRISTOWN

Today, Morristown is primarily residential, but the town and its surrounding area were developed thanks to the iron industry, so desperately needed during the Revolutionary War. George Washington and his army spent two winters here, operating throughout the area until the fall of 1781. Morristown was the site of the first successful experiments with the telegraph by Samuel F.B. Morse and Stephen Vail. Cartoonist Thomas Nast, writers Bret Harte and Frank Stockton and millionaire Otto Kahn all lived here.
Information: Historic Morris Visitors Center, 6 Court St., Morristown, 973-631-5151; www.morristourism.org

WHAT TO SEE AND DO

Acorn Hall
68 Morris Ave., Morristown,
973-267-3465;
www.acornhall.org
(1853) Victorian Italianate house; original furnishings, reference library, restored garden. Monday, Thursday, Sunday; group tours by appointment.

Fosterfields Living Historical Farm
73 Kahdena Rd., Morristown,
973-326-7645
Turn-of-the-century living history farm (200 acres). Self-guided trail; displays, audiovisual presentations, workshops, farming demonstrations; restored Gothic Revival house. Visitor Center. April-October: Wednesday-Sunday.

Frelinghuysen Arboretum
53 E. Hanover Ave., Morristown,
973-326-7600
Features 127 acres of forest and open fields, natural and formal gardens, spring and fall bulb displays, labeled collections of trees and shrubs, Braille trail. Gift shop. Grounds Daily.

Historic Speedwell
333 Speedwell Ave., Morristown,
973-540-0211
Home and factory of Stephen Vail, iron master, who in 1818 manufactured the engine for the *S.S. Savannah,* the first steamship to cross the Atlantic. In 1838, Alfred Vail (Stephen's son) and Samuel F.B. Morse perfected the telegraph and first publicly demonstrated it here in the factory. Displays include period furnishings in the mansion, exhibit on Speedwell Iron Works, exhibits on history of the telegraph; water wheel, carriage house and granary. Gift shop. Picnic area. May-September: Sunday, Thursday.

Macculloch Hall Historical Museum
45 Macculloch Ave., Morristown,
973-538-2404;
www.macullochhall.org

Restored 1810 house and garden; home of George P. Macculloch, initiator of the Morris Canal, and his descendants for more than 140 years. American, European decorative arts from the 18th and 19th centuries. Illustrations by Thomas Nast. Garden. Wednesday, Thursday and Sunday afternoons.

Morris Museum
6 Normandy Heights Rd., Morristown,
971-971-3700;
www.morrismuseum.org
Art, science and history exhibits. Musical, theatrical events; lectures and films. (Tuesday-Sunday.) Free admission Thursday afternoons.

Schuyler-Hamilton House
5 Olyphant Place, Morristown,
973-267-4039
(1760) Former home of Dr. Jabez Campfield. Alexander Hamilton courted Betsy Schuyler here. Period furniture; colonial garden. Sunday afternoons; other times by appointment.

HOTELS
★★★The Madison Hotel
1 Convent Rd., Morristown,
973-285-1800, 800-526-0729;
www.themadisonhotel.com
Family-owned since 1951, this Georgian-style hotel offers individually appointed guest rooms that combine Victorian style with modern comforts, including high-speed Internet access. Rod's Steak and Seafood Grille serves diners in two turn-of-the-century Pullman cars. New York City is just an hour-long train ride away via the nearby Convent Station stop of the Midtown Direct Train.
200 rooms. Complimentary continental breakfast. **$$**

★★★The Westin Governor Morris
2 Whippany Rd., Morristown,
973-539-7300, 800-937-8461;
www.westin.com/morristown
Accommodations at the Westin Governor Morris are comfortable and contemporary, with wireless high-speed Internet access, spacious work desks with ergonomic chairs, luxurious bath amenities and Westin's signature Heavenly Beds and Heavenly Showers. 230 rooms. **$$$**

RESTAURANTS
★★Caffe La Bella
61 E. Main St., Morristown,
856-234-7755
Italian menu. Lunch, dinner, Sunday brunch. Children's menu. Reservations recommended. **$$**

★★Rod's Steak and Seafood Grille
Hwy. 124, Convent Station,
973-539-6666;
www.rodssteak-seafoodgrill.com
Seafood, steak menu. Breakfast, lunch, dinner, Sunday brunch. Bar. Children's menu. Business casual attire. Reservations recommended. Valet parking. **$$$**

MORRISTOWN NATIONAL HISTORICAL PARK
Morristown National Historic Park was created by an Act of Congress in 1933, the first national historical park to be established and maintained by the federal government. Its three units cover more than 1,600 acres, and all but Jockey Hollow and the New Jersey Brigade Area are within Morristown's limits. The Continental Army's main body stayed here in the winter of 1779-1780.

Headquarters and museum (daily 9 a.m.-5 p.m.); Jockey Hollow buildings (summer: daily; rest of year schedule varies, phone ahead).
Information: Chief of Interpretation, 30 Washington Place, Morristown,
973-539-2016

WHAT TO SEE AND DO

Ford Mansion
10 Washington Place, Morristown National Historical Park, Morristown, 973-539-2085
One of the finest early houses in Morristown was built in 1772-74 by Colonel Jacob Ford, Jr., who produced gunpowder for American troops during the Revolutionary War. His widow rented the house to the army for General and Mrs. Washington when the Continental Army spent the winter of 1779-1780 here.

Fort Nonsense
Ann St., Morristown, 908-766-8215
Its name came long after residents had forgotten the real reason for earthworks constructed here in 1777. Overlook commemorates fortifications which were built at Washington's order to defend military supplies stored in the village.

Jockey Hollow
10 Washington Place, Morristown National Historical Park, 973-543-4030
The site of the Continental Army's winter quarters in 1779-80 and the 1781 mutiny of the Pennsylvania Line. Signs indicate locations of various brigades. There are typical log huts and an officer's hut, among other landmarks. Demonstrations of military and colonial farm life (summer). Visitor center has exhibits and audiovisual programs.

Wick House
30 Washington St., Morristown National Historical Park, Morristown, 973-543-4030
Farmer Henry Wick lived here with his wife and daughter. Used as quarters by Major General Arthur St. Clair in 1779-1780. Restored with period furnishings.

MOUNT HOLLY

120

The rock formation after which this old Quaker town was named is more a mound than a mountain: it stands only 183 feet high. For two months in 1779, Mount Holly was the capital of the state. Today, it is the seat of Burlington County.

WHAT TO SEE AND DO

John Woolman Memorial
99 Branch St., Mount Holly, 609-267-3226
(1783) John Woolman, the noted Quaker abolitionist whose "Journal" is still appreciated today, owned the property on which this small, three-story red brick house was built; garden. Picnicking. Wednesday-Friday; also by appointment.

Mansion at Smithville
801 Smithville Rd., Mount Holly, 609-265-5068
(1840) Victorian mansion and village of inventor/entrepreneur Hezekiah B. Smith; home of the "Star" hi-wheel bicycle. Guided tours. May-October, Wednesday and Sunday. Victorian Christmas tours December; fee.

Mount Holly Library
307 High St., Mount Holly, 609-267-7111; www.mtholly.lib.nj.us
Chartered in 1765 by King George III, the library is currently housed in Georgian mansion built in 1830. Historic Lyceum contains original crystal chandeliers, blue marble fireplaces, boxwood gardens; archives date to original 1765 collection. July-August: Tuesday-Thursday; rest of year: Monday-Saturday, limited hours.

RESTAURANTS

★★Charley's Other Brother
1383 Monmouth Rd., Eastampton Township, 609-261-1555; www.charleysotherbrother.com
American menu. Lunch, dinner. Bar. Children's menu. Casual attire. Reservations recommended. $$

NEW BRUNSWICK

On the south bank of the Raritan River, New Brunswick is both a college town and a diversified commercial and retail city. Rutgers University, the eighth-oldest institution of higher learning in the country and the only state university with a colonial charter, was founded in 1766 as Queens College and opened in 1771 with a faculty of one—aged 18. Livingston College, Cook College and Douglass College (for women), all part of the university, are also located here. The headquarters for Johnson & Johnson is located downtown. Joyce Kilmer, the poet, was born in New Brunswick; his house, at 17 Joyce Kilmer Avenue, is open to visitors.

Information: Middlesex County Regional Chamber of Commerce, One Distribution Way, Monmouth Junction, 732-821-1700; www.mcrcc.org

WHAT TO SEE AND DO

Buccleuch Mansion
George St. and Easton Ave., New Brunswick, 732-745-5094
Built in 1739 by Anthony White, son-in-law of Lewis Morris, a colonial governor of New Jersey. Period rooms. June-October: Sunday afternoons. Under 10 only with adult.

Crossroads Theatre
7 Livingston Ave., New Brunswick, 732-545-8100
Professional African-American theater company offering plays, musicals, touring programs and workshops. October-May: Wednesday-Sunday.

George Street Playhouse
9 Livingston Ave., New Brunswick, 732-246-7717;
www.georgestplayhouse.org
Regional theater; six-show season of plays and musicals; touring Outreach program for students. Cafe, Cabaret. Tuesday-Sunday.

Hungarian Heritage Center
300 Somerset St., New Brunswick, 732-846-5777
Museum of changing exhibits that focus on Hungarian folk life, fine and folk art; library, archives. Tuesday-Sunday.

New Jersey Museum of Agriculture
103 College Farm Rd., New Brunswick, 732-249-2077;
www.agriculturemuseum.org
Large collection of farm implements covers three centuries of farming history.

Interactive science and history exhibits. Tuesday-Sunday.

Rutgers-The State University of New Jersey
126 College Ave., New Brunswick, 732-932-1766;
www.rutgers.edu
(1766) (50,000 student) Multiple campuses include 30 colleges serving students at all levels through postdoctoral studies; main campus on College Ave.
  On campus:

Geology Museum
George and Somerset streets, New Brunswick, 732-932-7243
Displays of New Jersey minerals, mammals, including a mastodon; Egyptian exhibit with mummy. Monday-Friday; call for weekend/summer hours.

Jane Voorhees Zimmerli Art Museum
George and Hamilton streets, New Brunswick, 732-932-7237;
www.zimmerlimuseum.rutgers.edu
Paintings from early 16th century through the present; changing exhibits. Tuesday-Friday, also Saturday and Sunday afternoons.

The Rutgers Gardens
112 Ryder's Lane (Rte. 1), New Brunswick, 732-932-8451;
www.rutgersgardens.rutgers.edu
Features extensive display of American holly. Daily.

★
★
★
★
☆

SPECIAL EVENTS

Middlesex County Fair
Cranbury-South River Rd., East Brunswick,
732-257-8858
August.

HOTELS

★★★Hilton East Brunswick
3 Tower Center Blvd., East Brunswick,
732-828-2000, 800-445-8667;
www.hilton.com
The Hilton East Brunswick offers spacious guest rooms with high-speed Internet access and the Hilton's Serenity Collection bedding that features pillow-top mattresses and luxurious bed linens. Nearby attractions include Princeton University, Six Flags Great Adventure Theme Park and outlet shopping.
405 rooms. Airport transportation available. **$$**

★★★Hyatt Regency New Brunswick
2 Albany St., New Brunswick,
732-873-1234, 800-233-1234;
www.hyatt.com
This property is located downtown on a six-acre lot, midway between New York and Philadelphia.
258 rooms. Tennis. **$$**

RESTAURANTS

★★Delta's
19 Dennis St., New Brunswick,
732-249-1551;
www.deltasrestaurant.com
American menu. Lunch, dinner. Bar. **$$**

★★★The Frog and the Peach
29 Dennis St., New Brunswick,
732-846-3216;
www.frogandpeach.com
Housed in a converted factory, this restaurant has been in business since 1983 and features painted brick walls and exposed ductwork. Entrees include summer mushroom and local chard strudel with goat cheese and Jersey tomato emulsion, and Moroccan-spiced lamb sirloin with corn and garlic flan, popcorn shoots and pine nut yogurt sauce.

American menu. Lunch, dinner. Bar. Children's menu. Casual attire. Reservations recommended. Outdoor seating. **$$$**

★★★La Fontana
120 Albany St.,
New Brunswick,
732-246-0360;
www.lafontanaristorante.com
Executive chef Oscar Romero and partner Jose Akena offer a traditional BYOB Italian experience, serving entrees such as veal valentino, lobster ravioli and steak au poivre.
Italian menu. Lunch, dinner. Bar. Children's menu. Business casual attire. Reservations recommended. Valet parking. **$$$**

★★Makeda Ethiopian Restaurant
338 George St.,
New Brunswick,
732-545-5115;
www.makedas.com
Ethiopian menu. Lunch, dinner. Bar. Casual attire. Reservations recommended. **$$**

★★The Old Bay
61-63 Church St.,
New Brunswick,
732-246-3111;
www.oldbayrest.com
French Creole menu. Lunch, dinner. Closed Sunday. Bar. Outdoor seating. **$$**

★★★Stage Left: An American Cafe
5 Livingston Ave.,
New Brunswick,
732-828-4444;
www.stageleft.com
Since 1992, Stage Left has been serving up creative American cuisine in a warm setting. Selections from an extensive wine list can be paired with menu options such as pistachio-studded organic free-range chicken breast, pan-roasted cod and apple cider-braised pork belly. Wine-tasting dinners with guest speakers and festive brunches are among the special events offered.
American menu. Lunch, dinner. Bar. Business casual attire. Reservations recommended. Valet parking. Outdoor seating. **$$$**

122

NEW JERSEY

NEWARK

Once a strict Puritan settlement, Newark has grown to become the largest city in the state and one of the country's leading manufacturing cities. Major insurance firms and banks have large offices in Newark, dominating the city's financial life. Newark was the birthplace of Stephen Crane (1871-1900), author of *The Red Badge of Courage,* and Mary Mapes Dodge (1838-1905), author of the children's book *Hans Brinker.* Newark is also an educational center with Newark College of Rutgers University, College of Medicine and Dentistry of New Jersey, New Jersey Institute of Technology, Seton Hall Law School and Essex County College.
Information: www.state.nj.us/travel

WHAT TO SEE AND DO

Minor Basilica of the Sacred Heart
89 Ridge St., Newark, 973-484-4600
French Gothic in design, it resembles the cathedral at Rheims. Hand-carved reredos. Daily.

New Jersey Historical Society
52 Park Place, Newark,
973-596-8500;
www.jerseyhistory.org
Museum with collections of paintings, prints, furniture, decorative arts. Reference and research library of state and local history; manuscripts, documents, maps. Tuesday-Saturday 10 a.m.-5 p.m.

New Jersey Performing Arts Center
1 Center St., Newark,
973-297-5857, 888-466-5722;
www.njpac.org
Home of the New Jersey Symphony Orchestra and host to many other performances.

Newark Museum
49 Washington St., Newark,
973-596-6550;
www.newarkmuseum.org
Museum of art and science, with changing exhibitions. American paintings and sculpture; American and European decorative arts; classical art; and more. Also here are the Junior Museum, Mini Zoo, Dreyfuss Planetarium, and the Newark Fire Museum. Special programs, lectures, concerts, cafe (lunch). Wednesday-Sunday noon-5 p.m.

Old Plume House
407 Broad St., Newark, 973-483-8202
Now the rectory of the adjoining House of Prayer Episcopal Church, it is thought to have

been standing as early as 1710, which would make it the oldest building in Newark.

Symphony Hall
1020 Broad St., Newark, 973-643-4550
(1925) A 2,811-seat auditorium; home of New Jersey State Opera and the New Jersey Symphony Orchestra; also here is the famous Terrace Ballroom.

The Wars of America
Broad St. and Park Place, Newark
Military Park, bounded by Broad St., Park Place, Rector St., Raymond Boulevard. Sculptured bronze group by Gutzon Borglum features 42 human figures representing soldiers in the major conflicts in U.S. history.
Other works by Borglum:

Bridge Memorial
Broad St. and Washington Place, Newark
This sculpture of a Native American and a Puritan stands on the site of a colonial marketplace.

Statue of Abraham Lincoln
Springfield Ave. and Market St., Newark
Essex County Courthouse.

HOTELS

★★★Marriott Newark Airport
Newark International Airport, Newark,
973-643-8500, 800-882-1037;
www.marriott.com
Located on the premises of Newark Airport, this Marriott features a connecting indoor/outdoor pool, complimentary coffee in the lobby, laundry and dry-cleaning, and babysitting services. The hotel's three restaurants—Mangiare di Casa, JW Prime Steakhouse and

123

IRONBOUND NEWARK

Once moribund, Newark is experiencing a renaissance. The city now offers fascinating history, modern facilities and some of the finest Spanish-Portugese dining around. This walk first covers the historic Ironbound section. Named for the surrounding railroads, this area has been the settling site for immigrants since the 1830s and is now home to about 40 ethnic groups. The walk then continues into the resurgent Four Corners/Military Park section.

Start at Pennsylvania Station, built in 1933 and beautifully decorated with Art Deco wall reliefs and ceiling sculptures. Walk east on Market Street, passing diminutive Mother Cabrini Park, site of a bust of Jose Marti, liberator of Cuba. Turn right onto Union Street. In one block, at Ferry Street, Our Lady of Mount Carmel Roman Catholic Church stands opposite at McWhorter Street. Originally opened in 1848, this building is now home to the Ironbound Educational and Cultural Center. Turn left onto Ferry Street. This is the commercial heart of the Ironbound, and is filled with shops and restaurants.

Turn right onto Prospect Street. Number 76 is the Gothic Revival-style Christ Episcopal Church, completed in 1850. Destroyed by vandalism and fire, it was restored in 1978 and now serves as the Chancery Professional Center. At the corner of Lafayette Street stands St. Joseph's Roman Catholic Church, circa 1858, now called Immaculate Heart of Mary. Its basement holds hidden catacombs that are replicas of those found in Rome, complete with crypts featuring wax likenesses of Spanish saints. Turn left on Lafayette and walk six blocks to Van Duren. Turn right two blocks to Independence Park. Covering 12 1/2 acres, this was one of the city's first neighborhood parks (circa 1896). Turn left on New York Avenue, go one block and turn right on Pulaski Street. Pass East Side High School, and come to St. Casimir's Roman Catholic Church, built in 1919 in the Italian Renaissance style. Continue to Chestnut Street and turn right. Five blocks down the road stand the remains of the Murphy Varnish Company, once comprising six major structures; note the carving of a Roman chariot carrying a can of Murphy Varnish on the west side of the building.

Follow Chestnut under the railroad and across McCarter Highway to Broad Street. Turn right and walk through the business district to the Prudential Building at the heart of the Four Corners Historic District. Among the many historic buildings are the National Newark Building (744 Broad St.), a 34-story neoclassical structure completed in 1930, and 1180 Raymond Boulevard, another Depression-era skyscraper. In two more blocks, Military Park appears. Walk on the left side of the park to the New Jersey Historical Society (52 Park Place), which has an on-site museum and is next door to the historic Robert Treat Hotel. At the end of the park on Center Street stands the architecturally stunning New Jersey Performing Arts Center. Opened in 1997, it has become a world-renowned performance space. Return on Center Street towards Military Park, turn left on Central Street and go two blocks to the Newark Museum (49 Washington St.), site of the largest collection of Tibetan art outside Tibet, the Dreyfus Planetarium and the historic 1885 Ballantine House.

NEW JERSEY

Chatfields English Pub—cater to all tastes. Area attractions include Ellis Island and the Statue of Liberty, the Jersey Gardens Outlet Mall and Six Flags Great Adventure.

591 rooms. Airport transportation available. **$$**

OCEAN CITY

Families from all over the country come to this popular resort year after year, as do conventions and religious conferences. In accordance with its founder's instructions, liquor cannot be sold here. Ocean City is an island that lies between the Atlantic Ocean and Great Egg Harbor. It has eight miles of beaches, more than two miles of boardwalk, an enclosed entertainment auditorium on the boardwalk and excellent swimming, fishing, boating, golf and tennis.

Information: Public Relations Department, City of Ocean City, Nineth and Asbury Ave., Ocean City, 609-525-9300

WHAT TO SEE AND DO

Ocean City Historical Museum
1735 Simpson Ave., Ocean City,
609-399-1801;
www.ocnjmuseum.org
Victorian furnishings and fashions; doll exhibit, local shipwreck, historical tours, research library. Gift shop. Monday-Saturday.

SPECIAL EVENTS

Boardwalk Art Show
Arts Center, 1735 Simpson Ave.,
Ocean City, 609-399-7628
International and regional artists. August.

Concerts
Music Pier, Hwys. 152 and 40, Ocean City,
732-316-1095
Pops orchestra and dance band. Monday-Wednesday, Sunday. Late June-September.

Flower Show
Music Pier, Ocean City
June.

Hermit Crab Race, Miss Crustacean Contest
Sixth Street Beach, Ocean City,
609-525-9300, 800-232-2465
Crab beauty pageant, races. Early August.

Night in Venice
Ocean City,
609-525-9300
Decorated boat parade. Mid-July.

HOTELS

★★Beach Club Hotel
1280 Boardwalk,
Ocean City,
609-399-8555;
www.ochotels.com
82 rooms. Closed December-April. Restaurant. Children's pool. Beach. **$$**

★★Port-O-Call Hotel
1510 Boardwalk,
Ocean City,
609-399-8812, 800-334-4546;
www.portocallhotel.com
99 rooms. **$**

★★Serendipity Bed & Breakfast
712 E. Nineth St.,
Ocean City,
609-399-1554, 800-842-8544;
www.serendipitynj.com
5 rooms. Children over 12 years only. Complimentary full breakfast. **$**

PARAMUS

Now a well-known shopping mecca with a handful of sizeable malls, Paramus was once a Dutch farm community. Beginning in the Revolutionary War, the city was an important hub of transportation and western Paramus was headquarters for the Continental Army. Paramus has grown as a residential community from 4,000 inhabitants in 1946 to more than 25,000 today.

Information: Chamber of Commerce, 58 E. Midland Ave., Paramus, 201-261-3344; www.paramuschamber.com

WHAT TO SEE AND DO

New Jersey Children's Museum
599 Valley Health Plaza,
Paramus,
201-262-5151;
www.njcm.com
Interactive displays on aviation, firefighting; TV studio, hospital. Gift shop. Daily.

Van Saun County Park
216 Forest Ave., Paramus,
201-262-2627

Fishing lake; bike trail, tennis (fee), horseshoes, shuffleboard, ice-skating, sledding, picnicking, concession, playgrounds, ball fields (permit). Zoo, train, pony rides (fees). Garden surrounding historic Washington Spring. Park. Daily.

HOTELS

★★Crowne Plaza Hotel At Paramus Park
601 From Rd., Paramus,
201-262-6900, 800-496-7621;
www.crowneplaza.com
120 rooms. $$

PARK RIDGE

RESTAURANTS

★★★The Park Steakhouse
151 Kinderkamack Rd., Park Ridge,
201-930-1300;
www.theparksteakhouse.com
This classic American steakhouse is a local favorite specializing in 21-day dry-aged

sirloins (done on premises) and a variety of fish entrees. The chef uses the freshest ingredients in the creative cuisine, and the wine list includes nearly 200 selections. Steak menu. Lunch, dinner. Bar. Children's menu. Business casual attire. Reservations recommended. Valet parking. $$$

PARSIPPANY

WHAT TO SEE AND DO

**Six Flags Great Adventure Theme Park/
Six Flags Wild Safari Animal Park**
1 Six Flags Blvd., Jackson,
732-928-1821
This family entertainment center includes a 350-acre drive-through safari park with more than 1,200 free-roaming animals from six continents, and 125-acre theme park featuring more than 100 rides, shows and attractions. Late March-late October; schedule varies.

HOTELS

★★Best Western Fairfield Executive Inn
216-234 Rte. 46 E, Fairfield,
973-575-7700, 800-937-8376;
www.bwfei.com
170 rooms. Complimentary full breakfast.
$

★Hampton Inn
1 Hilton Ct., Parsippany,
973-267-7373, 800-445-8667;
www.hampton-inn.com
Pool, wireless Internet. $

★★★Hilton Parsippany
1 Hilton Court, Parsippany,
973-267-7373, 800-445-8667;
www.parsippany.hilton.com
The Hilton Parsippany is located 25 minutes from the Newark International Airport and 27 miles from New York.
509 rooms. $$

★★Prime Hotel & Suites Fairfield
690 Rte. 46 E, Fairfield,
973-227-9200, 800-496-7621;
www.crowneplaza.com
204 rooms. $$

PATERSON

Named after Governor William Paterson, this city owes its present and historic eminence as an industrial city to Alexander Hamilton. He was the first man to realize the possibility of harnessing the Great Falls of the Passaic River for industrial purposes. As Secretary of the Treasury, he helped form the Society for Establishment of Useful Manufactures in 1791 and a year later, was instrumental in choosing Paterson as the site of its initial ventures. Paterson was the country's major silk-producing town in the late 1800s. Today, it is a diversified industrial center. The area surrounding the Great Falls is now being restored and preserved as a historic district.

Information: Great Falls Visitor Center, 65 McBride Ave., across from the Great Falls, Paterson, 973-279-9587 or Special Events Office, 72 McBride Ave., Paterson, 973-523-9201

WHAT TO SEE AND DO

American Labor Museum-Botto House National Landmark
83 Norwood St., Haledon, 973-595-7953

The history of the working class is presented through restored period rooms, changing exhibits and ethnic gardens. Tours, seminars and workshops are offered. Wednesday-Saturday afternoons.

Garret Mountain Reservation
Rifle Camp Rd. and Mountain Ave., Paterson, 973-881-4832

A 575-acre woodland park on a 502-foot-high plateau. Fishing pond (stocked with trout), boat dock, rowboats, paddleboats; trails, stables, picnic groves.

Great Falls Historic District Cultural Center
65 McBride Ave., Paterson, 973-279-9587; www.patersongreatfalls.org

Includes 77-foot-high falls, park and picnic area, renovated raceway system, restored 19th-century buildings.

Also here is:

Paterson Museum
Thomas Rogers Building, 2 Market St., Paterson, 973-881-3874; www.thepatersonmuseum.org

Contains shell of original 14-foot submarine invented by John P. Holland in 1878. Paterson-Colt gun collection (1836-1840), mineral display, exhibits on Paterson history, including the silk and locomotive industries. Curtiss-Wright airplane engines; changing art exhibits. Tuesday-Sunday.

Lambert Castle
3 Valley Rd., Paterson, 973-247-0085; www.lambertcastle.com

Built by an immigrant who rose to wealth as a silk manufacturer. The 1893 castle of brownstone and granite houses a local-history museum; restored period rooms, art-history gallery, library. Wednesday, Friday, Sunday.

Rifle Camp Park
Rifle Camp Rd., West Paterson, 973-881-4832

This 158-acre park is 584 feet above sea level. Includes nature and geology trails, nature center with astronomical observatory, walking paths, fitness course. Picnic areas.

PENNSVILLE

WHAT TO SEE AND DO

Fort Mott State Park
454 Fort Mott Rd., Pennsville,
856-935-3218;
www.state.nj.us/dep/parksandforests/
parks/fortmott.html
A 104-acre park at Finns Point; established in 1837 as a defense of the port of Philadelphia. North of the park is Finns Point National Cemetery, where more than 2,500 Union and Confederate soldiers are buried. Fishing, ferry ride, picnicking, playground, overlook.

RESTAURANTS

★★J. G. Cook's Riverview Inn
60 Main St., Pennsville,
856-678-3700;
www.riverviewinn.net
Lunch, dinner. Closed Monday. Bar. Children's menu. Outdoor seating. **$$$**

POINT PLEASANT BEACH

RESTAURANTS

★★Marlins Cafe
1901 Ocean Ave., Point Pleasant Beach,
732-714-8035

American menu. Lunch, dinner. Bar. Children's menu. Casual attire. **$$**

PRINCETON

In 1776, the first State Legislature of New Jersey met in Princeton University's Nassau Hall. Washington and his troops surprised and defeated a superior British Army in the 1777 Battle of Princeton. From June to November 1783, Princeton was the new nation's capital. Around the same time, Washington was staying at Rockingham in nearby Rocky Hill, where he wrote and delivered his famous "Farewell Orders to the Armies."

Princeton's life is greatly influenced by the university, which opened here in 1756; at that time it was known as the College of New Jersey. In 1896, on the 150th anniversary of its charter, the institution became Princeton University. Woodrow Wilson, the first president of the university who was not a clergyman, held the office from 1902-1910. Princeton is also the home of the Institute for Advanced Study, where Albert Einstein spent the last years of his life.

Information: Chamber of Commerce, 216 Rockingham Row, Princeton, 609-520-1776;
www.princetonchamber.org

WHAT TO SEE AND DO

Bainbridge House
158 Nassau St.,
Princeton,
609-921-6748
(Circa 1766) Birthplace of commander of the *U.S.S. Constitution* during War of 1812. Changing exhibits on Princeton history; research library (Tuesday, Saturday; fee). Museum shops. Also offers walking tours of historic district (Sunday; fee).

Kuser Farm Mansion and Park
Newkirk Ave., Princeton,
609-890-3630
Farm and 1890s summer mansion of Fred Kuser; more than 20 rooms and open and include many original furnishings. Grounds consist of 22 acres with original buildings including coachman's house, chicken house, tennis pavilion. Park with picnic areas, quoit courts, lawn bowling, walking trails; formal garden, gazebo. Tours May-November:

Thursday-Sunday; February-April: Saturday and Sunday; limited hours, call for schedule and holiday closings. Self-guided tour maps of grounds. Special programs, lectures and video evenings throughout the year.

Morven
55 Stockton St., Princeton,
609-924-8144
(Circa 1750). House of Richard Stockton, signer of the Declaration of Independence. April-October: Wednesday-Friday, Sunday.

Princeton Battle Monument
Monument Dr. and Stockton St.,
Princeton
The work of Frederick W. MacMonnies, this 50-foot block of Indiana limestone commemorates the famous 1777 battle when George Washington's troops defeated the British.

Princeton Cemetery
Witherspoon and Wiggens streets,
Princeton,
609-924-1369
Buried in the Presidents' Plot are 11 university presidents, including Aaron Burr, Sr., Jonathan Edwards and John Witherspoon. Monument to Grover Cleveland and grave of Paul Tulane, in whose honor Tulane University was named.

Princeton University
1 Nassau Hall, Princeton,
609-258-3603;
www.princeton.edu
(1746) (4,500 undergraduate students, 1,650 graduate students.) An Ivy League college that has been coeducational since 1969. A campus guide service shows the visitor points of interest on the main campus. Daily.
   On campus:

McCarter Theatre
91 University Place, Princeton,
608-258-2787, 888-278-7932;
www.mccarter.org
Professional repertory company performs classical and modern drama; concerts, ballet; other special programs year-round.

Nassau Hall
Princeton University, Princeton,
609-258-3000
(1756) Provided all college facilities, classrooms, dormitories, library and prayer hall for about 50 years. New Jersey's first legislature met here in 1776, and the Continental Congress met here in 1783, when Princeton was the capital. During the Revolution, it served as a barracks and hospital for Continental and British troops.

The Putnam Sculptures
One of the largest modern outdoor sculpture showcases in the country, with 19 sculptures on display throughout the campus, including pieces by Picasso, Moore, Noguchi, Calder and Lipchitz.

Woodrow Wilson School of Public and International Affairs
Princeton,
609-258-4831
Designed by Minoru Yamasaki; reflecting pool and "Fountain of Freedom" by James Fitzgerald.

HOTELS
★★★Hyatt Regency Princeton
102 Carnegie Center, Princeton,
609-987-1234, 800-233-1234;
www.hyatt.com
This hotel is nestled on 16 acres of landscaped property just one mile from the city's business center and near the Princeton Junction Train Station. Guests receive a complimentary shuttle to anywhere within a five-mile radius of the property.
348 rooms. Airport transportation available. **$$**

★★Nassau Inn
10 Palmer Square, Princeton,
609-921-7500, 800-862-7728;
www.nassauinn.com
203 rooms. Complimentary continental breakfast. **$$**

★★★Peacock Inn
20 Bayard Lane, Princeton,
609-924-1707;
www.peacockinn.com

This colonial structure was built in the 1700s and was once the home to a number of prominent members of the Princeton community, including John Deare, a member of the 1783 Continental Congress. Each guest room is named after a previous owner. Rooms like Swain and Lindsay feature four-poster queen beds, down quilts, fireplaces and full baths with tubs, while the Deare includes an antique French double bed. The inn's restaurant, Le Plumet Royal, features a delectable menu that includes maple-seared duck breast and roasted rack of lamb. Princeton University is just two blocks away.
17 rooms. Complimentary continental breakfast. **$$**

★★The Princeton Premier Hotel
4355 Rte. 1 S, Princeton,
609-452-2400;
www.princetonpremier.com
241 rooms. **$$**

★★★Princeton Marriott Hotel & Conference Center at Forrestal
100 College Rd. E,
Princeton,
609-452-7800, 800-943-6709;
www.marriott.com

RED BANK
Formed in 1870, Red Bank is a historic community on the shores of the Navesink River in New Jersey's Monmouth County.

HOTELS
★★Courtyard by Marriott
245 Half Mile Rd., |Red Bank,
732-530-5552, 800-321-2211;
www.courtyard.com
146 rooms. High-speed Internet access. Bar. **$$**

RESTAURANTS
★★2 Senza Ristorante
2 Bridge Ave., Building 5, Red Bank,
732-758-0999;
www.2senza.com
Italian, Mediterranean menu. Lunch, dinner. Closed Monday. Children's menu. Casual attire. Outdoor seating. **$$**

Located on 25 wooded acres, this newly renovated hotel offers a full-service spa, health club, pool and jogging and recreational facilities.
290 rooms. Airport transportation available. **$**

RESTAURANTS
★★Alchemist and Barrister
28 Witherspoon, Princeton,
609-924-5555;
www.alchemistandbarrister.com
Lunch, dinner, Sunday brunch. Bar. Outdoor seating. **$$$**

★★★Tre Piani
120 Rockingham Row, Princeton,
609-452-1515;
www.trepiani.com
In its dining room, bistro and banquet space, Tre Piani (meaning three floors in Italian) serves entrees such as grilled filet mignon with wild mushroom ragu and a crispy potato and cheese galette; prosciutto-wrapped tuna loin with white bean stew and cherry tomatoes; and breast of Muscovy duck with duck confit and walnut risotto.
Italian, Mediterranean menu. Lunch, dinner. Bar. Casual attire. Outdoor seating. **$$$**

★★★Fromagerie
26 Ridge Rd., Rumson,
732-842-8088;
www.fromagerierestaurant.com
This romantic French restaurant first opened in 1972. Classical French cuisine is paired with an award-winning selection of wines, some of which may be sampled during special gourmet wine dinners.
French menu. Lunch, dinner. Bar. Jacket required. Valet parking. **$$$**

★Gaetano's
10 Wallace St., Red Bank,
732-741-1321;
www.gaetanosrebank.com

Italian menu. Lunch, dinner. Casual attire. Outdoor seating. **$$**

★**Little Kraut**
115 Oakland St.,
Red Bank,
732-842-4830
German menu. Dinner. Closed Monday. Bar. Children's menu. Casual attire. Outdoor seating. **$$**

★★★**Molly Pitcher Inn**
88 Riverside Ave.,
Red Bank,
732-747-2500, 800-221-1372;
www.mollypitcher-oysterpoint.com

Located in a waterfront hotel on the banks of the Navensink river, this sophisticated restaurant serves up dishes like country duck with smoked bacon, roasted pearl onions and cous cous or salmon with California avocado mashed potatoes and overnight tomatoes.
Breakfast, lunch, dinner, Sunday brunch. Bar. Children's menu. Jacket required. **$$**

★★★**The Raven & the Peach**
740 River Rd., Fair Haven,
732-747-4666
Guests will enjoy dining at this popular, casual restaurant.
French menu. Lunch, dinner. Bar. Children's menu. Valet parking. Outdoor seating. **$$$**

RUTHERFORD

WHAT TO SEE AND DO

Fairleigh Dickinson University-Rutherford Campus
W. Passaic and Montross avenues,
Rutherford,
201-692-7032
(1942) (2,300 students.) On campus is the Kingsland House (1670), in which George Washington stayed in August 1783; and the Castle, an 1888 copy of Chateau d'Amboise in France.

Meadowlands Racetrack
50 Hwy. 120,
East Rutherford,
201-935-8500;
www.meadowlands.com
The suburban leafy Meadowlands complex offers fine thoroughbred racing from September-mid-December and harness racing for the remainder of the year. Wednesday-Sunday.

New Jersey Devils (NHL)
Continental Airlines Arena,
50 Hwy. 120 N,
East Rutherford,
800-653-3845;
www.nhl.com/devils
Professional hockey team.

New Jersey Nets (NBA)
Continental Airlines Arena,
50 Hwy. 120,
East Rutherford,
201-935-8888;
www.nba.com/nets
Professional basketball team.

New York Giants (NFL)
Giants Stadium, 50 Hwy. 120,
East Rutherford,
201-583-7000;
www.giants.com
Professional football team.

New York Jets (NFL)
The Meadowlands, 50 Hwy. 120,
East Rutherford,
201-583-7000;
www.newyorkjets.com
Professional football team.

New York Red Bulls (MLS)
Giants Stadium, 50 Hwy. 120,
East Rutherford,
201-583-7000;
http://web.mlsnet.com/t107
Professional soccer team.

NEW JERSEY

HOTELS

★**Fairfield Inn**
850 Paterson Plank Rd.,
East Rutherford,
201-507-5222, 800-228-2800;
www.fairfieldinn.com
141 rooms. Complimentary continental breakfast. **$**

★★★**Sheraton Meadowlands Hotel And Conference Center**
2 Meadowlands Plaza,
East Rutherford,
201-896-0500, 800-325-3535;
www.sheraton.com
Located just across the river, this newly renovated hotel is only minutes from Manhattan. Many guest rooms offer views of the city's sparkling skyline. Grab a cup of coffee from the full-service Starbucks on site before heading out to shop at the nearby outlets, or hunker down in the Chairman's Grill for a hearty bite before the Giants game. 443 rooms. Airport transportation available. **$$**

SKYLANDS AT RINGWOOD STATE PARK

Skylands, the official state garden of New Jersey, covers 96 acres, with Skylands Manor House at its center. The Tudor-style manor house, circa 1922, holds an outstanding collection of antique stained-glass medallions set in leaded windows. Guided house tours are offered one Sunday each month from March through December (973-962-9534).

The walking here is largely on marked dirt paths, with some paved drives and paths. Start at the Visitors Center/Carriage House and pick up a self-guided tour brochure. Walk first to the right (in the general direction of Parking Lot A), skirting the manor house counter-clockwise. The Winter Garden contains New Jersey's largest Jeffery pine, a century-old upright beech and an elegant weeping beech. The Japanese umbrella pine is distinctive for its dark green needles. Also on display here are Atlas cedars and an Algerian fir, a tree that produces seven-inch-tall, purple standing cones.

Walk around the house along the lawn to the Terrace Garden. This garden comprises five terraces, each with its own particular ambience. Continue past a pair of Sweet Bay Magnolias to the third level. Here the centerpiece is a rectangular reflecting pool that in summer displays water lilies and tropical fish. Surrounding it is a large collection of azaleas and rhododendrons that bloom in many colors. Next comes the Summer Garden, home to annuals and day lilies, followed by the final terrace level, the Peony Garden.

Walk to the left into the Lilac Garden, which peaks in mid-May. Step onto Maple Avenue, the paved lane, and walk back toward the house. On the right, you'll see the Perennial Garden. A constant flow of color is maintained here from March until November. Just beyond that stands the Annual Garden, a frequently changing formal garden centered on a 16th-century Italian marble well. Move from there to the right, turn around and walk along Crab Apple Vista, a 1,600-foot grassy corridor of 166 Carmine crab apple trees that erupts into full bloom in early- to mid-May. At the end of the Vista stands a series of sculptures known as the Four Continents Statues and to the left, a collection of horse chestnut trees.

Turn left at the horse chestnut trees, and another world appears, revealing woodland paths that travel past swan ponds and through a bog. The paths also travel through a cactus collection, a wildflower garden and a heather garden and end at a colorful yet formal Rhododendron Display Garden. From here, follow East Cottage Road as it winds its way back to the Carriage House.

SALEM

Salem is said to be the oldest English settlement on the Delaware River. The town and its surrounding area have more than 60 18th-century houses and buildings, as well as many points of historical interest. In the Friends Burying Ground on Broadway stands the 600-year-old Salem Oak, under which John Fenwick, the town's founder, signed a treaty with the Lenni-Lenape tribe.

Information: Salem County Chamber of Commerce, 91A S. Virginia Ave., Carneys Point, 856-299-6699; www.salemcountynj.gov

WHAT TO SEE AND DO

Alexander Grant House
79-83 Market St., Salem,
856-935-5004
(1721) Headquarters of Salem County Historical Society. Twenty rooms with period furniture; Wistarburg glass, Native American relics, dolls, paintings; genealogy library; stone barn. Tuesday-Friday afternoons; also open the second Saturday afternoon of each month.

SCOTCH PLAINS

RESTAURANTS

★★★Stage House Inn
366 Park Ave., Scotch Plains,
908-322-4224;
www.stagehouserestaurant.com
A local favorite, this establishment offers lightened versions of classic French dishes, beautifully presented and full of flavor. Guests enjoy the simple, refined atmosphere and the casual patio dining.
American menu. Lunch, dinner. Bar. Business casual attire. Reservations recommended. Outdoor seating. $$$

SEASIDE PARK

WHAT TO SEE AND DO

Island Beach State Park
Seaside Park,
732-793-0506;
www.state.nj.us/dep/parksandforests/parks/island.html
This strip of land (3,002 acres) is across the water, north of Long Beach Island and faces Barnegat Lighthouse. There are two natural areas (Northern Area and Southern Area) and a recreational zone in the center. Excellent swimming and fishing in Atlantic Ocean (seasonal). Nature tours. Picnicking. Daily.

HOTELS

★★Windjammer Motor Inn
First and Central avenues,
Seaside Park,
732-830-2555;
www.windjammermotorinn.com
39 rooms. $

SECAUCUS

HOTELS

★★Holiday Inn Harmon Meadow Sportplex
300 Plaza Dr., Secaucus,
201-348-2000, 888-465-4329;
www.holiday-inn.com/secaucusnj
161 rooms. $

SHORT HILLS

WHAT TO SEE AND DO

Cora Hartshorn Arboretum and Bird Sanctuary
324 Forest Dr. S, Short Hills,
973-376-3587;
http://hartshornarboretum.org
A 17-acre sanctuary with nature trails; guided walks. Stone House Museum with nature exhibits (late September-mid-June: Tuesday, Thursday and Saturday). Grounds daily.

Paper Mill Playhouse
Brookside Dr. and Old Shore Hills Rd.,
Millburn, 973-376-4343;
www.papermill.org/papermill.html
State Theater of New Jersey. A variety of plays, musicals and children's theater (Wednesday-Sunday); matinees (Thursday, Saturday and Sunday).

HOTELS

★★★Hilton Short Hills
41 John F. Kennedy Pkwy., Short Hills,
973-379-0100, 800-445-8667;
www.hiltonshorthills.com

Executives visiting the New York metropolitan area appreciate this hotel's proximity to Manhattan, New Jersey's businesses and Newark airport—yet this hotel is not just a destination for corporate travelers. Located across from the fabulous Short Hills Mall, the Hilton Short Hills is also a favorite stomping ground for shopaholics. A beauty salon keeps guests properly primped, while a fitness center and pool are a boon for fitness enthusiasts.
308 rooms. Airport transportation available. **$$**

RESTAURANTS

★★★The Dining Room
41 John F. Kennedy Pkwy.,
Short Hills,
973-379-0100;
www.hilton.com
American, French menu. Dinner. Closed Sunday. Bar. Jacket required. Valet parking. **$$$**

SHREWSBURY

WHAT TO SEE AND DO

Allen House
400 Sycamore Ave., Shrewsbury,
732-462-1466
(Circa 1750) Lower floor restored as tavern of the Revolutionary period; traveler's bedrooms upstairs.

HOTELS

★★★Shadowbrook
Rte. 35, Shrewsbury,
732-747-0200, 800-634-0078;
www.shadowbrook.com

Established in 1942, this restaurant is set in an authentic Georgian mansion. Catering for weddings is their specialty, with bridal suites, attended restrooms and beautiful gardens for cocktail parties or receptions.
Dinner. Closed Monday. Bar. Children's menu. Jacket required. Valet parking. **$$$**

SOMERS POINT

RESTAURANTS

★★Crab Trap
2 Broadway, Somers Point,
609-927-7377;
www.thecrabtrap.com

Seafood menu. Lunch, dinner. Bar. Children's menu. Casual attire. Outdoor seating. On the bay. **$$**

★Gregory's
900 Shore Rd., Somers Point,
609-927-6665;
www.gregorysbar.com
Seafood menu. Lunch, dinner, late-night.
Bar. Children's menu. Casual attire. Out-
door seating. **$$**

★★Mac's
908 Shore Rd., Somers Point,
609-927-2759;
www.macsrestaurant.com
Italian, American menu. Dinner. Bar. Chil-
dren's menu. Casual attire. Reservations
recommended. **$$$**

SOMERSET

HOTELS
★★Doubletree Hotel
200 Atrium Dr., Somerset,
732-469-2600, 800-222-8733;
www.somerset.doubletree.com
361 rooms. **$$**

★★★Marriott Somerset
110 Davidson Ave., Somerset,
732-560-0500, 800-228-9290;
www.marriott.com

Sleep comfortably on the Marriott Somer-
set's 300 thread-count sheets. And if you
can pull the kids away from the hotel's
connecting indoor/outdoor pool, you can
visit nearby attractions, including Six Flags
Great Adventure, golf courses and Rutgers
University. The Garden State Exhibit Cen-
ter and Ukrainian Cultural Center are adja-
cent to the hotel.
440 rooms. **$$**

SOMERVILLE
Information: Somerset County Chamber of Commerce, 64 W. End Ave.,
Somerville,
908-725-1552;
www.somersetcountychamber.com

WHAT TO SEE AND DO
Duke Gardens
Rte. 206 S, Somerville,
908-722-3700
Features 11 gardens under glass, including
colonial, desert, Italian, Asian, English and
tropical; 45-minute guided tour (October-
May: daily). No high heels, no cameras.
Reservations required; contact Duke Gar-
dens Foundation (Monday-Friday).

Old Dutch Parsonage State Historic Site
38 Washington Place, Somerville,
908-725-1015
(1751) Moved from its original location, this
brick building was the home of the Reverend

Jacob Hardenbergh from 1758-1781. Who
founded Queens College, now Rutgers
University. Some furnishings and memorabilia on display. Wednesday-Sunday;
hours may vary.

Wallace House State Historic Site
38 Washington Place,
Somerville,
908-725-1015
General and Mrs. Washington made their
headquarters here immediately after the
house was built in 1778, while the army
was stationed at Camp Middlebrook. Period
furnishings. Wednesday-Sunday; hours
may vary.

★
★
★
★
★

SPRING LAKE

HOTELS

★★★Hewitt Wellington Hotel
200 Monmouth Ave.,
Spring Lake,
732-974-1212;
www.hewittwellington.com
Situated on Spring Lake in the town of the same name, this Victorian-style hotel offers well-appointed rooms and suites with wireless Internet access, along with a wraparound porch on which guests can relax. Those who wish to explore the area will find golf courses and tennis courts just a short distance away as well as unique shops and restaurants.
29 rooms. Children over 12 years only. **$$**

★★Spring Lake Inn
104 Salem Ave., Spring Lake,
732-449-2010;
www.springlakeinn.com
16 rooms. Complimentary full breakfast. **$$**

SPECIALTY LODGINGS

Ashling Cottage
106 Sussex Ave., Spring Lake,
732-449-3553, 888-274-5464;
www.ashlingcottage.com
Ashling Cottage was built in 1877 with materials from the Philadelphia Bicentennial agricultural exhibit by James Hulett, a prominent Philadelphia architect.
11 rooms. Closed November-March. Children over 14 years only. Complimentary full breakfast. Victorian-style frame house (1877). **$$**

Chateau Inn and Suites
500 Warren Ave.,
Spring Lake,
732-974-2000, 877-974-5253;
www.chateauinn.com
The Chateau Inn and Suites offers high-speed Interet access, bathrooms with imported marble and flat-screen televisions, along with wood-burning fireplaces and patios or balconies.
36 rooms. Renovated Victorian hotel (1888). Overlooks parks, lake. **$$**

Normandy Inn
21 Tuttle Ave., Spring Lake,
732-449-7172, 800-449-1888;
www.normandyinn.com
Found on the National Register of Historic Places, the Normandy Inn offers guests a true Victorian experience. All guest rooms include antiques, private baths and high-speed Internet access and some feature four-poster Tester beds, Jacuzzis, fireplaces and private porches. The inn's complimentary bicycles are great for exploring all that the scenic Spring Lake area has to offer.
18 rooms. Complimentary full breakfast. Built as a private residence in 1888; 19th-century antiques. **$$**

The Sandpiper Inn
7 Atlantic Ave., Spring Lake,
732-449-6060, 800-824-2779;
www.sandpiperinn.com
The Sandpiper Inn features a wraparound porch and a glass-enclosed heated pool.
15 rooms. Complimentary full breakfast. Opposite beach. **$$**

White Lilac Inn
414 Central Ave., Spring Lake,
732-449-0211;
www.whitelilac.com
Set on a tree-lined street just a few blocks from the Atlantic Ocean, the White Lilac Inn features wraparound porches on each level and uniquely themed rooms with in-room fireplaces and period furnishings. Each morning, breakfast is served in the dining area and on the enclosed porch.
9 rooms. Closed January. Children over 14 years only. Complimentary full breakfast. **$$**

RESTAURANTS

★★The Black Trumpet
7 Atlantic Ave.,
Spring Lake,
732-449-4700;
www.theblacktrumpet.com
American menu. Lunch, dinner. Casual attire. Reservations recommended. **$$**

★★★Mill Inn
101 Old Mill Rd., Spring Lake,
732-449-1800;
www.themillatslh.com
For more than 60 years, the Mill has been a popular New Jersey dining destination, serving contemporary American cuisine such as fresh seafood and prime aged steaks.

On special nights, the Mill features supper club events with comedians and musicians, as well as big band nights.
American menu. Lunch, dinner. Closed Monday. Bar. Children's menu. Casual attire. Reservations recommended. Valet parking. Outdoor seating. **$$**

STANHOPE

WHAT TO SEE AND DO
Waterloo Village Restoration
525 Waterloo Rd., Stanhope,
973-347-0900
Known as the Andover Forge during the Revolutionary War, this was once a busy town on the Morris Canal. The 18th-century buildings include Stagecoach Inn, houses, craft barns, gristmill, apothecary shop, general store. Music festival during

summer (fee). Mid-April-mid-November: Wednesday-Sunday.

RESTAURANTS
★★The Black Forest Inn
249 Rte. 206 N, Stanhope,
973-347-3344;
www.blackforestinn.com
German, Continental menu. Lunch, dinner. Closed Tuesday. Bar. Casual attire. **$$**

STONE HARBOR
Information: Stone Harbor Chamber of Commerce, 212 96th St., Stone Harbor, 609-368-6101 or Cape May County Chamber of Commerce, 609-465-7181; www.capemaycountychamber.com

WHAT TO SEE AND DO
Wetlands Institute
1075 Stone Harbor Blvd.,
Stone Harbor, 609-368-1211;
www.wetlandsinstitute.org
Environmental center focusing on coastal ecology. Also includes observation tower, marsh trail, aquarium, films and guided walks (July and August: daily). Book-store. Mid-May-mid-October: daily; rest of year, Tuesday-Saturday; two weeks in late December-early January.

SPECIAL EVENTS
Sail into Summer Boat Show
Stone Harbor,
609-368-6101
Pleasure boating, family entertainment, musicians, food. First weekend in May.

Wings 'n Water Festival
1075 Stone Harbor Blvd., Stone Harbor, 609-368-1211
Arts and crafts, entertainment, seafood. Third full weekend in September.

STRATHMERE

RESTAURANTS
★★Deauville Inn
201 Willard Rd.,
Strathmere,
609-263-2080;
www.deauvilleinn.com

Seafood, steak menu. Lunch, dinner, late-night. Closed Tuesday-Wednesday in October-March. Bar. Children's menu. Casual attire. Reservations recommended. Valet parking. Outdoor seating. **$$$**

★
★
★
★
★

TEANECK

HOTELS

★★★Marriott Glenpointe
100 Frank W. Burr Blvd.,
Teaneck,
201-836-0600, 800-992-7752;
www.marriott.com
On-site dining options at the Marriott Glenpointe include elegant Tuscan cuisine at the Grille Restaurant and light American fare at Glen Lounge. For a day of total relaxation, guests can head to The Spa at Glenpointe, while golf enthusiasts have a choice of seven nearby courses.
347 rooms. **$$**

TOMS RIVER

Information: Toms River-Ocean County Chamber of Commerce, 1200 Hooper Ave., Toms River,
732-349-0220; www.oc-chamber.com

WHAT TO SEE AND DO

Cooper Environmental Center
1170 Cattus Island Blvd., Toms River,
732-270-6960
A 530-acre facility with three-mile bay front. Boat tours (summer; free); 7 miles of marked trails, picnicking (grills), playground. Nature center. Daily.

HOTELS

★★Holiday Inn Toms River
290 Little League World Champions Blvd. (Hwy. 37 E), Toms River,
732-244-4000, 888-465-4329;
www.holidayinn.com
122 rooms. **$**

★★Ramada Inn
2373 Rte. 9, Toms River,
732-905-2626;
www.ramada.com
154 rooms. Complimentary continental breakfast. Restaurant, bar. Tennis. **$**

RESTAURANTS

★The Old Time Tavern
Dover Mall Rte. 166,
Toms River,
732-349-2387;
www.theoldtimetavern.com
American menu. Lunch, dinner. Bar. Children's menu. Casual attire. **$$**

TRENTON

The capital of New Jersey since 1790, Trenton is one of the fastest growing business and industrial areas in the country and a leading rubber-manufacturing center since colonial times.
Information: Mercer County Chamber of Commerce, 214 W. State St., Trenton, 609-393-4143; www.mercerchamber.org

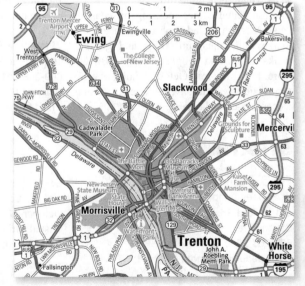

WHAT TO SEE AND DO

College of New Jersey
Trenton,
609-771-1855;
www.trenton.edu
(1855) (6,150 students.) A 250-acre wooded campus with two lakes. Tours of campus.
On campus is the:

College Art Gallery
Trenton,
609-771-2652
February-May and September-December: Monday-Friday, Sunday.

New Jersey State Museum
205 W. State St.,
Trenton,
609-292-6464;
www.newjerseystatemuseum.org
Adjacent to Capitol. Tuesday-Sunday.
Includes:

Auditorium
205 W. State St., Trenton
Lectures, films, music, children's theater. Some fees.

Main Building
Fine art, cultural history, archaeology and natural science exhibits. Tuesday-Sunday.

Planetarium
New Jersey State Museum,
205 W. State St., Trenton,
609-292-6303
One of few Intermediate Space Transit planetaria (duplicates motions of space vehicles) in the world. Programs (weekends; July-August: Tuesday-Sunday). Over four years only, except children's programs. Tickets 30 minutes in advance.

Old Barracks Museum
Barrack St., Trenton,
609-396-1776;
www.oldbarracks.org
One of the finest examples of colonial barracks in the U.S. Built between 1758 and 1759, it housed British, Hessian and Continental troops during the Revolutionary War. Museum contains restored soldiers' squad room, antique furniture, ceramics, firearms, dioramas. Guides in period costumes. Daily.

Sesame Place
Trenton,
215-752-7070
A family play park featuring characters from "Sesame Street."

Washington Crossing State Park
355 Washington Crossing-Pennington Rd.,
Titusville,
609-737-0623;
www.state.nj.us/dep/parksandforests/
parks/washcros.html
This 996-acre park commemorates the famous crossing on Christmas night, 1776, by the Continental Army, under the command of General George Washington. Natural trails. Picnicking, playground. Visitor center and nature center (Wednesday-Sunday); open-air summer theater (fee). Standard fees.
Also in park is:

Ferry House State Historic Site
355 Washington Crossing, Trenton,
609-737-2515
This building sheltered Washington and some of his men on December 25, 1776, after they had crossed the Delaware from the Pennsylvania side. It is believed that the strategy to be used for the attack on Trenton was discussed here. Restored as a living history colonial farmhouse; special programs throughout the year. Wednesday-Sunday.

William Trent House
15 Market St., Trenton,
609-989-3027;
www.williamtrenthouse.org
(1719) Trenton's oldest house is an example of Georgian architecture. It was the home of Chief Justice William Trent, for whom the city was named. Colonial garden. Daily, afternoons.

NEW JERSEY

★
★
★
★

SPECIAL EVENTS

Reenactment of Crossing of the Delaware
Washington Crossing State Park,
355 Washington Crossing Rd., Trenton
Departs on the afternoon of December 25.

Trenton Kennel Club Dog Show
Mercer County Park, Old Trenton and
S. Post Rds., W. Windsor Township;
www.trentonkennelclub.net/shows.html
Mercer County Central Park. Early May.

HOTELS

★★★Lafayette Yard Marriott
1 W. Lafayette St., Trenton,
609-421-4000, 888-796-4662;
www.marriott.com
Like all Marriott hotels, the Lafayette Yard offers guest rooms with luxurious linens, fluffy comforters and pillows and a host of amenities including high-speed Internet access. Archives Restaurant offers an American menu for breakfast, lunch and dinner, while the Archives Bar and Lounge features lighter fare.
197 rooms. Airport transportation available. $$

RESTAURANTS

★★Marsilio's
541 Roebling Ave.,
Trenton,
609-695-1916;
www.marsilios.com
Italian menu. Lunch, dinner. Closed Sunday. Bar. Children's menu. Business casual attire. Reservations recommended. Valet parking. $$

VERNON
Information: Vernon Township Municipal Building, 21 Church St., Vernon,
973-764-4055

WHAT TO SEE AND DO

Action Park
200 Rte. 94, Vernon,
973-827-2000, 888-767-0762;
www.mountaincreek.com
Theme park includes 75 self-operative rides, shows and attractions. Action Park has more than 40 water rides, including river rides and Tidal Wave Pool; also Grand Prix racecars, bungee jumping, miniature golf, children's park; food, picnic area. Three daily shows, weekend festival series. Mid-June-Labor Day: daily; late May-mid-June, Thursday-Sunday.
    Also here is:

Mountain Creek Ski Resort
200 NJ 94, Vernon,
973-827-2000, 888-767-0762;
www.mountaincreek.com
Gondola; four quad, triple, double chairlifts; three surface lifts, rope tow; school, rentals, snowmaking; cafeterias, restaurants, bars, night club; nursery. Forty-three runs; vertical drop 1,040 feet. December-March: daily Night skiing. Spa, country club (daily).

HOTELS

★★★Mineral Hotel and Spa
2 Chamonix Dr., Vernon,
973-827-5996;
www.crystalgolfresort.com
Located in the Kittaninny Mountains just an hour from New York City, Minerals Hotel and Spa offers 175 guest rooms, all of which include unlimited access to the sports club on site.
201 rooms. Golf, 100 holes. Ski in/ski out. $$

WARREN

HOTELS

★★★Somerset Hills Hotel
200 Liberty Corner Rd., Warren,
908-647-6700, 800-688-0700;
www.shh.com
Visitors will find that this hotel, located in the Watchung Mountains, combines the service of a country inn with the facilities, entertainment and accommodations expected from a full-service hotel.
111 rooms. Complimentary full breakfast. **$$**

WAYNE

Wayne is the home of William Paterson University of New Jersey (1855).
Information: Tri-County Chamber of Commerce, 2055 Hamburg Turnpike, Wayne, 973-831-7788;
www.tricounty.org

WHAT TO SEE AND DO

Dey Mansion
199 Totowa Rd.,
Wayne,
973-696-1776
(circa 1740) Restoration of Washington's headquarters (1780); period furnishings. Guided tours. Picnic tables. Wednesday-Sunday.

Ringwood State Park
Rte. 23, Ringwood,
973-962-7031
Ringwood State Park lies in upper Passaic County, near the town of Ringwood, within the heart of the Ramapo Mountains. Consisting of 6,196 acres, the park can be reached by routes 23 and 511 from the west and Route 17 and Sloatsburg Road from the east. Standard fees are charged for each section Memorial Day-Labor Day.

Ringwood Manor Section
This section features a 51-room mansion containing a collection of Americana; relics of iron-making days (1740); formal gardens. Interpretive tours. Fishing in Ringwood River. Picnic facilities nearby. Tours Wednesday-Sunday.

Shepherd Lake Section
A 541-acre wooded area has trap and skeet shooting all year (fee). The 74-acre Shepherd Lake provides a swimming beach and bathhouse, fishing, boating (ramp). Picnicking.

Skylands Section
Located here is a 44-room mansion modeled after an English baronial house (open to the public on select days). The gardens (90 acres) surrounding the manor house comprise the only botanical garden in the state park system (guided tours upon request; 973-962-7527). This 1,119-acre section also offers fishing, hunting, hiking, mountain biking.

Terhune Memorial Park (Sunnybank)
Terhune Dr. and Lamereux, Wayne,
973-694-1800
Estate of the late Albert Payson Terhune, author of "Lad, a Dog" and many other books about his collies. Scenic garden; picnic area. Daily.

Van Riper-Hopper (Wayne) Museum
533 Berdan Ave., Wayne,
973-694-7192
(Circa 1786) Dutch Colonial farmhouse with 18th- and 19th-century furnishings, local historical objects, herb garden, bird sanctuary.
Also here is:

Mead Van Duyne House
530 Berdan Ave., Wayne,
973-694-7192
Restored Dutch farmhouse.

★
★
★
★
★

WEST ORANGE

Information: West Orange Chamber of Commerce,
973-731-0360;
www.westorange.com

WHAT TO SEE AND DO

Eagle Rock Reservation

Prospect and Eagle Rock avenues,
West Orange,
973-268-3500;
www.eaglerockreservation.org

A 644-foot elevation in the Orange Mountains; visitors see a heavily populated area that stretches from the Passaic River Valley east to New York City. Hiking trails, picnicking, bridle paths. Restaurant. Daily.

Edison National Historic Site

Main St. and Lake Side Ave.,
West Orange,
973-324-9973;
www.nps.gpv/edis

Here is:

Edison Laboratory

Main St. and Lakeside Ave.,
West Orange,
973-736-5050

Built by Edison in 1887, this was his laboratory for 44 years. During that time, he was granted more than half of his 1,093 patents (an all-time record). Here he perfected the phonograph, motion picture camera and electric storage battery. One-hour lab tour (no video cameras, strollers) includes the chemistry lab and library; demonstrations of early phonographs. Visitor center has exhibits; films. Daily.

Turtle Back Zoo

560 Northfield Ave.,
West Orange,
973-731-5800;
www.turtlebackzoo.com

This 20-acre park features animals in natural surroundings; sea lion pool; miniature train ride (one mile). Picnicking, concessions. Daily; limited schedule December-March.

Adjacent is:

South Mountain Arena

560 Northfield Ave.,
West Orange,
973-731-3828

Indoor ice rink. Hockey games, special events.

RESTAURANTS

★★★Highlawn Pavilion

Eagle Rock Reservation,
West Orange,
973-731-3463;
www.highlawn.com

This restaurant offers a picturesque view of the Manhattan skyline. The building, built in 1909, was restored and opened as a restaurant in 1986. A French rotisserie and Italian brick wood-burning oven bring out the flavors of the American cuisine.
American menu. Lunch, dinner, late-night. Bar. Jacket required. Reservations recommended. Valet parking. Outdoor seating.
$$$

★★★The Manor

111 Prospect Ave.,
West Orange,
973-731-2360;
www.themanorrestaurant.com

One of the most well-known (and most formal) restaurants in New Jersey, the Manor offers dishes such as cilantro-sesame-seed-coated halibut filet, pan-seared veal tournados and lobster bisque.
American menu. Lunch, dinner, Sunday brunch. Closed Monday. Bar. Jacket required. Reservations recommended. Valet parking. **$$$**

142

NEW JERSEY

WHITEHOUSE

RESTAURANTS

★★★The Ryland Inn
Hwy. 22 W, Whitehouse,
908-534-4011;
www.therylandinn.com
Using ingredients culled from his seven acres of gardens, chef-owner Craig Shelton creates a simple, seasonal French cuisine at this country-estate restaurant. The decor ranges from homey to hunting lodge, and the wine list is long and varied.
French menu. Dinner. Bar. Children's menu. Jacket required. Reservations recommended. Valet parking. $$$$

WILDWOOD AND WILDWOOD CREST

Wildwood's busy boardwalk extends for approximately two miles along the five miles of protected sandy beach it shares with North Wildwood and Wildwood Crest, two neighboring resorts. The area offers swimming, waterskiing, ocean and bay fishing, boating, sailing, bicycling, golf, tennis and shuffleboard.
Information: Greater Wildwood Chamber of Commerce, 3306 Pacific Ave., Wildwood, 609-729-4000; www.gwcoc.com

WHAT TO SEE AND DO

Boat trips
Capt Sinn's Dock, 6006 Park Blvd.,
Wildwood Crest,
609-522-3934
Sightseeing and whale-watching cruises aboard "Big Flamingo." July-November: daily Also aboard the "Big Blue Sightseer." June-September: daily.

HOTELS

★Armada by the Sea
6503 Ocean Ave.,
Wildwood Crest,
609-729-3000, 800-399-3001;
www.armadamotel.com
56 rooms. Closed October-mid-April. $$

★★El Coronado Motor Inn
8501 Atlantic Ave.,
Wildwood Crest,
609-729-1000, 800-227-5302;
www.elcoronado.com
113 rooms. Closed November-April. Restaurant. Children's activity center. $

★Fleur De Lis
6105 Ocean Ave., Wildwood Crest,
609-522-0123;
www.fleurdelismotel.com
44 rooms. Closed mid-October-mid-April. On beach. $

★Jolly Roger Motel
6805 Atlantic Ave.,
Wildwood Crest,
609-522-6915, 800-337-5232;
www.jollyrogermotel.com
74 rooms. Closed late September-mid-May. Children's activity center. $

★Nassau Inn
6201 Ocean Ave., Wildwood Crest,
609-729-9077, 800-336-9077;
www.nassauinnmotel.com
56 rooms. Closed mid-October-April. On beach. $

★★Pan American Hotel
5901 Ocean Ave., Wildwood Crest,
609-522-6936;
www.panamericanhotel.com
78 rooms. Closed mid-October-mid-May. Children's activity center. $$

★★Port Royal Hotel
6801 Ocean Ave., Wildwood Crest,
609-729-2000;
www.portroyalhotel.com
100 rooms. Closed mid-October-April. Children's activity center. $$

NEW JERSEY

SPECIALTY LODGINGS

Candlelight Inn
2310 Central Ave.,
North Wildwood,
609-522-6200, 800-992-2632;
www.candlelight-inn.com
10 rooms. No children allowed. Complimentary full breakfast. Queen Anne/Victorian-style house (circa 1905); restored. **$$**

RESTAURANTS

★★Garfield's Giardino Ristorante
3800 Pacific Ave., Wildwood,
609-729-0120
Italian, seafood menu. Dinner. Bar. Children's menu. **$$**

144

PENNSYLVANIA

FROM ITS EASTERNMOST TIP NEAR BORDENTOWN, NEW JERSEY, TO ITS STRAIGHT WESTERN boundary with Ohio and West Virginia, Pennsylvania's 300-mile stride across the country covers a mountain-and-farm, river-and-stream, mine-and-mill topography. Its cities, people and resources are just as diverse. In the eastern part of the state, Philadelphia is a treasure house of tradition and historical shrines; in the west, Pittsburgh is a mighty museum of our nation's industrial heritage. Pennsylvania miners dig nearly all the anthracite coal in the United States and still work some of the oldest iron mines in the country. Oil employees work more than 19,000 producing wells, and 55,000 farm families make up 20 percent of the Pennsylvania work force.

The state is a leader in cigar leaf tobacco, apples, grapes, ice cream, chocolate products, mushrooms and soft drinks, plus factory and farm machinery, electronics equipment, scientific instruments, watches, textile machines, railroad cars, ships, assorted metal products and electrical machinery.

Pennsylvania has also been a keystone of culture. The first serious music in the colonies was heard in Bethlehem; today, both Pittsburgh and Philadelphia have well-known symphonies. Celebrated art galleries, museums and more than 140 institutions of higher learning (including the oldest medical school in the United States at the University of Pennsylvania) are based here.

Swedes made the first settlement on this fertile land at Tinicum Island in the Delaware River in 1643. The territory became Dutch in 1655 and British in 1664. After Charles II granted William Penn a charter that made him proprietor of "Pennsylvania," the Quaker statesman landed here in 1682 and invested the land with his money and leadership. Commercial, agricultural and industrial growth came quickly.

The Declaration of Independence was signed in Pennsylvania, and the Constitution was drafted here.

Information: www.state.pa.us

 SPOTLIGHT

★ Benjamin Franklin founded the Philadelphia Zoo, the first zoo in the United States.

PENNSYLVANIA

ALLENTOWN

Situated in the heart of Pennsylvania Dutch country, Allentown is conveniently accessible via a network of major highways. Allentown was originally incorporated as Northamptontown. The city later took the name of its founder, William Allen, a Chief Justice of Pennsylvania. Allentown was greatly influenced by the Pennsylvania Germans who settled the surrounding countryside and helped the city become the business hub for a rich agricultural community.

Information: Lehigh Valley Convention & Visitors Bureau, 840 Hamilton St., Allentown, 610-882-9200, 800-747-0561; www.lehighvalleypa.org

WHAT TO SEE AND DO

Cedar Crest College
100 College Dr., Allentown, 610-437-4471, 800-360-1222; www.cedarcrest.edu

(1867) (1,700 women.) An 84-acre campus that includes nationally registered William F. Curtis Arboretum (tours); chapel with stained-glass windows portraying outstanding women in history; art galleries, sculpture gardens, museum and theater. Campus tours.

Dorney Park and Wildwater Kingdom
3830 Dorney Park Rd., Allentown, 610-395-3724; www.dorneypark.com

This amusement and water park is one of the country's oldest. A former fish hatchery, the 200-acre park is home to nearly 100 rides, 11 water slides and four roller coasters. Little ones can discover turtle fountains and squirt guns. Bigger kids can climb and play on a submarine. Older kids may want to torpedo through an enclosed tube or float slowly down a 1,600-foot winding river. Just an hour from Philadelphia, the park also features song and dance revues and 40 food locations, including two air-conditioned, dine-in restaurants. Daily; closed November-April.

Frank Buchman House
117 N. 11th St., Allentown, 610-435-1074

Constructed in 1892, this three-story row house, typical of Allentown's inner city, is an example of Victorian architecture; period rooms. Saturday and Sunday afternoons; also by appointment.

Lehigh County Museum
432 W. Walnut St., Allentown, 610-435-1074; www.lchs.museum

Exhibits illustrate economic, social and cultural history of the county. Monday-Saturday, Sunday afternoons.

Liberty Bell Shrine
622 Hamilton, Allentown, 610-435-4232

Reconstructed Zion's church has shrine in basement area where Liberty Bell was hidden in 1777; contains a full-size replica of the original bell; other historical exhibits,

PENNSYLVANIA

art collection. February-April: Wednesday-Saturday afternoons; May-November: Monday-Saturday afternoons.

Lock Ridge Furnace Museum
525 N. Franklin St., Allentown,
610-435-4664
Exhibits on the development of the U.S. iron and steel industry. May-September: Saturday and Sunday afternoons; also by appointment.

Muhlenberg College
2400 W. Chew St., Allentown,
484-664-3100;
www.muhlenberg.edu
(1848) (2,000 students.) Founded by the Lutheran Church to honor patriarch of Lutheranism in America. On campus is the Gideon F. Egner Memorial Chapel, an example of Gothic architecture. Also here is the Center for the Arts, a dramatic building designed by renowned architect Philip Johnson, which houses the Muhlenberg Theater Association. Campus tours.

Saylor Park Cement Industry Museum
245 N. Second, Coplay,
610-435-4664
Outdoor historic site featuring remains of cement kilns.

Trexler Memorial Park
Cedar Crest Blvd. and Broadway, Allentown,
610-437-7628
Spring outdoor bulb display (April-May). Gross Memorial Rose Garden (at peak second week June): Trout Nursery and Fish-for-Fun stream. Picnic areas. Band concerts June-August.

Trexler-Lehigh County Game Preserve
5150 Game Preserve Rd., Allentown,
610-799-4171;
www.lvzoo.org
A 1,200-acre zoo, petting farm and wilderness tour that is home to more than 350 animals. Scenic overlooks; picnic area. April-October: daily.

Trout Hall
414 W. Walnut St., Allentown,
610-435-4664
(1770) Oldest house in city, Georgian Colonial; restored. Period rooms, museum. Guided tours. April-November: Tuesday-Sunday afternoons; also by appointment.

SPECIAL EVENTS
Das Awkscht Fescht
Macungie Memorial Park, Allentown,
610-967-2317;
www.awkscht.com
2,500 antique, classic and special-interest autos; entertainment, food, fireworks. First weekend in August.

Drum Corps International-Eastern Regional Championship
J. Birney Crum Stadium,
21st and Linden Streets, Allentown,
610-966-5344;
www.dci.org
Drum and bugle corps competition. September.

Great Allentown Fair
Fairgrounds, 17th and Chew Streets, Allentown,
610-435-7469;
www.allentownfair.com
Farm and commercial exhibits, rides, games, food, entertainment. Late August-early September.

Mayfair Festival of the Arts
Allentown,
610-437-6900;
www.mayfairfestival.org
Allentown parks. Family arts festival with 150 free musical performances; crafts and food. Monday and Thursday-Sunday, Memorial Day weekend.

HOTELS
★Comfort Inn
3712 Hamilton Blvd., Allentown,
610-437-9100, 877-424-6423
122 rooms. Complimentary continental breakfast. Airport transportation available. $

147

PENNSYLVANIA

★Crowne Plaza
904 Hamilton Mall,
Allentown,
610-433-2221, 877-424-4225;
www.crowneplaza.com
224 rooms. Airport transportation available. **$**

★★Four Points by Sheraton
3400 Airport Rd.,
Allentown,
610-266-1000;
www.fourpoints.com
147 rooms. **$**

★Hampton Inn
7471 Keebler Way,
Allentown,
610-391-1500, 800-426-7866;
www.hamptoninn.com
124 rooms. Complimentary continental breakfast. Airport transportation available. **$**

RESTAURANTS
★★Aladdin Restaurant
651 Union Blvd., Allentown,
610-437-4023
Middle Eastern menu. Lunch, dinner. Closed Monday, children's menu. Casual attire. **$$**

★★Bay Leaf
935 W. Hamilton St., Allentown,
610-433-4211;
www.allentownbayleaf.com
Thai menu. Lunch, dinner. Closed Sunday. Bar. **$$**

★★Federal Grill
536 Hamilton St., Allentown,
610-776-7600;
www.federalgrill.com
Seafood menu. Lunch, dinner. Saturday-Sunday brunch. Bar. Reservations recommended. Outdoor seating. **$$**

ALTOONA

148

The rough, high Alleghenies ring this city, which was founded by the Pennsylvania Railroad. Altoona expanded rapidly after 1852, when the difficult task of spanning the Alleghenies with track, linking Philadelphia and Pittsburgh, was completed. The railroad shops still offer substantial employment for residents of the city and Blair County.
Information: Allegheny Mountains Convention & Visitors Bureau, One Convention Center Dr., Altoona,
814-943-4183, 800-842-5866;
www.alleghenymountains.com

WHAT TO SEE AND DO
Baker Mansion Museum
3500 Oak Lane,
Altoona,
814-942-3916
(1844-1848) Stone Greek Revival house of early ironmaster; now occupied by Blair County Historical Society. Hand-carved Belgian furniture of the period; transportation exhibits, gun collection, clothing, housewares. Memorial Day-Labor Day: Tuesday-Sunday; mid-April-Memorial Day and Labor Day-October: Saturday-Sunday.

Canoe Creek State Park

Altoona,
814-695-6807

Approximately 950-acre park features 155-acre lake. Swimming beach, fishing, boating (launches, rentals); hiking, picnicking (reservations for pavilion), cross-country skiing, sledding, ice boating, ice skating, cabins.

Delgrossos Park

Altoona,
814-684-3538

More than 30 rides and attractions include antique carousel, miniature golf and pony rides. Also here are arcade games, picnic pavilions and restaurant. May-September: Tuesday-Sunday.

Fort Roberdeau

Altoona,
814-946-0048;
www.fortroberdeau.org

Reconstructed Revolutionary War fort with horizontal logs; contains blacksmith shop, barracks, storehouse, powder magazine. Costumed guides; weekend reenactments. Visitor center. Picnicking, nature trails. May-October: daily.

Horseshoe Curve Visitors Center

Altoona,
814-946-0834

World-famous engineering feat, carrying main-line Conrail and Amtrak trains around western grade of 91 feet per mile. Curve is 2,375 feet long and has a central angle of 220 degrees. Funicular runs between interpretive center and observation area. Gift shop. April-December: daily.

Lakemont Park

700 Park Ave.,
Altoona,
814-949-7275;
www.lakemontpark.com

An amusement park with more than 30 rides and attractions; home of the nation's oldest wooden roller coaster; water park, miniature golf, entertainment. May-September: closed Monday-Tuesday.

Prince Gallitzin State Park

Highway 53 and Beaver Valley Rd.,
Flinton,
814-674-1000

Approximately 6,200 acres; 26 miles of shoreline on 1,600-acre lake. Swimming beach, fishing, boating (rentals, mooring, launching, marina); hiking trails, horseback riding, x-country skiing, snowmobiling, iceskating, ice fishing; picnicking, snack bar, store, laundry facilities, tent and trailer sites, cabins. Standard fees.

Railroader's Memorial Museum

1300 Nineth Ave.,
Altoona,
814-946-0834,
888-428-6662;
www.railroadcity.com

Exhibits feature railroad artifacts, art and theme displays. Railroad rolling stock, steam and electric locomotive collections. Daily.

Wopsononock Mountain

Altoona

Lookout provides view of six-county area from height of 2,580 feet; offers one of the best views in the state.

SPECIAL EVENTS

Blair County Arts Festival

Penn State Altoona Campus,
3000 Ivyside Park, Altoona,
814-949-2787

Arts, crafts, hobbies on display. Mid-May.

Keystone Country Festival

Lakemont Park, 700 Park Ave.,
Altoona

Arts and crafts, music, food. Contact Convention and Visitors Bureau for details. Weekend after Labor Day.

Railfest

1300 Nineth Ave.,
Altoona,
814-946-0834

A celebration of Altoona's rich rail heritage. October.

149

PENNSYLVANIA

★
★
★
★
★

HOTELS

★★Ramada Inn
1 Sheraton Dr., Altoona,
814-946-1631, 800-311-5192;
www.ramada.com
215 rooms. Complimentary continental breakfast. Airport transportation available.
$

RESTAURANTS

★★Allegro
3926 Broad Ave.,
Altoona,
814-946-5216, 800-372-5524;
www.allegro-restaurant.com
American, Italian menu. Dinner. Closed Sunday. Bar. Children's menu. **$$**

AMBRIDGE

Founded by the American Bridge Company, this city rests on part of the site of Old Economy Village. In 1825, under the leadership of George Rapp, the Harmony Society established a communal pietistic colony that was important in the industrial life and development of western Pennsylvania for many decades. Despite its spiritual emphasis, Old Economy Village enjoyed a great material prosperity; farms were productive, craft shops were busy and factories made textiles widely acclaimed for their quality. Surplus funds financed railroads and industrial enterprises throughout the upper Ohio Valley. After celibacy was adopted and unwise investments were made, the community's productivity decreased. Officially dissolved in 1905, the remains of the community were taken over by the Commonwealth of Pennsylvania in 1916.
Information: Beaver County Recreation & Tourism Department, 121 Brady's Run Rd., Beaver Falls, 724-891-7030, 800-342-8192;
www.visitbeavercounty.com

WHAT TO SEE AND DO

Old Economy Village
270 16th St., Ambridge,
724-266-4500;
www.oldeconomyvillage.com
Seventeen original Harmony Society buildings located on six acres, restored and filled with furnishings of the community. Included are the communal leader's 32-room Great House, the Feast Hall, the Grotto in the Gardens, wine cellars, a five-story granary, shops, dwellings and community kitchens. Cobblestone streets link the buildings. Special festivals and events. Tuesday-Sunday.

SPECIAL EVENTS

Nationality Days
Ethnic cultural displays, foods, native music, dancing. Mid-May.

BEAVER FALLS

Founded as Brighton, the town changed its name for the falls in the Beaver River. The plates from which U.S. currency is printed are made in Beaver Falls. Geneva College (1848) is located here.
Information: Beaver County Recreation & Tourism Department,
121 Brady's Run Rd., Beaver Falls,
724-891-7030, 800-342-8192; www.visitbeavercounty.com

HOTELS

★Beaver Valley Motel
7257 Big Beaver Blvd., Beaver Falls,
724-843-0630, 800-400-8312;
www.bvmotel.com
27 rooms. **$**

★★Conley Inn
7099 Big Beaver Blvd., Beaver Falls,
724-843-9300, 800-345-6819
56 rooms. **$**

★★Holiday Inn
7195 Eastwood Rd.,
Beaver Falls,
724-846-3700, 800-282-0244;
www.holidayinn.com
156 rooms. **$**

RESTAURANTS
★★Wooden Angel
308 Leopard Lane, Beaver,
724-774-7880;
www.wooden-angel.com
Seafood menu. Lunch, dinner. Closed
Sunday-Monday. Bar. **$$$**

BEDFORD

Fort Bedford was a major frontier outpost in pre-Revolutionary War days. After the war, it became an important stopover along the route of western migration. Garrett Pendergrass, the second settler here, built Pendergrass's Tavern, which figures in a number of novels by Hervey Allen.

Information: Bedford County Conference & Visitors Bureau, 131 S. Juliana St., Bedford, 814-623-1771, 800-765-3331; www.bedfordcounty.net

WHAT TO SEE AND DO

Bedford County Courthouse
230 S. Juliana St., Building 2,
Bedford,
814-623-4807
Federal-style building constructed in 1828 has unique hanging spiral staircase; oldest courthouse still in operation in Pennsylvania. Monday-Friday.

Fort Bedford Park and Museum
Fort Bedford Dr., Bedford,
814-623-8891, 800-259-4284;
N end of Juliana St., park along
Raystown River
Log blockhouse, erected during Bedford's bicentennial. Contains large-scale replica of original fort, displays of colonial antiques and relics, Native American artifacts. May-late October: daily.

Old Bedford Village
220 Sawblade Rd.,
Bedford,
814-623-1156, 800-238-4347;
www.oldbedfordvillage.com
More than 40 authentic log and frame structures (1750-1851) house historical exhibits; crafts demonstrations, operating pioneer farm. Many special events throughout the year. Memorial Day weekend-Labor Day, closed Wednesdays; September-October: Thursday-Sunday.

SPECIAL EVENTS

Civil War Reenactment
Old Bedford Village. Early September.

Fall Foliage Festival Days
141 S. Juliana St.,
Bedford
Entertainment, ethnic foods, antique cars, more than 350 craft booths. First two full weekends in October.

HOTELS

★★Best Western Bedford Inn
4517 Business 220,
Bedford,
814-623-9006, 800-752-8592;
www.bestwestern.com
105 rooms. **$**

★★Quality Inn
4407 Business 220,
Bedford,
814-623-5188, 877-424-6423;
www.choicehotels.com
66 rooms. Complimentary continental breakfast. **$**

RESTAURANTS

★★Ed's Steak House
4476 Business 220, Bedford,
814-623-8894
Seafood, steak menu. Breakfast, lunch, dinner. Bar. Children's menu. **$$**

LAUREL HIGHLANDS

As the name suggests, the Laurel Highlands—spread across the Allegheny Mountains in southwestern Pennsylvania—is a region of lofty, wooded ridges, farm valleys, and streams and lakes, many boasting swimming beaches. Here and there you come upon covered bridges. Early on, the beauty of the setting drew many travelers—and it continues to do so. Today, the Highlands serve as a year-round playground, where you can raft, kayak, fish, swim, ski and bicycle.

This two-day, 150-mile drive meanders though the Highlands while visiting several important historic sites. This is a one-way trip between Bedford in the east and Uniontown in the west. You can drive in either direction, but we'll begin at Bedford, just off the Pennsylvania Turnpike. Stop in Bedford at the Old Bedford Village, which preserves more than 40 original farm buildings and other structures in a village-like cluster. One that catches the eye is the eight-sided schoolhouse built nearby in 1851. Called an Eight Square, the octagon shape had a specific purpose: it gave every student an equal share of window light and proximity to the pot-bellied stove in the center. In summer, craftsmen demonstrate blacksmithing, barrel-making, broom-making and other pioneer skills.

From Bedford, take I-99 North to State Route 56 northwest to Johnstown. Two sites here capture the horror of the Johnstown Flood of 1889, which struck the small, steel manufacturing city with a sudden ferocity that left 2,200 people dead. Just east of the city, the National Park Service operates the Johnstown Flood National Memorial. It overlooks the dry basin of what was once a man-made lake that emptied when heavy rains collapsed an earthen dam. In town, the Johnstown Flood Museum illustrates the damage wrought by the flood and Johnstown's determination to rebuild.

Ahead on the drive, two reconstructed 18th-century forts, Fort Ligonier in Ligonier and Fort Necessity National Battlefield near Farmington, recount British colonial efforts to wrest the Ohio River Valley west of the Alleghenies from French control. Both forts played a role in the ultimate defeat of the French at Fort Duquesne, which became the site of Pittsburgh. Ligonier is the more imposing of the two forts, but Fort Necessity may be more memorable. To reach it, take Route 271 West from Johnstown to Ligonier, and plan to spend the night there. To reach Fort Necessity, head two miles southeast on US 30 to Route 381 to Farmington, and turn right on US 40. At Fort Necessity, a modest ring of stakes thrusting from the earth marks the site of George Washington's only military surrender, a lesson that surely must have aided him two decades later as commander of the Continental Army.

The route from Ligonier to Farmington edges past Fallingwater, architect Frank Lloyd Wright's masterpiece on Bear Run. The structure, stair-stepping down a wooded mountainside, combines architecture and nature in a glorious piece of artwork. A stop here is a must, but allow at least three hours to take an escorted tour and to walk the grounds. Exhibits at the Entrance Pavilion explain the construction of the house, built in 1936 as a mountain retreat for a wealthy Pittsburgh department store owner. Inside the house, you'll learn about Wright's daring use of new construction materials and his fascination with the possibilities of space. Short in stature, Wright designed the house with surprisingly low ceilings.

A couple of miles down the road, the village of Ohiopyle is a center for whitewater rafting. Sign up for thrills, or watch helmet-clad rafters arriving or departing on upper and lower stretches of the Youghiogheny River (also called the "Yock"). From Fort Necessity, continue west on US 40 to Uniontown to conclude this tour. Approximately 150 miles.

BELLEFONTE

When Talleyrand, the exiled French minister, saw the Big Spring here in 1794, his exclamation—"Beautiful fountain"—gave the town its name. Bellefonte is perched on seven hills at the southeast base of Bald Eagle Mountain.

Information: Bellefonte Intervalley Area Chamber of Commerce, Train Station, 320 W. High St., Bellefonte, 814-355-2917; www.bellefontechamber.org

WHAT TO SEE AND DO

Black Moshannon State Park
814-342-5960
Approximately 3,450 acres. Swimming beach, fishing, boating (rentals, mooring, launching); hunting, hiking, cross-country skiing, snowmobiling, ice skating, ice fishing, ice boating; picnicking, snack bar, tent and trailer sites, cabins.

Centre County Library and Historical Museum
200 N. Allegheny St., Bellefonte, 814-355-1516; www.centrecountylibrary.org

Local historical museum includes central Pennsylvania historical and genealogical books, records. Monday-Saturday.

RESTAURANTS

★★Gamble Mill Restaurant
160 Dunlap St., Bellefonte, 814-355-7764; www.gamblemill.com
American menu. Lunch, dinner. Closed Sunday. Bar. **$$**

BETHLEHEM

Bethlehem Steel products have put this city on the map, but Bethlehem is also known for its Bach Festival, for its historic district, and for Lehigh University (1865) and Moravian College (1807).

Not surprisingly, Bethlehem has earned itself the nickname, "America's Christmas city." Moravians, members of a very old Protestant denomination, assembled here on Christmas Evening 1741 in a log house that was part stable, which was the only building in the area at the time. Singing a hymn that praised Bethlehem, they found a name for their village. Their private musical performance also was the first of many in Bethlehem; string quartets and symphonies were heard here before any other place in the colonies.

The Lehigh Canal's 1829 opening kicked off the area's industrialization, along with the development of the borough of South Bethlehem (1865), which was incorporated into Bethlehem in 1917.

Information: Bethlehem Tourism Authority, 52 W. Broad St., Bethlehem, 610-868-1513, 800-360-8687; www.bethlehem.info

WHAT TO SEE AND DO

Apothecary Museum
424 Main St., Bethlehem, 610-867-0173
Original fireplace (1752), where prescriptions were compounded; collection of artifacts includes retorts, grinders, mortars and pestles, scales, blown-glass bottles, labels and a set of Delft jars (1743); herb and flower garden. By appointment.

Brethren's House
Church and Main Streets, Bethlehem, 610-861-3916
(1748) Early residence and shop area for single men of the Moravian Community. Now serves Moravian College as its Center for Music and Art.

PENNSYLVANIA

Central Moravian Church

40 W. Church St.,
Bethlehem
(1806) Federal-style with hand-carved detail, considered foremost Moravian church in the U.S. Noted for its music, including a trombone choir in existence since 1754.

God's Acre

Church and Market Streets,
Bethlehem
(1742-1910) Old Moravian cemetery following Moravian tradition that all gravestones are laid flat, indicating that all are equal in the sight of God.

Hill-to-Hill Bridge

Joins old and new parts of the city and provides excellent view of historic area, river and Bethlehem Steel plant.

Historic Bethlehem Inc's 18th-Century Industrial Quarter

459 Old York Rd., Bethlehem,
610-691-0603
Ohio Road and Main St. (pedestrian entrance); Old York Road and Union Boulevard (parking lot entrance). Guided tours July-August: Saturday; late November-late December, weekends).

Tour of area includes:

Goundie House

501 Main St., Bethlehem
(1810) Restored Federal-style brick house has period-furnished rooms and interpretive exhibits.

Luckenbach Mill

459 Old York Rd., Bethlehem
(1869) Restored gristmill contains contemporary craft gallery and museum shop; also the offices of Bethlehem Area Chamber of Commerce and Historic Bethlehem Inc. Interpretive display here is included in guided tour.

Springhouse

459 Old York Rd., Bethlehem

(1764) Reconstruction on site of original spring that served Moravian community as a water source from the time of settlement in 1741 until 1912.

Tannery

459 Old York Rd., Bethlehem
(1761) Exhibits Moravian crafts, trades and industries. Includes a working model of the original oil mill.

Waterworks

459 Old York Rd., Bethlehem
(1762) Reconstructed 18-foot wooden waterwheel and pumping mechanisms.

Kemerer Museum of Decorative Arts

459 Old York Rd., Bethlehem,
610-691-6055, 800-360-3687
Exhibits include art, Bohemian glass, toys, prints, china; regional German folk art from 1750-1900; Federal furniture, period room settings. April-December: Thursday-Sunday.

Moravian Museum (Gemein Haus)

66 W. Church St.,
Bethlehem,
610-867-0173
(1741) This five-story log building is the oldest structure in the city; docents interpret the history and culture of early Bethlehem and the Moravians. 45-minute tour. Tuesday-Sunday; closed January.

Old Chapel

Heckewelder Place, adjacent to Moravian Museum, Bethlehem
(1751) Once called the "Indian chapel" because so many Native Americans attended the services, this stone structure, the second church for the Moravian congregation, is still used frequently. May be toured only in combination with Moravian Museum community walking tour.

SPECIAL EVENTS

Bach Festival

Packer Church, 18 University Dr.,
Bethlehem,

★
★
★
★
★

610-866-4382
Lehigh University campus. One of the country's outstanding musical events. Famous artists and the Bach Choir of Bethlehem participate. Mid-late May.

Christmas
52 W. Broad St.,
Bethlehem,
610-868-1513, 800-360-8687
Bethlehem continues more than two centuries of Christmas tradition with candlelight, music and a number of special events. Moravians sing their own Christmas songs intermingled with Mozart and Handel. A huge "Star of Bethlehem" shines from the top of South Mountain and the Hill-to-Hill Bridge has special lighting. The community "Putzes," a Moravian version of nativity scenes, are open to the public daily. Thousands of people post their Christmas cards from Bethlehem. Night Light Tours of city's Christmas displays and historical areas are offered (December) by the Bethlehem Tourism Authority. Reservations suggested.

Live Bethlehem Christmas Pageant
Bethlehem,
610-867-2893
Scores of volunteers (garbed in biblical costumes) and live animals (including camels, horses, donkey and sheep) join together to re-create the nativity story; narrated. First weekend in December.

Moravian College Alumni Association Antiques Show
Johnston Hall, Moravian College Campus, 1200 Main St., Bethlehem,
610-861-1366
Early June.

Musikfest
25 W. Third St., Bethlehem,
610-861-0678
Nine-day festival celebrating Bethlehem's rich musical and ethnic heritage. More than 600 performances (most free) of all types of music including folk, big-band, jazz, country-western, chamber, classical, gos-

pel, rock, swing. Also children's activities. Late August.

Shad Festival
Bethlehem,
610-691-0603
Historic Bethlehem's 18th-century Industrial Quarter. Old-fashioned planked shad bake (reservations required for dinner), exhibits, demonstrations. First Sunday in May.

HOTELS
★★Best Western Hotel
300 Gateway Dr.,
Bethlehem,
610-866-5800;
www.bestwestern.com
192 rooms. Airport transportation available. $

★Comfort Inn
3191 Highfield Dr., Bethlehem,
610-865-6300, 877-424-6423;
www.choicehotels.com
116 rooms. Complimentary continental breakfast. $

Wydnor Hall Inn
3612 Old Philadelphia Pike,
Bethlehem,
610-867-6851, 800-839-0020
5 rooms. Complimentary continental breakfast. European-style inn that was built in 1895. $

RESTAURANTS
★★Cafe
221 W. Broad St.,
Bethlehem,
610-866-1686
International menu. Lunch, dinner. Closed Sunday-Monday. Reservations recommended. $$

★Eastern Chinese
3926 Linden St.,
Bethlehem,
610-868-0299
Chinese menu. Lunch, dinner. Bar. Reservations recommended. $$

155

PENNSYLVANIA

★★Inn of the Falcon
1740 Seidersville Rd.,
Bethlehem,
610-868-6505;
www.innofthefalcon.com
American menu. Dinner. Closed Sunday. Bar. Building built in 1800s. Reservations recommended. **$$**

★★★Main Street Depot
61 W. Lehigh St., Bethlehem,
610-868-7123;
www.mainstreetdepotrestaurant.com
On the National Registry of Historic Buildings, the location out of which the Main Street Depot now operates was built in 1873 and served as a station for the Jersey Central railroad. Grab a depot burger at the bar, or sit down for dinner and enjoy an entrée like butter rum chicken with cashews, coconut and fresh pineapple over rice or filet mignon wrapped in bacon and served with asparagus and béarnaise.

American menu. Lunch, dinner. Closed Sunday. Bar. Reservations recommended. **$$$**

★★Minsi Trail Inn
626 Stefko Blvd., Bethlehem,
610-691-5613;
www.minsitrailinn.com
American, Greek menu. Lunch, dinner. Sunday brunch. Bar. Children's menu. Reservations recommended. **$$**

156 BIRD-IN-HAND

This Pennsylvania Dutch farming village got its name from the signboard of an early inn.
Information: Pennsylvania Dutch Convention and Visitors Bureau, 501 Greenfield Rd., Lancaster, 717-299-8901, 800-723-8824; www.padutchcountry.com

WHAT TO SEE AND DO
Abe's Buggy Rides
2596 Old Philadelphia Pike, Bird-in-Hand,
717-392-1794;
www.abesbuggyrides.com
A tour through Amish country in an Amish family carriage. Monday-Saturday.

Amish Country Tours
3121 Old Philadelphia Pike (Highway 340), Bird-In-Hand, 717-768-3600
Tours of Amish farmlands and Philadelphia.

Bird-in-Hand Farmers' Market
Hwy. 340 and Maple Ave., Bird-in-Hand,
717-393-9674;
www.birdinhandfarmersmarket.com
Indoor market with a wide variety of Pennsylvania Dutch foods and gifts.

July-October: Wednesday-Saturday; April-June and November: Wednesday, Friday and Saturday; rest of year: Friday and Saturday.

Weavertown One-Room Schoolhouse
2916 Old Philadelphia Pike, Bird-in-Hand,
717-768-3976
Life-size animated re-creation of activities at a one-room schoolhouse. Early April-October: daily; March and November: weekends.

HOTELS
★★★Bird-in-Hand Family Inn
2740 Old Philadelphia Pike, Bird-In-Hand,
717-768-8271, 800-665-8780;
www.bird-in-hand.com/familyinn
In the small town of Bird-in-Hand, this quiet inn offers a comfortable escape. Guests are welcome to visit the inn's petting zoo,

picnic pavilion and playground, or to take complimentary two-hour tours of Amish farmland.

100 rooms. Restaurant. Tennis. **$**

SPECIALTY LODGINGS
Greystone Manor Bed and Breakfast
2658 Old Philadelphia Pike,
Bird-in-Hand,
717-393-4233;
www.800padutch.com/greystone

This inn was built in the mid-1880s and is used today as a heritage lodging site. Situated on eight acres of landscaped property, the inn offers guests Victorian charm and style for a relaxing stay.

10 rooms. Closed January. Complimentary full breakfast. Victorian mansion built in 1883. **$**

Village Inn
2695 Old Philadelphia Pike,
Bird-in-Hand,
717-293-8369, 800-914-2473;
www.bird-in-hand.com/villageinn

3 story. Closed early December-early February. Children over 13 years old only. Complimentary continental breakfast. Built in 1734 as inn on Old Philadelphia Pike. Victorian interior ambience. **$**

RESTAURANTS
★Plain and Fancy Farm
3121 Old Philadelphia Pike,
Bird-in-Hand,
717-768-4400;
www.plainandfancyfarm.com

Pennsylvania Dutch menu. Lunch, dinner. Children's menu. **$$**

BLAKESLEE

WHAT TO SEE AND DO
Fern Ridge Campgrounds
Hwy. 115, Blakeslee,
570-646-2267

More than 200 shaded tent and RV campsites with water, electric hook-ups, picnic tables and fire rings. Heated pool, hot showers, volleyball, basketball, horseshoes, mountain biking, fishing stream and playground available. Convenience store with groceries, propane, ice and firewood. Laundry. Dump station and pump-out service. Rental cabins also available.

Jack Frost
Hwy. 940, Blakeslee,
570-443-8425

Two triple, five double chairlifts; patrol, school, rentals, snowmaking; cafeteria, restaurant, bar; nursery. Longest run approximately 1/2 mile; vertical drop 600 feet. December-March: daily. Half-day rate.

WT Family Camping
Hwy. 115, Blakeslee,
570-646-9255;
www.wtfamily.com

This clean, friendly campground a couple of miles south of Pocono Raceway has plenty of activities for the entire family. The wooded sites have picnic tables and fire rings. RV, trailer and tent sites; full hook-ups. Propane station, restrooms, convenience store, ice, wood. Outdoor pool, miniature golf.

BLOOMSBURG

On the north bank of the Susquehanna River, Bloomsburg was a center for mining, transportation and industry during the 19th and early 20th centuries. While it remains a manufacturing town, Bloomsburg retains the relaxed atmosphere of earlier days with its lush scenery and covered bridges. In nearby Orangeville, Fishing Creek offers trout, bass and pickerel.

Information: Columbia-Montour Visitors Bureau, 121 Papermill Rd., Bloomsburg, 570-784-8279, 800-847-4810; www.cmtpa.org

WHAT TO SEE AND DO

Bloomsburg University of Pennsylvania
400 Second St., Bloomsburg,
570-389-4316;
www.bloomu.edu
(1839) (6,600 students.) On campus are Carver Hall (1867); the Harvey A. Andruss Library (1966); Haas Center for the Arts (1967) with 2,000-seat auditorium and art gallery; McCormick Center for Human Services (1985); Redman Stadium and Nelson Field House. Tours (academic year, Monday-Friday).

Historic District
Bounded by West, Fifth, First,
Lake Streets, Bloomsburg,
570-784-7703
More than 650 structures spanning architectural styles from Georgian to Art Deco. Center of town.

The Children's Museum
2 W. Seventh St., Bloomsburg,
570-389-9206;
www.the-childrens-museum.org
This museum has more than 50 hands-on activities that aim to make learning about our world and the environment fun. The museum has a new theme each year, and most of the exhibits change as well. Mid-June-mid-December: Tuesday-Saturday.

SPECIAL EVENTS

Bloomsburg Theatre Ensemble
Alvina Krause Theatre, 226 Center St.,
Bloomsburg, 570-784-8181;
www.bte.org

Three to four weeks of performances for each of six plays. Main stage October-June (special performances rest of year).

Covered Bridge & Arts Festival
I-80, exit 35. Tours of covered bridges; apple butter boil; weaving, old-fashioned arts and crafts. Early October.

HOTELS

★Budget Host Patriot Inn
6305 Columbia Blvd.,
Bloomsburg,
570-387-1776, 800-873-1180;
www.budgethost.com
48 rooms. $

★★★Inn at Turkey Hill
991 Central Rd.,
Bloomsburg,
570-387-1500;
www.innatturkeyhill.com
This inn's 1839 brick farmhouse offers two guest bedrooms with whirlpool tubs. Sixteen additional rooms are available on the property. Visit the inn's gazebo, duck pond and two resident ducks.
18 rooms. Complimentary continental breakfast. Airport transportation available. $

Magee's Main Street Inn
20 W. Main St.,
Bloomsburg,
570-784-3200, 800-331-9815
8 rooms. Complimentary full breakfast. $

BRADFORD
When oil was discovered in Bradford in the late 1800s , the price of land jumped from about six cents to $1,000 an acre, and wells appeared on front lawns, in backyards and even in a cemetery. An oil exchange was established in 1877, two years after the first producing well was brought in. A Ranger District office of the Allegheny National Forest is located here.
Information: Bradford Area Chamber of Commerce, 10 Marilyn Horne Way, Bradford, 814-368-7115; www.bradfordpa.com

WHAT TO SEE AND DO

Bradford Landmark Society
45 E. Corydon St., Bradford,
814-362-3906;
www.bradfordlandmark.org

Headquartered in restored bakery; local history exhibits, period rooms. Monday, Wednesday and Friday.

Crook Farm
Seaward Ave. Exit, Bradford,
814-362-3906;
Near the Tuna Crossroad
(1848) Original home of Erastus and Betsy
Crook; restored to the 1870s period. May-
September: Tuesday-Friday afternoons,
also Saturday by appointment.

Carpenter Shop
(Circa 1870) Reconstruction of original;
old hand tools.

Old Barn
(Circa 1870) Identical to the original;
moved to Crook Farm in 1981 and rebuilt
on the site of the original barn.

Old One-Room Schoolhouse #8
(1880) Authentic structure where classes
are still held occasionally.

SPECIAL EVENTS
Crook Farm Country Fair
Crook Farm, Seaward Ave.,
at Tuna Crossroad, Bradford,
914-362-3906
Arts and crafts, exhibits, entertainment, food.
Last weekend in August.

HOTELS
★★Best Western Bradford Inn
100 S. Davis St.,
Bradford,
814-362-4501;
www.bestwestern.com
120 rooms. $

★★★Glendorn
1000 Glendorn Dr.,
Bradford,
814-362-6511, 800-843-8568;
www.glendorn.com
Set on 1,280 acres, this one-time private
estate offers a sophisticated twist on the
traditional wooded retreat. A long, private
drive welcomes visitors to this hideaway,
where guests enjoy walks in the woods,
canoe and fishing trips, hiking and biking
adventures, and a host of other outdoor
pursuits. The accommodations in the Big
House reflect a warm, country house spirit,
while the cabin suites have a rugged charm.
Fine dining is a hallmark of this country
lodge, with hearty country breakfasts, delicious lunches and four-course prix-fixe
dinners.
18 rooms. Children over 12 years only.
$$$$

BRISTOL
Bristol, founded in 1681, was on the main thoroughfare from Philadelphia to New York.
It has been frequented by famous visitors including Joseph Bonaparte, brother of Napoleon
and General Lafayette. There are homes dating from the 1700s, most of which have been
restored.
Information: Bucks County Conference and Visitors Bureau, 152 Swamp Rd.,
Doylestown, 215-345-4552, 800-836-2825;
www.buckscountycvb.org

WHAT TO SEE AND DO
Grave of Captain John Green
St. James Protestant Episcopal Church
Burial Ground, Cedar and Walnut Streets,
Bristol
Grave of U.S. Navy captain who piloted
the Columbia around the world in 1787-
1789 on first such voyage by vessel flying
American flag.

Pennsbury Manor
400 Pennsbury Memorial Rd., Bristol,
215-946-0400;
www.pennsburymanor.org
Reconstruction of William Penn's 17th-
century country manor; formal and kitchen
gardens; livestock. Craft demonstrations;
hands-on workshops. April-November:
Tuesday-Sunday.

159

PENNSYLVANIA

★
★
★
★
★

BROOKVILLE

Information: Brookville Area Chamber of Commerce, 175 Main St., Brookville, 814-849-8448; www.brookvillechamber.com

WHAT TO SEE AND DO

Clear Creek State Park
Brookville,
814-752-2368
Approximately 1,600 acres. Swimming beach, fishing, canoeing; hiking trails, cross-country skiing, picnicking, playing field, camping, cabins. Nature center; interpretive activities.

SPECIAL EVENTS

Western Pennsylvania Laurel Festival
Brookville,
814-849-4751
Third week in June.

HOTELS

★Holiday Inn Express
235 Allegheny Blvd.,
Brookville,
814-849-8381, 800-315-2621;
www.holidayinn.com
68 rooms. Complimentary continental breakfast. $

RESTAURANTS

★★Meeting Place
209 Main St., Brookville,
814-849-2557
American menu. Breakfast, lunch, dinner. Closed Sunday. Bar. Children's menu. $$

BRYN MAWR

WHAT TO SEE AND DO

Harriton House
500 Harriton Rd.,
Bryn Mawr,
610-525-0201;
www.haritonhouse.org
(1704) Early American domestic architecture of the Philadelphia area. Originally 700-acre estate, now 16 1/2 acres. House of Charles Thomson, Secretary of the Continental Congresses; restored to early 18th-century period. Nature park. Wednesday-Saturday; Sunday by appointment.

RESTAURANTS

★★Wild Onion
900 Conestoga Rd., Bryn Mawr,
610-527-4826;
www.thewildonion.com
Seafood menu. Lunch, dinner. Bar. Children's menu. $$

BUTLER

Robert Morris of Philadelphia, financier of the Revolutionary War, once owned the hills in which Butler now sits. The city is named for General Richard Butler, who died in the St. Clair Indian Expedition. During the 1930s, the Butler-based American Austin Company—later called American Bantam Company—pioneered the development of small, lightweight cars in America and invented the prototype of the jeep.

Information: Butler County Chamber of Commerce, 101 E. Diamond St., Butler, 724-283-2222; www.butlercountychamber.com

HOTELS

★★Conley Resort
740 Pittsburgh Rd., Butler,
724-586-7711, 800-344-7303;
www.conleyresort.com
56 rooms. 150-foot indoor water park. $

★Fairfield Inn By Marriott Butler
200 Fairfield Lane,
Butler,
724-283-0009, 800-228-2800;
www.fairfieldinn.com
75 rooms. $

CAMBRIDGE SPRINGS

HOTELS
★★★Riverside Inn
1 Fountain Ave., Cambridge Springs,
814-398-4645, 800-964-5173;
www.theriversideinn.com
Opened in 1885, this inn continues to provide excellent service to its visitors. The inn is found nestled in a quiet and peaceful area overlooking French Creek. Guests will enjoy golf, swimming, tennis and other activities.
74 rooms. Closed January-mid-April. Complimentary full breakfast. **$**

CANADENSIS

SPECIALTY LODGINGS
Brookview Manor Inn
2960 Hwy. 447, Canadensis,
570-595-2451, 800-585-7974;
www.brookviewmanor.com
Brookview Manor Inn sits on five acres in the Pocono Mountains and is surrounded by 200 acres of privately owned forests. Relax in a rocking chair on the inn's wraparound porch. Or head out to shop at the area's wide selection of outlet stores and antiques shops.
10 rooms. Children over 12 years only. Complimentary full breakfast. **$$**

RESTAURANTS
★★★Pump House Inn
Hwy. 390 N,
Canadensis,
570-595-7501
Located in a big house in the country, the Pump House pleases diners with well-prepared American fare and congenial service. There are a variety of specials that change every night.
American, French menu. Lunch, dinner. Bar. Closed Monday. **$$**

161

CARLISLE
In the historically strategic Cumberland Valley, Carlisle was a vital point for Native American fighting during the Revolutionary and Civil wars.

The Carlisle Barracks is one of the oldest military posts in America. Soldiers mounted guard here as early as 1750 to protect the frontier. In 1794 President Washington reviewed troops assembled here to march against the "Whiskey Rebels," and troops went from the Barracks to the Mexican and Civil wars. The Barracks was reopened in 1920 as the Medical Field Service School. It is now home to the U.S. Army War College. George Ross, James Wilson and James Smith, all signers of the Declaration of Independence, lived in Carlisle, as did Molly Pitcher.
Information: Greater Area Chamber of Commerce, 212 N. Hanover St., Carlisle, 717-243-4515; www.carlislechamber.org

WHAT TO SEE AND DO
Carlisle Barracks
22 Ashburn Dr., Carlisle,
717-245-3611
Army War College, senior school in U.S. Army's educational system. Includes the U.S. Army Military History Institute and Hessian Powder Magazine Museum (1777), built by prisoners captured at the Battle of Trenton. The Carlisle Indian Industrial School (1879-1918) was one of the first institutions of higher learning for Native Americans. Also includes the Omar Bradley Museum, containing a collection of personal and military memorabilia of the five-star general. Jim Thorpe and other famous Native American athletes studied here. Military History Institute and the Omar Bradley Museum (Monday-Friday; closed federal holidays). Post/grounds. (daily; closed federal holidays).

PENNSYLVANIA

★
★
★
★
☆

Cumberland County Historical Society and Hamilton Library Association
21 N. Pitt St., Carlisle,
717-249-7610;
www.historicalsociety.com
Woodcarvings, furniture, silver, tools, redware, ironware, tall-case clocks, coverlets, paintings by local artisans; mementos of the Carlisle Indian School; special exhibits and programs. Library contains books, tax lists, early photographs, genealogical material. Tuesday-Saturday, Monday evenings.

Dickinson College
242 W. High St., Carlisle,
717-243-5121;
www.dickinson.edu
(1773) (1,900 students.) Tenth college chartered in U.S. President James Buchanan was a graduate. On campus is "Old West" (1804), a building registered as a National Historic Landmark that was designed by Benjamin Henry Latrobe, one of the designers of the Capitol in Washington. Tours of campus.
Also here is:

The Trout Gallery
West High St.,
Carlisle,
717-245-1711
Emil R. Weiss Center for the Arts. Permanent and temporary exhibits. September-mid-June: Tuesday-Saturday.

Grave of Molly Pitcher
In Old Graveyard, E. South St.,
Carlisle
(Mary Ludwig Hays McCauley) Soldiers in the Battle of Monmouth (June 1778) gave Molly her nickname because of her devotion to her husband and others who were fighting by bringing them pitchers of water. When her husband was wounded, Molly took his place at a cannon and continued fighting for him.

Pine Grove Furnace State Park
1212 Pine Grove Rd., Carlisle,
717-486-7575

Pre-Revolutionary iron, slate and brick works were in this area. Approximately 696 acres. Swimming beaches, fishing, boating (rentals, mooring, launching); hunting, hiking, bicycling (rentals), cross-country skiing, ice skating, ice fishing; picnicking, snack bar, store, tent and trailer sites. Visitor center. Lodging available.

HOTELS
★★**Allenberry Resort Inn**
1559 Boiling Springs Rd.,
Boiling Springs,
717-258-3211, 800-430-5468;
www.allenberry.com
69 rooms. Airport transportation available.
$

★★**Clarion Hotel**
1700 Harrisburg Pike, Carlisle,
717-243-1717, 800-692-7315;
www.hotelcarlisle.com
270 rooms. **$**

★**Days Inn**
101 Alexander Spring Rd., Carlisle,
717-258-4147, 800-329-7466;
www.daysinn.com
130 rooms. Complimentary continental breakfast. Airport transportation available. **$**

★★**Holiday Inn**
1450 Harrisburg Pike, Carlisle,
717-245-2400, 800-315-2621;
www.holidayinn.com
100 rooms. **$**

★**Quality Inn**
1255 Harrisburg Pike, Carlisle,
717-243-6000, 877-424-6423;
www.qualityinn.com
96 rooms. Complimentary continental breakfast. **$**

RESTAURANTS
★★**Boiling Springs Tavern**
Front and First Streets, Boiling Springs,
717-258-3614
American menu. Lunch, dinner. Closed Sunday-Monday. Bar. Children's menu. Old stone structure (1832), originally an inn. **$$**

162

PENNSYLVANIA

★
★
★
★
★

★★California Cafe
38 W. Pomfret St., Carlisle,
717-249-2028;
www.calcaf.com

California, French menu. Lunch, dinner. Closed Memorial Day weekend. **$$**

CHADDS FORD

WHAT TO SEE AND DO

Barns-Brinton House
630 Baltimore Pike, Chadds Ford,
610-388-7376
(1714) Authentically restored 18th-century tavern, now a house museum furnished in the period. Guides in colonial costume offer interpretive tours; domestic art demonstrations. May-September: weekends.

Brandywine Battlefield
1491 Baltimore Pike, Chadds Ford,
610-459-3342
The Battle of the Brandywine (1777) took place here and around Chadds Ford—a decisive battle for Washington—includes Lafayette's quarters and Washington's headquarters. Visitor center with exhibits; tours of historic buildings; museum shop. Picnicking. March: weekends; April-November: Tuesday-Sunday; December-February: Thursday-Sunday.

Brandywine River Museum
Hwy. 1, Chadds Ford,
610-388-2700;
www.brandywinerivermuseum.org
Converted 19th-century gristmill houses largest collection of paintings by Andrew Wyeth and other Wyeth family members; also collections of American illustration, still life and landscape painting. Nature trail, wildflower gardens; restaurant, museum shop, guided tours. Daily.

Chaddsford Winery
632 Baltimore Pike, Chadds Ford,
610-388-6221;
www.chaddsford.com
Tours of boutique winery, housed in renovated old barn; view of production process; tasting room. Tours; tastings. Schedule varies.

John Chadds House
1736 Creek Road,
Chadds Ford,
610-388-7376;
www.chaddsfordhistory.org
Stone building (circa 1725) is fine example of early 18th-century Pennsylvania architecture; authentically restored and furnished as a house museum. Narrated tours by guides in colonial costume; baking demonstrations in beehive oven. May-September: Saturday-Sunday; also by appointment.

HOTELS

★Brandywine River Hotel
Highways 1 and 100, Chadds Ford,
610-388-1200, 800-274-9644;
www.brandywineriverhotel.com
40 rooms. Complimentary continental breakfast. Airport transportation available. **$**

163

PENNSYLVANIA

CHAMBERSBURG
Named for Colonel Benjamin Chambers, a Scottish-Irish pioneer, this is an industrial county seat amid peach and apple orchards. John Brown had his headquarters here. During the Civil War, Confederate cavalry burned down the town, destroying 537 buildings after the citizens refused to pay an indemnity of $100,000.
Information: Chamber of Commerce, 75 S. Second St., 717-264-7101.
Information is also available at the Visitors Station, 1235 Lincoln Way E, Chambersburg, 717-261-1200; www.chambersburg.org

WHAT TO SEE AND DO

Capitol Theatre
159 S. Main St.,
Chambersburg,
717-263-0202;
www.thecapitoltheatre.org
This 1927 movie house presents performances ranging from classical concerts to big bands; theatrical presentations. Features a 1928 Moller pipe organ. Call for performances and fees.

The Old Jail
175 E. King St., Chambersburg,
717-264-1667
Jail complex (1818) restored and renovated for use as the Kittochtinny Historical Society's Museum and Library. An 1880 cell block houses community cultural activities, art and historical exhibits. Also on grounds are Colonial, Fragrance and Japanese gardens; 19th-century barn; agricultural museum. Cultural programs (May-October). Tours. May-November: Thursday-Saturday.

SPECIAL EVENTS

ChambersFest
Emil R. Weiss Center for the Performing Arts,
Caledonia State Park, 75 S. Second St.,
Chambersburg,
717-264-7101
Civil War festival with crafts, food, reenactments, parade of pets. July.

Franklin County Fair
Rod and Gun Club Farm,
5995 Warm Springs, Chambersburg,
717-369-4100

CHAMPION

SPECIAL EVENTS

Seven Springs Wine and Food Festival
777 Waterwheel Dr., Champion,
814-352-7777, 800-452-2223;
www.7springs.com
Sample some of the best local producers have to offer and drink from the complimentary

Arts and crafts displays, needlework, home and dairy products, state turkey-calling contest, tractor pull, agricultural and livestock exhibits, entertainment. Third full week in August.

Totem Pole Playhouse
Caledonia State Park, 9555
Golf Course Rd., Fayetteville,
717-352-2164;
www.totempoleplayhouse.org
Resident professional theater company performs dramas, comedies and musicals in 453-seat proscenium theater. Tuesday-Sunday evenings; matinees Wednesday, Saturday-Sunday. June-August.

HOTELS

★Hampton Inn
955 Lesher Rd.,
Chambersburg,
717-261-9185, 800-486-7866;
www.hamptoninn.com
124 rooms. Complimentary continental breakfast. $

★★Quality Inn
1095 Wayne Ave.,
Chambersburg,
717-263-3400;
www.qualityinnchambersburg.com
139 rooms. $

RESTAURANTS

★★Copper Kettle
1049 Lincoln Way E (Highway 30),
Chambersburg,
717-264-3109
Seafood, steak menu. Dinner. Closed Sunday. Bar. Children's menu. $$

wine glass given to you with the price of admission. With easy access from the Pennsylvania turnpike, you can head to Champion to stomp grapes or simply enjoy the cuisine of the Keystone State. Third weekend in August.

HOTELS

Road 1, County Line Rd., Champion,
814-352-7777, 866-437-1300;
www.7springs.com
405 rooms. Check-in 5 p.m. Children's
activity center. Airport transportation available. **$$**

RESTAURANTS

★★★Helen's

777 Waterwheel Dr., Champion,
814-352-7777;
www.7springs.com
Though the menu changes with the seasons,
it leans towards classics.
American menu. Lunch, dinner. Bar. Reservations recommended. **$$$**

CHESTER

The oldest settlement in the state, Chester was established by the Swedish Trading Company as Upland. William Penn came to Upland in 1682 to begin colonization of the land granted to him by King Charles II. He renamed the settlement in honor of Chester, a Quaker center in Cheshire, England. The first Assembly here adopted Penn's framework of government, enacted the first laws and organized the county of Chester—from which Delaware County broke off in 1789. On the Delaware River, 15 miles southwest of Philadelphia, Chester is a busy port and home of shipyards where every type of vessel has been built for the navy and merchant marine.
Information: Delaware County Convention & Tourist Bureau, 200 E. Estate St., Media, 610-565-3679, 800-343-3983; www.brandywinecvb.org

WHAT TO SEE AND DO

Penn Memorial Landing Stone

Front and Penn Streets, Chester,
610-447-7881
Marks spot where William Penn first landed October 28, 1682.

Widener University

3800 Vartan Rd., Chester,
610-499-4000;
www.widener.edu

(1821) (7,000 students.) On campus are Old Main, a national historic landmark, and the University Art Museum, with a permanent collection of 19th- and 20th-century American Impressionist and European academic art as well as contemporary exhibits September-May: Tuesday-Saturday; June and August: Monday-Thursday; closed July. Also here is Wolfgram Memorial Library. Campus tours.

CLARION

Once the forests were so thick and tall here that, according to tradition, the wind in the treetops sounded like a distant clarion. Today many campers and sports and outdoors enthusiasts enjoy the beauty and recreation that the Clarion area offers.
Information: Clarion Area Chamber of Business and Industry, 41 S. Fifth Ave., Clarion, 814-226-9161; www.clarionpa.com

WHAT TO SEE AND DO

Clarion County Historical Society

18 Grant St., Clarion,
814-226-4450
Museum housed in mid-19th century Sutton-Ditz house. Contains exhibits on county industry and business; Victorian bedroom and parlor; genealogical and historical library (researchers may call

ahead for appointment other than regular hours); changing exhibits. April-December: Tuesday, Thursday and Friday afternoons.

SPECIAL EVENTS

Autumn Leaf Festival

Parade, carnival, autorama, scholarship pageants, concerts, flea market, craft shows. Late September-early October.

Spring Fling
Concerts, food concessions, games, entertainment. Early May.

HOTELS
★★**Holiday Inn**
45 Holiday Inn Dr., Clarion,
814-226-8850, 800-596-1313;
www.holidayinn.com
122 rooms. Airport transportation available. **$**

CLARK

HOTELS
★★★**Tara Country Inn**
2844 Lake Rd., Clark,
724-962-2992, 800-782-2803;
www.tara-inn.com

★**Super 8**
I-80 and Route 68, Clarion,
814-226-4550, 800-800-8000;
www.super8.com
99 rooms. Complimentary continental breakfast. **$**

Inspired by *Gone With the Wind,* this pillared inn brings Southern charm and hospitality to the northeast.
27 rooms. No children allowed. **$$$**

CLARKS SUMMIT

HOTELS
★★**Inn At Nichols Village**
1101 Northern Blvd., Clarks Summit,
570-587-1135, 800-642-2215;
www.nicholsvillage.com

135 rooms. Airport transportation available. 12 acres include over 1,000 rhododendrons; forestland. **$**

CLEARFIELD
The old and important Native American town of Chinklacamoose occupied this site until it was burned in 1757. Coal and clay mining and more than 20 diversified plants producing school supplies, firebrick, fur products, precision instruments, electronic products and sportswear now occupy what used to be cleared fields.
Information: Clearfield Chamber of Commerce, 125 E. Market St., 814-765-7567;
www.clearfieldchamber.com

WHAT TO SEE AND DO
Parker Dam
28 Fairview Rd.,
Clearfield,
814-765-0630
Approximately 950 acres in Moshannon State Forest. Swimming beach, fishing, boating (launch, rentals); hiking, cross-country skiing, snowmobiling, sledding, ice skating, ice fishing, snack bar, tent and trailer sites, cabins. Nature center.

S. B. Elliott State Park
814-765-7271

Approximately 300 acres in the heart of the Moshannon State Forest; entirely wooded; display of mountain laurel in season. Fishing in small mountain streams surrounding the park. Hiking, snowmobile trails, tent and trailer sites, cabins. Standard fees.

SPECIAL EVENTS
Clearfield County Fair
Clearfield County Fairgrounds, Mill Road and Turnpike Ave., Clearfield,
814-765-4629;
www.clearfieldcountyfair.com
Late July-early August.

High Country Arts & Craft Fair
814-765-9804
S. B. Elliott State Park. Sunday after July 4.

HOTELS

★Days Inn
Rte. 879 and I-80, Clearfield,
814-765-5381, 800-329-7466;
www.daysinn.com

119 rooms. Complimentary continental breakfast. $

COATESVILLE

WHAT TO SEE AND DO

Hibernia County Park
1 Park Ave., Coatesville,
610-384-0290
Once the center of an iron works community, it is now the largest of the county parks, encompassing 800 acres of woodlands and meadows. The west branch of the Brandywine Creek, Birch Run and a pond are stocked with trout; hiking trails, picnicking, tent and trailer camping. Park features Hibernia Mansion; portions of house date from 1798, period furnishings. Tours of mansion. Memorial Day-Labor Day: Sunday; fee.

SPECIAL EVENTS

Hibernia Mansion Christmas Tours
Hibernia County Park, 1 Park Ave.,
Coatesville
First week in December.

Old Fiddlers' Picnic
Hibernia County Park, 1 Park Ave.,
Coatesville
Second Saturday in August.

167

PENNSYLVANIA

CONNELLSVILLE

George Washington once owned land in the region, and many places are named in his honor. The restored Crawford Cabin near the river was the home of Colonel William Crawford, surveyor of these properties and Washington's surveying pupil.

Northwest of town in Perryopolis, the town square is named for Washington, who some believe planned the design of the town.

Information: Greater Connellsville Chamber of Commerce, 923 W. Crawford Ave.,
724-628-5500; www.greaterconnellsville.org

WHAT TO SEE AND DO

Fallingwater (Kaufmann Conservation on Bear Run)
Hwy. 381 S., Mill Run, Connellsville,
724-329-8501;
www.wpconline.org/fallingwaterhome.htm
One of the most famous structures of the 20th century, Fallingwater, designed by Frank Lloyd Wright in 1936, is cantilevered on three levels over a waterfall; interior features Wright-designed furniture, textiles and lighting, as well as sculpture by modern masters; extensive grounds are heavily wooded and planted with rhododendron, which blooms in early July. Visitor center with self-guided orientation program, concession, gift shop. Guided tours. Mid-March-Thanksgiving: Tuesday-Sunday; winter: Saturday-Sunday. No children under age 6; child-care center. Reservations required.

m o b i l t r a v e l g u i d e . c o m

SPECIALTY LODGINGS

Newmyer House
507 S. Pittsburgh St., Connellsville,
724-626-0141

Restored Queen Anne-style mansion built in 1892; antiques.
4 rooms. Children over 12 years only. Complimentary full breakfast. **$**

CORNWALL

The Cornwall Ore Banks were a major source of magnetic iron ore for nearly 250 years.
Information: Pennsylvania Rainbow Region Vacation Bureau, 625 Quentin Road, Lebanon, 717-272-8555; www.visitlebanoncounty.com

WHAT TO SEE AND DO

Cornwall Iron Furnace
Rexmont Rd. and Boyd St., Cornwall,
717-272-9711;
www.cornwallironfurnace.org
In operation 1742-1883. Open pit mine; 19th-century Miners Village still occupied. Furnace building houses "great wheel" and 19th-century steam engine. Visitor center, exhibits, book store. Tuesday-Sunday.

Historic Schaefferstown
Hwy. 419 N, Schaefferstown, Cornwall,
717-949-2244;
www.hsimuseum.org
An 18th-century farm established by Swiss-German settlers. Village square with authentic log and stone and half-timber buildings; site of first waterworks in U.S. (1758), still in operation. Schaeffer Farm Museum has Swiss Bank House and Barn (1737); early farm tools; colonial farm garden. The museum north of the square has antiques and artifacts of settlers. House and museum (open during festivals; also June-September, by appointment).

SPECIAL EVENTS

Historic Schaefferstown Events
www.hsimuseum.org
Events during the year include Cherry Fair, fourth Saturday in June; Folk Festival, mid-July; Harvest Fair & Horse Plowing Contest, second weekend in September.

168

DANVILLE

Information: Columbia-Montour Visitors Bureau, 316 Mill St., Danville, 570-275-8185

WHAT TO SEE AND DO

PP & L Montour Preserve
700 Preserve Rd., Danville,
570-437-3131
Fishing, boating (no gasoline motors) on 165-acre Lake Chillisquaque. Hiking and nature trails, picnicking. Birds of prey exhibit in visitor center; scheduled programs (daily, fee for some).

HOTELS

★★★**Pine Barn Inn**
1 Pine Barn Place, Danville,
570-275-2071, 800-627-2276;
www.pinebarninn.com
This quiet inn is only a 20-minute drive from downtown and the lake. Behind its comfortably rustic exterior, it displays a modern touch with amenities such as Jacuzzi tubs and complimentary, wireless high-speed Internet access.
65 rooms. Check-out 1 p.m. Restaurant, bar. **$**

★**Quality Inn**
15 Valley West Rd., Danville,
570-275-5100, 877-424-6423;
www.choicehotels.com
77 rooms. **$**

RESTAURANTS

★★**Pine Barn Inn**
1 Pine Barn Place, Danville,
570-275-2071;
www.pinebarninn.com
Seafood, steak menu. Breakfast, lunch, dinner. Sunday brunch. Bar. Children's menu. Converted 19th-century barn. Outdoor seating. **$$**

DELAWARE WATER GAP NATIONAL RECREATION AREA

It is difficult to believe that the quiet Delaware River could carve a path through the Kittatinny Mountains, which are nearly 1/4 of a mile high at this point. Conflicting geological theories account for this natural phenomenon. The prevailing theory is that the mountains were formed after the advent of the river, rising up from the earth so slowly that the course of the Delaware was never altered.

Despite the speculation about its origin, there is no doubt about the area's recreational value. A relatively unspoiled area along the river boundary between Pennsylvania and New Jersey, stretching approximately 35 miles from Matamoras to an area just south of I-80, the site of the Delaware Water Gap is managed by the National Park Service.

Trails and overlooks offer scenic views. Also here are canoeing and boating, hunting and fishing; camping is nearby at the Dingmans Campground within the recreation area. Swimming and picnicking at Smithfield and Milford beaches. Dingmans Falls and Silver Thread Falls, two of the highest waterfalls in the Poconos, are near here. Several 19th-century buildings are in the area, including Millbrook Village (several buildings open May-October) and Peters Valley. The visitor center is located off I-80 in New Jersey, at Kittatinny Point (April-November: daily; rest of year, Saturday and Sunday only), 570-426-2452. Park headquarters are in Bushkill.
Information: www.nps.gov/dewa

DENVER/ADAMSTOWN

Just off the Pennsylvania Turnpike, Denver and Adamstown are in the center of an active antique marketing area, which preserves its Pennsylvania German heritage.
Information: Pennsylvania Dutch Convention and Visitors Bureau, 501 Greenfield Rd., Lancaster, 717-299-8901, 800-723-8834; www.padutchcountry.com

★
★
★
★
★

WHAT TO SEE AND DO

Stoudt's Black Angus
Route 272, Adamstown,
717-484-4386;
PA Turnpike exit 21 to just beyond Adamstown,
www.stoudtsbeer.com
More than 350 dealers display quality antiques for sale. Sunday.

SPECIAL EVENTS

Bavarian Summer Fest
Adamstown,
717-484-4385
Oompah bands, schuhplattler dance groups; Oktoberfest atmosphere. Includes special events, German folklore, German food, displays, shops. Early August-Labor Day: Friday-Sunday, October: Sunday only.

HOTELS

★★Black Horse Lodge & Suites
2180 N. Reading Rd., Denver,
717-336-7563, 800-610-3805;
www.blackhorselodge.com
74 rooms. Complimentary full breakfast. Restaurant, bar. **$**

★★Holiday Inn
1 Denver Rd., Denver,
717-336-7541, 800-315-2621;
www.holidayinn.com
110 rooms. **$**

SPECIALTY LODGINGS

Inns of Adamstown
62 W. Main St., Adamstown,
717-484-0800, 800-594-4808;
www.adamstown.com

Two inns (Adamstown Inn and Amethyst Inn); built in 1925; Victorian decor; antiques, family heirlooms.

9 rooms. Children over 12 years only. Complimentary continental breakfast. **$**

RESTAURANTS

★★**Black Horse**

2180 N. Reading Rd., Denver, 717-336-6555; www.blackhorselodge.com

Seafood, steak menu. Dinner. Bar. Children's menu. **$$$**

DONEGAL

WHAT TO SEE AND DO

Seven Springs Mountain Resort Ski Area

Donegal,
800-452-2223;
www.7springs.com

Three quad, five triple chairlifts; two rope tows, six-passenger high-speed chair; patrol, school, rentals, snowmaking; cafeteria, restaurant, bar, lodge. Longest run 1 1/4 miles; vertical drop 750 feet. Night skiing. (December-March: daily) Alpine slide (May-September: daily). Hotel and conference center; summer activities include 18-hole golf, tennis, rope course, horseback riding and swimming.

HOTELS

★**Days Inn**

Hwy. 31, Donegal,
724-593-7536, 800-329-7466;
www.daysinn.com

50 rooms. Complimentary continental breakfast. **$**

DOWNINGTOWN

Settled by emigrants from Birmingham, England, Downingtown honors Thomas Downing, who erected a log cabin here in 1702. The borough was first called Milltown, after the mill built here by Roger Hunt in 1765. The town, with its many historically interesting homes, retains much of its colonial charm. Jacob Eichholtz, a leading early American portrait artist, was born here.

Information: Chester County Conference and Visitors Bureau, 400 Exton Square Pkwy., Exton, 610-280-6145, 800-228-9933; www.brandywinevalley.com

HOTELS

★★★**Sheraton Great Valley Hotel**

707 Lancaster Pike,
Downingtown,
610-524-5500, 800-325-3535;
www.sheraton.com

Located in Chester County, this full-service hotel is conveniently located near area attractions and corporate offices. Historic Philadelphia is about 30 miles away, and Exton Square and King of Prussia Mall are nearby. Guests can get comfortable in the spacious guest rooms, which feature large work desks and the Sheraton Sweet Sleeper Beds (also available for dogs). The hotel offers a complimentary shuttle service to the surrounding area for guests who would like to see the sites or need a ride to the office. The White Horse Tavern, a historic 18th-century farmhouse, serves traditional American fare. Guests can also find a bite to eat or a drink at the casual Chesterfields Lounge, located just off the main lobby. 198 rooms. **$$**

DOYLESTOWN (BUCKS COUNTY)

Information: Bucks County Conference and Visitors Bureau, 152 Swamp Rd., Doylestown, 215-345-4552, 800-836-2825; www.buckscountycvb.org

WHAT TO SEE AND DO

Covered Bridges

Descriptive list, map of 11 bridges in Bucks County may be obtained at Bucks County Tourist Commission.

James A. Michener Art Museum

138 S. Pine St.,
Doylestown,
215-340-9800;
www.michenerartmuseum.org

This museum, a former prison modeled after the Eastern State Penitentiary in Philadelphia, is as large as a football field and was named for Doylestown's most famous son, the Pulitzer Prize-winning writer James Michener. He supported the arts and dreamed of a regional art museum dedicated to preserving, interpreting and exhibiting the art and cultural heritage of the Bucks County region. The museum is now home to more than 2,500 paintings, sculptures, drawings and photographs, as well as stained glass collections and an outdoor gallery paying homage to the local landscape. Tuesday-Sunday.

Mercer Mile

Three reinforced-concrete structures built between 1910-1916 within a one-mile radius by Dr. Henry Chapman Mercer, archaeologist, historian, a major proponent of the Arts and Crafts movement in America. They include:

Fonthill Museum

525 E. Court St., Doylestown,
215-348-9461

Concrete castle of Henry Chapman Mercer, displays his collection of tiles and prints from around the world. Guided tours (times vary).

Mercer Museum

84 S. Pine St.,
Doylestown,
215-345-0210;
www.mercermuseum.org

In this towering castle built in 1969, visitors will find implements, folk art and furnishings of early America before mechanization. See a Conestoga wagon, a whaling boat, carriages and an antique fire engine. Fifty thousand pieces of more than 60 early American crafts and varying trade tools on display. Daily.

The Moravian Pottery and Tile Works

130 Swamp Rd., Doylestown,
215-345-6722

This historic landmark is a working history museum in which visitors can witness tiles produced by hand. Visitors may purchase tiles made on site in the tile shop. Daily.

DU BOIS

At the entrance to the lowest pass of the Allegheny Range, Du Bois is a transportation center—once the apex of huge lumbering operations. Destroyed by fire in 1888, the town was rebuilt on the ashes of the old community and today ranks as one of the 12 major trading centers in the state.

Information: Du Bois Area Chamber of Commerce, 31 N. Brady St., Du Bois, 814-371-5010; www.duboispachamber.com

HOTELS

★★Clarion Hotel

1896 Rich Hwy., Du Bois,
814-371-5100, 877-424-6423;
www.choicehotels.com

160 rooms. Airport transportation available. $

★Hampton Inn

1582 Bee Line Hwy.,
Du Bois,
814-375-1000, 800-426-7866;
www.hamptoninn.com

96 rooms. Complimentary continental breakfast. $

EASTON

Easton is part of a larger metropolitan area, the Lehigh Valley, which also includes Allentown and Bethlehem. Lafayette College, with its beautiful campus and the historic Great Square is of interest.

Information: Two Rivers Area Chamber of Commerce, 1 S. Third St., Easton, 610-253-4211

WHAT TO SEE AND DO

National Canal Museum
30 Centre Square, Easton, 610-559-6613;
www.canals.org
Exhibits include photographs, models, documents and artifacts from the era of mule-drawn canal boats in the 1800s; electronic map and audiovisual programs. Changing exhibits. Memorial Day-Labor Day: daily; rest of year, Tuesday-Sunday.

Crayola Factory
Two Rivers Landing, 30 Centre Square, Easton, 610-515-8000, 800-272-9652;
www.crayola.com/factory
This isn't the main factory, which is several miles away, but it explains well how crayons and markers are manufactured. There are lots of colorful interactive exhibits and plenty of opportunities to draw and color to your heart's content. Hours vary.

Hugh Moore Park
S. 25th St., Easton, 610-250-6700
Restored Lehigh Canal; mule-drawn canal boat rides (early May-Labor Day: daily; early-late September: weekends) Also hiking, picnicking; boat rentals in park. Park daily.

The Great Square
Center of business district. Now called Center Square. Dominated by Soldiers' and Sailors' Monument. Bronze marker shows replica of Old Courthouse, which stood until 1862 on land rented from the Penns for one red rose a year. From Old Courthouse steps, the Declaration of Independence was read on July 8, 1776, when the Easton Flag, the first Stars and Stripes of the united colonies, was unfurled here.

Lafayette College
Hwy. 22 and Hwy. 78, Easton, 610-250-5000;
www.lafayette.edu
(1826) (2,000 students.) Bronze statue of Lafayette by Daniel Chester French in front of college chapel; American historical portrait collection in Kirby Hall of Civil Rights. Tour of campus.

Northampton County Historical Society
101-107 S. Fourth St., Easton, 610-253-1222;
www.northamptonctymuseum.org
Changing exhibits; library; museum. Monday-Friday.

RESTAURANTS

★★Pearly Baker's Ale House
11 Centre Square, Easton, 610-253-9949;
www.pearlybakers.net
International menu. Lunch, dinner. Closed Monday. Bar. Children's menu. Reservations recommended. Outdoor seating. **$$**

EDINBORO

HOTELS
★★Edinboro Inn Resort and Conference Center
401 W. Plum St., Edinboro, 814-734-5650;
www.edinboroinn.com
105 rooms. **$**

EMMAUS

RESTAURANTS
★★The Farmhouse
1449 Chestnut St., Emmaus, 610-967-6225;
www.thefarmhouse.com

American menu. Dinner. Closed Sunday-Monday. Bar. Outdoor seating. **$$$**

EPHRATA
Information: Chamber of Commerce, 16 E. Main St., Ephrata, 717-738-9010;
www.ephrata-area.org

WHAT TO SEE AND DO
Ephrata Cloister
632 W. Main St., Ephrata,
717-733-6600;
www.ephratacloister.org
Buildings stand as a monument to an unusual religious experiment. In 1732 Conrad Beissel, a German Seventh-Day Baptist, began to lead a hermit's life here. Within a few years he established a religious community of recluses, with a Brotherhood, a Sisterhood and a group of married "householders." The members of the solitary order dressed in concealing white habits; the buildings (1735-1749) were without adornment, the halls were narrow, the doorways were low, and board benches served as beds and wooden blocks as pillows. Their religious zeal and charity, however, proved to be their undoing. After the Battle of Brandywine, the cloistered community nursed the Revolutionary sick and wounded but contracted typhus, which decimated their numbers. Celibacy also contributed to the decline of the community, but the Society was not formally dissolved until 1934. An orientation exhibit and video prepare each visitor for their journey back through time. Craft demonstrations (summer). Daily.

Museum and Library of the Historical Society of Cocalico Valley
249 W. Main St., Ephrata,
717-733-1616
Italianate Victorian mansion contains period displays, historical exhibits, genealogical and historical research library (fee) on Cocalico Valley area and residents. Monday, Wednesday, Thursday, Saturday.

SPECIAL EVENTS
Street Fair
717-733-4451;
www.ephratafair.org
One of largest in the state. Last full week in September.

SPECIALTY LODGINGS
The Inns at Doneckers
318-324 N. State St., Ephrata,
717-738-9502, 800-377-2206;
www.doneckers.com
35 rooms. Complimentary continental breakfast. Restored clockmaker's house (1777). Hand-cut stenciling. **$**

Smithton Bed & Breakfast Country Inn
900 W. Main St., Ephrata,
717-733-6094, 877-755-4590;
www.historicsmithtoninn.com
17 rooms. Complimentary full breakfast. Historic stone inn (1763). **$**

RESTAURANTS
★★★The Restaurant at Doneckers
333 N. State St., Ephrata, 717-738-9501;
www.doneckers.com
Guests can opt for a formal atmosphere amidst antiques and artwork in the main dining room, or a more casual setting in the bistro. Entrees include sautéed trout on black beluga lentils with roast garlic and a saffron-roasted red pepper broth or filet mignon with a crispy truffled risotto cake, celery gremolata and Malmsey Madeira sauce. Check for special events, such as theme dinners and wine tastings.
American, French menu. Lunch, dinner. Closed Wednesday, Sunday. Bar. Children's menu. **$$$**

173

PENNSYLVANIA

ERIE

The third-largest city in Pennsylvania, Erie is the state's only port on the Great Lakes and boasts a wealth of natural beauty and fascinating historical tales. Visitors enjoy Presque Isle State Park, with its seven miles of sandy beaches, hiking and biking trails. Downtown offers cultural and entertainment options including Broadway shows, classical ballet, philharmonic performances and comedy clubs. Explore acres of vineyards at local wineries, take in a play at the Erie Playhouse or the Roadhouse Theater, cheer for the AA Seawolves Baseball or the Otters

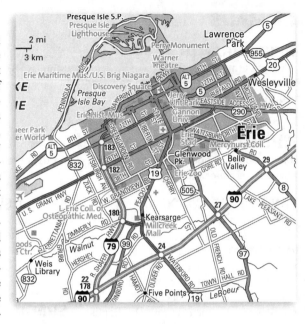

OHL professional hockey team, splash around at northwest Pennsylvania's only indoor water park, or strap on your skis for downhill or cross-country fun.

The lake and city take their name from the Erie tribe, who were killed by the Seneca about 1654. On the south shore of Presque Isle Bay, Commodore Oliver Hazard Perry built his fleet, floated the ships across the sandbars and fought the British in the Battle of Lake Erie (1813). Fort Presque Isle, built by the French in 1753 and destroyed by them in 1759, was rebuilt by the English, burned by Native Americans, and rebuilt again in 1794 by Americans.

Information: Erie Area Convention and Visitors Bureau, 208 E. Bayfront Pkwy., Erie, 814-454-7191, 800-524-3743; www.visiterriepa.com

WHAT TO SEE AND DO

Bicentennial Tower
7 Dobbins Landing, Erie,
814-455-6055
Commemorating Erie's 200th birthday, this 187-foot tower features two observation decks with an aerial view of the city, bay and Lake Erie. Concessions in tower lobby. April-September: daily; rest of year, call for schedule. Free admission Tuesday.

Erie Art Museum
411 State St., Erie,
814-459-5477;
www.erieartmuseum.org
Temporary art exhibits in a variety of media; regional artwork and lectures in the restored Greek Revival Old Customs House (1839). Art

classes, concerts, lectures and workshops are also offered. Tuesday-Saturday, also Sunday afternoons. Free admission Wednesday.

Erie Zoo
423 W. 38th St., Erie,
814-868-3651;
www.eriezoo.org
Zoo houses more than 300 animals, including gorillas, polar bears and giraffes; children's zoo (May-September); one-mile tour of grounds on Safariland Express Train (fee). Indoor ice rink. September-March.

Firefighters Historical Museum
428 Chestnut St., Erie,
814-456-5969
More than 1,300 items of firefighting memorabilia are displayed in the old #4

PENNSYLVANIA

Firehouse. Exhibits include fire apparatus dating from 1823, alarm systems, uniforms, badges, ribbons, helmets, nozzles, fire marks and fire extinguishers; fire safety films are shown in the Hay Loft Theater. May-October: Saturday-Sunday.

Gridley's Grave

Lakeside Cemetery, 1718 E. Lake Rd., Erie, 814-459-8200

Final resting place of Captain Charles Vernon Gridley, to whom, at the Battle of Manila Bay in 1898, Admiral Dewey said, "You may fire when ready, Gridley." Gridley died in Japan; his body was returned here for burial. Four old Spanish cannons from Manila Harbor, built in 1777, guard the grave. Offers view of peninsula, Lake Erie and entrance to Erie Harbor from cliff by Gridley Circle.

Land Lighthouse

2 Lighthouse St., Erie, 814-452-3937

(1867) The first lighthouse on the Great Lakes was constructed on this site in 1813.

Misery Bay

NE corner of Presque Isle Bay, Erie

State monument to Perry; named after Perry defeated British and the fleet suffered cold and privations of a bitter winter.

Presque Isle State Park

1 Peninsula Dr., Erie, 814-833-7424; www.presqueisle.org

Peninsula stretches seven miles into Lake Erie and curves back toward city. Approximately 3,200 acres of recreation and conservation areas. Swimming, fishing, boating (rentals, mooring, launching, marina); hiking, birding, trails, cross-country skiing, ice skating, ice fishing, ice boating, picnicking, concessions. Visitor center, environmental education and interpretive programs.

Waldameer Park & Water World

220 Peninsula Dr., Erie, 814-838-3591; www.waldameer.com

At entrance to Presque Isle State Park. Rides, midway, kiddieland, water park, picnic area, food, dance pavilion. Memorial Day-Labor Day: Tuesday-Sunday; open Monday holidays.

Watson-Curtze Mansion

356 W. Sixth St., Erie, 814-871-5790

Housed in 1890s Victorian mansion. Museum features regional history and decorative arts exhibits, restored period rooms, changing exhibits (Wednesday-Sunday afternoons). Also planetarium with shows Saturday afternoons.

Wayne Memorial Blockhouse

560 E. Third St., Erie, 814-871-4531

On grounds of State Soldiers' and Sailors' Home. Replica of blockhouse in which General Anthony Wayne died December 15, 1796, after becoming ill on a voyage from Detroit. He was buried at the foot of the flagpole; later, his son had the body disinterred and the remains moved to Radnor. Memorial Day-Labor Day: daily.

HOTELS

★Comfort Inn

3041 W. 12th St., Erie, 814-835-4200, 877-424-6423; www.choicehotels.com

100 rooms. Complimentary continental breakfast. Airport transportation available. **$**

★★Downtown Erie Hotel

18 W. 18th St., Erie, 814-456-2961, 800-832-9101; www.downtowneriehotel.com

133 rooms. Complimentary full breakfast. Airport transportation available. **$**

★Glass House Inn

3202 W. 26th St., Erie, 814-833-7751, 800-956-7222; www.glasshouseinn.com

30 rooms. Complimentary continental breakfast. **$**

★Quality Inn & Suites
8040 Perry Hwy., Erie,
814-864-4911, 877-424-6423;
www.qualityinn.com
107 rooms. Complimentary continental breakfast. Airport transportation available. **$**

RESTAURANTS
★★Pufferbelly
414 French St., Erie,
814-454-1557;
www.thepufferbelly.com

Restored firehouse (1907). Dinner. Sunday brunch. Bar. Outdoor seating. **$$**

★★The Stonehouse Inn
4753 W. Lake Rd., Erie,
814-838-9296;
www.stonehouse-inn.com
International/fusion menu. Dinner. Closed Sunday-Monday; also Holy Week. Bar. Business casual attire. Reservations recommended. **$$$**

ERWINNA

HOTELS
★★★Evermay on the Delaware
889 River Rd., Erwinna,
610-294-9100, 877-864-2365
Built in the 1700s, this inn is situated on 25 acres of pastures, woodlands and gardens, and close to antique shops, galleries, historic sites, parks and much more.
18 rooms. Children over 13 years only. Complimentary continental breakfast. Restaurant. **$$**

★★★Golden Pheasant Inn
763 River Rd., Erwinna,
610-294-9595, 800-830-4474;
www.goldenpheasant.com
Located an hour and a half from New York City and 20 minutes outside of Philadelphia, this provincial and romantic weekend hideaway sits between the Delaware River and the Pennsylvania Canal.
6 rooms. Complimentary continental breakfast. **$**

RESTAURANTS
★★★Evermay
889 River Rd.,
Erwinna,
610-294-9100, 877-864-2365
This formal carriage house serves sumptuous meals in a beautiful country setting.
American menu. Dinner. Closed Monday-Thursday. Bar. Casual attire. **$$$**

★★★Golden Pheasant Inn
763 River Rd.,
Erwinna,
610-294-9595;
www.goldenpheasant.com
Enjoy entrees such as roasted pheasant with apple and calvados sauce or grilled petite lamb chops with a roasted shallot and mint sauce.
French menu. Dinner. Sunday brunch. Closed Monday. Bar. **$$**

EXTON

HOTELS
★★★Duling-Kurtz House & Country Inn
146 S. Whitford Rd., Exton,
610-524-1830;
www.duling-kurtz.com
Rich in history and comfort, this small inn offers a homey, elegant atmosphere for relaxation. The Duling-Kurtz House was

built in 1783 and is located within walking distance of shopping, the train station and more.
20 rooms. Complimentary continental breakfast. **$**

PENNSYLVANIA

★★Inn At Chester Springs

815 N. Pottstown Pike,
Exton,
610-363-1100, 888-253-6119;
www.innatchestersprings.com
225 rooms. Restaurant, bar. Airport transportation available. $

RESTAURANTS

★★Duling-Kurtz House

146 S. Whitford Rd., Exton,
610-524-1830;
www.duling-kurtz.com
French menu. Lunch, dinner. Bar. Valet parking Friday, Saturday. Seven dining rooms. $$$

FARMINGTON

WHAT TO SEE AND DO

Braddock's Grave

200 Caverns Park Rd., Farmington
Granite monument marks burial place of British General Edward Braddock, who was wounded in battle with French and Native American forces on July 9, 1755, and died four days later.

Laurel Caverns

200 Caverns Park Rd., Farmington,
724-438-2070, 800-515-4150;
www.laurelcaverns.com
Colored lighting, unusual formations. Indoor miniature golf. Repelling (fee). Guided tours. Exploring trips. May-October: daily.

HOTELS

★★★★Nemacolin Woodlands Resort & Spa

1001 Lafayette Dr., Farmington,
724-329-8555, 866-344-6957;
www.nemacolin.com
Tucked away in Pennsylvania's scenic Laurel Highlands, this comprehensive resort offers a multitude of recreational opportunities, from the Hummer driving club, equestrian center and shooting academy to the adventure and activities centers, culinary classes and art museums. Two golf courses and a renowned golf academy delight players, while special activities entertain children and teenagers. Grand European style defines the guest accommodations at Chateau LaFayette, while the Lodge maintains a rustic charm. Families enjoy the spacious accommodations in the townhouses, while the luxury homes add a touch of class to group travel. 220 rooms. Children's activity center. $$$

★★★Summit Inn Resort

101 Skyline Dr.,
Farmington,
724-438-8594, 800-433-8594;
www.summitinnresort.com
Located at the peak of Mount Summit, the Summit Inn Resort offers sparkling panoramic views of the surrounding counties. The 1907 inn is an architecture lover's dream: it's located near Frank Lloyd Wright's Fallingwater and has its own spot on the National Register of Historic Places. 100 rooms. Closed early November-mid-April. Atop Mount Summit. $

SPAS

★★★★Woodlands Spa at Nemacolin Resort

1001 LaFayette Dr., Farmington,
724-329-8555, 800-422-2736;
www.nemacolin.com
Famed interior designer Clodagh created the look of this spa using natural materials and the guiding properties of feng shui, the ancient Chinese philosophy of balancing the forces of nature. Achieving inner tranquility is the mission here, and the treatments embrace this guiding principle. An extensive massage menu includes favorites such as Swedish, sports, aromatherapy, shiatsu and deep tissue as well as Eastern methods such as reflexology and reiki. From Japanese citrus and Balinese hibiscus to German chamomile and Greek mint, the body scrubs embody international personalities. Fitness and nutrition consultations help you gain insight into your body and its needs. The onsite spa restaurant makes healthy eating easier. $$

177

PENNSYLVANIA

★
★
★
★
★

FOGELSVILLE

HOTELS
★★★The Glasbern Inn
2141 Pack House Rd., Fogelsville,
610-285-4723;
www.glasbern.com
Stay in rustic luxury, amidst antique furnishings and all of the contemporary comforts.

Built in the late 1800s on 100 acres near Allentown, the inn is housed in an old farm and includes a renovated farmhouse, barn, gate house and carriage house. 37 rooms. Complimentary full breakfast. $

FORT WASHINGTON
Information: Valley Forge Convention & Visitors Bureau, 600 W. Germantown Pike, Plymouth Meeting, 610-834-1550; www.valleyforge.org

WHAT TO SEE AND DO
Fort Washington State Park
500 Bethlehem Pike, Fort Washington,
215-646-2942
Commemorates the site of Washington's northern defense line against the British in 1777. Fishing, hiking, ball fields, picnicking.

The Highlands
7001 Sheaff Lane, Fort Washington,
215-641-2687;
www.highlandshistorical.org
(1796) Late-Georgian mansion on 43 acres built by Anthony Morris, active in both state and federal government. Formal gardens and crenellated walls built circa 1845. Tours. Monday-Friday.

Hope Lodge
553 Bethlehem Pike, Fort Washington,
215-646-1595;
www.ushistory.org
(Circa 1745) Colonial Georgian mansion; headquarters for Surgeon General John Cochran after Battle of Germantown. Historic furnishings, paintings, ceramics. Tuesday-Sunday.

RESTAURANTS
★★Palace of Asia
285 Commerce Dr.,
Fort Washington,
215-646-2133
Indian menu. Lunch, dinner. Brunch. Bar. Reservations recommended. $$

FRANKLIN
A series of French and British forts was erected in this area. The last one, Fort Franklin, was razed by local settlers who used the stone and timber in their own buildings. Old Garrison took its place in 1796 and later served as the Venango County Jail. In 1859, James Evans, a blacksmith, made tools to drill an oil well, bringing an oil boom to the area. For years, oil was the area's dominant industry.
Information: Franklin Area Chamber of Commerce, 1259 Liberty St., Franklin, 814-432-5823, 888-547-2377; www.franklin-pa.org

WHAT TO SEE AND DO
DeBence Antique Music World
1261 Liberty St.,
Franklin,
814-432-5668
Features nickelodeons, band organs, calliopes, German organs, a variety of music boxes, many other items. Unique "see and

hear" museum. Guided tours. Mid-March-December: Tuesday-Sunday.

Hoge-Osmer House
301 S. Park St., Franklin,
814-437-2275
(Circa 1865) Museum owned by Venango County Historical Society; displays materials

and artifacts relating to Venango County history; period furnishings, research library. House open May-December: Tuesday-Thursday and Saturday; rest of year, Saturday. Inquire for genealogy library hours.

Pioneer Cemetery
Otter and 15th Streets, Franklin
(1795-1879) Self-guided walking tour booklets can be purchased at the Chamber of Commerce.

Venango County Court House
1168 Liberty St., Franklin 814-432-9500
(1868) Unique styling; contains display of Native American artifacts. Monday-Friday.

SPECIAL EVENTS
Applefest
1259 Liberty St., Franklin,
814-432-5823, 888-547-2377;
www.franklinapplefest.com

Apple pie-baking contest, arts and crafts, entertainment, classic car show, 5-K race, horse-drawn buggy rides. First full weekend in October.

Franklin Silver Cornet Band Concerts
City Park
Thursday, mid-June-August.

Rocky Grove Fair
July.

SPECIALTY LODGINGS
Lamberton House Bed and Breakfast
1331 Otter St.,
Franklin,
814-432-7908, 866-632-7908;
www.lambertonhouse.com
5 rooms. Complimentary full breakfast. Historic building (1874). **$**

GETTYSBURG
Because of the many historical attractions in this town, visitors may want to stop in at the Gettysburg Convention & Visitors Bureau for complete information about bus tours, guide service (including a tape-recorded and self-guided tour) and help in planning their visit here.
Information: Convention & Visitors Bureau,
102 Carlisle St., Gettysburg, 717-334-6274, 800-337-5015; www.gettysburg.travel

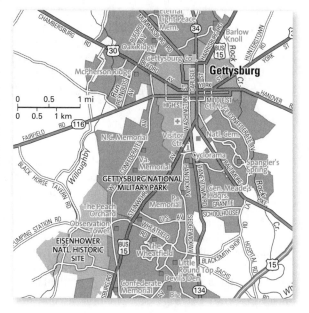

WHAT TO SEE AND DO
A. Lincoln's Place
571 Steinwehr Ave., Gettysburg,
717-334-6049
Live portrayal of the 16th president; 45 minutes. Mid-June-Labor Day: Monday-Friday.

Boyd's Bear Country
75 Cunningham Rd.,
Gettysburg,
717-630-2600, 866-367-8338;
www.boydsbearcountry.com
"The World's Most Humungous Teddy Bear Store" features four floors of bears

A TOWN GRIPPED BY WAR

In July 1863 a three-day Civil War battle unfolded about a mile outside Gettysburg, a small rural community. Gettysburg suffered greatly in the battle.

This one-mile walking tour visits several of the well-preserved buildings that withstood the conflict. Begin at Lincoln Square, the commercial heart of Gettysburg. Abraham Lincoln stayed at the David Wills House, now a small museum at No. 12, the night before he delivered the "Gettysburg Address" in the National Cemetery nearby. Just outside the door is an odd, life-size statue of Lincoln, dressed somberly, appearing to help a visitor dressed in a colorful sweater and corduroys—known to the town's residents as the "Perry Como statue" because of the tourist's strange garb.

Head south on Baltimore Street to Nos. 242-246, the Jennie Wade Birthplace. Wade, the only civilian killed in the battle, was supposedly shot by a Confederate soldier while baking bread and biscuits for Union troops in her sister's house nearby. Between the two homes, stop at the Schriver House at 309 Baltimore. Built for George Schriver and his family, the house contains a garret that was occupied by Confederate sharpshooters who poked still-visible holes in the wall for their rifles. Now a museum, the Schriver House details life in the town during and immediately after the battle.

Across the street at No. 304, formerly the Methodist parsonage, note the shell near the second story window in front. The parson's daughter, Laura, was said to have narrowly escaped injury when a shell crashed through the brick wall into her room. Later, the shell was placed in the hole to mark the spot.

Return to Lincoln Square via Washington Street. At the corner of West Middle Street, pause in front of the Michael Jacobs House at No. 101. A meteorologist, Jacobs recorded the weather throughout his life, leaving important details of the battle's weather and cloud conditions to posterity.

PENNSYLVANIA

(plus rabbits, moose and other furry friends) in a giant barn. At the Boyd's Teddy Bear Nursery, kids can adopt their very own baby bear; personalize your bear at the Make-N-Take-Craft Center. Live entertainment every weekend adds to the merriment. Restaurant; museum. Daily 10 a.m.-6 p.m.

Eisenhower National Historic Site
Rural Route 9, Gettysburg

General Lee's Headquarters
401 Buford Ave.,
Gettysburg,
717-334-3141;
www.civilwarheadquarters.com
Robert E. Lee planned Confederate strategy for the Gettysburg battle in this house;

contains collection of historical items from the battle. Mid-March-mid-November: daily.

Gettysburg Battle Theatre
571 Steinwehr Ave.,
Gettysburg,
717-334-6100
Battlefield diorama with 25,000 figures; 30-minute film and electronic maps program showing battle strategy. March-November: daily.

Gettysburg College
300 N. Washington St.,
Gettysburg,
717-337-6000;
www.gettysburg.edu

(1832) (2,000 students.) Liberal arts; oldest Lutheran-affiliated college in the U.S. Pennsylvania Hall was used as Civil War hospital; Eisenhower House and statue on grounds. Tour of campus.

Gettysburg Scenic Rail Tours
**Washington St.,
Gettysburg,
717-334-6932**
A 22-mile round trip to Aspers on a steam train. Also charter trips and special runs. June: Thursday-Sunday; July-August: Tuesday-Sunday; September: Saturday-Sunday afternoons.

Ghosts of Gettysburg Candlelight Walking Tours
**271 Baltimore St.,
Gettysburg,
717-337-0445;
www.ghostsofgettysburg.com**
Armed with tales from Mark Nesbitt's "Ghosts of Gettysburg" books, knowledgeable guides lead 1 1/4-hour tours through sections of town that were bloody battlefields 130 years ago. March and November: weekends; April-October: daily.

Hall of Presidents and First Ladies
**789 Baltimore St.,
Gettysburg,
717-334-5717**
Costumed life-size wax figures of all the presidents and reproductions of their wives' inaugural gowns. Mid-March-November: daily.

Land of Little Horses
**125 Glenwood Dr.,
Gettysburg,
717-334-7259;
www.landoflittlehorses.com**
A variety of performing horses—all in miniature. Continuous entertainment; indoor arena; exotic animal races. Saddle and wagon rides. Picnic area, snack bar, gift shop. April-August: daily; September-October: weekends.

Lincoln Room Museum
**12 Lincoln Square, Gettysburg,
717-334-8188**
Preserved bedroom in Wills House; collection of Lincoln items; huge plaque inscribed with Gettysburg Address. April-November: daily.

Lincoln Train Museum
**425 Steinwehr Ave., Gettysburg,
717-334-5678**
Museum features more than 1,000 model trains and railroad memorabilia; Lincoln Train Ride—simulated trip of 15 minutes. March-November: daily.

Lutheran Theological Seminary
**61 Seminary Ridge, Gettysburg,
717-334-6286;
www.ltsg.edu**
(1826) (250 students.) Oldest Lutheran seminary in the United States; cupola on campus used as Confederate lookout during battle. Old Dorm, now home of Adams County Historical Society, served as hospital for both Union and Confederate soldiers.

National Civil War Wax Museum
**297 Steinwehr Ave., Gettysburg,
717-334-6245;
www.gettysburgmuseum.com**
Highlights Civil War era and Battle of Gettysburg. March-December: daily; rest of year: Saturday and Sunday.

Schriver House
**309 Baltimore St., Gettysburg,
717-337-2800;
www.schriverhouse.com**
Built prior to the Civil War, this two-story brick house was used by Confederate sharpshooters, who knocked still-visible holes in the garret walls through which to aim their weapons. Private owners have restored and furnished the house as a period museum; the 30-minute guided tour details the Schriver family's experience during the battle, as well as the experience of other townspeople. April-November: daily; December, February-March: weekends.

181

PENNSYLVANIA

★
★
★
★
★

Soldiers' National Museum
777 Baltimore St., Gettysburg,
717-334-4890
Dioramas of major battles, with sound;
Civil War collection. March-November:
daily; schedule may vary.

SPECIAL EVENTS

Apple Blossom Festival
South Mountain Fairgrounds,
35 Carlisle St., Gettysburg,
Early May.

Apple Harvest Festival
South Mountain Fairgrounds,
218 Mercer St., Gettysburg
Demonstrations, arts and crafts, guided
tours of orchard, mountain areas. First and
second weekends in October.

Civil War Heritage Days
Gettysburg
Lectures by historians, Civil War collec-
tors' show, entertainment, fireworks. Late
June-early July.

HOTELS

★Best Inn
301 Steinwehr Ave., Gettysburg,
717-334-1188, 800-237-8466;
www.gettysburgbestinn.com
77 rooms. Complimentary continental
breakfast. **$**

★★Best Western Gettysburg Hotel
1 Lincoln Square, Gettysburg,
717-337-2000, 866-378-1797;
www.bestwestern.com
96 rooms. **$**

★★★The Herr Tavern and Publick House
900 Chambersburg Rd., Gettysburg,
717-334-4332, 800-362-9849;
www.herrtavern.com
Built in 1815, this inn served as the first
Confederate hospital during the Battle of
Gettysburg. Guest rooms have been mod-
ernized with a light touch that hasn't marred
their quaint, historic charm.
16 rooms. Children over 12 years only.
Complimentary continental breakfast. **$$**

★Holiday Inn Express
869 York Rd., Gettysburg,
717-337-1400, 800-315-2621;
www.hiexpress.com
51 rooms. Complimentary continental
breakfast. **$**

★Quality Inn
401 Buford Ave., Gettysburg,
717-334-3141, 877-424-6423;
www.choicehotels.com
45 rooms. Complimentary continental
breakfast. **$**

SPECIALTY LODGINGS

Baladerry Inn
40 Hospital Rd., Gettysburg,
717-337-1342, 800-220-0025;
www.baladerryinn.com
9 rooms. Children over 12 years only. Com-
plimentary full breakfast. **$**

Battlefield Bed and Breakfast Inn
2264 Emmitsburg Rd., Gettysburg,
717-334-8804, 888-766-3897;
www.gettysburgbattlefield.com
Built in 1809, this Civil War inn is located
on the Gettysburg battlefield. Guests can
enjoy a carriage ride and a historic dem-
onstration with real muskets, cannons and
cavalry.
8 rooms. Complimentary full breakfast.
Check-in 2:30-8 p.m. **$$**

Brafferton Inn
44 York St., Gettysburg,
717-337-3423, 866-337-3427;
www.brafferton.com
14 rooms. Children over eight years only.
Complimentary full breakfast. **$**

The Gaslight Inn
33 E. Middle St.,
Gettysburg,
717-337-9100, 800-914-5698;
www.thegaslightinn.com
This bed-and-breakfast is located in the
center of historic Gettysburg, near shopping, restaurants and local attractions.
9 rooms. Children over 11 years only.
Complimentary full breakfast. **$$**

James Gettys Hotel

27 Chambersburg St.,
Gettysburg,
717-337-1334, 800-900-5275;
www.jamesgettyshotel.com
11 rooms, all suites. Complimentary continental breakfast. $$

RESTAURANTS

★★Dobbin House Tavern

89 Steinwehr Ave.,
Gettysburg,
717-334-2100;
www.dobbinhouse.com
American menu. Lunch, dinner. Closed first Monday in January and second Monday in June. Bar. Children's menu. Business casual attire. Reservations recommended. $$$

★★Farnsworth House Inn

401 Baltimore St., Gettysburg,
717-334-8838;
www.farnsworthhouseinn.com/
dining-room.html
American menu. Dinner. Children's menu. Outdoor seating. $$

★Gingerbread Man

217 Steinwehr Ave., Gettysburg,
717-334-1100;
www.thegingerbreadman.net
American menu. Lunch, dinner. Bar. Children's menu. $$

★★★Herr Tavern and Publick House

900 Chambersburg Rd., Gettysburg,
717-334-4332, 800-362-9849;
www.herrtavern.com
This restaurant is housed in the historic country inn of the same name, which served as the first Confederate hospital during the Battle of Gettysburg. Guests here are treated to friendly, pleasant service and an appetizing menu of American-inspired fare that includes some Mediterranean influences. Because most ingredients are obtained from local farmers, the menu frequently changes. Past dishes included shrimp and scallops in red pepper fondue with baby spinach and fettuccine; and Black Angus filet mignon with port wine demi-glace and a stuffed potato. American menu. Lunch, dinner. Bar. Children's menu. Business casual attire. Reservations recommended. $$$

183

PENNSYLVANIA

GETTYSBURG NATIONAL MILITARY PARK

The hallowed battlefield of Gettysburg, the site of one of the Civil War's most decisive battles and immortalized by Lincoln's Gettysburg Address, is preserved by the National Park Service. The town itself is still a college community, as it was more than a hundred years ago on July 1-3, 1863, when General Robert E. Lee led his Confederate Army in its greatest invasion of the North. The defending Northerners, under Union General George Meade, repulsed the Southern assault after three days of fierce fighting, which left 51,000 men dead, wounded or missing.

The Gettysburg National Military Park has more than 35 miles of roads through 5,900 acres of the battlefield area. There are more than 1,300 monuments, markers and tablets of granite and bronze, as well as 400 cannons.

Visitors may wish to tour the battlefield with a Battlefield Guide, licensed by the National Park Service (two-hour tour; fee). The guides escort visitors to all points of interest and sketch the movement of troops and details of the battle. Or visitors may wish to first orient themselves at the Electric Map at the Visitor Center; then using the park folder, the battlefield can be toured without a guide. Audio cassettes are also available for self-guided tours.

The late President Dwight D. Eisenhower's retirement farm, a National Historic Site, adjoins the battlefield. It is open to the public on a limited-tour basis. All visitors must obtain tour tickets at the information center, located at the lobby of the Visitor Center-Electric Map building. Transportation to the farm is by shuttle (fee).

Information: Gettysburg National Military Park, 97 Taneytown Road,
Gettysburg, 717-334-1124; www.nps.gov/gett

WHAT TO SEE AND DO

The Angle
Spot where Pickett's Charge was repulsed on July 3, referred to as "high water mark" of the Confederacy.

Culp's Hill
Site of longest sustained fighting during battle.

Cyclorama Center
97 Taneytown Rd., Gettysburg
Adjacent to visitor center. Instructive film and exhibits: 356-foot Cyclorama painting of Pickett's Charge. Daily.

Devil's Den
Stronghold of Confederate sharpshooters following its capture during action on the second day.

East Cemetery Hill
Rallying point for Union forces on first day of battle. Scene of fierce fighting on evening of second day.

Eisenhower National Historic Site
(Visitor Center) 97 Taneytown Rd.,
Gettysburg,
717-338-9114
Farm and home of the 34th President of the United States and his wife, Mamie. Tour of grounds and home (1 1/2-2 hours). Self-guided tours explore the farm and skeet range. Reception Center houses exhibits and bookstore; 11-minute video is shown. Access to site is by shuttle only, from the National Park Service Visitor Center. Daily.

Eternal Light Peace Memorial
On Oak Ridge. Erected in 1938 and dedicated by President Roosevelt to "peace eternal in a nation united."

Gettysburg National Cemetery
Site of Lincoln's Gettysburg Address.

Little Round Top
Key Union position during second and third days of battle.

Memorials to State Units
Includes Pennsylvania State Monument, with names of more than 34,500 Pennsylvanian soldiers who participated in the battle.

Seminary Ridge
Main Confederate battle line.

Visitor Center-Electric Map-Gettysburg Museum of the Civil War
35 Carlisle St., Gettysburg
Visits to the park should begin here. Park information, including a self-guided auto tour, and guides may be obtained at the center. Story of battle told on 750-square-foot electric map surrounded by 525 seats (every 45 minutes; fee). Gettysburg Museum of the Civil War has an extensive collection of Civil War relics (free). Daily.

Wheatfield and Peach Orchard
Scene of heavy Union and Confederate losses on the second day of fighting.

Whitworth Guns on Oak Hill
Only breech-loading cannon used here.

GREENSBURG
Greensburg was named for Revolutionary General Nathanael Greene.
Information: Laurel Highlands Visitors Bureau, 120 E. Main St., Ligonier, 724-238-5661; www.laurelhighlands.org

WHAT TO SEE AND DO

Historic Hanna's Town
951 Old Salem Rd.,
Greensburg,
724-836-1800
Costumed tour guide tells story of Hanna's Town, site of first court west of Alleghenies. Includes reconstructed courthouse, tavern, jail and stockaded fort; picnic area. June-August: Tuesday-Sunday; May, September and October: weekends only.

Lincoln Highway Heritage Corridor
114 S. Market St.,
Greensburg,
724-238-9030;
www.lhhc.org
A 140-mile stretch of Hwy 30 extending from Greensburg to Chambersburg. Pass through and explore countless historical and recreational areas. Driving guide available (fee).

Westmoreland County Courthouse
Main and Pittsburgh Streets,
Greensburg,
724-830-3000
Building in style of Italian Renaissance; restored in 1982. Monday-Friday.

GWYNEDD

HOTELS
★★★William Penn Inn
US 202 & Sumneytown Pike,
Gwynedd,
215-699-9272;
www.williampenninn.com
4 rooms. Complimentary continental breakfast. $

HANOVER

Hanover was once known as "McAllisterstown" (for founder Colonel Richard McAllister) and "Rogue's Harbor" (for its lack of law enforcement). Here, on June 30, 1863, Confederate General J. E. B. Stuart's cavalry tangled with Union forces under Generals Kilpatrick and Custer. The battle prevented Stuart from reaching Gettysburg in time to function as "the eyes of Lee's army."

Among the products of the town's diversified industry are books, wirecloth, yarns, furniture, industrial machinery, textiles and foods, including the famous pretzel maker, Snyder's of Hanover.

Information: Hanover Area Chamber of Commerce, 146 Carlisle St., Hanover, 717-637-6130; www.hanoverchamber.com

WHAT TO SEE AND DO
Codorus State Park
1066 Blooming Grove Rd., Hanover
Approximately 3,300 acres. Swimming pool, fishing in 1,275-acre Lake Marburg, boating (rentals, mooring, launching, marina); hunting, hiking, bridle trails, cross-country skiing, snowmobiling, sledding, ice skating, ice boating, ice fishing, picnicking, mountain biking, snack bar, tent and trailer sites.

Conewago Chapel
30 Basilica Dr., Hanover,
717-637-2721
(1741) Oldest stone Catholic church in the U.S. Designated Sacred Heart Basilica in 1962. Cemetery dates from 1752. Daily.

Westmoreland Museum of American Art
221 N. Main St., Greensburg,
724-837-1500;
www.wmuseumaa.org
18th-, 19th- and early 20th-century American paintings, sculpture, furniture and decorative arts. 19th- and early 20th-century southwestern Pennsylvania paintings. Extensive toy collection. Lectures, guided tours. Wednesday-Sunday.

HOTELS
★★Four Points by Sheraton
100 Sheraton Dr. (Route 30E), Greensburg,
724-836-6060, 800-325-3535;
www.sheraton.com
146 rooms. $

RESTAURANTS
★★William Penn Inn
US 202 and Sumneytown Pike,
Gwynedd, 215-699-9272;
www.williampenninn.com
American menu. Lunch, dinner. Sunday brunch. Bar. Originally built as a tavern (1714); antiques. $$$

★
★
★
★
★

Neas House Museum
113 W. Chestnut St.,
Hanover,
717-632-3207

Neas House (circa 1783), restored Georgian mansion, serves as local history museum. May-November: Tuesday-Friday. Special events. Spring, summer, late December.

Utz Quality Foods, Inc
900 High St., Hanover,
717-637-6644;
www.utzsnacks.com

Producers of potato chips and snack foods. Glass-enclosed tour gallery overlooks production area; push-to-talk audio program and closed-circuit TV monitors. Monday-Thursday.

SPECIALTY LODGINGS

The Beechmont Bed and Breakfast Inn
315 Broadway, Hanover,
717-632-3013, 800-553-7009;
www.thebeechmont.com

Built in 1834, this bed-and-breakfast is located just 14 miles outside of Gettysburg. It offers four large guest rooms and three suites, each furnished with fine antiques. Breakfast can be enjoyed in the dining room, on the porch or in the rooms. 7 rooms. Children over 12 years only. Complimentary full breakfast. $

HARRISBURG

This mid-state metropolis holds what many consider the finest capitol building in the nation. Other showplaces include the city's riverside park (known as City Island), Italian Lake, unique museum and beautiful Forum.

Harrisburg's location was viewed in 1615 by Etienne Brul on a trip down the Susquehanna, but more than a century passed before John Harris, the first settler, opened his trading post here. His son established the town in 1785. The cornerstone of the first capitol building was laid in 1819.

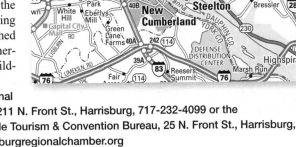

Information: Capital Regional Chamber of Commerce, 3211 N. Front St., Harrisburg, 717-232-4099 or the Harrisburg-Hershey-Carlisle Tourism & Convention Bureau, 25 N. Front St., Harrisburg, 717-231-7788; www.harrisburgregionalchamber.org

WHAT TO SEE AND DO

Capitol Hill Buildings
N. Third and Walnut Streets,
Harrisburg,
717-787-6810

Clustered in a 45-acre complex, the major buildings are:

Capitol
Third and State Streets, Harrisburg

(Dedicated 1906) Italian Renaissance building covers two acres and has 651 rooms; 26,000-ton, 272-foot dome, imitating that of St. Peter's in Rome, dominates city skyline. Includes murals by Abbey and Okley. Tours. Daily.

Finance Building
Ceiling murals by Maragliotti, Eugene Savage; mural in south vestibule illustrates "The Collection of Taxes." Monday-Friday.

Forum Building
Includes auditorium below constellation-bedecked ceiling; walls review man's progress through time. Main lobby boasts a Maragliotti ceiling. General and law libraries.

North Office Building
Map inscribed on main lobby floor shows state highways, seals of Pennsylvania cities.

South Office Building
Colorful murals by Edward Trumbull depict "Penn's Treaty with the Indians" and "The Industries of Pittsburgh."

The State Museum of Pennsylvania
Third and North Streets,
Harrisburg,
717-787-4980
www.statemuseumpa.org
A six-story circular building housing four stories of galleries, authentic early country store, Native American life exhibit, technological and industrial exhibits, collection of antique autos and period carriages; planetarium; natural history and geology exhibits and one of the world's largest framed paintings, Rothermel's "The Battle of Gettysburg." Planetarium has public shows (Saturday and Sunday; fee). Tuesday-Sunday.

Dauphin County Courthouse
Front and Market Streets,
Harrisburg,
717-255-2741
Seven imposing courtrooms; outline map on floor of main foyer pictures borough and township boundaries. Monday-Friday.

Fort Hunter Park
Historic 37-acre property; site of British-built fort erected in 1754 to combat mounting threats prior to the French and Indian War. In 1787, the land was purchased and became a farm that eventually grew into a self-sufficient village. The Pennsylvania Canal runs through the park; on the grounds are historic buttonwood trees dating from William Penn's time, a 19th-century boxwood garden and picnic area. Outstanding feature of park is:

Fort Hunter Mansion
5300 N. Front St., Harrisburg,
717-599-5751;
www.forthunter.org
Federal-style stone mansion, built in three sections. Front stone portions were built in 1786 and 1814; rear wooden portion built in 1870. Spacious mansion displays period furnishings, clothing, toys and other artifacts. Guided tours. May-December: Tuesday-Sunday.

Italian Lake
N. Third and Division Streets,
Harrisburg
Bordered with flowers, shrubs and shade trees in summer.

John Harris Mansion
219 S. Front St., Harrisburg,
717-233-3462
Home of city's founder, now Historical Society of Dauphin County headquarters. Stone house has 19th-century furnishings, library (Monday-Thursday; fee), collection of county artifacts. Tours April-December: Monday-Thursday.

Reservoir Park
Walnut and N. 19th Streets,
Harrisburg
View of east end of city, five nearby counties.

Riverfront Park
Four miles along Susquehanna River, with park promenade flanking Front Street, concrete walk along river.

Rockville Bridge
(1902) A 3,810-foot stone-arch bridge; 48 spans carry four tracks of Penn Central Railroad main line.

PENNSYLVANIA

★
★
★
★
★

SPECIAL EVENTS

Eastern Sports & Outdoor Show
State Farm Show Complex,
2301 N. Cameron, Harrisburg,
717-787-5373
Early-mid-February.

Kipona
Boating and water-related activites. Labor
Day weekend.

Pennsylvania National Horse Show
1509 Cedar Cliff Dr., Harrisburg,
717-975-3677
Ten days in mid-October.

Pennsylvania State Farm Show
State Farm Show Complex,
2301 N. Cameron St.,
Harrisburg,
717-787-5373
State fair. Early-mid-January.

HOTELS

★★**Best Western Harrisburg/Hershey Hotel & Suites**
300 N. Mountain Rd.,
Harrisburg,
717-652-7180;
www.bestwestern.com
49 rooms. $

★★★**Crowne Plaza**
23 S. Second St.,
Harrisburg,
717-234-5021, 800-496-7621;
www.crowneplaza.com
A smart choice for families and budget travelers, this full-service hotel is near all the attractions of Harrisburg but doesn't leave the wallet empty. HersheyPark is minutes away, as are Chocolate World, the Carlisle Fairgrounds, the National Civil War Museum and the Capitol Complex. Restaurant Row (a collection of more than 30 restaurants, clubs, pubs and shops) is literally outside the front door and should not be missed. After a busy day, a nap in one of the contemporary guest rooms is the answer.
261 rooms. Airport transportation available. $

★**Days Inn**
3919 N. Front St., Harrisburg,
717-233-3100, 800-329-7466;
www.daysinn.com
116 rooms. Complimentary continental breakfast. Children's activity center.$

★★**Four Points by Sheraton**
800 E. Park Dr., Harrisburg,
717-561-2800, 800-325-3535;
www.starwoodhotels.com
174 rooms. Airport transportation available. $

★**Hampton Inn**
4230 Union Deposit Rd., Harrisburg,
717-545-9595, 800-426-7866;
www.hamptoninn.com
145 rooms. Complimentary continental breakfast. Airport transportation available. $

★★★**Hilton Harrisburg and Towers**
1 N. Second St., Harrisburg,
717-233-6000, 800-445-8667;
www.harrisburg.hilton.com
This elegant, family-friendly hotel is located in the heart of historic Harrisburg and is connected to the Whitaker Center by an enclosed walkway. Although the standard guest rooms are well-appointed, guests who choose to upgrade to Tower Level rooms will enjoy upgraded amenities including access to a private lounge that serves complimentary continental breakfast and evening hors d'oeuvres. The hotel also offers three restaurants, as well as a seasonal (summer) restaurant.
341 rooms. Airport transportation available. $$

★★**Radisson Penn Harris Hotel & Convention Center**
1150 Camp Hill Bypass, Camp Hill,
717-763-7117, 800-333-3333;
www.radisson.com
250 rooms. Airport transportation available. $

★★★**Sheraton Harrisburg Hershey Hotel**
4650 Lindle Rd., Harrisburg,
717-564-5511, 800-325-3535;
www.sheraton.com

188

PENNSYLVANIA

★
★
★
★
★

Minutes from downtown Harrisburg and the airport, this full-service hotel is also near many attractions such as Hershey Park, Hershey Chocolate World, historic Gettysburg, the Pennsylvania Dutch Country and the State Museum of Pennsylvania. The traditional-style guest rooms are spacious and include large work desks. The Dog and Pony Restaurant serves breakfast, lunch and dinner in a casually elegant setting, and the Dog and Pony Pub is a nice place for a nightcap.

348 rooms. Airport transportation available. **$**

HAWLEY

A major attraction in this Pocono resort area is man-made Lake Wallenpaupack, offering summer recreation and winter recreation nearby.

Information: Pocono Mountains Vacation Bureau, 1004 Main St., Stroudsburg, 570-424-6050, 800-762-6667; www.poconos.org

WHAT TO SEE AND DO

Gravity Coach

Car used on Pennsylvania Gravity Railroad (22 inclined planes between Hawley and Scranton, 1850-1885).

Lake Wallenpaupack

Hwy. 6, Hawley, 570-226-2141

One of the largest man-made lakes in the state (5,600 acres), formed by the damming of Wallenpaupack Creek. Swimming beach (Memorial Day-Labor Day; fee), fishing, boating, water sports; ice fishing, camping. The information center is 1/2 mile NW on Hwy. 6 at Hwy. 507. Daily.

PPL Wallenpaupack

126 PPL Dr., Hawley, 570-226-3702

Hydroelectric facilities, dam; recreation area. Superintendent's office has information on campgrounds, hiking trails, picnic groves (Monday-Friday); observation point. Daily.

HOTELS

★Gresham's Lake View Motel

Hwy. 6, Hawley, 570-226-4621; www.greshems.net

21 rooms. **$**

★★★Settlers Inn at Bingham Park

4 Main Ave., Hawley, 570-226-2993, 800-833-8527; www.thesettlersinn.com

The Settlers Inn, a Craftsmen mountain lodge, was built in 1927. Guests can request in-room massages, or champagne and flowers to greet them upon their arrival.

23 rooms. Complimentary full breakfast. Restaurant. Airport transportation available. **$**

RESTAURANTS

★★The Settlers Inn

4 Main Ave., Hawley, 570-226-2993; www.thesettlersinn.com

Seafood menu. Lunch, dinner. Sunday brunch. Bar. Children's menu. **$$**

HAZLETON

On top of Spring Mountain, Hazleton calls itself the highest city in Pennsylvania. Rich agricultural land surrounds it, and its early and rapid economic growth was spurred by the rich anthracite coal reserves found in the area. Although coal dominated the town's economy during the 19th century, today there are many diversified industries located here.

Information: Greater Hazleton Chamber of Commerce, 1 S. Church St., Hazleton, 570-455-1508; www.hazletonchamber.org

PENNSYLVANIA

HOTELS

★Best Western Genetti Lodge
Hwy. 309 and RR1, Hazleton,
570-454-2494, 800-780-7234;
www.bestwestern.com
85 rooms. Complimentary continental
breakfast. Laundry services. **$**

★★Ramada Inn
Route 309 N,
Hazleton,
570-455-2061, 800-272-6232;
www.ramada.com
107 rooms. **$**

HERSHEY

One of America's most fascinating success stories, this planned community takes its name from founder M. S. Hershey, who established his world-famous chocolate factory here in 1903, then built a town around it. The streets have names like Chocolate and Cocoa and streetlights are shaped like chocolate kisses. But there's more than chocolate here. Today, Hershey is known as one of the most diverse entertainment and resort areas in the eastern United States. Hershey is also known as the "golf capital of Pennsylvania" and has a number of well-known golf courses.

Information: Hersheypark, 100 W. Hersheypark Dr., Hershey,
800-HERSHEY (information) or 800-533-3131 (reservations); www.800hershey.com

WHAT TO SEE AND DO

Founders Hall
801 Spartan Lane, Hershey, 717-520-2000
Campus center of Milton Hershey School, noted for its striking rotunda. Daily.

Hershey Gardens
170 Hotel Rd., Hershey,
717-534-3492;
www.hersheygardens.org
From mid-June to first frost, 8,000 rose plants bloom on 23 acres. Tulip garden (mid-April-mid-May); chrysanthemums and annuals; butterfly house featuring 400-500 butterflies; six theme gardens. Daily.

Hershey Museum
170 W. Hershey Park Dr., Hershey,
717-534-3439;
www.hersheymuseum.org
Pennsylvania German, Native American, Eskimo collections; displays of Stiegel glass; "Apostolic Clock" depicting life of Christ; Milton Hershey history. Daily.
    Adjacent is:

Hersheypark Arena
100 Hershey Park Dr., Hershey,
717-534-3911
Capacity 10,000; professional hockey, basketball, ice skating, variety shows, concerts.

Hershey's Chocolate World
800 Hershey Park Dr., Hershey,
717-534-4900;
www.hersheys.com/chocolateworld
Tour via automated conveyance; simulates steps of chocolate production from cacao bean plantations through chocolate-making in Hershey. Also tropical gardens, shopping village. Daily.

Hershey Park
100 W. Hershey Park Dr., Hershey,
800-437-7439;
www.800hershey.com
This 110-acre theme park includes Rhine Land, Tudor Square, Dutch crafts barn; more than 60 rides include six roller coasters; live family shows. Mid-May-Labor Day: daily; May and September: selected weekends.
    Also here is:

Hersheypark Stadium/Star Pavilion
100 W. Hershey Park Dr., Hershey,
717-534-3911
Sports and entertainment events.

Seltzer's Lebanon Bologna Company
230 N. College St.,
717-838-6336
Outdoor wooden smokehouses since 1902. Monday-Saturday.

Zoo America

100 W. Hershey Park Dr., Hershey,
717-534-3860;
www.zooamerica.com
An 11-acre environmental zoo depicting
five climatic regions of North America;
home to more than 200 animals. Daily.
Combination admission with Hersheypark
available.

SPECIAL EVENTS

Antique Automobile Club
National fall rally. Second weekend in
October.

Chocolate Lovers' Weekend
Hotel Hershey, 100 Hotel Rd., Hershey
February.

Christmas Candylane
Hersheypark, 100 W. Hershey Park Dr.,
Hershey
Hersheypark is transformed into "Christmas
Candylane" to mark the beginning of the
Christmas season. Mid-November-December.

Hersheypark Balloonfest
Hersheypark, 100 W. Hershey Park Dr.,
Hershey, 717-534-3900
October.

HOTELS

★Days Inn
350 W. Chocolate Ave., Hershey,
717-534-2162, 800-329-7466;
www.daysinn.com/hershey06452
100 rooms. Complimentary continental
breakfast. Airport transportation available.

★★★Hershey Lodge and Convention Center
W. Chocolate Ave. and University Dr.,
Hershey,
717-533-3311, 800-437-7439;
www.hersheypa.com
The Hershey Lodge stays true to its name,
with chocolate-themed décor in every guest
room and special Hersheypark privileges
including discounted tickets and early
access to certain rides. Kids can even check
themselves in at their own check-in desk
and greet the friendly Hershey's product

characters who might make an appearance
in the lobby.
665 rooms. High-speed, wireless Internet
access. Five restaurants, three bars. Children's activity center. Airport transporta-
tion available. Tennis. **$$**

★★★★The Hotel Hershey
One Hotel Rd., Hershey,
717-533-2171, 800-437-7439;
www.hersheys.com
Perched atop a hill overlooking town, the
Hotel Hershey sits on 300 acres of formal
gardens, fountains and reflecting pools.
Instead of mints, you'll find chocolate kisses
on your pillow at evening turndown. Recre-
ational opportunities abound, from 72 holes
of golf, six miles of nature trails, basketball,
volleyball and tennis courts to the pools and
fitness center. Rest your sweet tooth with a
meal at the Fountain Cafe, or grab snacks
and light meals at the coffeehouse or fire-
side lounge. The Spa at Hotel Hershey is
a wonderfully sinful place, with whipped
cocoa baths and chocolate fondue wraps.
234 rooms. Children's activity center. Ski
in/ski out. Airport transportation available.
Skiing. **$$$**

★Spinners Inn
845 E. Chocolate Ave., Hershey,
717-533-9157, 800-800-5845;
www.spinnersinn.com
52 rooms. Complimentary continental
breakfast. **$**

SPAS

★★★The Spa at the Hotel Hershey
100 W. Hersheypark Dr., Hershey,
717-533-2171, 800-437-7439;
www.spaathotelhershey.com
The Spa at Hotel Hershey doesn't skimp
on using its signature luscious ingredi-
ent. Chocolate reigns at this spa, from the
chocolate bean polish and whipped cocoa
bath to the chocolate fondue wrap and the
chocolate scrub. The facility includes an
inhalation room, a quiet room for meditation, soaking tubs, steam rooms, saunas
and signature showers for hydrotherapy
treatments.

★
★
★
★
★

RESTAURANTS

★★★Circular Dining Room
One Hotel Rd., Hershey,
717-534-8800, 800-437-7439;
www.hersheypa.com
This elegant dining destination is tucked away in the Hotel Hershey. Its circular design—the idea of founder Milton S. Hershey—affords all guests, no matter where they are seated, unobstructed views of the exquisite formal gardens and reflecting pools from the room's soaring windows. The contemporary American menu is as refined as the restaurant's surroundings, and changes seasonally to ensure only the freshest and most flavorful ingredients are used. Past menus have included cocoa-braised beef short ribs, pulled pork shoulder with house-made sauerkraut, and grilled beef filet with truffled dauphinoise potatoes. Decadent desserts feature many choices for chocolate lovers, like warm chocolate soufflé, chocolate and blood orange bombe, and the Chocolate Evolution, a tasting of chocolate. American menu. Breakfast, lunch, dinner. Sunday brunch. Children's menu. Jacket required (dinner. Sunday brunch). **$$$**

★★Dimitri's
1311 E. Chocolate Ave.,
Hershey,
717-533-3403
Greek. Lunch, dinner. Closed Sunday. Bar. Children's menu. **$$$**

★★Union Canal House
107 S. Hanover St., Hershey,
717-566-0054, 888-566-5867;
www.unioncanalhouse.com
American menu. Dinner. Closed Sunday. Bar. Children's menu. Business casual attire. Reservations recommended. **$$$**

HONESDALE

Named in honor of Philip Hone, a mayor of New York City and first president of the Delaware & Hudson Canal Company, Honesdale was for many years the world's largest coal storage center, shipping millions of tons of anthracite. A gravity railroad brought coal here in winter; in spring it was reshipped by canal boats to tidewater. The Stourbridge Lion, first steam locomotive to operate in the United States (1829), was used by the Delaware & Hudson Canal Company, but when the rail bed proved too weak, mule power replaced the steam engine. Today, Honesdale manufactures textile products, business forms and furniture, and is surrounded by dairy farms in the beautiful rolling countryside.
Information: Wayne County Chamber of Commerce, 303 Commercial St., Honesdale, 570-253-1960, 800-433-9008; www.waynecountycc.com

WHAT TO SEE AND DO

Replica of the Stourbridge Lion
Main St., Honesdale
Original is in Smithsonian Institution First steam locomotive to operate in the U.S. (1829).

Stourbridge Rail Excursions
Scenic rail excursions from Honesdale to Lackawaxen, centering on the change of seasons, with entertainment and activities. Contact the Chamber of Commerce for schedule, fees.

Triple W Riding Stable
Honesdale, 570-226-2620, 800-540-2620
A 181-acre horse ranch in the NE range of Pocono Mountains. Variety of trail rides for beginners or advanced riders; 1/2- and full-day trips; overnight camping trips. Hay and sleigh rides (seasonal; by appointment). Daily.

Wayne County Historical Society Museum
810 Main St.,
Honesdale,
570-253-3240;
www.waynehistorypa.org
Delaware and Hudson-Canal exhibit, Native American exhibit. April-December: Wednesday-Saturday.

HOPEWELL FURNACE NATIONAL HISTORIC SITE

Hopewell, an early industrial community, was built around a charcoal-burning cold-blast furnace, which made pig iron and many other iron products from 1771-1883. Nearby mines and forests supplied ore and charcoal for the furnace. The National Park Service has restored the buildings, and interpretive programs emphasize the community's role in the history of American industry. Hopewell is surrounded by French Creek State Park.

The Visitor Center has a museum and audiovisual program on iron-making and community life. Self-guided tour includes charcoal house, blacksmith shop, office store and more. Stove molding and casting demonstrations (late June-Labor Day; fee). Captioned slide program for the hearing impaired; Braille map and large-print pamphlets for the visually impaired; wheelchair access. daily; closed winter holidays.
2 Mark Bird Lane, Elverson, 610-582-8773;
www.berksweb.com/historic.html

HOPWOOD

RESTAURANTS
★★★Chez Gerard Authentic French Restaurant
1187 National Pike, Highway 40 E, Hopwood, 724-437-9001;
www.chezgerard.net
Chez Gerard is located in the historic Hopwood House, which dates to 1790. The all-French staff prides itself on providing the most authentic French experience, serving entrees such as magret de canard aux deux facons (grilled and smoked duck breasts with a plum and ginger reduction, grilled marinated zucchini and potato au gratin). French menu. Lunch, dinner. Sunday brunch. Closed Tuesday. Bar. Children's menu. Outdoor seating. $$$

★★Sunday Porch
Hwy. 40 E, Hopwood, 724-439-5734
Lunch, dinner. Closed Monday. Children's menu. $$

HUNTINGDON
Founded on the site of an Oneida village in the Juniata Valley, Huntingdon was first called Standing Stone for a 14-foot etched stone pillar venerated by Native Americans.
Information: Huntingdon County Visitors Bureau, Seven Points Rd., Hesston, 814-658-0060, 800-729-7869; www.raystown.org

WHAT TO SEE AND DO
Greenwood Furnace State Park
Hwy 305 and Broadmountain Rd., Huntingdon,
814-667-1800
Remains of Greenwood Works, last iron furnace to operate in area (circa 1833-1904); restored stack. Approximately 400 acres. Swimming beach, fishing; hiking, snowmobiling, ice skating, ice fishing, picnicking, playground, snack bar, store, tent and trailer sites. Visitor center, interpretive program.

Lincoln Caverns
Hwy. 22, Huntingdon,
814-643-0268
The one-hour tour of two caves includes Frozen Niagara, Diamond Cascade; visitor center and gift shop. April-November: daily; March and December, weekends only.

INDIANA
Named after the area's Native American population, this borough was established on 250 acres donated for a county seat by George Clymer of Philadelphia, a signer of the

PENNSYLVANIA

★
★
★
★
★

Declaration of Independence. Indiana University of Pennsylvania (1875) is located here. This is also the birthplace of actor Jimmy Stewart.

Information: Indiana County Tourist Bureau, 2334 Oakland Ave., Indiana, 724-463-7505; www.visitindianacountypa.org

WHAT TO SEE AND DO

County Parks
Indiana,
724-463-8636

Blue Spruce park covers 420 acres. Fishing for bass, perch, catfish and crappie; boating (rowboat, canoe rentals); winter sports area, picnicking, grills, playground. Daily. Pine Ridge covers 630 acres. Trout fishing; hiking, picnicking. Nature study. Daily. Hemlock Lake park covers 200 acres. Fishing; small game hunting, hiking, ice skating. Nature study, photography. Daily.

Jimmy Stewart Museum
Indiana Public Library Building, third floor, 845 Philadelphia St., Indiana, 724-349-6112, 800-835-4669; www.jimmy.org

Highlights the namesake's accomplishments on film, radio and TV. His roles as a military hero, civic leader, family man and world citizen are woven into displays, film presentations and gallery talks. Fifty-seat vintage theater. Daily.

HOTELS

★★Best Western University Inn
1545 Wayne Ave., Indiana, 724-349-9620, 888-299-9620; www.bestwestern.com
107 rooms. $

★★Holiday Inn
1395 Wayne Ave., Indiana, 724-463-3561, 800-315-2621; www.holidayinn.com
159 rooms. $

JIM THORPE

The twin towns, Mauch Chunk (Bear Mountain) and East Mauch Chunk, built on the sides of a narrow gorge of the Lehigh River, merged in 1954 and adopted the name of Jim Thorpe, the great Native American athlete. This, together with a "nickel-a-week" plan whereby each man, woman and child paid five cents to promote the community and attract industry, gave the area (formerly dependent on coal mining) a new lease on economic life. Little has changed in appearance after more than a century; a walking tour will reveal 19th-century architecture.

Information: Carbon County Tourist Promotion Agency Information Center, Jim Thorpe, 570-325-3673; 888-JIM-THORPE

WHAT TO SEE AND DO

Asa Packer Mansion Museum
Packer Hill, Jim Thorpe, 570-325-3229; www.asapackermansionmuseum. homestead.com

Former showplace home of founder of Lehigh Valley Railroad and Lehigh University, one of state's wealthiest men. Packer's house, treasures and money were left to the borough. June-November: daily; April-May: weekends; closed first two weeks in December.

Jim Thorpe Memorial
A 20-ton granite mausoleum built in memory of the 1912 Olympic champion.

Blue Mountain Sports
34 Susquehanna St., Jim Thorpe, 570-325-2700, 800-599-4421; www.bikejimthorpe.com

Blue Mountain Sports offers whitewater rafting, kayaking and mountain biking services.

Old Jail Museum
128 W. Broadway, Jim Thorpe, 570-325-5259

Built in 1871, the Old Jail, which was an active prison until January 1995, contains 28 original cells, warden's living quarters and 16 dungeon cells. Famous for hangings of the Molly Maguires, a group of rebel union organizers. Late May-early November.

Stone Row
Race St., Jim Thorpe
Sixteen town houses built by Asa Packer for the engineers on his railroad; reminiscent of Philadelphia's Elfreth's Alley. Some are stores open to the public.

Also here is:

St. Mark's Church
Jim Thorpe,
570-325-2241
Has Tiffany windows and copy of reredos from Windsor Castle. June-October: Wednesday-Saturday afternoons.

Whitewater Rafting
On upper and lower gorges of Lehigh River.

Jim Thorpe River Adventures, Inc
1 Adventure Lane, Jim Thorpe,
570-325-2570
March-November: daily

Pocono Whitewater Adventures
RR 903, Jim Thorpe, 570-325-3655
Also bike tours. March-November: daily.

SPECIAL EVENTS
Fall Foliage Festival
Arts and crafts, food, entertainment. Scenic three-hour train rides. Second weekend in October.

Laurel Blossom Festival
Arts and crafts, entertainment, food, steam train rides. Second weekend in June.

SPECIALTY LODGINGS
Harry Packer Mansion
1 Packer Hill Rd., Jim Thorpe, 570-325-8566;
www.murdermansion.com
This mansion's ornate, brick facade served as a model for the haunted mansion at Disney World, but its regal, lived-in quality is elegant and inviting. The interior features 15-foot ceilings, marble fireplaces and gilded mirrors. The mansion hosts special events and murder mystery weekends.
13 rooms. Children over 12 years only. Complimentary full breakfast. **$**

★
★
★
★
★

JOHNSTOWN
On May 31, 1889, a break in the South Fork Dam that impounded an old reservoir 10 miles to the east poured a wall of water onto the city, causing the disastrous "Johnstown Flood." The death toll rose to 2,209 and property damage totaled $17 million. The city has been flooded 22 times since 1850, most recently in 1977.

Founded by a Swiss Mennonite, Joseph Johns, the city is now the center of Cambria County's iron and steel industry, producing iron and steel bars, railroad cars, parts and railroad supplies.

Information: Greater Johnstown/Cambria County Convention & Visitors Bureau, 416 Main St., Johnstown, 814-536-7993, 800-237-8590; www.visitjohnstownpa.com

WHAT TO SEE AND DO

Conemaugh Gap
Located at the W end of the city.
Gorge, seven miles long and 1,700 feet deep, cuts between Laurel Hill Ridge and Chestnut Ridge.

Inclined Plane Railway
Vine St. and Roosevelt Blvd., Johnstown, 814-536-1816
Joins Johnstown and Westmont. Ride is on steep (72 percent grade) passenger incline with 500-foot ascent. Counterbalanced cable cars take 50 passengers and two automobiles each. Daily.

Johnstown Flood Museum
304 Washington St., Johnstown, 814-539-1889
Museum depicts history of Johnstown, with permanent exhibits on 1889 Johnstown Flood; Academy Award-winning film, photographs, artifacts, memorabilia. Daily.

Johnstown Flood National Memorial
733 Lake Rd., Johnstown, 814-495-4643
Commemorates 1889 Johnstown Flood; preserved remnants of the South Fork Dam. Visitor center with exhibits, 30-minute movie. Daily.

HOTELS

★Comfort Inn
455 Theatre Dr., Johnstown, 814-266-3678;
www.choicehotels.com
117 rooms. Complimentary continental breakfast. Airport transportation available. $

★★Holiday Inn
250 Market St., Johnstown, 814-535-7777, 800-443-5663;
www.holidayinn.com
164 rooms. Airport transportation available. $

★Sleep Inn
453 Theatre Dr., Johnstown, 814-262-9292, 877-424-6423;
www.sleepinn.com
62 rooms. Complimentary continental breakfast. Airport transportation available. $

RESTAURANTS

★★Surf N' Turf
100 Valley Pike, Johnstown, 814-536-9250
Seafood, steak menu. Dinner. Bar. Children's menu. $$

KANE

Situated on a lofty plateau, Kane offers hunting, fishing and abundant winter sports. Summers are cool and winters are bracing. Allegheny National Forest is to the north, west and south; there are scenic drives through 4,000 acres of virgin timber. General Thomas L. Kane of "Mormon War" fame settled here and laid out the community, which prospered as a lumber and railroad town. General Ulysses Grant was once arrested here for fishing without a license.

Information: Seneca Highlands Tourist Association, junction Highways 770 W. and 219, Custer City, 814-368-9370; www.visitanf.com

WHAT TO SEE AND DO

Thomas L. Kane Memorial Chapel
30 Chestnut St., Kane, 814-837-9729
(1878) Built as a chapel for the new town under the direction of General Kane, a Civil War hero and humanitarian who championed the persecuted Mormons. Visitor center includes film of General Kane's life; small museum. Tuesday-Saturday.

Twin Lakes
Kane, 814-723-5150
Swimming (fee), fishing; hiking, picnicking, camping (fee).

KEMPTON

WHAT TO SEE AND DO
Hawk Mountain Sanctuary
1700 Hawk Mountain Rd., Kempton,
610-756-6961
Hawk and eagle flights visible with binoculars from lookouts mid-August-mid-December; museum, bookstore.

Wanamaker, Kempton & Southern, Inc
42 Community Center Dr., Kempton,
610-756-6469;
www.kemptontrain.com

A six-mile, 40-minute round trip on steam or diesel train along the Ontelaunee Creek at the foot of Hawk Mountain. Model railroad (Sunday), antique shop. Snack bar, picnic area. Steam train (July-August and October: Saturday and Sunday afternoons; May and June: Sunday afternoons). Diesel train (June and September: first and third Saturday afternoons only). Also special events throughout the year.

KENNETT SQUARE

Information: Chester County Conference and Visitors Bureau, 400 Exton Square Pkwy., Exton, 610-280-6145, 800-228-9933 or the Southeastern Chester County Chamber of Commerce, 206 E. State St., Kennett Square, 610-444-0774; www.scccc.com

WHAT TO SEE AND DO
Longwood Gardens
Route 1, Kennett Square,
610-388-1000;
www.longwoodgardens.org
Longwood Gardens is a stately horticultural display garden created by Pierre S. du Pont, offering more than 1,000 acres of indoor and outdoor gardens, woodlands and meadows. Lovers of living things are treated to greenhouses heated year-round, more than 10,000 different types of plants, spectacular fountains, flower shows and gardening demonstrations. Children's programs are available as well. The Orangery and Exhibition Hall are centerpieces, with a sunken marble floor flooded with reflective water. Daily.

SPECIALTY LODGINGS
Kennett House Bed and Breakfast
503 W. State St., Kennett Square,
610-444-9592, 800-820-9592;
www.kennetthouse.com

4 rooms. Complimentary full breakfast. American Foursquare house built in 1910; Victorian decor. $

RESTAURANTS
★★Kennett Square Inn
201 E. State St.,
Kennett Square,
610-444-5687;
www.kennettinn.com
Lunch, dinner. Bar. Restored country inn (1835). $$$

★★Terrace
Longwood Gardens,
Kennett Square,
610-388-6771;
www.longwoodgardens.org
Lunch, dinner. Closed January-March. Bar. Children's menu. Outdoor seating. Admission to Longwood Gardens required. $$

★
★
★
★
★

KING OF PRUSSIA
Originally named Reeseville for the Welsh family that owned the land, the town renamed itself after the local inn, which is still standing.
Information: Valley Forge Convention & Visitors Bureau, 600 W. Germantown Pike, Plymouth Meeting, 610-834-1550; www.valleyforge.org

WHAT TO SEE AND DO

King of Prussia Mall

160 N. Gulph Rd., King of Prussia,
610-265-5727;
www.kingofprussiamall.com

The king of malls on the eastern seaboard is located just 18 miles west of central Philadelphia. Bloomingdales, Neiman Marcus, Nordstrom, Macy's, Lord & Taylor, JCPenney, Sears and Strawbridge's anchor this mall, and its 365 specialty shops and 40 restaurants will keep you from staying in one place too long.

HOTELS

★Best Western The Inn At King Of Prussia

127 S. Gulph Rd., Hwy. 202 N, King of Prussia,
610-265-4500, 800-780-7234;
www.bestwestern.com

168 rooms. Complimentary continental breakfast. Airport transportation available. **$**

★★Crowne Plaza

260 Mall Blvd., King of Prussia,
610-265-7500, 800-496-7621;
www.crowneplaza.com
225 rooms. **$**

★★Doubletree Hotel

640 W. Germantown Pike, Plymouth Meeting,
610-834-8300, 800-222-8733;
www.doubletree.com

252 rooms, all suites. Airport transportation available. **$$**

★Holiday Inn Express Hotel & Suites King Of Prussia

260 N. Gulph Rd., King of Prussia,
610-768-9500, 800-315-2621

210 rooms. Complimentary continental breakfast. **$**

★★★Radnor Hotel

591 E. Lancaster Ave., Saint Davids,
610-688-5800, 800-537-3000;
www.radnorhotel.com

171 rooms. Airport transportation available. **$$**

★Springhill Suites

430 Plymouth Rd., Plymouth Meeting,
610-940-0400;
www.marriott.com

201 rooms. Complimentary continental breakfast. **$**

RESTAURANTS

★★Creed's

499 N. Gulph Rd., King of Prussia,
610-265-2550;
www.creedskop.com

Seafood, steak menu. Lunch, dinner. Closed Sunday; also first week in July. Bar. **$$**

★★Lotus Inn

402 W. Swedesford Road, Berwyn,
610-725-8888

Chinese, Japanese menu. Lunch, dinner. Bar. Children's menu. Reservations recommended. **$$**

KULPSVILLE

Information: Valley Forge Country Convention & Visitors Bureau, 600 W. Germantown Pike, Plymouth Meeting, 610-834-1550; www.valleyforge.org

WHAT TO SEE AND DO

Morgan Log House

850 Weikel Rd., Kulpsville,
215-368-2480;
www.morganloghouse.org

(1695) Built by the grandfather of General Daniel Morgan and Daniel Boone, this is the oldest and finest surviving medieval-style log house in the country. Partially restored; authentic early 18th-century furnishings. It exhibits fine, early antiques, including 18th-century Pennsylvania furniture. Guided tours. April-December: weekends; other times by appointment.

RESTAURANTS

★★Mainland Inn

17 Main St., Kulpsville,
215-256-8500;
www.themainlandinn.com

Seafood menu. Lunch, dinner. Sunday brunch. Bar. **$$$**

KUTZTOWN

Home of a popular folk festival, Kutztown is named for its founder, George Kutz. The town's population includes many descendants of the Pennsylvania Germans.

WHAT TO SEE AND DO

Crystal Cave Park

963 Crystal Cave Rd., Kutztown, 610-683-6765; www.crystalcavepa.com

Discovered in 1871; crystal formations, stalactites, stalagmites, natural bridges—all enhanced by indirect lighting. Also museum (July-September); nature trail; miniature golf (July-September; fee); theater. Cafe, rock shop, gift shop. Tours. March-November: Daily.

SPECIAL EVENTS

Folk Festival

Festival Grounds, Kutztown, 215-679-9610

Celebration of Pennsylvania Dutch folk culture; quilts, music, dancing and food of Plain and Fancy Dutch. Craftspeople make baskets, brooms, rugs, toleware and other handcrafts. Late June-early July.

RESTAURANTS

★★New Smithville Country Inn

10425 Old Route 22, Kutztown, 610-285-2987

Breakfast, lunch, dinner. Closed Memorial Day, Labor Day. Bar. Children's menu. $$

LAHASKA

WHAT TO SEE AND DO

Peddler's Village

Hwys. 202 and 263, Lahaska, 215-794-4000; www.peddlersvillage.com

This 18th-century-style country village with 42 acres of landscaped gardens and winding brick paths makes a great day trip from Philadelphia. Browse through a selection of more than 70 specialty shops for handicrafts, toys, accessories, leather goods, collectibles and gourmet foods. Take the kids for a ride on an antique carousel, or take advantage of the many free family events and seasonal festivals. Daily.

Also in village is:

Carousel World

Peddlers Village Shop #165, Lahaska, 215-794-8960

Learn about history of the carousel in turn-of-the-century park. Antique carousel rides.

SPECIAL EVENTS

Scarecrow Festival

Peddler's Village, between Highways 202 and 263, Lahaska, 215-794-4000

Scarecrow making, pumpkin painting. Jack-o-lantern and gourd art contest. Square dancing, entertainment. September.

Teddy Bear's Picnic

Peddler's Village, between Highways 202 and 263, Lahaska, 215-794-4000

Teddy bear vendors, parades, competitions. "Bear clinic" for "hurt" bears. Appraisals. Music. July.

HOTELS

★★★Golden Plough Inn

41 Peddlersvillage, Lahaska, 215-794-4004; www.peddlersvillage.com

72 rooms. Complimentary continental breakfast. $

RESTAURANTS

★★Cock N' Bull

Hwys. 202 and 263, Lahaska, 215-794-4000; www.peddlersvillage.com

Steak menu. Dinner. Bar. Casual attire. Reservations recommended. $$

PENNSYLVANIA

★

★

★

★

LAKE HARMONY

WHAT TO SEE AND DO

Big Boulder
Hwy. 940 and Moseywood Rd.,
Lake Harmony, 570-722-0100
Five double, two triple chairlifts; patrol, school, rentals, snowmaking; cafeteria, bar, nursery, lodge. Night skiing. Longest run approximately 3/4 mile; vertical drop 475 feet. December-March: daily.

HOTELS

★★Ramada
Hwy. 940, off I-80,
Lake Harmony,
570-443-8471, 800-251-2610;
www.ramada.com
138 rooms. Airport transportation available.
$

LAKEVILLE

WHAT TO SEE AND DO

Claws 'N Paws Wild Animal Park
1475 Ledgedale Rd., Lakeville,
570-698-6154
A zoo in the woods with more than 100 species of exotic animals. Petting zoo with tame deer, lambs and goats. Farmyard area. Parrot, reptile shows; zookeeper talks (schedule varies). Picnicking, snack bar. May-October: daily.

HOTELS

★★Caesars Cove Haven
Hwy. 590, Lakeville,
570-226-2101
276 rooms. Complimentary continental breakfast. Airport transportation available.
$$

PENNSYLVANIA

★
★
★
★
★

LANCASTER

Lancaster blends the industrial modern, the colonial past and the Pennsylvania Dutch present. It is in the heart of the Pennsylvania Dutch Area, one of the East's most colorful tourist attractions. To fully appreciate the area, visitors should leave the main highways and travel on country roads, which Amish buggies share with automobiles. Lancaster was an important provisioning area for the armies of the French and Indian and Revolutionary wars. Its crafters turned out fine guns, which brought the city fame as the "arsenal of

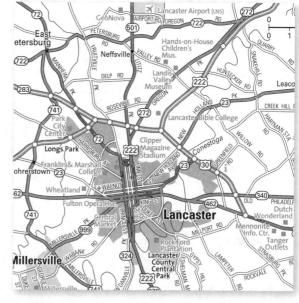

the Colonies." When Congress, fleeing Philadelphia, paused here on September 27, 1777, the city was the national capital for one day. It was the state capital from 1799 to 1812.

Information: Pennsylvania Dutch Convention & Visitors Bureau, 501 Greenfield Rd., Lancaster, 717-299-8901, 800-723-8824; www.padutchcountry.com

PENNSYLVANIA DUTCH AREA

In the 18th century, great waves of immigrants from Germany's Rhineland and Palatinate settled in Pennsylvania, first near Philadelphia and then farther west. Because they retained their customs and speech, and developed bountiful farms, the Pennsylvania Dutch (corruption of the German "Deutsch") and their communities are one of the state's greatest tourist attractions.

Descendants of Pennsylvania's original German immigrants all share tremendous vigor, family devotion, love of the Bible and belief in thrift and hard work. Many of the plain people—Amish, Old Order Mennonites and Bretren (Dunkards)—still live much as they did a century ago. Married men wear beards, black coats and low-crowned hats. Women wear bonnets and long, simple dresses. They drive horses and buggies rather than cars, work long hours in the field and shun the use of modern farm machinery, and turn to the Bible for guidance. Despite their dated methods, they are master farmers, among the first to rotate crops and practice modern fertilization methods. Their harvests are among the best in the country.

Many Amish regard photographs as "graven images." Visitors should not take pictures of individuals without their permission.

Information: www.padutch.com

WHAT TO SEE AND DO

Amish Farm and House
2395 Lincoln Hwy. E, Lancaster,
717-394-6185;
www.amishfarmandhouse.com
Typical Amish farm in operation. Lecture on the Amish and tour through early 19th-century stone buildings furnished and decorated as old-order Amish household; waterwheels, windmill, hand-dug well, carriages, spring wagon, sleighs. Daily.

Brunswick Tours
2102 Lincoln Hwy. E, Lancaster,
717-397-7541
Private guide and auto tape tours.

Dutch Wonderland
2249 Lincoln Hwy. E, Lancaster,
866-386-2839;
www.dutchwonderland.com
Family fun park with rides, botanical gardens, diving shows, shops. Monorail (fee). Memorial Day-Labor Day: daily; Mid-May-Memorial Day and after Labor Day-October: Saturday and Sunday.

National Wax Museum of Lancaster County
2251 Lincoln Hwy. E,
Lancaster,
717-393-3679
Figures re-create Lancaster County's history from the 1700s to present. Daily.

Franklin and Marshall College
Race and College Avenues,
Lancaster,
717-291-3981;
www.fandm.edu
(1787) (1,810 students.) Liberal arts college. Rothman Gallery showcases Pennsylvania-German artifacts: quilts, Fraktur and stoneware. More than 200 varieties of trees, plants and shrubs on grounds. Tours of campus.
Also here are:

Joseph R. Grundy Observatory
Lancaster,
717-291-4136
Holds 11-inch refractor and 16-inch reflecting telescope demonstrations.

PENNSYLVANIA

★
★
★
★
★

North Museum of Natural History and Science
400 College Ave., Lancaster,
717-291-3941;
www.northmuseum.org
General science and natural history; planetarium shows (Saturday and Sunday); children's Discovery Room; film series; monthly art exhibits. Tuesday-Sunday.

Fulton Opera House
12 N. Prince St., Lancaster,
717-394-7133
(1852) One of the oldest American theaters; many legendary people have performed here. It is believed that more than one ghost haunts the theater's Victorian interior. Professional regional theater; home of community theater, opera and symphony organizations.

Hans Herr House
1849 Hans Herr Dr., Lancaster,
717-464-4438;
www.hansherr.org
(1719) Example of medieval Germanic architecture; served as an early Mennonite meetinghouse and colonial residence of the Herr family. Mennonite rural life exhibit; blacksmith shop. House tours. April-November: Monday-Saturday; rest of year by appointment.

Heritage Center Museum of Lancaster County
13 W. King St., Lancaster,
717-299-6440;
www.lancasterheritage.com
(1795) Houses examples of early Lancaster County arts and crafts. Furniture, tall clocks, quilts, needlework, silver, pewter, rifles. Mid-April-early January: Tuesday-Saturday.

Historic Lancaster Walking Tour
100 S. Queen St.,
Lancaster,
717-392-1776
A 90-minute tour of historic downtown area. Costumed guide narrates 50 points of architectural or historic interest covering six square blocks. April-October: two tours daily Friday-Saturday, one tour daily Monday-Thursday and Sunday; rest of year, by appointment.

Historic Rock Ford
881 Rockford Rd., Lancaster,
717-392-7223;
www.rockfordplantation.org
(1794) Preserved home of General Edward Hand, Revolutionary War commander, member of Continental Congress. April-October: Tuesday-Friday and Sunday.

James Buchanan's Wheatland
1120 Marietta Ave., Lancaster,
717-392-8721;
www.wheatland.org
(1828) Residence of President James Buchanan from 1848 to 1868; restored Federal mansion with period rooms containing American Empire and Victorian furniture and decorative arts. Guided tours. April-October: daily; November: Friday-Monday. Christmas candlelight tours early December.

Landis Valley Museum
2451 Kissel Hill Rd., Lancaster,
717-569-0401;
www.landisvalleymuseum.org
Interprets Pennsylvania German rural life. Largest collection of Pennsylvania German objects in U.S.; craft and living history demonstrations (May-October); farmsteads, tavern, country store among other exhibit buildings. March-December: daily.

Mennonite Information Center
2209 Millstream Rd., Lancaster,
717-299-0954
Tourist information; interpretation of Mennonite and Amish origins beliefs. Free video. Monday-Saturday.
Also here is:

Hebrew Tabernacle Reproduction
2209 Millstream Rd., Lancaster,
717-299-0954
Tours Monday-Saturday.

Muddy Run LLC
Lancaster,
717-284-4325
Covers 700 acres with 100-acre lake for boating (rentals; no power boats), fishing;

picnicking, playgrounds, snack bar, concession, camping. Park April-early November.

Robert Fulton Birthplace
Lancaster,
717-548-2679
Robert Fulton, a great inventor and accomplished artist, is best known for having built the steamboat Clermont, which in 1807 successfully made a trip up the Hudson River against winds and strong current. This little stone house, where Fulton was born, was nearly destroyed by fire about 1822; now refurbished. Memorial Day-Labor Day: Saturday and Sunday.

The Watch and Clock Museum
514 Poplar St., Lancaster,
717-684-8261;
www.nawcc.org/museum/museum.htm
National Association of Watch and Clock Collectors living museum of timepieces and related tools and memorabilia. Over 8,000 items representing the 1600s to the present. Extensive research library. Special exhibitions. April-November: Tuesday-Sunday; December-March, Tuesday-Saturday.

SPECIAL EVENTS
Harvest Days
Landis Valley Museum,
2451 Kissel Hill Rd.,
Lancaster,
717-569-0401
Demonstrations of more than 80 traditional craft and harvest-time activities. Columbus Day weekend.

Old-Fashioned Sunday
1120 Marietta Ave., Lancaster,
717-392-8721
On grounds of Wheatland. Festivities include entertainment, magic show and 19th-century activities. Mid-May.

Sheep Shearing
Animal Farm and House, 2395 Lincoln Hwy. E, Lancaster, 717-394-6185
Last Thursday and Friday in April, first Friday in October.

Victorian Christmas Week
Wheatland, 1120 Marietta Ave., Lancaster,
717-392-8721
Early December.

HOTELS
★★Best Western Eden Resort Inn & Suites
222 Eden Rd., Lancaster,
717-569-6444;
www.bestwestern.com
276 rooms. Airport transportation available. $

★★Days Inn
30 Keller Ave.,
Lancaster,
717-299-5700, 800-329-7466;
www.daysinn.com
193 rooms. $

★Garden Spot Motel
2291 Lincoln Hwy. E,
Lancaster,
717-394-4736;
www.gardenspotmotel.com
19 rooms. Closed December-March. $

★Hershey Farm Motor Inn
240 Hartman Bridge Rd., Ronks,
717-687-8635, 800-827-8635;
www.hersheyfarm.com
59 rooms. Complimentary full breakfast. $

★★Hilton Garden Inn Lancaster
101 Granite Run Dr.,
Lancaster,
717-560-0880, 877-782-9444
156 rooms. $

★★Holiday Inn
24 S. Willowdale Dr., Lancaster,
717-293-9500, 800-524-3817;
www.holidayinn.com
113 rooms. $

★★Holiday Inn
521 Greenfield Rd., Lancaster,
717-299-2551;
www.holidayinn.com
189 rooms. $

203

PENNSYLVANIA

★★Hotel Brunswick
151 Queen St., Lancaster,
717-397-4800, 800-821-9258;
www.hotelbrunswick.com
222 rooms. $

★★Willow Valley Resort
2416 Willow St., Pike, Lancaster,
717-464-2711, 800-444-1714;
www.willowvalley.com
342 rooms. Restaurant. Airport transportation available. $

SPECIALTY LODGINGS
Australian Walkabout Inn Bed and Breakfast
837 Village Rd., Lancaster, 717-464-0707;
www.walkaboutinn.com
8 rooms. Children over 10 years only. Complimentary full breakfast. $$

Country Living Inn
2406 Old Philadelphia Pike, Lancaster,
717-295-7295;
www.countrylivinginn.com
34 rooms. $

King's Cottage
1049 E. King St., Lancaster,
717-397-1017, 800-747-8717;
www.kingscottagebb.com
This bed-and-breakfast is nestled in the center of scenic Lancaster County. It provides a perfect location for travelers looking to explore Pennsylvania Dutch Country. The inn is a Spanish-style mansion providing a comfortable stay for travelers.
8 rooms. Children over 12 years only. Complimentary full breakfast. $$

O'Flaherty's Dingeldein House
1105 E. King St.,
Lancaster,
717-293-1723, 800-779-7765;
www.dingeldeinhouse.com
7 rooms. Complimentary full breakfast. Airport transportation available. $

RESTAURANTS
★★D & S Brasserie
1679 Lincoln Hwy. E,
Lancaster,
717-299-1694;
www.dandsbrasserie.com
American menu. Lunch, dinner. Bar. House built in 1925; original woodwork, fireplaces. Outdoor seating. $$$

★★★Haydn Zug's
1987 State St.,
East Petersburg,
717-569-5746;
www.haydnzugs.com
Owner and Chef Terry Lee hails from Petersburg. With its award-winning wine list and exceptional cuisine, Lee's restaurant makes a day journey worthwhile. Winner of the Wine Spectator Award of Excellence. American menu. Lunch, dinner. Closed Sunday-Monday. Bar. Casual attire. Reservations recommended. $$

★★Olde Greenfield Inn
595 Greenfield Rd.,
Lancaster,
717-393-0668;
www.theoldegreenfieldinn.com
American menu. Dinner. Bar. Children's menu. Casual attire. Outdoor seating. $$$

LEBANON
This industrial city, steeped in German traditions, is the marketplace for colorful Lebanon County. Many Hessians were confined here after the Battle of Trenton. Today, Lebanon bologna factories and food processing are important to the city's economy.
Information: Pennsylvania Rainbow Region Vacation Bureau,
625 Quentin Rd., Lebanon, 717-272-8555; www.visitlebanoncounty.com

WHAT TO SEE AND DO

Coleman Memorial Park

Hwy. 72 and N. 12th St.,
Lebanon,
717-228-4470

This 100-acre former estate has swimming pool (Memorial Day-Labor Day: daily; fee); tennis courts, athletic fields, picnic facilities. Fee for some activities. Park. Daily.

Daniel Weaver Company

15th Ave. and Weavertown Rd.,
Lebanon,
717-274-6100, 800-932-8377

Manufacturers, since 1885, of Weaver's Famous Lebanon Bologna and other wood-smoked gourmet meats; smoked in 100-year-old outdoor smokehouses. Samples. Tours. Monday-Saturday.

Stoevers Dam Recreational Area

943 Miller St., Lebanon,
717-228-4470

A 153-acre park with 52-acre lake for fishing, boating (electric motors only), canoeing; 1 1/2-mile trail for jogging, hiking and bicycling; primitive camping (permit only; fee). Nature trails; nature barn (April-October: Tuesday-Sunday; winter, by appointment). Community park. Daily.

Stoy Museum of the Lebanon County Historical Society

924 Cumberland St.,
Lebanon,
717-272-1473

Local historical museum containing 30 permanent room and shop displays on three floors of house built in 1773 and used as first county courthouse; research library. Tours. Monday-Friday, Sunday; closed Monday and Sunday of holiday weekends.

HOTELS

★★Quality Inn

625 Quentin Rd.,
Lebanon,
717-273-6771, 800-626-8242;
www.choicehotels.com
130 rooms. $

LEWISBERRY

WHAT TO SEE AND DO

Gifford Pinchot State Park

2200 Rosstown Rd.,
Lewisberry,
717-432-5011

Approximately 2,300 acres; 340-acre lake. Fishing, boating (rentals, mooring, launching). Hunting; hiking cross-country skiing, ice skating, ice fishing, ice boating. Picnicking, store. Tent and trailer sites, cabins. Nature center, interpretive center. Standard fees.

Ski Roundtop

925 Roundtop Rd.,
Lewisberry,
717-432-9631,
800-767-4766;
www.skiroundtop.com

Two quad, triple, two double chairlifts; two J-bars, one magic carpet, two tubing lifts; patrol, school, rentals, snowmaking; cafeteria, nursery. Longest run 4,100 feet; vertical drop 600 feet. Mid-November-mid-March: daily.

★
★
★
★
★

LEWISBURG

Home of Bucknell University (1846), this college community also has light industry. The Native American village of Old Muncy Town was located nearby before the region was opened by Ludwig (Lewis) Doerr.

Information: Susquehanna Valley Visitors Bureau, Rural Route 3, 81 Hafer Rd., Lewisburg, 570-524-7234, 800-525-7320; www.svvb.com

WHAT TO SEE AND DO
Packwood House Museum
15 N. Water St.,
Lewisburg,
570-524-0323;
www.packwoodhousemuseum.com
A three-story, 27-room log and frame building begun in the late 18th century. Former hostelry houses a wide-ranging collection of Americana, period furnishings, textiles and decorative arts. Changing exhibits; museum shop. Tours. Tuesday-Saturday.

Slifer House Museum
80 Magnolia Dr., Lewisburg,
570-524-2245
Elaborate three-story, 20-room Victorian mansion. First and second floors have been restored, complete with Victorian parlor, dining room, library and five bedrooms. April-late December: Tuesday-Sunday; rest of year: Tuesday-Friday afternoons, also by appointment.

HOTELS
★Best Western Country Cupboard Inn
Route 15 N, Lewisburg,
570-524-5500, 800-780-7234;
www.bestwestern.com
106 rooms. Complimentary continental breakfast. $

RESTAURANTS
★Country Cupboard
101 Hafer Rd., Lewisburg,
570-523-3211
Breakfast, lunch, dinner. Children's menu. Country dining. $$

LEWISTOWN
Surrounded by rich farmland and beautiful forested mountain ranges, Lewistown lies in the scenic Juniata River Valley in the heart of central Pennsylvania. Lewistown retains the charm of its rustic surroundings, which yearly attract thousands of sportsmen and outdoor enthusiasts to the area's fine hunting, fishing and camping facilities. A large Amish population that thrives on the farmland of the Kishacoquillas Valley has contributed greatly to the area's culture and heritage.
Information: Juniata Valley Area Chamber of Commerce, 1 W. Market St., Lewistown, 717-248-6713, 877-568-9739; www.juniatarivervalley.org

WHAT TO SEE AND DO
Reeds Gap State Park
Lewistown, 717-667-3622
Approximately 200 acres. Swimming pool, fishing; hiking, picnicking, snack bar. Tent sites only.

HOTELS
★★Clarion Hotel
13015 Furguson Valley Rd., Burnham,
717-248-4961, 877-424-6423;
www.choicehotels.com
119 rooms. $

LIGONIER
Fort Ligonier, built in 1758 by the British, was the scene of one of the key battles of the French and Indian War. It also served as a supply base during Pontiac's War in 1763.
Information: Ligonier Valley Chamber of Commerce, Town Hall, 120 E. Main St., Ligonier, 724-238-4200; www.ligonier.com

WHAT TO SEE AND DO
Fort Ligonier
Hwys. 30 and 711,
Ligonier,
724-238-9701
Reconstructed 18th-century British fort; includes buildings with period furnishings. Museum houses outstanding French and Indian War collection, 18th-century artifacts; introductory film. May-October: daily.

PENNSYLVANIA

Idlewild Park

Hwy. 30 E, Ligonier,
724-238-3666
Amusement rides, entertainment, picnicking, children's play area, water park. Memorial Day-late August: Tuesday-Sunday.
   Adjacent is:

Story Book Forest

US 30 E, Ligonier,
724-238-3666
Admission included with Idlewild Park. Children's park with animals, people and buildings portraying nursery rhymes. Memorial Day-late August: Tuesday-Sunday.

SPECIAL EVENTS
Fort Ligonier Days

120 E. Main St., Ligonier,
724-238-4200
Living history program of the French and Indian War. Parade, 150 juried crafters, food and special events. Usually second weekend in October.

Ligonier Highland Games and Gathering of the Clans of Scotland

Idlewild Park, Ligonier,
724-238-3666
Sports, massed pipe bands, Highland dancing competitions, Scottish fiddling; sheep dog, wool spinning and weaving demonstrations; genealogy booth. Scottish fair. First Saturday after Labor Day.

Ligonier Ice Fest

Ligonier,
724-238-4200
Professional ice sculptures on the Diamond and in front of businesses; collegiate ice-carving competition. Super Bowl weekend, January.

HOTELS
★★Ramada

216 W. Loyalhanna St., Ligonier,
724-238-9545, 800-272-6232;
www.ramada.com
66 rooms. $

LIMERICK

Information: Valley Forge Convention & Visitors Bureau, 600 W. Germantown Pike, Plymouth Meeting, 610-834-1550; www.valleyforge.org

WHAT TO SEE AND DO
Spring Mountain Ski Area

Limerick,
610-287-7900;
www.springmountain-fun.com
Triple, three double chairlifts; two rope tows; patrol, school, rentals, snowmaking; cafeteria, lodge. Longest run 1/2 mile; vertical drop 420 feet. Also camping available. (fee; hook-ups). Mid-December-mid-March: daily.

LOCK HAVEN

Founded on the site of pre-Revolutionary Fort Reed, the community takes its name from two sources. The lock of the Pennsylvania Canal once crossed the West Branch of the Susquehanna River here and the town was once a "haven" for the rafts and lumberjacks of nearby logging camps. Near the geographic center of the state, the town today is a center of commerce and small industry.

Information: Clinton County Tourist Promotion Agency, Court House Annex, 151 Susquehanna Ave., Lock Haven, 570-893-4037; www.clintoncountyinfo.com

WHAT TO SEE AND DO
Bucktail Natural Area

Scenic area extends from mountain rim to mountain rim for 75 miles from Lock Haven north to Renovo and west to Emporium. Connecting the three towns and weaving through the park is Highway 120, an outstanding drive through mountain scenery.

Historic site west of Renovo commemorates Bucktail Trail, which served pioneers and Civil War volunteers. Fishing.

Bull Run School House
Lock Haven, 570-893-4037
(1899) Only remaining one-room schoolhouse in county; fully restored with all of its original equipment. Waterbury clock, bell. Hours vary.

Heisey Museum
362 E. Water St., Lock Haven,
570-748-7254;
www.clintoncountyhistory.com
Victorian house museum; early 1800s kitchen; ice house containing logging, farming and canal artifacts. Tuesday-Friday; also by appointment.

Hyner View
At 2,000 feet, "Laurel Drive to the top of the world" provides panoramic view of valley, river, highway and forest. Site of state and national hang gliding competitions.

SPECIALTY LODGINGS
Victorian Inn Bed and Breakfast
402 E. Water St., Lock Haven,
570-748-8688, 888-653-8688;
www.victorianinnbnb.com
12 rooms. No children allowed. Complimentary full breakfast. Built in 1859; garden atrium. $

LUMBERVILLE

SPECIALTY LODGINGS
1740 House
3690 River Rd. Route 32,
Lumberville,
215-297-5661;
www.1740house.com
25 rooms. Complimentary full breakfast. $$

RESTAURANTS
★★Cuttalossa Inn
3478 River Rd. (PA 32), Lumberville,
215-297-5082;
www.cuttalossainn.com
American menu. Lunch, dinner. Closed Sunday; also three weeks in January. Bar. Outdoor seating. $$$

MANHEIM
Baron Henry William Stiegel founded Manheim and started manufacturing the flint glassware that bore his name. In 1770 he owned the town; by 1774 he was in debtor's prison, the victim of his own generosity and his poor choice of business associates. After his imprisonment, he made a meager living teaching here.
Information: Manheim Area Chamber of Commerce, 13 E. High St., Manheim, 717-665-6330; www.manheimchamber.com

WHAT TO SEE AND DO
Mount Hope Estate & Winery
2775 Lebanon Rd., Manheim,
717-665-7021
Restored sandstone mansion was originally built in the Federal style (circa 1800), then increased its size to 32 rooms with an extension built in 1895, which changed the house's style to Victorian. Turrets, winding walnut staircase, hand-painted 18-foot ceilings, Egyptian marble fireplaces, grand ballroom, crystal chandeliers; greenhouse, solarium, gardens. Wine tasting in billiards room. Daily.

Zion Lutheran Church
2 S. Hazel St., Manheim,
717-665-5880;
www.zionmanheim.com
(1891) Victorian-Gothic structure built on site of original church; Stiegel donated the ground (1772) in exchange for one red rose from the congregation every year. Monday-Friday.

SPECIAL EVENTS

Pennsylvania Renaissance Faire
83 Mansion House Rd.,
Manheim
Mt. Hope Estate and Winery. A 16th-century village is created in the acres of gardens surrounding the mansion. Eleven stages includes a jousting arena with capacity of 6,000. Highlights includes medieval jousting tournament, trial and dunking, human chess match, knighthood ceremonies. August-mid-October: weekends.

Rose Festival
Celebration during which a Stiegel descendant accepts annual rent of one red rose for church grounds. Second Sunday in June.

MEADVILLE

David Mead—Revolutionary War ensign, tavern-keeper and major general in the War of 1812—and his brothers established Mead's Settlement in 1788. Colonel Lewis Walker started the manufacture of "hookless slide fasteners" here; since 1923 these fasteners (now known as zippers) have been the leading local industry. The city is also a major producer of yarn and thread, and is home to many tool-and-die manufacturers.
Information: Crawford County Convention & Visitors Bureau, 16709 Conneaut Lake Rd., Meadville, 814-333-1258, 800-332-2338; www.visitcrawford.org

WHAT TO SEE AND DO

Allegheny College
485 Chestnut St.,
Meadville,
814-332-3100;
www.allegheny.edu
(1815) (1,850 students.) Bentley Hall (1820) is a fine example of Federalist architecture. Also on campus are Bowman, Penelec and Megahan Art Galleries. Library has colonial, Ida Tarbell and Lincoln collections. Tours of campus.

Baldwin-Reynolds House Museum
411 Chestnut St.,
Meadville,
814-333-9882
(1841-1843) Restored mansion of Henry Baldwin, congressman and U.S. Supreme Court justice. First and second floors refurbished in period; basement exhibits 19th-century kitchen and Land Office. Also on grounds is 1890 doctor's office. Elaborate landscaping on three-acre grounds feature pond and icehouse. Tours. Late May-Labor Day: Wednesday-Sunday.

Colonel Crawford Park
Meadville,
814-724-6879
Within park is Woodcock Creek Lake. Swimming (fee), fishing, boating; hunting, nature trail, picnicking, camping (fee). Park. Memorial Day-Labor Day: daily.

SPECIAL EVENTS

Crawford County Fair
Dickson Rd.,
Meadville,
814-337-2154
Third week in August.

HOTELS

★Days Inn
18360 Conneaut Lake Rd., Meadville,
814-337-4264, 800-329-7466;
www.daysinn.com
163 rooms. **$**

MEDIA

Information: Delaware County Convention & Visitors Bureau, 200 E. State St., Media, 610-565-3679, 800-343-3983; www.brandywinecvb.org

PENNSYLVANIA

WHAT TO SEE AND DO

Ridley Creek State Park
Media, 610-892-3900
Approximately 2,600 acres of woodlands and meadows. Fishing, hiking, bicycling, sledding, picnicking, playground.
Within park is:

Colonial Pennsylvania Plantation
Media, 610-566-1725
A 200-year-old farm is a living history museum that re-creates the life of a typical farm family of the late 1700s. Period tools and methods are used to perform seasonal and daily chores. Tours. Tuesday-Friday, by appointment. Visitors may participate in some activities. Mid-April-November: Saturday and Sunday.

Tyler Arboretum
515 Painter Rd., Media,
610-566-5431;
www.tylerarboretum.org
Approximately 650 acres of ornamental and native plants. Outdoor "living museum" with a 20-mile system of trails; special fragrant garden and bird garden; notable trees planted in the 1800s; bookstore. Guided walks and educational programs each week.

RESTAURANTS

★★D'Ignazio's Towne House
117 Veterans Square, Media,
610-566-6141;
www.townehouse.com
Italian, seafood menu. Dinner. Bar. Children's menu. Singing maitre'd. $$

MENDENHALL

HOTELS

★★Mendenhall Hotel
323 Kennett Pike, Mendenhall,
610-388-2100;
www.mendenhallinn.com
70 rooms. Complimentary continental breakfast. Airport transportation available. $

SPECIALTY LODGINGS

Fairville Inn
506 Kennett Pike, Mendenhall,
610-388-5900, 877-285-7772;
www.fairvilleinn.com
15 rooms. No children allowed. Complimentary continental breakfast. Built in 1826; antiques, period decor. View of surrounding countryside. $$

RESTAURANTS

★★Mendenhall Inn
Hwy. 52, Mendenhall, 610-388-1181;
www.mendenhallinn.com
American, French menu. Dinner. Sunday brunch. Bar. Children's menu. Business casual attire. Reservations recommended. Valet parking. $$$

MERCER

Information: Mercer Area Chamber of Commerce, 143 N. Diamond St., Mercer, 724-662-4185; www.mercerareachamber.com

WHAT TO SEE AND DO

Magoffin House Museum
119 S. Pitt St., Mercer,
724-662-3490
(1821) Houses collection of Native American artifacts, pioneer tools, furniture, children's toys, clothing; military items. Some original furnishings, memorabilia. Special collection of artifacts from John Goodsell's trip to the North Pole with Peary in 1908-1909, as well as early maps, historic records; restored print shop. Tuesday-Saturday.

SPECIAL EVENTS

Penn's Woods West-Folk & Arts Festival
545 W. Butler St., Mercer,
412-662-1490
Fine arts and country crafts. 130 artisans, live entertainment and demonstrations, children's activities, home-cooked food. Mid February.

Wayne County Fair
545 W. Butler St.,
Mercer
Exhibits, livestock, horse racing. First full week in August.

HOTELS
★★Howard Johnson
835 Perry Hwy., Mercer,
724-748-3030, 800-542-7674;
www.hojo.com
102 rooms. Amish craft shop in lobby. $

MERCERSBURG

HOTELS
★★★Mercersburg Inn
405 S. Main St.,
Mercersburg,
717-328-5231;
www.mercersburginn.com
Located between the civil war battlefield and other historic sites, the Mercersburg Inn is a 15-room turn-of-the-century Georgian mansion. Golf courses, tennis facilities, skiing, fly fishing, mountain biking and hiking trails are all located within a short distance.
15 rooms. Complimentary full breakfast. $

RESTAURANTS
★★★Mercersburg Inn
405 S. Main St., Mercersburg,
717-328-5231;
www.mercersburginn.com
Built in 1909, this Georgian-style mansion resides in a charming, 230-year-old village. With both a prix fixe and an a la carte menu, the inn's restaurant serves entrees such as sautéed skate ala menuiere with capers, preserved lemon and caramelized onion risotto or rosemary lemon Cornish hen with roasted fingerling potatoes.
French menu. Dinner. Closed Sunday-Wednesday. Bar. Reservations recommended. $$$

MIDDLETOWN

RESTAURANTS
★★★Alfred's Victorian Restaurant
38 N. Union St., Middletown,
717-944-5373;
www.alfredsvictorian.com
Housed in a picturesque, 1888-Victorian brownstone, this 30-year-old restaurant offers five intimate dining rooms each with authentically restored design elements and period decor. The menu shows a northern Italian influence and offers 30 different entrees including lobster tail and filet mignon.
American, Italian menu. Lunch, dinner. Closed early January. Bar. Business casual attire. Reservations recommended. Outdoor seating. $$$

MILFORD
The borough of Milford was settled by Thomas Quick, a Hollander. Noted forester and conservationist Governor Gifford Pinchot lived here. His house, Grey Towers, is near the town.
Information: Pocono Mountains Vacation Bureau, 1004 Main St., Stroudsburg, 570-424-6050, 800-762-6667; www.poconos.org

WHAT TO SEE AND DO
Canoeing, Rafting, Kayaking and Tubing
Kittatinny Canoes. Milford,
570-828-2338, 800-356-2852
Trips travel down the Delaware River. Camping. Mid-April-October: daily.

Dingmans Falls and Silver Thread Falls
Milford,
570-588-2451
Part of Delaware Water Gap National Recreation Area. Two of the highest waterfalls in the Pocono Mountains; many rhododendrons bloom in July.

Grey Towers
151 Grey Tower Dr., Milford,
570-296-6401
(1886) A 100-acre estate originally built as summer house for philanthropist James W. Pinchot; became residence of his son, Gifford Pinchot, "father of American conservation," governor of Pennsylvania and first chief of USDA Forest Service. Now site of Pinchot Institute for Conservation Studies. Tours. Memorial Day weekend-Labor Day weekend: daily; after Labor Day-Veterans Day: afternoons Monday and Friday-Sunday; rest of year, by appointment; occasionally closed for conferences.

HOTELS
★★★Cliff Park Inn
155 Cliff Park Rd.,
Milford,
570-296-6491, 800-225-6535;
www.cliffparkinn.com
The Clifford Park Inn is located on 500 acres overlooking the Delaware River. With 14 guestrooms, three restaurants, seven miles of hiking trails, a nine-hole golf course and free wireless Internet access, this inn might encourage you to extend your stay. Nearby activities include cross-country skiing, hiking trails, swimming and more.
18 rooms. Classic country inn; originally a farmhouse built 1820. **$**

★Myer Motel
600 Hwys. 6 and 209,
Milford,
570-296-7223, 800-764-6937;
www.myermotel.com
20 rooms. **$**

MONTGOMERYVILLE

HOTELS
★Comfort Inn
PA 309, 678 Bethlehem Pike,
Montgomeryville,
215-361-3600, 877-424-6423;
www.choicehotels.com
84 rooms. Complimentary continental breakfast. **$**

RESTAURANTS
★★★Joseph Ambler Inn
1005 Horsham Rd., Montgomeryville,
215-362-7500;
www.josephamblerinn.com
Complex combinations of local fare and European cuisine make up the innovative menu at this rustic country inn. Executive Chef Meg Votta and her team offer entrees such as grilled day boat scallops with sweet corn, potato and bacon chowder and tarragon butter; and Lancaster County roast half chicken with citrus, a rosemary and garlic rub, creamed potatoes and summer beans.
Dinner. Bar. In 1820s stone barn. Outdoor seating. **$$$**

MOUNT JOY

WHAT TO SEE AND DO
Bube's Brewery
102 N. Market St.,
Mount Joy,
717-653-2056;
www.bubesbrewery.com
Historic brewery built before the Civil War is the only brewery left in the country that has remained intact since the mid-1800s; now operates as a restaurant. Guided tours take visitors 43 feet below the street into the brewery's aging vaults

and passages, built from a cave and later part of the Underground Railroad; narrator tells history of brewery and explains methods of producing beer in a Victorian-age brewery. Tours Memorial Day-Labor Day: daily. Restaurant open all year. Free tour included with reservations for Catacombs restaurant.

Donegal Mills Plantation & Inn
Mount Joy,
717-653-2168
Historic village and resort dating from 1736. Mansion, bake house, gardens; restaurant and lodging (year-round). Plantation tours March-December: Saturday and Sunday afternoons.

RESTAURANTS
★★Catacombs at Bube's Brewery
102 N. Market St.,
Mount Joy,
717-653-2056;
www.bubesbrewery.com
American menu. Lunch, dinner. Bar. Outdoor seating. Guided tours. $$$

★★Groff's Farm Restaurant
650 Pinkerton Rd.,
Mount Joy,
717-653-2048;
www.groffsfarmgolfclub.com
Dinner. Closed weekdays January-mid-February. Children's menu. Reservations recommended. $$

MOUNT POCONO
One of the many thriving resort communities in the heart of the Pocono Mountains, Mount Pocono offers recreation year-round in nearby parks, lakes and ski areas.
Information: Pocono Mountains Vacation Bureau, 1004 Main St., Stroudsburg, 570-424-6050, 800-762-6667; www.poconos.org

WHAT TO SEE AND DO
Memorytown, USA
Grange Rd., Mount Pocono,
570-839-1680
Old-time village includes hex shop, country store, store with artifacts, ice-cream parlor; paddle-boats, entertainment, lodging, restaurant and tavern. Summer festivals. Fee for some activities. Daily.

Mount Airy Lodge Ski Area
42 Wood Land, Mount Pocono,
800-441-4410;
www.mountairylodge.com
Two double chairlifts; patrol, school, rentals, snowmaking; cafeteria, restaurant, bar, nursery, lodge. Longest run 1,800 feet; vertical drop 250 feet. Also country trails. Mid-December-late March.

Mount Pocono Campground
30 Edgewood Rd., Mount Pocono,
570-839-8950;
www.mtpoconocampground.com
Enjoy campsites for every need on 42 wooded acres in sunny or shaded locations.

RV, trailer and tent sites; full hook-ups (with cable), water and electrical hook-ups, electrical hook-ups, or no hook-ups. Convenience store; outdoor pool, children's pool; hiking, playground, volleyball court, picnic areas, game room.

Pocono Knob
Excellent view of surrounding countryside.

Summit Lanes
3 Park Dr. E, Pocono Summit,
570-839-9635;
www.summitlanes.com
Summit Lanes is a terrific bowling center with 36 new state-of-the-art synthetic lanes and automatic scorers with color monitors. It also has a billiards area, food court, pro shop, lounge and video game room. Daily; glow bowling Saturday 9:30 p.m.-2 a.m.

HOTELS
★★★Caesars Paradise Stream
Hwy. 940, Mount Pocono,
570-226-2101, 800-432-9932;
www.caesarsparadisestream.com

213

For that honeymoon experience for which the Poconos are so well known, Caesars is the place to stay. These are all-inclusive resorts, with heart-shaped tubs, round beds and champagne glass-shaped whirlpools that offer a romantic contrast to a day at the races. Big-name entertainers often appear at Caesars.

164 rooms. No children allowed. Restaurant, bar. Tennis. **$$$**

★★★Crescent Lodge
191 Paradise Valley, Mt. Pocono,
570-595-7486, 800-392-9400;
www.crescentlodge.com

Nestled in the heart of the Pocono Mountains, the Cresecnt Lodge is elegant and welcoming. Guests enjoy uniquely furnished guest rooms, with some offering sunken jacuzzis, private patios and sundecks overlooking the well-maintained grounds.

31 rooms. Complimentary continental breakfast. **$**

★★★Pocono Manor Inn and Golf Club
Hwy. 314, Pocono Manor,
570-839-7111, 800-233-8150;
www.poconomanor.com

Less than two hours from New York, this "Grand Lady of the Mountains" has been in business since 1902. Its rooms are well-appointed and tasteful, in keeping with its spot on the National Register of Historic Places.

Golf, horseback riding, swimming and tennis are all available on the 3,100-acre estate, as are fishing, clay shooting and more.

255 rooms. Children's activity center. **$$**

★★★Skytop Lodge
1 Skytop, Mt. Pocono,
570-595-7401, 800-345-7759;
www.skytop.com

Skytop Lodge is the ultimate mountain getaway for outdoor enthusiasts, with an 18-hole golf course, seven tennis courts, a clay shooting range, indoor and outdoor pools and fly fishing in the natural streams found throughout the property. This retreat in the heart of the Poconos is easily accessed from New York or Philadelphia. Accommodations are offered within the historic hotel, four-bedroom cottages, or the intimate golf course inn. The continental menu at the Windsor Dining Room (jacket required) draws a crowd, while more casual dining is available at the Lake View Dining Room and the Tap Room.

185 rooms. Children's activity center. Beach. **$$$$**

RESTAURANTS
★Tokyo Teahouse
Hwy. 940, Pocono Summit,
570-839-8880;
www.tokyoteahouse.us

Japanese menu. Lunch, dinner. Closed Tuesday. **$$**

NEW CASTLE

At the junction of the Shenango, Mahoning and Beaver rivers, New Castle was long an important Native American trading center; the Delawares used it as their capital. Today the fireworks and plastics industries have become an integral part of the community.

Information: Lawrence County Tourist Promotion Agency, Celli Central Station, 229 S. Jefferson, New Castle, 724-654-8408, 888-284-7599; www.visitlawrencecounty.com

WHAT TO SEE AND DO
Greer House
408 N. Jefferson,
New Castle,
724-658-4022

Turn-of-the-century restored mansion houses the Lawrence County Historical Society. Museum has extensive Shenango and Castleton china collections, Sports Hall of Fame, fireworks room. Archives, workshops and speakers. Tuesday-Saturday; also by appointment.

Hoyt Institute of Fine Arts
124 E. Leasure Ave., New Castle,
724-652-2882

Cultural arts center housed in two early 20th-century mansions on four acres of landscaped grounds; permanent art collection, changing exhibits, period rooms, performing arts programs, classes. Tours. Tuesday-Saturday.

Living Treasures Animal Park
Hwy. 422, New Castle,
724-924-9571
Pet and feed over 100 species from around the world. Memorial Day-Labor Day: daily; May, September, October: weekends.

McConnell's Mill State Park
New Castle,
724-368-8091
Approximately 2,500 acres. Century-old mill surrounded by beautiful landscape and scenery. Fishing, hunting, whitewater boating. Hiking. Picnicking, store. Historical center, interpretive program.

Scottish Rite Cathedral
614 Center Ave.,
New Castle,
724-654-6683
On hillside; six 32-foot columns dominate city's skyline. Large auditorium; ballroom. Local Masonic headquarters. Tours by appointment.

HOTELS
★Comfort Inn
1740 New Butler Rd., New Castle,
724-658-7700, 877-424-6423;
www.choicehotels.com
79 rooms. Complimentary continental breakfast. $

RESTAURANTS
★★The Tavern
108 N. Market St., New Wilmington,
724-946-2020
Lunch, dinner. Closed Tuesday. $$

NEW HOPE

The river village of New Hope was originally the largest part of a 1,000-acre land grant from William Penn to Thomas Woolrich of Shalford, England. In the 20th century, the area gained fame as the home of artists and literary and theatrical personalities.
Information: Information Center, 1 W. Mechanic St., New Hope, 215-862-5880, or Bucks County Conference and Visitors Bureau, 152 Swamp Road, Doylestown, 215-345-4552, 800-836-2825;
www.buckscounty.travel

PENNSYLVANIA

WHAT TO SEE AND DO
Coryell's Ferry
22 S. Main St., New Hope,
215-862-2050
Passenger and charter rides aboard the Major William C. Barnett, a 65-foot Mississippi-style stern-wheel riverboat, on the Delaware River. Memorial Day-Labor Day: daily; call for extended season.

Ghost Tours
Main and Ferry Streets, New Hope,
215-957-9988
Follow a lantern-led walk to learn about the area's ghosts. October: Friday and Saturday evenings; June-September: Saturday evening only.

New Hope & Ivyland Railroad
32 W. Bridge St., New Hope,
215-862-2332;
www.newhoperail.com
A nine-mile, 50-minute narrated train ride through Bucks County. Reading Railroad passenger coaches from the 1920s depart from restored 1890 New Hope Station. Early April-November: daily; December: special Santa Train Friday-Sunday; rest of year: weekends.

Parry Barn
S. Main St., New Hope
Opposite mansion. (1784) Owned by New Hope Historical Society; operated as commercial art gallery.

★
★
★
★
★
☆

BUCKS COUNTY

Over the years, literary references to Bucks County, just north of Philadelphia, have been plentiful, and with good reason. Manhattan literati, including Broadway's Moss Hart and George S. Kaufman, and the acerbic writer Dorothy Parker, have favored this woodland retreat along the Delaware River for decades. Though estate-sized homes are popping up in the privileged realm, the rumpled landscape still retains the look of a Currier and Ives print. Stately, old fieldstone houses stand beneath towering trees, and stalks of ripening corn march across the fields. Nearby, the wide and peaceful Delaware flows quietly past.

A one-day, 75-mile loop out of New Hope provides a rewarding glimpse of Bucks County's scenic and cultural appeal. Begin in New Hope. A colonial-era ferry crossing on the main road between Philadelphia and New York, the town is dotted with old stone structures sandwiched between the river and the Delaware Canal. Shops here are worth visiting; several feature exquisite handmade crafts of local and national artisans. Many visitors come simply to stroll the old streets and enjoy the cafés, pubs and ice cream parlors. You can hike or bicycle on the canal tow path. If you're in town on Saturday or Tuesday morning, drop by Rice's Market on Greenhill Road, a 10-minute drive northwest of New Hope. Set in a 30-acre field, the market is the next best thing to an old-fashioned county fair. More than 200 vendors haul in booths selling merchandise such as produce, plants and flowers, crafts, furniture pieces and clothing, often at bargain prices.

To see more of the county, return to New Hope and take River Road (SR 32) north. The road winds alongside the Delaware River for about 25 miles to Kintnersville. Quaint river towns, mostly a cluster of old homes, dot the route. The stretch of road between New Hope and Lumberville passes a river setting that in the early years of the century, drew a number of landscape artists who formed a colony of Pennsylvania Impressionists in the hamlet of Phillips Mill. You can't miss it; River Road makes a sharp turn here. Today, their work can be seen in a permanent exhibit called Visual Heritage of Bucks County at the James A. Michener Art Museum in Doylestown, ahead on this drive.

In Kintnersville, take Route 611, the Lackawanna Trail, south to Doylestown. Visit the Michener Museum, which also features an exhibit detailing the Broadway and Hollywood legends who have lived in the county. Save time for the three castle-like structures that archeologist and historian Henry Chapman Mercer bequeathed his hometown. Turrets, towers and parapets adorn the buildings, all built between 1908 and 1916 in a free-form style of reinforced concrete. The Moravian Pottery and Tile Works, which resembles a Spanish-colonial mission, houses Mercer's innovative tile factory. On the same 70-acre grounds stands Fonthill, Mercer's 44-room mansion, a fairy-tale creation of strange nooks and crannies adorned with decorative titles from his factory and around the world. A mile away, the seven-story Mercer Museum houses an important collection of furnishings, folk art and implements of early America. Conclude this drive by returning to New Hope via Routes 202 and 179. Approximately 75 miles.

PENNSYLVANIA

Parry Mansion Museum

S. Main and Ferry Streets,
New Hope,
215-862-5652

(1784) Restored stone house built by Benjamin Parry, prosperous merchant and mill owner. Eleven rooms on view, restored and furnished to depict period styles from late 18th to early 20th centuries. May-December: Friday-Sunday; also by appointment.

SPECIAL EVENTS

New Hope Arts and Crafts Festival

1 W. Mechanic St.,
New Hope,
215-862-5880

Contemporary and traditional crafts. Painting, photography, sculpture. October.

HOTELS

★★★Hotel du Village

2535 N. River Rd.,
New Hope,
215-862-9911;
www.hotelduvillage.com

Simple and intimate, Hotel du Village offers 20 cozy guest rooms, two tennis courts, a pool and a restaurant that specializes in French country cuisine. Tennis. $

★★★The Inn at Bowman's Hill

518 Lurgan Rd.,
New Hope,
215-862-8090;
www.theinnatbowmanshill.com

The Inn at Bowman's Hill consists of stone and stucco buildings sitting on five acres of well-manicured grounds. An 80-foot stream runs out front, and the property adjoins the Bowman's Hill Wildflower Preserve. The decor and furnishings are rustic but very upscale, with lots of natural wood. Guest rooms are intimate, with gas fireplaces and large whirlpool tubs. Guests can enjoy a three-course gourmet breakfast in the breakfast room or in their own rooms, and afternoon snacks are offered from 3 to 7 p.m.
6 rooms. No children allowed. Complimentary full breakfast. $$$

★★★The Mansion Inn

9 S. Main St., New Hope,
215-862-1231;
www.themansioninn.com

This grand 1865 Baroque Victorian mansion is located along a tranquil canal in the center of downtown New Hope, within walking distance to numerous shops and restaurants, as well as the Michener Art Museum. The stately building welcomes guests with its garden, gazebo, refreshing outdoor pool and beautifully decorated Empire/French Victorian rooms.
7 rooms. Children over 14 years only. Complimentary full breakfast. Restaurant, bar. $$

SPECIALTY LODGINGS

1870 Wedgwood Inn of New Hope

111 W. Bridge St., New Hope,
215-862-3936;
www.1870wedgwoodinn.com

Built in 1870, this inn features antiques and a large Wedgwood collection. Carriage rides are available.
12 rooms. Complimentary full breakfast. $

Aaron Burr House

80 W. Bridge St., New Hope,
215-862-2343;
www.new-hope-inn.com

5 rooms. Complimentary full breakfast. Built in 1873. $

Fox and Hound Bed and Breakfast of New Hope

246 W. Bridge St., New Hope,
215-862-5082, 800-862-5082;
www.foxhoundinn.com

8 rooms. Children over 12 years only. Complimentary continental breakfast. Stone manor house built in 1850. $

Pineapple Hill Bed and Breakfast

1324 River Rd.,
New Hope,
215-862-1790, 888-866-8404;
www.pineapplehill.com

8 rooms. Complimentary full breakfast. Built in 1790. $

217

PENNSYLVANIA

RESTAURANTS

★★Centre Bridge Inn
2998 N. River Rd., New Hope,
215-862-9139;
www.centrebridgeinn.com
International/Fusion menu. Dinner. Closed
Monday-Tuesday. Bar. Business casual
attire. Reservations recommended (weekends). Valet parking (weekends). Outdoor
seating. **$$$**

★★★The Champagne Room
9 S. Main St., New Hope,
215-862-1231;
www.themansioninn.com
Situated in the Mansion Inn, this casual yet
stately restaurant offers continental cuisine
in candlelit dining rooms. Along with a sig-
nature champagne cocktail, the restaurant
serves entrees including pan-seared sea
scallops with lobster ravioli, porcini mush-
rooms, cream sauce and sautéed organic
spinach or a pan-seared rack of lamb chops
with coriander and cumin served over yel-
low beet Yukon gold mash and topped with
goat cheese, crispy shoestring sweet pota-
toes and port wine demi-glaze.
Continental menu. Lunch, dinner. Closed
Tuesday; open weekends only in January-
April. Bar. Business casual attire. Reser-
vations recommended. Outdoor seating.
$$$

★★The Inn at Phillips Mill
2590 N. River Rd., New Hope,
215-862-9919

French menu. Dinner. Closed four weeks in
January/early February. Casual attire. Res-
ervations recommended. Outdoor seating.
No credit cards accepted. **$$$**

★★★Odette's
S. River Rd., New Hope,
215-862-2432;
www.odettes.com
Odette's, originally built in 1794 as a barge-
man's inn, overlooks the Delaware River
and is a short drive from the downtown
New Hope area. A piano bar is featured
nightly in the tavern area, and frequent cab-
aret shows are also offered. Guests can dine
in one of four riverside dining areas while
enjoying such dishes as gorgonzola strip
steak, seared yellowfish tuna and sauteed
chicken breast.
American menu. Lunch, dinner. Sunday
brunch. Bar. Children's menu. Reservations
recommended. Valet parking. **$$$**

★Spotted Hog
Hwys. 202 and 263,
New Hope,
215-794-4040;
www.peddlersvillage.com
Breakfast, lunch, dinner. Bar. Children's
menu. **$$**

NEW STANTON
Information: Laurel Highlands Visitors Bureau, Town Hall, 120 E. Main St.,
Ligonier, 724-238-5661; www.laurelhighlands.org

WHAT TO SEE AND DO

L. E. Smith Glass Co
1900 Liberty St., New Stanton,
724-547-3544;
www.lesmithglass.com
Reproductions of several styles of antique
handcrafted glass. Tours. Children under
six years not admitted on tour. Monday-
Friday; closed first two weeks in July.

HOTELS

★★Days Inn
127 W. Byers Ave.,
New Stanton,
724-925-3591, 800-329-7466;
www.daysinn.com
135 rooms. **$**

NORRISTOWN

William Penn, Jr., owner of the 7,600-acre tract around Norristown, sold it to Isaac Norris and William Trent for 50 cents an acre in 1704. It became a crossroads for colonial merchants and soldiers; Washington's army camped nearby. Dutch, German, Swedish, Welsh and English immigrants all left their mark on the city. Today Norristown is still a transportation hub.

Information: Valley Forge Convention and Visitors Bureau, 600 W. Germantown Pike, Plymouth Meeting, 610-834-1550; www.valleyforge.org

WHAT TO SEE AND DO

Elmwood Park Zoo
1661 Harding Blvd.,
Norristown,
610-277-3825;
www.elmwoodparkzoo.org
Features extensive North American waterfowl area; cougars, bobcats, bison, elk; outdoor aviary; children's zoo barn; museum with exhibit on animal senses. Daily.

HOTELS

★★★Sheraton Bucks County Hotel
400 Oxford Valley Rd., Norristown,
215-547-4100, 800-325-3535;
www.sheraton.com
187 rooms. Restaurant, bar. **$$**

RESTAURANTS

★★★The Jefferson House
2519 DeKalb Pike, Norristown,
610-275-3407
American menu. Lunch, dinner. Sunday brunch. Bar. Children's menu. **$$$**

NORTH EAST

When Pennsylvania bought the tract containing North East from the federal government in 1778, the state gained 46 miles of Lake Erie frontage, a fine harbor and some of the best Concord grape terrain in the nation.

Information: Chamber of Commerce, 21 S. Lake St., North East, 814-725-4262; www.nechamber.org

WHAT TO SEE AND DO

Heritage Wine Cellars
12162 E. Main Rd., North East,
814-725-8015;
www.heritagewine.biz
Guided tours; wine tastings. Daily.

Mazza Vineyards
11815 E. Lake Rd., North East,
814-725-8695;
www.mazzawines.com
Guided tours; wine tastings. Daily.

Penn-Shore Vineyards and Winery
10225 E. Lake Rd., North East,
814-725-8688;
www.pennshore.com
Guided tours; wine tastings. Daily.

SPECIAL EVENTS

Cherry Festival
Concessions, rides, games, parade. Mid-July.

Wine Country Harvest Festival
21 S. Lake St.,
North East,
814-725-4262
Gravel Pit Park and Gibson Park. Arts and crafts, bands, buses to wineries, food. Last full weekend in September.

OIL CITY

Spreading on both sides of Oil Creek and the Allegheny River, Oil City was born of the oil boom. Oil refining and the manufacture of oil machinery are still its major occupations today. Nearby are natural gas fields.

Seven miles northwest stood the famous oil-boom town of Pithole, now a ghost town. In 1865, Pithole expanded from a single farmhouse to a population of more than 10,000 in five months as its first oil well brought in 250 barrels a day. When the oil began to run out, the town fell to pieces.

HOTELS

★★Arlington Hotel
1 Seneca St., Oil City,
814-677-1221, 877-677-1222;
www.oilcityhotel.com
106 rooms. $

PHILADELPHIA

In the mid-18th century, it was the second-largest city in the English-speaking world. Today, Philadelphia is the second-largest city on the East Coast and the fifth largest in the country. Here, in William Penn's City of Brotherly Love, the Declaration of Independence was written and adopted, the Constitution was molded and signed, the Liberty Bell was rung, Betsy Ross was said to have sewn her flag and Washington served most of his years as president.

This is the city of "firsts," including the first American hospital, medical college, women's medical college, bank, paper mill, steamboat, zoo, sugar refinery, daily newspaper, U.S. mint and public school for black children (1750).

The first Quakers, who came here in 1681, lived in caves dug into the banks of the Delaware River. During the first year, 80 houses were raised; by the following year, William Penn's "greene countrie towne" was a city of 600 buildings. The Quakers prospered in trade and commerce, and Philadelphia became the leading port in the colonies. Its leading citizen for many years was Benjamin Franklin.

The fires of colonial indignation burned hot and early in Philadelphia. Soon after the Boston Tea Party, a protest rally of 8,000 Philadelphians frightened off a British tea ship. In May 1774, when Paul Revere rode from Boston to Philadelphia to report Boston's harbor had been closed, all of Philadelphia went into mourning. The first and second Continental Congresses convened here, and Philadelphia became the headquarters of the Revolution. After the Declaration of Independence was composed and accepted by Congress the city gave its men, factories and shipyards to the cause. But British General Howe and 18,000 soldiers poured in on September 26, 1777, to spend a comfortable and social winter here while Washington's troops endured the bitter winter at Valley Forge. When the British evacuated the city, Congress returned. Philadelphia continued as the seat of government until 1800, except for a short period when New York City held the honor. Since those historic days, Philadelphia has figured prominently in the country's politics, economy and culture.

More than 1,400 churches and synagogues grace the city. There are over 25 colleges, universities and professional schools in Philadelphia as well. Fine restaurants are in abundance, along with exciting nightlife to top off an evening. Entertainment is offered by the world-renowned Philadelphia Orchestra, theaters, college and professional sports, outstanding parks, recreation centers and playgrounds. Shoppers may browse major department stores and hundreds of specialty and antique shops.

Information: Convention & Visitors Bureau, 1515 Market St., Philadelphia, 215-636-3300; www.pcvb.org

WHAT TO SEE AND DO

Nineth Street Italian Market
Nineth St., between Wharton and Fitzwater, Philadelphia,
215-923-5637;
www.phillyitalianmarket.com
Sip on Italian gourmet coffee, inhale imported cheeses or treat yourself to a cannoli. With more than 100 merchants selling their wares, this is the largest working outdoor market in the United States. Pining choices range from fine Italian dining to lunch counters to an outdoor snack tent. Tuesday-Sunday.

Academy of Music
Broad and Locust Streets, Philadelphia,
215-893-1999;
www.academyofmusic.org
(1857) City's opera house, concert hall; home of Philadelphia Orchestra, Philly Pops, Opera Company of Philadelphia and Pennsylvania Ballet.

Academy of Natural Sciences Museum
1900 Ben Franklin Parkway, Philadelphia,
215-299-1000;
www.acnatsci.org
(1812) Dinosaurs, Egyptian mummies, animal displays in natural habitats, live animal programs, hands-on children's museum. Daily.

African-American Museum Philadelphia
701 Arch St., Philadelphia,
215-574-0380;
www.aampmuseum.org
Built to house and interpret African-American culture. Changing exhibits; public events include lectures, workshops, films and concerts. Tuesday-Sunday.

American Swedish Historical Museum
1900 Pattison Ave., Philadelphia,
215-389-1776;
www.americanswedish.org
From tapestries to technology, the museum celebrates Swedish influence on American life. Special exhibits on the New Sweden Colony. Research library, collections. Tuesday-Friday 10 a.m.-4 p.m., Saturday-Sunday from noon.

Antique Row
From Nineth to 17th streets along Pine St., Philadelphia
Dozens of antique, craft and curio shops.

Arch Street Meetinghouse
Fourth and Arch Streets, Philadelphia,
215-627-2667;
www.archstreetfriends.org
(1804) Perhaps the largest Friends meetinghouse in the world. Exhibits, slide show, tours. Daily except Sunday.

Atwater Kent Museum of Philadelphia
15 S. Seventh St., Philadelphia,
215-685-4830;
www.philadelphiahistory.org
Hundreds of fascinating artifacts, toys and miniatures, maps, prints, paintings and photographs reflect the city's social and cultural history. Wednesday-Sunday 1 p.m.-5 p.m.

Betsy Ross House
239 Arch St., Philadelphia,
215-686-1252;
www.betsyrosshouse.org
Where the famous seamstress is said to have made the first American flag. Upholsterer's shop, memorabilia. Flag Day ceremonies, June 14. April-September: daily; October-March: closed Mondays.

Blue Cross River Rink
Festival Pier at Penn's Landing, Columbus Blvd. and Spring Garden St., Philadelphia, 215-925-7465;
www.riverrink.com
Few outdoor ice skating rinks are as well-located as this one along the Delaware River. Visitors have a great vantage point from which to view the Benjamin Franklin Bridge and the Philadelphia skyline. This Olympic-size rink, at 200 feet x 85 feet, can accommodate 500 skaters. After a hearty skate, warm yourself in the heated pavilion, which features a video game area and concessions. November-February: daily.

Burial Ground of Congregation Mikveh Israel
Spruce and Eighth Streets, Philadelphia
(1738) Graves of Haym Salomon, Revolutionary War financier and Rebecca Gratz, probable model for Rebecca of Sir Walter Scott's "Ivanhoe."

Centipede Tours
1315 Walnut St., Philadelphia,
215-735-3123;
www.centipedeinc.com
Candlelight strolls (1 1/2 hours) through historic Philadelphia and Society Hill areas led by guides in 18th-century dress; begins and ends at City Tavern. Mid-May-Mid-October: Saturday. Reservations preferred.

Christ Church and Burial Ground
Second and Market Streets, Philadelphia,
215-922-1695;
www.oldchristchurch.org
(Episcopal) Patriots, Loyalists and heroes have worshiped here since 1695. Sit in pews once occupied by Washington, Franklin and Betsy Ross. Burial ground resting place of Benjamin Franklin, his wife, Deborah and six other signers of the Declaration of Independence. March-December: daily; rest of year: Wednesday-Sunday.

City Hall
Broad and Market Streets, Philadelphia,
215-686-2840
A granite statue of William Penn stands 510 feet high above the heart of the city on top of this municipal building, which is larger than the Capitol. It's known as Penn Square, and was designated by Penn as the location for a building of public concerns. It also functions as Philadelphia's City Hall. One of the finest examples of French Second-Empire architectural style, constructing this building with the tallest statue (37,000 feet) in the world on its top took 30 years. Penn's famous hat is more than seven feet in diameter, and the brim creates a two-foot-wide track. There are more than 250 sculptures around this marble, granite and limestone structure, 20 elevators, and a four-faced, 50-ton clock. Monday-Friday.

Civil War and Underground Railroad Museum of Philadelphia
1805 Pine St., Philadelphia,
215-735-8196;
www.cwurmuseum.org
Four-story brick 19th-century townhouse filled with 18,000 books and periodicals dealing with Civil War. Unique collection of arms, uniforms, flags of the period, memorabilia and artifacts begun in 1888 by former officers of the Union Army. Exhibits on Lincoln, Grant and Meade; Thursday-Saturday 11 a.m.-4:30 p.m.; other days, by appointment.

Cliveden
6401 Germantown Ave., Philadelphia,
215-848-1777;
www.cliveden.org
(1767) A 2 1/2-story stone Georgian house built as a summer home by Benjamin Chew, Chief Justice of colonial Pennsylvania. On October 4, 1777, British soldiers used the house as a fortress to repulse Washington's

★
★
★
★
★

attempt to recapture Philadelphia. Used as the Chew family residence for 200 years; many original furnishings. A National Trust for Historic Preservation property. April-December: Thursday-Sunday afternoons.

Deshler-Morris House
5442 Germantown Ave., Philadelphia,
215-596-1748;
www.nps.gov/demo
(1772-1773) Residence of President Washington in the summers of 1793, 1794; period furnishings, garden. Friday-Sunday afternoons, or by appointment.

Edgar Allan Poe National Historic Site
532 N. Seventh St., Philadelphia,
215-597-8780;
www.nps.gov/edal
Where Poe lived before his move to New York in 1844. The site is the nation's memorial to the literary genius of Edgar Allan Poe. Exhibits, slide show, tours and special programs. Wednesday-Sunday 9 a.m.-5 p.m.

Electric Factory
421 N. Seventh St., Philadelphia,
215-569-9400;
www.electricfactory.com
This all-ages live music venue offers accessibility to lesser-known bands, though Tori Amos, Garbage, Brian Setzer and other well-known artists have played here. Arrive early to set a bar table in the upstairs balcony overlooking the stage. Daily.

Elfreth's Alley
126 Elfreth's Alley, Philadelphia,
215-574-0560;
www.elfrethsalley.org
Philadelphians still live in these Georgian- and Federal-style homes along cobblestoned Elfreth's Alley, the nation's oldest continued-use residential street. A few homes have been converted into museums, offering guided tours, a quaint gift shop and hand-crafted memorabilia. Culture and architecture appreciators will pick up all sorts of historical facts through photos and the collections. March-October: Monday-Sunday, November-February: Thursday-Saturday.

Fairmount Park
4231 N. Concourse Dr., Philadelphia,
215-683-0200;
www.phila.gov/fairpark
At 8,900 acres, Fairmount Park is the largest city park in America. It is home to 100 miles of beautifully landscaped paths for walking and horseback riding. Cyclists love to bike along the Pennypack and Wissahickon trails. Walkers stroll or power-hike in Valley Green alongside the ducks. In-line skaters and rowing and sculling enthusiasts at Boathouse Row enjoy the sights along the Schuykill River on Kelly Drive. Within the park are the Philadelphia Zoo, the Shofuso Japanese House, the Philadelphia Museum of Art, the outdoor festival center Robin Hood Dell and the Philadelphia Orchestra's summer amphitheater (Mann Music Center), as well as 127 tennis courts and numerous picnic spots. The park contains America's largest collection of authentic colonial homes, features majestic outdoor sculptures, and includes Memorial Hall, the only building remaining from the 1876 Centennial Exhibition. Daily.
In park are:

Colonial Mansions
4231 N. Concourse Dr., Philadelphia,
215-683-0200
Handsome 18th-century dwellings in varying architectural styles, authentically preserved and furnished, include Mount Pleasant (1761) (Tuesday-Sunday); Cedar Grove (1756) (Tuesday-Sunday); Strawberry Mansion (1797) (Tuesday-Sunday); Sweetbriar (1797) (Monday, Wednesday-Sunday); Lemon Hill (1799) (Wednesday-Sunday); Woodford (1756) (Tuesday-Sunday); Laurel Hill (1760) (Wednesday-Sunday). Further details and guided tours from Park Houses office at Philadelphia Museum of Art.

Japanese Exhibition House
Fairmount Park Horticulture Center,
Horticultural Dr., Philadelphia,
215-878-5097;
www.shofuso.com
Re-creates a bit of Japan, complete with garden, pond, bridge. May-October: Tuesday-Sunday.

223

PENNSYLVANIA

Philadelphia Museum of Art

N. 26th St. and Pennsylvania Ave.,
Philadelphia,
215-763-8100;
www.philamuseum.org

Modeled after a Greco-Roman temple, this massive museum amplifies the beauty of more than 300,000 works of art, and offers spectacular natural views. From the top of the steps outside (made famous by Sylvester Stallone in "Rocky"), visitors discover a breathtaking view of the Ben Franklin Parkway toward City Hall. Inside, the collections span 2,000 years and many more miles. There's a lavish collection of period rooms, a Japanese teahouse and a Chinese palace hall. Art lovers will also find Indian and Himalayan pieces, European decorative arts, Medieval sculptures, Impressionist and Post-Impressionist paintings, and modern and contemporary works in many media. Tuesday-Sunday: daily and Friday evenings.

Philadelphia Orchestra

260 S. Broad St. #1600, Philadelphia,
215-893-1999

The internationally renowned Philadelphia Orchestra has distinguished itself through a century of acclaimed performances, historic international tours and best-selling recordings. Performances are held at the Kimmel Center for the Performing Arts at Broad and Spruce Streets; the Mann Center for the Performing Arts, 52nd Street and Parkside Avenue; Saratoga Performing Arts Center in upstate New York; and annually at New York's Carnegie Hall.

Philadelphia Zoo

3400 W. Girard Ave., Philadelphia,
215-243-1100;
www.philadelphiazoo.org

The Philadelphia Zoo may have been America's first zoo—it was home to the nation's first white lions and witnessed its first successful chimpanzee birth—but you'll see no signs of old age here. Over the last century, the zoo has transformed itself into a preservation spot for rare and endangered animals, and a garden and wildlife destination point. The zoo is home to 1,600 live animals, from red pandas to Rodrigues fruit bats. Take a pony, camel or elephant ride; feed nectar to a parrot in a walk-through aviary; or engage with a playful wallaby. Pedal a boat around Bird Lake. Or take a soaring balloon 400 feet up on the country's first passenger-carrying Zooballoon. March-November: daily; December-February: daily.

Fireman's Hall Museum

147 N. Second St., Philadelphia,
215-923-1438;
www.firemanshall.org

Collection of antique firefighting equipment; displays and exhibits of fire department history since its beginning in 1736; library. Tuesday-Saturday daily and the first Friday of every month until 9 p.m.

First Presbyterian Church

201 S. 21st St., Philadelphia,
215-567-0532;
www.fpcphila.org

This more than 300-year-old church was designed in the Victorian Gothic style, combining French and English medieval Gothic cathedral motifs with massive details, flamboyant decoration and mixed materials, including granite, sand-toned brick, six types of marble, terra-cotta and stone. No plaster was used anywhere within the original building, a matter of some architectural significance toward the end of the 19th century. Call ahead to arrange visit.

Fort Mifflin

Fort Mifflin Road and Enterprise Ave.,
Philadelphia,
215-685-4167

Fort Mifflin, a Revolutionary War fort strategically located in the Delaware River at the mouth of the Schuylkill, is a complex of 11 restored buildings. Here, you can climb into a bombproof enclosure used to shelter troops; witness the uniform and weapons demonstrations that take place throughout the year; explore the 4-foot-thick walls of the Arsenal, soldiers barracks, officers quarters and blacksmith's shop; or simply enjoy the spectacular view of Philadelphia

PENNSYLVANIA

and the Delaware from the Northeast Bastion. Self-guided and one-hour guided tours are available. April-November: Wednesday-Sunday.

Franklin Institute Science Museum
222 N. 20th St., Philadelphia,
215-448-1200;
www.sln.fi.edu
This 300,000-square-foot science museum complex and memorial hall brings biology, earth science, physics, mechanics, aviation, astronomy, communications and technology to life with a variety of highly interactive exhibits honoring Philadelphia's mechanical inventor Ben Franklin. (A 30-foot marble statue of Franklin sits in a Roman Pantheon-inspired chamber known as the Benjamin Franklin National Memorial.) The kids can play tic-tac-toe with a strategically adept computer, climb into the cockpit of an Air Force jet trainer, or test water quality in the Mandell Center, located in a 38,000-square-foot garden. Stargazers can witness the birth of the universe, see galaxies form, or discover wondrous nebulae under the Fels Planetarium dome. Budding physicists and bike fanatics will appreciate the 28-foot-high bicycle perched on a one-inch cable demonstrating gyroscopic stability in the Sky Bike exhibit. Daily.

Franklin Mills Mall
1455 Franklin Mills Cir., Philadelphia,
215-632-1500;
www.simon.com
Bargain hunters will feel like they've hit the jackpot in the more than 200 discount stores in this mega-shopping complex, just 15 miles outside Center City Philadelphia, which touts itself as Pennsylvania's most visited attraction. Shoppers will find outlets of such well-known retailers as Kenneth Cole, Tommy Hilfiger, Casual Corner, The Gap, Old Navy, Nine West, Neiman Marcus, Saks Fifth Avenue and Marshalls. There is no sales tax on apparel in Pennsylvania, which makes slashed prices even more appealing. If you don't want to fight for a parking spot, take advantage of the daily shuttle services from area hotels, airport and train stations. Monday-Saturday 10 a.m.-9:30 p.m., Sunday 11 a.m.-7 p.m.

Free Library
Logan Square, 1901 Vine St., Philadelphia,
215-686-5322;
www.library.phila.gov
Large central library with over nine million indexed items in all fields. Rare books, maps, theater scripts and orchestral scores; automobile reference collections; changing exhibits. Daily.

Gloria Dei Church National Historic Site
Columbus Blvd. and Christian St.,
Philadelphia,
215-389-1513;
www.nps.gov/glde
(1700) The state's oldest church. Memorial to John Hansen, president of the Continental Congress under the Articles of Confederation. Daily.

Historic Bartram's Garden
54th St. and Lindbergh Blvd., Philadelphia,
215-729-5281;
www.bartramsgarden.org
Pre-Revolutionary home of John Bartram, the royal botanist to the colonies under George III, naturalist and plant explorer. The 18th-century stone farmhouse, barn, stable and cider mill overlook the Schuylkill River. Museum shop. Daily.

Historical Society of Pennsylvania
1300 Locust St., Philadelphia,
215-732-6200;
www.hsp.org
Museum exhibit features first draft of Constitution, 500 artifacts and manuscripts, plus video tours of turn-of-the-century urban and suburban neighborhoods. Research library and archives house historical and genealogical collections. Tuesday-Friday daily and Wednesday evening.

Independence National Historical Park
Third and Chestnut Streets, Philadelphia,
215-965-2305;
www.nps.gov/inde

PENNSYLVANIA

The park has been called "America's most historic square mile." The Independence Visitor Center at 6th & Market streets has a tour map, information on all park activities and attractions, and a 30-minute film entitled "Independence." Unless otherwise indicated, all historic sites and museums in the park are open daily and are free.

Bishop White House
309 Walnut St., Philadelphia
(1786-1787) House of Bishop William White, first Episcopal Bishop of Pennsylvania. Restored and furnished. Free tickets at park's Visitor Center. Admission by tour only.

Carpenters' Hall
320 Chestnut St., Philadelphia
(1770) Constructed as guild hall; meeting site of First Continental Congress (1774). Historical museum since 1857; still operated by Carpenters Co. Contains original chairs; exhibits of early tools. Tuesday-Sunday, daily.

Congress Hall
Sixth and Chestnut Streets, Philadelphia, 215-965-2305
Congress met here during the last decade of the 18th century. House of Representatives and Senate chambers are restored.

Declaration House
701 Market St.,
Philadelphia,
215-965-2305
Reconstructed house on the site of the writing of the Declaration of Independence by Thomas Jefferson; two rooms Jefferson rented have been reproduced. Short orientation and movie about Jefferson, his philosophy on the common man, and the history of the house.

First Bank of the United States
Third and Walnut Streets, Philadelphia
(1797-1811) Organized by Alexander Hamilton; country's oldest bank building; exterior restored. Closed to the public.

Franklin Court
316-322 Market St., Philadelphia,
215-965-2305
The site of Benjamin Franklin's house has been developed as a tribute to him; area includes working printing office and bindery, underground museum with multimedia exhibits, an archaeological exhibit and the B. Franklin Free Post Office.

Independence Hall
Fifth and Chestnut Streets,
Philadelphia,
215-965-2305;
www.nps.gov/inde
Built in the mid-1700s, Independence Hall is the site of the first public reading of the Declaration of Independence. It also played host to large political rallies during the country's founding years. It is considered a fine example of Georgian architecture. Visitors often find the Hall a good first stop for their tour of Independence National Historic Park, which includes the Liberty Bell, Congress Hall, Old City Hall and Carpenters' Hall. The building is open for tours only. Admission by tour only. Daily.

Independence Square
Known as State House Yard in colonial times. Contains Independence Hall, Congress Hall, Old City Hall and Philosophical Hall.

Liberty Bell
Liberty Bell Center,
Market and Sixth Streets, Philadelphia,
215-965-2305
An international icon and one of the most venerated stops in Independence Park, this mostly copper symbol of religious freedom, justice and independence is believed to hang from its original yoke. Daily.

Library Hall
105 S. Fifth St., Philadelphia,
215-440-3400
Reconstruction of Library Company of Philadelphia (1789-1790). Open to scholars. Monday-Friday.

★
★
★
★
★

Merchant's Exchange

Third and Walnut Streets, Philadelphia
Designed by William Strickland, this building is one of the East's finest examples of Greek Revival architecture. Exterior restored; now houses regional offices of the National Park Service. Closed to the public.

Museum Shop (Pemberton House)

Chestnut St., Philadelphia,
215-965-2307
Reconstruction of Quaker merchant's house; now shop with items relating to historic sites.

New Hall Military Museum

Fourth and Chestnut Streets, Philadelphia,
215-965-2305
This reconstruction houses the U.S. Marine Corps Memorial Museum, featuring exhibits on the early history of the Marines, and the Army-Navy Museum. Wednesday-Sunday 3 p.m.-5 p.m.

Old City Hall

Fifth and Chestnut Streets, Philadelphia
(1789) Built as City Hall, but was also home of first U.S. Supreme Court, 1791-1800. Exterior restored. Interior depicts the judicial phase of the building.

Philosophical Hall

104 S. Fifth St., Philadelphia
(1785-1789) Home of the American Philosophical Society, oldest learned society in America (1743), founded by Benjamin Franklin. Not open to the public.

Thaddeus Kosciuszko National Memorial

301 Pine St., Philadelphia,
215-597-8974;
www.nps.gov/thko
House of Polish patriot during his second visit to the United States (1797-1798). He was one of the 18th century's greatest champions of American and Polish freedom and one of the first volunteers to come to the aid of the American Revolutionary Army. Exterior and second-floor bedroom have been restored. Wednesday-Sunday afternoons.

Todd House

Fourth and Walnut Streets, Philadelphia
(1775) House of Dolley Payne Todd, who later married James Madison and became First Lady; 18th-century furnishings depict middle-class Quaker family life. Free tickets at park's Visitor Center. Admission by tour only.

Independence Seaport Museum

211 S. Columbus Blvd., Philadelphia,
215-413-8655;
www.phillyseaport.org
Maritime enthusiasts of all ages will appreciate the creative interactive exhibits about the science, history and art of boat building along the region's waterways at the Independence Seaport Museum. Oral histories of the men and women who have lived and worked here take visitors through immigration, commerce, defense, industry and the recreational aspects of boats. You can watch how builders assemble a boat, walk (or crawl) through a full-size replica of a Delaware River Shad Skiff, or pull shapes through a 10-foot tank of water to examine drag-affecting speed. Daily.

Jeweler's Row

Seventh and Sansom Streets, Philadelphia
Largest jewelry district in the country other than New York City. More than 300 shops, including wholesalers and diamond cutters.

John Heinz National Wildlife Refuge at Tinicum

8601 Lindbergh Blvd.,
Philadelphia,
215-365-3118;
www.fws.gov/northeast/heinz
Largest remaining freshwater tidal wetland in the state, protecting more than 1,000 acres of wildlife habitat. Area was first diked by Swedish farmers in 1643; Dutch farmers and the colonial government added dikes during the Revolutionary War. More than 280 species of birds and 13 resident mammal species. Hiking, bicycling, nature observation, canoeing on Darby Creek; fishing. Daily 8:30 a.m.-4 p.m.

227

PENNSYLVANIA

★
★
★
★
★

Laff House Comedy Club
221 South St., Philadelphia,
215-440-4242;
www.laffhouse.com
This humor hub located on the city's artsy and alternative South Street hosts comedy events all week.

Manayunk
Philadelphia,
215-482-9565;
www.manayunk.com
This historic district, just seven miles from Center City, makes a great destination point or place to hang out. Old rail lines, canal locks and textile mills dot this quaint town. Joggers, walkers, hikers and off-road cyclists will enjoy traveling the towpath that edges the town while their shop-a-holic counterparts check out the more than 70 boutiques and galleries.

Masonic Temple
1 N. Broad St., Philadelphia,
215-988-1900;
www.pagrandlodge.org
Philadelphia's Masonic Temple was designed for the Fraternal Order of Freemasons, of which Benjamin Franklin and George Washington were members. The interior houses seven different halls, including the Gothic Hall, Oriental Hall and the better-known Egyptian Hall. It showcases treasures of freemasonry, including a book written by Franklin and Washington's Masonic apron. Open for tours only. Tuesday-Friday.

Morris Arboretum of the University of Pennsylvania
100 E. Northwestern Ave., Philadelphia,
215-247-5777;
www.upenn.edu/arboretum
(1887). Public garden with more than 14,000 accessioned plants on 166 acres; special garden areas such as Swan Pond, Rose Garden and Japanese gardens. Tours. Daily.

Mummer's Museum
1100 S. Second St., Philadelphia,
215-336-3050;
www.riverfrontmummers.com

Participatory exhibits and displays highlighting the history and tradition of the Mummer's Parade. Costumes and videotapes of past parades. Free outdoor string band concerts (May-September: Tuesday evenings, weather permitting); 20 string bands, different every week. Tuesday-Sunday; closed Monday, and Sunday in July-August.

Mutter Museum
19 S. 22nd St., Philadelphia,
215-563-3737;
www.collphyphil.org/muttpg1.shtml
This collection of one-of-a-kind, hair raising medical curiosities includes President Cleveland's jawbone; the thorax of John Wilkes Booth; a plaster cast of Siamese twins; human bones shattered by bullets; a liver in a jar; and a drawer full of buttons, coins and teeth removed from human stomachs without surgery. Located at the esteemed College of Physicians of Philadelphia, the gallery holds an internationally revered collection of creepy anatomical and pathological specimens, medical instruments and illustrations. Daily 10 a.m.-5 p.m. and Friday evening.

National Museum of American Jewish History
Independence Mall East, 55 N. Fifth St., Philadelphia,
215-923-3811;
www.nmajh.org
The museum presents experiences and educational programs that preserve, explore, and celebrate the history of Jews in America. Sunday-Friday: daily.

Old Pine Street Presbyterian Church
412 Pine St., Philadelphia,
215-925-8051;
www.oldpine.org
(1768) Colonial church and graveyard, renovated in 1850s in Greek Revival style. Daily.

Old St. George's United Methodist Church
235 N. Fourth St., Philadelphia,
215-925-7788;
www.historicstgeorges.org

(1769) Oldest Methodist Church in continuous service in the United States. Colonial architecture; collection of Methodist memorabilia; has only Bishop Asbury bible and John Wesley chalice cup in America. Daily.

Old St. Mary's Church
252 S. Fourth St., Philadelphia,
215-923-7930
(1763) Commodore John Barry, "father of the US Navy," is interred in graveyard behind the city's first Catholic cathedral. Daily.

Penn's Landing
Columbus Blvd. and Spruce St.,
Philadelphia

USS Olympia
Columbus Blvd. and Walnut St.,
Philadelphia,
215-925-5439
Commodore Dewey's flagship during Spanish-American War; restored. Naval museum has weapons, uniforms, ship models and naval relics of all periods. Also here is World War II submarine, *USS Becuna*. Daily.

Pennsylvania Academy of Fine Arts
118 N. Broad St., Philadelphia,
215-972-7600;
www.pafa.org
This is the nation's oldest art museum and school of fine arts. Within the Gothic Victorian structure are paintings, works on paper and sculptures by American artists ranging from colonial masters to contemporary artists. Many of the nation's finest artists, including Charles Willson Peale, Mary Cassatt, William Merritt Chase and Maxfield Parrish, were founders, teachers or students here. Sunday 11 a.m.-5 p.m., Tuesday-Saturday 10 a.m.-5 p.m.

Pennsylvania Ballet
1101 S. Broad St., Philadelphia,
215-336-2000;
www.paballet.org
This company with a George Balanchine influence includes a varied repertoire of ballets ranging from classics like "The Nutcracker" to original works. Performances are held at the Academy of Music and the Merriam Theatre.

Pennsylvania Hospital
Eighth and Spruce Streets, Philadelphia
(1751) First in country, founded by Benjamin Franklin.

Pentimenti Gallery
145 N. Second St., Philadelphia,
215-625-9990;
www.pentimenti.com
Exhibiting works of art in all modes ranging from figurative to abstract by local, regional and international artists. Wednesday-Saturday.

Philadelphia 76ers (NBA)
Wachovia Complex, 3601 S. Broad St.,
Philadelphia,
www.nba.com/sixers
Professional basketball team.

Philadelphia Carriage Company
500 N. 13th St., Philadelphia,
215-922-6840;
www.philacarriage.com
Guided tours via horse-drawn carriage covering Society Hill and other historic areas; begin and end on Fifth St. at Chestnut. Daily, weather permitting.

Philadelphia Eagles (NFL)
Lincoln Financial Field, 11th St. and Pattison Ave., Philadelphia,
215-463-2500;
www.philadelphiaeagles.com
Professional football team.

Philadelphia Flyers (NHL)
Wachovia Complex, 3601 S. Broad St.,
Philadelphia, 215-336-2000
Professional hockey team.

Philadelphia Phillies (MLB)
Citizens Bank Park, 1 Citizens Bank Way,
Philadelphia, 215-463-5000;
www.philadelphiaphillies.com
Professional baseball team.

229

PENNSYLVANIA

Philadelphia Soft Pretzel

The famous Philadelphia soft pretzel is a hand-rolled, freshly baked, coarsely salted, buttery, golden-brown comfort food in a paper bag. A Philadelphia pretzel's texture is as vital as its taste: not too dry and certainly not too moist. Aficionados claim that Amish girls in hairnets sell the best ones, at Fisher's in Reading Terminal Market. But serious pretzel hunters can also find these chewy twists of dough, considered to be the country's oldest snack food, in food carts at city intersections, family-owned restaurants and the airport. Try one with a dollop or two of yellow mustard.

Please Touch Museum for Children

210 N. 21st St., Philadelphia,
215-963-0667;
www.pleasetouchmuseum.org

A group of artists, educators and parents conceived of this award-winning, interactive exploratory learning center for children ages one to seven in 1976. The safe, hands-on learning laboratory has since become a model for children's museums nationwide. Story lovers will enjoy having tea with the Mad Hatter or hanging out with Max in the forest where the wild things are. Children who don't want to sit still can board the life-size bus or shop at the miniature supermarket. The ones who like to get their hands dirty can engage in science experiments. Creature lovers can interact with fuzzy human-made barnyard animals. And the entertainment-minded can see themselves on television or audition for a news anchor position. Daily.

Reading Terminal Market

12th and Arch Streets, Philadelphia,
215-922-2317;
www.readingterminalmarket.org

The nation's oldest continuously operating farmers' market is alive—and thriving—in downtown Philadelphia. An indoor banquet for the senses, the market offers an exhilarating array of baked goods, meats, poultry, seafood, produce, flowers and Asian, Middle Eastern and Pennsylvania Dutch foods. Locals recommend the family-run stands, three of which are descendants of the original market. Monday-Saturday 8 a.m.-6 p.m., Sunday 9 a.m.-4 p.m.

Rita's Water Ice

239 South St., Philadelphia,
215-629-3910;
www.ritasice.com

The best water ice is not a solid and not quite a liquid, and visitors to Philadelphia will find it at Rita's. With locations throughout the city and surrounding area, Rita's is the city's favorite for frozen water ice, offering a changing selection of smooth, savory water ice, as well as ice cream and gelati. Daily.

Rittenhouse Square

1800 Walnut St., Philadelphia,
www.rittenhouserow.org

In the blocks that surround this genteel urban square in Philadelphia's most fashionable section of town are exclusive shops, restaurants and cafes. Discover what's new at chic boutiques—Francis Jerome, Sophy Curson, Nicole Miller, Ralph Lauren—or experience department store shopping of old at the historic Wanamaker's building, which is now a Lord & Taylor.

Rodin Museum

22nd St. and Franklin Pkwy., Philadelphia,
215-763-8100;
www.rodinmuseum.org

This museum, built in the Beaux Arts style, houses more than 200 sculptures created by Auguste Rodin (1840-1917) and is considered the largest collection of his works outside his native France. "The Thinker," Rodin's most famous piece, greets visitors outside at the gateway to the museum. Tours available. Tuesday-Sunday 10 a.m.-5 p.m.

Schuylkill Center for Environmental Education

8480 Hagy's Mill Rd., Philadelphia,
215-482-7300;
www.schuylkillcenter.org

A 500-acre natural area with more than seven miles of trails; discovery room; gift shop/bookstore. Daily.

Sesame Place
100 Sesame Rd., Philadelphia,
215-752-7070;
www.sesameplace.com

Shops at the Bellevue
200 S. Broad St., Philadelphia,
215-875-8350
Beaux Arts architecture of the former Bellevue Stratford Hotel has been preserved and transformed; it now contains offices, a hotel and a four-level shopping area centered around an atrium court. Monday-Saturday 10 a.m.-5 p.m., Wednesday to 8 p.m.

Society Hill Area
Seventh and Lombard Streets, Philadelphia,
www.ushistory.org/tour/tour_sochill.htm
Secret parks, cobblestone walkways and diminutive alleys among beautifully restored brick colonial townhouses make this historic area a treasure for visitors. A popular, daily, 30-minute walking tour will inspire history fans as well architecture lovers. Highlights along the way include a courtyard designed by I. M. Pei; gardens planted by the Daughters of the American Revolution; a sculpture of Robert Morris, one of the signers of the Declaration of Independence; Greek Revival-style architecture now home to the National Portrait Gallery; and the burial ground of Revolutionary War soldiers. In the summer months, the area hosts outdoor arts festivals in Headhouse Square. It's also home to some of Philadelphia's finest restaurants.

Athenaeum of Philadelphia
219 S. Sixth St., Philadelphia,
215-925-2688;
www.athenaonline.org
Landmark example of Italian Renaissance architecture (1845-1847); restored building has American neoclassical-style decorative arts, paintings, sculpture; research library; furniture and art from the collection of Joseph Bonaparte, King of Spain and older brother of Napoleon; changing exhibits of architectural drawings, photos and rare books. Tours by appointment. Monday-Friday.

Physick House
321 S. Fourth St., Philadelphia,
215-925-7866
(1786) House of Dr. Philip Sung Physick, "father of American surgery," from 1815-1837. Restored Federal-style house with period furnishings; garden. Thursday-Sunday afternoons.

Powel House
244 S. Third St., Philadelphia,
215-627-0364;
www.powellhouse.org
(1765) Georgian townhouse of Samuel Powel, last colonial mayor of Philadelphia and first mayor under the new republic. Period furnishings, silver and porcelain; garden. Tours. Thursday-Sunday afternoons.

South Street District
South St., Philadelphia,
www.south-street.com
On South Street, the young and hip will enjoy the search for thrift store finds and a fashion show of the pierced and tattooed sort. The rest can rifle through dusty rare books or cruise the art galleries. These blocks at the southern boundary of the city—as well as the numbered streets just off of it—are chock full of offbeat shops, cafes, street musicians and water ice stands, all within walking distance of Penn's Landing and Society Hill. For a Philadelphia signature treat, visitors of all tastes should not miss the cheesesteaks at Jim's Steaks.

St. Peter's Church
Third and Pine Streets, Philadelphia,
215-925-5968;
www.stpetersphila.org
(1761 Episcopal) Georgian colonial architecture; numerous famous people buried in churchyard.

Stenton House
4601 N. 18th St., Philadelphia,
215-329-7312;
www.stenton.org
(1723-1730) Mansion built by James Logan, secretary to William Penn. Excellent example of Pennsylvania colonial architecture,

231

PENNSYLVANIA

furnished with 18th- and 19th-century antiques. General Washington spent August 23, 1777, here and General Sir William Howe headquartered here for the Battle of Germantown. Colonial barn, gardens, kitchen. April-December: Tuesday-Saturday afternoons; rest of year: by appointment.

Temple University
Cecil B Moore Ave. and Broad St., Philadelphia,
215-204-7000;
www.temple.edu
(1884) (33,000 students) Undergraduate, professional and research school. Walking tours of campus.

The Bourse
S. Fifth St., 111 S. Independence Mall E, Philadelphia
(1893-1895) Restored Victorian building houses shops and restaurants. Daily.

The Five Spot
5 S. Bank St., Philadelphia,
215-574-0070;
www.phillytown.com/fivespot.htm
Originally opened as a swing club during the late-1990s swing trend, The Five Spot is now a live music and dance club that features everything from rock music and live DJs to salsa and swing. Daily.

The Gallery
Nineth and Market Streets, Philadelphia,
215-925-7162;
www.galleryatmrketeast.com
Concentration of 250 shops and restaurants in a four-level mall with glass elevators, trees, fountains and benches. Daily.

The Trocadero Theatre
1003 Arch St., Philadelphia,
215-922-5483;
www.thetroc.com
This former 1870s opera house hosted vaudeville, burlesque and Chinese movies before it became the beautiful, contemporary live music venue that it is today. The theater now hosts many well-known rock and pop artists, as well as the annual eight-hour Philadelphia Pop Festival held in June, which highlights local bands. On Movie Mondays, the theater holds free screenings (on its original screen) of such classic movies as *Apocalypse Now* and *Escape from New York.*

University of Pennsylvania
32nd and Walnut Streets, Philadelphia,
215-898-5000;
www.upenn.edu
(1740) (23,000 students) On campus are the restored Fisher Fine Arts Library (215-898-8325); Annenberg Center for performing arts (215-898-6791), University Museum of Archaeology and Anthropology and the Institute of Contemporary Art, located at 36th and Sansom streets Wednesday-Sunday; 215-898-7108; fee.
Also here is:

University of Pennsylvania Museum of Archaeology and Anthropology
3260 South St., Philadelphia,
215-898-4000;
www.museum.upenn.edu
World-famous archaeological and ethnographic collections developed from the museum's own expeditions, gifts and purchases; features Chinese, Near Eastern, Greek, ancient Egyptian, African, Pacific and North, Middle and South American materials; library. Restaurant, shops. Tuesday-Sunday; closed Sunday in summer.

U.S. Mint
Fifth and Arch Streets, Philadelphia,
215-408-0114;
www.usmint.gov
Produces coins of all denominations. Gallery affords visitors an elevated view of the coinage operations. Medal making may also be observed. Audiovisual, self-guided tours. Rittenhouse Room on the mezzanine contains historic coins, medals and other exhibits. Monday-Friday 9 a.m.-3 p.m.

Wagner Free Institute of Science
1700 W. Montgomery Ave., Philadelphia,
215-763-6529;
www.pacscl.org/wagner

PENNSYLVANIA

Victorian science museum with more than 50,000 specimens illustrating the various branches of the natural sciences. Dinosaur bones, fossils, reptiles and rare species are all mounted in the Victorian style. Reference library and research archives. Tuesday-Friday.

Walnut Street Theatre
825 Walnut St., Philadelphia,
215-574-3550;
www.wstonline.org
(1809) America's oldest theater. The Walnut Mainstage offers musicals, classical and contemporary plays. Two studio theaters provide a forum for new and avant-garde works.

Washington Square
Walnut and Sixth Streets, Philadelphia
Site where hundreds of Revolutionary War soldiers and victims of the yellow fever epidemic are buried. Life-size statue of Washington has tomb of Revolutionary War's Unknown Soldier at its feet.

Across the street is:

Philadelphia Savings Fund Society Building
(1816) Site of oldest savings bank in the U.S. Not open to the public.

Wok N' Walk Tours of Philadelphia Chinatown
1002 Arch St., Philadelphia,
215-928-9333;
www.josephpoon.com
Considered one of the best culinary tours in the country, Joseph Poon's Wok N Walk Tour is rich with Chinese history and culture as well as calories. This two-and-a-half-hour tour begins at Poon's Asian restaurant. (Be sure to try Chef Poon's trademark potato carvings.) Walkers are treated to a tai chi demonstration, a peek at Poon's state-of-the-art kitchen and a vegetable carving lesson. Along the tour, you visit a Chinese herbal medicine expert, a fortune cookie factory and a Chinese noodle shop and best of all, snack on free samples from a Chinese bakery in one of the city's more vibrant ethnic communities. Daily.

SPECIAL EVENTS
Army-Navy Football Game
www.usna.edu/libexhibits/archives/
armynavy/armynavygames.htm
First Saturday in December.

CoreStates US Pro Cycling Championship
Broad and Walnut Streets,
Philadelphia
At 156 miles, it's the longest (and richest) single-day cycling event in the country. Mid-June.

Delaware Valley First Fridays
In the Old City, Second and Third Streets,
from Market to Race, Philadelphia,
www.dvfirstfridays.com
First Fridays is a citywide cultural event that takes place at rotating venues with alternating formats on the first Friday of every month, with socializing and networking as goals. Galleries, shops, theaters, restaurants and sidewalks in the Old City area along Second and Third streets from Market to Race have hosted record label release parties, live concerts, comedy shows, children's festivals, fashion shows and vendor expositions. Proceeds go to African-American charitable organizations. First Friday of every month.

Elfreth's Alley Fete Days
126 Elfreth's Alley, Philadelphia,
215-574-0560;
www.elfrethsalley.org
Homes open to the public, costumed guides, demonstrations of colonial crafts; food, entertainment. Second weekend in June.

Head House Open Air Craft Market
Pine and Second Streets,
Philadelphia
Crafts demonstrations, children's workshops. June-August: Saturday and Sunday.

Horse racing
Philadelphia Park, 3001 Street Rd.,
Bensalem,
215-639-9000;
www.philadelphiapark.com
Flat racing at Philadelphia Park.

Mann Center for the Performing Arts
Fairmount Park, 5201 Parkside Ave.,
Philadelphia,
215-546-7900;
www.manncenter.org
Orchestra performs late June-July: Monday, Wednesday and Thursday. Also popular music attractions. Late May-September.

Mummer's Parade
Philadelphia,
215-336-3050;
www.mummers.com
The Mummers Parade is Philadelphia's version of New Orleans' Mardi Gras or Spain's Carnivale. It is an annual tradition to dress in outlandish costumes and noisily parade down the streets of Philadelphia on New Year's Day (the word "mummer" comes from an old French word that means to wear a mask). January 1.

Opera Company of Philadelphia
Academy of Music, Broad and
Locust Streets,
Philadelphia,
215-893-3600;
www.operaphilly.com
October-April.

PECO Energy Jazz Festival
2301 Market St.,
Philadelphia,
215-841-4000, 800-537-7676
Jazz concerts around the city. Early-mid-February.

Penn Relays
Franklin Field, 235 S. 33rd St.,
Philadelphia,
215-898-6151;
www.thepennrelays.com
These races originally served as a way to dedicate Franklin Field to the University of Pennsylvania. That was in 1895. Today, the Penn Relays hold the record for being the longest uninterrupted amateur track meet in the country. Thousands of men and women, ranging in age from eight to 80, have competed. More than 400 races take place, one every five minutes. Last weekend in April.

Philadelphia Flower Show
Pennsylvania Convention Center,
12th and Arch Streets, Philadelphia,
215-988-8899;
www.theflowershow.com
The country's first formal flower show took place here in 1829 in the city's Masonic Hall on Chestnut Street. More than 150 years later, exotic and rare flowers are still on display in the Pennsylvania Convention Center. Flower lovers will be dazzled by more than 275,000 flowers from Africa, Germany, Japan, England, France, Holland, Italy and Belgium. Early March.

Philadelphia Open House
325 Walnut St., Philadelphia,
215-928-1188
House and garden tours in different neighborhoods; distinguished selection of over 150 private homes, gardens, historic sites. Many tours include lunches, candlelight dinners, or high teas. Late April-early June.

Robin Hood Dell East
Fairmount Park, 33rd and Ridge Streets,
Philadelphia,
215-685-9560;
www.delleast.org
Top stars in popular music stage outdoor concerts. July-August.

The Book and the Cook
1528 Walnut St., Philadelphia,
215-545-5353;
www.thebookandthecook.com
Sample fine cuisine as world-famous cookbook authors team up with the city's most respected chefs to create culinary delights. Wine tastings, market tours, film festival. March.

HOTELS
★Best Western Independence Park Hotel
235 Chestnut St., Philadelphia,
215-922-4443, 800-780-7234;
www.independenceparkhotel.com
36 rooms. Complimentary continental breakfast. **$$**

★★Courtyard by Marriott
21 N. Juniper St., Philadelphia,
215-496-3200, 800-321-2211;
www.courtyard.com
498 rooms. Airport transportation available.
$$

★★Doubletree Hotel
237 S. Broad St.,
Philadelphia,
215-893-1600, 800-222-8733;
www.doubletree.com
434 rooms, Airport transportation available. **$**

★★Embassy Suites Center City
1776 Benjamin Franklin Pkwy.,
Philadelphia,
215-561-1776, 800-362-2779;
www.embassysuites.com
288 rooms, all suites. Complimentary full breakfast. Airport transportation available.
$$

★★★★Four Seasons Hotel Philadelphia
1 Logan Square,
Philadelphia,
215-963-1500, 866-516-1100;
www.fourseasons.com/philadelphia
Located on historic Logan Square, this hotel puts the city's museums, shops and businesses within easy reach. The eight-story Four Seasons is a Philadelphia institution in itself, from its dramatic Swann Fountain to its highly rated Fountain Restaurant, considered one of the better dining establishments in town. The rooms and suites are a celebration of Federalist decor, and some accommodations incorporate deep soaking tubs. City views of the Academy of Natural Science, Logan Square and the tree-lined Ben Franklin Parkway provide a sense of place for some guests, while other rooms offer tranquil views over the inner courtyard and gardens. The Four Seasons spa focuses on nourishing treatments, while the indoor pool resembles a tropical oasis with breezy palm trees and large skylights.
364 rooms. Airport transportation available. **$$$**

★★Hilton Garden Inn Philadelphia Center City
1100 Arch St., Philadelphia,
215-923-0100, 877-782-9444;
www.hiltongardeninn.com
279 rooms. Airport transportation available.
$$

★★★The Hilton Inn At Penn
3600 Sansom St., Philadelphia,
215-222-0200, 800-774-1500;
www.theinnatpenn.com
Experience a distinctly collegiate environment at this hotel, located in the middle of the University of Pennsylvania's campus, not far from the city's central business district. Travelers find the Inn at Penn easily accessible from I-76, Amtrak's 30th Street Station, and the Philadelphia International Airport. The Penne Restaurant and Wine Bar features regional Italian cuisine with fresh pasta made daily, while the University Club at Penn serves up breakfast and brunch favorites daily.
238 rooms. **$$**

★★★Hyatt Regency Philadelphia at Penn's Landing
201 S. Columbus Blvd., Philadelphia,
215-928-1234, 800-233-1234;
www.hyatt.com
Located in the Penn's Landing area of Philadelphia, this Hyatt property offers unobstructed views of the Delaware River. Major historic attractions and many shops and restaurants are within walking distance. Travelers can take advantage of the indoor pool and fitness center after a busy day of work or play, or head to the restaurant for a relaxing dinner.
345 rooms. **$$$**

★★★The Latham Hotel
135 S. 17th St., Philadelphia,
215-563-7474, 877-528-4261;
www.lathamhotel.com
This charming hotel is a favorite of guests looking for an intimate setting in downtown Philly. It is near Rittenhouse Square and close to Walnut Street, Philadelphia's main shopping area.

235

PENNSYLVANIA

★
★
★
★
★

139 rooms. Airport transportation available. **$**

★★★Loews Philadelphia Hotel
1200 Market St.,
Philadelphia,
215-627-1200, 800-235-6397;
www.loewshotels.com

This 1930s National Historic Landmark building (formerly the Pennsylvania Savings Fund Society), is situated across from the Market East train station and the convention center. The modern, Art Deco guest rooms feel spacious with their 10-foot ceilings. Upscale amenities include 300-thread-count linens, Bloom toiletries (with natural plant and herb extracts), flat-screen televisions and large work areas with ergonomic chairs. There are three floors of Concierge Level rooms, which include entry to the private library and lounge. Guests can keep up with their workouts in the nicely equipped Balance Spa & Fitness center—a 15,000-square-foot-space including a full-service spa, fitness room and heated indoor lap pool.
581 rooms. Children's activity center. **$$$**

★★★Omni Hotel At Independence Park
401 Chestnut St., Philadelphia,
215-925-0000, 888-444-6664;
www.omnihotels.com

Situated in the downtown area, only 10 minutes from Philadelphia International Airport and just a stone's throw from historic sights like the Liberty Bell and Independence Hall, the Omni offers an ideal location for both business and leisure trips to Philadelphia. Each well-appointed guest room combines old-world elegance with modern day luxury. Feather pillows, comfortable bath robes, 27" TVs with cable and executive desks are found in all rooms, while the ultra-plush penthouse suite features marble baths, Jacuzzi tubs and a parlor room with 20-foot cathedral ceilings, multiple sitting areas and a dining table. A courteous staff, on hand to assist with everything from laundry and dry-cleaning services to business needs, makes kids feel welcome with the Omni Sensational Kids program.
150 rooms. **$$$**

★★★Park Hyatt Philadelphia
Broad and Walnut Streets,
Philadelphia,
215-893-1234, 800-464-9288;
www.parkphiladelphia.hyatt.com

This elegant hotel was built in 1904 and is listed on the National Historic Register. Beautiful, early 20th-century architecture reflects the building's history, yet guests are pampered with a number of modern amenities and comforts. Goose-down duvets are found in each guest room along with luxurious linens, large televisions, DVD players, mini bars and plush bathrobes.
172 rooms. **$$$**

★★★Penn's View Hotel
Front and Market Streets,
Philadelphia,
215-922-7600, 800-331-7634;
www.pennsviewhotel.com

Located in historic Old City Philadelphia, near Penn's Landing and the Delaware River, Penn's View Hotel is on the National Historic Register. The decor here is European/Chippendale, but guest rooms have a slightly more modern feel. Guests looking for a smaller hotel with more personal touches will find this property especially appealing.
51 rooms. Complimentary continental breakfast. Airport transportation available. **$**

★★★Philadelphia Airport Marriott
One Arrivals Rd., Philadelphia,
215-492-9000, 800-228-9290;
www.marriott.com

This well-maintained Marriott property is situated within the Philadelphia Airport. It is physically connected to Terminal B, sharing the same parking garage. Sports complexes are close by, and historic downtown Philadelphia are just a short drive away.
419 rooms. Airport transportation available. Airport. **$$$**

236

PENNSYLVANIA

★★★Philadelphia Marriott Downtown
1201 Market St., Philadelphia,
215-625-2900, 800-320-5744;
www.philadelphiamarriott.com

Guests are assured a comfortable and relaxing stay at the Marriott Philadelphia Downtown. When not outdoors exploring nearby attractions like the Liberty Bell, Independence Park, the Franklin Institute and the waterfront area, guests can work out in the hotel's fitness center or take advantage of the indoor pool, whirlpool and sauna. There's also a number of dining options, from Steakhouse to Sushi.
1,408 rooms. Airport transportation available. $$$

★★★The Radisson Plaza Warwick Hotel
1701 Locust St., Philadelphia,
215-735-6000, 800-201-1718;
www.radisson.com/philadelphia

Just one block from Rittenhouse Park, this property is close to shopping, restaurants, performing arts and museums. It is also convenient to the universities. Listed on the National Register of Historic Places, the 1926 hotel has an English Renaissance theme, with guest rooms providing a more contemporary feel.
301 rooms. $$

★★★The Rittenhouse Hotel and Condominium Residences
210 W. Rittenhouse Square,
Philadelphia,
215-546-9000, 800-635-1042;
www.rittenhousehotel.com

This intimate hotel occupies a particularly enviable address across from the leafy Rittenhouse Square and among the prestigious townhouses of this exclusive area. The accommodations are among the most spacious in the city and are decorated with a sophisticated flair. Guests at the Rittenhouse are treated to the highest levels of personalized service. From the mood-lifting decor of the gracious Cassatt Lounge and the striking contemporary style of Lacroix to the rowing memorabilia of Boathouse Row Bar and the traditional steakhouse feel of Smith & Wollensky, the Rittenhouse Hotel also

provides memorable dining experiences to match every taste.
98 rooms. $$$$

★★★The Ritz-Carlton, Philadelphia
Ten Avenue of the Arts, Philadelphia,
215-523-8000, 800-241-3333;
www.ritzcarlton.com

This one-time home to Girard and Mellon Banks was designed in the 1900s by the architectural firm of McKim, Mead and White, and was inspired by Rome's Pantheon. Marrying historic significance with trademark Ritz-Carlton style, this Philadelphia showpiece boasts handsome decor. Impressive marble columns dominate the lobby. The rooms and suites are luxurious, while Club Level accommodations offer private lounges filled with five food and beverage selections daily. Dedicated to exceeding visitors expectations, the Ritz-Carlton even offers a pillow menu, a bath butler and other unique services. Dining options are plentiful, and the Sunday jazz brunch is a local favorite.
300 rooms. Airport transportation available. $$$

★★★Sheraton Society Hill
One Dock St., Philadelphia,
215-238-6000, 800-325-3535;
www.sheraton.com/societyhill

The Sheraton Society Hill offers affordable comfort in downtown Philadelphia, just steps from Independence Hall, Society Hill, the Liberty Bell, the Philadelphia Zoo and the Pennsylvania Convention Center. Wireless Internet access is available throughout the hotel.
365 rooms. Airport transportation available. $$

★★★Sheraton University City
36th and Chestnut Streets,
Philadelphia,
215-387-8000, 800-325-3535;
www.starwoodhotels.com

Perfect for visitors to the University of Pennsylvania, this Sheraton is located in the midst of an eclectic university environment. The hotel's early American decor and lobby

237

PENNSYLVANIA

★

★

★

★

☆

fireplace give it a cozy feel, and the friendly staff makes a stay here even more pleasant. A "pet suitcase," which includes a bed, bowls, mat, brush, toys and treat, is available for cats and dogs.
316 rooms. **$$**

★★★Sofitel Philadelphia
120 S. 17th St., Philadelphia,
215-569-8300, 800-763-4835;
www.sofitel.com
Modern French style permeates the Sofitel Philadelphia. This elegant hotel sits on the former site of the Philadelphia Stock Exchange, and its downtown Center City location makes it ideal for both business and leisure travelers. Warm and inviting, the accommodations welcome with a variety of thoughtful touches, such as fresh flowers and plush towels. Comfortable chic defines the lobby bar, La Bourse, while the bistro fare and unique setting of Chez Colette recall the romance of 1920s Paris.
306 rooms. **$$$**

238 SPECIALTY LODGINGS

Alexander Inn
Spruce and 12th Streets,
Philadelphia,
215-923-3535, 877-253-9466;
www.alexanderinn.com
48 rooms. Complimentary continental breakfast. **$**

Rittenhouse Square B&B
1715 Rittenhouse Square, Philadelphia,
215-546-6500, 877-791-6500;
www.rittenhouse1715.com
This renovated 1900s carriage house affords guests a choice of 10 deluxe rooms in an ideal setting just off of Rittenhouse Square, one of the city's most fashionable locations. Rooms feature marble bathrooms, telephone and cable TV and workstations with Internet access. Guests are made comfortable with 24-hour concierge service, nightly turndown service, a nightly complimentary wine and snack reception, and continental breakfast served in the cafe.
10 rooms. Complimentary continental breakfast. **$$**

Thomas Bond House
129 S. Second St., Philadelphia,
215-923-8523, 800-845-2663;
www.winston-salem-inn.com/philadelphia/index.htm
Perfect for history buffs and ideally situated in charming Old City Philadelphia, this beautiful bed-and-breakfast is actually a part of the Independence National Historic Park. The house, on the National Register of Historic Places, has a warm and inviting atmosphere and antique furnishings, and is close to many important historical sites, great shopping and fine dining.
12 rooms. Complimentary continental breakfast. Airport transportation available. **$**

RESTAURANTS

★★★Azalea
401 Chestnut St., Philadelphia,
215-925-0000;
www.omnihotels.com
Just a block from historic Independence Hall and the Liberty Bell, this restaurant at the Omni Hotel at Independence Park is a restful spot to enjoy a meal. The decor is stylishly eclectic, and the menus are rooted in classic French technique, featuring contemporary touches and international accents. Dishes range from comfortingly rich (house-made herb spaetzle baked with Gruyere and Emmantal cheeses and assorted summer vegetables) to heart-healthy (mustard-glazed salmon over golden whipped potatoes with a sauce ver jus and baby bok choy). Sunday brunch is popular here, where live piano, harp or guitar music sets an elegant tone.
Continental menu. Breakfast, lunch, dinner. Sunday brunch. Closed Monday. Bar. Children's menu. Business casual attire. Reservations recommended. Valet parking. **$$$**

★★★Bistro Romano
120 Lombard St., Philadelphia,
215-925-8880;
www.bistroromano.com
When you walk into this cozy Italian restaurant located in the Society Hill area, one of the first things you see is the majestic

oak bar from the City of Detroit III, a 1912 side wheel passenger steamer. There is also a beautiful painting from the ship of a sea nymph in the stairwell that leads downstairs to the romantic dining room. Besides the beautiful decor, Bistro Romano is well known for its tableside Caesar salad, homemade ravioli and award-winning tiramisu. Italian menu. Dinner. Bar. Children's menu. Business casual attire. Reservations recommended. **$$**

★★★Brasserie Perrier
1619 Walnut St., Philadelphia,
215-568-3000;
www.brasserieperrier.com

Brasserie Perrier, the laid-back, younger sibling of Le Bec-Fin, is a terrific spot for first-rate modern French fare with Italian and Asian influences. In traditional French brasserie style, you'll find plats du jour, steak frites, and frise aux lardons among other perfectly prepared standards. The kitchen also departs from the traditional brasserie-style menu, offering creative takes on pasta and entrees painted with eclectic flavors from around the globe. If you love choucroute, make sure to call ahead and find out which day it is one of the plats du jours. The impressive wine list is mostly French, but filled with offerings that will not only fit all budgets, but all tastes as well. French menu, Pacific-Rim/Pan-Asian menu. Lunch, dinner. Bar. Business casual attire. Reservations recommended. Valet parking. Outdoor seating. **$$$**

★★★Buddakan
325 Chestnut St., Philadelphia,
215-574-9440;
www.buddakan.com

Slick, sexy and spectacular, Buddakan is one of Philadelphia's hottest spots for dining, drinking and lounging. Whether you're seated in the shadow of the restaurant's 10-foot gilded Buddha at the elevated communal table or at one of the other more intimate tables for two in chairs backed with black-and-white photo portraits, you will never guess that this den of fabulousness was once a post office. If your mail carrier

were feasting on Buddakan's brand of splashy Asian fusion fare, like lobster fried rice with Thai basil and saffron, or crisp pizza topped with seared tuna and wasabi, you can be sure that the mail would never arrive on time. Entrees are meant for sharing. A nice way to kick off the evening is with the signature Buddalini, a sexy sipper made from Champagne, Cointreau and fresh mango juice. Pan-Asian menu. Lunch, dinner. Bar. Business casual attire. Reservations recommended. Valet parking. **$$$**

★★Cafe Spice
35 S. Second St., Philadelphia,
215-627-6273;
www.cafespice.com
Indian menu. Lunch, dinner, brunch. Bar. Casual attire. Reservations recommended. Outdoor seating. **$$**

★★★Chez Colette
120 S. 17th St., Philadelphia,
215-569-8300;
www.sofitel.com
Black-and-white photos decorate the walls in this brasserie, jazz plays in the background, and the staff and menus are both bilingual—French and English. All the pastries, breads and desserts are made on premise. For breakfast, try the fruit sushi. French menu. Breakfast, lunch, dinner. Sunday brunch. Bar. Business casual attire. Reservations recommended. Valet parking. **$$$**

★★City Tavern
138 S. Second St., Philadelphia,
215-413-1443;
www.citytavern.com
American menu. Lunch, dinner. Closed Monday in January. Bar. Children's menu, outdoor seating. **$$$**

★★Dark Horse
421 S. Second St., Philadelphia,
215-928-9307;
www.darkhorsepub.com
American menu. Lunch, dinner. Sunday brunch. Closed Monday. Bar. Children's menu. **$$**

PENNSYLVANIA

★★★Deux Cheminees

1221 Locust St., Philadelphia,
215-790-0200

Featuring classic and regional French cuisine in five beautifully appointed dining rooms, Deux Cheminees ("two fireplaces") is a testament to the fact that some traditions endure for good reason. Located in two 19th-century townhouses, the formal restaurant offers fixed-price, five-course menus and special value three-course dinners for early diners. This is the place for foie gras, pates and terrines, sweetbreads and escargot. The house specialty, rack of lamb for two, is roasted to order and served with truffle-filled sauce Perigord.
French menu. Dinner. Closed Sunday-Monday. Business casual attire. Reservations recommended. **$$$$**

★Famous Fourth Street Delicatessen

700 S. Fourth St., Philadelphia,
215-922-3274

Deli menu. Breakfast, lunch, dinner, brunch. Closed Rosh Hashanah, Yom Kippur. Casual attire. **$$**

★★Felicia's

1148 S. 11th St., Philadelphia,
215-755-9656

Italian menu. Dinner. Closed Monday. Bar. Valet parking. **$$**

★★Fez

620 S. Second St., Philadelphia,
215-925-5367;
www.fezrestaurant.com

Middle Eastern menu. Dinner. Casual attire. Reservations recommended. **$$**

★★Fork

306 Market St., Philadelphia,
215-625-9425;
www.forkrestaurant.com

American menu. Lunch, dinner. Sunday brunch. Bar. Business casual attire. Reservations recommended. Outdoor seating. **$$$**

★★★★Fountain Restaurant

1 Logan Square, Philadelphia,
215-963-1500;
www.fourseasons.com/philadelphia

The Fountain is the stunning flagship restaurant of the Four Seasons Hotel Philadelphia. The wine list, which covers all of France as well as Germany, Italy, the United States, Australia, New Zealand and South America, is just one of the highlights of dining here. The kitchen often uses ingredients from local producers and includes the farms' names on the menu, so you'll know which farmer planted your baby greens and where your beets were picked. As you'll see here, the best ingredients really do make a difference. Vegetarian items are available on request, and the kitchen offers several selections that are marked nutritionally balanced, healthier fare.
American menu, French menu. Breakfast, lunch, dinner. Sunday brunch. Bar. Children's menu. Jacket required. Reservations recommended. Valet parking. **$$$**

★Geno's Steaks

1219 S. Nineth St., Philadelphia,
215-389-0659;
www.genossteaks.com

American menu. Breakfast, lunch, dinner. Late-night. Casual attire. Outdoor seating. **$**

★★Italian Bistro of Center City

211 S. Broad St., Philadelphia,
215-731-0700;
www.italianbistro.com

Italian menu. Lunch, dinner. Bar. Children's menu. Casual attire. Reservations recommended. **$$**

★★Jack's Firehouse

2130 Fairmount Ave., Philadelphia,
215-232-9000;
www.jacksfirehouse.com

American menu. Lunch, dinner. Sunday brunch. Bar. Children's menu. Casual attire. Outdoor seating. **$$**

★★★Jake's Restaurant

4365 Main St., Philadelphia, 215-483-0444;
www.jakesrestaurant.com

Located in Manayunk, Philadelphia's funky, high-energy, artsy neighborhood, Jake's Restaurant is a lively spot to meet friends for drinks and stay for dinner. Chef/owner

240

PENNSYLVANIA

Bruce Cooper's chic regulars make a habit of staying all night, savoring his unique brand of stylish, regional American food. While at the bar, go for one of Jake's wild house cocktails or take a chance on a unique microbrew. The kitchen is in sync with its customers' desire for both fun and flavor in their food. For instance, on a recent visit, the prix fixe menu was titled Jake's Clam Bake, which featured a popular four-course clam bake-style shellfish menu paired with wine. American menu. Lunch, dinner. Sunday brunch. Bar. Business casual attire. Reservations recommended. Valet parking. Outdoor seating. $$$

★★Joseph Poon
1002 Arch St., Philadelphia,
215-500-9774;
www.josephpoon.com
Asian fusion menu. Lunch, dinner. Closed Monday; also Chinese New Year. Bar. $$

★★★★Lacroix at the Rittenhouse
210 W. Rittenhouse Square, Philadelphia,
215-790-2533;
www.rittenhousehotel.com
Set in the stately Rittenhouse Hotel, Lacroix is a restaurant of understated elegance. The kitchen plays up fresh local ingredients with a delicate French hand, while guests dine in posh, sophisticated luxury and enjoy views of the charming Rittenhouse Square. While acclaimed chef Jean-Marie Lacroix has retired, the kitchen is still in able hands under the direction of Chef Matthew Levin. The flexible tasting menu is the best option here, where diners can choose three, four or five-courses, and desserts are generously provided as a gift from the chef. The Sunday Brunch (where the buffet is set up in the kitchen) is a particular Philadelphia favorite. French menu. Breakfast, lunch, dinner. Sunday brunch. Bar. Children's menu. Jacket required. Reservations recommended. Valet parking. $$$

★★★Le Bar Lyonnais
1523 Walnut St., Philadelphia,
215-567-1000;
www.lebecfin.com

Since Georges Perrier added Le Bar Lyonnais to his internationally renowned Le Bec-Fin restaurant in 1990, the bar has achieved status as one of Philadelphia's best French bistros, winning kudos for its comfortable setting and accessible menu. The decor is subdued and casual with dark wallpaper, dark woods, soft lighting and marble-topped tables. The bistro has featured dishes such as a cassolette of snails in champagne and hazelnut butter sauce, grilled Dover sole with herb gnocchi in beurre blanc and veal tenderloin with calves liver and onions. This lower-level bar is a great choice for diners who want to sample some of Le Bec-Fin's signature dishes without paying for a prix fixe menu. French bistro menu. Lunch, dinner. Closed Sunday. Bar. Business casual attire. Reservations recommended. Valet parking. $$$

★★★★★Le Bec-Fin
1523 Walnut St.,
Philadelphia,
215-567-1000;
www.lebecfin.com
Still sparkling from its 2002 renovation, Georges Perrier's Le Bec-Fin, which opened in 1970, remains a shining star for haute French cuisine. The room is a bastion of civility with fresh flowers, glass chandeliers, amber lighting and finely dressed tabletops. Perrier's talented team brings out the brilliance in classic dishes while offering several new creations destined to be classics. Perrier's signature crab cake with haricot verts is divine and joins an exciting menu divided between Les Entrees (appetizers); an impressive and unusual selection of Les Poissons (fish), depending on availability; and an equally terrific assortment of Les Viandes (meats), also listed according to season and availability. French menu. Lunch, dinner. Closed Sunday. Bar. Jacket required. Reservations recommended. Valet parking. $$$$

★★★Le Castagne Ristorante
1920 Chestnut St., Philadelphia,
215-751-9913;
www.lecastagne.com

PENNSYLVANIA

★
★
★
★
★
★

This contemporary Italian restaurant offers a menu that concentrates on northern Italian dishes, and in season, a pre-theater menu is offered. Everything is made in-house including—breads, pastas, sauces and desserts. Some dessert and fish selections are prepared tableside.
Italian menu. Lunch, dinner. Closed Sunday. Bar. Business casual attire. Reservations recommended. Outdoor seating. $$$

★Manayunk Brewery and Restaurant
4120 Main St., Philadelphia,
215-482-8220;
www.manayunkbrewery.com
American menu. Lunch, dinner. Late-night, Sunday brunch. Bar. Children's menu. Business casual attire. Reservations recommended. Valet parking. Outdoor seating. $$

★Manayunk Diner
3720 Main St., Philadelphia,
215-483-4200
American menu. Breakfast, lunch, dinner. Bar. Children's menu. Casual attire. Outdoor seating. $$

★★★Monte Carlo Living Room
150 South St., Philadelphia,
215-925-2220;
www.montecarlolivingroom.com
Chef Raymond Brown's weekly menus represent fine, contemporary Italian cuisine at its best. A starter duet of foie gras and sweetbreads is coupled with Firelli pears and aged balsamic vinegar, and the roasted lamb entree is fragrant with sage and paired with cranberry beans and Barolo sauce. Cheese course selections are well thought out, and the desserts are creative.
Italian menu. Dinner. Closed Sunday. Bar. Business casual attire. Reservations recommended. Valet parking. Outdoor seating. $$$

★★★Moonstruck
7955 Oxford Ave., Philadelphia,
215-725-6000;
www.moonstruckrestaurant.com
Formerly known as Ristorante DiLullo, this elegantly casual northern Italian gem has been doing business for more than 20 years. Menus let customers choose among a wide range of antipasti, primi piatti (pasta appetizers), secondi piatti (second courses) and piatti tradizionale (traditional classics). The latter menu section features one special dish per night, ranging from Friday's caciucco, a bouillabaisse of seafood and fish, to Tuesday's osso buco.
Italian menu. Dinner. Bar. Children's menu. Business casual attire. Reservations recommended. $$$

★★★Morimoto
723 Chestnut St., Philadelphia,
215-413-9070;
www.morimotorestaurant.com
Japanese fusion cuisine from Iron Chef Masaharu Morimoto of New York's Nobu fame (he was executive chef at Nobu Matsuhisa's restaurant for six years) pulsates with life and creativity. His Philadelphia outpost, stunningly shaped by local restaurant impresario Stephen Starr, is Morimoto's first restaurant in the United States. Ceilings undulate, booths change color and the sushi bar at the back never stops bustling. The best way to challenge your taste buds is to select one of Morimoto's omakase (multicourse tasting) menus.
Japanese menu. Lunch, dinner. Bar. Business casual attire. Reservations recommended. $$$

★★★Moshulu Restaurant
401 S. Columbus Blvd., Philadelphia,
215-923-2500;
www.moshulu.com
Moshulu is a stunning South Seas-inspired restaurant housed in a 100-year-old, 394-foot, four-masted sailing ship. Its several dining rooms are elegantly decorated with rattan chairs, cane furniture, dark mahogany and Polynesian artwork. The kitchen, headed by Executive Chef Ralph Fernandez, churns out creative, delicious dishes that will keep you coming back for more.
American menu. Lunch, dinner. Bar. Business casual attire. Reservations recommended. Valet parking. Outdoor seating. $$$

★

★

★

★

★

★★★Overtures
609 E. Passyunk Ave., Philadelphia,
215-627-3455

Chef/proprietor Peter LamLein has been creating his finely tuned menus of French/ Mediterranean fare for Philadelphians for more than a decade. The setting is elegantly Empire, with murals on the garden room walls and additional paintings by pastry chef Ron Weisberg throughout. There's a nice selection of la carte dishes, including an appetizer of fresh anchovies in lemon oil with garlic and roasted peppers, and an entree of veal sweetbreads in hazelnut crumbs with orange Cognac sauce. But the best values are LamLein's fixed-price menus—$50 for four courses and $20.07 (the price matches the year) for three courses—three nights a week. Bring your own alcoholic beverages, as there is no bar. Fresh juices and mixers are stocked, however, and the waitstaff will uncork and pour your wines.

French, Mediterranean menu. Dinner. Closed Monday. Business casual attire. Reservations recommended. **$$$**

★★Paloma
6516 Castor Ave., Philadelphia,
215-533-0356

French, Mexican menu. Dinner. Closed Sunday-Monday; last week of August-first week of September. Bar. Business casual attire. Reservations recommended. **$$$**

★★★Pasion!
211 S. 15th St., Philadelphia,
215-875-9895

Award-winning chef Guillermo Pernot's passion is Nuevo Latino cuisine, a melding of ancient cooking influences plumbed from Mexico, Central America and South America with fun, contemporary stylings. Known for his meal-starting ceviches (five different versions are featured daily), Pernot is equally creative with main courses, such as a plantain and wasabi pea-crusted salmon with creamy fufu and recao beurre blanc sauce.

Latin American menu. Dinner. Closed Sunday in summer. Bar. Business casual attire. Reservations recommended. **$$$**

★★Philadelphia Fish & Co
207 Chestnut St., Philadelphia,
215-625-8605;
www.philadelphiafish.com

Seafood menu. Lunch, dinner. Bar. Children's menu. Business casual attire. Reservations recommended. Outdoor seating. **$$$**

★★The Plough & the Stars
123 Chestnut St., Philadelphia,
215-733-0300;
www.ploughstars.com

Continental menu. Lunch, dinner, brunch, late-night. Bar. Children's menu. Business casual attire. Reservations recommended. Outdoor seating. **$$$**

★Rangoon Burmese Restaurant
112 N. Nineth St., Philadelphia,
215-829-8939

Burmese menu. Lunch, dinner. Casual attire. **$$**

★★★Ristorante Panorama
14 N. Front St., Philadelphia,
215-922-7800;
www.pennsviewhotel.com

Panorama is part of the boutique-style Penn's View Hotel. The beautiful dining room features marble floors, a wall of windows and murals throughout. The cuisine is gutsy, old-world Italian, featuring dishes such as paillard of beef rolled in garlic, cheese, egg and herbs, slow-cooked in tomato sauce, and served with house-made gnocchi. But this place is known for its wine. Daily wine lists offer from 22 to 26 different flights (five wines per flight), plus dozens more by-the-glass options. The quality, made possible by the restaurant's cruvinet preservation and dispensing system, is exceptional, earning Panorama numerous "Best Wines by the Glass" awards from national food magazines.

Italian menu. Lunch, dinner. Bar. Business casual attire. Reservations recommended. Valet parking. **$$$**

★★★Ruth's Chris Steak House
260 S. Broad St., Philadelphia,
215-790-1515, 800-544-0808;
www.ruthschris.com

★
★
★
★

Ruth's Chris is a top choice of many steak lovers. With a menu that highlights aged prime Midwestern beef that's broiled at 1800 degrees and drizzled with butter, how could it not be? Dark wood accents and comfortable leather booths give the room a club-like steakhouse feel.

Steak menu. Dinner. Bar. **$$$**

★★★The Saloon

750 S. Seventh St., Philadelphia,
215-627-1811;
www.saloonrestaurant.net

Richard Santore has been operating this venerable establishment in Philadelphia's Bellavista neighborhood, bordering Center City and South Philly, for nearly 40 years. The food is classic Italian fare, served for lunch and dinner. Appetizers include poached pear and gorgonzola salad with roasted walnuts, baby greens and red onion with pear vinaigrette. Fettuccini Lobster Amatriciana is a toss of house-made fettuccini with lobster, bacon, onion, fresh tomato and pecorino cheese in tomato sauce. Daily dinner specials range from beef carpaccio drizzled with truffle essence and served with fava beans to a double veal chop marinated in white wine, pan seared and served with Yukon gold potatoes.

Italian, Steak menu. Lunch, dinner. Closed Sunday; also one week in early July. Bar. Business casual attire. Valet parking. No credit cards accepted. **$$$**

★★Serrano

20 S. Second St., Philadelphia,
215-928-0770;
www.tinangel.com

International menu. Dinner. Closed last week in August-first week in September. Bar. Business casual attire. Reservations recommended. **$$**

★South Street Diner

140 South St.,
Philadelphia,
215-627-5258

American, Italian, Greek menu. Breakfast, lunch, dinner. Late-night. Children's menu. Casual attire. **$$**

★★★★Striped Bass

1500 Walnut St., Philadelphia,
215-732-4444;
www.stripedbassrestaurant.com

Set in a former brokerage house, Striped Bass boasts towering 28-foot ceilings, red marble columns and a high-energy open kitchen presided over by a 16-foot striped bass made of iron. The menu showcases virtually every fish in the sea. If it once swam, you'll find it on the menu. A magnificent raw bar tempts diners with briny oysters, sweet clams and plump, juicy shrimp. Save room for the raw fish selection: a shimmering array of tartars, ceviches and carpaccios deliciously tinged with Asian (wasabi, ginger, miso), Latin American (cilantro, chilies, lime) and Italian (olive oil, herbs, pine nuts) flavors.

Seafood menu. Dinner. Bar. Business casual attire. Reservations recommended. Valet parking. **$$$**

★★★Susanna Foo

1512 Walnut St., Philadelphia,
215-545-8800;
www.susannafoo.net

Thanks to the plethora of greasy Chinese takeout joints, Chinese food has been much maligned over the years. But at Susanna Foo, a Zen-like dining oasis, the delicious, traditional cuisine of China sheds its unfortunate reputation and gains the respect it deserves. For years, chef/owner Susanna Foo has been dressing up the dishes of her native land with sophisticated French flair and modern, global accents. Foo's dim sum can be a meal on their own. The entrees are equally mouthwatering, especially the famous tea-smoked Peking duck breast. You may never be able to order takeout again.

Chinese, French menu. Lunch, dinner. Bar. Business casual attire. Reservations recommended. **$$$**

★★★Swann Cafe

1 Logan Square, Philadelphia,
215-963-1500, 866-516-1100;
www.fourseasons.com/philadelphia

Named for the spectacular Logan Square fountain in front of the Four Seasons Hotel Philadelphia, Swann Cafe is the more accessible of the hotel's exceptional restaurants. Menus are overseen by Executive Chef Martin Hamann, and range from light and lovely dishes such as an appetizer ragout of forest mushrooms and asparagus tips to a zesty sandwich of pulled osso buco with aged provolone and spicy pepper and onion relish on a Stirato roll.

American menu. Lunch, dinner. Bar. Children's menu. Casual attire. Reservations recommended. Valet parking. **$$$**

★★★Tangerine
232 Market St., Philadelphia,
215-627-5116;
www.tangerinerestaurant.com
This Middle Eastern-themed restaurant in the heart of Olde City Philadelphia features a menu that blends flavors from the Mediterranean, France, Spain, Italy and Africa. An appetizer of harissa-spiced gnocchi is sweetened with dates and paired with celery root. Pistachio-crusted duck breast is served with creamy onions, seared foie gras and port-poached pear.

Mediterranean menu. Dinner. Bar. Business casual attire. Reservations recommended. Valet parking. **$$$**

★★Umbria
7131 Germantown Ave.,
Philadelphia,
215-242-6470
International menu. Dinner. Closed Sunday-Tuesday. Business casual attire. Reservations recommended. **$$**

★★★Vetri
1312 Spruce St., Philadelphia,
215-732-3478;
www.vetriristorante.com

Chef Mark Vetri learned to prepare rustic Italian cuisine (think: rabbit loin and sweetbreads wrapped in pancetta with morels, and baby goat poached in milk and then oven roast to crispness) from Italy's best chefs and then brought his skills home to Philly. Ensconced in the tiny, 35-seat space once occupied by other pinnacle establishments (Le Bec-Fin, Chanterelle), Vetri is intent on creating likewise legendary meals. The wine list has been nationally lauded, and the service is seamless. On Saturdays, indulge in Vetri's five- or seven-course fixed-price menus (not available during the summer).

Italian menu. Dinner. Closed Sunday; two weeks in January and three weeks in August; also Saturday in summer. Business casual attire. Reservations recommended. **$$$$**

★★White Dog Cafe
3420 Sansom St.,
Philadelphia,
215-386-9224;
www.whitedog.com
American, vegetarian menu. Lunch, dinner, brunch. Bar. Children's menu. Business casual attire. Reservations recommended. Outdoor seating. **$$$**

★★Zocalo
3600 Lancaster Ave.,
Philadelphia,
215-895-0139;
www.zocalophilly.com
Mexican menu. Lunch, dinner. Closed Sunday. Bar. Children's menu. Casual attire. Reservations recommended. Outdoor seating. **$$**

PENNSYLVANIA

PHOENIXVILLE

RESTAURANTS
★★Seven Stars Inn
263 Hoffecker Rd., Phoenixville,
610-495-5205;
www.sevenstarsinn.com

Seafood menu. Dinner. Closed Monday; holidays. Bar. Children's menu. **$$$**

PITTSBURGH

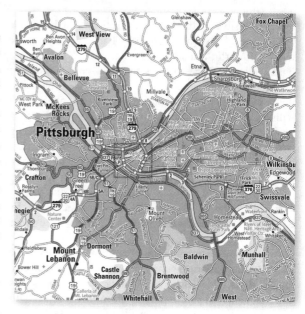

Pittsburgh has become one of the most spectacular civic redevelopments in America, with modern buildings, clean parks and community pride. The new Pittsburgh is a result of a rare combination of capital-labor cooperation, public and private support, enlightened political leadership, and imaginative, venturesome community planning. Its $1-billion international airport was designed to be the most user-friendly in the country.

After massive war production, Pittsburgh labored to eliminate the 1930s image of an unsophisticated mill town. During the 1950s and 1960s, Renaissance I began, a $500-million program to clean the city's air and develop new structures such as Gateway Center, the Civic Arena and Point State Park. The late 1970s and early 1980s ushered in Renaissance II, a $3-billion expansion program reflecting the movement away from industry and toward high technology.

Today Pittsburgh has completed this dramatic shift from industry to a diversified base including high technology, health care, finance and education and continues its transition to a services-oriented city.

Pittsburgh's cultural personality is expressed by the Pittsburgh Symphony Orchestra, Pittsburgh Opera, Pittsburgh Ballet, Phipps Conservatory and the Carnegie Museums of Pittsburgh, which include the Museum of Natural History and the Museum of Art. The city has 25 parks, 45 "parklets," 60 recreation centers and 27 swimming pools.

Born of frontier warfare in the shadow of Fort Pitt, the city is named after the elder William Pitt, the great British statesman. Its strategic military position was an important commercial asset, and Pittsburgh soon became a busy river port and transit point for the western flow of pioneers.

Industry grew out of the West's need for manufactured goods; foundries and rolling mills were soon producing nails, axes, frying pans and shovels. The Civil War added tremendous impetus to industry, and by the end of the war, Pittsburgh was producing half the steel and one-third of the glass made in the country. Captains of industry and finance such as Thomas Mellon, Andrew Carnegie and Henry Clay Frick built their industrial empires in Pittsburgh. The American Federation of Labor was born here (1881) because the city has been the scene of historic clashes between labor and management.

Information: Greater Pittsburgh Convention & Visitors Bureau, Liberty Ave. at Gateway center, 425 Sixth Ave., Pittsburgh, 800-366-0093; www.visitpittsburgh.com

PENNSYLVANIA

WHAT TO SEE AND DO

Alcoa Building
425 Sixth Ave., Pittsburgh
Pioneer in aluminum for skyscraper construction, exterior work was done from inside; no scaffolding was required. Draped in aluminum waffle, 30 stories high; considered to be one of the country's most daring experiments in skyscraper design.

Allegheny County Courthouse
Grant St. and Fifth Ave., Pittsburgh
One of the country's outstanding Romanesque buildings, the two-square-city-block structure was designed by Henry Hobson Richardson in 1884. Monday-Friday.

Andy Warhol Museum
117 Sandusky St., Pittsburgh,
412-237-8300;
www.warhol.org
The most comprehensive single-artist museum in the world. More than 500 works. Tuesday-Sunday.

Benedum Center for the Performing Arts
719 Liberty Ave., Pittsburgh,
412-456-6666
Expansion and restoration of the Stanley Theater, a movie palace built in 1928. Gilded plasterwork, 500,000-piece crystal chandelier, and a nine-story addition to backstage area make this an exceptional auditorium with one of the largest stages in the country. The center is home to Pittsburgh Ballet Theatre, the Pittsburgh Dance Council, the Pittsburgh Opera and Civic Light Opera. Free guided tours (by appointment).

Carnegie Mellon University
5000 Forbes Ave., Pittsburgh,
412-268-2000;
www.cmu.edu
(1900) (7,900 students.) Founded by Andrew Carnegie. Composed of seven colleges. Tours of campus.

Carnegie Museums of Pittsburgh
4400 Forbes Ave., Pittsburgh,
412-622-3360;
www.carnegiemuseums.org
Public complex built by industrialist Andrew Carnegie. Tuesday-Sunday.

Carnegie Museum of Art
412-622-3131;
www.cmoa.org
Possibly America's first modern art museum, as Carnegie urged the gallery to exhibit works dated after 1896. Collection of Impressionist and Post-Impressionist paintings; Hall of Sculpture; Hall of Architecture; films, videos.

Carnegie Museum of Natural History
412-622-3131;
www.carnegiemnh.org
Houses one of the most complete collections of dinosaur fossils. Exhibits include Dinosaur Hall, Polar World, Hillman Hall of Minerals and Gems, the Walton Hall of Ancient Egypt; changing exhibits.

Library of Pittsburgh
412-622-3114;
www.clpgh.org
Central branch contains more than 4 1/2 million books. Houses first department of science and technology established in a U.S. public library.

Music Hall
412-622-1906
Home to Mendelssohn Choir, Pittsburgh Chamber Music Society and River City Brass Band. Elaborate gilt and marble foyer; walls of French eschallion, 24 pillars made of green stone and a gold baroque ceiling.

Carnegie Science Center
One Allegheny Ave., Pittsburgh,
412-237-3400;
www.carnegiesciencecenter.org
Learning and entertainment complex has more than 40,000 square feet of exhibit galleries that demonstrate how human activities are affected by science and technology. U.S.S. Requin, moored in front of the center, is a World War II diesel-electric submarine; tours (40 minutes) demonstrate the electronic, visual and voice communication devices on board.

PENNSYLVANIA

Henry Buhl Jr. Planetarium and Observatory is a technologically sophisticated interactive planetarium with control panels at every seat. Also here are the 350-seat Rangos Omnimax Theater and the Health Sciences Amphitheater. Restaurant, gift shop. Daily.

County Parks
Pittsburgh, 412-350-2455
South Park, 12 miles S on Highway 88. North Park, 14 miles N on Highway 19. Boyce Park, 14 miles E on I-376, Highway 22. Settler's Cabin Park, 9 miles W on I-279, Highway 22. Swimming, fishing, boating. Bicycling (rentals), ball fields, golf, tennis. Cross-country skiing, downhill skiing, ice skating (winter, daily). Picnicking. Parks open daily. Fees for activities. Attractions for each park vary.

Frick Art and Historical Center
7227 Reynolds St., Pittsburgh,
412-371-0600;
www.frickart.org
Museum complex built on grounds of estate once belonging to industrialist Henry Clay Frick; gardens, carriage house museum, greenhouse, cafe and restored children's playhouse that now serves as a visitor's center. Tuesday-Sunday.

Clayton, the Henry Clay Frick Home
7227 Reynolds St., Pittsburgh
A restored four-story Victorian mansion with 23 rooms; only remaining house of area in East End once known as "Millionaire's Row." Some original dcor and personal mementos of the Fricks' Tours; reservation recommended.

The Frick Art Museum
7227 Reynolds St., Pittsburgh,
412-371-0600;
www.frickart.org
Collection of Helen Clay Frick, daughter of Henry Clay Frick, includes Italian Renaissance, Flemish and French 18th-century paintings and decorative arts. Italian and French furniture, Renaissance bronzes, tapestries, Chinese porcelains. Also changing exhibits; concerts, lectures.

Frick Park
Beechwood Blvd. and English Lane, Pittsburgh,
412-422-6536
Covers 476 acres, largely in natural state; nature trails wind through ravines and over hills; also nature center (2005 Beechwood Boulevard), tennis courts, picnic areas, playgrounds. Daily.

Gateway Center
420 Fort Duquesne Blvd., Pittsburgh,
412-392-6000
Complex includes four skyscrapers of Trizec Properties, Inc. Gateway Center Plaza, a two-acre open-air garden over underground parking garage, has lovely walks, three fountains, more than 90 types of trees and 100 varieties of shrubs and seasonal flowers. Monday-Friday.

Guided Bus and Walking Tours
1 Station Square, Suite 450,
Pittsburgh, 412-471-5808;
www.phlf.org
Offered through the Pittsburgh History and Landmarks Foundation.

Hartwood Acres
215 Saxonburg Blvd.,
Pittsburgh,
412-767-9200
(1929) A 629-acre re-creation of English country estate; Tudor mansion with many antiques; formal gardens, stables. Tours (Tuesday-Sunday). Also music and theater events during summer.

Duquesne Incline
220 Grandview Ave.,
Pittsburgh,
412-381-1665
Built 1877; restored and run by community effort; observation deck. Free parking at lower station. Daily.

Monongahela Incline
Pittsburgh,
412-442-2000
Panoramic views from observation deck. Daily.

248

James L. Kelso Bible Lands Museum

616 N. Highland Ave., Pittsburgh,
412-362-5610

Artifacts and displays from the ancient Near East, especially Palestine. Call for hours.

Mellon Arena

66 Mario Lemieux Place, Pittsburgh,
www.mellonarena.com

This $22-million all-weather amphitheater accommodates 17,500 people. Retractable roof can fold up within 2 1/2 minutes.

Museum of Photographic History

531 E. Ohio, Pittsburgh, 412-231-7881;
www.photoantiquities.org

Photo gallery and museum. Selections from 100,000 antique photographic images. Closed Sundays, Tuesdays.

National Aviary

700 Arch St., Allegheny Commons West,
Pittsburgh, 412-323-7235;
www.aviary.org

The Aviary is home to one of the world's premier bird collections and is the only indoor bird facility independent of a larger zoo in North America. Daily.

Pittsburgh Children's Museum

10 Children's Way, Pittsburgh,
412-322-5058;
www.pittsburghkids.org

Hands-on exhibits. and silkscreen studio; storytelling, regularly scheduled puppet shows, live performances; two-story climber. Daily.

Pittsburgh Penguins (NHL)

Mellon Arena,
66 Mario Lemieux Place, Pittsburgh,
412-323-1919;
www.penguins.nhl.com

Professional hockey team.

Pittsburgh Pirates (MLB)

PNC Park, 115 Federal St.,
Pittsburgh,
412-323-5000;
www.pittsburgh.pirates.mlb.com

Professional baseball team.

Pittsburgh Steelers (NFL)

Heinz Field, 600 Stadium Circle,
Pittsburgh, 412-432-7800;
www.steelers.com

Professional football team.

Pittsburgh Zoo & Aquarium

1 Wild Place, Pittsburgh,
412-665-3639;
www.pittsburghzoo/com

More than 70 acres containing nearly 6,000 animals, children's farm (late May-October), discovery pavilion, reptile house, tropical and Asian forests, African savanna and aqua zoo. Merry-go-round and train rides (fee). Highland Park covers 75 acres and has tennis courts, picnic grounds, shelters (some require permit), twin reservoirs, swimming pool (fee). Daily.

Point State Park

Fort Duquesne and
Fort Pitt boulevards, Pittsburgh,
412-471-0235

Point where the Allegheny and Monongahela rivers meet to form the Ohio. A 150-foot fountain symbolizes the joining of the rivers. There are military drills with fifes and drums, muskets and cannon (May-Labor Day, some Sunday afternoons).

Block House of Fort Pitt

Fort Duquesne and
Fort Pitt boulevards, Pittsburgh

Last remaining building of original fort (1767). Wednesday-Sunday.

Fort Pitt Museum

101 Commonwealth Place Pittsburgh,
412-281-9284;
www.fortpittmuseum.com

Built on part of original fort. Exhibits on early Pittsburgh and Fort Pitt. Wednesday-Sunday.

PPG place

Market Square, Pittsburgh

Designed by Philip Johnson, this is Pittsburgh's most popular Renaissance II building. PPG Place consists of six separate buildings designed in a postmodern, Gothic

249

PENNSYLVANIA

skyscraper style. Shopping and a food court can be found in Two PPG Place.

Riverview Park
Swimming pool (mid-June-Labor Day: daily; fee); tennis courts (April-November: daily); picnic shelter (May-September, permit required). Also playgrounds, parklet; nature, jogging trail. Fee for some activities.

Allegheny Observatory
159 Riverview Ave., Pittsburgh,
412-321-2400;
www.pitt.edu
Slides, tour of building. Maintained by University of Pittsburgh. Children under 12 years only with adult. Reservation required. April-October: Thursday-Friday.

Rodef Shalom Biblical Botanical Garden
4905 Fifth Ave., Pittsburgh,
412-621-6566;
www.rodefshalom.org/who/garden
The natural world of ancient Israel is re-created here in settings that specialize in plants of the Bible. A waterfall, desert and stream all help simulate the areas of the Jordan, Lake Kineret and the Dead Sea. Tours (by appointment). Special programs and exhibits. June-mid-September: Sunday-Thursday; Saturday hours limited.

Sandcastle Water Park
1000 Sandcastle Dr., Pittsburgh,
412-462-6666;
www.sandcastlewaterpark.com
The city's down-by-the-riverside water park has 15 slides, adult and kiddie pools; boardwalk, food. First Saturday in June-Labor Day: Daily.

Schenley Park
5000 Forbes Ave., Pittsburgh,
412-687-1800
Picnic areas, 18-hole golf course, lighted tennis courts; swimming pool; ice skating (winter); softball fields, running track, nature trails; bandstand (summer; free). Fee for some activities. Daily.
Also in park is:

Phipps Conservatory
Schenley Park, 1 Schenley Park, Pittsburgh,
412-622-6914;
www.conservatory.org
Constantly changing array of flowers; tropical gardens; outstanding orchid collection. Children's Discovery Garden with interactive learning opportunities. Seasonal flower shows. Daily, Tuesday-Saturday evenings.

Senator John Heinz Regional History Center
1212 Smallman St., Pittsburgh,
412-454-6000;
www.pghhistory.org
In Chatauqua Ice Warehouse (1898). Preserves 300 years of region's history with artifacts and extensive collection of archives, photos. Houses the Historical Society of Western Pennsylvania and Pittsburgh Sports Museum. Library Tuesday-Saturday. Daily.

Soldiers and Sailors Memorial Hall and Military History Museum
At Bigelow Boulevard, 4141 Fifth Ave., Pittsburgh,
412-621-4253;
www.soldiersandsailorshall.org
Auditorium has Lincoln's Gettysburg Address inscribed above stage; flags, weapons, uniforms, memorabilia from U.S. wars. Monday-Saturday: daily.

Station Square
1 Station Square, 450 Landmarks Building, Pittsburgh,
412-471-5808;
www.stationsquare.com
This 40-acre area features shopping, dining and entertainment in and among the historic buildings of the P & LE Railroad. Shopping in warehouses that once held loaded railroad boxcars. Daily.

Tour-Ed Mine and Museum
748 Bull Creek Rd., Pittsburgh,
724-224-4720;
www.tour-edmine.com
Complete underground coal mining operation; sawmill, furnished log house

(1789), old company store; historical mine museum, shelters; playground. May-Labor Day week: Daily.

Two Mellon Bank Center
Grant St. and Fifth Ave., Pittsburgh
Formerly the Union Trust Building, its Flemish-Gothic style was modeled after a library in Louvain, Belgium. Interior has a glass rotunda.

University of Pittsburgh
Fifth Ave. and Bigelow Blvd.,
Pittsburgh,
412-624-4141;
www.pitt.edu
(1787) (33,000 students.) Tours of Nationality Rooms in Cathedral of Learning. Campus of 70 buildings on 125 acres.

Cathedral of Learning
4200 Fifth Ave.,
Pittsburgh,
412-624-6000
(1935). Unique skyscraper of classrooms, stretching its Gothic-Moderne architecture 42 floors high (535 feet); vantage point on 36th floor. Surrounding a three-story Gothic commons room are an Early American Room and 24 Nationality Rooms, each reflecting the distinctive culture of the ethnic group that created and furnished it. Tours. Daily.

Heinz Chapel
Fifth and Bellefield avenues,
Pittsburgh,
412-624-4157;
www.heinzchapel.pitt.edu
Tall stained-glass windows; French Gothic architecture. Monday-Thursday, Saturday-Sunday.

Henry Clay Frick Fine Arts Building
Schenley Plaza, 104 Frick Fine Arts,
Pittsburgh,
412-648-2400
Glass-enclosed cloister; changing exhibits; art reference library. September-mid-June: daily; rest of year: Monday-Friday; closed university holidays.

Stephen Foster Memorial
4301 Forbes Ave., Pittsburgh,
412-624-4100
Auditorium/theater. Collection of the Pittsburgh-born composer's music and memorabilia. Said to be one of the most elaborate memorials ever built to a musician. Monday-Saturday, also Sunday afternoons.

U.S. Steel Tower
Grant St. and Seventh Ave., Pittsburgh
The tallest building in Pittsburgh, and 35th tallest in the nation. Ten exposed triangular columns and an exterior paneling of steel make up its construction.

SPECIAL EVENTS
Phipps Conservatory Flower Shows
Schenley Park, 1 Schenley Dr.,
Pittsburgh,
412-622-6914
Spring, summer, fall and holidays.

Pittsburgh Irish Festival
Chevrolet Amphitheatre, Station Square,
1 Station Square, Pittsburgh,
412-422-1113;
www.pghirishfest.org
Irish foods, dances and entertainment. Early or mid-September.

Pittsburgh Public Theater
621 Penn Ave., Pittsburgh,
412-316-1600;
www.ppt.org
City's largest resident professional company. September-June.

Pittsburgh Symphony Orchestra
Heinz Hall for the Performing Arts,
600 Penn Ave., Pittsburgh,
412-392-4900;
www.pittsburghsymphony.org
Classical, pop and family concerts. September-May.

Three Rivers Regatta
www.pghregatta.com
Water, land and air events; water shows and speedboat races. Last weekend in July and first weekend in August.

251

PENNSYLVANIA

★
★
★
★
★

Three Rivers Arts Festival
707 Penn Ave., Pittsburgh,
412-281-8723;
www.artsfestival.net
Juried, original works of local and national
artists: paintings, photography, sculpture,
crafts and videos; artists' market in outdoor plazas. Ongoing performances include
music, dance and performance art. Special
art projects, film festival, food; children's
activities. Early-mid-June.

HOTELS

★★Doubletree Hotel
1 Bigelow Square, Pittsburgh,
412-281-5800, 800-222-8733;
www.doubletree.com
311 rooms. Complimentary continental
breakfast. **$**

★★★Hilton Pittsburgh
600 Commonwealth Place, Pittsburgh,
412-391-4600;
www.hilton.com
713 rooms. Airport transportation available. **$**

★★★Marriott Pittsburgh City Center
112 Washington Place, Pittsburgh,
412-471-4000;
www.marriott.com
402 rooms. **$$**

★★★Omni William Penn Hotel
530 William Penn Place, Pittsburgh,
412-281-7100, 888-444-6664;
www.omnihotels.com
This hotel, built in 1916, fuses historic
charm with modern luxury in the heart of
downtown Pittsburgh. The rooms and suites
are tastefully and elegantly appointed with
a distinguished style. Executives on the go
appreciate the hotel's complete business
and fitness centers; families adore the Omni
Kids Program; and leisure visitors enjoy the
spa and salon services and proximity to
the city's leading stores. The hotel offers a
variety of convenient and tempting dining
choices, from Starbucks to pub food at the
Palm Court and Tap Room, to fine dining at
the Terrace Room.

596 rooms. Airport transportation available.
$$

★Quality Suites
700 Mansfield Ave., Pittsburgh,
412-279-6300, 877-424-6423;
www.choicehotels.com
151 rooms. Complimentary full breakfast.
Airport transportation available. Chalet-
style buildings. **$**

★★★Renaissance Pittsburgh Hotel
107 Sixth St., Pittsburgh,
412-562-1200;
www.renaissancehotels.com
Housed in the classic Fulton Building downtown, this hotel is an architectural stunner
in the city's renowned Cultural District.
Stroll across the Roberto Clemente Bridge
to reach North Shore destinations.
300 rooms. **$$**

★★★Sheraton Station Square Hotel
7 Station Square Drive, Pittsburgh,
412-261-2000, 800-255-7488;
www.sheraton.com
In the heart of Station Square, a major
nightlife destination, this riverfront hotel is
convenient to sightseeing, North Shore des-
tinations and the Gateway Clipper Fleet.
292 rooms. **$$**

★★★The Westin Convention Center Pittsburgh
1000 Penn Ave., Pittsburgh,
412-281-3700;
www.westin.com
The Westin Convention Center is located
in the heart of Pittsburgh's business and
cultural districts, and connected to the new
David L. Lawrence Convention Center by a
skywalk. Complimentary transportation to
local attractions is available.
616 rooms. **$$**

SPECIALTY LODGINGS

The Inn on Negley
703 S. Negley Ave., Pittsburgh,
412-661-0631;
www.innonnegley.com
Historic building (1884).

8 rooms. Children over 12 years only. Complimentary full breakfast. **$$**

The Priory Inn
614 Pressley St., Pittsburgh,
412-231-3338
This European-style inn with a fountain and floral arrangements in the courtyard was previously a haven for Benedictine monks (1888).
24 rooms. Complimentary continental breakfast. **$**

RESTAURANTS

★★1902 Landmark Tavern
24 Market Square,
Pittsburgh,
412-471-1902
Italian, American menu. Lunch, dinner. Closed Sunday. Bar. **$$**

★Abruzzi's Restaurant
52 S. Tenth St.,
Pittsburgh,
412-431-4511
Italian menu. Dinner. Bar. Casual attire. **$$**

★★★Cafe Allegro
51 S. 12th St.,
Pittsburgh,
412-481-7788;
www.cafeallegropittsburgh.com
This restaurant's several intimate dining areas draw crowds for Mediterranean fare. Try uncomplicated dishes like fish cooked en papillote.
Italian menu. Dinner. Bar. Valet parking. **$$**

★★Cafe at the Frick
7227 Reynolds St., Pittsburgh,
412-371-0600;
www.frickart.org
Lunch. Closed Monday. Outdoor seating. **$**

★★★Carlton
500 Grant St., Pittsburgh,
412-391-4099;
www.thecarltonrestaurant.com
American menu. Lunch, dinner. Closed Sunday. Bar. Children's menu. **$$$**

★★Casbah
229 S. Highland Ave.,
Pittsburgh,
412-661-5656;
www.bigburrito.com/casbah
Mediterranean menu. Lunch, dinner. Bar. Casual attire. Outdoor seating. **$$**

★★The Church Brew Works
3525 Liberty Ave.,
Pittsburgh,
412-688-8200;
www.churchbrew.com
American menu. Dinner. Bar. Outdoor seating. **$$**

★★★Cliffside
1208 Grandview Ave.,
Pittsburgh,
412-431-6996
American menu. Dinner. Bar. Valet parking. **$$**

★★★Common Plea
308 Ross St., Pittsburgh,
412-697-3100;
www.commonplea-restaurant.com
With its dark paneling, glass wall and subdued lighting, this restaurant caters to the legal crowd.
Seafood menu. Lunch, dinner. Bar. Valet parking (dinner). **$$**

★★Cozumel
5507 Walnut St.,
Pittsburgh,
412-621-5100
Mexican menu. Lunch, dinner. Bar. Children's menu. Casual attire. **$**

★★D'Imperio's
3412 William Penn Highway,
Pittsburgh,
412-823-4800
American, Italian menu. Lunch, dinner. Closed Sunday. Bar. Children's menu. **$$$**

★Dave and Andy's Ice Cream Parlor
207 Atwood St., Pittsburgh,
412-681-9906
$

★
★
★
★
★

★**Deja vu Lounge**
2106 Penn Ave.,
Pittsburgh,
412-434-1144;
www.dejavulive.net
American, Pan-Asian menu. Lunch, dinner.
Late-night. Closed Sunday. Bar. Casual
attire. Outdoor seating. **$$**

★★**Georgetown Inn**
1230 Grandview Ave.,
Pittsburgh,
412-481-4424;
www.georgetowninn.com
Seafood, steak menu. Lunch, dinner. Bar.
$$$

★★★**Grand Concourse**
1 Station Square,
Pittsburgh,
412-261-1717;
www.muer.com
Converted railroad station on the river
serves a legendary Sunday brunch.
International menu. Lunch, dinner. Sunday
brunch. Bar. Children's menu. Outdoor
seating. **$$$**

★★**India Garden**
328 Atwood St.,
Pittsburgh,
412-682-3000;
www.indiagarden.net
Indian menu. Lunch, dinner. **$**

★★**Kaya**
2000 Smallman St.,
Pittsburgh,
412-261-6565;
www.bigburrito.com/kaya
Caribbean menu. Dinner. Bar. Outdoor
seating. **$$$**

★★**Le Mont**
1114 Grandview Ave.,
Pittsburgh,
412-431-3100;
www.lemontpittsburgh.com
American menu. Dinner. Bar. Valet park-
ing. **$$$**

★★★**Le Pommier**
2104 E. Carson St., Pittsburgh,
412-431-1901;
www.lepommier.com
Located in the oldest storefront in the area
(1863), Le Pommier bills serves French-
American bistro entrees such as cauliflower
sautéed in brown butter with a roasted
cauliflower-gruyere sauce and fresh oregano
in puff pastry.
French menu. Lunch, dinner. Closed Sunday.
Bar. Valet parking (Friday-Saturday).
Outdoor seating. **$$**

★★**Max's Allegheny Tavern**
537 Suismon St.,
Pittsburgh,
412-231-1899;
www.maxsalleghenytavern.com
German menu. Lunch, dinner. Bar. **$$**

★★**Mezzanotte Cafe**
4621 Liberty Ave.,
Pittsburgh,
412-688-8070;
www.mezzanottecafe.com
Italian menu, Mediterranean menu. Lunch,
dinner. Closed Sunday. Bar. Casual attire.
$$

★★**Monterey Bay Fish Grotto**
1411 Grandview Ave.,
Pittsburgh,
412-481-4414;
www.montereybayfishgrotto.com
Lunch, dinner. Children's menu. **$$$**

★★**Old Europe**
1209 E. Carson St., Pittsburgh,
412-488-1700
Eastern European menu. Dinner. Bar.
Casual attire. **$$**

★**Penn Brewery**
800 Vinial St., Troy Hill,
Pittsburgh,
412-237-9402;
www.pennbrew.com
German menu. Lunch, dinner. Closed
Sunday. Bar. Children's menu. Outdoor
seating. **$$**

254

PENNSYLVANIA

★★Piccolo Mondo
661 Andersen Dr., Pittsburgh,
412-922-0920;
www.piccolo-mondo.com
Italian menu. Lunch, dinner. Closed Sunday
except Mother's Day. Bar. Children's menu.
Jacket required. **$$**

★Primanti Brothers
46 18th St., Pittsburgh,
412-263-2142;
www.primantibros.com
American, Italian menu. Dinner. **$**

★★Rico's
1 Rico Lane, Pittsburgh,
412-931-1989
Italian, American menu. Lunch, dinner.
Closed Sunday. Bar. Jacket required. Valet
parking. **$$$**

★★★Soba
5847 Ellsworth Ave., Pittsburgh,
412-362-5656;
www.bigburrito.com/soba
A modern interior with a two-story waterfall, plush seating, tropical wood tones and
mellow lighting serves as the perfect backdrop for Soba's sophisticated Asian fusion
cuisine. Recent small-plate selections have
included crispy tofu with lemongrass sauce
and Vietnamese chicken spring rolls, while
pad Thai, bacon-dusted sea scallops with
sweet miso sake and scallion honey sauces,
and filet mignon with chili-garlic mashed
potatoes and wild mushroom ragout have
been featured as large plate choices. A few
soups, salads and bowls round out the
menu. An ambitious wine list with selections that span the globe is also offered,
along with a number of sakes, martinis and
cocktails.
Pan-Asian menu. Dinner. Bar. Outdoor
seating. **$$$**

★★★Steelhead Brasserie and Wine Bar
112 Washington Place, Pittsburgh,
412-394-3474;
www.thesteelhead.com
This casual American brasserie features
artistically prepared cuisine that highlights

fresh seafood like Prince Edward Island
mussels, seared ahi tuna and oysters. The
menu also includes certified Angus beef
strip steak, filet mignon and a porterhouse
pork chop. On a daily basis, a special soup,
pasta, pizza and grilled fresh fish dish
are offered, all of which can be perfectly
paired with a selection from the adventur-
ous wine list.
American, seafood menu. Lunch, dinner.
Children's menu. **$$$**

★★Sushi Two
2122 E. Carson St.,
Pittsburgh,
412-431-7874
Japanese menu. Lunch, dinner. Bar. **$$$**

★★Tambellini
860 Saw Mill Run Blvd., Pittsburgh,
412-481-1118
American menu. Lunch, dinner. Closed
Sunday. Bar. Children's menu. Valet parking
dinner. **$$**

★★Tessaro's
4601 Liberty Ave.,
Pittsburgh,
412-682-6809
American, Mexican menu. Lunch, dinner.
Closed Sunday. Bar. **$$**

★★Thai Place
5528 Walnut St.,
Pittsburgh,
412-687-8586;
www.thaiplacepgh.com
Thai menu. Lunch, dinner. Bar. Casual attire.
$$

★★★Tin Angel
1200 Grandview Ave.,
Pittsburgh,
412-381-1919;
www.tinangel.com
Located in a prime spot on Grandview
Avenue, Tin Angel boasts wonderful views
of downtown Pittsburgh in a candlelit
setting.
Seafood, steak menu. Closed Sunday. Bar.
$$$

255

PENNSYLVANIA

★

★

★

★

★

PITTSBURGH INTERNATIONAL AIRPORT AREA

HOTELS

★Hampton Inn
1420 Beers School Rd., Coraopolis,
412-264-0020, 800-426-7866;
www.hamptoninn.com
129 rooms. Complimentary continental breakfast. Airport transportation available. **$**

★★★Hyatt Regency Pittsburgh International Airport
1111 Airport Blvd.,
Pittsburgh,
724-899-1234, 800-633-7313;
www.hyatt.com
336 rooms. **$**

RESTAURANTS

★★★Hyeholde
190 Hyeholde Dr., Moon Township,
412-264-3116;
www.hyeholde.com
Don a jacket and tie for this long-standing outpost of English-country elegance 20 minutes from downtown Pittsburgh. The game and seafood menu and manor-like setting of rich tapestries, exposed wood beams and candlelight are a popular choice for special events.
International menu. Lunch, dinner. Closed Sunday. Valet parking. Outdoor seating. Herb garden. **$$$**

POTTSTOWN

An iron forge operating in 1714 at Manatawny Creek, about three miles north of Pottstown, was the first industrial establishment in the state. The borough was established by John Potts, an ironmaster, on land William Penn had earlier deeded to his son, John. Today, the community is the commercial and cultural hub for an area with a population of 130,000. Nearly 200 modern industries are located here.
Information: TriCounty Area Chamber of Commerce, 135 High St., Pottstown, 610-326-2900; www.tricopa.com

WHAT TO SEE AND DO

Pottsgrove Manor
W. King St. and Hwy. 100, Pottstown,
610-326-4014
(1752) Newly restored house of John Potts, 18th-century ironmaster and founder of Pottstown; outstanding example of early Georgian architecture and furniture. Includes recently discovered slave quarters and Potts's office. Slide orientation. Museum shop. Tuesday-Sunday.

Ringing Rocks Roller Rink
1500 Ringing Rocks Park, Pottstown,
610-323-6560
Roller skating (Friday-Sunday; fee); nature trails, picnicking, interesting rock formations. Daily.

SPECIAL EVENTS

Duryea Day Antique & Classic Auto Show
Boyertown Community Park,
28 Warwick St., Pottstown

Antique autos, trucks and other vehicles; displays, arts and crafts, flea market with automotive memorabilia, activities, Pennsylvania Dutch food. Labor Day weekend.

HOTELS

★Best Western Pottstown Inn
1600 Industrial Hwy.,
Pottstown,
610-327-3300;
www.bestwestern.com
20 rooms. Complimentary continental breakfast. **$**

★Comfort Inn
99 Robinson St.,
Pottstown,
610-326-5000, 800-879-2477;
www.choicehotels.com
121 rooms. Complimentary continental breakfast. **$**

QUAKERTOWN

Once a station on the Underground Railroad, Quakertown still retains some of its colonial appearance. In 1798, angered by what they considered an unfair federal tax, Quakertown housewives started greeting tax assessors with pans of hot water. The "hot water" rebellion cooled down when federal troops arrived, but the town switched political parties (from Federalist to Jeffersonian) almost en masse.

Information: Upper Bucks County Chamber of Commerce, 2170 Portzer Rd., Quakertown, 215-536-3211, or Bucks County Conference and Visitors Bureau, 152 Swamp Rd., Doylestown, 215-345-4552, 800-836-2825; www.ubcc.org

RESTAURANTS

★★Brick Tavern Inn
2460 Old Bethlehem Park, Quakertown
215-538-0865;
www.bricktavern.org

American menu. Lunch, dinner. Bar. Casual attire. $$

READING

A city of railroads and industry famous for its superb pretzels, Reading was the second community in the United States to vote a Socialist government into office; however, the city has not had such a government for many years. The character of this unofficial capital of Pennsylvania Dutch land reflect the love of music and the thrift and vigor of the "Dutch."

William Penn purchased the land now occupied by Reading from the Lenni-Lenape Native Americans and settled his two sons, Thomas and Richard, on it.

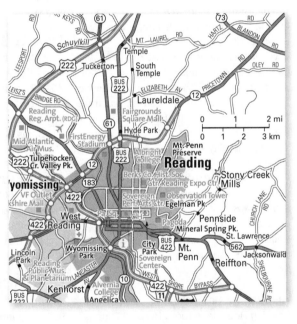

They named it Reading (fern meadow) for their home in England. During the Revolution, the citizens of Reading mustered troops for the Continental army, forged cannon and provided a depot for military supplies and a prison for Hessians and British. The hundreds of skilled German craftspeople, plus canal and railroad transportation, ignited Reading's industrial development.

Information: Reading & Berks County Visitors Bureau, 352 Penn St., Reading, 610-375-4085, 800-443-6610; www.readingberkspa.com

WHAT TO SEE AND DO

Berks County Heritage Center
2201 Tulpehocken Rd.,
Reading,
610-374-8839

Historical interpretive complex. Here are the Gruber Wagon Works (1882), where finely crafted wagons were produced for farm and industry; Wertz's Red Bridge (1867), the longest single-span covered

PENNSYLVANIA

bridge in the state; Deppen Cemetery, with graves of Irish workers who died of "swamp fever" while building the Union Canal; C. Howard Hiester Canal Center, with its collection of canal artifacts. Tours of wagon works and canal center; orientation slide program. May-October: Tuesday-Sunday.

Conrad Weiser Homestead
28 Weiser Lane, Reading,
610-589-2934;
www.conradweiserhomestead.org
(1729) Restored and furnished house of colonial "ambassador" to the Iroquois nation; springhouse, gravesite, visitor center, picnicking in 26-acre park. Wednesday-Sunday.

Daniel Boone Homestead
400 Daniel Boone Rd., Reading,
610-582-4900;
www.danielboonehomestead.org
Birthplace of Daniel Boone in 1734. Approximately 570 acres; includes Boone House, barn, blacksmith shop and sawmill. Picnicking. Nature trails. Youth camping. Visitor's center. March-December: Tuesday-Sunday.

Historical Society of Berks County
940 Centre Ave., Reading,
610-375-4375;
www.berkhistory.org
Local history exhibits; decorative arts, antiques, transportation displays. Tuesday-Saturday.

Mid-Atlantic Air Museum
Reading Regional Airport, Hwy. 183 and Van Reed Rd., Reading,
610-372-7333;
www.maam.org
Aviation museum dedicated to the preservation of vintage aircraft; planes are restored to flying condition by volunteers. Collection of 40 airplanes and helicopters; 20 on public display, including Martin 4-0-4 airliners, B-25 bomber and others. Daily.

Outlet Shopping
801 N. Nineth St., Reading,
610-375-4085, 800-443-6610

More than 300 factory outlet stores can be found at five different shopping complexes. Contact Visitors Bureau.

Reading Public Museum and Art Gallery
500 Museum Rd.,
Reading,
610-371-5850;
www.readingpublicmuseum.org
In 25-acre Museum Park with stream. Exhibits of art and science. Tuesday-Sunday.
Adjacent is:

Planetarium
500 Museum Rd., Reading,
610-371-5854
Changing exhibits. Star and laser light shows.

HOTELS
★★Best Western Dutch Colony Inn & Suites
4635 Perkiomen Ave., Reading,
610-779-2345, 800-828-2830;
www.bestwestern.com
71 rooms. $

★Comfort Inn
2200 Stacy Dr., Reading,
610-371-0500, 877-424-6423;
www.choicehotels.com
60 rooms. Complimentary continental breakfast. Airport transportation available. $

RESTAURANTS
★★Alpenhof Bavarian
903 Morgantown Rd., Reading,
610-373-1624
American, German menu. Lunch, dinner. Bar. Outdoor seating. $$

★★Antique Airplane
4635 Perkiomen Ave., Reading,
610-779-2345
Breakfast, lunch, dinner. Bar. Children's menu. Casual elegance; aviation theme. $$

★★★Green Hills Inn
2444 Morgantown Road, Reading,
610-777-9611

258

PENNSYLVANIA

The owner of this small-town spot has big-city pedigree: He was a student of Georges Perrier, owner of Philadelpia's renowned La Bec-Fin.

French, American menu. Dinner. Closed Sunday. **$$$**

RENOVO

WHAT TO SEE AND DO
Kettle Creek
Hwy. 62, Renovo,
570-923-6004
Approximately 1,600 acres. Winds through beautiful valley developed as tourist area. Swimming beach, fishing, boating (mooring, launching); hunting, hiking, bridle trail, snowmobiling, sledding, ice skating, picnicking, playground, tent and trailer sites (electric hookups). Standard fees.

SPECIAL EVENTS
Flaming Foliage Festival
Renovo, 570-923-2411
Includes parade, craft show and contest for festival queen. Second weekend in October.

SAYRE

HOTELS
★★Best Western Grand Victorian Inn
255 Spring St., Sayre,
570-888-7711, 800-627-7972;
www.bestwestern.com
100 rooms. **$**

SCRANTON
The first settlers here found a Monsey Native American village on the site. In 1840, George and Seldon Scranton built five iron furnaces using the revolutionary method of firing with anthracite coal instead of charcoal. Manufacture of iron and steel remained important industries until 1901, when the mills moved to Lake Erie to ease transportation problems.

After World War II, Scranton thoroughly revamped its economy when faced with depletion of the anthracite coal mines, which for more than a century had fired its forges. Scranton's redevelopment drew nationwide attention and served as a model for

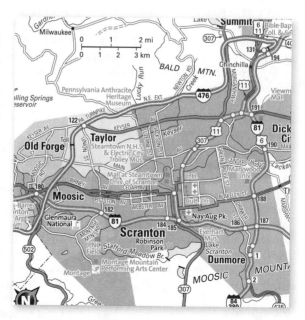

problem cities elsewhere. Today, Scranton is the home of electronic and printing industries and is host to several major trucking firm terminals.
Information: Visitors Bureau Montage Mountain Rd., Scranton, 570-963-6363, 800-229-3526; www.visitnepa.org

WHAT TO SEE AND DO

Catlin House
232 Monroe Ave., Scranton,
570-344-3841;
www.lackawannahistory.org
(1912) Headquarters of Lackawanna Historical Society; period furnishings (colonial-1900s), historic exhibits, antiques; research library (fee). Tours available (fee). Tuesday-Friday, also Saturday afternoons.

Houdini Museum
1433 N. Main Ave., Scranton,
570-342-5555;
www.houdini.org
This museum is devoted to the career and life of the great magician Harry Houdini. Tours, films featuring Houdini himself and a magic show (with live animals) are all included. Daily.

Lackawanna County Stadium
235 Montage Mountain Rd., Scranton,
570-969-2255
Open-air stadium/civic arena seats 11,000. Home of AAA baseball, high school and college football and marching band competitions. April-November.

Montage Ski Area
1000 Montage Mountain Rd., Scranton,
570-969-7669;
www.skimontage.com
Quad, double, three triple chairlifts; school, rentals, snowmaking; bar, restaurant, lodge. Vertical drop 1,000 feet. Night skiing. More than 130 acres of trails set in 400 acres of mountainside. Early December-late March: daily, Summer activities include water slides, batting cages, amphitheater (June-Labor Day).

Nay Aug Park
Arthur Ave. and Mulberry St., Scranton,
570-348-4186

More than 35 acres with memorials to pioneer days. Picnicking, swimming pool (fee), walking trail, refreshment stands, and the "Pioneer," a gravity railroad car dating back to 1850; weekend concerts (summer). Daily.

In park is:

Anthracite Heritage Museum
Keyser Ave. and Bald Mountain Rd., Scranton,
570-963-4804;
www.anthracitemuseum.org
History and culture of anthracite region. Other affiliated parts of the complex are the Iron Furnaces; Museum of Anthracite Mining, with emphasis on the technology of the industry, and the 19th-century miners' village of Eckley, near Hazleton. Daily.

Everhart Museum
1901 Mulberry St., Scranton,
570-346-7186;
www.everhart-museum.org
Permanent collections includes 19th- and 20th-century American art; Dorflinger glass; Native American, Asian and primitive art; natural history displays, including Dinosaur Hall. Gift shop. Tuesday-Sunday.

Lackawanna Coal Mine Tour
McDade Park, Keyser Ave., Scranton,
570-963-6463, 800-238-7245
The tour of this underground coal mine provides a realistic glimpse of the working lives of anthracite miners in an earlier time. A five-minute ride in a coal-mine car takes you into the cool and damp mine, and the ensuing hour-long tour will enlighten you about the hazards and harsh conditions faced by miners, as well as the unfortunate pit ponies, who lived permanently in the mine. April-November: Daily.

Scranton Iron Furnaces
159 Cedar Ave., Scranton,
570-963-3208
Partially restored site of four anthracite-fired iron furnaces built 1848-1857 and used until 1902. Visitor center, outdoor exhibits. Self-guided tours (daily). Guided tours. Late May-early September: Monday-Thursday.

Steamtown National Historic Site
Lackawanna and Cliff Streets, Scranton,
888-693-9391;
www.nps.gov/stea
Site with large collection of steam locomotives and other memorabilia located in an authentic freight yard. Steam train ride through yard (Memorial Day-December: daily). 25-mile train excursion July 4-mid-October: Saturday and Sunday.

HOTELS
★★Clarion Hotel
300 Meadow Ave.,
Scranton,
570-344-9811, 800-347-1551;
www.choicehotels.com
125 rooms. Airport transportation available. $

SELLERSVILLE

RESTAURANTS
★★Washington House
136 N. Main St., Sellersville,
215-257-3000;
www.washingtonhouse.net

★Hampton Inn
22 Montage Mountain Rd.,
Scranton,
570-342-7002, 800-426-7866;
www.hamptoninn.com
129 rooms. Complimentary continental breakfast. Airport transportation available. $

★★Radisson Lackawanna Station Hotel Scranton
700 Lackawanna Ave.,
Scranton,
570-342-8300;
www.radisson.com
145 rooms. Airport transportation available. Located in the historic Lackawanna train station building. $

RESTAURANTS
★Cooper's Seafood House
701 N. Washington Ave.,
Scranton,
570-346-6883;
www.coopers-seafood.com
American menu. Lunch, dinner. Bar. Children's menu. $$

American menu. Lunch, dinner. Late-night. Bar. Children's menu. Casual attire. $$

★
★
★
★
★

SHAWNEE ON DELAWARE
Information: Pocono Mountains Vacation Bureau Inc., 1004 Main St., Stroudsburg,
717-424-6050, 800-762-6667;
www.poconos.org

WHAT TO SEE AND DO
Shawnee Mountain Ski Area
Hollow Rd.,
Shawnee on Delaware,
570-421-7231;
www.shawneemt.com

Quad, triple, seven double chairlifts; patrol, school, rentals, snowmaking; cafeteria, bar, nursery. 23 slopes and trails; longest run one mile; vertical drop 700 feet. Night skiing. Half-day rates. Late November-March: daily.

Shawnee Place Play & Water Park

Hollow Rd., Shawnee on Delaware,
570-421-7231

Kids can jump in a pool of plastic balls, swing on a cable glide, climb on cargo nets, glide down water slides and splash in a wading pool. Magic shows, picnics, video games, snack bar. Mid-June-early September: daily; late May-mid-June, weekends only.

HOTELS

★★Shawnee Inn And Golf Resort

1 River Rd.,
Shawnee on Delaware,
570-424-4000, 800-742-9633;
www.shawneeinn.com

103 rooms. Children's activity center. **$$**

SOMERSET

James Whitcomb Riley described the countryside in his poem "Mongst the Hills of Somerset," starting the poem by saying, "Mongst the Hills of Somerset, I wish I were a'roamin' yet." The county offers fishing, swimming, boating, hiking, biking, camping, skiing and ice skating.

Information: Somerset County Chamber of Commerce, 601 N. Center Ave., Somerset, 814-445-6431; www.shol.com/smrst/somrst.htm

WHAT TO SEE AND DO

Kooser State Park

Somerset,
814-445-8673

Approximately 220 acres, this park contains a four-acre lake with fishing and a swimming beach (Memorial Day-Labor Day). The park also offers cross-country skiing and sledding in winter and picnicking and camping in summer (tent and trailer sites, cabins).

Laurel Hill State Park

1454 Laurel Hill Park Rd., Somerset,
814-445-7725

Approximately 3,900 acres. Swimming beach, snack bar, boating (mooring, launching). Hiking, hunting; snowmobiling, ice fishing. Picnicking snack bar. Tent and trailer sites.

Mount Davis

Somerset,
724-238-9533

Highest point in state (3,213 feet).

Somerset Historical Center

10649 Somerset Pike,
Somerset,
814-445-6077

Museum exhibits on rural life; outdoor display includes log house, log barn, covered bridge, sugarhouse. Bus tour (fee). Tuesday-Saturday.

SPECIAL EVENTS

Maple Festival

Festival Park, 120 Meyers Ave.,
Somerset,
814-634-0213

April.

Mountain Craft Days

Somerset Historical Center,
10649 Somerset Pike, Somerset,
814-445-6077

More than 150 traditional craft demonstrations, antique exhibits; entertainment. Early September.

Somerfest

Laurel Arts/Phillip Dressler Center for the Arts, 214 Harrison Ave.,
Somerset,
814-443-2433

German festival: dancing, competitions, entertainment, food, tours. Mid-July.

HOTELS

★Quality Inn

215 Ramada Rd., Somerset,
814-443-4646, 877-424-6423;
www.choicehotels.com

152 rooms. **$**

★★★Inn at Georgian Place
800 Georgian Place Dr., Somerset,
814-443-1043;
www.theinnatgeorgianplace.com
11 rooms. Children over 5 years only. Complimentary full breakfast. Georgian mansion built in 1915; chandeliers, marble foyer. **$**

SPECIALTY LODGINGS
Bayberry Inn Bed and Breakfast
611 N. Center Ave., Somerset,
814-445-8471;
www.bayberry-inn.com
11 rooms. Children over 12 years only. Complimentary continental breakfast. Brick house built 1902. **$**

RESTAURANTS
★★Oakhurst Tea Room
2409 Glades Pike, Somerset,
814-443-2897;
www.oakhursttearoom.com
American menu. Lunch, dinner, Sunday brunch. Closed Monday. Bar. Children's menu. Outdoor seating. **$$**

★★Pine Grill
800 N. Center Ave., Somerset,
814-445-2102;
www.pinegrill.com
Breakfast, lunch, dinner. Bar. Children's menu. Opened 1941. **$**

SOUTH STERLING

HOTELS
★★★French Manor
50 Huntington Rd., South Sterling,
570-676-3244, 877-720-6090;
www.thefrenchmanor.com
French chateau-style with Spanish slate roof. Great Hall has two floor-to-ceiling fireplaces. 9 rooms. No children allowed. Restaurant. Airport transportation available. **$$**

★★★Sterling Inn
Hwy. 191, South
Sterling,
570-676-3311, 800-523-8200;
www.sterlinginn.com
Built in the 1850s; country and Victorian suites.
54 rooms. Airport transportation available. **$**

SPRUCE CREEK

WHAT TO SEE AND DO
Indian Caverns
Hwy. 45, Spruce Creek,
814-632-7578;
www.indiancaverns.com
Indian Caverns was first excavated by Harold and Leonore Wertz just before the beginning of the Great Depression. When their expedition uncovered arrowheads and human remains, it became clear the site belonged to the Mohawk and Algonquin peoples. Today, the site is preserved and includes areas used for rituals of fire and sacrifice, carvings hundreds of years old, and even a former hideout for notorious criminal David Lewis. Still on some of the walls are examples of American Indian picture writing. April-May, September-November: Thursday-Sunday; June-August: daily.

ST. MARY'S

HOTELS
★★★Towne House Inn
138 Center St.,
Saint Mary's,
814-781-1556, 800-851-1180
57 rooms. Complimentary continental breakfast. Stained glass, antiques in seven historic (1890s) townhouses. **$**

STATE COLLEGE

Not surprisingly, State College is the home of Pennsylvania State University. In the beautiful Nittany Valley, the borough is surrounded by farmland famous for its production of oats and swine. Iron ore was discovered just east of town in 1790, and many iron furnaces later sprang up.

Information: Centre County Convention & Visitors Bureau, 800 E. Park Ave., State College, 16803, 814-231-1400, 800-358-5466; www.visitpennstate.org

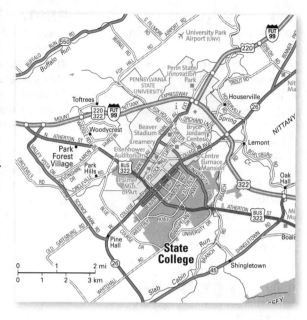

WHAT TO SEE AND DO

Mount Nittany Vineyard & Winery
300 Houser Rd., State College, 814-466-6373; www.mtnittanywinery.com
Stone-faced, chalet-style building nestled on southern slopes of Mount Nittany. Tasting room offers variety of wines and view of large pond, vineyard and mountains. Group tastings (by appointment). Friday-Sunday; closed January.

Pennsylvania State University
College and Atherton Streets, State College, 814-865-4700
(1855) (41,000 students.) Approximately 760 major buildings on a 15,984-acre campus; it is the land grant institution of Pennsylvania.

On campus are:

Ag Hill, The College of Agriculture
College and Atherton Streets, State College
Showplace for state's dairy industry including the dairy center, off Park Road near stadium, with five herds of cows, automatic milking equipment (daily). The creamery, Curtain Road, has retail salesroom for cheeses, milk, cream, ice cream (daily). Also test flower gardens off Park Road near East Halls. July-September.

Earth and Mineral Sciences Museum
Steidle Building, Pollock Rd., State College, 814-865-6427
Exhibitions of ores, gems and fossils; automated displays; art gallery. Monday-Friday.

Old Main
College and Atherton Streets, State College, 814-865-2501
(1929) Present building, on site of original Old Main (1863), uses many of the original stones; topped by lofty bell tower. Here are Henry Varnum Poor's land grant frescoes. Monday-Friday.

Whipple Dam State Park
State College, 814-667-3808
Approximately 250 acres. Swimming beach, fishing, hunting, boating (launching, mooring). Hiking, Snowmobiling, ice skating, ice fishing. Picnicking, snack bar.

SPECIAL EVENTS

Central Pennsylvania Festival of the Arts
403 S. Allen St. #201,
State College,
814-237-3682;
www.arts-festival.com
Open-air display of visual and performing arts, indoor exhibits, demonstrations of arts and crafts; food booths. Mid-July.

Centre County Grange Fair
Centre Hall, 237 Hoffer St.,
State College,
814-364-9674
Exhibits, livestock show, rides, concessions, entertainment. Last week in August.

HOTELS

★★★Atherton Hotel
125 S. Atherton St. (US 322 Business),
State College,
814-231-2100, 800-832-0132;
www.athertonhotel.net
This inn is located 1/2 mile from Penn State. The Anthropology Museum, Historic Boalsburg Village and Palmer Museum of Art are also nearby.
150 rooms. Airport transportation available. **$**

★★Autoport Motel & Restaurant
1405 S. Atherton St.,
State College,
814-237-7666, 800-932-7678;
www.autoport.statecollege.com
86 rooms. **$**

★★Days Inn
240 S. Pugh St.,
State College,
814-237-7666, 800-932-7678;
www.daysinn.com
184 rooms. Complimentary continental breakfast. Airport transportation available. **$**

★Hampton Inn
1101 E. College Ave.,
State College,
814-231-1590, 800-426-7866;
www.hamptoninn.com
121 rooms. Complimentary continental breakfast. Airport transportation available. **$**

★★★The Nittany Lion Inn
200 W. Park Ave.,
State College,
814-865-8500;
www.pshs.psu.edu/nittanylioninn/
nlhome.asp
237 rooms. Restaurant, bar. Airport transportation available. Located on the main campus of Penn State. **$**

★★★Toftrees Resort And Four Star Golf Club
1 Country Club Lane,
State College,
814-234-8000, 800-458-3602;
www.toftrees.com
This "home among the trees" sits in 1,500 wooded acres and offers private patios and balconies from which guests can enjoy the view.
113 rooms. Airport transportation available. Mediterranean dcor. **$**

★★★Carnegie House
100 Cricklewood Dr.,
State College,
814-234-2424, 800-229-5033;
www.carnegiehouse.com
When you've conquered the links, stow your golf gear in your cozy guest room, relax in a deep library chair and have a celebratory drink. Carnegie House offers packages for golf and Penn State football weekends.
22 rooms. Complimentary continental breakfast. Restaurant. Airport transportation available. Decor and ambiance is reminiscent of Scotland. **$**

RESTAURANTS

★★Tavern
220 E. College Ave.,
State College,
814-238-6116;
www.thetavern.com
Dinner. Bar. Children's menu. **$$**

★
★
★
★
★

STRASBURG

WHAT TO SEE AND DO

Choo-Choo Barn, Traintown, USA
Hwy. 741 E, Strasburg,
717-687-7911;
www.choochoobarn.com

A 1,700-square-foot layout of Lancaster County in miniature, featuring 20 operating trains and more than 150 animated and automated figures and vehicles. Gift shop. Picnicking. Mid-March-December: daily.

Mill Bridge Village
S Ronks and Soudersburg roads, Strasburg,
717-687-8181, 800-645-2744;
www.millbridge.com

Restored historic colonial mill village with operating water-powered gristmill (1738), covered bridge; country crafts include broom-making, quilting, candlemaking, blacksmithing; quilt log cabin; Amish kitchen exhibit; music boxes and nickelodeons; horse-drawn hay and carriage rides; 1890s playground; picnicking. Amish house and schoolhouse tour available. Oktoberfest (October weekends). Camp resort (early April-October: daily; fee). Village (early April-November: daily).

National Toy Train Museum
300 Paradise Lane, Strasburg,
717-687-8976

Trains from the 1880s to present; live operating layouts; movies; rare, unusual and specialty trains. May-October: daily; April and November-December: Saturday-Sunday.

Strasburg Railroad
Hwy. 741 E, Strasburg,
717-687-7522;
www.strasburgrailroad.com

Railroad runs 4 1/2 miles to Paradise. Picnic stop. This 160-year-old line uses late 19th-century coaches, various steam locomotives. April-October: daily; winter, weekends.

Adjacent is:

Railroad Museum of Pennsylvania
300 Gap Rd., Strasburg,
717-687-8628;
www.rrmuseumpa.org

More than 50 locomotives, freight and passenger cars dating from 1825; audio-visual exhibits; railroading memorabilia. Picnicking. April-October: daily; rest of year: Tuesday-Sunday.

HOTELS

★★★Netherlands Inn & Spa
1 Historic Dr., Route 896, Strasburg,
717-687-7691;
www.netherlandsinn.com

101 rooms. Complimentary full breakfast.
$

STROUDSBURG

Information: Pocono Mountains Vacation Bureau, Inc., 1004 Main St., Srroudsburg, 570-424-6050, 800-762-6667; www.poconos.org

WHAT TO SEE AND DO

Canoeing
Stroudsburg, 570-421-0180

Canoe trips on the Delaware River; equipment provided; also transportation to and from the river. (May-October.)

Delaware Water Gap KOA
233 Hollow Rd., East Stroudsburg,
570-223-8000, 800-562-0375;
www.koa.com

This KOA campground has both wooded and open sites. Electrical hook-ups, propane station. Laundry services, convenience store, outdoor pool, playground, game room, organized activities.

Quiet Valley Living Historical Farm
1000 Turkey Hill Rd., Stroudsburg,
570-992-6161;
www.quietvalley.org

A log house (1765) with kitchen and parlor added 1892; 12 other original or reconstructed buildings. Demonstrations of seasonal farm activities. Farm animals, garden, gift shop. Guided tours with costumed guides, 1 1/2-2 hours. Late June-Labor Day: Tuesday-Sunday.

Stroud Mansion
900 Main St., Stroudsburg,
570-421-7703
(18th century). Built by founder of city; houses Historical Society of Monroe County. Historical artifacts, genealogical records. Tours. Tuesday-Friday, also Sunday afternoons.

HOTELS
★★Best Western Pocono Inn
700 Main St., Stroudsburg,
570-421-2200, 888-508-2378;
www.bestwestern.com
90 rooms. Complimentary continental breakfast. Laundry services. $

★★Caesars Brookdale
Hwy. 611 and Brookdale Rd.,
Scotrun,
570-839-8844, 800-233-4141;
www.caesarspoconoresorts.com
119 rooms. Children's activity center. $$

★★Shannon Inn
US Route 209 and State Route 447,
Stroudsburg,
570-424-1951, 800-424-8052;
www.sharoninn.com

120 rooms. Complimentary continental breakfast. $

RESTAURANTS
★Arlington Diner
834 N. Nineth St.,
Stroudsburg,
570-421-2329
American menu. Breakfast, lunch, dinner. Children's menu. Casual attire. $$

★Brownie's in the Burg
700 Main St.,
Stroudsburg,
570-421-2200;
www.browniesintheburg.com
American menu. Breakfast, lunch, dinner. Bar. Casual attire. $$

★Sarah Street Grill
550 Quaker Alley, Stroudsburg,
570-424-9120;
www.sarahstreetgrill.com
American, sushi menu. Lunch, dinner. Bar. Children's menu. Casual attire. Outdoor seating. $$

★★Stone Bar Inn
Hwy. 209, Stroudsburg,
570-992-6634;
www.stonebar.com
American menu. Dinner. Bar. Children's menu. Reservations recommended. Outdoor seating. $$

SWARTHMORE

WHAT TO SEE AND DO
Swarthmore College
500 College Ave., Swarthmore,
610-328-8000;
www.swarthmore.edu
(1864) (1,320 students.) Coeducational; on wooded 330-acre campus are Friends Historical Library and Peace Collection, an art gallery, concert hall, performing arts center, observatory, terraced grass amphitheater, and more. Symposia, exhibits, music and dance programs are open to the public.

TITUSVILLE

Titusville spreads from the banks of Oil Creek, so called because of the oil that appeared on its surface. Edwin L. Drake drilled the first successful oil well in the world on August 27, 1859. Overnight, Titusville became the center of the worldwide oil industry.

Information: Titusville Area Chamber of Commerce, 202 W. Central Ave., Titusville, 814-827-2941; www.titusvillechamber.com

WHAT TO SEE AND DO

Drake Well Museum
E. Bloss and Allen St. Exit,
Titusville,
814-827-2797
Site of world's first oil well; operating replica of Drake derrick and engine house; picnic area. Museum contains dioramas, working models, life-size exhibits depicting history of oil. May-October: daily; November-April: Tuesday-Saturday, also Sunday afternoons.

HOTELS

★★Cross Creek Resort
Route 8 S,
Titusville,
814-827-9611, 800-461-3173;
www.crosscreekresort.com
94 rooms. **$**

TOWANDA

On the north branch of the Susquehanna River, Towanda takes its name from a Native American word meaning "where we bury the dead."

In 1793, the Asylum Company purchased 1,600 acres of these wild valleys as a refuge for Marie Antoinette of France, should she escape to America. "La Grande Maison," a queenly house, was built. French noblemen settled here and a thriving community (called Azilum) was planned. The colony was unsuccessful and most of its founders returned to France. Many of their descendants, however, still live in Bradford County.

Information: Endless Mountains Visitors Bureau, 712 Route 6E, Tunkhannock, 570-836-5431, 800-769-8999; www.endlessmountains.org

WHAT TO SEE AND DO

David Wilmot's Burial Place
Riverside Cemetery, William and Chestnut Streets, Towanda
Congressman (1845-1851), senator (1861-1863), leader of the Free Soil Party, Wilmot introduced the Wilmot Proviso in Congress, which would have required the U.S. to outlaw slavery in any lands purchased from Mexico. This was an important factor in the dissension between North and South that led to the Civil War.

French Azilum
Route 456, Towanda,
570-265-3376
Site of colony for refugees from the French Revolution (1793-1803). Three cabins with crafts, tool exhibits; log cabin museum (1793); Laporte House (1836), built by son of one of colony's founders, reflects elegant French influence. Special events. Guided tours. June-August: Wednesday-Sunday; May, September-October: Saturday, Sunday.

TUNKHANNOCK

HOTELS

★★Shadowbrook Inn and Resort
615 Route 6 E,
Tunkhannock,
570-836-2151, 800-955-0295;
www.shadowbrookresort.com
73 rooms. Complimentary continental breakfast. **$**

RESTAURANTS

★Fireplace
1111 PA 6W,
Tunkhannock
570-836-9662;
www.tunkhannock.com/thefireplace
Lunch, dinner. Bar. Children's menu. **$$**

UNIONTOWN

Coal and its byproducts made Uniontown prosperous, but with the decline in coal mining, the city has developed a more diverse economic base. First known as Union, this city has been the Fayette County seat since 1784. Uniontown was a hotbed of the Whiskey Rebellion, and federal troops were sent here in 1794.

Information: Laurel Highlands Visitors Bureau, 120 E. Main St., Ligonier, 724-238-5661; www.laurelhighlands.org

WHAT TO SEE AND DO

Fort Necessity National Battlefield
1 Washington Pkwy.,
Farmington,
724-329-5512
(1754) The site of Washington's first major battle and the opening battle of the French and Indian War (1754). This land was known as the Great Meadows. A portion was later purchased by Washington, who owned it until his death. A replica of the original fort was built on the site following an archaeological survey in 1953. Picnic area (mid-spring-late fall).

Included in the admission fee is:

Visitor Center
Exhibits on battle at Great Meadows; audiovisual program. Daily.

Friendship Hill National Historic Site
1 Washington Pkwy., Uniontown,
724-329-5512;
www.nps.gov/frhi
Preserves the restored home of Albert Gallatin, a Swiss immigrant who served his adopted country, in public and private life, for nearly seven decades. Gallatin made significant contributions to our young Republic in the fields of finance, politics, diplomacy and scholarship. He is best known as the Treasury Secretary under Jefferson and Madison. Exhibits, audiovisual program and audio tour provide information. Daily.

Jumonville Glen
200 Caverns Park Rd., Uniontown
Site of skirmish between British and French forces that led to the battle at Fort Necessity. Mid-April-mid-October.

River tours
Whitewater rafting on the Youghiogheny River; some of the wildest and most scenic in the eastern U.S. Cost includes equipment and professional guides. Age limits are imposed because of level of difficulty.

Mountain Streams & Trails Outfitters
Uniontown,
724-329-8810, 800-723-8669
Also on the Youghiogheny, Big Sandy, Cheat and Tygart's Valley rivers. Also rentals of whitewater rafts, canoes, trail bikes.

White Water Adventurers
Uniontown,
800-992-7238

PENNSYLVANIA

Wilderness Voyageurs
Uniontown,
800-272-4141;
www.wilderness-voyageurs.com
Trips on the lower and middle Youghiogheny. Also bicycle, canoe rentals; kayak and canoe lessons.

HOTELS
★★Holiday Inn
700 W. Main St.,
Uniontown,
724-437-2816, 800-465-4329;
www.holidayinn.com
179 rooms. $

SPECIALTY LODGINGS
Inne at Watson's Choice
234 Balsinger Rd.,
Uniontown,
724-437-4999, 888-820-5380;
www.watsonschoice.com

7 rooms. No children allowed. Complimentary full breakfast. $

RESTAURANTS
★★★Coal Baron
7606 National Pike,
Uniontown,
724-439-0111
Small and intimate, this 20-year-old restaurant offers a broad, continental menu. A painting of a coal tipple adorns the dining room wall, in honor of the establishment's name.
American menu. Lunch, dinner. Closed Monday. Bar. Children's menu. Jacket required. Valet parking. $$

VALLEY FORGE NATIONAL HISTORICAL PARK
Two thousand soldiers died here from hunger, disease and cold, but General George Washington and his beleaguered army ultimately triumphed over the British in 1778. Today, Valley Forge has come to symbolize American perseverance and sacrifice on a lush, hilly, 3,600-acre expanse with rich historical significance and beautiful scenery. Visitors can tour the park by car or bus and see Washington's restored stone headquarters, log soldier huts, bronze statues and monuments, and weapons and equipment used during the American Revolution. You can even learn how Washington's soldiers were taught to load and fire their muskets. The visitors center features exhibits, artifacts, a gift shop and an 18-minute film. Choose from a 16-mile walking trail, 10-mile horse trails, a bike path or a 10-mile self-guided tour. Picnic areas are available as well. Daily 9 a.m.-5 p.m.
Information: 610-783-1077; www.nps.gov/vafo

WHAT TO SEE AND DO
Auto Tape Tour
Valley Forge,
610-783-5788
Self-guided tour dramatizes Washington's winter encampment. Bookstore (two-hour tape rental, May-October, daily)

Bus Tour
Valley Forge,
610-783-5788

Narrated tour (approximately 90 minutes) includes stops at historic sites. Tours leave from Visitor Center. June-Labor Day: tour departures every 1/2-hour; Labor Day-October: weekends only.

National Memorial Arch
Built in 1917 to commemorate Washington's army. Inscribed in the arch is a quote from General Washington: "Naked and starving as they are, we cannot enough

admire the incomparable patience and fidelity of the soldiery."

Soldier Life Program
Interpreters present programs detailing camp life of the Continental Army soldier (offered at various times during the year).

Visitor Center
Hwy. 23 and Gulph Rd.,
Valley Forge,
610-783-1077
Information, exhibits, audiovisual program, tour maps. Bus tours depart from here. Daily.

Washington Headquarters
Park staff will provide information about the house where Washington lived for six months and which served as military headquarters for the Continental Army during that time. Daily. Fee charged April-November.

Washington Memorial Chapel
Hwy. 23, Valley Forge,
610-783-0120
Private property within park boundaries. Stained-glass windows depict the story of the New World, its discovery and development; hand-carved oak choir stalls, Pews of the Patriots and Roof of the Republic bearing the State Seal of all the states. Also part of the chapel is the 58 cast-bell Washington Memorial National Carillon, with bells honoring states and territories.

RESTAURANTS
★★★Kennedy-Supplee Mansion
1100 W. Valley Forge Rd.,
Valley Forge,
610-337-3777;
www.kennedysupplee.com
Enjoy the classic American fare in one of eight dining rooms of this 1850s mansion. American menu. Lunch, dinner. Closed Sunday. Bar. Jacket required (dinner). Valet parking. $$$

WARREN
At the junction of the Allegheny and Conewango rivers, Warren is the headquarters and gateway of the famous Allegheny National Forest. Named for General Joseph Warren, an American patriot killed in the Battle of Bunker Hill, the town was once the point where great flotillas of logs were formed for the journey to Pittsburgh or Cincinnati.
Information: Warren County Chamber of Commerce, 308 Market St.,
Warren, 814-723-3050 or Travel Northern Alleghenies, 315 Second St.,
Warren, 814-726-1222;
www.warrenpachamber.com

WHAT TO SEE AND DO
Allegheny National Forest
222 Liberty St.,
Warren,
814-723-5150
More than 510,000 acres S and E on Hwys. 6, 62, located in Warren, Forest, McKean and Elk counties. Black bear, whitetail deer, wild turkey, a diversity of small birds and mammals; streams and reservoirs with trout, walleye, muskellunge, northern pike and bass; rugged hills, quiet valleys, open meadows, dense forest. These lures, plus swimming, boating, hiking, camping and picnicking facilities, draw more than 2 million visitors a year. Hundreds of campsites; fees are charged at some recreation sites.

In forest are:

Buckaloons Recreation Area
Klondike,
Bradford,
814-362-4613
Site of former Native American village on the banks of the Allegheny River. Boat launching. Picnicking. Camping (fee). Seneca Interpretive Trail.

Kinzua Dam and Allegheny Reservoir
1205 Kinzua Rd., Warren,
814-726-0661
Dam (179 feet high, 1,897 feet long) with 27-mile-long lake. Swimming, fishing, boating (ramps, rentals; fees). Picnicking, overlooks. Camping (fee). Kinzua Dam Visitor Center has displays. Kinzua Point Information Center, 4 miles NE of dam, 814-726-1291. Some fees. (It is possible that the Highway 59 bridge, 1 1/2 miles E of Kinzua Dam, will be closed; phone ahead for information.)

WASHINGTON

Originally a Native American village known as Catfish Camp, the village of Bassettown became Washington during the Revolution. During the Whiskey Rebellion, the town was a center of protest against the new federal government's tax. The arrival of federal troops quieted the rebellious farmers. Washington and Jefferson College (1781) is located here.
Information: Washington County Tourism Promotion Agency, Franklin Mall,
1500 W. Chestnut St., Washington,
724-228-5520, 800-531-4114;
www.washpatourism.org

WHAT TO SEE AND DO

David Bradford House
175 S. Main St., Washington,
724-222-3604
(1788) Restored frontier home of a leader of the Whiskey Rebellion. May-mid-December: Wednesday-Saturday, limited hours, also Sunday afternoons.

LeMoyne House
49 E. Maiden St.,
Washington,
724-225-6740
(1812) Abolitionist's home, built by the LeMoyne family, was a stop on the underground railroad; period furnishings, paintings, library; gardens; museum shop. Administered by Washington County Historical Society. January-ebruary: Tuesday-Friday; March-December: Tuesday-Saturday.

Pennsylvania Trolley Museum
1 Museum Rd., Washington,
724-228-9256;
www.pa-trolley.org
Museum displays include more than 35 trolley cars dating from 1894. Scenic trolley ride; car barn and trolley-restoration shop; visitor center and gift shop with exhibit, video presentation and picnic area. June-August: daily; April-May and September-December: weekends.

HOTELS

★★Holiday Inn
340 Racetrack Rd.,
Washington,
724-222-6200, 800-465-4329;
www.holidayinn.com
138 rooms. Airport transportation available. Meadows Racetrack is adjacent. **$**

WASHINGTON CROSSING HISTORIC PARK

In a blinding snowstorm on Christmas night 1776, George Washington and 2,400 soldiers crossed the Delaware River from the Pennsylvania shore and marched to Trenton, surprising the celebrating Hessian mercenaries and capturing the city. Washington's feat was a turning point of the Revolutionary War. Tuesday-Sunday.
Information: 215-493-4076

WHAT TO SEE AND DO

Area of Embarkation
Marked by tall granite shaft supporting Washington's statue.

Bowman's Hill Wildflower Preserve
New Hope,
215-862-2924

272

Pennsylvania's native plants come into focus at this 100-acre preserve located 40 miles northeast of Philadelphia. Hike or walk along woodland, a meadow, a creek or an arboretum. Botanic enthusiasts will discover 1,000 species of trees, shrubs, ferns, vines and herbaceous wildflowers. There are many contemplative places for meditation and study, scenic picnic spots and several historic sites within hiking distance. Head five miles south to Washington Crossing Historic Park (215-493-4076), where George Washington crossed the Delaware River in 1776. Bowman's Hill Tower, a lookout commemorating the American Revolution, offers a view of the Delaware River and rolling countryside one mile on foot or by car (215-862-3155). Nearby is New Hope, a perfect place for antiquing, art gallery hopping, shopping, or taking a mule barge ride on the Delaware Canal. Daily.

Concentration Valley
Where Washington assembled troops for raid on Trenton.

McConkey Ferry Inn
(1752) Restored as historic house. Sold in 1777 to Benjamin Taylor, whose descen-dents established the 19th-century village of Taylorsville.

Memorial Building
1112 River Rd., Washington Crossing, 215-493-4076
Near Point of Embarkation. Houses copy of Emanuel Leutze's painting, "Washington Crossing the Delaware." Movie shown five times a day.

Memorial Flagstaff
Bowman's Hill. Marks graves of unknown Continentals who died during encampment.

SPECIAL EVENTS
The Crossing
1112 River Rd., Washington Crossing, 215-493-4076
Reenactment of Washington's crossing of the Delaware River, Christmas night in 1776. December.

SPECIALTY LODGINGS
Inn to the Woods
150 Glenwood Dr., Washington Crossing, 215-493-1974, 800-574-1974; www.inn-bucks.com
6 rooms. Children over 12 years only. Complimentary full breakfast. $$

WAYNE

HOTELS
★★Courtyard by Marriott
1100 Drummers Lane, Wayne, 610-687-6700, 800-320-5748; www.courtyard.com
150 rooms. $

★★★Wayne Hotel
139 E. Lancaster Ave., Wayne, 610-687-5000, 800-962-5850; www.waynehotel.com
Located 18 miles west of Philadelphia, this restored property reflects the elegance of a time past with its wraparound porch and antique reproduction furnishings. Individually decorated guest rooms feature voice mail, data ports and direct dial tele-phones.
38 rooms. Complimentary continental breakfast. Airport transportation available. Restored Victorian building (1906) with ornate furnishings, antiques. $

★★★Wyndham Valley Forge Hotel
888 Chesterbrook Blvd., Wayne, 610-647-6700, 877-999-3223; www.wyndham.com
229 rooms. Airport transportation avail-able. $$

RESTAURANTS

★★★Taquet
139 E. Lancaster Ave.,
Wayne,
610-687-5005;
www.taquet.com
This elegant Main Line restaurant prides itself on serving local products prepared with a French sensibility. Entrees include Norwegian salmon with tamarind barbeque glaze and vegetable couscous or Nebraska center-cut beef filet mignon with a cabernet wine reduction. French menu. Lunch, dinner. Closed Sunday. Bar. Outdoor seating. $$

★★Town and Country Grille
888 Chesterbrook Blvd.,
Wayne,
610-647-6700;
www.wyndham.com
Breakfast, lunch, dinner. Sunday brunch. Bar. Children's menu. Country furnishings. $$

WELLSBORO

Wellsboro is the gateway to Pennsylvania's "canyon country." Settled largely by New Englanders, the area yields coal, natural gas, hardwoods, maple syrup and farm products.
Information: Wellsboro Area Chamber of Commerce, 114 Main St., Wellsboro, 570-724-1926; www.wellsboropa.com

WHAT TO SEE AND DO

Auto tours
There are more than a million acres of forests, mountains and streams to be explored. The Wellsboro Area Chamber of Commerce has published a map of three tours.

Red Arrow Tour
Follows Highway 660 SW 10 miles from Wellsboro to Leonard Harrison State Park. Lookout Point, near the parking area, has large picnic area nearby. Path winds one mile from park to bottom of gorge, through shady glens, past waterfalls.

White Arrow Tour
Leads from the Switchbacks (1 1/2 miles W of Bradley Wales Park), three miles S to Leetonia, once a prosperous lumber village, now occupied by State Forest Rangers; then W & N to Cushman View, Wilson Point Road, Lee Fire Tower, Cedar Run Mountain Road and Highway 6; approximately 75 miles.

Yellow Arrow Tour
Leads from Leonard Harrison State Park, back on Highway 660, NW on Highway 362, then 1/4 mile W on Highway 6 to Colton Point Road for views of the canyon and Four Mile Run Country. At Colton Point State Park (observation points, picnic shelters, fireplaces) the arrows follow Pine Creek S on old lumbering railroad tracks, converted into roadways called the "Switchbacks," to Bradley Wales Park overlooking Tiadaghton, the next lookout point on Pine Creek. From here continue S on W Rim Road to Blackwell. From Blackwell, NE on Highway 414 to Morris, then N on Highway 287 to Wellsboro—a circle of 65 miles.

Robinson House Museum
120 Main St., Wellsboro,
570-724-6116
(Circa 1820) Houses turn-of-the-century artifacts; genealogical library. Monday-Friday afternoons.

Ski Sawmill Family Resort
Wellsboro,
570-353-7521, 800-532-7669;
www.skisawmill.com
Chairlift, three T-bars; patrol, school, rentals, snowmaking; cafeteria, restaurant, bar. Longest run 3,250 feet; vertical drop 515 feet. December-March: daily Year-round activities.

★

★

★

★

★

SPECIAL EVENTS

Pennsylvania State Laurel Festival
114 Main St.,
Wellsboro,
Week-long event includes parade of floats, marching musical and precision units, antique cars, laurel queen contestants; crowning of the queen; arts and crafts; children's pet and hobby parade, exhibits and displays. Mid-June.

HOTELS

★Canyon Motel
18 East Ave.,
Wellsboro,
570-724-1681, 800-255-2718;
www.canyonmotel.com
31 rooms. Complimentary continental breakfast. **$**

Kaltenbach's Bed and Breakfast
Stony Fork Rd.,
Wellsboro,
570-724-4954, 800-772-4954;
www.kaltenbachsinn.com
10 rooms. Complimentary full breakfast. **$**

★★Penn Wells Hotel & Lodge
62 Main St., Wellsboro,
570-724-2111, 800-545-2446;
www.pennwells.com
73 rooms. **$**

★Sherwood Motel
2 Main St.,
Wellsboro,
570-724-3424, 800-626-5802;
www.sherwoodmotel.org
42 rooms. **$**

WEST CHESTER

In the heart of three Pennsylvania Revolutionary War historic sites—Brandywine, Paoli and Valley Forge—West Chester today is a university and residential community with fine examples of Greek Revival and Victorian architecture.
Information: Chester County Tourist Bureau, 601 Westtown Rd., West Chester, 610-344-6365, 800-228-9933; www.brandywinevalley.com

HOTELS

★★Holiday Inn
943 S. High St.,
West Chester,
610-692-1900, 800-465-4329;
www.holidayinn.com
143 rooms. Airport transportation available. **$**

RESTAURANTS

★★Gilmore's
133 E. Gay St., West Chester,
610-431-2800;
www.gilmoresrestaurant.com
French menu. Dinner. Closed Sunday, Monday; also one week in winter and one week in summer. **$$$**

WEST CONSHOHOCKEN

HOTELS

★★★Marriott Philadelphia West
111 Crawford Ave.,
West Conshohocken,
610-941-5600, 800-237-3639;
www.marriott.com

This hotel is located just miles from the Valley Forge National Park, Philadelphia Zoo, Museum of Art and Franklin Institute, as well as many other local points of interest. 286 rooms. Airport transportation available. **$$**

WHITE HAVEN

Information: Pocono Mountains Vacation Bureau, 1004 Main St., Stroudsburg, 570-424-6050, 800-762-6667; www.poconos.org

WHAT TO SEE AND DO

Hickory Run State Park

Hickory Run,
White Haven,
570-443-0400

Approximately 15,500 acres of scenic area. Swimming beach, fishing, hunting; hiking; cross-country skiing, snowmobiling, sledding, ice skating, ice fishing. Picnicking, playground, snack bar, store. Tent and trailer sites. Standard fees.

HOTELS

★Comfort Inn

Hwy. 940, White Haven,
570-443-8461, 877-424-6423;
www.choicehotels.com
123 rooms. $

★★Mountain Laurel Resort and Spa

I-80 at PA Turnpike NE exit,
White Haven,
570-443-8411;
www.mountainlaurelresort.com
250 rooms. Children's activity center. Airport transportation available. $$

RESTAURANTS

★★★Powerhouse

1 Powerhouse Rd., off I-80, exit 273,
White Haven,
570-443-4480

This restaurant is popular for its Italian-American menu. Its brick walls and exposed pipes and valves remind diners of its earlier function as a coal-fueled power plant. American, Italian menu. Lunch (Sunday), dinner. Bar. Reservations recommended (weekends). $$

WILKES BARRE

Named in honor of two members of the British Parliament who championed individual rights and supported the colonies, Wilkes-Barre and the Wyoming Valley were settled by pioneers from Connecticut. Pennsylvania and Connecticut waged the Pennamite-Yankee War, the first phase ending in 1771 with Connecticut in control of the valley. It was later resumed until Connecticut relinquished its claims in 1800. Wilkes-Barre was burned by the Native Americans and Tories during the Revolution and again by Connecticut settlers protesting the Decree of Trenton (1782), in which Congress favored Pennsylvania's claim to the territory. Discovery of anthracite coal in the valley sparked the town's growth after Judge Jesse Fell demonstrated that anthracite could be burned in a grate without forced draft.

Information: Northeast Pennsylvania Convention & Visitors Bureau, 99 Glenmaura National Blvd., Scranton, 800-229-3526; www.visitnepa.org

HOTELS

★★Best Western East Mountain Inn & Suites
2400 E. End Blvd.,
Wilkes Barre,
570-822-1011, 800-780-7234;
www.bestwestern.com
156 rooms. Airport transportation available. **$**

★Hampton Inn
1063 Hwy. 315,
Wilkes Barre,
570-825-3838, 800-426-7866;
www.hamptoninn.com
123 rooms. Complimentary continental breakfast. **$**

★★Holiday Inn
880 Kidder St., Wilkes Barre,
570-824-8901, 888-466-9272;
www.holidayinn.com
120 rooms. **$**

★★★Woodlands Inn & Resort
1073 Hwy. 315, Wilkes Barre,
570-824-9831, 800-762-2222;
www.thewoodlandsresort.com
The Woodlands Inn & Resort offers urban warriors a chance to bask in the simple joys of nature. This wooded resort on 40 acres in the foothills of the Poconos is a perfect place to spend a vacation, a romantic getaway or even a corporate retreat. Golf and skiing are a short distance away, and the resort offers five nightclubs, bars and lounges, with live jazz and dancing.
179 rooms. Airport transportation available. **$**

RESTAURANTS

★★Saber Room
94 Butler St., Wilkes Barre,
570-829-5743;
www.saberroom.com
American menu. Lunch, dinner. Closed Sunday. Bar. Reservations recommended. **$$**

WILLIAMSPORT

Now famous as the birthplace of Little League baseball, Williamsport was once known as the "lumber capital of the world." In 1870, a log boom extended seven miles up the Susquehanna River, and 300 million feet of sawed lumber were produced each year. When the timber was exhausted, the city developed diversified industry and remained prosperous. The historic district of Williamsport, known as "millionaire's row," includes homes of former lumber barons.
Information: Lycoming County Tourist Promotion Agency, 454 Pine St., Williamsport, 800-358-9900

WHAT TO SEE AND DO

"Hiawatha"
Williamsport,
800-248-9287
Sightseeing trips down Susquehanna River aboard replica of an old-fashioned paddlewheel riverboat. Public cruises May-October: Tuesday-Sunday.

Little League Baseball International Headquarters
Route 15, Williamsport,
570-326-1921
Summer baseball camp and Little League World Series Stadium are here. Monday-Friday.
    Adjacent is:

Little League Baseball Museum
Hwy. 15,
Williamsport,
570-326-3607
Memorial Day-Labor Day: daily; rest of year: Monday, Thursday-Sunday.

Little Pine State Park
Williamsport,
570-753-6000
Approximately 2,000 acres. Swimming beach, fishing, boating (ramps, mooring); hunting; cross-country skiing, snowmobiling, sledding, ice skating, ice fishing. Picnicking, playground, store. Tent and trailer sites (electric hook-ups). Interpretive program.

★
★
★
★
★

Thomas T. Thaber Museum of the Lycoming County Historical Society

858 W. Fourth St., Williamsport,
570-326-3326;
www.lycominglineage.com
Exhibits on regional history from 10,000
B.C. to present. Exhibits include Native
American, frontier era; canals, steam fire
engine and hose cart; military history; general
store, blacksmith shop, woodworker's
shop, gristmill, crafts and industry;
Victorian parlor and furnished period
rooms; wildlife, sports and Little League;
lumber business. May-October: daily; rest
of year: Tuesday-Sunday.

Within museum is:

Shempp Toy Train Collection

Extensive toy train collection. More than
350 train sets on display, including the entire
Lionel collection. Two detailed running
displays allow visitors to start trains, blow
whistles. Twelve unique trains include
an American Flyer #3117 and Lionel
"Super #381."

SPECIAL EVENTS

Little League World Series

Teams from all over the world compete.
Third week in August.

Lycoming County Fair

More than 50 acres of amusements, commercial
displays, livestock judging, demolition
derbies, grandstand entertainment,
food. Mid-July.

Victorian Sunday

House tours, flower show, entertainment.
Second Sunday in June.

HOTELS

★★Best Western Williamsport Inn

1840 E. Third St., Williamsport,
570-326-1981;
www.bestwestern.com
170 rooms. $

★★Holiday Inn

100 Pine St., Williamsport,
570-327-8231, 800-315-2621;
www.holidayinn.com
148 rooms. Airport transportation available. $

★★Genetti Hotel & Suites

200 W. Fourth St., Williamsport,
570-326-6600, 800-321-1388;
www.genetti.com
206 rooms. Airport transportation available.
$

WILLOW GROVE

WHAT TO SEE AND DO

Bryn Athyn Cathedral

1000 Cathedral Rd., Bryn Athyn,
215-947-0266;
www.brynathyncathedral.org
Outstanding example of Gothic architecture.
Free guided tours April-November:
Tuesday-Sunday.

On grounds adjacent is:

Glencairn Museum

1001 Cathedral Rd., Willow Grove,
215-938-2600
Romanesque building features medieval
sculpture and one of the largest privately
owned collections of stained glass in the
world; also Egyptian, Greek, Roman,
ancient Near East and Native American collections.
Monday-Friday by appointment.

HOTELS

★★Courtyard by Marriott

2350 Easton Rd., Willow Grove,
215-830-0550;
www.courtyard.com
149 rooms. Airport transportation available.
$$

★Hampton Inn

1500 Easton Rd., Willow Grove,
215-659-3535, 800-426-7866;
www.hamptoninn.com
150 rooms. Complimentary continental
breakfast. Airport transportation available. $

WYOMISSING

HOTELS

★★Inn At Reading
1040 N. Park Rd., Wyomissing,
610-372-7811, 800-383-9713;
www.innatreading.com
250 rooms. Airport transportation available.
$

★★Sheraton Reading Hotel
1741 W. Papermill Rd., Wyomissing,
610-376-3811;
www.sheratonreadingpa.com
254 rooms. Airport transportation available.
$

YORK

York claims to be the first capital of the United States. The Continental Congress met here in 1777 and adopted the Articles of Confederation, using the phrase "United States of America" for the first time. The first Pennsylvania town founded west of the Susquehanna River, York was and is still based on an agricultural and industrial economy. The city is dotted with 17 historical markers and 35 brass or bronze tablets marking historical events or places. There are more than 10 recreation areas in the county.

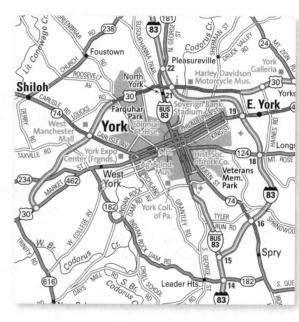

Information: Convention and Visitors Bureau, 1 Market Way East, York, 673-2429, or the Visitors Information Center, 1618 Toronita St., York, 717-843-6660; www.yorkpa.org

WHAT TO SEE AND DO

Bob Hoffman Weightlifting Hall of Fame
3300 Board Rd., York,
717-767-6481;
www.yorkbarbell.com
Weightlifting section honors Olympic weightlifters, powerlifters, bodybuilders and strongmen; displays include samples of Iron Game artifacts, memorabilia and photos. Monday-Saturday.

Central Market House
34 W. Philadelphia St., York,
717-848-2243
Opened in March 1888. Over 70 vendors offer fresh produce, homemade baked goods, regional handcrafts and specialty items. Tuesday, Thursday, Saturday.

Fire Museum of York County
757 W. Market St., York,
717-843-0464
Turn-of-the-century firehouse preserves two centuries of firefighting history; from leather bucket brigades to hand-drawn hose carts and pumps, horse-drawn equipment and finally to motorized equipment; artifacts and memorabilia; fire chief's office and firefighter's sleeping quarters are re-created, complete with brass slide pole. April-October: Saturday and second Sunday every month; also by appointment.

Friends Meeting House
135 W. Philadelphia St.,
York,
717-843-2285
(1766) Original virgin pine paneling;
restored. Regular meetings are still held
here. By appointment.

Harley-Davidson, Inc
1425 Eden Road,
York,
717-848-1177
Guided tour through motorcycle assembly
plant and the Rodney Gott Antique Motorcycle Museum. Children under 12 and cameras not permitted on plant tour. Plant and
museum combination tour Monday-Friday.
Museum tour Saturday.

Historical Society of York County
250 E. Market St.,
York,
717-848-1587
Includes library with genealogical records
(Tuesday-Saturday; fee for nonmembers).
Museum features exhibits on the history of
York County. Combination ticket for all his-
toric sites maintained by the society. Daily.
    Sites include:

Bonham House
152 E. Market St., York,
717-848-1587
(Circa 1875). Historic house reflects life in
late 19th century. By appointment.

General Gates' House
157 W. Market St.,
York
(1751) It was here that Lafayette gave a
toast to Washington, marking the end of
a movement to replace him. Also here are
Golden Plough Tavern (1741), one of the
earliest buildings in York, which reflects
the Germanic background of many of the
settlers in its furnishings and half-timber
architecture, and the Bobb Log House
(1811), furnished with painted and grained
furniture. Tuesday-Saturday.

Warrington Friends Meeting House
(1769; expanded in 1782) Fine example of
early Quaker meetinghouse.

York County Colonial Court House
W. Market St. and N. Pershing Ave.,
York, 717-848-1587;
www.yorkheritage.org
Replica of 1754 original. Exhibits include
multimedia presentation of Continental
Congress's adoption of the Articles of Confederation, audiovisual story of 1777-1778
historic events; original printer's copy of
Articles of Confederation, historic documents and artifacts. Tours. Daily.

SPECIAL EVENTS
River Walk Art Festival
1 Market Way W, York
Along Codorus Creek at York County
Colonial Court House. Late August.

HOTELS
★Best Western Westgate Inn
1415 Kenneth Rd., York,
717-767-6931;
www.bestwestern.com
105 rooms. Complimentary continental
breakfast. $

★Hampton Inn
1550 Mt. Zion Rd., York,
717-840-1500, 800-426-7866;
www.hamptoninn.com
144 rooms. Complimentary continental
breakfast. $

★★Holiday Inn
2000 Loucks Rd., York,
717-846-9500, 800-465-4329;
www.holidayinn.com
181 rooms. $

★★The Yorktowne Hotel
48 E. Market St., York,
717-848-1111;
www.yorktowne.com
122 rooms. Airport transportation available. $

PENNSYLVANIA

RESTAURANTS

★★★Accomac Inn
6330 S. River Dr., York,
717-252-1521;
www.accomac.com
This elegant country restaurant comes complete with white tablecloths and tableside preparation.
French menu. Dinner. Sunday brunch. Bar. $$$

★★San Carlo's
333 Arsenal Rd., U.S. 30,
York,
717-854-2028;
www.sancarlosrestaurant.com
American menu. Dinner. Bar. Children's menu. Renovated 175-year-old barn; original fieldstone walls. $$

PENNSYLVANIA

★

★

★

★

★

VIRGINIA

lovers—of nature, history, art, fine dining and family fun. The first of the Southern states stays true to its tourism slogan, "Virginia is for lovers," four words that just might be vague enough to encapsulate all that Virginia has to offer.

The state is best known for its prominent role in U.S. history, and strong ties with the past are readily apparent. More than 1,600 historical markers dot its 55,000 miles of paved roads. More than 100 historic buildings are open all year; hundreds more welcome visitors during the statewide Historic Garden Week (usually the last week in April).

Permanent English settlement of America began in Jamestown in 1607 and started a long line of Virginia "firsts:" the first legislative assembly in the Western Hemisphere (1619); the first armed rebellion against royal government (Bacon's Rebellion, 1676); the first stirring debates, in Williamsburg and Richmond, which left pre-Revolutionary America echoing Patrick Henry's inflammatory "Give me liberty, or give me death!" Records show that America's first Thanksgiving was held December 4, 1619, on the site of what is now Berkeley Plantation.

To Virginia the nation owes its most cherished documents: Thomas Jefferson's Declaration of Independence, George Mason's Bill of Rights and James Madison's Constitution. The Old Dominion was the birthplace of George Washington and seven other U.S. presidents.

Ironically, the state so passionately involved in creating a new nation was very nearly the means of its destruction. Virginia was the spiritual and physical capital of the Confederacy; the Army of Northern Virginia was the Confederacy's most powerful weapon, General Robert E. Lee its greatest commander. More than half the fighting of the Civil War took place in Virginia; and here, in the courthouse of the quaint little village of Appomattox, the war finally came to an end.

When chartered in 1609, the Virginia territory included about one-tenth of what is now the United States; the present state ranks 36th in size, but the remaining area is remarkably diverse. Tidewater Virginia—the coastal plain—is low, almost flat, arable land cut by rivers and bays into a magnificent system of natural harbors. Inland lies the gentle, rolling Piedmont, covering about half the state. Virginia's leading tobacco area, the Piedmont also produces apples, corn, wheat, hay and dairy products. West of the Piedmont rise the Blue Ridge Mountains; high, rugged, upland plateaus occur to the south. Farther west is the Valley of Virginia, which is actually a series of valleys. The best known valley is the Shenandoah, which contains some of the richest—and once the bloodiest—land in the nation. Civil War fighting swept the valley for four years; Winchester changed hands 72 times. To the southwest are the Appalachian Plateaus, a rugged, forested region of coal mines.

For the vacationer today, the state offers colonial and Civil War history at every turn, seashore and mountain recreation year-round, caverns in the west and the Dismal Swamp in the southeast, and the Skyline Drive, one of the loveliest scenic drives in the East.

Capital: Richmond

Web Site: www.virginia.org

282

VIRGINIA

★ SPOTLIGHT

★ The Pentagon building in Arlington is the largest office building in the world.

ABINGDON

Daniel Boone passed through this area in 1760 and dubbed it "Wolf Hill" after a pack of wolves from a nearby cave disturbed his dogs. Wolf Hill had long been a crossing for buffalo and Native Americans; Boone later used it for his own family's westward migration. Later, Black's Fort was built here and the community adopted that name. Now known as Abingdon, this summer resort in the Virginia Highlands just north of Tennessee is Virginia's largest burley tobacco market and a livestock auction center.

Information: Abingdon Convention & Visitors Bureau, 335 Cummings St., Abingdon, 800-435-3344; www.abingdon.com

WHAT TO SEE AND DO

Abingdon Historic District
Abingdon,
276-676-2282, 800-435-3440
Listed on the National Register of Historic Places, this 20-block district features buildings that date from the 1700s. The historically significant structures aren't the only draw: the area has dozens of shops and galleries.

Callebs Cove Campground
25136 Whitaker Hollow Rd., Abingdon,
276-475-5222;
www.callebscovecampground.com
55 sites with full hook-ups.

Grayson Highlands State Park
Abingdon,
276-579-7092, 800-933-7225;
www.dcr.virginia.gov/state_parks/gra.shtml
Within this 4,935-acre park are rugged peaks, some more than 5,000 feet; alpine scenery. Hiking, horse trails, picnicking, camping, visitor center, interpretive programs, pioneer life displays (June-August). Adjacent to Mount Rogers National Recreation Area. Daily. Standard fees.

Riverside Campground
18496 N. Fork River Rd., Abingdon,
276-628-5333
Campers will enjoy the live music and bingo hall. 96 sites, full hook-ups; 68 sites, water and electric hook-ups. Pool.

Virginia Creeper National Recreation Trail
Abingdon,
276-676-2282, 800-435-3440;
www.vacreepertrail.org

Hikers, bicyclists, equestrians, and anyone who wants to enjoy a good hike will find one on this 34-mile scenic railroad bed converted into a recreational facility. There are numerous shuttle and bike rental facilities nearby.

White's Mill
12291 White's Mill Rd., Abingdon,
276-628-2960;
www.whitesmill.org
White's Mill is a still-functioning grist and flour mill built in 1790. Just 4 1/2 miles from Abingdon, this Virginia Historic Landmark is one of the only water-powered mills in existence in southwestern Virginia. Watch as corn becomes cornmeal, and don't forget to take home a sample. Nearby is the working Blacksmith Shop. Wednesday-Sunday 10 a.m.-6 p.m.

Wolf Lair Village & Campground
19091 County Park Rd., Abingdon,
276-628-3680;
www.wolflairvillagecampground.com
This campground is a half-mile from South Holston Lake and includes: 48 sites, full hook-ups, 15/30-amp service. Pool, water slide, diving board; miniature golf.

SPECIAL EVENTS

Barter Theatre
127 W. Main St., Abingdon,
540-628-3991;
www.bartertheatre.com
America's oldest, longest-running professional repertory theater. Founded during the Depression on the theory that residents would barter their abundant crops for first-rate professional entertainment. Designated

283

VIRGINIA

★
★
★
★

State Theatre of Virginia in 1946. Barter Players perform March-December. Children's theater June-August.

Virginia Highlands Festival
208 W. Main St., Abingdon,
276-623-5266;
www.vahighlandsfestival.org
Exhibits, demonstrations of rustic handicrafts; plays, musical entertainment; historical reenactments and house tours, antique market. Early-mid-August.

HOTELS

★Comfort Inn
170 Old Jonesboro Rd., Abingdon,
276-676-2222, 877-424-6423;
www.choicehotels.com
80 rooms. Complimentary continental breakfast. $

★Days Inn
887 Empire Dr. S.W.,
Abingdon,
276-628-7131, 800-329-7466;
www.daysinn.com
99 rooms. $

★★★The Martha Washington Inn
150 W. Main St.,
Abingdon,
276-628-3161, 888-888-5252;
www.marthawashingtoninn.com
Experience Southern hospitality at its finest in this historic inn, built as a private residence for a Virginia general in 1832. The original architecture has been painstakingly maintained, with wood floors, crystal chandeliers and plaster detailing. Meals served in the Dining Room are innovative and well prepared. 62 rooms. $$$

ALEXANDRIA

★
★
★
★
☆

A group of English and Scottish merchants established a tobacco warehouse at the junction of Hunting Creek and the "Potowmack" River in the 1740s. The little settlement prospered, and 17 years later surveyor John West, Jr., and his young assistant, George Washington, arrived and "laid off in streets and 84 half-acre lots" the town of Alexandria. Among the first buyers on the July morning in 1749 when the lots were offered for public sale were Lawrence Washington and his brother Augustus, William Ramsay, the Honorable William Fairfax, and John Carlyle. Erecting handsome town houses, these gentlemen soon brought a lively and cosmopolitan air to Alexandria with parties, balls and horse racing. George Washington made his home here, as did George Mason and Robert E. Lee.

In 1789, Virginia ceded Alexandria to the District of Columbia, but in 1846, the still Southern-oriented citizens asked to return to the Old Dominion, which Congress allowed.

During the Civil War, Alexandria was cut off from the Confederacy when Union troops occupied the town to protect Potomac River navigation. Safe behind Union lines, the city escaped the dreadful destruction experienced by many other Southern towns. Today, Alexandria has developed into a trade, commerce, transportation and science center.
Information: Convention/Visitors Association, 421 King St., Alexandria, 703-838-4200, 800-388-9119; www.funside.com

WHAT TO SEE AND DO

Alexandria Black History Resource Center
638 N. Alfred St.,
Alexandria,
703-838-4356
Photographs, letters, documents and artifacts relate the history of African-Americans in Alexandria. Tuesday-Saturday.

Athenaeum
201 Prince St., Alexandria,
703-548-0035;
www.nvfaa.org
Greek Revival structure (1851) built as a bank now houses the Fine Arts Association. Art shows, dance performances. Wednesday-Friday and Saturday-Sunday afternoons.

GEORGE WASHINGTON'S PLANTATIONS

Ask any historically knowledgeable American to name George Washington's home, and the answer you might get is Mount Vernon, just south of Alexandria, Virginia. This is only partly correct. In his youth, Washington lived on two other plantations, both of which, like Mount Vernon, now honor the country's first president.

Each unique home tells of a different aspect of his life. All three can be visited in a one-day, 170-mile round-trip. Make sure to get an early start, and begin in Alexandria, a Potomac River port long before the Capitol at Washington, D.C. was conceived. Paralleling the Potomac, the scenic Mount Vernon Parkway winds south for about 10 miles to Mount Vernon, a sprawling estate Washington inherited at the age of 20 from a half-brother. Here, you can tour his stately white mansion, enjoy the Potomac views, walk among the 18th-century farm fields and gardens, and pay homage at his and Martha's tombs. At Mount Vernon, you'll learn about Washington the farmer, the soldier and the statesman. Plan to spend much of the morning at the estate.

Next, head south to Washington's two childhood homes. The first stop is Popes Creek Plantation, which is officially called the George Washington Birthplace National Monument. From Mount Vernon, take State Route 235 West to Highway 1 South and follow the signs to I-95 South to Fredericksburg, about 40 miles. In Fredericksburg, take State Route three east for about 36 miles. Make a left turn onto State Route 204, which ends at the plantation in about two miles. This is where Washington was born on February 22, 1732. Unlike Mount Vernon, nothing remains of the original house except a few foundation bricks and grand Potomac River views. And yet the 550-acre park—re-created in part as a colonial farm with fields, pastures and livestock—does a fine job of exploring Washington's origins. His great-grandfather, John, an English seaman, settled in the area in 1657, prospered and was eventually buried in the park. You can tour Memorial House, a Colonial-style farmhouse similar to one that might have stood on the property in 1732. Nearby are other reconstructed period farm buildings and a large herb garden. Walking trails trace the river's shoreline past a grove of towering cedars, and a shaded picnic area is provided. Packing a picnic is a good idea since the park has no food service.

Next head to Fredericksburg's Ferry Farm, where Washington's family moved when he was six. At the city outskirts, bear right onto Business Route 3. A sign to Ferry Farm will indicate a U-Turn at a stoplight. It is at Ferry Farm that Washington might have chopped down a cherry tree—wild cherries still grow on the property—and where he might have tossed a coin across the Rappahannock River. Archeological digs, sometimes open to visitors, are underway, and a small museum describes Washington's childhood here. Return to Alexandria via Route 3 and I-95 North. Conclude your day there with dinner in early American style at Gadsby's Tavern, built in 1792. Approximately 170 miles.

285

VIRGINIA

★

★

★

★

★

Atlantic Kayak
1201 N. Royal St., Alexandria,
703-838-9072, 800-297-0066;
www.atlantickayak.com

See the capital's sights from a new perspective: as a kayaker on the Potomac. Atlantic Kayak runs short trips that include a brief lesson; all equipment is included and no experience is required. Sunset and moonlight tours are especially beautiful. Another outing takes you to the Dyke Marsh Wildlife Area, where you'll see ospreys and great blue herons. On July 4, take a tour to view the fireworks. April-October: daily.

Boyhood Home of Robert E. Lee
607 Oronoco St., Alexandria,
703-548-8454

Federalist architecture. Famous guests include Washington and Lafayette.

Carlyle House
121 N. Fairfax St., Alexandria,
703-549-2997

(1753) This stately stone mansion built in Palladian style was the site of a 1755 meeting between General Edward Braddock and five British colonial governors to plan the early campaigns of the French and Indian War. Tuesday-Sunday.

Christ Church
118 N. Washington St., Alexandria,
703-549-1450;
www.historicchristchurch.org

(1773) Washington and Robert E. Lee were pewholders. Fine Palladian window; interior balcony; wrought-brass and crystal chandelier brought from England. Structure is extensively restored but has changed little since it was built. Exhibit, gift shop at Columbus Street entrance. Monday-Saturday, also Sunday afternoons.

Doorways to Old Virginia
221 King St., Alexandria,
757-482-4848;
www.chesapeakejubilee.org

Offers guided walking tours of the historic district. March-October: Friday-Sunday, evenings.

Fort Ward Museum and Historic Site
4301 W. Braddock Rd., Alexandria,
703-838-4848

Restored Union Fort from the Civil War; museum contains a Civil War collection. Museum. Tuesday-Sunday. Park, picnicking. Daily to sunset.

Gadsby's Tavern Museum
134 N. Royal St., Alexandria,
703-838-4242

(1770, 1792) Frequented by Washington and other patriots. Combines two 18th-century buildings; interesting architecture. Tuesday-Sunday.

George Washington Masonic National Memorial
101 Callahan Dr., Alexandria,
703-683-2007;
www.gwmemorial.org

American Freemasons' memorial to their most prominent member, this 333-foot-high structure houses a large collection of objects that belonged to George Washington, which were collected by his family or the masonic lodge where he served as the first Master. Guided tours explore a replica of Alexandria-Washington Lodge's first hall, a library, museum and an observation deck on the top floor. Daily 9 a.m.-4 p.m.

King Street
Street is lined with trendy restaurants, shops and fine antique stores.

Lee-Fendall House
614 Oronoco St., Alexandria,
703-548-1789

(1785) Built by Phillip Richard Fendall and occupied by the Lee family for 118 years. Both George Washington and Revolutionary War hero "Light Horse Harry" Lee were frequent visitors to the house. Remodeled in 1850, the house is furnished with Lee family belongings. Tuesday-Saturday 10 a.m.-4 p.m., Sunday 1-4 p.m., weekend hours may vary.

The Lyceum
201 S. Washington St., Alexandria,
703-838-4994

286

VIRGINIA

Museum, exhibitions; Virginia travel information (limited). Daily.

Old Presbyterian Meeting House
321 S. Fairfax St., Alexandria,
703-549-6670
(1774) Tomb of the unknown soldier of the Revolution is in the churchyard. Monday-Friday.

Sightseeing Boat Tours
Potomac Riverboat Company,
Alexandria, 703-684-0580;
www.potomacriverboatco.com
Tours of the Alexandria waterfront. Contact the Potomac Riverboat Company.

Stabler-Leadbeater Apothecary Museum
105 S. Fairfax St., Alexandria,
703-838-3852
(1792) Largest collection of apothecary glass in its original setting in the country; more than 1,000 apothecary bottles. Original building is now a museum of early pharmacy; collection of old prescriptions, patent medicines, scales and other 18th-century pharmacy items. George Washington, Robert E. Lee, and John Calhoun were regular customers. Daily.

Torpedo Factory Arts Center
105 N. Union St., Alexandria,
703-838-4565;
www.torpedofactory.org
Renovated munitions plant houses an artists' center with more than 160 professional artists of various media. Studios, cooperative galleries, school. Also the home of Alexandria Archaeology offices, lab, and museum; 703-838-4399. Daily 10 a.m.-5 p.m.

Walking Tour of Historic Sites
221 King St., Alexandria,
703-838-4200
Start at the Visitor Center in Ramsay House (circa 1725), which is the oldest house in Alexandria and has been used as a tavern, grocery store and cigar factory. Here, you can obtain special events information and a free visitors' guide, and purchase block tickets good for reduced admission to three of the city's historic properties. Guided

walking tours depart from here (spring-fall, weather permitting). The bureau also issues free parking permits, tour and highway maps, and hotel, dining, and shopping information. Daily.

One block N on Fairfax St. is:

SPECIAL EVENTS

George Washington Birthday Celebrations
Events include a race and a Revolutionary War reenactment; climaxed by a birthday parade on the federal holiday. February.

House Tours
221 King St., Alexandria,
703-838-4200
Tours depart from the Ramsay House. Fine colonial and Federalist houses are open to the public: Historic Garden Week (April); Hospital Auxiliary Tour of Historic Houses (September); Scottish Christmas Walk (December). Tickets, additional information at Alexandria Convention/Visitors Association.

Red Cross Waterfront Festival
123 N. Alfred St., Alexandria,
703-549-8300;
www.waterfrontfestival.org
Commemorates Alexandria's maritime heritage. Features "tall ships," blessing of the fleet, river cruises, races, arts and crafts, exhibits, food, a variety of music, and fireworks. June.

Scottish Christmas Walk
Ramsay House, 221 King St.,
Alexandria,
703-548-0111, 800-388-9119
Parade, house tour, concerts, greens and heather sales, and a dinner/dance to emphasize city's Scottish origins. First Saturday in December.

Virginia Scottish Games
Ramsay House, 221 King St.,
Alexandria,
703-838-4200;
www.vascottishgames.org
Athletic competition, Highland dance and music, antique cars, displays and food. Fourth weekend in July.

★
★
★
★
★

HOTELS

★Best Western Old Colony Inn
1101 N. Washington St.,
Alexandria,
703-739-2222, 800-780-7234;
www.bestwestern.com
49 rooms. Complimentary full breakfast. Airport transportation available. **$**

★Hampton Inn
4800 Leesburg Pike,
Alexandria,
703-671-4800;
www.hamptoninn.com
130 rooms. Complimentary continental breakfast. **$**

★★★Hilton Alexandria Mark Center
5000 Seminary Rd., Alexandria,
703-845-1010;
www.hilton.com
The lakeside Hilton Alexandria Mark Center is situated near the central business district of Washington, D.C., and the shops and galleries of Old Town. This elegant atrium hotel sits adjacent to a 43-acre botanical preserve and offers views of the Captiol. Guests looking for on-site activities can work out in the 24-hour fitness center, take a swim in the heated indoor/outdoor pool, or take in a game of tennis on one of the two outdoor (lighted) tennis courts.
495 rooms. Airport transportation available. **$**

★★★Morrison House Boutique Hotel
116 S. Alfred St., Alexandria,
703-838-8000, 866-324-6628;
www.morrisonhouse.com
Just down the river from the Capitol, this Federal-style mansion presents visitors with a peaceful alternative to the bustling city. Decorative fireplaces, four-poster mahogany beds and silk sofas fill the guest rooms, all furnished in early American decor. But the amenities are decidedly 21st century, with oversized marble bathrooms and luxurious Frette linens. The Grille attracts a smart, casual set with its clubby ambience and live piano music. Don't miss the exceptional Elysium, where menus are banished

and the dishes are determined by the chef's conversations with each patron.
45 rooms. **$$**

★★Old Town Hotel
480 King St., Alexandria,
703-549-6080, 800-368-5047
227 rooms. Complimentary continental breakfast. Airport transportation available. **$$**

★★Radisson Hotel Old Town Alexandria
901 N. Fairfax St.,
Alexandria,
703-683-6000;
www.radisson.com
258 rooms. Airport transportation available. **$**

★★★Sheraton Suites Old Town Alexandria
801 N. St. Asaph St.,
Alexandria,
703-836-4700, 800-325-3535;
www.sheraton.com
Just steps from the Potomac River, this hotel offers an easy commute from both Ronald Reagan Washington National Airport and D.C.
247 rooms, all suites. Airport transportation available. **$$**

RESTAURANTS

★★Bilbo Baggins
208 Queen St., Alexandria,
703-683-0300;
www.bilbobaggins.net
American menu. Lunch, dinner, Sunday brunch. Bar. Children's menu. **$$**

★★Bistrot Laf Fayette
1118 King St., Alexandria,
703-548-2525
French menu. Lunch, dinner. Closed Sunday. Bar. Casual attire. **$$$**

★★Chart House
1 Cameron St., Alexandria,
703-684-5080; www.chart-house.com
Seafood menu. Lunch, dinner, Sunday brunch. Bar. Children's menu. Outdoor seating. **$$$**

288

VIRGINIA

★★★Chez Andree
10 E. Glebe Rd., Alexandria,
703-836-1404;
www.chezandree.com
Chez Andree, family-owned for more than 40 years, offers country French cuisine in three different dining rooms. Originally a railroad bar that catered to the Potomac Yards, the restaurant now serves specials such as duck l'orange and rack of lamb to hungry diners. French menu. Lunch, dinner. Closed Sunday. Bar. Reservations recommended. **$$**

★Copeland's of New Orleans
4300 King St., Alexandria,
703-671-7997
Cajun/Creole menu. Lunch, dinner, Sunday brunch. Bar. Children's menu. Outdoor seating. **$**

★Faccia Luna
823 S. Washington St., Alexandria,
703-838-5998;
www.faccialuna.com
American, Italian menu. Lunch, dinner. Bar. Children's menu. Outdoor seating. **$$**

★★Fish Market
105 King St., Alexandria,
703-836-5676;
www.fishmarketoldtown.com
Seafood menu. Lunch, dinner. Bar. Children's menu. Casual attire. **$$**

★★Gadsby's Tavern
138 N. Royal St., Alexandria,
703-548-1288
American menu. Lunch, dinner, Sunday brunch. children's menu. Outdoor seating. **$$**

★★Geranio
722 King St., Alexandria,
703-548-0088;
www.geranio.net
Italian menu. Lunch, dinner. Casual attire. **$$**

★★★The Grille
116 S. Alfred St., Alexandria,
703-838-8000, 800-367-0800;
www.morrisonhouse.com

The Grille in the Morrison House Boutique Hotel lets diners create their very own Flight of Food based on what the chef has purchased from local markets and farmers that day. Instead of a dinner menu, you'll be presented with a wine list, followed by a personal visit from the chef to discuss what you're in the mood to eat. He'll give you the list of ingredients, and you work together to develop the menu. After dinner, a butler will escort you to the parlor for an after-dinner drink or a wonderful, aromatic pot of special-blend loose tea made for the Morrison House Boutique Hotel.
International menu. Breakfast, dinner. Bar. Children's menu. Casual attire. **$$$**

★★Il Porto
121 King St., Alexandria,
703-836-8833;
www.ilportoristorante.com
Italian menu. Lunch, dinner. Bar. Children's menu. Casual attire. Reservations recommended. **$$**

★★★La Bergerie
218 N. Lee St., Alexandria,
703-683-1007;
www.labergerie.com
In a historic brick warehouse, La Bergerie serves up French dishes, including roasted wild rockfish on mussel and salmon caviar risotto with a saffron vanilla sauce, roasted wild boar chop with kimchi cabbage, burgundy carrots and a sweet and sour sauce, along with a daily prix-fixe menu.
French menu. Lunch, dinner. Closed Sunday except Mother's Day. Reservations recommended. **$$**

★★Landini Brothers
115 King St., Alexandria,
703-836-8404;
www.landinibrothers.com
Italian menu. Lunch, dinner. Bar. Reservations recommended. 1790s building. **$$**

★★Le Gaulois
1106 King St., Alexandria,
703-739-9494

VIRGINIA

★
★
★
★
★

French menu. Lunch, dinner. Casual attire. Reservations recommended. Outdoor seating. **$$**

★★Le Refuge
127 N. Washington St., Alexandria,
703-548-4661;
www.lerefugealexandria.com
French menu. Lunch, dinner. Closed Sunday. Bar. Reservations recommended. **$$$**

★Mango Mike's
4580 Duke St., Alexandria,
703-370-3800;
www.mangomikes.com
Caribbean menu. Lunch, dinner, Sunday brunch. Bar. Children's menu. Outdoor seating. **$**

★★Monroe's
1603 Commonwealth Ave., Alexandria,
703-548-5792;
www.munroesrestaurant.com
Italian menu. Dinner, Sunday brunch. Bar. Children's menu. Reservations recommended. Outdoor seating. Contemporary trattoria with large murals. **$$**

★★R. T.'s
3804 Mt. Vernon Ave., Alexandria,
703-684-6010
Cajun/Creole menu. Lunch, dinner. Bar. Children's menu. **$$**

★★Tempo
4231 Duke St., Alexandria,
703-370-7900;
www.temporestaurant.com
Italian, French menu. Lunch, dinner, Sunday brunch. Bar. Reservations recommended. Outdoor seating. **$$**

★★Thai Hut
408 S. Van Dorn St., Alexandria,
703-823-5357
Thai menu. Lunch, dinner. **$**

★★Union Street Public House
121 S. Union St., Alexandria,
703-548-1785;
www.usphalexandria.com
American menu. Lunch, dinner, Sunday brunch. Bar. Children's menu. **$$**

★★Villa d'Este
600 Montgomery St., Alexandria,
703-549-9477
Italian menu. Lunch, dinner. Bar. Reservations recommended. **$$$**

★★The Wharf
119 King St.,
Alexandria,
703-836-2834;
www.wharfrestaurant.com
Seafood menu. Lunch, dinner. Bar. Children's menu. Late 18th-century building. **$$**

APPOMATTOX COURT HOUSE NATIONAL HISTORICAL PARK

The series of clashes between General Ulysses S. Grant and General Robert E. Lee that started with the Battle of the Wilderness (May 5, 1864) finally ended here on Palm Sunday, April 9, 1865, in the little village of Appomattox.

A week earlier, Lee had evacuated besieged Petersburg and headed west in a desperate attempt to join forces with General Johnston in North Carolina. Ragged and exhausted, decimated by desertions, without supplies, and beset by Union forces at every turn, the once-great Army of Northern Virginia launched its last attack at dawn on April 9. By 10 a.m., it was clear that further bloodshed was futile; after some difficulty in getting a message to Grant, the two antagonists met in the parlor of the McLean House. By 3 p.m., the generous surrender terms had been drafted and signed. The war was over. Three days later, 28,231 Confederate soldiers received their parole here.

The 1,743-acre park includes the village of Appomattox, restored and reconstructed to appear much as it did in 1865. Uniformed park rangers or interpreters in period dress answer questions about the residents and events. (Daily; closed holidays November-February.) Golden Eagle Passport accepted. Audiovisual programs, Braille guide folders, audio guide, and large-print folder available for the hearing and visually impaired.
Information: Superintendent, Hwy. 24, Appomattox, 434-352-8987; www.nps.gov/apco.

WHAT TO SEE AND DO

Appomattox Courthouse Building
Reconstructed building houses visitor center, museum; audiovisual slide program (every half-hour, second floor). Self-guided tour of village begins here and includes:

Clover Hill Tavern and Outbuildings
(1819) Oldest structure in village Bookstore, rest rooms.

Confederate Cemetery

County Jail
(1870) Furnished.

McLean House and Outbuildings
Reconstruction of house where Generals Lee and Grant met on April 9, 1865.

Meek's Store and Meek's Storehouse
With period furnishings.

Stacking of Arms
On the fourth anniversary of the firing on Fort Sumter, which triggered the outbreak of war, Confederate soldiers laid down their weapons here.

Woodson Law Office
With period furnishings.

Holliday Lake State Park
Rte. 2, Appomattox,
434-248-6308
Approximately 250 acres in Buckingham-Appomattox State Forest. Swimming beach, bathhouse, fishing, boating (launch, rentals) on 150-acre lake; hiking trails, picnicking, concession, tent and trailer sites. Visitor center, interpretive programs. Standard fees. Park (daily); most activities, including camping (Memorial Day-Labor Day).

291

ARLINGTON COUNTY (RONALD REAGAN WASHINGTON-NATIONAL AIRPORT AREA)

Information: www.mwaa.com/national/index.htm

WHAT TO SEE AND DO

Arlington Farmers' Market
N. Courthouse Rd. and N. 14th St.,
Arlington,
703-228-6423;
www.arlingtonfarmersmarket.com
Irresistibly fresh berries, peaches, and heirloom tomatoes are just some of the pleasures available at this lively market, which has been featuring the produce of farmers within 125 miles of Arlington since 1979. Don't miss the grass-fed meats, specialty goat cheeses, and unusual varieties of familiar fruits and vegetables (one longtime vendor grows 35 different types of apples). Saturday.

Arlington National Cemetery
Arlington,
703-979-0690;
www.arlingtoncemetery.org
The solemn grounds of Arlington National Cemetery are a profoundly stirring sight. Gentle hills are studded as far as the eye can see with white stones marking the graves of more than 260,000 Americans who served in the nation's military, from the American Revolution to more recent conflicts. Many visitors stop at the Tomb of the Unknowns, which contains the unidentified remains of servicemen killed in the world wars and the Korean War, and provides quiet tribute to anonymous sacrifice. Most also pay their

respects at the eternal flame marking the granite-paved gravesite of President John F. Kennedy and his wife, Jacqueline, and that of Robert F. Kennedy nearby.

Also located here are:

Arlington House, the Robert E. Lee Memorial
Arlington,
703-557-0613
National memorial to Robert E. Lee. Built between 1802 and 1818 by George Washington Parke Custis, Martha Washington's grandson and foster son of George Washington. In 1831 his daughter, Mary Anna Randolph Custis, married Lieutenant Robert E. Lee; six of the seven Lee children were born here. As executor of the Custis estate, Lee took extended leave from the U.S. Army and devoted his time to managing and improving the estate. It was the Lee homestead for 30 years before the Civil War. On April 20, 1861, following the secession of Virginia, Lee made his decision to stay with Virginia. Within a month, the house was vacated. Some of the family possessions were moved for safekeeping, but most were stolen or destroyed when Union troops occupied the house during the Civil War. In 1864, when Mrs. Lee could not appear personally to pay property tax, the estate was confiscated by the federal government; a 200-acre section was set aside for a national cemetery. (There is some evidence that indicates this was done to ensure the Lee family could never again live on the estate.) G. W. Custis Lee, the general's son, later regained title to the property through a Supreme Court decision and sold it to the U.S. government in 1883 for $150,000. Restoration of the house to its 1861 appearance was begun in 1925. The Classic Revival house is furnished with authentic pieces of the period, including some Lee family originals. From the grand portico with its six massive, faux-marble Doric columns there is a panoramic view of Washington, D.C. Daily.

Memorial Amphitheatre
This impressive white marble edifice is used for ceremonies such as Memorial Day, Easter sunrise and Veterans Day services.

Tomb of the Unknowns
On November 11, 1921, the remains of an unknown American soldier of World War I were entombed here. A memorial was erected in 1932 with the inscription "Here rests in honored glory an American soldier known but to God." On Memorial Day 1958, an unknown warrior who died in World War II and another who died in the Korean War were laid beside him. On Memorial Day 1984, an unknown soldier from the Vietnam War was interred here. Sentries stand guard 24 hours a day; changing of the guard is every hour on the hour October-March, every 30 minutes April-September.

Crystal City Shops
Crystal Dr., Arlington,
703-922-4636;
www.thecrystalcityshops.com
Crystal City, a mixed-use residential and commercial development, has an underground shopping complex and a lot of street-level activity. It's currently being upgraded to provide more of a Main Street feel, with outdoor cafes as well as improved landscaping and opportunities for window-shopping. You'll find jewelry and gift shops, men's and women's apparel, books and home furnishings, as well as a Japanese steakhouse, two American steakhouses, and a Legal Sea Foods. Daily.

Fashion Centre at Pentagon City
1100 S. Hayes St., Arlington,
703-415-2400;
www.fashioncentrepentagon.com
The Ritz-Carlton Hotel's presence dictates a glamorous tone at this huge, glittering mall, anchored by Macy's and Nordstrom and home to more than 150 other tantalizing shops and restaurants. Women's fashion and accessories stores include Betsey Johnson and MAC Cosmetics. For home furnishings, check out Crate & Barrel and Williams-Sonoma. Daily.

Freedom Park
1101 Wilson Blvd.,
Arlington,
703-284-3544

292

VIRGINIA

★
★
★
★
★

Nearly 1,000 feet in length, the park occupies a never-used bridge. The park also features a memorial to the journalists killed in the line of duty and various icons of freedom.

Iwo Jima Statue
On Arlington Blvd.,
near Arlington National Cemetery
Marine Corps War Memorial depicts raising of the flag on Mount Suribachi, Iwo Jima, February 23, 1945; this is the largest sculpture ever cast in bronze. Sunset Parade concert with performances by U.S. Marine Drum and Bugle Corps, U.S. Marine Corps Color Guard, and the Silent Drill Team (late May-late August, Tuesday evenings).

Newseum
1101 Wilson Blvd., Arlington,
703-284-3700, 888-639-7386
This 72,000-square-foot interactive museum of news takes visitors behind the scenes to see and experience how and why news is made. Be a reporter or newscaster; relive great news stories through multimedia exhibits; see today's news as it happens on a block-long video wall. Wednesday-Sunday.

The Pentagon
Jefferson Davis Hwy.,
Washington Blvd., and I-395,
Arlington,
703-695-1776;
www.defenselink.mil/pubs/pentagon
With some 6 million square feet of floor area, this is one of the largest office buildings in the world. It houses the offices of the Department of Defense.

SPECIAL EVENTS
Arlington County Fair
3308 S. Stafford St., Arlington,
703-920-4556;
www.arlingtoncountyfair.com
Countywide fair; arts, crafts, international foods, children's activities. August.

Army 10-miler
The Pentagon, Arlington,
202-685-3361;
www.armytenmiler.com
America's largest 10-mile road race, attracting thousands of military and civilian runners. Early October.

Marine Corps Marathon
Route 110 and Marshall Dr., Arlington,
800-786-8762;
www.marinemarathon.com
Cheer on your favorite runner at the Marine Corps Marathon. The 26-mile, 385-yard route starts and ends near the Iwo Jima Memorial and winds through Arlington, Georgetown and D.C., passing the Capitol, the Pentagon and other inspiring sights along the way. The Marine Corps Marathon 5K race, organized in conjunction with the Special Olympics competition, starts at the Memorial at 9:10 a.m. Late October.

Memorial Day Service Ceremony
Arlington National Cemetery,
Arlington
Wreaths placed at the Tomb of the Unknown Soldier. The National Symphony Orchestra gives a free concert later in the evening on the lawn of the Capitol. Memorial Day.

HOTELS
★★Arlington Court Hotel
1200 N. Courthouse Road,
Arlington,
703-524-4000;
www.arlingtoncourthotel.com
392 rooms. **$**

★★Courtyard by Marriott
2899 Jefferson Davis Hwy., Arlington,
703-549-3434, 800-321-2211;
www.courtyard.com
272 rooms. Airport transportation available. Airport. **$$**

★★★Crowne Plaza Hotel
1480 Crystal Dr., Arlington,
703-416-1600, 800-227-6963;
www.cpnationalairport.com
This Crowne Plaza Hotel is conveniently located near the attractions of Washington, D.C., Ronald Reagan National Airport and many businesses. Comfortable guest rooms

293

VIRGINIA

★
★
★
★
★

feature two-line phones, 25-inch TVs and work desks.
308 rooms. Airport transportation available. **$$**

★★Embassy Suites
1300 Jefferson Davis Hwy.,
Arlington,
703-979-9799, 800-362-2779;
www.embassysuites.com
267 rooms, all suites. Complimentary full breakfast. Airport transportation available. **$$**

★Hampton Inn
2000 Jefferson Davis Hwy.,
Arlington,
703-418-5901, 800-329-7466;
www.hamptoninn.com
247 rooms. Airport transportation available. **$**

★★★Hilton Arlington
950 N. Stafford St.,
Arlington,
703-528-6000, 800-695-7487;
www.hiltonarlington.com
This centrally located hotel is connected by a skybridge to the Ballston Common Mall and National Science Foundation Office Complex. The contemporary guest rooms feature Hilton's Serenity Bed and amenities such as Crabtree & Evelyn toiletries, in-room coffee makers and complimentary weekday newspapers.
209 rooms. **$$**

★★★Hyatt Arlington
1325 Wilson Blvd.,
Arlington,
703-525-1234, 800-233-1234;
www.arlington.hyatt.com
This hotel is located in the Rosslyn neighborhood across the bridge from Washington, D.C., and close to the Arlington National Cemetery. Sitting among businesses, shops and restaurants, the Hyatt Arlington is within walking distance of the Metro and Georgetown.
304 rooms. Airport transportation available. **$$**

★★★Marriott Crystal City At Reagan National Airport
1999 Jefferson Davis Hwy.,
Arlington,
703-413-5500;
www.crystalcitymarriott.com
This conveniently located, boutique-style hotel has an underground walkway that gives guests access to the Metro system, the Crystal City shopping mall and the surrounding metropolitan area. A curved staircase in the lobby leads you to guest rooms that feature Revive, Marriott's new bed with 300 thread-count linens, and high-speed Internet service.
343 rooms. Airport transportation available. Airport. **$$**

★★★★The Ritz-Carlton, Pentagon City
1250 S. Hayes St.,
Arlington,
703-415-5000, 800-241-3333;
www.ritzcarlton.com
Five minutes from Washington National Airport, the Ritz-Carlton, Pentagon City offers tailored elegance, with feather beds, Egyptian cotton linens, updated technology and luxurious club-level accommodations. Massages and personal fitness assessments are available at the fitness center. Afternoon tea takes on a whimsical edge with the Winnie the Pooh children's tea service in the Lobby Lounge, and the Grill never ceases to delight diners with its all-day dining.
366 rooms. Airport transportation available. **$$$**

★★★Sheraton Crystal City Hotel
1800 Jefferson Davis Hwy.,
Arlington,
703-486-1111, 800-862-7666;
www.sheraton.com/crystalcity
Just across the river from Washington, D.C., the Sheraton Crystal City Hotel offers complimentary shuttle service to and from local businesses and Ronald Reagan Washington National Airport.
210 rooms. Airport transportation available. **$$**

★

★

★

★

★

RESTAURANTS

★★Alpine
4770 Lee Hwy., Arlington,
703-528-7600
Italian menu. Lunch, dinner. Closed Monday. Bar. Business casual attire. Reservations recommended. Valet parking. **$$$**

★★Bistro Bistro
4021 S. 28th St., Arlington,
703-379-0300;
www.bistro-bistro.com
French bistro menu. Lunch, dinner, Sunday brunch. Bar. Children's menu. Casual attire. Reservations recommended. Outdoor seating. **$$**

★Cafe Dalat
3143 Wilson Blvd., Arlington,
703-276-0935
Vietnamese menu. Lunch, dinner. Closed Chinese New Year. Casual attire. Outdoor seating. **$$**

★★Carlyle Grand Cafe
4000 S. 28th St., Arlington,
703-931-0777;
www.greatamericanrestaurants.com/carlyle/cm.htm
American menu. Lunch, dinner, Sunday brunch. Bar. Children's menu. Casual attire. Outdoor seating. **$$**

★Faccia Luna
2909 Wilson Blvd., Arlington,
703-276-3099;
www.faccialuna.com
Italian menu. Lunch, dinner. Bar. Children's menu. Casual attire. Outdoor seating. **$$**

★★★The Grill
1250 S. Hayes St.,
Arlington,
703-412-2762;
www.ritzcarlton.com/en/properties/pentagoncity/dining/thegrill/default.htm
The Grill at the Ritz-Carlton Pentagon City offers upscale American classics in a warm, clubby dining room decked out in mahogany wood. The seasonal menu features dishes such as lobster, filet mignon, foie gras, caviar and oysters. Weekends are busy for the Grill, as it houses one of the best brunches in the area.
American menu. Breakfast, lunch, dinner, brunch. Bar. Children's menu. Casual attire. Reservations recommended. Valet parking. **$$$**

★★J. W.'s Steakhouse
1401 Lee Hwy.,
Arlington,
703-524-6400;
www.marriott.com
Steak menu. Dinner, Sunday brunch. Bar. Business casual attire. Reservations recommended. **$$$**

★★La Cote d'Or Cafe
2201 W. Moreland St.,
Arlington,
703-538-3033;
www.lacotedorcafe.com
French menu. Lunch, dinner, Sunday brunch. Closed Monday. Bar. Business casual attire. Reservations recommended. Outdoor seating. **$$$**

★★Little Viet Garden
3012 Wilson Blvd.,
Arlington,
703-522-9686
Vietnamese menu. Lunch, dinner. Bar. Casual attire. Reservations recommended. Outdoor seating. **$$**

★Matuba
2915 Columbia Pike, Arlington,
703-521-2811;
www.matuba-sushi.com
Japanese menu. Lunch, dinner. Closed Sunday. Casual attire. **$$**

★Red Hot and Blue
1600 Wilson Blvd.,
Arlington,
703-276-7427;
www.redhotandblue.com
Barbecue menu. Lunch, dinner. Bar. Children's menu. Casual attire. **$$**

★
★
★
★
★

★Silver Diner
3200 Wilson Blvd., Arlington,
703-812-8600;
www.silverdiner.com
American menu. Breakfast, lunch, dinner, late-night. Children's menu. Casual attire. **$$**

★★★Tivoli
1700 Moore St., Arlington,
703-524-8900;
www.tivolirestaurant.net
This three-story northern Italian restaurant is named after the well-known cultural center in Rome. Located in a high-end indoor mall, it sits directly above the Rosslyn Metro Station. The decor features wood, marble and brass in the dining room. The large bar, which is located downstairs, is a great place for a drink before dinner. A prix fixe menu is offered every night, and entrees include cannelloni filled with grilled vegetables in a saffron sauce and sautéed filets of trout with jumbo lump crab meat.
Italian menu. Lunch, dinner. Closed Sunday. Bar. Business casual attire. Reservations recommended. **$$$**

★Village Bistro
1723 Wilson Blvd.,
Arlington,
703-522-0284;
www.villagebistro.com
American, French menu. Lunch, dinner. Bar. Casual attire. Reservations recommended. Outdoor seating. **$$**

★★Woo Lae Oak
1500 S. Joyce St., Arlington,
703-521-3706;
www.woolaeoak.com
Korean menu. Lunch, dinner. Casual attire. Reservations recommended. **$$$**

ASHLAND

Ashland was founded when the president of the Richmond, Fredericksburg and Potomac Railroad bought land here. He dug a well, struck mineral water and started a health resort called Slash Cottage (wilderness acres were called "slashes"). A thriving village grew up and was named after Henry Clay's Kentucky estate. In 1866, the railroad company gave land to the Methodist Church and induced the church to move Randolph-Macon College here. A section of early 1900s houses along the railroad tracks has been set aside as a historic district.
Information: Ashland/Hanover Visitor Information Center, 112 N. Railroad Ave., Ashland, 804-752-6766, 800-897-1479; www.vatc.org

WHAT TO SEE AND DO

Americamps Richmond North
11322 Air Park Rd., Ashland,
804-798-5298, 800-628-2802;
www.americamps.com
Americamps is a wooded campground. 146 sites, 116 water and electrical hook-ups, 87 sewer hook-ups; 30 tent sites. Convenience store, pool, playground, game room.

Randolph-Macon College
204 Henry St., Ashland,
804-752-7305;
www.rmc.edu
(1830) (1,100 students.) Coeducational, liberal arts, Methodist-affiliated college. Historic buildings include Washington-Franklin Hall, Old Chapel, and Pace Hall.

SPECIALTY LODGINGS

Henry Clay Inn
114 N. Railroad Ave., Ashland,
804-798-3100, 800-343-4565;
www.henryclayinn.com
This inn, an authentic reproduction of a Georgian Revival, is near the historic areas of Williamsburg, Charlottesville and Fredericksburg.
11 rooms. Complimentary continental breakfast. **$**

RESTAURANTS

★★Ironhorse
100 S. Railroad Ave., Ashland,
804-752-6410
American, International menu. Lunch, dinner. Closed Sunday. Bar. Business casual attire. Reservations recommended. **$$**

BASYE

Information: Bryce Resort, Basye, 540-856-2121, 800-821-1444; www.bryceresort.com

WHAT TO SEE AND DO

Bryce Resort

1982 Fairway Dr., Basye,
540-856-2121, 800-821-1444;
www.bryceresort.com

Bryce Resort sits in the Shenandoah Valley, with Stony Creek winding through its golf course, coming into play on seven different holes. This par-71 course is just a shade under 6,300 yards from the championship tees, and the challenging distance is never more evident than on the 575-yard opening hole. The course is played moderately, with about 30,000 rounds going off each year, but it's kept in great condition, and the teaching pros on staff are always willing to help even the most inexperienced golfer.

Bryce Resort Ski Area

1982 Fairway Dr., Basye,
800-821-1444

Day and night skiing. Two double chairlifts, three surface lifts; patrol, school, rentals, snowmaking; ski shop, restaurant, cafeteria, bar. Longest run 2,750 feet; vertical drop 500 feet. Mid-December-mid-March: daily. In summer: Fishing, swimming, boating; horseback riding, golf, tennis, hiking, grass skiing. Fee for activities.

BEAVERDAM

WHAT TO SEE AND DO

Patrick Henry Home

16120 Chiswell Lane, Beaverdam,
804-227-3500

The 1719 Scotchtown was American Revolution-era hero Patrick Henry's home from 1771 to 1778. It was also the girlhood home of Dolly Madison. Fine colonial architecture. April-October: Thursday-Saturday 10 a.m.-4:30 p.m., Sunday 1:30-4:30 p.m.

BIG STONE GAP

This rugged mountain country gave author John Fox, Jr., his inspiration for "Trail of the Lonesome Pine" and "Little Shepherd of Kingdom Come," best-selling novels of the early 1900s. The town lies at the junction of three forks of the Powell River, which cuts a pass through Stone Mountain.

Information: Lonesome Pine Tourist Information Center, 619 Gilley Ave., Big Stone Gap, 276-523-2060; www.thelonesomepine.net

WHAT TO SEE AND DO

John Fox, Jr., House & Museum

118 Shawnee Ave. E., Big Stone Gap,
276-523-2747

Occupied from 1888 by John Fox, Jr. Memorabilia and original furnishings. Guided tours. June-September: Wednesday-Sunday.

June Tolliver House

Jerome St. and Clinton Ave., Big Stone Gap,
276-523-4707

Heroine in "Trail of the Lonesome Pine" lived here; period furnishings; now an arts and crafts center; restored 1890 house. Daily.

Southwest Virginia Museum

10 W. 1st St.,
Big Stone Gap,
276-523-1322;
www.swvamuseum.org

Four-story mansion contains exhibits dealing with life in southwestern Virginia during original coal boom of the 1890s; also Native Americans of the area and early pioneers. Daily, closed Mondays except from Memorial Day-Labor Day.

VIRGINIA

★
★
★
★

"Trail of the Lonesome Pine"
Big Stone Gap,

540-523-1235;
www.trailofthelonesomepine.org
Outdoor musical drama. Late June-Labor
Day: Thursday-Saturday.

BLACKSBURG

The Washington and Jefferson national forests, which lie to the northwest, provide a colorful backdrop of azaleas, flowering dogwood, and redbud in spring and brilliant hardwoods in fall. Virginia Polytechnic Institute and State University (Virginia Tech) is a source of employment for the town. The forests' Blacksburg Ranger District office is located here.
Information: Blacksburg Regional Chamber of Commerce,
1995 S. Main St., Blacksburg, 540-522-4503, 800-288-4061;
www.blacksburg-chamber.com

WHAT TO SEE AND DO
Mountain Lake
110 Southpark Dr., Blacksburg,
550-552-4641
A resort lake, particularly inviting in late June and early July, when azaleas and rhododendron are in bloom.

Smithfield Plantation
460 Bypass and Highway 314, Blacksburg,
540-231-3947;
www.smithfieldplantation.org
Home of Colonel William Preston and three governors. Restored pre-Revolutionary house; original woodwork. Architectural link between Tidewater and Piedmont plantations of Virginia and those of the Mississippi Valley. Grounds restored by Garden Club of Virginia. April-November: daily, closed Wednesdays.

HOTELS
★Comfort Inn
3705 S. Main St., Blacksburg,
540-951-1500, 800-424-6423;
www.comfortinnblacksburg.com
80 rooms. Complimentary continental breakfast. Airport transportation available. **$**

298

VIRGINIA

BLUE RIDGE PARKWAY

Winding 469 mountainous miles between the Shenandoah and Great Smoky Mountains national parks (about 217 miles are in Virginia), the Blue Ridge Parkway represents a different concept in highway travel. It is not an express highway (speed limit 45 miles per hour) but a road intended for leisurely travel. All towns are bypassed. Travelers in a hurry would be wise to take state and U.S. routes, where speed limits are higher.

The parkway follows the Blue Ridge Mountains for about 355 miles, then winds through the Craggies, Pisgahs and Balsams to the Great Smokies. Overlooks, picnic and camp sites, visitor centers, nature trails, fishing streams and lakes, and points of interest are numerous and well-marked. Accommodations are plentiful in cities and towns along the way. Food availability is limited on the parkway.

The parkway is open all year, but the best time to drive it is between April and November. Some sections are closed by ice and snow for periods in winter and early spring. Fog may be present during wet weather. The higher sections west of Asheville to Great Smoky Mountains National Park and north of Asheville to Mount Mitchell may be closed January through March due to hazardous driving conditions.
Information: 828-298-0398; www.nps.gov/blri

WHAT TO SEE AND DO

Camping
Tent and trailor sites at Otter Creek, Peaks of Otter, Roanoke Mountain, Rocky Knob, Doughton Park, Julian Price Memorial Park, Linville Falls, Crabtree Meadows and Mount Pisgah. May-October. 14-day limit, June-Labor Day. No electricity; pets on leash only; water shut off with first freeze, usually late October. Fee/site/night. Primitive winter camping at Linville Falls when roads are passable.

Fishing
Rainbow, brook, brown trout and small-mouth bass in streams and lakes. State licenses required.

Interpretive Programs
Mile 60.8, 86, 169, Blue Ridge Parkway
Outdoor talks (mid-June-Labor Day) at Otter Creek (mile 60.8), Peaks of Otter (mile 86), Rocky Knob (mile 169). Obtain schedules at Parkway Visitor Centers.

Elk Run Trail
Mile 86. Forest, plant, animal community.

Greenstone Trail
Mile 8.8. Of geologic interest.

Mabry Mill Trail
Mile 176. Old-time mountain industry.

Mountain Farm Trail
Mile 5.8. Typical mountain farm, reconstructed.

Rocky Knob Trail
Mile 168. Leads to overlook of Rock Castle Gorge.

Trail of the Trees
Mile 63.6. Leads to overlook of James River.

Visitor Centers
Blue Ridge Parkway, Floyd,
828-259-0398, 800-727-5928;
www.blueridgeparkway.org

Exhibits, travel information, interpretive publications. Daily during peak travel season.
  Center's include:

Humpback Rocks Visitor Center
Mile 5.8, Blue Ridge Parkway
Pioneer mountain farm, park ranger.

Mabry Mill
Mile 176, Blue Ridge Parkway
Old-time mountain industry, including tannery exhibits, picturesque mill, blacksmith shop.

Peaks of Otter Visitor Center
Mile 86, Blue Ridge Parkway
Wildlife exhibits, park ranger.

Rocky Knob Information Station
Mile 169, Blue Ridge Parkway
Information, exhibits, park ranger.

HOTELS
★★Doe Run Lodge Resort and Conference Center
Blue Ridge Parkway, Mile Post 189, Fancy Gap,
276-398-2212, 800-325-6189;
www.doerunlodge.com
47 rooms. $

★★Peaks Of Otter Lodge
85554 Blue Ridge Parkway,
Bedford,
540-586-1081, 800-542-5927;
www.peaksofotter.com
63 rooms. $

RESTAURANTS
★★Peaks of Otter
Mile Post 86,
Blue Ridge Parkway,
540-586-1081;
www.peaksofotter.com
American menu. Breakfast, lunch, dinner, Sunday brunch. Bar. Children's menu. Casual attire. $$

BOOKER T. WASHINGTON NATIONAL MONUMENT

The 1861 property inventory of the Burroughs plantation listed, along with household goods and farm implements, the entry "1 Negro boy (Booker)—$400." Freed in 1865, the boy and his family moved to Malden, West Virginia. There, while working at a salt furnace and in coal mines, the youngster learned the alphabet from "Webster's Blueback Spelling Book." Later, by working at the salt furnace before school, then going to work at the mine after school, he got the rudiments of an education. When he realized that everyone else at the school roll call had two names, he chose Washington for his own.

At age 16 he started the 500-mile trip from Malden to Hampton Institute, where he earned his way. He taught at Malden for two years, attended Wayland Seminary, and returned to Hampton Institute to teach. In July 1881, he started Tuskegee Institute in Alabama with 30 pupils, two run-down buildings and $2,000 for salaries. When Washington died in 1915 the Institute had 107 buildings and more than 2,000 acres, and was assessed at more than $500,000.

The 224-acre monument includes most of the original plantation. A 1/4-mile self-guided plantation trail passes reconstructed farm buildings, a slave cabin, crops and animals of the period; there is also a 1 1/2-mile self-guided Jack-O-Lantern Branch nature trail. Picnic facilities. Visitor Center has an audiovisual program, exhibits depicting his life Daily.
Information: 12130 Booker T. Washington Hwy., Hardy, 540-721-2094; www.nps.gov/bowa

BOYCE

RESTAURANTS

★★★L'Auberge Provencal
Route 340 S., Boyce,
540-837-1375, 800-638-1702;
www.laubergeprovencale.com
This country inn has earned a reputation for fine cuisine served with detailed, personal attention. Innkeeper/chef Alain Borel, from Avignon, and his wife, Celeste, provide an authentic, garden-inspired menu.
French menu. Dinner. Closed Monday-Tuesday. Bar. Outdoor seating. $$$

BREAKS INTERSTATE PARK

The "Grand Canyon of the South," where the Russell Fork of the Big Sandy River plunges through the mountains, is the major focus of this 4,600-acre park on the Kentucky-Virginia border. From the entrance, a paved road winds through an evergreen forest and then skirts the canyon rim. Overlooks provide a spectacular view of the "Towers," a huge pyramid of rocks. Within the park are extraordinary rock formations, caves, springs, a profusion of rhododendron and of course, the 5-mile-long, 1,600-foot-deep gorge.

The visitor center houses historical and natural exhibits, including a coal exhibit (April-October: daily). Laurel Lake is stocked with bass and bluegill. Swimming pool, pedal boats; hiking, bridle and mountain bike trails, picnicking, playground, camping (April-October, fee); motor lodge, cottages (year-round), restaurant, gift shop. Park (daily); facilities (April-late December: daily).
Information: 276-865-4413, 800-982-5122; www.breakspark.com

HOTELS

★★Breaks Interstate
Hwy. 1, Breaks,
540-865-4414, 800-982-5122;
www.breakspark.com

34 rooms. Closed late December-March.
Woodland setting; overlooks Breaks Canyon.
$

BRISTOL

Essentially a city in two states, Bristol is actually two cities—Bristol, Tennessee, and Bristol, Virginia—sharing the same main street and the same personality. Each has its own government and city services. Together they constitute a major shopping center. Named for the English industrial center, Bristol is an important factory town in its own right. These cities carry on the pioneer tradition of an ironworks established here about 1784 which made the first nails for use on the frontier. Bristol also has the distinction of being the "Official Birthplace of Country Music."
Information: 423-989-4850; www.bristolchamber.org

WHAT TO SEE AND DO

Antiques
State St. and Commonwealth Ave.,
Bristol,
More than 20 large antiques shops are within a half-mile of these two perpendicular streets in downtown Bristol. Those searching for eclectic collectibles and furniture rave about the selection.

Birthplace of Country Music Alliance Museum
Bristol Mall, I-81, exit 1, Bristol,
276-645-0111;
www.birthplaceofcountrymusic.org
Country music pioneers like Jimmie Rodgers, the Carter Family, Jim and Jesse, and Tennessee Ernie Ford all got their starts in Bristol. Every Thursday night, local pickers and singers gather to perform and produce a live radio show from the mall.

Bristol White Sox
Devault Memorial Stadium,
1501 Euclid Ave., Bristol,
276-669-6859;
www.bristolsox.com
This minor league team is affiliated with the Chicago White Sox. June-August

Rocky Mount Historic Site
200 Hyder Hill Rd., Bristol,
423-538-7396;
www.rockymountmuseum.com

Features the 2 1/2-story log house (1770) that served from 1790 to 1792 as capital under William Blount, governor of the Territory of the United States South of the River Ohio. Restored to its original simplicity; 18th-century furniture. On grounds are restored log kitchen, slave cabin, barn, blacksmith shop and smokehouse. March-mid-December: Tuesday-Saturday 11:00 a.m.-5:00 p.m.

HOTELS

★Comfort Inn
2368 Lee Hwy.,
Bristol,
276-466-3881, 877-424-6423;
www.choicehotels.com
60 rooms. Complimentary continental breakfast. **$**

★La Quinta Inn
1014 Old Airport Rd.,
Bristol,
276-669-9353, 800-531-5900;
www.laquinta.com
123 rooms. Complimentary continental breakfast. **$**

★★Ramada
2221 Euclid Ave.,
Bristol,
276-669-7171, 800-272-6232;
www.ramada.com
123 rooms. **$**

★
★
★
★
★

BROOKNEAL

WHAT TO SEE AND DO

Patrick Henry National Memorial (Red Hill)
1250 Red Hill Rd., Brookneal,
434-376-2044;
www.redhill.org

Last home and burial place of Patrick Henry. Restoration of family cottage, cook's cabin, smokehouse, stable, kitchen. Patrick Henry's law office. Museum and gift shop on grounds. Interpretive video. Daily.

CAPE CHARLES

The Chesapeake Bay Bridge-Tunnel (17.6 miles long) leads from Cape Charles (12 miles south of the town) to Virginia Beach/Norfolk. There is a scenic stop, gift shop, restaurant and fishing pier (bait available).
Information: Chesapeake Bay Bridge & Tunnel District, Cape Charles, 757-331-2960, ext. 20; www.cbbt.com

CASANOVA

HOTELS

★★★**Poplar Springs**
9245 Rogues Rd., Casanova,
540-788-4600, 800-490-7747;
www.poplarspringsinn.com

22 rooms. Complimentary continental breakfast. **$$$**

VIRGINIA

CENTREVILLE

HOTELS

★★**Springhill Suites**
5920 Trinity Pkwy., Centreville,
703-815-7800, 888-287-9400;
www.springhillsuites.com
136 rooms, all suites. Complimentary continental breakfast. **$**

RESTAURANTS

★★**Sweetwater Tavern**
14250 Sweetwater Lane,
Centreville,
703-449-1100
Lunch, dinner. Bar. Children's menu. **$$**

CHANTILLY

RESTAURANTS

★★★**Palm Court**
14750 Conference Center Dr.,
Chantilly,
703-818-3522;
www.westfieldspalmcourt.com
Housed in the Marriott Westfields Resort, this restaurant's menu is a throwback to the days of tableside dining. The buffet-style Sunday brunch is an extravaganza with tuxedo-clad waiters, mimosas and an unending array of sweets.
American menu. Breakfast, lunch, dinner, Sunday brunch. Bar. Children's menu. Reservations recommended. Valet parking. **$$$**

CHARLES CITY

SPECIALTY LODGINGS

Edgewood Bed And Breakfast
4800 John Tyler Memorial Hwy.,
Charles City,
804-829-2962, 800-296-3343;
www.edgewoodplantation.com
This Gothic home built in 1870 houses a collection of country primitives. It is famous for its ghost, which has been experienced by generations of occupants. The property includes a gristmill that once ground corn for both the Union and Confederate armies.
8 rooms. Children over 12 years only. Complimentary full breakfast. **$$**

North Bend Plantation Bed and Breakfast
12200 Weyanoke Rd., Charles City,
804-829-5176;
www.northbendplantation.com
4 rooms. Complimentary full breakfast. **$**

Piney Grove at Southhall's Plantation
16920 Southall Plantation Lane,
Charles City,
804-829-2480;
www.pineygrove.com
5 rooms. Complimentary full breakfast. Two historic farmhouses (circa 1800). **$**

RESTAURANTS

★★**Indian Fields Tavern**
9220 John Tyler Memorial Hwy.,
Charles City,
804-829-5004
American menu. Lunch, dinner. Closed Monday in January-February. Bar. Business casual attire. Reservations recommended. Outdoor seating. **$$$**

CHARLOTTESVILLE

Popularly known as the number one small city in the South, Charlottesville is famous as the home of Thomas Jefferson, the third president of the United States, and the University of Virginia, which Jefferson founded and designed.

Charlottesville offers much more than history. The downtown pedestrian mall streetscape at the center of the historic district is alive with more than 120 shops and 30 restaurants, outdoor cafes, theaters, bookstores and a skating rink. Charlottesville is also able to brag about its beautiful parks, top-notch museums, and award-winning wineries and outstanding entertainment.

The area's historic attractions include Monticello, Michie Tavern, Ash Lawn-Highland (James Monroe's home) and Montpelier. Constructed sculptures from the Art in Place program stand along the roadways. A myriad of scenic byways, hiking trails and river paths run throughout the area, as does the Blue Ridge Parkway, considered by some to be America's most beautiful drive.

Information: Charlottesville/Albemarle Convention & Visitors Bureau,
600 College Dr., Charlottesville,
804-977-1783, 877-386-1102; www.pursuecharlottesville.com

★
★
★
★
★

WHAT TO SEE AND DO
Albemarle County Courthouse
Court Square, Charlottesville
North wing was used in 1820s as a "common temple" shared by Episcopalian, Methodist, Presbyterian and Baptist sects, one Sunday a month to each but with all who wished attending each week. Jefferson, Monroe, and Madison worshipped here.

Ash Lawn-Highland
1000 James Monroe Pkwy.,
Charlottesville,
434-293-9539;
www.ashlawnhighland.org
(1799) Built on a site personally selected by Thomas Jefferson, this 535-acre estate was the home of President James Monroe (1799-1823). The estate is now owned by Monroe's alma mater, the College of William and Mary. This early 19th-century working plantation offers guided tours of the house with Monroe possessions, spinning and weaving demonstrations, old boxwood gardens, peacocks, picnic spots. Daily.

George Rogers Clark Memorial
W. Main and Jefferson Park Ave.,
Charlottesville
Brother of William Clark and soldier on the frontier, this intrepid explorer who opened up the Northwest Territory was an Albemarle County native son.

Historic Michie Tavern
683 Thomas Jefferson Pkwy.,
Charlottesville,
434-977-1234;
www.michietavern.com
(Circa 1784) Located near Jefferson's Monticello. Visitors dine on hearty Midday Fare in the Tavern's Ordinary, where servers in period attire greet them. Afterwards, a tour of the original tavern features living history where guests participate in 18th-century activities, including a lively Virginia dance. Daily.

Lewis and Clark Monument
Midway Park, Ridge and Main Streets,
Charlottesville

Memorial to Jefferson's secretary, Meriwether Lewis, who explored the Louisiana Territory with his friend William Clark.

Monticello
Charlottesville,
434-984-9822;
www.monticello.org
Located on a mountaintop, Monticello is one of the most beautiful estates in Virginia and is considered a classic of American architecture. The house was designed by Thomas Jefferson and built over the course of 40 years, symbolizing the pleasure he found in "putting up and pulling down." Jefferson moved into the first completed outbuilding of his new home in 1771, although construction continued until 1809. Most of the interior furnishings are original. Tours of the restored orchard, vineyard, 1,000-foot-long vegetable garden, and Mulberry Row, once the site of plantation workshops. Jefferson died at Monticello on July 4, 1826, and was buried in the family cemetery. The Thomas Jefferson Memorial Foundation maintains the house and gardens. Daily.

Monticello Visitors Center
Hwy. 20 S. and I-64, Charlottesville,
434-984-9822
Personal and family memorabilia; architectural models and drawings; "Thomas Jefferson: The Pursuit of Liberty," a 35-minute film, shown twice daily. Daily.

Robert E. Lee Monument
1st and Jefferson Streets, Charlottesville

"Stonewall Jackson on Little Sorrel"
Adjacent to courthouse,
Charlottesville

University of Virginia
914 Emmet St. N.,
Charlottesville,
434-924-1019;
www.virginia.edu
(1819) (18,100 students.) Founded by Thomas Jefferson and built according to his plans. Handsome red brick buildings

with white trim, striking vistas, smooth lawns, and ancient trees form the grounds of Jefferson's "academical village." The serpentine walls, one brick thick, which Jefferson designed for strength and beauty, are famous. Room 13, West Range, occupied by Edgar Allan Poe as a student, is displayed for the public. Walking tours start at the Rotunda. Daily; closed three weeks mid-December-early January.

Walking tour
VA 20, Charlottesville,
434-977-1783
The Charlottesville/Albemarle Information Center, located on Highway 20 S in the Monticello Visitors Center Building, has information for a walking tour of historic Charlottesville.

SPECIAL EVENTS
Dogwood Festival
Parade, lacrosse and golf tournaments, carnival. Nine days mid-April.

Founder's Day
(Jefferson's Birthday) Commemorative ceremonies. April 13.

Garden Week
Some fine private homes and gardens in the area are open. Mid-late April.

HOTELS
★Best Western Cavalier Inn
105 N. Emmet St.,
Charlottesville,
434-296-8111, 800-987-8376;
www.bestwesterncavalierinn.com
118 rooms. Complimentary continental breakfast. Airport transportation available. $

★★★Boar's Head Inn
200 Ednam Dr.,
Charlottesville,
434-296-2181, 800-476-1988;
www.boarsheadinn.com
Located in the Blue Ridge Mountains, this resort welcomes guests to visit the past and enjoy the present. Guests can visit past

presidential homes, stroll through local wineries or enjoy a panoramic view by hot-air balloon.
170 rooms. Children's activity Airport transportation available. $$

★★Doubletree Hotel
990 Hilton Heights Rd.,
Charlottesville,
434-973-2121, 800-222-8799;
www.charlottesville.doubletree.com
240 rooms. Airport transportation available. $

★English Inn of Charlottesville
2000 Morton Dr.,
Charlottesville,
434-971-9900, 800-786-5400;
www.wytestone.com
88 rooms. Complimentary full breakfast. Airport transportation available. $

★Hampton Inn
2035 India Rd., Charlottesville,
434-978-7888, 800-426-7866;
www.hamptoninn.com
123 rooms. Complimentary continental breakfast. Airport transportation available. $

★★★Omni Charlottesville Hotel
235 W. Main St.,
Charlottesville,
434-971-5500, 888-444-6664;
www.omnihotels.com
Located on a downtown pedestrian mall, the Omni Charlottesville Hotel is within walking distance of the government buildings. Guest rooms in this four-diamond luxury hotel offers views of the Blue Ridge Mountains and historic Charlottesville.
211 rooms. $

★★★Silver Thatch Inn
3001 Hollymead Dr., Charlottesville,
434-978-4686, 800-261-0720;
www.silverthatch.com
Built in 1780, this clapboard home is full of history and is one of the oldest buildings in the area. Guest rooms are named for Virginia-born presidents.

★
★
★
★
★

7 rooms. Children over 14 years only. Complimentary full breakfast. **$$**

SPECIALTY LODGINGS

200 South Street Inn
200 W. South St., Charlottesville,
434-979-0200, 800-964-7008;
www.southstreetinn.com
19 rooms. Complimentary continental breakfast. Check-in 2-8:30 p.m. Built 1856; antiques. **$$**

Inn at Monticello
Route 20 S., 1188 Scottsville Rd.,
Charlottesville,
434-979-3593, 877-735-2982;
www.innatmonticello.com
Guests can choose to relax by a fireplace in winter or sit on the porch in summer at this country manor house built in the mid-1800s. Guest rooms are decorated with period antiques and reproductions.

5 rooms. Children over 12 years only. Complimentary full breakfast. **$$**

RESTAURANTS

★★Aberdeen Barn
2018 Holiday Dr., Charlottesville,
434-296-4630;
www.aberdeenbarn.com
Steak menu. Dinner. Bar. Children's menu. Business casual attire. Reservations recommended. **$$**

★★C & O
515 E. Water St., Charlottesville,
434-971-7044;
www.candorestaurant.com
French menu. Dinner, late-night. Closed one week after December 25 and one week at the end of summer. Bar. Children's menu. Business casual attire. Reservations recommended. Outdoor seating. **$$$**

★★Ivy Inn
2244 Old Ivy Rd.,
Charlottesville,
434-977-1222;
www.ivyinnrestaurant.com
American menu. Dinner. Closed Sunday. Bar. Victorian-style house (1804); fire-

places. Business casual attire. Reservations recommended. Outdoor seating. **$$**

★★L'Avventura
220 W. Market St.,
Charlottesville,
434-977-1912;
www.vinegarhilltheatre.com
Italian menu. Dinner. Closed Sunday-Monday. Bar. Casual attire. Reservations recommended. Outdoor seating. **$$**

★★Maharaja
139 Zan Rd.,
Charlottesville,
434-973-1110;
diningmenus.com
Indian. Lunch, dinner. Bar. Casual attire. Reservations recommended. Outdoor seating. **$$**

★★★Old Mill Room
US 250 W. (200 Ednam Dr.),
Charlottesville,
434-972-2230, 800-476-1988;
www.boarsheadinn.com
This dining room is located in the Boar's Head Inn at the University of Virginia. Dishes such as apple balsamic-glazed copper river salmon with cauliflower mousse and celeriac-apple salad are prepared with vegetables from the restaurant's garden.
American menu. Breakfast, lunch, dinner. Bar. Valet parking. Outdoor seating, Children's menu. Business casual attire. Reservations recommended. **$$$**

★★★OXO
215 W. Water St., Charlottesville,
434-977-8111;
www.oxorestaurant.com
French menu. Lunch, dinner. Bar. Business casual attire. Reservations recommended. Outdoor seating. **$$$**

CHESAPEAKE

For beach lovers who seek a vacation off the beaten path, Chesapeake is an excellent choice. You'll be minutes away from 18th-century America, the oceanfront boardwalk of Virginia Beach, theme parks and more. The active Atlantic Intra-coastal Waterway, home to a myriad of birds and wildlife, is complemented by the 49,000-acre Great Dismal Swamp National Wildlife Refuge managed by the Nature Conservancy. Bring your binoculars, your camera and your lifelong checklist of birds.

Farther up the coast, the Back Bay National Wildlife Refuge encompasses a series of barrier islands that feature large sand dunes, maritime forests, freshwater marshes and ponds populated with large flocks of wintering waterfowl. Move through the bay on the unique trolley designed not to disturb the wildlife, kayak on the waterway itself or stroll on the more than 19 miles of hiking trails at First Landing State Park.

Information: Chesapeake Conventions & Tourism Bureau, 3815 Bainbridge Blvd., Chesapeake, 757-502-4898, 888-889-5551; www.visitchesapeake.com

WHAT TO SEE AND DO

Northwest River Park

1733 Indian Creek Rd.,
Chesapeake,
757-421-3145

Approximately eight miles of hiking/nature trails wind through this 763-acre city park. Fishing, boating, canoeing (ramp, rentals); picnicking (shelters), playground, nine-hole miniature golf, camping, tent and trailer sites (April-December: daily; fee). Shuttle tram. Daily. Fragrance trail for the visually impaired.

SPECIAL EVENTS

Chesapeake Jubilee

City Park, 1500 Mount Pleasant Rd.,
Chesapeake,
757-482-4848;
www.chesapeakejubilee.org

National and regional entertainment, carnival, food booths, fireworks. Third weekend in May.

HOTELS

★Comfort Suites

1550 Crossways Blvd., Chesapeake,
757-420-1600, 877-424-6423;
www.choicehotels.com

124 rooms. All suites. Complimentary continental breakfast. **$**

★★Red Roof Inn

724 Woodlake Dr.,
Chesapeake,
757-523-1500, 800-733-7663;
www.redroofinn.com
229 rooms. **$**

RESTAURANTS

★★Kyoto

1412 Greenbriar Pkwy.,
Chesapeake,
757-420-0950

Japanese menu. Lunch, dinner. Bar. Children's menu. Casual attire. Reservations recommended. **$$**

★★Locks Pointe

136 N. Battlefield Blvd.,
Chesapeake,
757-547-9618

Seafood menu. Lunch, dinner, Sunday brunch. Closed Monday. Bar. Children's menu. Casual attire. Reservations recommended. Outdoor seating. On Intracoastal Waterway; dockage. **$$**

VIRGINIA

CHINCOTEAGUE

Oysters, wild ponies and good fishing are the stock in trade of this small island, connected with Chincoteague National Wildlife Refuge by a bridge and to the mainland by 10 miles of highway. The oysters, many of them grown on the hard sand bottoms off Chincoteague from seed or small oysters brought from natural beds elsewhere, are among the best in the

East. Commercial fishing has always been the main occupation of the islanders, but now catering to those who fish for fun is also economically important.

Chincoteague's wild ponies are actually small horses, but when full-grown they are somewhat larger and more graceful than Shetlands. They are thought to be descended from horses that swam ashore from a wrecked Spanish galleon, their limited growth caused by generations of marsh grass diet.

Information: Chamber of Commerce, 6733 Maddox Blvd., Chincoteague, 757-336-6161; www.chincoteaguechamber.com

WHAT TO SEE AND DO

Assateague Island
8586 Beach Rd., Chincoteague, 757-336-6577;
www.nps.gov/asis
A 37-mile barrier island, Assateague has stretches of ocean and sand dunes, forest and marshes that create a natural environment unusual on the East Coast. Sika deer, a variety of wildlife, and countless birds, including the peregrine falcon (autumn), can be found here, but wild ponies occasionally roaming the marshes offer the most exotic sight for visitors. Nature and auto trails; interpretive programs. Swimming (bathhouse), lifeguards in summer, surf fishing; camping, hike-in and canoe-in camp sites and day-use facilities. Picnicking permitted in designated areas; cars are limited to designated roads. No pets allowed. Obtain information at Toms Cove Visitor Center (spring-fall: daily) and at Chincoteague Refuge Visitor Center (daily). Access for the disabled to all facilities.

Captain Barry's Back Bay Cruises & Expeditions
6174 Landmark Plaza, Chincoteague, 757-336-6508;
www.captainbarry.bigstep.com
Includes Bird Watch Cruise, Back Bay Expedition, Champagne Sunset Cruise, Moonlight Excursions, and Fun Cruise. Trips vary from one to four hours. Reservations recommended.

Oyster and Maritime Museum of Chincoteague
7125 Maddox Blvd., Chincoteague, 757-336-6117
Museum contains diorama, aquarium, shellfish industry interpretation. Also has the Wyle Maddox Library. May-August: daily; September-October: Saturday and Sunday.

Refuge Waterfowl Museum
7059 Maddox Blvd., Chincoteague, 757-336-5800
Rotating displays of antique decoys and hunting tools. Decoy making and waterfowl art. Call ahead for hours. Daily.

SPECIAL EVENTS

Chincoteague Power Boat Regatta
Memorial Park, Chincoteague, 757-336-6161
Late June.

Easter Decoy & Art Festival
Chincoteague Combined School, 4586 Main St., Chincoteague, 757-336-6161
Easter weekend.

Oyster Festival
6733 Maddox Blvd., Chincoteague,
Columbus Day weekend.

Pony Penning
Chincoteague, 757-336-6161
The "wild" ponies are rounded up on Assateague Island, then swim the inlet to Chincoteague, where foals are sold at auction before the ponies swim back to Assateague. Carnival amusements. Last Wednesday and Thursday in July.

Waterfowl Week
8231 Beach Rd., Chincoteague
National Wildlife Refuge open to vehicles during peak migratory waterfowl populations. Late November.

HOTELS

★Best Western Chincoteague Island
7105 Maddox Blvd., Chincoteague,
757-336-6557, 800-553-6117;
www.bestwestern.com
53 rooms. Complimentary continental breakfast. At entrance to Assateague National Seashore. **$**

★Comfort Suites Chincoteague
4195 Main St., Chincoteague,
757-336-3700, 877-424-6423;
www.choicehotels.com
87 rooms. **$**

★★Island Motor Inn Resort
4391 Main St., Chincoteague,
757-336-3141;
www.islandmotorinn.com
60 rooms. **$**

★Refuge Inn
7058 Maddox Blvd., Chincoteague,
757-336-5511, 800-257-0034;
www.refugeinn.com
72 rooms. Children's activity center. Near wildlife refuge and national seashore. Chincoteague ponies on grounds. **$**

SPECIALTY LODGINGS

Cedar Gables Seaside Inn
6095 Hopkins Lane, Chincoteague,
757-336-6860, 888-491-2944;
www.cedargable.com
This waterfront bed-and-breakfast inn overlooks Oyster Bay and the Chincoteague Wildlife Refuge. All rooms open to waterfront decks and offer breathtaking views of Assateague Island. The rooms have cable TV, fireplaces and Jacuzzis. Nearby guests can enjoy the beach, wildlife refuge, fishing, biking and hiking.
4 rooms. Closed one week in late December. Children over 14 years only. Complimentary full breakfast. **$$**

Miss Molly's Inn
4141 Main St.,
Chincoteague,
757-336-6686, 800-221-5620;
www.missmollysinn.com
Marguerite Henry stayed here while writing "Misty of Chincoteague." In historic building (1886) with a library, sitting room.
7 rooms. Children over 4 years only. Complimentary full breakfast. **$**

Watson House
4240 Main St., Chincoteague,
757-336-1564, 800-336-6787;
www.watsonhouse.com
5 rooms. Children over 10 years only. Complimentary full breakfast. Victorian residence (1874). **$**

RESTAURANTS

★Don's Seafood
4113 Main St.,
Chincoteague Island,
757-336-5715;
www.donsseafood.com
Seafood menu. Lunch, dinner, late-night. Closed Sunday in fall and winter. Bar. Children's menu. Casual attire. **$$**

★Steamers Seafood
6251 Maddoc Blvd., Chincoteague,
757-336-5478
Seafood menu. Dinner. Closed December. Children's menu. Casual attire. **$$**

CLARKSVILLE

Information: Clarksville Lake Country Chamber of Commerce, 105 2nd St., Clarksville, 434-374-2436, 800-557-5582; www.clarkesvilleva.com

WHAT TO SEE AND DO

Occoneechee State Park
Clarksville,
434-374-2210;
www.dcr.virginia.gov/state_parks/occ.shtml
Approximately 2,700 acres under development; long shoreline on John H. Kerr Reservoir (Buggs Island Lake). Fishing, boat launching; hiking, picnic shelters, tent and trailer sites (hookups, season varies). Amphitheater; interpretive programs. Standard fees. Daily.

★
★
★
★
★

Prestwould
429 Prestwould Dr., Clarksville,
434-374-8672
(1795) Manor house built by Sir Peyton Skipwith; rare French scenic wallpaper; original and period furnishings; restored gardens. Mid-April-October: daily; rest of year, by appointment.

SPECIAL EVENTS
Native American Heritage Festival and Powwow
Occoneechee State Park, 105 2nd St., Clarksville,
434-374-2210
Native American music, dances, crafts. Second weekend in May.

CLIFTON

RESTAURANTS
★★Heart-in-Hand
7145 Main St.,
Clifton,
703-830-4111;
www.heartinhandrestaurant.com
Lunch, dinner, Sunday brunch. Converted general store (circa 1870). Outdoor seating. **$$**

Virginia Lake Festival
Occoneechee State Park, 105 2nd St., Clarksville,
434-374-2210
Juried arts and crafts show, beach music, dancers, gymnasts. Fun Run, antique car show, sailboat race, hot-air balloons. Food vendors. Third weekend in July.

HOTELS
★Best Western On The Lake
103 2nd St.,
Clarksville,
434-374-5023;
www.bestwestern.com
50 rooms. Complimentary continental breakfast. **$**

★★★Hermitage Inn
7134 Main St., Clifton,
703-266-1623;
www.hermitageinnrestaurant.com
A historic clapboard inn is the setting for an intimate dining experience. Mediterranean menu. Dinner, Sunday brunch. Closed Monday; July 14. **$$$**

CLIFTON FORGE
The town, named after a tilt-hammer forge that operated profitably for almost 100 years, is at the southern tip of the Shenandoah Valley, just west of the Blue Ridge Parkway.
Information: Alleghany Highlands Chamber of Commerce, 501 E. Ridgeway St., Clifton Forge, 540-862-4969, 888-430-5786; www.ahchamber.com

WHAT TO SEE AND DO
C & O Historical Society Archives
312 E. Ridgeway St.,
Clifton Forge,
540-862-2210
Includes C & O Railroad artifacts, old blueprints for cars and engines, books, models, collection of photos. Monday-Saturday.

Douthat State Park
Clifton Forge,
540-862-8100;
www.dcr.virginia.gov/state_parks/dou.shtml
Nearly 4,500 acres, high in the Allegheny Mountains, with 50-acre lake. Swimming beach, bathhouse, trout fishing (fee/day), boating (Memorial Day-Labor Day; rentals, some electric and water hook-ups; launching, electric motors only); hiking, self-guided trails, picnicking, restaurant, concession, camping (fee), tent and trailer sites (March-September; no hookups), cabins (all year). Visitor center, interpretive programs. Standard fees. Daily.

Iron Gate Gorge
Perpendicular walls of rock rise from banks of Jackson River. James River Division of C & O Railroad and U.S. 220 pass through gorge. Restored chimney of old forge is here.

COLONIAL NATIONAL HISTORICAL PARK

In its four independent areas—Cape Henry Memorial, the Colonial Parkway, Jamestown and Yorktown Battlefield—America as we know it began. Jamestown, Yorktown and Williamsburg (not a National Park Service area) are connected by the Colonial Parkway. Abundant in natural as well as historical wealth, the park boundaries enclose more than 9,000 acres of forest woodlands, marshes, shorelines, fields, and a large variety of wildlife.
Information: Route 17 and Goosley Rd., Jamestown, 757-898-3400; www.nps.gov/colo

COVINGTON

Named for its oldest resident, Covington developed from a small village on the Jackson River. It is located in the western part of Virginia known as the Allegheny Highlands. The James River Ranger District office of the Washington and Jefferson national forests is located here.
Information: Alleghany Highlands Chamber of Commerce, 501 E. Ridgeway St., Clifton Forge, 540-962-2178, 888-430-5786; www.ahchamber.com

WHAT TO SEE AND DO

Humpback Bridge

Erected in 1857, this 100-foot-long structure was made of hand-hewn oak held together with locustwood pins. In use until 1929, it is now maintained as part of a five-acre state highway wayside and is the only surviving curved-span covered bridge in the United States.

Lake Moomaw

Covington,
540-962-2214
This 12-mile-long lake has a rugged shoreline of more than 43 miles set off by towering mountains. It is surrounded by the Gathright Wildlife Management Area and portions of the Washington and Jefferson national forests. Boating, swimming, fishing, waterskiing; picnicking, camping (fee). Visitor center. April-October: daily.

HOTELS

★★Best Western Mountain View

820 E. Madison St.,
Covington,
540-962-4951, 800-937-8376;
www.bestwestern.com
76 rooms. Complimentary full breakfast. **$**

311

CULPEPER

Volunteers from Culpeper, Fauquier and Orange counties marched to Williamsburg in 1777 in answer to Governor Patrick Henry's call to arms. Their flag bore a coiled rattlesnake with the legends "Don't Tread on Me" and "Liberty or Death."

In the winter of 1862-1863, churches, homes and vacant buildings in Culpeper were turned into hospitals for the wounded from the battles of Cedar Mountain, Kelly's Ford and Brandy Station. Later, the Union Army had headquarters here.

Today, Culpeper is a light industry and trading center for a five-county area, with a healthy agriculture industry.
Information: Chamber of Commerce, 109 S. Commerce St., Culpeper, 540-825-8628; www.culpepervachamber.com

WHAT TO SEE AND DO

Dominion Wine Cellars

1 Winery Ave., Culpeper,
540-825-8772
Tours and tasting. Daily.

HOTELS

★★Best Western Culpeper Inn

791 James Madison Rd. S., Culpeper,
540-825-1253
158 rooms. **$**

★**Comfort Inn**
890 Willis Lane, Culpeper,
540-825-4900, 877-424-6423;
www.choicehotels.com
49 rooms. Complimentary continental breakfast. **$**

SPECIALTY LODGINGS
Fountain Hall Bed and Breakfast
609 S. East St., Culpeper,
540-825-8200, 800-298-4748;
www.fountainhall.com

This charming bed and breakfast is located on the foothills of the Blue Ridge Mountains in historic downtown Culpeper. The Colonial Revival house (1859) was converted and now offers uniquely decorated rooms. Guests can relax in one of the spacious parlors or go off to discover the many historic sites and bike trails nearby.

6 rooms. Complimentary full breakfast. **$**

DANVILLE

This textile and tobacco center blends the leisurely pace of the Old South with the modern tempo of industry. It is one of the nation's largest brightleaf tobacco auction markets. Dan River Inc. houses the largest single-unit textile mill in the world. Nancy Langhorne, Viscountess Astor, the first woman to sit in the British House of Commons, was born in Danville in 1879.
Information: Danville Welcom Center, 645 River Park Dr., Danville, 434-793-4636;
www.visitdanville.com

WHAT TO SEE AND DO
"Wreck of the Old 97" Marker
Riverside Dr. (Hwy. 58), Danville, between N. Main and Locust Lane, overpass
Site of celebrated train wreck (September 27, 1903), made famous by a folk song.

Danville Historic District
Ridge and High Streets, Danville,
www.visitdanville.com
Take a self-guided walking tour of Danville's Historic District, including old tobacco buildings and Millionaires Row, with its eclectic mix of architectural styles dating from pre-Civil War times.

Danville Museum of Fine Arts and History
975 Main St., Danville,
434-793-5644;
www.danvillemuseum.org
Home of Major W. T. Sutherlin; built in 1857. President Jefferson Davis and his cabinet fled to Danville after receiving news of General Lee's retreat from Richmond. It was during this time that the Sutherlin mansion served as the last capital of the Confederacy. Victorian restoration in historical section of house (parlor, library and Davis bedroom). Rotating art exhibits by national and regional artists. Tuesday-Friday 10 a.m.-5 p.m., Saturday-Sunday 2-5 p.m.

Danville Science Center
677 Craghead St., Danville,
434-791-5160;
www.dsc.smv.org
Hands-on museum for the entire family. Located in a restored Victorian train station. Daily.

Tobacco auctions
635 Main St., Danville,
434-793-5422
Several huge warehouses ring with the chants of tobacco auctioneers. August-early-November: Monday-Thursday; closed Labor Day, Columbus Day, Veterans Day.

SPECIAL EVENTS
Danville Harvest Jubilee
125 S. Floyd St., Danville,
434-799-5200
Celebration of tobacco harvest season. Late-August-September.

★
★
★

Festival in the Park
125 S. Floyd St., Danville,
434-793-4636
Arts, crafts, entertainment. Third weekend in May.

HOTELS
★Holiday Inn Express
2121 Riverside Dr.,
Danville,
434-793-4000, 800-282-0244;
www.hiexpress.com

DUFFIELD

WHAT TO SEE AND DO
Natural Tunnel State Park
Hwy. 871, Duffield,
276-940-2674;
www.dcr.virginia.gov/state_parks/
nat.shtml
Consists of 648 acres. Giant hole chiseled through Purchase Ridge by Stock Creek; pinnacles or "chimneys." Railroad and stream are accommodated in this vast

98 rooms. Complimentary continental breakfast. **$**

★★Stratford Inn
2500 Riverside Dr.,
Danville,
434-793-2500, 800-326-8455;
www.stratfordinn.com
151 rooms. Complimentary full breakfast. **$**

tunnel—100 feet or more in diameter, 850 feet long. Tunnel, visitor center with exhibits. Swimming, pool, fishing; hiking, picnicking, concession, camping, tent and trailer sites (Memorial Day-Labor Day). Interpretive programs. Chairlift. Park (daily); tunnel and most activities (Memorial Day-Labor Day: daily). Standard fees.

DULLES INTERNATIONAL AIRPORT AREA
Information: www.metwashairports.com/dulles

WHAT TO SEE AND DO
Reston Town Center
11900 Market St., Reston,
703-689-4699;
www.restontowncenter.com
A 20-acre urban development incorporating elements of a traditional town square. Includes more than 50 retail shops and restaurants, movie theater complex, office space and hotel.

SPECIAL EVENTS
Fountain Square Holiday Celebration
Reston Town Center,
Freedom Dr., Reston,
Choral groups, puppeteers, magicians, ice shows, dancers, parade. Thanksgiving-December 24.

Fountain Square Ice Rink
Reston Town Center,
1830 Discovery St., Reston,

Outdoor public ice rink. Mid-November-mid-March.

Northern Virginia Fine Arts Festival
Reston Town Center,
11921 Freedom Dr. #980, Reston,
703-471-9242;
www.restonarts.org/festival
Art sale, children's activity area, barbecue. Mid-May.

Oktoberfest
Reston Town Center,
11921 Freedom Dr. #980, Reston,
Biergarten with authentic German music, food. Mid-September.

Summer Concerts
Reston Town Center,
11921 Freedom Dr. #980, Reston,
Saturday evenings June-August; also Thursday evenings in July.

HOTELS

★Comfort Inn
200 Elden St., Herndon,
703-437-7555, 800-228-5150;
www.choicehotels.com
103 rooms. Complimentary continental breakfast. Airport transportation available. **$**

★★Crowne Plaza
2200 Centreville Rd., Herndon,
703-471-6700;
www.cpdulles.com/herndon.html
205 rooms. Complimentary continental breakfast. Airport transportation available. **$**

★★Holiday Inn
45425 Holiday Dr., Sterling,
703-471-7411, 800-465-4329;
www.holidayinn.com
296 rooms. Airport transportation available. **$$**

★★★Hyatt Regency Reston
1800 President's St., Reston,
703-709-1234, 800-633-7313;
www.hyatt.com
Located in the heart of Fairfax County's technology hub, this property offers resort-like ambience in a suburban setting. The oversized guest rooms offer flat-screen TVs, ergonomic desk chairs and wireless high-speed Internet access.
514 rooms. Airport transportation available. **$$**

★★★Marriott Suites Dulles Worldgate
13101 Worldgate Dr., Herndon,
703-709-0400, 800-228-9290;
www.marriott.com
This all-suite hotel located in the Dulles Technology Corridor is just minutes from the airport and corporate offices. After a long day at the office or at play, guests can relax in their spacious suites with high-speed Internet access and luxury bedding. The hotel and surrounding area offer an indoor/outdoor pool, biking and jogging trails, tennis, squash, bowling and miniature golf. There is also a Starbucks kiosk onsite. 253 rooms, all suites. Airport transportation available. **$$**

★★★Sheraton Reston Hotel
11810 Sunrise Valley Dr., Reston,
703-620-9000, 800-325-3535;
www.sheraton.com
Located just 20 minutes from Washington, D.C., and near shopping, various corporate headquarters and Reston Town Center, this contemporary hotel is a smart choice for both business and leisure travelers. Each spacious guest room features the famous Sheraton Sweet Sleeper Bed with a pillow-top mattress, individual climate control and a large work area. Golf-lovers can get a game in at the adjacent Reston National Golf Course. 301 rooms. **$$**

★★★Westfields Marriott Washington Dulles Hotel
14750 Conference Center Dr., Chantilly,
703-818-0300, 800-635-5666;
www.marriott.com
Located within 10 miles of the National Air and Space Museum and the Wolf Trap Center for Performing Arts, the Westfields Marriott Washington Dulles Hotel offers spacious accommodations and the Signature Fred Couples Golf Club.
340 rooms. Airport transportation available. **$$**

RESTAURANTS

★★Clyde's
11905 Market St., Reston,
703-787-6601;
www.clydes.com
American, seafood menu. Lunch, dinner, Sunday brunch. Bar. Outdoor seating. **$$**

★★Fortune
1428 N. Point Village Center, Reston,
703-318-8898
Chinese menu. Lunch, dinner. Reservations recommended. **$$**

★★★Palm Court
14750 Conference Center Dr., Chantilly,
703-818-3522;
www.westfieldspalmcourt.com
In the Westfields Marriott Hotel, this restaurant offers a buffet-style Sunday Brunch

314

VIRGINIA

★

★

★

★

★

with tuxedo-clad waiters, mimosas and an unending array of sweets.
American menu. Breakfast, lunch, dinner, Sunday brunch. Bar. Children's menu. Reservations recommended. Valet parking. **$$**

★★★Russia House
790 Station St.,
Herndon,
703-787-8880;
www.russiahouserestaurant.com
This contemporary restaurant features Russian artwork. The aristocratic dining experience includes dishes such as beef stroganoff or puff pastry with lamb, vegetables and tarragon sauce.

★Tortilla Factory
648 Elden St.,
Herndon,
703-471-1156;
www.thetortillafactory.com
Mexican menu. Lunch, dinner. Children's menu. Homemade tortillas. **$$**

HILTONS

WHAT TO SEE AND DO
The Carter Fold
Hiltons,
276-386-6054;
www.carterfamilyfold.org
The Carter Family homestead offers an old-time country music and bluegrass concert often by top country music performers every Saturday at 7:30 p.m. The Fold was established by the children of A. P. and Sara Carter to carry on the musical and performing traditions established by their parents. In keeping with the traditional music style, no electrified instruments are used. There's lots of dancing and fun for the entire family; no alcohol permitted.

FAIRFAX

Fairfax, nestled in northern Virginia in the shadow of Washington, D.C., is a quaint, historic town, which has become a government center, home to many major corporations and a thriving technology industry.
Information: Fairfax County Convention & Visitors Bureau, 8300 Boone Blvd., 703-790-3329, 703-550-2450 (visitor center), 800-732-4732; www.visitfairfax.org

WHAT TO SEE AND DO
County Parks
12055 Government Center Pkwy., Fairfax,
703-324-8700;
www.fairfaxcounty.gov/parks

Burke Lake
7315 Ox Rd.,
Fairfax Station,
703-323-6601;
www.fairfaxcounty.gov/parks/burkelake
Consists of 888 acres. Fishing, boating (ramp, rentals); picnicking, playground, concession, miniature train, carousel (summer: daily; early May and late September: weekends), 18-hole and par-three golf, camping (May-September; seven-day limit). Beaver Cove Nature Trail; fitness trail. Fee for activities. Daily.

Lake Fairfax
1400 Lake Fairfax Dr., Reston,
703-471-5415;
www.fairfaxcounty.gov/parks/lakefairfax
Pool, boat rentals, fishing, excursion boat; picnicking, carousel, miniature train (late May-Labor Day: daily), camping (daily, closed Christmas; seven-day limit; electric additional fee). Fee for activities. Daily.

George Mason University
4400 University Dr., Fairfax,
703-993-1000;
www.gmu.edu
(1957) (24,000 students.) This state-supported university started as a branch of the University of Virginia. Performing Arts Center features concerts, theater, dance;

★
★
★
★
☆

Fenwick Library maintains largest collection anywhere of material pertaining to Federal Theatre Project of the 1930s. Research Center for Federal Theatre Project contains 7,000 scripts, including unpublished works by Arthur Miller, sets and costume designs, and oral history collection of interviews with former Federal Theatre personnel. Monday-Friday.

Regional Parks
5400 Ox Rd.,
Fairfax Station,
703-352-5900;
www.nvrpa.org

Algonkian
47001 Fairway Dr.,
Fairfax,
703-450-4655;
www.nvrpa.org/parks/algonkian
An 800-acre park on the Potomac River; swimming (Memorial Day-Labor Day; fee), fishing, boating (ramp); golf, miniature golf, picnicking, vacation cottages, meeting and reception areas.

Bull Run
7700 Bull Run Dr.,
Fairfax,
703-631-0550;
www.nvrpa.org/parks/bullrun
Consists of 1,500 acres. Themed swimming pool (Memorial Day-Labor Day: daily; fee); camping (one to four persons, fee; electricity available; reservations accepted, 703-631-0550); concession, picnicking, playground, miniature golf, public shooting center, nature trail. Mid-March-December.

Sully
3601 Sully Rd.,
Fairfax,
703-437-1794;
www.fairfaxcounty.gov/parks/sully
(1794) Restored house of Richard Bland Lee, brother of General "Light Horse Harry" Lee; some original furnishings; kitchen-washhouse, log house store, smokehouse on grounds. Guided tours. Monday, Wednesday-Sunday.

SPECIAL EVENTS
Antique Car Show
3601 Sully Rd., Fairfax,
703-437-1794
Four hundred antique cars, flea market and music. June.

Quilt Show
3601 Sully Rd., Fairfax,
703-437-1794
Quilts for sale, quilting demonstrations and antique quilts on display. September.

Taste of the Town
Selected restaurants offer sample-size specialties. Last weekend in June.

HOTELS
★Comfort Inn University Center
11180 Fairfax Blvd., Fairfax,
703-591-5900, 877-424-6423;
www.choicehotels.com
205 rooms. Complimentary continental breakfast. Airport transportation available. $

★★★Hyatt Fair Lakes
12777 Fair Lakes Circle, Fairfax,
703-818-1234;
www.hyatt.com
Minutes from Washington Dulles Airport, this striking high-rise hotel in the wooded Fair Lakes Office Park offers large guest rooms. This property features a column-free ballroom and a towering atrium lobby. 316 rooms. Airport transportation available. $$

RESTAURANTS
★★Artie's
3260 Old Lee Hwy., Fairfax,
703-273-7600;
www.greatamericanrestaurants.com
American menu. Lunch, dinner, late-night, Sunday brunch. Bar. Children's menu. Casual attire. $$

★Blue Ocean
9440 Main St., Fairfax,
703-425-7555;
www.izakayablueocean.com
Japanese menu. Lunch, dinner. $$

★★Bombay Bistro
3570 Chain Bridge Rd.,
Fairfax,
703-359-5810;
www.bombaybistro.com
Indian menu. Lunch, dinner, brunch. Bar. Outdoor seating. **$$**

★★★LaRue 123 at the Bailiwick Inn
4023 Chain Bridge Rd., Fairfax,
703-691-2266;
www.larue123.com
This Federal-style inn and restaurant, on the National Register of Historic Places, offers French-American cuisine in a quaint, romantic space. Visit for one of the seasonal wine dinners or for traditional English high tea in one of the intimate parlors. American, Mediterranean, seafood menu. Lunch, dinner. Closed Monday, Tuesday. Reservations recommended. Outdoor seating. **$$$**

★P. J. Skidoo's
9908 Lee Hwy.,
Fairfax,
703-591-4515;
www.pjskidoos.com
American menu. Lunch, dinner, Sunday brunch. Bar. Children's menu. Outdoor seating. **$$**

FALLS CHURCH

Falls Church is a pleasant, cosmopolitan suburb of Washington, D.C., just over the Arlington County line, graced with many interesting old houses. This was a crossover point between the North and the South through which pioneers, armies, adventurers and merchants passed.

Information: Greater Falls Church Chamber of Commerce, 417 W. Broad St., Falls Church, 703-532-1050; www.fallschurchchamber.org

WHAT TO SEE AND DO

The Falls Church
115 E. Fairfax St., Falls Church,
703-532-7600;
www.thefallschurch.org
(1769) Episcopal. This building replaced the original wooden church built in 1732. Served as a recruiting station during the Revolutionary War; abandoned until 1830; used during the Civil War as a hospital and later as a stable for cavalry horses. Restored according to original plans with gallery additions in 1959. Monday-Friday, Sunday. Worship services Wednesday noon and Sunday at 8 a.m. and noon.

Fountain of Faith
7400 Lee Hwy.,
Falls Church,
Memorial dedicated to the four chaplains—two Protestant, one Jewish, one Catholic—who were aboard the *U.S.S. Dorchester* when it was torpedoed off Greenland in 1943. They gave their life jackets to four soldiers on deck who had none.

HOTELS

★★★Marriott Fairview Park
3111 Fairview Park Dr.,
Falls Church,
703-849-9400;
www.marriott.com
Sitting on a park-like setting, this property offers jogging paths through woods and around a lake.
394 rooms. **$$**

RESTAURANTS

★★Bangkok Steakhouse
926 W. Broad St.,
Falls Church,
703-534-0095;
www.bangkokbluesrestaurant.com
Thai, Laotian menu. Lunch, dinner. **$$**

★★★Duangrat's
5878 Leesburg Pike,
Falls Church,
703-820-5775;
www.duangrats.com
Thai menu. Lunch, dinner. Bar. **$$**

VIRGINIA

★
★
★
★
★

★★★Haandi
1222 W. Broad St., Falls Church,
703-533-3501;
www.haandi.com

The accolades are plentiful for this fine dining restaurant, renowned as one of the best in the region. The depth of flavor and unique spices found in each dish are unmatched. Entrees include keasar chicken khorma, barbecued chunks of boneless chicken breast marinated in saffron and cooked in a creamy curry sauce.
Indian menu. Lunch, dinner. **$$**

★★Peking Gourmet Inn
6029 Leesburg Pike (Hwy. 7), Falls Church,
703-671-8088;
www.pekinggourmet.com

Chinese menu. Lunch, dinner. Reservations recommended. **$$**

★★Pilin Thai
116 W. Broad St. (Hwy. 7),
Falls Church,
703-241-5850;
www.pilinthairestaurant.com

Thai menu. Lunch, dinner. Bar. Reservations recommended. **$$**

★★Secret Garden Beewon
6678 Arlington Blvd.,
Falls Church,
703-533-1004

Korean, Japanese menu. Lunch, dinner. Bar. Reservations recommended. **$$**

FARMVILLE

Longwood College's Jeffersonian buildings provide architectural interest in downtown Farmville.

WHAT TO SEE AND DO

Twin Lakes State Park
Farmville,
434-392-3435;
www.dcr.virginia.gov/state_parks/
twi.shtml

More than 250 acres of state forest; two lakes. Swimming, bathhouse, fishing, boating (rentals, launching electric motors only); hiking, bicycle and self-guided trails; picnicking, playground, concession, camping, hook-ups, tent and trailer sites, cabins (March-December); pavilion.

HOTELS

★Comfort Inn
Hwy. 15 and 460 Bypass, Farmville,
434-392-8163, 877-424-6423;
www.choicehotels.com

51 rooms. Complimentary continental breakfast. **$**

FREDERICKSBURG

One of the seeds of the American Revolution was planted here when a resolution declaring independence from Great Britain was passed on April 29, 1775. George Washington went to school in Fredericksburg, his sister Betty lived here and his mother, Mary Ball Washington, lived and died here. James Monroe practiced law in town. Guns for the Revolution were manufactured here, and four of the most savage battles of the Civil War were fought nearby.

Captain John Smith visited the area in 1608 and gave glowing reports of its possibilities for settlement. In 1727, the General Assembly directed that 50 acres of "lease-land" be laid out and the town called Fredericksburg, after the Prince of Wales.

Ships from abroad sailed up the Rappahannock River to the harbor—ampler then than now—to exchange their goods for those brought from "upcountry" by the great road wagons and river carriers. The town prospered.

The Civil War left Fredericksburg ravaged. Situated midway between Richmond and Washington, it was a recurring objective of both sides; the city changed hands seven times and the casualties were high.

Even so, many buildings put up before 1775 still stand. Proudly aware of their town's place in the country's history, the townspeople keep Fredericksburg inviting with fresh paint, beautiful lawns and well-kept gardens.

Information: Visitor Center, 706 Caroline St., Fredericksburg, 540-373-1776, 800-678-4748; www.fredericksburgva.com

FREDERICKSBURG'S PRESIDENTIAL LEGACY

Midway between Washington and Richmond, the old colonial river port of Fredericksburg earned the dubious nickname of battlefield city in the Civil War, as the site of four major battles between 1862 and 1864. As a result, many visitors overlook its colonial antecedents and its unique status as the hometown of both George Washington and James Monroe.

This one-hour, one-mile stroll down its quiet tree-shaded streets is an introduction to this presidential legacy. Begin by visiting the Fredericksburg Visitor Center at 706 Caroline Street. Walk north along Caroline Street, the Historic District's attractive main street, which is lined with interesting shops and cafes. At George Street, turn left one block to Charles Street, and then go right to 908 Charles, the James Monroe Museum. As a young man, Monroe practiced law in an office on this site. The museum displays rich pieces of furniture he took with him to the White House as the country's fifth president.

Continue north on Charles Street to Lewis Street and turn left onto Washington Avenue. Turn right a half block to Kenmore Plantation, the lovely mansion and garden at 2101 Washington. Built in 1752, it was the home of Betty Lewis, George Washington's sister, and her husband Fielding Lewis, a financier and gun manufacturer who aided the Revolutionary cause. The house is particularly noted for its richly decorated, hand-molded ceilings.

From Kenmore, retrace your steps on Lewis Street for three blocks to Charles Street. At 1200 Charles Street stands the Mary Washington House, which George Washington bought for his mother in 1772 so she could be more easily looked after by daughter Betty. Though George, who lived 40 miles north at Mount Vernon, was a dutiful son, his mother often accused him of neglect, a story told at the museum.

Continue east on Lewis to Caroline Street, and turn north (left) to the Rising Sun Tavern at 1306, the tour's conclusion. Built in 1760 as a private home by Charles Washington, George's younger brother, it has been restored to the 18th-century tavern it became in 1792.

VIRGINIA

WHAT TO SEE AND DO

Belmont (The Gari Melchers Estate and Memorial Gallery)

224 Washington St.,
Fredericksburg,
540-654-1015

Residence from 1916 to 1932 of American-born artist Gari Melchers (1860-1932), best known for his portraits of the famous and wealthy, including Theodore Roosevelt, William Vanderbilt and Andrew Mellon and as an important impressionist artist of the period. The artist's studio comprises the nation's largest collection of his works, housing more than 1,800 paintings and drawings. The site is a registered National and State Historic Landmark and includes a 27-acre estate, frame house built in the late 18th century and enlarged over the years, and a stone studio built by Melchers. Owned by the state of Virginia, Belmont is administered by Mary Washington College. Daily.

Confederate Cemetery

Willilam St. and Washington Ave.,
Fredericksburg

There are 2,640 Confederate Civil War soldiers buried here, some in graves marked "Unknown."

Fredericksburg Area Museum (Town Hall)

907 Princess Anne St.,
Fredericksburg,
540-371-3037;
www.famcc.org

(1814) Museum and cultural center interpret the history of Fredericksburg area from its first settlers to the 20th century. Changing exhibits. Children's events. Daily.

Fredericksburg Masonic Lodge #4, AF and AM

Princess Anne and Hanover Streets,
Fredericksburg,
540-373-5885;
www.masoniclodge4.com

Washington was initiated into this Lodge November 4, 1752; the building, dating from 1812, contains relics of his initiation and membership; authentic Gilbert Stuart portrait; 300-year-old Bible on which Washington took his Masonic oath. Monday-Saturday, also Sunday afternoons.

George Washington's Ferry Farm

268 Kings Hwy., Fredericksburg,
540-370-0732

The site of George Washington's boyhood home. Once a tobacco plantation, it now serves as an archaeological dig and a nature preserve. Guided tours. Daily.

Hugh Mercer Apothecary Shop

1020 Caroline St., Fredericksburg,
540-373-3362

This 18th-century medical office and pharmacy offers exhibits on the medicine and methods of treatment used by Dr. Hugh Mercer before he left to join the Revolutionary War as brigadier general. Authentic herbs and period medical instruments. Daily.

James Monroe Museum

908 Charles St., Fredericksburg,
540-654-1043

As a young lawyer, James Monroe lived and worked in Fredericksburg from 1786 to 1789, and even served on Fredericksburg's City Council. This museum houses one of the nation's largest collections of Monroe memorabilia, articles and original documents. Included are the desk bought in France in 1794 during his years as ambassador and used in the White House for signing of the Monroe Doctrine, formal attire worn at Court of Napoleon, and more than 40 books from Monroe's library; also garden. The site is a National Historic Landmark owned by the Commonwealth of Virginia and administered by Mary Washington College. Daily.

Kenmore Inn

1201 Washington Ave., Fredericksburg,
540-373-3381;
www.kenmore.org

(1752) Considered one of finest restorations in Virginia; former home of Colonel Fielding Lewis, commissioner of Fredericksburg gunnery, who married George Washington's only sister, Betty. On an original grant of 863 acres, Lewis built a magnificent home; three rooms have full decorative molded plaster ceilings. Diorama of 18th-century Fredericksburg. Daily; closed January, February.

Mary Washington College
1301 College Rd., Fredericksburg, 540-654-1000, 800-468-5614; www.umw.edu
(1908) (3,700 students.) Coeducational liberal arts and sciences institution that offers historic preservation, computer science, and business administration. College also includes 275 acres of open and wooded campus; red brick, white-pillared buildings. President of the college occupies Brompton (private), house built in 1830 on land sold to Fielding Lewis in 1760 and expanded by a later owner, Colonel John Lawrence Marye. Campus tours.

Mary Washington House
1200 Charles St., Fredericksburg, 540-373-1569
Bought by George for his mother in 1772; she lived here until her death in 1789. Here she was visited by General Lafayette. Some original furnishings. Boxwood garden. Daily.

Mary Washington Monument
Washington Ave. and Pitt St., Fredericksburg,
Where Mrs. Washington often went to rest and pray, and where she is buried.

Masonic Cemetery
George and Charles Streets, Fredericksburg,
One of nation's oldest Masonic burial grounds.

Old Slave Block
William and Charles Streets, Fredericksburg,
Circular block of sandstone about three feet high from which ladies mounted their horses and slaves were auctioned in antebellum days.

Presbyterian Church
Princess Anne and George Streets, Fredericksburg,
540-373-7057; www.fredericksburgpc.org

(1833) Cannonballs in the front pillar and other damages inflicted in 1862 bombardment. Pews were torn loose and made into coffins for soldiers. Clara Barton, founder of the American Red Cross, is said to have nursed wounded here. A plaque to her memory is in the churchyard. Open on request (Monday-Friday, Sunday).

Rising Sun Tavern
1306 Caroline St., Fredericksburg, 540-371-1494
(Circa 1760) Washington's youngest brother Charles built this tavern, which became a social and political center and stagecoach stop. Restored and authentically refurnished as an 18th-century tavern; costumed tavern staff, English and American pewter collection. Daily.

Sailor's Creek Battlefield Historic State Park
State Routes 307 N. and 17, Fredericksburg, 434-392-3435; www.dcr.virginia.gov/state_parks/sai.shtml
The site of last major battle of the Civil War on April 6, 1865, preceding Lee's surrender at Appomattox by three days. Auto tour.

St. George's Episcopal Church and Churchyard
Princess Anne and George Streets, Fredericksburg, 540-373-4133; www.stgeorgesepiscopal.net
Patrick Henry, uncle of the orator, was the third rector. Headstones in the churchyard bear the names of illustrious Virginians. Daily.

St. James House
1300 Charles St., Fredericksburg, 540-373-1569
Frame house built in 1760s, antique furnishings, porcelain and silver collections; landscaped gardens. Open Historic Garden Week in April and first week in October; other times by appointment.

321

VIRGINIA

★
★
★
★
★

SPECIAL EVENTS

Christmas Candlelight Tour
604 William St. #A,
Fredericksburg,
540-371-4504
Historic homes open to the public; carriage rides; Christmas decorations and refreshments of the Colonial period. First weekend in December.

Historic Garden Week
Private homes open. Mid-late April.

Market Square Fair
Entertainment, crafts demonstrations, food. Mid-May.

Quilt Show
Exhibits at various locations. Demonstrations and sale of old and new quilts. September.

HOTELS

★★Holiday Inn Select Fredericksburg
2801 Plank Rd.,
Fredericksburg,
540-786-8321, 800-282-0244;
www.holidayinn.com
195 rooms. Airport transportation available. $

★★Ramada Inn South Fredericksburg
5324 Jefferson Davis Hwy.,
Fredericksburg,
540-898-1102, 800-311-5192;
www.ramadainn.com
195 rooms. $

SPECIALTY LODGINGS

Fredericksburg Colonial Inn
1707 Princess Anne St.,
Fredericksburg,
540-371-5666;
www.fci1.com
Located at the north end of Fredericksburg, this lodging is several blocks from the Rappahannock River and approximately seven blocks from the historic Olde Towne center. Guest rooms feature furnishings and decor that reflect the Civil War period.
27 rooms. Complimentary continental breakfast. $

Kenmore Inn
1200 Princess Anne St.,
Fredericksburg,
540-371-7622;
www.kenmoreinn.com
This historic bed-and-breakfast, which dates to the early 19th century, is located at the northern end of Olde Towne Fredericksburg and several blocks from the Rappahannock River. The two-story white brick building features a broad staircase leading to the guest rooms, which are uniquely furnished and decorated.
9 rooms. Complimentary full breakfast. $$

Richard Johnston Inn
711 Caroline St., Fredericksburg,
540-899-7606, 877-557-0770;
www.therichardjohnstoninn.com
Easily accessible from Interstate 95, this historic inn (1787) is located in the heart of Fredericksburg's Olde Towne historic district. Each guest room is unique in decor and furnishings, with a mix of antiques and period reproductions.
9 rooms. Complimentary continental breakfast. $

RESTAURANTS

★★Renato
422 William St.,
Fredericksburg,
540-371-8228;
www.ristoranterenato.com
Italian menu. Lunch, dinner. Business casual attire. Reservations recommended. Valet parking. Outdoor seating. $$$

FREDERICKSBURG AND SPOTSYLVANIA NATIONAL MILITARY PARK

WHAT TO SEE AND DO

Chancellorsville Visitor Center

120 Chatham Lane,
Fredericksburg and Spotsylvania National
Military Park,
540-786-2880
Slide program, museum with exhibits;
dioramas. Daily.

Chatham Manor

120 Chatham Lane,
Fredericksburg and Spotsylvania National
Military Park,
540-371-0802
Georgian brick manor house, owned by a
wealthy planter, was converted to Union
headquarters during two of the battles of
Fredericksburg. The house was eventually
used as a hospital where Clara Barton and
Walt Whitman nursed the wounded. Daily.

Fredericksburg and Spotsylvania National Military Park

Lafayette Blvd. and Sunken Road,
Fredericksburg,
540-373-6122;
www.nps.gov/frsp
Visitor Center on Old US 1.

Fredericksburg Visitor Center

Lafayette Blvd. (Highway 1) and Sunken
Road, Fredericksburg and Spotsylvania
National Military Park,
540-373-6122

Information and directions for various parts
of park. Tours should start here. Daily.
Center includes:

Fredericksburg National Cemetery

Lafayette Blvd. and Sunken Road,
Fredericksburg,
More than 15,000 Federal interments; almost
13,000 unknown.

Museum

1900 E. Kanawha,
Fredericksburg,
Slide program, diorama, exhibits. Same days
as Visitor Center.

Old Salem Church

(1844) Building used as a field hospital and
refugee center. Scene of battle on May 3-4,
1863.

Stonewall Jackson Shrine

120 Chatham Lane, Fredericksburg and
Spotsylvania National Military Park,
804-633-6076
Plantation office where on May 10, 1863,
Confederate General Jackson, ill with pneu-
monia and with his shattered left arm ampu-
tated, murmured, "Let us cross over the
river, and rest under the shade of the trees,"
and died. Mid-June-Labor Day: daily;
April-mid-June, after Labor Day-October:
Monday, Tuesday, Friday-Sunday; rest of
year: Monday, Saturday-Sunday.

★
★
★
★
★

FRONT ROYAL

Once known as "Hell Town" for all the wild and reckless spirits it attracted, Front Royal
was a frontier stop on the way to eastern markets. The present name is supposed to have
originated in the command, "Front the royal oak," given by an English officer to his
untrained mountain militia recruits.

Belle Boyd, the Confederate spy, worked here extracting military secrets from Union
officers. It is said that she invited General Nathaniel Banks, whose regiment was occupying the town, and his officers to a ball once. Later she raced on horseback to tell General
Jackson what she had learned. The next morning (May 23, 1862), the Confederates attacked
and captured nearly all of the Union troops, providing Jackson one of his early victories in
the famous Valley Campaign.

Front Royal was a quiet village until the entrance to Shenandoah National Park and the beginning of Skyline Drive opened in 1935, just one mile to the south. With millions of motorists passing through every year, the town has grown rapidly. The production of automotive finishes, limestone and cement contributes to the town's economy, but the tourism industry remains one of its largest.

Information: Chamber of Commerce of Front Royal-Warren County, 104 E. Main St., Front Royal, 540-635-3185, 800-338-2576; www.frontroyalchamber.com

WHAT TO SEE AND DO

Belle Boyd Cottage
101 Chester St., Front Royal,
540-636-1446

Relocated to its present site, the two-story cottage has been restored to reflect life in Front Royal between 1840 and 1860. For a two-year period during the Civil War, Belle Boyd stayed in this cottage while visiting relatives and used the opportunity to spy on Union troops occupying the town. This modest dwelling was also used to house wounded soldiers of both armies. May-August: Monday-Saturday; September-April: Monday-Friday.

Jackson's Chase Golf Course
65 Jackson's Chase Dr.,
Front Royal,
540-635-7814;
www.jacksonschase.com

Jackson's Chase is built on a tract of land that was used by Confederate General "Stonewall" Jackson to chase Union forces through the Shenandoah Valley and into the eventual first Battle of Winchester. The course itself incorporates the area's rolling terrain into plateau fairways and holes lined with water. Holes three through eight surround a small area being developed for homes with one-acre lots, for those who wish to live in full view of history and the links.

Shenandoah Valley Golf Club
134 Golf Club Circle, Front Royal,
540-636-4653;
www.svgcgolf.com

Nestled into the Blue Ridge Mountains, Shenandoah Valley offers 27 holes and has hosted such prestigious tournaments as the PGA Tour's Kemper Open. If you want to play, make sure to reserve a tee time at least a week in advance. Once you do, you'll be happy with a course that is very affordable and playable for most any golfer.

Sky Meadows State Park
11012 Edmonds Lane, Front Royal,
540-592-3556;
www.dcr.virginia.gov/state_parks/
sky.shtml

A 1,862-acre park. Fishing pond; hiking and bridle trails, picnicking, primitive walk-in camping. Visitor center; programs. Daily.

Skyline Caverns
10344 Stonewall Jackson Hwy.,
Front Royal,
540-635-4545, 800-296-4545;
www.skylinecaverns.com

Extensive, rare, intricate flowerlike formations of calcite (anthodites); sound and light presentation; 37-foot waterfall; clear stream stocked with trout (observation only). Electrically lighted; 54 F year-round. Miniature train provides trip through surrounding wooded area (Monday-Friday: year round; daily. March-mid-November: Snack bar; gift shop. Cavern tours start every few minutes. Daily.

Warren Rifles Confederate Museum
95 Chester St., Front Royal,
540-636-6982

Historic relics and memorabilia of War between the States. Mid-April-October: daily; rest of year, by appointment.

SPECIAL EVENTS

Festival of Leaves
Main and Chester Streets,
Front Royal,
540-636-1446

Arts and crafts, demonstrations; historic exhibits; parade. Second weekend in October.

324

VIRGINIA

Virginia Mushroom and Wine Festival
Mushrooms, wine and cheese. Entertainment. Third Saturday in May.

Warren County Fair
540-635-5821,
www.warrencountyfair.com
Entertainment, livestock exhibits and sale, contests. First week in August.

Warren County Garden Tour
Garden Club sponsors tours of historic houses and gardens. Mid-late April.

HOTELS
★★Quality Inn
10 S. Commerce Ave., Front Royal,
540-635-3161, 877-424-6423;
www.choicehotels.com
107 rooms. $

GALAX

Galax is named for the pretty evergreen with heart-shaped leaves that florists use in various arrangements. It grows in the mountainous regions around Galax and is gathered for sale all over the United States. Nearby are three mountain passes: Fancy Gap, Low Gap and Piper's Gap.
Information: Galax-Carroll-Grayson Chamber of Commerce,
405 N. Main St., Galax, 276-236-2184; www.gcgchamber.com

WHAT TO SEE AND DO
Jeff Matthews Memorial Museum
606 W. Stuart Dr., Galax,
276-236-7874
Two authentically restored log cabins (1834 and 1860s). Relocated to present site and furnished with items used in the period in which the cabins were inhabited. Also houses collection of photos of Civil War veterans, artifacts and memorabilia of the area; covered wagon; farm implements. Restored log cabin used as a blacksmith's shop. Wednesday-Sunday.

Recreation
Swimming, boating, fishing on New River; hunting and hiking. Canoeing and other activities can be found at:

Cliffview Trading Post
442 Cliffview Road, Galax,
276-238-1530
Bike rentals (Tuesday-Saturday) and horse rentals (April-November: Tuesday-Saturday); trail rides in New River Trail State Park.

SPECIAL EVENTS
Old Fiddler's Convention
Felts Park,
276-236-8541;
www.oldfiddlersconvention.com
Folk songs, bands and dancing. Second week in August.

GEORGE WASHINGTON BIRTHPLACE NATIONAL MONUMENT

George Washington, first child of Augustine and Mary Ball Washington, was born February 11, 1732 (celebrated February 22) at his father's estate on Popes Creek on the south shore of the Potomac. The family moved in 1735 to Little Hunting Creek Plantation (later called Mount Vernon), then in 1738 to Ferry Farm near Fredericksburg. The 538-acre monument includes much of the old plantation land. Daily.
www.nps.gov/gewa

WHAT TO SEE AND DO

Colonial Farm
1732 Popes Creek Rd.,
George Washington Birthplace National
Monument,
804-224-1732
"Living" farm designed to show 18th-century
Virginia plantation life; livestock, colonial
garden, several farm buildings, furnished
colonial kitchen, household slave quarters
and spinning and weaving room.

Family Burial Ground
1732 Popes Creek Rd.,
George Washington Birthplace National
Monument,
804-224-1732
Site of 1664 home of Colonel John
Washington, first Washington in Virginia
and great-grandfather of the first president.
Washington's ancestors are buried here.

Picnic Area
1732 Popes Creek Rd., George Washington
Birthplace National Monument,
804-224-1732

Visitor Center
1732 Popes Creek Rd.,
George Washington Birthplace National
Monument,
804-224-1732
Orientation film; museum exhibits.

Memorial House
1732 Popes Creek Rd.,
George Washington Birthplace National
Monument,
804-224-1732
Original house burned (1779) and was
never rebuilt. The Memorial House is not a
replica of the original; it represents a com-
posite of typical 18th-century Virginia plantation house. Bricks were handmade from
nearby clay. Furnishings are typical of the
times.

326 GLEN ALLEN

HOTELS
★Springhill Suites
9701 Brook Rd., Glen Allen,
804-266-9403, 800-287-9400;
www.marriott.com/ricsh

136 rooms. Complimentary continental
breakfast. $$

GLOUCESTER

In the spring, acres of daffodil blooms make this area a treat for the traveler. This
elm-shaded village is the commercial center of Gloucester (GLOSS-ter) County. There are
many old landmarks and estates nearby, including the birthplace of Walter Reed, at the
junction of Highways 614 and 616.
Information: Chamber of Commerce, 6688 Main St., Gloucester,
804-693-2425; www.gloucestervacc.com

WHAT TO SEE AND DO

County Courthouse
6489 Main St., Gloucester,
804-693-4042
(18th century) Part of Gloucester Court
House Circle Historic District. Portraits
of native sons in the courtroom; plaques
memorializing Nathaniel Bacon, leader in
the rebellion of 1676, first organized resis-
tance to British authority, and Major Walter

Reed, surgeon and conqueror of yellow
fever. Monday-Friday.

Rosewell Historic Ruins
6549 Main St., Gloucester,
804-693-2585
Three-story Georgian mansion's brick-
work was put in place over 250 years ago.
Majestic ruins hint at projecting pavilions,
arched windows and stone-capped chimney

stacks. Tours by appointment. April-October: Sunday; winter by appointment.

Virginia Institute of Marine Science, College of William and Mary
1208 Greate Rd., Gloucester Point, 804-684-7000;
www.vims.edu

Small marine aquarium and museum display local fish and invertebrates; marine science exhibits, bookstore. Monday-Friday.

GREAT DISMAL SWAMP NATIONAL WILDLIFE REFUGE

Harriet Beecher Stowe found Virginia's Dismal Swamp a perfect setting for her antislavery novel *Dred* (1856); modern hunters, fishermen and naturalists find the area fits their ambition just as well. From its northern edge just southwest of Norfolk, the swamp stretches almost due south like a great ribbon, 25 miles long and 11 miles wide. Centuries of decaying organic matter have created layers of peat so deep that fires would sometimes smolder under the surface for weeks.

Creation of the refuge began in 1973 when the Union Camp Corporation donated 49,100 acres of land to the Nature Conservancy, which in turn conveyed it to the Department of Interior. The refuge was officially established through the Dismal Swamp Act of 1974 and is managed for the primary purpose of protecting and preserving a unique ecosystem. The refuge now consists of over 107,000 acres of forested wetlands that have been greatly altered by drainage and logging operations.

Near the center is Lake Drummond, 3,100 acres of juniper water, which is water that combines the juices of gum, cypress and maple with a strong infusion of juniper or white cedar. The chemical mix added by the tree resins results in a water that remains sweet, or fresh, indefinitely. In the days of long sailing voyages, when ordinary water became foul after a few weeks, this "dark water" was highly valued.

The Great Dismal Swamp has also been commercially exploited for its timber, particularly cypress and cedar. A company organized by George Washington and several other businessmen bought a large piece of the swamp and used slave labor to dig the Dismal Swamp Canal, which both facilitated drainage of timber land and provided a transportation route in and out of the swamp.

Animal and bird life continues to abound in this eerie setting. There are white-tailed deer and rarely observed black bear, foxes, bobcats and a large number of snakes, including copperheads, cottonmouths and rattlesnakes. Birding is popular in the swamp from April-June; the peak of spring migration is mid-April-mid-May.
Information: Refuge Manager, 3100 Desert Rd., Suffolk, 757-986-3705; www.fws.gov/northeast/greatdismalswamp

327

VIRGINIA

GREAT FALLS

WHAT TO SEE AND DO

Colvin Run Mill Historic Site
10017 Colvin Run Rd., Great Falls,
703-759-2771;
www.fairfaxcounty.gov/parks/crm
Tours of historical gristmill. General store, miller's house exhibit, barn and grounds (free). Daily, closed Tuesdays.

RESTAURANTS

★★★**Dante**
1148 Walker Rd., Great Falls, 703-759-3131
A historic Victorian home (previously a dairy farm and "lying-in" hospital) is the setting for this romantic restaurant. There are several small dining areas, each with its own unique decor, but all are charming—one

room even has an entire wall displaying wine bottles. The authentic northern Italian menu offers items such as rabbit legs, osso buco and homemade ravioli. Don't leave without trying the layered chocolate cake (filled with a chocolate mousse) with a cup of espresso. Italian menu. Lunch, dinner. Bar. Business casual attire. Reservations recommended. Outdoor seating. **$$$**

★★★Fiore Di Luna
1025 Seneca Rd.,
Great Falls,
703-444-4060;
www.fiorediluna.com

Fiore di Luna is a simple but elegant Northern Italian restaurant, serving dishes such as butternut squash gnocchi with a robiola cheese sauce, julienne celery, amaretti cookies and parmesan cheese or Grimaud farm-raised Muscovy duck breast with baby green and red Brussels sprouts, white polenta timbale and parsley puree. Italian menu. Lunch, dinner. Closed Monday. Bar. Business casual attire. Reservations recommended. Outdoor seating. **$$$**

★★★L'Auberge Chez Francois
332 Springvale Rd., Great Falls,
703-759-3800;
www.laubergechezfrancois.com

Rich, hearty dishes at this Alsatian-themed restaurant are served by dirndl-clad waitresses and waiters in red vests with gold buttons. Located outside the Great Falls area, this charming farmhouse restaurant is set along a winding, two-lane road. Outside, it is surrounded by flowers and an herb garden, a gazebo and fountains on the terrace. The inside is cozy with wood beams, wood burning fireplaces and stained glass panels. The Haeringer family focuses on traditional Alsatian French cuisine and offers a prix fixe menu. French menu. Dinner. Closed Monday. Children's menu. Business casual attire. Reservations recommended. Outdoor seating. **$$$**

★★★Le Relais
1025-I Seneca Rd., Great Falls,
703-444-4060

French menu. Lunch, dinner. Closed Monday. Bar. Outdoor seating. **$$$**

★★★Serbian Crown
1141 Walker Rd., Great Falls,
703-759-4150;
www.serbiancrown.com

Russian and French cuisines are fearlessly combined to create an elegant menu at this special-occasion restaurant. Beef stroganoff, stuffed cabbage rolls, marinated wild boar and duck braised in sauerkraut are just a few of the items that keep diners coming back for more. Various live entertainment such as a violinist, Gypsy music and a sing-along piano bar add to the unique ambience. French, International menu. Lunch, dinner, late-night. Bar. Business casual attire. Reservations recommended. **$$$**

HAMPTON

Hampton is the oldest continuous English-speaking community in the United States (Jamestown, settled in 1607, is a national historical park, but not a town). The settlement began at a place then called Kecoughtan, with the building of Fort Algernourne as protection against the Spanish. In the late 1600s and early 1700s, pirates harassed the area. Finally in 1718, the notorious brigand Blackbeard was killed by Lieutenant Robert Maynard and organized piracy came to an end here.

Hampton was shelled in the Revolutionary War, sacked by the British in the War of 1812, and burned in 1861 by retreating Confederates to prevent its occupation by Union forces. Only the gutted walls of St. John's Church survived the fire. The town was rebuilt after the Civil War by its citizens and soldiers. Computer technology, manufacturing, aerospace research and commercial fishing are now big business here.

Langley Air Force Base, headquarters for the Air Combat Command, Fort Monroe, head-quarters for the U.S. Army's Training and Doctrine Command, and the NASA Langley Research Center are located here.

Information: Hampton Visitor Center, 120 Old Hampton Lane, Hampton, 757-722-1222, 800-487-8778; www.hampton.va.us

WHAT TO SEE AND DO

Air Power Park and Aviation History Center

413 W. Mercury Blvd., Hampton, 23666 (Highway 258), 757-727-1163

Over 50 indoor and outdoor exhibits feature real fighter aircraft, missiles and rockets; local aviation history and model aircraft exhibits. Picnicking, playground. Daily.

Bluebird Gap Farm

60 Pine Chapel Rd., Hampton, 757-727-6739

This 60-acre farm includes barnyard zoo; indigenous wildlife such as deer and wolves; antique and modern farm equipment and farmhouse artifacts. Picnicking, playground. Wednesday-Sunday.

Buckroe Beach

22 Lincoln St., Hampton, 757-850-5134

Swimming; public park, concerts. Lifeguards. Memorial Day-Labor Day.

Fort Monroe

First fort here was a stockade called Fort Algernourne (1609); the second, Fort George, though built of brick, was destroyed by a hurricane in 1749; present fort was completed about 1834.

Here are:

Casemate Museum

20 Bernard Rd., Hampton, 757-788-3391

Provides insight on heritage of the fort, Old Point Comfort and the Army Coast Artillery Corps. Museum offers access to a series of casemates and a walking tour of the fort. Jefferson Davis casemate contains cell in which the Confederacy's president was confined on false charges of plotting to kill Abraham Lincoln. Museum features Civil War exhibits, military uniforms and assorted artwork, including three original Remington drawings, along with audiovisual programs. Scale models of coast artillery guns and dioramas represent the role of the coast artillery from 1901 to 1946. Daily.

Chapel of the Centurion

(1858) One of the oldest churches on the Virginia peninsula. Woodrow Wilson worshiped here occasionally.

Hampton Carousel

602 Settlers Landing Rd., Hampton, 757-727-6381

(1920) Completely restored in 1991, antique carousel is housed in its own pavilion and features 48 hand-carved horses. June-September: daily; October-November, Friday-Sunday; December-end of May, closed.

Hampton University

Cemetery Rd. and Frissell Ave., Hampton, 757-727-5253; www.hamptonu.edu

(1868) (6,100 students.) Founded by Union Brigadier General Samuel Chapman Armstrong, chief of the Freedman's Bureau, to prepare the youth of the South, regardless of color, for the work of organizing and instructing schools in the Southern states; many blacks and Native Americans came to be educated. Now Virginia's only coeducational, nondenominational, four-year private college. The Hampton choir is famous. It "sang up" a building, Virginia-Cleveland Hall, in 1870 on a trip through New England and Canada, raising close to $100,000 at concerts.

On campus are:

Emancipation Oak

The Emancipation Proclamation was read here.

329

VIRGINIA

★
★
★
★
★

Hampton University Museum

Huntington Building, Cemetery Road and Frissell Ave., Hampton,
757-727-5308;
www.museum.hamptonu.edu
Collection of ethnic art; Native American and African artifacts; contemporary African-American works; paintings by renowned artists. Daily; closed Sundays.

Miss Hampton II Harbor Cruises

764 Settlers Landing Rd.,
Hampton,
757-722-9102, 888-757-2628;
www.misshamptoncruises.com
Narrated three-hour cruise includes a stop at Fort Wool, a Civil War island fortress. April-October.

Settlers Landing Monument

Marks approximate site of first settlers' landing near Strawberry Banks in 1607. Painting by Sidney King depicts visit to Kecoughtan by colonists en route to Jamestown. Daily.

St. John's Church and Parish Museum

W. Queens Way and Franklin St.,
Hampton,
757-722-2567;
www.stjohnshampton.org
(1728) Fourth site of worship of Episcopal parish established in 1610. Bible dating from 1599; communion silver from 1618; Colonial Vestry Book; taped historical message. Daily.

Virginia Air and Space Center and Hampton Roads History Center

600 Settlers Landing Rd.,
Hampton,
757-727-0900, 800-296-0800;
www.vasc.org
Exhibits show the historical link between Hampton Roads' seafaring past and space-faring future. Exhibits include 19 full-sized air- and spacecraft, the *Apollo 12* Command Module, a moon rock and rare NASA artifacts. Films shown in 283-seat IMAX theater. Daily.

SPECIAL EVENTS

Hampton Bay Days

Hampton,
757-727-6122;
www.baydays.com
Arts and crafts, rides, science exhibits; entertainment. Mid-September.

Hampton Cup Regatta

Mill Creek,
Hampton,
800-800-2202;
www.hamptoncupregatta.org
Inboard hydroplane races. Mid-August.

Hampton Jazz Festival

Hampton Coliseum, 1000 Coliseum Dr.,
Hampton,
757-838-4203
Three days late June.

HOTELS

★Quality Inn

1813 W. Mercury Blvd.,
Hampton,
757-838-8484, 877-424-6423;
www.qualityinn.com
131 rooms. Complimentary continental breakfast. Airport transportation available. **$**

★★Radisson Hotel Hampton

700 Settlers Landing,
Hampton,
757-727-9700, 888-201-1718;
www.radisson.com/hamptonva
172 rooms. Airport transportation available. On Hampton River. **$**

RESTAURANTS

★Sammy and Nick's

2718 W. Mercury Blvd.,
Hampton,
757-838-9100
American menu. Breakfast, lunch, dinner. Children's menu. Casual attire. **$**

HARRISONBURG

Originally named Rocktown due to the limestone outcroppings prevalent in the area, Harrisonburg became the county seat of Rockingham County when Thomas Harrison won a race against Mr. Keezle of Keezletown, three miles east. They had raced on horseback to Richmond to file their respective towns for the new county seat.

Harrisonburg is noted for good hunting and fishing, recreational opportunities, beautiful scenery and turkeys. The annual production of more than five million turkeys, most of them processed and frozen, has made Rockingham County widely known. This is a college town with three 4-year universities. Much of the Washington and Jefferson national forests are here.
Information: Harrisonburg Tourism Center, 212 S. Main St., Harrisonburg, 540-432-8935; www.harrisonburgtourism.com

WHAT TO SEE AND DO

Caverns
www.uvrpa.org
There are several caverns within 24 miles of Harrisonburg.
They include:

Grand Caverns Regional Park
Dogwood Ave., Grottoes,
540-249-5705, 888-430-2283
Known for its immense underground chambers and spectacular formations. Visited by Union and Confederate troops during the Civil War. Unique shield formations. Electrically lighted; 54 F. Park facilities include a swimming pool, tennis courts, miniature golf, picnic pavilions and hiking and bicycle trails. Guided tours. April-October: daily; November-March: weekends.

Eastern Mennonite University
1200 Park Rd., Harrisonburg,
540-432-4000;
www.emu.edu
(1917) (1,350 students.) Many Mennonites live in this area. On campus is an art gallery, planetarium (shows by appointment, free), natural history museum and the Menno Simons Historical Library, containing many 16th-century Mennonite volumes (school year, Monday-Saturday). Campus tours.

James Madison University
800 S. Main St., Harrisonburg,
540-568-6211;
www.jmu.edu
(1908) (15,000 students.) Campus tours through Visitor Center, 540-568-5681.
On campus is:

Miller Hall Planetarium and Sawhill Art Gallery
800 S. Main, Harrisonburg,
540-568-3621

Lincoln Homestead
Brick house, the rear wing of which was built by Abraham Lincoln's grandfather, and where his father was born. Main portion of the house was built about 1800 by Captain Jacob Lincoln. Private.

Shenandoah Valley Folk Art and Heritage Center
115 Bowman Rd., Harrisonburg,
540-879-2681;
www.heritagecenter.com
Featured is the Stonewall Jackson Electric Map that depicts his Valley Campaign of 1862. The 12-foot vertical relief map fills an entire wall and lets visitors see and hear the campaign, battle by battle. Also displays of Shenandoah Valley history, artifacts. Monday-Saturday.

Virginia Quilt Museum
301 S. Main St., Harrisonburg,
540-433-3818;
www.vaquiltmuseum.org
Resource center for the study of quilts and quilting. Thursday-Monday.

SPECIAL EVENTS

Natural Chimneys Jousting Tournament
Natural Chimneys Regional Park,
94 Natural Chimneys Lane, Harrisonburg
America's oldest continuous sporting event, held annually since 1821. "Knights" armed with lances charge down an 80-yard track and attempt to spear three small

rings suspended from posts. Each knight is allowed three rides at the rings, thus a perfect score is nine rings. Ties are run off using successively smaller rings. Third Saturday in June and August.

Rockingham County Fair
4808 S. Valley Pike, Harrisonburg
Mid-August.

HOTELS
★Comfort Inn
1440 E. Market St., Harrisonburg,
540-433-6066, 800-424-6423;
www.choicehotels.com
102 rooms. Complimentary continental breakfast. **$**

★Hampton Inn
85 University Blvd., Harrisonburg,
540-432-1111, 800-426-7866;
www.hamptoninn.com

163 rooms. Complimentary continental breakfast. **$**

★★The Village Inn
4979 S. Valley Pike,
Harrisonburg,
540-434-7355, 800-736-7355;
www.thevillageinn.info
37 rooms. Children's activity **$**

RESTAURANTS
★★Village Inn Restaurant
4979 South Valley Pike,
Harrisonburg,
540-434-7355, 800-736-7355;
www.thevillageinn.travel
American menu. Breakfast, lunch, dinner. Closed Sunday. Children's menu. Casual attire. **$$**

HOPEWELL

Hopewell, the second permanent English settlement in America, has been an important inland port since early times, with its fine channel 28-feet deep and 300-feet wide. It was the birthplace of statesman John Randolph of Roanoke. Edmund Ruffin, an early agricultural chemist who fired the first shot at Fort Sumter, was born near here.

"Cittie Point," at the junction of the James and Appomattox rivers, finally became one of Virginia's big cities during World War I when an E. I. du Pont de Nemours Company dynamite plant on Hopewell Farm supplied guncotton to the Allies.
Information: Hopewell Area-Prince George Chamber of Commerce, 210 N. 2nd Ave., Hopewell, 804-458-5536

WHAT TO SEE AND DO
City Point Unit of Petersburg National Battlefield
Cedar Lane and Pecan Ave., Hopewell,
804-458-9504
Grant's headquarters during the siege of Petersburg and largest Civil War supply depot. Includes Appomattox Manor, home to one family for 340 years; Grant's headquarters were on the front lawn. Many other buildings. Daily.

Flowerdew Hundred
1617 Flowerdew Hundred Rd., Hopewell,
804-541-8897;
www.flowerdew.org

Outdoor museum on the site of an early English settlement on the south bank of the James River. Originally inhabited by Native Americans, settled by Governor George Yeardley in 1618. Thousands of artifacts dating from the prehistoric period through the present have been excavated and are on exhibit in the museum. A replicated 19th-century detached kitchen and working 17th-century-style windmill are open to visitors. Exhibits, interpretive tours. Picnicking. Monday-Friday.

Merchants Hope Church
11500 Merchants Hope Rd.,
Hopewell,
804-458-6197

(1657) Given the name of a plantation that was named for a barque plying between Virginia and England. The exterior has been called the most beautiful colonial brickwork in America. Oldest operating Protestant church in the country. Open by request.

SPECIAL EVENTS
Hooray for Hopewell Festival
Arts and crafts, food, entertainment, children's rides. Third weekend in September.

Prince George Country Heritage Fair
Arts and crafts; educational exhibits and demonstrations; music, food, children's rides, hayrides. Last weekend in April.

HOTELS
★Quality Inn
4911 Oaklawn Blvd., Hopewell,
804-458-1500, 877-424-6423;
www.qualityinn.com
115 rooms. Complimentary continental breakfast. **$**

HOT SPRINGS
A Ranger District office of the Washington and Jefferson national forests is located here.

WHAT TO SEE AND DO
The Homestead Ski Area
Hwy. 220, Hot Springs,
540-839-3860, 866-354-4653;
www.thehomestead.com
Double chairlift, T-bar, J-bar, baby rope tow; patrol, school, rentals, snowmaking; cafeteria, bar. Curling, ice skating rink Thanksgiving-March.

HOTELS
★★★The Homestead
Hwy. 220, Hot Springs,
540-839-1766, 866-354-4653;
www.thehomestead.com
Founded 10 years before the American Revolution, The Homestead is one of America's finest resorts. For more than two centuries, presidents and other notables have flocked to this idyllic mountain resort on 15,000 acres in the scenic Allegheny Mountains. From the fresh mountain air and natural hot springs to the legendary championship golf, this Georgian-style resort is the embodiment of a restorative retreat. A leading golf academy sharpens skills, while three courses challenge players. America's oldest continuously played tee is located here at the Old Course. Guests take to the waters as they have done for 200 years, while the spa incorporates advanced therapies for relaxation and rejuvenation. 506 rooms. Children's activity center. Ski in/ski out. Airport transportation available. Ski. **$$**

★★★The Homestead Spa
Hwy. 220, Hot Springs,
540-839-1766;
www.thehomestead.com
The Homestead Spa at the Homestead Resort grows out of a healing tradition nearly as old as the Allegheny Mountains themselves: taking the waters that bubble up from the ground in Hot Springs, Virginia. For thousands of years, native peoples and the Europeans who came after them have soaked in these mineral-rich waters, easing rheumatism and dozens of other aches and ailments. The Homestead is a National Historic Landmark, a spa since 1766. The octagonal wooden building atop the hot springs is even older, built in 1761 and essentially unchanged. A 75-year-old Thomas Jefferson came to the Gentleman's Pool House to soak several times a day during his Homestead visit in 1818. Today, men can still retreat to the Jefferson Pools, while women have their own 1836 Ladies' Pool House atop another spring. Treatments have become more exotic over time, encompassing reflexology and Ayurvedic head massage, alpha beta skin peels and banana-and-coconut hair therapy. The spa still values the time-tested mineral baths and salt scrubs of the past, often combined with fresh-picked flowers and herbs from the mountains that hug the Homestead. **$$**

VIRGINIA

★
★
★
★
★

SPECIALTY LODGINGS

Vine Cottage Inn
7402 Sam Snead Hwy.,
Hot Springs,
540-839-2422, 800-410-9755;
www.vinecottageinn.com
15 rooms. Closed two weeks in March. Complimentary full breakfast. Built in 1894; family-oriented Victorian inn. **$**

RESTAURANTS

★Country Cafe
Route 220 S., Hot Springs,
540-839-2111

American menu. Breakfast, lunch, dinner. Closed Monday, children's menu. Casual attire. **$$**

★★Sam Snead's Tavern
220 Main St.,
Hot Springs,
540-839-7666;
www.thehomestead.com
American menu. Dinner. Bar. Children's menu. Business casual attire. Reservations recommended. **$$$**

IRVINGTON

WHAT TO SEE AND DO

Historic Christ Church
420 Christ Church Rd., Irvington,
804-438-6855;
www.christchurch1735.org
(1735) Built by Robert Carter, ancestor of eight governors of Virginia, two presidents, three signers of the Declaration of Independence, a chief justice, and many others who served the country with distinction. Restored; original structure and furnishings, triple-decker pulpit. Built on site of earlier wooden church (1669); family tombs. Tours. Daily.

On the grounds is:

Carter Reception Center
420 Christ Church Rd., Irvington
Narrated video presentation; museum with artifacts from Corotoman, home of Robert Carter, and from the church construction; photographs of the restoration. Guides. April-November: daily.

HOTELS

★★★Tides Inn
480 King Carter Dr.,
Irvington,
804-438-5000, 800-843-3746;
www.tidesinn.com
Bordered by the Chesapeake Bay, Potomac River and Rappahannock River, and with views of gentle Carters Creek, water figures largely in the experience here. A 64-slip marina is a boater's paradise. Golf, tennis, croquet, biking, blissing out in the spa, and exploring the nearby historic sites are just some of the ways guests fill their days while staying here. Dining runs the gamut from the elegant setting at the Dining Room and dinner river cruises on the "Miss Ann" to the casual atmospheres of Commodores, Cap'n B's and the Chesapeake Club.
106 rooms. Closed January-mid-March. Children's activity center. **$$**

JAMESTOWN (COLONIAL NATIONAL HISTORICAL PARK)

On May 13, 1607, in this unpromising setting, the first permanent English settlement in the New World was founded. From the beginning, characteristics of the early United States were established: self-government, industry, commerce, the plantation system and a diverse populace, originally made up of men of English, German, African, French, Italian, Polish and Irish descent.

Nothing of the 17th-century settlement remains above ground except the Old Church Tower. Since 1934, however, archaeological exploration by the National Park Service has made the outline of the town clear. Cooperative efforts by the Park Service and the Association for the Preservation of Virginia Antiquities (which owns 22.5 acres of the island, including the Old Church Tower) have exposed foundations and restored streets, property ditches, hedgerows, fences and the James Fort site from 1607. Markers, recorded messages, paintings and monuments are everywhere. Entrance station (daily). Information: 757-229-1733; www.nps.gov/jame

WHAT TO SEE AND DO

Confederate Fort
(1861) One of two Civil War fortifications on the island.

Dale House
1367 Colonial Pkwy., Jamestown (Colonial National Historical Park)
Archaeological laboratory. A viewing area is open to the public.

First Landing Site
Colonial Historic Pkwy. and Jamestown Rd., Jamestown (Colonial National Historical Park)
Fixed by tradition as point in river, about 200 yards from present seawall, upriver from Old Church Tower.

Glasshouse
Colonial National Historic Pkwy. and Jamestown Rd., Jamestown (Colonial National Historical Park)
Colonists produced glass here in 1608. Demonstration exhibits, glassblowing Daily.

James Fort Site
Colonial Historic Pkwy. and Jamestown Rd., Jamestown
Excavation of first fort (1607) can be viewed between seawall and Old Church Tower.

Memorial Church
Colonial National Historic Pkwy. and Jamestown Rd., Jamestown (Colonial National Historical Park)
Built in 1907 by the National Society of the Colonial Dames of America over foundations of original church. Within are two foundations alleged to be of earlier churches, one from 1617 that housed the first assembly.

New Towne
1367 Colonial Pkwy, Jamestown (Colonial National Historical Park)
Area where Jamestown expanded around 1620 may be toured along "Back Streete" and other original streets. Section includes reconstructed foundations indicating sites of Country House, Governor's House, homes of Richard Kemp, builder of one of the first brick houses in America, Henry Hartwell, a founder of College of William and Mary, and Dr. John Pott and William Pierce, who led the "thrusting out" of Governor John Harvey in 1635.

Old Church Tower
Only standing ruin of the 17th-century town. Believed to be part of the first brick church (1639). Has 3-foot-thick walls of handmade brick.

Tercentenary Monument
Erected by the United States (1907) to commemorate 300th Jamestown anniversary. Other monuments include Captain John Smith statue (by William Couper), Pocahontas Monument (by William Ordway Partridge), House of Burgesses Monument (listing members of first representative legislative body in America).

Trails
Three- and five-mile auto drives provide access to entire area. Visitor center has 45-minute auto drive and town site tape tours available.

Visitor Center
Colonial National Historic Pkwy. and Jamestown Rd., Jamestown (Colonial National Historical Park),
Guide leaflets, introductory film and exhibits. Post office. Daily.

335

VIRGINIA

★
★
★
★
★

COLONIAL PARKWAY

The Colonial Parkway is a 23-mile link between the three towns that formed the "cradle of the nation:" Jamestown, Williamsburg and Yorktown. It starts at the Visitor Center at Jamestown, passes through Williamsburg (the Colonial Williamsburg Information Center is near the north underpass entrance), and ends at the Visitor Center in Yorktown.

At turnouts and overlooks along the route, information signs note historic spots such as Glebeland, Kingsmill, Indian Field Creek, Powhatan's Village, Fusilier's Redoubt, and others. A free picnic area is provided during the summer at Ringfield Plantation, midway between Williamsburg and Yorktown. The parkway is free to private vehicles, and the speed limit is 45 miles per hour. There are no service stations along the way.

SPECIAL EVENTS

First Assembly Day
Commemorates first legislative assembly in 1619. Late July.

Jamestown Weekend
Commemorates arrival of first settlers in 1607; special tours and activities. Mid-May.

KESWICK

HOTELS

★★★Keswick Hall At Monticello
701 Club Dr., Keswick,
434-979-3440, 800-274-5391;
www.keswick.com

Keswick Hall's 600-acre estate, set at the foot of the Blue Ridge Mountains, offers visitors individually designed guest rooms that reflect a modern interpretation of early American style, with overstuffed furniture, club chairs, Aubusson carpets and canopied four-poster beds. Views over the magnificent formal gardens are particularly coveted. The rolling hills of the Shenandoah Valley invite exploration and the historic halls of Monticello are only minutes away, but this resort also entices its guests with a variety of recreational opportunities. The members-only Keswick Hall, adjacent to the hotel, presents an exclusive opportunity for guests to enjoy its indoor/outdoor pool, tennis courts, fitness facility, spa services and 18-hole Arnold Palmer golf course.

48 rooms. Children's activity center. Airport transportation available. $$$$

RESTAURANTS

★★★Main Dining Room
701 Club Dr., Keswick,
434-979-3440;
www.keswick.com

"A feast for the eyes" best describes the chef's classically inspired culinary creations, most appropriate given the formal dining room's trompe l'oeil wall murals and expansive garden views.

American menu. Breakfast, dinner. Bar. Children's menu. Casual attire. Reservations recommended. Valet parking. Outdoor seating. $$$

LANCASTER

The family of Mary Ball Washington, mother of George Washington, were early settlers of this area. Washington's maternal ancestors are buried in the churchyard of St. Mary's Whitechapel Church five miles west of Lancaster.

WHAT TO SEE AND DO

Lancaster County Courthouse Historic District

Sycamore trees surround this area around the antebellum courthouse (1860). Marble obelisk is one of the first monuments erected to Confederate soldiers (1872).

Mary Ball Washington Museum and Library Complex

8346 Mary Ball Rd., Lancaster,
804-462-7280;
www.mbwm.org

Contains the Old Clerk's Office (1797), the Old Jail (1819), Lancaster House (1800), the headquarters and main museum building. Also Virginia genealogical research center. Museum Tuesday-Friday; Library Wednesday-Saturday.

LEON

RESTAURANTS

★★★The Grille at Prince Michel

154 Winery Lane, Leon,
540-547-9720, 800-800-9463;
www.princemichel.com

Meals are served on gold-rimmed china in a refined setting to create a romantic dining experience.

St. Mary's Whitechapel Church

5940 White Chapel Rd., Warsaw,
804-462-5908

(1740-1741) Church where Mary Ball and her family worshiped; many of the tombstones bear the Ball name.

SPECIALTY LODGINGS

Inn at Levelfield

10155 Mary Ball Rd., Lancaster,
804-435-6887, 800-238-5578;
www.innatlevelefields.com

This 1857 antebellum landmark homestead is situated on 54 acres, with 12 acres of lawn and 42 acres of timberland. The building features a double-tiered portico and four massive chimneys, as well as a 1,000-foot driveway.

6 rooms. Complimentary full breakfast. **$**

American menu. Lunch, dinner, brunch. Closed Monday-Wednesday. Children's menu. Business casual attire. Reservations recommended. Outdoor seating. **$$**

LEESBURG

Originally named Georgetown for King George II of England, this town was later renamed Leesburg, probably after Francis Lightfoot Lee, a signer of the Declaration of Independence and a local landowner. Leesburg is located in a scenic area of rolling hills, picturesque rural towns and thoroughbred horse farms, where point-to-point racing and steeplechases are popular.

Information: Loudoun County Visitors Center, 222 Catocin Circle, S.E., Leesburg, 703-771-2170, 800-752-6118; www.visitloudoun.org

WHAT TO SEE AND DO

Ball's Bluff Battlefield

Ball Bluff Rd., Leesburg,
703-737-7800;
www.nvrpa.org/parks/ballsbluff/

One of the smallest national cemeteries in the U.S. marks site of the third armed engagement of the Civil War. On October 21, 1861, four Union regiments suffered catastrophic losses while surrounded by Confederate forces; the Union commander, a U.S. senator and presidential confidant,

was killed here along with half his troops, while attempting to recross the Potomac River. Oliver Wendell Holmes, Jr., later to become a U.S. Supreme Court justice, was wounded here.

Loudoun Museum

16 Loudoun St. S.W., Leesburg,
703-777-7427;
www.loudounmuseum.org

Century-old restored building contains exhibits and memorabilia of the area; audiovisual presentation "A Special Look at Loudoun." Brochures, information about Loudoun County; walking tours; self-guided tour booklets (fee). Daily; closed January.

Morven Park
17263 Southern Planter Lane, Leesburg, 703-777-2414;
www.morvenpark.org
Originally the residence of Thomas Swann, early Maryland governor, the estate was enlarged upon by Westmoreland Davis, governor of Virginia from 1918 to 1922. The 1,200-acre park includes a 28-room mansion, boxwood gardens, Winmill Carriage Museum with more than 70 horse-drawn vehicles, Museum of Hounds and Hunting with video presentation and artifacts depicting the history of fox hunting, and Morven Park International Equestrian Center. April-November: Friday-Monday afternoons.

Oatlands
20850 Oatlands Plantation Lane, Leesburg, 703-777-3174;
www.oatlands.org
(1803) A 261-acre estate; Classical Revival mansion, built by George Carter, was the center of a 5,000-acre plantation; house was partially remodeled in 1827, which was when the front portico was added. Most of the building materials, including bricks and wood, came from or were made on the estate. Interior furnished with American, English and French antiques; reflects period between 1897 and 1965 when the house was owned by Mr. and Mrs. William Corcoran Eustis, prominent Washingtonians. Formal garden has some of the finest boxwood in U.S. Farm fields provide equestrian area for races and horse shows. April-December: daily.

Vineyard and Winery Tours
Leesburg,
800-752-6118

Waterford
Leesburg,
703-771-2170
Eighteenth-century Quaker village, designated a National Historic Landmark, has been restored as a residential community. An annual homes tour (first full weekend in October) has craft demonstrations, exhibits, traditional music. Waterford Foundation has brochures outlining self-guided walking tours.

SPECIAL EVENTS

August Court Days
108 South St. S.E., Leesburg,
703-777-2420
Reenactment of the opening of the 18th-century judicial court. Festivities resemble a country fair with craft demonstrations, games, entertainers on the street. Third weekend in August.

Christmas at Oatlands
20850 Oatlands Plantation Lane, Leesburg,
www.oatlands.org
Candlelight tours, 1800s decorations, refreshments. Mid-November-December: Saturday evenings.

Homes and Gardens Tour
703-777-2420
Sponsored by Garden Club of Virginia. Mid-late April.

Loudoun Hunt Pony Club Horse Trials
Morven Park International Equestrian Institute, 4173 Tutt Lane, Leesburg, 703-777-2890;
www.morvenpark.org/equine
Competition in combined training: dressage, cross-country and stadium jumping. Late March.

Sheep Dog Trials
Oatlands, 20850 Oatlands Plantation Lane, Leesburg
May.

Wine Festival
Morven Park, 17263 Southern Planter Lane, Leesburg,
703-823-1868, 866-877-3343;
www.virginiawinefestival.org
Many wineries participate; includes seminar for home/commercial wine growers; grape-stomping, waiters' race, jousting tournament, music, wine tastings, awards presentations. September.

338

VIRGINIA

HOTELS

★Days Inn
721 E. Market St., Leesburg,
703-777-6622, 800-329-7466;
www.daysinn.com
81 rooms. Complimentary continental breakfast. **$**

★★Holiday Inn
1500 E. Market St., Leesburg,
703-771-9200, 800-282-0244;
www.holidayinn.com
126 rooms. Airport transportation available.
Colonial mansion (1773). **$**

★★★Lansdowne Resort
44050 Woodridge Pkwy., Leesburg,
703-729-8400, 877-509-8400;
www.lansdowneresort.com
The stylishly streamlined Lansdowne Resort, which comprises a nine-story tower and two five-story wings, recently underwent a $55 million renovation. Guest rooms are reminiscent of a country manor, elegant but casual, with lush woodland views.
305 rooms. Children's activity center. Airport transportation available. **$$**

★★★Leesburg Colonial Inn
19 S. King St., Leesburg,
703-777-5000, 800-392-1332;
www.leesburgcolonialinn.com
Bordered by the majestic Blue Ridge Mountains and the Potomac River, this circa 1830 inn is located in the heart of historic Leesburg (just 25 miles from Washington, D.C.). The inn is decorated in 18th-century American style. Each guest room features individual climate controls, cable television,
antique poster beds, hardwood floors, fine rugs and period pieces. Some rooms also have whirlpool tubs and fireplaces. A full gourmet breakfast is offered each morning in the dining room.
10 rooms. Complimentary full breakfast. Restaurant. Airport transportation available. **$**

SPECIALTY LODGINGS

Norris House Inn
108 Loudoun St. S.W., Leesburg,
703-777-1806, 800-644-1806;
www.norrishouse.com
Located in the historic district of Leesburg, this rambling colonial house dates from 1760. Filled with antiques and plenty of charm, both the common rooms and guest rooms are comfortable and relaxing. The Stone House Tea Room serves an elegant afternoon tea.
6 rooms. Complimentary full breakfast. Airport transportation available. **$**

RESTAURANTS

★★Green Tree
15 S. King St., Leesburg,
703-777-7246
Lunch, dinner, Sunday brunch. Authentic 18th-century recipes. Windows open to street. **$$**

★★Leesburg Colonial Inn
19 S. King St.,
Leesburg,
703-777-5000;
www.leesburgcolonialinn.com
American menu. Lunch, dinner. Bar. Children's menu. Outdoor seating. **$$**

★

★

★

★

★

LEXINGTON

Lexington was home to two of the greatest Confederate heroes: Robert E. Lee and Thomas J. "Stonewall" Jackson. Both are buried here. Sam Houston, Cyrus McCormick and James Gibbs (inventor of the sewing machine) were born nearby.

Set in rolling country between the Blue Ridge and Allegheny mountains, this town is the seat of Rockbridge County. Lexington is known for attractive homes, trim farms, fine old mansions and two of the leading educational institutions in the Commonwealth: Washington and Lee University and Virginia Military Institute.

Information: Visitors Bureau, 106 E. Washington St., Lexington,
540-463-3777, 877-453-9822; www.lexingtonvirginia.com

WHAT TO SEE AND DO
Goshen Pass
Scenic mountain gorge formed by Maury River. Memorial to Matthew Fontaine Maury is here.

Lexington Carriage Company
106 E. Washington St., Lexington,
540-463-5647;
www.lexcarriage.com
Approximately 45-minute narrated horse-drawn carriage tours of historic Lexington. Groups of 10 or more by appointment only. April-October: daily, weather permitting. Tours depart across street from Visitor Center.

Stonewall Jackson House
8 E. Washington St., Lexington,
540-463-2552;
www.stonewalljackson.org
Only home owned by Confederate General Stonewall Jackson, restored to its appearance of 1859-1861. Many of the furnishings were once owned by Jackson. Interpretive slide presentation and guided tours (1/2 hour). Restored gardens; shop. Daily.

Stonewall Jackson Memorial Cemetery
White and Main Streets, Lexington
General Jackson and more than 100 other Confederate soldiers are buried here.

★ Virginia Horse Center
487 Maury River Rd., Lexington,
540-464-2950;
www.horsecenter.org
Sprawling across nearly 400 acres, the Center provides a versatile site for numerous horse-related functions year-round: shows, clinics, auctions, festivals. Fees vary.

Virginia Military Institute
Letcher Ave., Lexington,
540-464-7207;
www.vmi.edu
(1839) (1,300 cadets.) State military, engineering, sciences and arts college. Coeducational since 1997. Stonewall Jackson taught here, as did Matthew Fontaine Maury, famed naval explorer and inventor. George Catlett Marshall, a general of the army and author of the Marshall Plan, was a graduate. Mementos of these men on display in VMI museum (daily). Dress parade (most Friday afternoons, weather permitting).

Located on the south end of the parade ground is:

George C. Marshall Museum
VMI Parade Ground, Lexington,
540-463-7103;
www.marshallfoundation.org
(1964) Displays on life and career of the illustrious military figure and statesman (1880-1959); World War I electric map and recorded narration of World War II; Marshall Plan; gold medallion awarded with his Nobel Prize for Peace (1953). Daily.

Washington and Lee University
W. Washington St., Lexington,
540-463-8400;
www.wlu.edu
(1749) (2,137 students.) Liberal arts university situated on an attractive campus with white colonnaded buildings; also includes Washington and Lee Law School. Founded as Augusta Academy in 1749; became Liberty Hall in 1776; name changed to Washington Academy in 1798 after receiving 200 shares of James River Canal Company stock from George Washington, and then to Washington College. General Robert E. Lee served as president from 1865-1870; soon after Lee's death in 1870 it became Washington and Lee University.

On campus is:

Lee Chapel
540-458-8768
Robert E. Lee is entombed here. Also houses Lee family crypt and museum, marble "recumbent statue" of Lee, portions of art collection of Washington and Lee families. Lee's office remains as he left it. Daily.

SPECIAL EVENTS
Garden Week in Historic Lexington
106 E. Washington St., Lexington,
804-644-7776;
www.vagardenweek.org

340

VIRGINIA

Tour of homes and gardens in the Lexington, Rockbridge County area. Mid-late April.

Holiday in Lexington
Lexington, 540-463-3777
Parade, plays, children's events. Early December.

Lime Kiln Arts Theater
14 S. Randolph St., Lexington,
540-463-7088;
www.theatreatlimekiln.com
Professional theatrical productions and concerts in outdoor theater. Memorial Day-Labor Day.

HOTELS
★★Best Western Inn At Hunt Ridge
25 Willow Springs Rd., Lexington,
540-464-1500, 800-780-7234;
www.bestwestern.com
100 rooms. $

★Comfort Inn Virginia Horse Center
62 Comfort Way, Lexington,
540-463-7311, 877-424-6423;
www.choicehotels.com

80 rooms. Complimentary continental breakfast. $

★Holiday Inn Express
850 N. Lee Hwy., Lexington,
540-463-7351, 800-282-0244;
www.holidayinnexpress.com
72 rooms. Complimentary continental breakfast. View of mountains. $

★★Maple Hall Country Inn
3111 N. Lee Hwy., Lexington,
540-463-6693, 877-463-2044;
www.lexingtonhistoricinns.com
21 rooms. Complimentary continental breakfast. $

RESTAURANTS
★Redwood
898 N. Lee Hwy., Lexington,
540-463-2168
American menu. Breakfast, lunch, dinner, brunch. Children's menu. $

LORTON

WHAT TO SEE AND DO
Gunston Hall
10709 Gunston Rd.,
Mason Neck,
703-550-9220;
www.gunstonhall.org
(1755-1759) The 550-acre estate of George Mason, framer of the Constitution and father of the Bill of Rights. Restored 18th-century mansion with period furnishings; reconstructed outbuildings; boxwood gardens on grounds; nature trail. Picnic area, gift shop. Daily.

Pohick Bay Regional Park
6501 Pohick Bay Dr., Lorton,
703-339-6104;
www.nvrpa.org/parks/pohickbay

Activities in this 1,000-acre park include swimming (Memorial Day-Labor Day), boating (ramp, rentals, fee); 18-hole golf, miniature and Fridaysbee golf, camping (7-day limit; electric hookups available; fee), picnicking. Park (all year). Fee charged for activities.

Pohick Episcopal Church
9301 Richmond Hwy.,
Lorton,
703-339-6572;
www.pohick.org
(1774) The colonial parish church of Mount Vernon and Gunston Hall. Built under the supervision of George Mason and George Washington; original walls; interior fully restored. Daily.

★
★
★
★
★

LURAY

This town's name is of French origin, and its fame comes from the caverns discovered here in 1878. Situated at the junction of Highways 211 and 340, Luray is nine miles away from, and within sight of, Shenandoah National Park and Skyline Drive. Park headquarters are located here. There are three developed recreation areas north and west of town in Washington and Jefferson national forests.

Information: Page County Chamber of Commerce, 46 E. Main St., Luray, 540-743-3915, 888-743-3915; www.luraypage.com

WHAT TO SEE AND DO

Luray Caverns
970 Hwy. 211/340 W., Luray,
540-743-6551;
www.luraycaverns.org

One of the largest caverns in the East. Huge underground rooms (one is 300-feet wide, 500-feet long, with a 140-foot ceiling) connected by natural corridors and paved walkways are encrusted with colorful rock formations, some delicate as lace, others massive. In one chamber is the world's only "stalacpipe" organ, which produces music of symphonic quality from stone formations. Indirect lighting permits taking of color photos within caverns. Temperature is 54 F. One-hour guided tours start about every 20 minutes. Daily.

Fee includes:

Car and Carriage Museum
Exhibits include 140 restored antique cars, carriages and coaches featuring history of transportation from 1625.

Luray Singing Tower
970 Hwy. 211/340 W., Luray,
540-743-6551

Houses 47-bell carillon; largest bell weighs 7,640 pounds. Features 45-minute recitals by celebrated carillonneur. June-August: Tuesday, Thursday and Sunday evenings; March-May and September-October: weekend afternoons. In park adjacent to caverns.

Luray Zoo
1087 Hwy. 211 W., Luray,
540-743-4113; www.lurayzoo.com

Features large reptile collection, exotic animals and tropical birds; petting zoo; live animal shows; life-sized dinosaur reproductions. Gift shop. Mid-April-October: daily.

Massanutten One-room School
Restored and furnished as it was in the 1800s. Period displays and pictures. By appointment.

SPECIAL EVENTS

Mayfest Street Festival
46 E. Main St., Luray
Entertainment, crafts. Third Saturday in May.

Page County Heritage Festival
Arts and crafts exhibits. Self-guided tour of churches and old homes. Columbus Day weekend.

HOTELS

★★Big Meadows Lodge
Skyline Dr., Mile 51, Luray,
540-999-2221, 800-999-4714;
www.visitshenandaoh.com

97 rooms. Closed December-mid-May. Children's activity center. Panoramic view of Shenandoah Valley. $

★★Days Inn
138 Whispering Hill Rd.,
Luray, 540-743-4521, 800-329-7466;
www.daysinn-luray.com

100 rooms. $

★Luray Caverns Motel West
1001 Hwy. 211 E., Luray,
540-743-4531;
www.luraycaverns.com

20 rooms. Complimentary continental breakfast. Check-in 2-11 p.m. Views of Blue Ridge Mountains. $

★★Skyland Lodge
Skyline Dr., Luray,
540-999-2211, 800-999-4714

177 rooms. Closed December-March. $

SPECIALTY LODGINGS

Cabins at Brookside
2978 Hwy. 211 E., Luray,
540-743-5698, 800-299-2655;
www.brooksidecabins.com
This vacation development located 4 1/2 miles from the entrance to Skyline Drive offers the privacy and seclusion of your own log cabin. The cabins have a plush country décor and front porches, and are set into the woods. A cozy restaurant on the property serves homestyle food.
9 rooms. **$**

Mayneview Bed and Breakfast
439 Mechanic St., Luray,
540-743-7921;
www.mayneview.com
This lovely inn sits in the heart of the Shenandoah Valley and has a wonderful wraparound porch. Visitors can take day trips to the famous Luray Caverns, the New Market Battlefield and several antique shops.
5 rooms. Complimentary full breakfast. Victorian building (1865). **$**

Woodruff House Bed and Breakfast
330 Mechanic St., Luray,
540-743-1494, 866-937-3466;
www.woodruffinns.com
Three 1800s Victorian houses make up this bed-and-breakfast located near many local attractions including the Shenandoah National Park, Luray Caverns and the George Washington National Forest.
10 rooms. Complimentary full breakfast. **$$$**

RESTAURANTS

★Brookside
2978 Hwy. 211 E., Luray,
540-743-5698, 800-299-2655;
www.brooksidecabins.com
American menu. Lunch, dinner, brunch. Closed four weeks in December. Children's menu. Casual attire. **$**

★Parkhurst
2547 Hwy. 211 W., Luray,
540-743-6009
American menu. Lunch, dinner. Casual attire. Outdoor seating. **$**

343

LYNCHBURG

Lynchburg is perched on hills overlooking the James River, which was for many years the city's means of growth. Today, Lynchburg is home to more than 3,000 businesses and diversified industries. Educational institutions located here include Lynchburg College, Randolph-Macon Women's College and Liberty University.

One of the first buildings in the town was a ferry house built by John Lynch. The same enterprising young man later built a tobacco warehouse, probably the first one in the country. During the Civil War, Lynchburg was

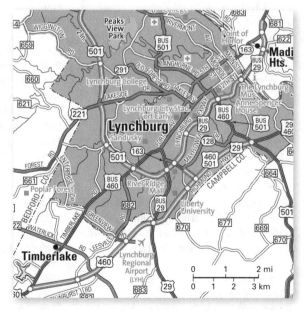

important as a supply base and hospital town. In June 1864, General Jubal A. Early successfully defended the town from an attack by Union forces. More than 2,200

Confederates are buried in the Confederate Cemetery, located within the Old City Cemetery.

Information: Visitors Information Center, 12th and Church Streets, Lynchburg, 434-522-9592, 800-732-5821; www.lynchburgchamber.org

WHAT TO SEE AND DO

Anne Spencer House
1313 Pierce St., Lynchburg,
434-845-1313
House of noted poet, only black woman and only Virginian to be included in the "Norton Anthology of Modern American and British Poetry." On grounds is Spencer's writing cottage "Edan Kraal." Many dignitaries have visited here. Museum with artifacts, memorabilia, period antique furnishings; formal garden. House by appointment; gardens daily.

Blackwater Creek Natural Area
Ruskin Freer Nature Preserve (115 acres) includes trails with plants; athletic area; bikeway winds past wildflower area and historical sites, ending downtown; Creekside Trunk Trail, natural grass trail with typical Piedmont species of plants, moist ravines, north-facing rocky bluffs. Daily.

Fort Early
Memorial and Fort avenues, Lynchburg
Defense earthwork for Lynchburg's closest battle during the Civil War. Confederates under General Jubal A. Early turned back forces under General David Hunter in 1864. Daily.

Old Court House Museum
901 Court St., Lynchburg,
434-455-6226;
www.lynchburgmuseum.org
(1855) Restored to original Greek Revival appearance. Three galleries have exhibits on early history of the area, highlighting Quaker settlement and role of tobacco; restored mid-19th-century courtroom. Daily.

Pest House Medical Museum
Old City Cemetery,
Fourth and Taylor Streets, Lynchburg,
434-847-1465
The 1840s white frame medical office of Quaker physician Dr. John Jay Terrell has been joined with Pest House quarantine hospital to typify the standard of medicine during the late 1800s. Original medical instruments include operating table, hypodermic needle, clinical thermometer and chloroform mask. Period furnishings on one side duplicate Dr. Terrell's office during the Civil War; other side represents quarantine hospital for Confederate soldiers in which Dr. Terrell volunteered to assume responsibility. Window displays with audio description. Tours (by appointment). Daily.

Point of Honor
112 Cabell St., Lynchburg,
434-455-6226;
www.pointofhonor.org
(1815) Restored mansion on Daniel's Hill above the James River, built by Dr. George Cabell, Sr., physician to Patrick Henry. Federalist style with octagon bay facade and finely crafted interior woodwork; period furnishings; gardens and grounds being restored. Daily.

Randolph-Macon Women's College
2500 Rivermont Ave., Lynchburg,
434-947-8000;
www.rmwc.edu
(1891) (748 women.) A 100-acre campus on historic Rivermont Ave near James River. First college for women in the South granted a Phi Beta Kappa chapter. Campus is interesting mixture of architecture including Vincent Kling design for Houston Chapel. Tours (by appointment).

On campus is:

Maier Museum of Art
2500 Rivermont Ave., Lynchburg,
434-947-8136
Collection is representative of 19th- and 20th-century American painting. Artists include Thomas Hart Benton, Edward Hicks, Winslow Homer, James McNeil Whistler, Mary Cassatt and Georgia

O'Keeffe. Changing exhibits. Academic year: Tuesday-Sunday afternoons.

Riverside Park
2270 Rivermont Ave., Lynchburg
Daily.
In park is:

Packet Boat "Marshall"
Mounted on a stone base, the boat carried the remains of Stonewall Jackson home to Lexington; for many years packets were the principal mode of transportation along the James River and Kanawha Canal.

South River Meeting House
5810 Fort Ave., Lynchburg,
434-239-2548
Completed in 1798, the stone building remained the site of Quaker worship and activity until the 1840s. John Lynch, founder of Lynchburg, and other early leaders of community are buried in adjacent historic cemetery. Daily.

HOTELS
★★Holiday Inn
601 Main St., Lynchburg,
434-528-2500, 800-282-0244;
www.hiselect.com/lynchburgva
241 rooms. Airport transportation available.
$

★Holiday Inn Express
5600 Seminole Ave., Lynchburg,
434-237-7771, 800-282-0244;
www.hiexpress.com
103 rooms. Complimentary continental breakfast. Airport transportation available. $

★★★Radisson Hotel Lynchburg
2900 Candler's Mountain Rd.,
Lynchburg,
434-237-6333, 800-333-3333;
www.radisson.com
Located at the foot of the Blue Ridge Mountains, this hotel sits on a unique, 10-acre, landscaped and wooded spread. The Natural Bridge, one of the seven natural wonders of the world, is easily accessible.
168 rooms. Airport transportation available.
$

RESTAURANTS
★★Crown Sterling
6120 Fort Ave.,
Lynchburg,
434-239-7744;
www.thecrownsterling.com
Steak menu. Dinner. Closed Sunday-Monday. Bar. Children's menu. Business casual attire. Reservations recommended. $$$

★★★Sachiko's Porterhouse
126 Old Graves Mill Rd.,
Lynchburg,
434-237-5655
Sachiko's Poerterhouse has been in business for 25 years, serving beef, lamb, chicken and seafood dishes, as well as pastries fresh from their in-house bakery.
American menu. Dinner. Closed Sunday; three weeks in January. Bar. Business casual attire. Reservations recommended. $$

★

★

★

★

★

MANASSAS
The Native Americans who had occupied this area for thousands of years were driven out under a treaty in 1722. Afterwards, settlement remained concentrated along the Potomac River until the coming of the railroad in 1858. The Manassas rail junction was vital to the South, and many troops were stationed along this line of communication. Control of this junction led to two major battles nearby.
Information: Prince William County/Manassas Conference & Visitors Bureau, 9431 West St., Manassas, 703-361-6599, 800-432-1792; www.visitpwc.com

NORTHERN VIRGINIA WINE COUNTRY

Virginia is home to more than 60 wineries, many of which produce award-winning vintages. Even California, home to some of America's most notable wines, cannot match everything done here: Several of Virginia's winemakers are producing new and different wines from grapes not yet grown on the West Coast.

In recent years, wine-tasting has become an inviting pastime for weekenders. Fortunately, many of the wineries are clustered conveniently to make a visit to three or four in half a day quite practical, though many visitors combine a sampling tour with a stay in a country inn that serves Virginia wines.

Part of the fun of visiting Virginia's wineries is that they tend to be located in out-of-the-way corners of the countryside. To get to them, drivers must negotiate winding back roads over which they might not otherwise travel. This one-day, 150-mile tour from Fairfax County (a Washington, D.C., suburb) traverses the scenic foothills of the Blue Ridge Mountains. Here and there it edges Shenandoah National Park, where a detour of a few miles will take you to one of the lofty overlooks along Skyline Drive, the famed ridge-top parkway. Begin the tour on I-66 West just north of Fairfax City. Near Manassas, stop at the Visitor Information Center to pick up the latest edition of Virginia Wineries Festival and Tour Guide. It lists the operating hours of the tasting rooms, many of which are open daily, some only on weekends. If Civil War history interests you, stop briefly at Manassas National Battlefield Park, which commemorates the first major clash between the North and South.

At Gainesville, head south on Highway 29 past Culpeper to the village of Leon; the Prince Michel Vineyards will be on the right. Begin your visit with a self-guided tour of the wine-making facility. This French-owned facility produces a very nice Chardonnay. Its gourmet restaurant, serving lunch and dinner, overlooks acres of vineyards draped across rolling hills. From St. Michel, continue south on Highway 29 to Madison, and turn right onto State Route 231 North. For about 20 miles, this stretch of the road is a Virginia Scenic Byway. On your left, the high, forested ridge rising overhead is Shenandoah National Park. On both sides of the road, stately plantation homes carry descriptive names. Just south of Sperryville, pick up Highway 522 North. In Sperryville, browse the sprawling Sperryville Antiques Market. Continue north on Highway 522 toward Front Royal, turning right at Route 635. For about a mile, the road glides beneath towering tree; Oasis Winery is on the right, best known for its sparkling wines. After your visit, return to Highway 522 and continue north to Front Royal. Head east (right) on Route 55 to Linden. Turn right onto Route 638 and proceed two miles to Linden. Perched atop a small hill, its outdoor deck offers gorgeous Blue Ridge views. Linden is one of Virginia's finest wineries, and one of the prettiest. Linden's Seyval, a dry white wine, is popular with wine fanciers looking for something new. Return to Route 55 and turn west (left) one mile to the entrance to I-66. Take I-66 east back to Fairfax. Approximately 150 miles.

WHAT TO SEE AND DO

The Manassas Museum
9101 Prince William St., Manassas,
703-368-1873

Museum features collections dealing with Northern Virginia Piedmont history from prehistoric to modern times, with special emphasis on Civil War. Tuesday-Sunday.

SPECIAL EVENTS

Prince William County Fair

9101 Prince William St., Manassas,
703-368-0173;
www.pwcfair.com
Carnival, entertainment, tractor pull, exhibits, contests. Mid-August.

HOTELS

★★Hotel Manassas

10800 Vandor Lane, Manassas,
703-335-0000
158 rooms. Complimentary continental breakfast. Restaurant, bar. Near Manassas (Bull Run) Battlefield. $

RESTAURANTS

★★★Carmello's and Little Portugal

9108 Center St., Manassas,
703-368-5522;
www.carmellos.com
At Carmello's and Little Portugal, Italian and Portuguese cuisine are beautifully combined to create generous contemporary dishes. The restaurant's intimate atmosphere makes it a popular spot for special occasions.
Italian, Spanish menu. Lunch, dinner. Bar. $$

★★Jake's

9412 Main St., Manassas,
703-330-1534;
www.jakesofmanassas.com
American menu. Lunch, dinner. Bar. Outdoor seating. Closed Mondays. $$

★★★Panino

9116 Mathis Ave., Manassas,
703-335-2566
Although off the beaten path, this chef-owned and-operated restaurant has for the past decade offered perhaps the best regional Italian cuisine outside the Beltway. Only the freshest of ingredients are used. Italian menu. Lunch, dinner. Closed Sunday. Reservations recommended. $$

MANASSAS (BULL RUN) NATIONAL BATTLEFIELD PARK

This 5,000-acre park was the scene of two major Civil War battles. More than 26,000 men were killed or wounded here in struggles for control of a strategically important railroad junction. The war's first major land battle was fought here on July 21, 1861, between poorly trained volunteer troops from both the North and South. The battle finally evolved into a struggle for Henry Hill, where "Stonewall" Jackson earned his nickname. With the outcome in doubt, Confederate reinforcements arrived by railroad from the Shenandoah Valley and turned the battle into a rout.

Thirteen months later (August 28-30, 1862), in the second battle of Manassas, General Robert E. Lee outmaneuvered and defeated Union General John Pope and cleared the way for a Confederate invasion of Maryland. Daily.
Information: US 29 and Highway 234, Manassas, 703-361-1339; www.nps.gov/mana

WHAT TO SEE AND DO

Chinn House Ruins

6511 Sudley Rd.,
Manassas (Bull Run)
National Battlefield Park
The house served as a field hospital in both engagements and marked the left of the Confederate line at First Manassas; also the scene of Longstreet's counterattack at Second Manassas.

Dogan House

6511 Sudley Rd., Manassas (Bull Run)
National Battlefield Park,
An original structure at Groveton, a village around which the battle of Second Manassas was fought.

Stone Bridge

6511 Sudley Rd., Manassas (Bull Run)
National Battlefield Park,

Where Union artillery opened the Battle of First Manassas; it afforded an avenue of escape for the Union troops after both First and Second Manassas.

Stone House
6511 Sudley Rd.,
Manassas (Bull Run)
National Battlefield Park,
703-361-1339
Originally a tavern (circa 1848), used as field hospital in both battles. Summer: daily.

Unfinished Railroad
6511 Sudley Rd.,
Manassas (Bull Run)
National Battlefield Park
Fully graded railroad bed, never completed, behind which Stonewall Jackson's men were positioned during the second battle.

Visitor Center
6511 Sudley Rd.,
Manassas (Bull Run)
National Battlefield Park,
703-361-1339;
www.nps.gov/mana
Hill affords view of much of the first battlefield. Information; self-guided tours start here (walking tour of First Manassas, directions for driving tour of Second Manassas). Markers throughout park explain various aspects of battles. Ranger-conducted tours (summer).

In the same building is:

Battlefield Museum
6511 Sudley Rd., Manassas (Bull Run)
National Battlefield Park
Exhibits reflect incidents of battles; audiovisual presentations offer orientation. Daily.

MARION

This popular vacation spot is surrounded by the George Washington and Jefferson national forests, abounding in game and birds and high enough to promise an invigorating climate. The seat of Smyth County, it was named for General Francis Marion, known during the American Revolution as the "Swamp Fox."

Information: Smyth County Chamber of Commerce, 214 W. Main St., Marion, 276-783-3161; www.smythchamber.org

WHAT TO SEE AND DO
Mount Rogers National Recreation Area
3714 Hwy. 16,
Marion,
276-783-5196
A 140,000-acre area includes Mount Rogers, the state's highest point (5,729 feet), mile-high open meadows known as "balds," and a great variety of animals and plants. Swimming, fishing; hunting, camping (fee at some areas), four visitor centers, approximately 400 miles of hiking, bicycle and bridle trails. Mount Rogers Scenic Byway (auto); Virginia Creeper Trail (hikers, bicycles, horses) follows an abandoned railroad grade through spectacular river gorges. Adjacent to New River Trails State Park. Visitor Center (daily all year). Mid-May-Mid-September: daily; rest of year: Monday-Friday. Some fees.

Hungry Mother State Park
2854 Park Blvd., Marion,
276-781-7400
More than 2,180 acres amid the mountains with a 108-acre lake; panoramic views. Swimming beach, bathhouse, fishing, boating (rentals, launching, electric motors only); hiking, self-guided trails, picnicking, restaurant, concession, tent and trailer sites (electrical hookups, late March-December), cabins (year round). Hilltop visitor center, interpretive programs.

SPECIAL EVENTS
Chilhowie Apple Festival
Mid-September.

Hungry Mother Arts and Crafts Festival
Hungry Mother State Park,
2854 Park Blvd., Marion
Mid-July.

Whitetop Ramp Festival
Mid-May.

HOTELS
★★**Econo Lodge Marion**
1424 N. Main St., Marion,
276-783-6031, 877-424-6423;
www.choicehotels.com
79 rooms. Complimentary continental breakfast. **$**

MARTINSVILLE
Martinsville was named for Joseph Martin, a pioneer who settled here in 1773. Henry County takes its name from Patrick Henry, who lived here. When Henry County Court first opened in October 1776, 640 residents pledged an oath of allegiance to the United States; 40 refused to renounce allegiance to England. Located near the beautiful Blue Ridge Mountains, this community is home to Bassett Furniture and E. I. du Pont de Nemours.
Information: Martinsville-Henry County Chamber of Commerce, 115 Broad St., Martinsville, 276-632-6401; www.martinsville.com

WHAT TO SEE AND DO
Philpott Lake
1058 Philpott Lake Rd.,
Martinsville,
276-629-2703
State's fourth-largest lake, formed by Philpott Dam, a U.S. Army Corps of Engineers project. Swimming, skin diving, waterskiing, boating, fishing; hunting, hiking, picnicking; four camping areas (April-October), one area free, some fees.

Virginia Museum of Natural History
21 Starling Ave.,
Martinsville,
276-634-4141;
www.vmnh.net
Younger kids will appreciate this small museum, housed in an old school. They'll enjoy exhibits featuring wild animals, butterflies, nature and science, along with a model of a giant sloth and a computer-activated, car-sized Triceratops. Monday-Saturday 10 a.m.-5 p.m., Sunday 1-5 p.m.

SPECIAL EVENTS
Blue Ridge Folklife Festival
Blue Ridge Farm Museum, Hwy. 40,
Martinsville, 540-365-4415
Gospel, blues and string band music; traditional regional crafts; quilt show, antique autos, steam and gas-powered farm equipment, regional foods. Sports events include horse-pulling and log-skidding contests, coon dog swimming and treeing contests. Late October.

Stock Car Races
Martinsville Speedway, Martinsville,
540-956-3151, 877-722-3849
Miller Genuine Draft 300, mid-March. Hanes 500, late April. Goody's 500, late September. Taco Bell 300, mid-October.

HOTELS
★★**Best Western Martinsville Inn**
1755 Virginia Ave., Martinsville,
276-632-5611, 800-780-7234;
www.bestwestern.com
97 rooms. **$**

349

VIRGINIA

MCLEAN
Information: Fairfax County Convention & Visitors Bureau, 1961 Chain Bridge Rd., Tyson's Corner, 703-752-9500, 800-732-4732; www.visitfairfax.org

WHAT TO SEE AND DO

Claude Moore Colonial Farm

6310 Georgetown Pike, McLean,
703-442-7557;
www.1771.org
Demonstration of 1770s low-income working farm; costumed interpreters work with crops and animals using 18th-century techniques. April-mid-December: Wednesday-Sunday weather permitting.

Great Falls Park

George Washington Memorial Pkwy.,
McLean,
703-285-2965;
www.nps.gov/grfa
Spectacular natural beauty is only 15 miles from the nation's capital at Great Falls Park, where the usually peaceful Potomac River narrows into a series of dramatically cascading rapids and 20-foot waterfalls before heading through Mather Gorge. Enjoy the view from a scenic overlook, and then explore some of the park's 15 miles of trails, which take you past the remains of the Patowmack Canal, part of an 18th-century engineering project backed by George Washington, among others. Daily 7 a.m.-dark.

Tysons Corner Center

1961 Chain Bridge Rd., McLean,
703-893-9400, 888-289-7667;
www.shoptysons.com
More than 250 stores, including Norstrom, Bloomingdale's and L.L.Bean. Monday-Saturday 10 a.m.-9:30 p.m., Sunday 11 a.m.-6 p.m.

HOTELS

★★Crowne Plaza

1960 Chain Bridge Rd., McLean,
703-893-2100, 877-424-4225;
www.crowneplaza.com
316 rooms. Airport transportation available. $$

★★★Hilton McLean Tysons Corner

7920 Jones Branch Dr., McLean,
703-847-5000, 800-445-8667;
www.mclean.hilton.com
Located close to the famous shopping area of Tyson Corners, this atrium-style hotel offers comfortable rooms, local shuttle service, a gift shop and live jazz Thursday through Saturday evenings. 458 rooms. $$

★★★★The Ritz-Carlton, Tysons Corner

1700 Tysons Blvd., McLean,
703-506-4300, 800-241-3333;
www.ritzcarlton.com
Only 15 miles from Washington, D.C., this northern Virginia hotel is a luxurious retreat from the bustle of the city center. Guest rooms feature luxurious fabrics, flat-screen televisions and down duvet-covered beds. The Ritz-Carlton Day Spa offers unique treatments such as coffee anti-cellulite wrap or the bamboo lemongrass body scrub. The adjacent Tysons Galleria and Tysons Mall have more than 320 shops and a movie theater. 398 rooms. Pets accepted, restrictions. Check-in 3 p.m., check-out noon. High-speed Internet access. Two restaurants, bar. Fitness room, spa. Indoor pool, whirlpool. $$$$

RESTAURANTS

★★Cafe Oggi

6671 Old Dominion Dr.,
McLean,
434-442-7360
Italian menu. Lunch, dinner. Reservations recommended. $$

★★Cafe Taj

1379 Beverly Rd.,
McLean,
703-827-0444;
www.mycafetaj.com
Indian menu. Lunch, dinner. Bar. Outdoor seating. $$

★★Da Domenico

1992 Chain Bridge Rd.,
McLean,
703-790-9000;
www.da-domenico.com
Italian menu. Lunch, dinner. Closed Sunday. Bar. Reservations recommended. $$

350

VIRGINIA

★
★
★
★
★

★★J Gilbert's Steakhouse
6930 Old Dominion Dr., McLean,
703-893-1034;
www.jgilbert.com
Seafood, steak menu. Lunch, dinner, Sunday brunch. Bar. Children's menu. Outdoor seating. **$$**

★★J. R.'s Goodtimes
8130 Watson St., McLean,
703-893-3390;
www.jrsbeef.com
Seafood menu. Lunch, dinner. Bar. Reservations recommended. **$$**

★★Kazan
6813 Redmond Dr., McLean,
703-734-1960
Middle Eastern menu. Lunch, dinner. Closed Sunday. Children's menu. **$$**

★★Pulcinella
6852 Old Dominion Dr.,
McLean,
703-893-7777;
www.pulcinellarestaurant.com
Italian menu. Lunch, dinner. Bar. **$$**

★★Tachibana
6715 Lowell Ave.,
McLean,
703-847-1771;
www.j-netusa.com/com/tachibana
Japanese menu. Lunch, dinner. Circular dining room. **$$$**

MIDDLETOWN

SPECIAL EVENTS

Battle of Cedar Creek Reenactment
Belle Grove, 8437 Valley Pike, Middletown,
540-869-2064, 888-628-1864;
www.cedarcreekbattlefield.org
Mid-October.

East Coast Surfing Championship
757-557-6140, 800-861-7873;
www.surfecsc.com
Fourth weekend in August.

Learning Weekend
8437 Valley Pike, Middletown,
Colonial Williamsburg. Family-oriented weekend of discovery on a single topic. March.

Washington's Birthday Celebration
8437 Valley Pike, Middletown
President's Day weekend.

Wayside Theatre
7853 Main St., Middletown,
540-869-1776;
www.waysidetheatre.org
Professional performances. Wednesday-Sunday. Reservations required. Late May-mid-October and December.

HOTELS

★★★Wayside Inn
7783 Main St.,
Middletown,
540-869-1797, 877-869-1797;
www.alongthewayside.com
Operating since 1797, this inn is located in the Shenandoah Valley at the foot of the Massanutten Mountains. Canopied beds, English, French and Oriental antiques, brocades, chintzes and silks decorate the property. Fresh cuisine is prepared and served in seven different dining rooms.
22 rooms. Complimentary continental breakfast. **$**

RESTAURANTS

★★Wayside Inn
7783 E. Main St. (Highway 11),
Middletown,
540-869-1797;
www.alongthewayside.com
American menu. Breakfast, lunch, dinner. Closed Monday-Tuesday in January and February. Bar. Children's menu. Sunday brunch. Casual attire. Reservations recommended. Outdoor seating. **$$**

351

MIDLOTHIAN

WHAT TO SEE AND DO

Southside Speedway
12800 Genito Rd.,
Midlothian,
804-744-2700;
www.southside-speedway.com
If you need to see some short track action,
this 1/3-mile asphalt oval is the ticket with
Late Model Sportsman, Modified and
Grand Stock racing on Friday nights. Heat
races begin at 7 p.m. with the first feature at
8 p.m. Closed on NASCAR race weekends.

RESTAURANTS

★★★Ruth's Chris Steak House
11500 Huguenot Rd., Midlothian,
804-378-0600;
www.sizzlingsteak.com
Located in the historic Bellgrade Plantation
House, this restaurant offers fine dining
with elegant Southern hospitality. Dine on
the patio or in a private room with period
furnishings and enjoy Ruth's Chris classic
menu.
Steak menu. Dinner. Bar. Business casual
attire. Reservations recommended. Outdoor
seating. **$$$**

MONTEREY

Information: Highland County Chamber of Commerce, Monterey,
540-468-2550; www.highlandcounty.org

SPECIAL EVENTS

Highland County Maple Festival
Monterey,
540-468-2550
Tours of sugar camps producing maple
syrup and maple sugar products. Juried craft
show; food, entertainment. Mid-March.

HOTELS

★★★Highland Inn
68 W. Main St., Monterey,
540-468-2143, 888-466-4682;

www.highlandinn.com
Known for 75 years as the landmark Hotel
Monterey, the Highland Inn maintains
its traditional hospitality while offering
upgraded amenities in the 1904 building.
A detailed, double-decker porch graces the
inn's façade, complete with rocking chairs
from which guests can enjoy a view of the
peaceful street.
18 rooms. Victorian building furnished with
period antiques. Built in 1904. **$**

★
★
★
★
★

MONTPELIER

WHAT TO SEE AND DO

Montpelier
11407 Constitution Hwy., Montpelier
Station,
540-672-2728;
www.montpelier.org
The former residence of James Madison,
fourth president of the United States.
Madison was the third generation of his
family to live on this extensive plantation.
He inherited Montpelier and enlarged it
twice. After his presidency, he and Dolley
Madison retired to the estate, which
Mrs. Madison sold after the president's

death to pay off her son's gambling debts.
In 1901, the estate was bought by William
du Pont, who enlarged the house, added
many outbuildings, including a private
railroad station, built greenhouses and
planted gardens. Today, under the stew-
ardship of the National Trust for Historic
Preservation, a long-term research and
preservation project has begun. Self-
guided tours of the arboretum, nature trails
and formal garden. April-October: daily
9:30 a.m.-5:30 p.m.; November-March:
daily 9:30 a.m.-4:30 p.m.; closed first
Saturday in November.

MONTROSS

WHAT TO SEE AND DO
Stratford Hall Plantation
Hwy. 3 E. and Hwy. 214, Montross,
804-493-8038;
www.stratfordhall.org
Boyhood home of Richard Henry Lee and Francis Lightfoot Lee and birthplace of General Robert E. Lee. Center of restored, working plantation is monumental Georgian house built circa 1735, famous for its uniquely grouped chimney stacks. Interiors span approximately a 100-year period and feature a Federal-era parlor and neoclassical paneling in the Great Hall. Flanking dependencies include kitchen, plantation office and gardener's house. Boxwood garden; 18th- and 19th-century carriages; working mill; visitor center with museum, video presentations. Plantation luncheon. Daily.

Westmoreland State Park
1650 State Park Rd., Hwy. 347,
Montross,
804-493-8821
Approximately 1,300 acres on Potomac River. Sand beach, swimming pool, bathhouse, fishing, boating (ramp, rentals); hiking trails, picnicking, playground, concession, camping, tent and trailer sites (March-November; dump station, electrical hookups), cabins (March-December). Visitor center, evening programs. Standard fees.

MOUNT JACKSON

HOTELS
★★Super 8 Motel Mount Jackson
250 Conicville Blvd.,
Mount Jackson,
540-477-2911, 800-800-8000;
www.super8.com
92 rooms. $

SPECIALTY LODGING
Widow Kip's Country Inn
355 Orchard Dr., Mount Jackson,
540-477-2400, 800-478-8714;
www.widowkips.com
This restored 1830 Victorian home is set on seven acres of rural countryside with a view of the Shenandoah River and the valley.
7 rooms. Complimentary full breakfast. $

MOUNT VERNON

WHAT TO SEE AND DO
Gristmill
Mount Vernon,
703-780-2000
This mill was reconstructed in 1930 on the original foundation of a mill George Washington operated on the Dogue Run. Visitor center, programs. April-October: daily.

Mount Vernon
George Washington Pkwy., Mount Vernon,
703-780-2000;
www.mountvernon.org
Touring Mount Vernon, George Washington's home for more than 45 years, gives visitors a fascinating glimpse of the world of landed gentry in 18th-century America, as well as the personal vision of the first U.S. president. Washington designed sections of the beautifully landscaped grounds himself, incorporating woods, meadows and serpentine walkways. He also added the red-roofed mansion's cupola, weather vane and two-story piazza, from which guests may enjoy an awe-inspiring view of the Potomac River. Explore the working areas of the estate, including the wash house, stable and kitchen; an audio tour describes the lives of some of the more than 300 slaves who lived and worked there. The house has been restored to its 1799 appearance, the year Washington died. He is buried on the estate with his wife, Martha. Daily; hours vary by season.

353

VIRGINIA

Woodlawn Plantation
9000 Richmond Hwy., Mount Vernon,
703-780-4000;
www.woodlawn1805.org
(1800-1805) In 1799, George Washington gave 2,000 acres of land as a wedding present to Eleanor Parke Custis, his foster daughter, who married his nephew, Major Lawrence Lewis. Dr. William Thornton, first architect of the U.S. Capitol, then designed this mansion. The Lewises entertained such notables as Andrew Jackson, Henry Clay and the Marquis de Lafayette. The house was restored in the early 1900s and later became the residence of a U.S. senator; 19th-century period rooms; many original furnishings. Formal gardens. March-December: Tuesday-Sunday.

Also here is:

Frank Lloyd Wright's Pope-Leighey House
9000 Richmond Hwy., Mount Vernon,
703-780-4000;
www.nationaltrust.org/woodlawn

(1940) Erected in Falls Church in 1940, the house was disassembled (due to the construction of a new highway) and rebuilt at the present site in 1964. Built of cypress, brick and glass, the house is an example of Wright's "Usonian" structures, which he proposed as a prototype of affordable housing for Depression-era middle-income families; original Wright-designed furniture. March-December: Tuesday-Sunday. Combination ticket for both houses available.

RESTAURANTS
★★**Mount Vernon Inn**
On the grounds of Mount Vernon,
Mount Vernon,
703-780-0011;
www.themountvernoninn.com
Lunch, dinner. Bar. Children's menu. **$$**

★
★
★
★
★

NATURAL BRIDGE
Native Americans worshiped at the stone bridge nature formed across a deep gorge. The town and county were both named after it. The limestone arch, 215 feet high, 90 feet long and 150 feet wide in some places, attracted the interest of Thomas Jefferson, who purchased the bridge and 157 surrounding acres from King George III for 20 shillings, about $2.49, in 1774. Fully appreciative of this natural wonder, Jefferson built a cabin for visitors and installed caretakers. His guest book reads like a colonial "Who's Who." Surveyed by George Washington and painted by many famous artists, the bridge easily accommodates Highway 11. The Glenwood Ranger District of the Washington and Jefferson National Forests has its office in Natural Bridge.
Information: Natural Bridge of Virginia, Hwy. 11 and Hwy. 130, P.O. Box 57, Natural Bridge, 540-291-2121, 800-533-1410; www.naturalbridgeva.com

WHAT TO SEE AND DO
Cave Mountain Lake Recreation Area
Natural Bridge,
540-291-2189
Swimming; picnicking, camping (fee). May-October.

Natural Bridge
Hwys. 11 and 130,
Natural Bridge,
540-291-2121, 800-533-1410
Self-guided tours (one hour). Daily. Ticket includes entrance to:

"Drama of Creation"
Musical presentation, viewed from beneath Natural Bridge, includes light show cast under and across arch. Nightly.

Caverns of Natural Bridge
Hwy. 11 and I-81, Natural Bridge
More than 300 feet below ground on three levels; streams, hanging gardens of formations, flowstone cascade, totem pole, colossal dome and more. One-mile guided tour (one hour). March-November: daily; December-February: weekends.

Natural Bridge Wax Museum
70 Wert Faulkner Hwy.,
Natural Bridge
Wax figures depicting local history; self-guided factory tours. March-November: daily; December-February: weekends.

Natural Bridge Zoo
Hwy. 11, Natural Bridge,
540-291-2420;
www.naturalbridgezoo.com

State's largest and most complete zoo with over 400 reptiles, birds and mammals. Petting area; safari shop; picnic grounds. March-November: daily.

HOTELS
★★Natural Bridge Inn & Conference Center
Hwy. 11, Natural Bridge,
540-291-2121, 800-533-1410;
www.naturalbridgeva.com
180 rooms. $

NEW CHURCH

HOTELS
★★★The Garden and the Sea Inn
4188 Nelson Rd., New Church,
757-824-0672, 800-824-0672;
www.gardenandseainn.com
This lovely Victorian inn offers romantically decorated rooms. The complimentary breakfast can be enjoyed in either the dining room overlooking the gardens or in the garden by the lily pond.
8 rooms. Closed late November-April, pets accepted. Complimentary full breakfast. $

RESTAURANTS
★★The Garden and the Sea Inn
4188 Nelson Rd.,
New Church,
757-824-0672 , 800-824-0672;
www.gardenandseainn.com
International menu. Dinner. Closed Monday-Wednesday; also Saturday after Thanksgiving-March. Business casual attire. Reservations recommended. $$

NEW MARKET
New Market, situated in the Shenandoah Valley, gained its niche in Virginia history on May 15, 1864, when, in desperation, Confederate General Breckinridge ordered the cadets from Lexington's Virginia Military Institute to join the battle against the forces of General Franz Sigel. The oldest was just 20, but they entered the fray fearlessly, taking prisoners and capturing a battery. Their heroism inspired the Confederate defeat of Sigel's seasoned troops.
Information: Shenandoah Valley Travel Association, New Market, 540-740-3132, 800-847-4878; www.visitshenandoah.org

WHAT TO SEE AND DO
Bedrooms of America
9386 Congress St.,
New Market,
540-740-3512
Authentic furnishings from William and Mary through Art deco periods. Antique dolls. Gift shop. Daily.

Endless Caverns
1800 Endless Caverns Rd., New Market,
540-896-2283, 800-544-2283;
www.endlesscaverns.com

Lighted display of unusual rock formations; stalagmites and stalactites, columns, shields, flowstone and limestone pendants, presented in natural color. Temperature 55 F summer and winter. Camping. Guided tours (75 minutes). Daily.

New Market Battlefield State Historical Park
8895 Collins Dr.,
New Market,
540-740-3101, 866-515-1864;
www.4vmi.edu/museum/nm

Site of Civil War Battle of New Market (May 15, 1864), in which 257 VMI cadets played a decisive role. Original Bushong farmhouse and outbuildings restored, period furnishings. Hall of Valor, exhibits, films. Scenic overlooks, walking tour. Daily.

Also here is:

New Market Battlefield Military Museum
9500 George R. Collins Dr., New Market,
540-740-8065
Located on actual site of Battle of New Market, the museum houses a private collection of more than 2,000 military artifacts and genuine, personal artifacts of the American soldier from 1776 to the present. Includes uniforms, weapons, battlefield diaries, medals, mementos; film (30 minutes). Bookshop has more than 500 titles, some antique. Union and Confederate troop position markers are on museum grounds. Mid-March-November: daily.

Shenandoah Caverns
261 Caverns Rd., New Market,
540-477-3115
Elevator lowers visitors 60 feet to large subterranean rooms, fascinating rock formations; snack bar, picnic areas. Interior a constant 54 F. Daily.

HOTELS
★Budget Inn
2192 Old Valley Pike,
New Market,
540-740-3105, 800-296-6835;
www.budgetinn.com
14 rooms. $

★★Shenvalee Golf Resort
9660 Fairway Dr.,
New Market,
540-740-3181, 888-339-3181;
www.shenvalee.com
42 rooms. $

NEWPORT NEWS

One of the three cities that make up the Port of Hampton Roads, Newport News has the world's largest shipbuilding company, Newport News Shipbuilding. During the two World Wars it was a vitally important point of embarkation and supply. The area still has many important defense establishments.

Newport News is located on the historic Virginia Peninsula between Williamsburg and Virginia Beach. The peninsula also contains Hampton, Yorktown and Jamestown, and it hosted some of the earliest landings in this country. The name "Newport News" is said to derive from the good "news" of the arrival of Captain Christopher Newport, who brought supplies and additional colonists to the settlement at Jamestown.

Information: Visitor Center, 13560 Jefferson Ave., Newport News,
757-886-7777, 888-493-7386; www.newport-news.org

WHAT TO SEE AND DO
Fort Eustis
213 Calhoun St., Newport News,
757-878-4920
Headquarters of U.S. Army Transportation Center. Self-guided auto tour available; brochures at Public Affairs Office (Building 213).

On grounds is:

US Army Transportation Museum
3 Newport News,
757-878-1115
Depicts development of Army transportation from 1776 to the present; "flying saucer,"

amphibious vehicles, trucks, helicopters. Gift shop. Tuesday-Sunday.

Historic Hilton Village
Warwick Blvd. and Main St.,
Newport News
Listed on the National Register of Historic Places, this village was built between 1918-1920 to provide wartime housing for workers at Newport News Shipbuilding. Architecturally significant neighborhood features 500 English cottage-style homes and antique and specialty shops.

Mariners' Museum

100 Museum Dr., Newport News,
757-596-2222;
www.mariner.org

Exhibits and displays represent international nautical history; ship models, figureheads, scrimshaw, paintings, decorative arts and small craft. The Age of Exploration Gallery chronicles advancements in shipbuilding, ocean navigation and cartography that led to early transoceanic exploration. The Chesapeake Bay Gallery exhibits Native American artifacts, workboats, racing shells, multimedia exhibits, a working steam engine and hundreds of artifacts and photos that tell the story of this body of water. Historical interpreters, research library; museum shop. A 550-acre park on the James River features five-mile Noland Trail with 14 pedestrian bridges; picnic area. Guided tours. Daily.

Newport News Park

13564 Jefferson Ave., Newport News,
757-886-7912, 800-203-8322

Facilities in this 8,065-acre park include freshwater fishing, canoes, paddleboats, boat rentals; history and nature trails, bicycle paths (rentals), archery, arboretum, discovery center, picnicking, Civil War earthworks, 188 campsites. All year. Some fees.

Peninsula Fine Arts Center

101 Museum Dr., Newport News,
757-596-8175;
www.pfac-va.org

Changing bimonthly exhibits ranging from national traveling exhibitions to regional artists; classes, workshops and special events. Children's hands-on activity area; museum shop. Daily.

Virginia Living Museum

524 J. Clyde Morris Blvd.,
Newport News,
757-595-1900;
www.thevlm.org

Exhibits on natural science; native Virginia, wildlife living in natural habitats; indoor and outdoor aviaries; aquariums; wildflower gardens; planetarium with daily shows; observatory; children's hands-on Discovery Center. Daily.

Virginia War Museum

9285 Warwick Blvd., Newport News,
757-247-8523;
www.warmuseum.org

More than 60,000 artifacts, including weapons, uniforms, vehicles, posters, insignias and accoutrements relating to every major U.S. military involvement from the Revolutionary War to the Vietnam War. Military history library and film collection. Civil War tours and educational programs available. Daily.

HOTELS

★Comfort Inn

12330 Jefferson Ave., Newport News,
757-249-0200, 877-424-6423;
www.newportnewscomfort.com

124 rooms. Complimentary full breakfast. Airport transportation available. **$**

★Hampton Inn

12251 Jefferson Ave., Newport News,
757-249-0001, 800-426-7866;
www.hamptoninn.com

120 rooms. Complimentary full breakfast. Airport transportation available. **$**

★★★Omni Newport News Hotel

1000 Omni Blvd.,
Newport News,
757-873-6664, 800-843-6664;
www.omnihotels.com

Located minutes from historic Williamsburg, the Omni Newport News Hotel offers comfortable accommodations with wireless high-speed Internet access. Enjoy its modern amenities after soaking in the area's history. 182 rooms. **$**

RESTAURANTS

★★Al Fresco

11710 Jefferson Ave., Newport News,
757-873-0644

Italian menu. Lunch, dinner. Closed Sunday. Bar. Children's menu. Business casual attire. Reservations recommended. Outdoor seating. **$$**

★

★

★

★

★

★★Das Waldcafe
12529 Warwick Blvd.,
Newport News,
757-930-1781
German menu. Lunch, dinner. Closed
Sunday. Bar. Casual attire. Reservations
recommended. **$**

★★Port Arthur
11137 Warwick Blvd.,
Newport News,
757-599-6474
Chinese menu. Lunch, dinner. Children's
menu. Casual attire. Reservations recommended. **$**

NORFOLK

This city is part of the Port of Hampton Roads, with a bustling trade center and many
historic, cultural and resort areas nearby. Harbor tours depart from Norfolk's downtown
waterfront.

In 1682, the General Assembly purchased 50 acres on the Elizabeth River from Nicholas
Wise for "ten thousand pounds of tobacco and caske." By 1736, the town that developed
was the largest in Virginia. On January 1, 1776, Norfolk was shelled by the British and
later burned by the colonists to prevent a British takeover. The battle between the Merrimac and the Monitor in Hampton Roads in March 1862 was followed by the city's fall
to Union forces in May of that year. In 1883, the first shipment of coal to the port by the
Norfolk and Western Railway (now Norfolk Southern) began a new era of prosperity for
the city.

Norfolk houses the largest naval facility in the world, and is headquarters for the United
States Navy's Atlantic Fleet and NATO's Allied Command Atlantic. Norfolk has shipbuilding and ship repair companies, consumer and industrial equipment manufacturers and
food-processing plants. The city ships coal, tobacco, grain, seafood and vegetables. It is
also the region's cultural center, home to the Virginia Opera, Virginia Symphony, Virginia
Waterfront International Arts Festival and Virginia Stage Company.

Old Dominion University (1930), Virginia Wesleyan College (1967), Norfolk State
University (1935) and Eastern Virginia Medical School (1973) are located in Norfolk.
Within a 50-mile radius are ocean, bay, river and marsh fishing, as well as hunting. Nearby
there are 25 miles of beaches. The 17.6-mile-long Chesapeake Bay Bridge-Tunnel between
Norfolk and the Delmarva Peninsula opened in 1964; toll for passenger cars is $10, includ-
ing passengers.

Information: Norfolk Convention and Visitors Bureau, 232 E. Main St., Norfolk,
757-441-1852, 800-368-3097; www.norfolkcvb.com

WHAT TO SEE AND DO

American Rover
Norfolk,
757-627-7245;
www.americanrover.com
This 135-foot, three-masted topsail passenger schooner cruises the "smooth waters" of
Hampton Roads historical harbor; spacious
sun decks, below-deck lounges, concessions. Tour passes historic forts, merchant
and U.S. Navy ships. Some tours pass the
naval base (inquire for tour schedule).
April-October, 1 1/2- and two-hour tours
daily.

"Carrie B" Harbor Tours
Norfolk,
757-393-4735;
www.carriebcruises.com
Departs from the Waterside. Replica of 19th-
century riverboat takes narrated 90-minute
tour of naval shipyard and inner harbor
(May-October: daily); narrated 2 1/2-hour
tour of naval base (May-October: daily);
and 2 1/2-hour sunset cruise to Hampton
Roads and naval base. Daily.

358

VIRGINIA

Chrysler Museum of Art

245 W. Olney Rd., Norfolk,
757-664-6200;
www.chrysler.org

Art treasures representing nearly every important culture, civilization and historical period of the past 4,000 years. Photography gallery; fine collection of Tiffany decorative arts and glass, includes the 8,000-piece Chrysler Institute of Glass. Wednesday-Sunday.

General Douglas MacArthur Memorial

City Hall Ave. and Bank St.,
Norfolk,
757-441-2965;
www.macarthurmemorial.org

Restored former city hall (1847) where MacArthur is buried. Nine galleries contain memorabilia of his life and military career. There are three other buildings on MacArthur Square: a theater where a film biography is shown, a gift shop, and the library/archives. Daily.

Hermitage Foundation Museum

7637 N. Shore Road, Norfolk,
757-423-2052;
www.hermitagefoundation.org

Guided tours of fine arts museum in Tudor-style mansion. Collections of tapestries, Chinese bronzes and jade, ancient glass. Thursday-Tuesday.

Hunter House Victorian Museum

240 W. Freemason St., Norfolk,
757-623-9814;
www.hunterhousemuseum.org

Built in 1894 and rich in architectural details, the house contains the Hunter family's collection of Victorian furnishings and decorative pieces, including a Renaissance Revival bedchamber suite, a nursery with children's playthings, an inglenook, and stained-glass windows; lavish period reproduction floor and wall coverings, lighting fixtures and drapery. Also exhibited is a collection of early-20th-century medical memorabilia. Tours begin every 30 minutes. April-December: Wednesday-Sunday.

Moses Myers House

331 Bank St., Norfolk,
757-333-6283

(1792) Excellent example of Georgian architecture; many pieces of original furniture, silver and china. Wednesday-Saturday.

Nauticus-The National Maritime Center

1 Waterside Dr.,
Norfolk,
757-664-1000, 800-664-1080;
www.nauticus.org

Interprets aspects from marine biology and ecology to exploration, trade and shipbuilding. Interactive computer exhibits allow visitors to navigate a simulated ocean voyage, design a model ship, pilot a virtual reality submarine, and view actual researchers at work in two working marine laboratories. Active U.S. Navy ships and scientific research vessels periodically moor at Nauticus and open to visitors. Also 350-seat, 70mm wide-screen theater; shark petting tank. Memorial Day-Labor Day: daily; rest of year: Tuesday-Sunday.

Also here is:

Hampton Roads Naval Museum

1 Waterside Dr., Norfolk,
757-322-2987;
www.hrnm.navy.mil

Interprets the extensive naval history of the Hampton Roads area; including detailed ship models, period photographs, archaeological artifacts, and a superior collection of naval prints and artwork. Daily.

Norfolk Botanical Garden

6700 Azalea Garden Rd., Norfolk,
757-441-5830;
www.norfolkbotanicalgarden.org

Azaleas, camellias, rhododendrons, roses (May-October), dogwoods and hollies on 155 acres. Japanese, Colonial, perennial and rose gardens; flowering arboretum; fragrance garden for the visually impaired; picnicking, restaurant and gift shop; tropical pavilion. Flowering displays best from early April-October. Gardens (daily; closed special events). Information center (daily). Narrated boat ride (30 minutes) and tram tours (daily).

359

VIRGINIA

★
★
★
★
★

Norfolk Naval Base and Norfolk Naval Air Station

Hampton Blvd. and I-564, Norfolk,
757-322-2330

The largest naval installation in the world. Ship visitors should check in at the Naval Base Pass Office on Hampton Blvd., opposite Gate 5. Naval base tours are also offered. Tour buses from Tour and Information Office, 9079 Hampton Blvd., Norfolk. April-October: daily.

"Spirit of Norfolk"

Norfolk,
757-625-1748, 866-304-2469;
www.spiritofnorfolk.com

Departs from the Waterside. Harbor cruise aboard 600-passenger cruise ship. Captain's narration highlights the harbor's famous landmarks, including Waterside Festival Marketplace, Portsmouth Naval Hospital, Old Fort Norfolk, Blackbeard's hiding place, Norfolk Naval Base, and downtown area's dynamic skyline. Luncheon cruise (Tuesday-Sunday); evening dinner cruise (Tuesday-Sunday); moonlight party cruise (Friday-Saturday, in season).

St. Paul's Episcopal Church

201 St. Paul's Blvd., Norfolk,
757-627-4353

(1739) Only building to survive burning of Norfolk in 1776. Monday-Saturday, also by appointment.

Virginia Zoological Park

3500 Granby St., Norfolk,
757-441-2374;
www.virginiazoo.org

A combination zoo, park and conservatory. Playground, tennis courts, basketball courts; picnic area, concession. Daily.

Waterside Festival Marketplace

333 Waterside Dr., Norfolk,
757-627-3300;
www.watersidemarketplace.com

A waterfront pavilion with more than 90 shops, restaurants. (Monday-Saturday 10 a.m.-9 p.m., Sunday noon-6 p.m.) Bordering the Waterside are the city's marina

and dock areas, where harbor tour vessels take on passengers.

Town Point Park

120 W. Main St., Norfolk,
757-441-2345

Home to Norfolk Festevents, the park hosts more than 100 free outdoor concerts, parties, dances, movies and festivals each year.

Willoughby-Baylor House

601 E. Freemason St., Norfolk,
757-441-1526

(1794) Restored town house with period furnishings; herb and flower garden adjacent. By appointment; inquire at Moses Myers House.

SPECIAL EVENTS

Festival in the Park

119 Park Ave., Norfolk,
757-625-1445

Art exhibits, crafts, sports, food, parade, entertainment. Two weekends beginning the Friday before Memorial Day.

Harborfest

Town Point Park, 120 W. Main St., Norfolk,
757-441-2345

Sailboat and speedboat races, tall ships, ship tours, waterskiing, military demonstrations, entertainment, children's activities, fireworks, seafood. First full weekend in June.

International Azalea Festival

Downtown and Norfolk Botanical Garden, Norfolk,
757-282-2801;
www.azaleafestival.org

To honor NATO. Parade, coronation ceremony, air show (held at Norfolk Naval Air Station), events, concerts, fair, ball, entertainment. Late April.

Virginia Children's Festival

Town Point Park, 120 W. Main St., Norfolk,
757-441-2345

More than 200 educational, creative and interactive activities; entertainment. Early October.

Virginia Opera
160 E. Virginia Beach Blvd.,
Norfolk,
757-623-1223, 866-673-7282;
www.vaopera.org
Harrison Opera House and other select locations. Statewide opera company; traditional and contemporary works. Features young American artists. October-April.

Virginia Symphony
Norfolk,
757-892-6366
Chrysler Hall and other select locations. Five performance series. September-May.

Virginia Waterfront International Arts Festival
Norfolk,
757-282-2800;
www.virginiaartsfest.com
Eighteen days of classical and contemporary music, dance, visual arts and theater performances. Late April-mid-May.

HOTELS

★★Best Western Center Inn
235 N. Military Hwy., Norfolk,
757-461-6600, 800-237-5517;
www.bestwestern.com
152 rooms. Complimentary continental breakfast. Airport transportation available. Near airport. $

★Best Western Holiday Sands Inn & Suites
1330 E. Oceanview Ave.,
Norfolk,
757-583-2621, 800-525-5156;
www.bestwestern.com
95 rooms. Complimentary continental breakfast. Airport transportation available. $

★Hampton Inn
1450 N. Military Hwy., Norfolk,
757-466-7474
130 rooms. Complimentary full breakfast. Airport transportation available. Airport. $

★★★Hilton Norfolk Airport
1500 N. Military Hwy., Norfolk,
757-466-8000, 800-445-8667;
www.norfolkhilton.com
Conveniently located two miles from Norfolk International Airport, this hotel is ideal for those visiting the business district or military installations.
254 rooms. Airport transportation available. $$

★★★Marriott Norfolk Waterside
235 E. Main St., Norfolk,
804-627-4200, 800-228-9290;
www.marriott.com
In Norfolk's historic district, the Marriott Norfolk Waterside offers well-appointed guest rooms and dining options such as Shula's 347 Steakhouse.
405 rooms. $$

Page House
323 Fairfax Ave., Norfolk,
757-625-5033, 800-599-7659;
www.pagehouseinn.com
This Georgian Revival mansion (1898), originally a family home and completely renovated in 1990, is located in the fashionable Ghent historic district. It offers distinctly decorated guest rooms.
7 rooms. Children under 12 years only by reservations. Check-in 2-9 p.m. $$

★Quality Inn
8051 Hampton Blvd., Norfolk,
757-451-0000, 877-424-6423;
www.comfortinn.com
119 rooms. Complimentary continental breakfast. $

361

VIRGINIA

★

★

★

★

★

★★★Sheraton Norfolk Waterside Hotel
777 Waterside Dr., Norfolk,
757-622-6664, 800-325-3535;
www.sheraton.com
Adjacent to Waterside Marketplace on the Elizabeth River, this landmark hotel affords great views of the harbor and downtown skyline. 445 rooms. **$**

RESTAURANTS
★★Baker's Crust
330 W. 21st St., Norfolk,
757-625-3600;
www.bakerscrust.com
Steak menu. Lunch, dinner. Bar. Children's menu. Casual attire. Outdoor seating. **$$**

★The Banque
1849 E. Little Creek Rd., Norfolk,
757-480-3600
Dinner. Closed Monday. Bar. Western decor. **$$**

★★ Freemason Abbey
209 W. Freemason St., Norfolk,
757-622-3966;
www.freemasonabbey.com
American, seafood menu. Lunch, dinner, Sunday brunch. Bar. Children's menu. Casual attire. Renovated church (1873); many antiques. **$$**

★★★La Galleria
120 College Place, Norfolk,
757-623-3939;
www.lagalleriaristorante.com
With its freestanding granite bar, live music and wood-burning oven, La Galleria is well-equipped to serve authentic Italian cuisine with European flair. This Norfolk restaurant serves dishes such as buccatini carbonara, tortellini mac and cheese and ham marsala. Desserts are made in-house.
Italian menu. Dinner. Closed Sunday and Monday. Bar. Business casual attire. Reservations recommended. Valet parking. **$$**

★★Monastery
443 Granby St., Norfolk,
757-625-8193
Czech, Eastern European menu. Dinner. Closed Mondays. Bar. Reservations recommended. **$$**

362

★
★
★
★

ORANGE
Orange and Orange county were named for William of Orange in 1734. Located in the Piedmont (foothills) of the Blue Ridge Mountains, Orange was settled by Germans under the leadership of Alexander Spotswood between 1714 and 1719. This is riding and hunting country, drawing its livelihood from farming, livestock and light industry. The county boasts many antebellum houses.

WHAT TO SEE AND DO
James Madison Museum
129 Caroline St.,
Orange,
540-672-1776;
www.jamesmadisonmus.org
Exhibits commemorating Madison's life and his contributions to American history; also Orange County history and Hall of Agriculture that includes an 18th-century homestead. March-December: daily; rest of year, Monday-Friday.

HOTELS
Greenock House Inn
249 Caroline St., Orange,
540-672-3625, 800-841-1253;
www.greenockhouse.com
This inn is located close to Monticello, Montpelier and Skyline Drive and offers activities that include biking, hiking,

antique shopping, boating and fishing. The inn comprises four buildings, including a century-old main house built by descendents of Thomas Jefferson. Verandas wrap around the building and look out over the wooded gardens.

5 rooms. Closed late December-early January. Complimentary full breakfast. **$**

Holladay House

155 W. Main St., Orange,
540-672-4893, 800-358-4422;
www.holladayhousebandb.com

6 rooms. Children over 12 only. Complimentary full breakfast. Federal-style residence (circa 1830). **$**

PARIS

HOTELS

★★★Ashby Inn

692 Federal St., Paris,
540-592-3900, 866-336-0099;
www.ashbyinn.com

This restored 1829 inn is charming and elegant. Guests should certainly make a point to dine in the restaurant, which features seasonal fare.

9 rooms. Complimentary full breakfast. Restaurant. **$$**

RESTAURANTS

★★★Ashby Inn

692 Federal St., Paris,
540-592-3900;
www.ashbyinn.com

Seasonal provisions inspire the simple, hearty menu that rivals those at trendy city restaurants. Look for garden-fresh tomatoes in the summer and wild game in the fall. Relax in a very warm, very country atmosphere.

American menu. Dinner, Sunday brunch. Closed Monday-Tuesday. Business casual attire. Reservations recommended. Outdoor seating. **$$$**

PETERSBURG

This city, Lee's last stand before Appomattox (1864-1865), was settled in 1645 when the General Assembly authorized construction of Fort Henry at the falls of the Appomattox River. In 1784, three separate towns united to become the single city of Petersburg. Between the Revolutionary War and Civil War, the town was a popular stopping place with a social life that for a time eclipsed that of Richmond.

Physically untouched during the early years of the Civil War (though the town sent 17 companies

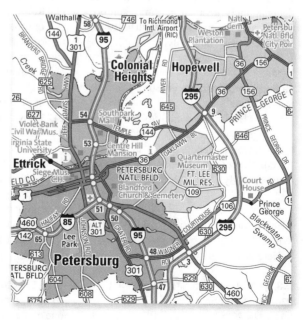

to the front), Petersburg in 1864 was the scene of Lee's final struggle against Grant. In April 1865, when Lee's supply routes were finally cut and he was forced to evacuate the city, the Confederacy collapsed. A week later Lee surrendered at Appomattox.

The shattered city made a new start after the war, showing amazing recuperative powers. Petersburg added 20 more industries in 20 years, between 1850 and 1870. Today, besides being a storehouse of colonial and Civil War history, Petersburg is a thriving industrial city. **Information: Petersburg Visitors Center, 425 Cockade Alley, Petersburg, 804-733-2402, 800-368-3595; www.petersburg-va.org**

WHAT TO SEE AND DO

Appomattox River Park
Petersburg,
804-733-2394
A 137-acre park with canal for canoeing or fishing; access to rapids; picnic area. Mid-April-October: daily.

Blandford Church and Cemetery
321 S. Crater Rd., Petersburg,
804-733-2396
Church (1735) and cemetery (1702); since 1901 a memorial to the Confederacy, has 15 Tiffany stained-glass windows. Daily.

Centre Hill Mansion
1 Centre Hill Ct., Petersburg,
804-733-2401
(1823) Federalist mansion visited by Presidents Tyler, Lincoln and Taft. Chandeliers, finely detailed carvings; antiques, 1886 Knabe Art grand piano with hollywood inlaid on rosewood. Daily.

Farmers Bank
19 Bollingbrook St., Petersburg,
804-733-2400
(1817) Banking memorabilia including original plates and press for printing Confederate currency. Tours depart from Visitor Center, Old Market Square. April-October: daily.

Fort Lee
Army training center in World War I and World War II.
Here is:

U.S. Army Quartermaster Museum
22nd St., Fort Lee,
804-734-4203;
www.qmmuseum.lee.army.mil

Uniforms, flags, weapons, equestrian equipment from 200 years of military service. Civil War and Memorial rooms. Tuesday-Sunday.

Lee Memorial Park
Petersburg,
804-733-2394
Facilities of this 864-acre park include lake (launch fee), fishing (fee; license required); game fields and courts (fee), picnic area. Daily; lake facilities closed mid-October-mid-April.
Also here is:

Lee's Retreat
Petersburg,
800-673-8732
A 98-mile driving tour follows route of General Robert E. Lee's retreat from Petersburg to Appomattox. Roadside pull-overs, signs and audio interpretation at important Civil War sites. For brochures, maps and audio tapes, contact the Petersburg Visitors Center.

Pamplin Park Civil War Site
6125 Boydton Plank Rd., Petersburg,
804-861-2408, 877-726-7546
Site of General Ulysses S. Grant's decisive victory over Confederate forces in 1865. This 422-acre park includes battle trails, reconstructed soldier huts, plantation home. Interpretive Center and museum. Guided tours available. Daily.
Also here is:

National Museum of the Civil War Soldier
6125 Boydton Plank Rd., Petersburg,
Exhibit on the Civil War's common soldier, one of the country's largest Civil War bookshops. Gift shop; restaurant.

364

VIRGINIA

Poplar Grove (Petersburg) National Cemetery

On self-guided tour of Petersburg National Battlefield. Of 6,315 graves, 4,110 are unidentified.

Siege Museum

15 W. Bank St., Petersburg,
804-733-2402

Greek Revival building houses exhibits describing the ten-month Civil War siege of Petersburg. Film "The Echoes Still Remain," with Joseph Cotten, is shown every hour on the hour. Daily.

St. Paul's Episcopal Church

110 N. Union, Petersburg,
804-733-3415;
www.stpaulspetersburg.com

(1856) Lee worshiped here during the siege of Petersburg (1864-1865). Open on request. Monday-Thursday.

Trapezium House

Market and High Streets, Petersburg,
804-733-2400

(1817) Built by eccentric Irish bachelor Charles O'Hara in the form of a trapezium, with no right angles and no parallel sides. O'Hara is said to have believed the superstitions of his West Indian servant, who thought that ghosts and evil spirits inhabited right angles. Tours depart from Siege Museum. April-October: daily.

HOTELS

★★Comfort Inn Prince George

5380 Oaklawn Blvd., Prince George,
804-452-0022;
www.choicehotels.com

Fitness center. High-speed internet.

★Days Inn

12208 S. Crater Rd., Petersburg,
804-733-4400, 877-512-4400;
www.daysinn.com

155 rooms. Complimentary continental breakfast. Children's activity center. $

★★Howard Johnson

12205 S. Crater Rd., Petersburg,
804-733-0600, 800-446-4656;
www.howardjohnson.com

137 rooms. Children's activity center. $

RESTAURANTS

★Alexander's

101 W. Bank St.,
Petersburg,
804-733-7134

American, Greek, Italian menu. Breakfast, lunch, dinner. Closed Saturday; week of July 4. Children's menu. In old town storefront. Casual attire. $$

PETERSBURG NATIONAL BATTLEFIELD

At the price of 70,000 Union and Confederate casualties, the campaign that spelled doom for the Confederacy occurred in a huge, 40-mile semicircle around Richmond and Petersburg.

After his unsuccessful attempt to take Richmond by frontal assault (at Cold Harbor, June 3, 1864), General Grant withdrew and attacked Petersburg. After four days of fighting and failing to capture the city, Grant decided to lay siege. Petersburg was the rail center that funneled supplies to Lee and Richmond.

The siege lasted 10 months, from June 15, 1864, to April 2, 1865, with the two armies in almost constant contact. When Petersburg finally fell, Lee's surrender was only a week away.

The park, more than 2,700 acres, preserves Union and Confederate fortifications, trenches and gun pits. Another unit of the battlefield, Five Forks Unit, is located 23 miles to the west. Park (daily). Living history programs daily during summer. Access for the disabled includes several paved trails and ramps to the Visitor Center.

Information: Superintendent, 1539 Hickory Hill Rd., Petersburg, 804-732-3531,
Golden Eagle, Golden Age and Golden Access Passports honored.
Route 36 and I-95, Petersburg; www.nps.gov/pete

WHAT TO SEE AND DO

Battery 5

Route 36 and I-95, Petersburg National Battlefield

Strongest original Confederate position, captured on opening day of battle. From here "the Dictator," a Union mortar, shelled Petersburg, 2 1/2 miles away. A similar mortar is nearby.

Battery 8

Route 36 and I-95, Petersburg National Battlefield

Confederate artillery position captured and used by Union as Fort Friend.

Battery 9

Route 36 and I-95, Petersburg National Battlefield

Confederate position on original line. Site of reconstructed Union camp and living history programs.

Colquitt's Salient

Section of Confederate defense line.

The Crater

Hole remaining after Union troops tunneled beneath Confederate artillery position and exploded four tons of powder (July 30, 1864). The resulting breach in Confederate lines failed as a major breakthrough. Several special monuments in vicinity.

Five Forks Unit

1539 Hickory Hill Rd., Petersburg National Battlefield, 804-265-8244

(1,115 acres) This road junction, beyond Lee's extreme right flank, led to the only remaining Confederate supply line, the South Side Railroad. The Battle of Five Forks (April 1, 1865) saw Union forces under General Philip H. Sheridan smash Confederates commanded by General George Pickett and gain access to the tracks beyond. On April 2, Grant ordered an all-out assault, crumbling Lee's right flank. Only a heroic stand by Confederate forces at Fort Gregg held off the Union advance while Lee evacuated Petersburg on the night of April 2. Visitor contact station (summer).

Fort Haskell

One of the points where Union troops stopped a desperate attempt by Lee to break the siege.

Fort Stedman

Lee's "last grand offensive" concentrated here (March 25, 1865). The battle lasted four hours; the Confederates failed to hold their breakthrough.

Gracie's Dam

Site of one of several Confederate dams intended to flood area between lines.

Harrison's Creek

First Grant (June 1864), then Lee (March 1865) had advances checked here.

Spring Garden

Heaviest Union artillery concentration during Battle of Crater was along this ridge.

Visitor Center

Information, exhibits; maps for self-guided tours. Self-guided tour starts near center building.

PORTSMOUTH

Connected to Norfolk by two bridge tunnels and a pedestrian ferry that cross the Elizabeth River, Portsmouth is part of the great Hampton Roads port, unrivaled for commercial shipping and shipbuilding activity. It is also the headquarters of the United States Coast Guard Atlantic Fleet.

★
★
★
★
★

In Gosport, long a part of Portsmouth, Scotsman Andrew Sprowle built a marine yard in 1767 that became a British naval repair station and after the Revolutionary War, a federal navy yard. Now called the Norfolk Naval Shipyard, it is the largest naval shipyard in the world. The Chesapeake, sister of the U.S.S, Constitution and one of the U.S. Navy's first warships, was built here. So was the Merrimac, which was seized by the Confederates, changed into an ironclad in 1861, and rechristened the CSS Virginia. The oldest dry dock (1831) here is still in use.

Information: Portsmouth Convention and Visitors Bureau, 505 Crawford St., Portsmouth, 757-393-5327, 800-767-8782; www.portsmouth.va.us

WHAT TO SEE AND DO

Hill House
221 North St., Portsmouth,
757-393-0241
Headquarters of the Portsmouth Historical Association. Built in early 1820s, this four-story English basement-style (with a raised basement) house contains original furnishings collected by generations of the Hill family. In near-original condition, the house has undergone only limited renovation through the years. Garden restored. April-December: Wednesday, Saturday-Sunday.

Historic Houses
6 Crawford Pkwy., Portsmouth,
757-393-5111
Portsmouth has over 300 years of history represented by more than 20 examples of colonial, Federal and antebellum houses. Among them is the Nivison-Ball House (circa 1730-1750), 417 Middle Street, where Andrew Jackson and General Lafayette were entertained. These houses are private and may be viewed only from the exterior. Obtain Olde Towne Portsmouth walking tour brochures with map and descriptions of churches, homes and old buildings from the Visitor Center at High Street Landing.

Monumental United Methodist Church
450 Dinwiddie St., Portsmouth,
757-397-1297;
www.monumentalumc.org
(1772) Methodist. Oldest Methodist congregation in the South; history room. Guided tour Monday-Friday, by appointment.

The Portsmouth Museums
221 High St., Portsmouth,
757-393-8983
Located in a four-block radius, the museum complex has facilities housing artistic, educational and historic exhibits. Memorial Day-Labor Day: daily.
    The complex includes:

Children's Museum of Virginia
221 High St., Portsmouth,
757-393-5258
More than 60 interactive activities in 12 areas; planetarium. Mid-June-Labor Day: Monday-Saturday, also Sunday afternoons.

Courthouse Galleries
420 High St., Portsmouth,
757-393-8543
Changing exhibits.

Lightship Museum
London Slip and Water St.,
Portsmouth,
757-393-8591
Built in 1915, commissioned in 1916 as "Lightship 101," it served 48 years in Virginia, Delaware and Massachusetts. Retired in 1964 and renamed Portsmouth.

Naval Shipyard Museum
2 High St., Portsmouth,
757-393-8591
Thousands of items of naval equipment, plus flags, uniforms, prints, maps and models, including models of the C.S.S. Virginia; the U.S. Ship-of-the-line Delaware, built in Portsmouth; and the first ship drydocked in the U.S.

367

VIRGINIA

★
★
★
★
★

Trinity Church
500 Court St.,
Portsmouth,
757-393-0431;
www.trinityportsmouth.org
Episcopal. Oldest church building (1762) and parish in Portsmouth. Legend says the church bell cracked while ringing out news of Cornwallis' surrender; it was later recast. Confederate Memorial window. Many colonial patriots are buried here. Open on request, Monday-Friday; office behind church in parish hall.

HOTELS
★★**Holiday Inn**
8 Crawford Pkwy.,
Portsmouth,
757-393-2573, 800-282-0244;
www.holidayinn.com
219 rooms. $

★★**Holiday Inn Old Towne Portsmouth**
8 Crawford Pkwy.,
Portsmouth,
757-393-2573, 800-860-7109;
www.ichotelsgroup.com
219 rooms. Fitness center. Outdoor pool. Restaurant. $$

★★★**Renaissance Portsmouth Hotel**
425 Water St.,
Portsmouth,
757-673-3000, 888-839-1775;
www.renaissanceportsmouth.com
254 rooms. $

RESTAURANTS
★★**Cafe Europa**
319 High St.,
Portsmouth,
757-399-6652
French, Italian menu. Lunch, dinner. Closed Sunday-Monday; also one week in spring. Bar. Business casual attire. Reservations recommended. Outdoor seating. $$$

★**The Circle**
3010 High St.,
Portsmouth,
757-397-8196
American menu. Lunch, dinner, brunch. Bar. Children's menu. Casual attire. $

★★**Island Grill**
8 Crawford Pkwy.,
Portsmouth,
757-393-2573, 800-860-7109;
www.ichotelsgroup.com
American. Breakfast, lunch, dinner.

368

RADFORD
★ Information: Chamber of Commerce, 1126 Norwood St., Radford, 540-639-2202;
www.radfordchamber.com

WHAT TO SEE AND DO
Claytor Lake State Park
4400 State Park Rd.,
Radford,
540-643-2500
Consists of 472 acres in wooded hills adjacent to 5,000-acre lake. Swimming, sand beach, bathhouse, fishing, boating (ramp, rentals, marina); hiking and bridle trails, picnicking, concession, tent and trailer sites (electrical hookups, April-September), cabins (March-early December). Visitor center, interpretive programs. Park office and visitor center in Howe House (1876-1879), built on land once settled by Dunkers (Dunkards), a religious sect that fled persecution in Germany in the 1720s.

HOTELS
★★**Best Western Radford Inn**
1501 Tyler Ave.,
Radford,
540-639-3000, 800-628-1955;
www.bestwestern.com
104 rooms. Complimentary continental breakfast. $

RICHMOND

Located at the falls of the James River, Richmond had to wait 170 years before becoming the state capital. Four hundred years later, with a history almost as old as Jamestown, the city blends its heritage with vibrant, contemporary commerce and trade. Its location, equidistant from the plantations of Tidewater Virginia and the Piedmont of central Virginia, gives the city a unique mix of heritage, culture and geography.

There have been few dull moments in Richmond's history. Native Americans and settlers fought over the ground on which it now stands. In 1775, Patrick Henry made his famous "liberty or death" speech in St. John's Church, and in 1780, the city was named capital of the state. British soldiers plundered it brutally in the Revolutionary War. As the capital of the Confederacy from 1861 to 1865, it was constantly in danger. Finally, in 1865, the city was evacuated and retreating Confederate soldiers burned the government warehouse. A portion of the rest of the city also went up in flames.

Richmond survived, and it now proudly exemplifies the modern South: industrially aggressive yet culturally aware, respectful of its own historical background yet receptive to new trends in architecture and modes of living.

Tobacco, paper, aluminum, chemicals, textiles, printing, publishing and machinery contribute to the city's economy. Richmond is also an educational center; Virginia Commonwealth University, Virginia Union University and the University of Richmond are based here.

Information: Convention and Visitors Bureau, 405 N. Third St., Richmond, 804-783-7450, 800-370-9004; www.visit.richmond.com

WHAT TO SEE AND DO

17th Street Farmers' Market

17th and Main Streets, Richmond, 804-646-0477; www.17thstreetfarmersmarket.com

This farmers' market is built at the site of a Native American trading village and features seasonal produce in Shockoe Bottom. April-December: Thursday, Saturday-Sunday.

Sixth Street Marketplace

Sixth St., Richmond, between Coliseum and Grace St., downtown

Restored area of shops, restaurants and entertainment.

Agecroft Hall

4305 Sulgrave Rd., Richmond, 804-353-4241; www.agecrofthall.com

Half-timbered Tudor manor built in the late 15th century near Manchester, England.

RICHMOND'S HISTORICAL LEGACY

Once the Civil War capital of the Confederacy, Richmond is brimming with historical attractions. This two-mile walking tour of the city center will take you past many Civil War landmarks, as well as the city's less-troubling claims to historical fame.

Begin your walk at the Virginia State Capitol, designed in 1785 by Thomas Jefferson, himself a state governor, in the style of a classical temple. Surrounded by Capitol Square's expanse of well-tended lawn, it commands the eye despite the modern-day structures that surround it. Step inside the Rotunda to see the famous life-size statue of George Washington.

From Capitol Square, walk north (right) on Nineth Street across Broad Street to the neighborhood once known as Court End, which now bustles with students and faculty of the Medical College of Virginia. At 818 East Marshall Street (intersecting 9th) stands the most important residence of Court End, the home of John Marshall, the distinguished chief justice of the U.S. Supreme Court from 1801 to 1835. Built in 1790, the two-story brick house where he lived for 45 years is a museum dedicated to his memory.

Although it's a seven-block detour, head west on Marshall Street to Second Street and turn north (right) two blocks to 110 East Leigh Street, the Maggie Walker National Historic Site. The modest two-story brick home on a quiet residential street, honors a woman of impressive ability. Despite physical handicaps, Walker became America's first female bank president, establishing the Penny Savings Bank in 1903 as a way of helping local African Americans during the Jim Crow period.

Double back via Marshall Street past the John Marshall House to the Valentine Museum at 1015 East Clay Street. A small, innovative museum with a contemporary outlook, it focuses on the people and history of Richmond. Conclude the tour a block down the street at 12th and East Clay at the adjacent Museum of the Confederacy and the White House of the Confederacy. Not surprisingly, the museum emphasizes Southern leaders, featuring mementos of General Robert E. Lee. The White House, a neoclassical mansion built in 1818, recounts the home life during the Civil War of Confederate President Jefferson Davis and his wife, Varina.

Disassembled, brought here and rebuilt during the late 1920s in a spacious setting of formal gardens and grassy terraces overlooking the James River. English furnishings from 16th and 17th centuries. Audiovisual presentation explains the history of the house. Tuesday-Sunday.

Canal Club
1545 E. Cary St., Richmond,
804-643-7407;
www.thecanalclub.com

Catch live music, especially blues and rock, or shoot a game of pool in Shockoe Bottom. A bonus: the interesting menu at The Under the Stage Cafe. Wednesday-Saturday.

Canal Walk
Enter at S. Fifth, Seventh, 14th, 15th, or 17th Streets
The Canal Walk meanders 1 1/4 miles through downtown and features a pedestrian bridge to Brown's Island. Richmond Canal Cruisers (804-649-2800) depart on

the hour from noon to 7 p.m. Wednesday to Saturday and from noon to 5 p.m. on Sunday from the Turning Basin between 14th and Virginia streets.

Capitol Square
Ninth and Grace Streets,
Richmond,
804-643-7407

Equestrian Statue of Washington
Ninth and Grace Streets,
Richmond
By Thomas Crawford; cast in Munich over an 18-year period. Base features allegorical representations of six famous Revolutionary War figures from Virginia.

Governor's Mansion
Ninth and Grace Streets,
Richmond,
804-371-2642
(1813) This two-story Federal-style house was built after the capital was moved from Williamsburg. Oldest governor's mansion in the U.S. still in use as a governor's residence. Tours (by appointment).

State Capitol
Ninth and Grace Streets,
Richmond,
804-698-1788
(1785-1788) Modeled after La Maison Carre, an ancient Roman temple at Némes, France, the Capitol was designed by Thomas Jefferson. In this building, where America's oldest continuous English-speaking legislative bodies still meet, is the famous Houdon statue of Washington. The rotunda features the first interior dome in the U.S.; Monday-Saturday, also Sunday afternoons.

Virginia State Library and Archives
800 E. Broad St.,
Richmond,
804-692-3500;
www.lva.lib.va.us
Outstanding collection of books, maps and manuscripts. Monday-Saturday.

Carytown
W. Cary St., Richmond, between
Blvd. St. and Thompson St.,
www.carytown.org
More than 250 shops and restaurants in this area include quirky clothing boutiques, antique shops, the city's best music store, and collectibles ranging from Christmas decorations to glass and dolls.

Church Hill Historic Area
Main and 21st Streets,
Richmond, bounded by Broad,
29th, Main,
and 21st Streets, E. of Capitol Square
Neighborhood of 19th-century houses, more than 70 of which predate Civil War. Some Church Hill houses are open during Historic Garden Week.
In center of Church Hill is:

Edgar Allan Poe Museum
1914-1916 E. Main St.,
Richmond,
804-648-5523, 888-213-2763;
www.poemuseum.org
Old Stone House portion is thought to be oldest structure in Richmond (1737). Three additional buildings house Poe mementos; James Carling illustrations of "The Raven;" scale model of the Richmond of Poe's time. Guided tours. Tuesday-Sunday.

St. John's Episcopal Church
25th and Broad Streets,
Richmond,
804-648-5015, 877-915-1775;
www.stjohnschurch.org
(1741) Where Patrick Henry delivered his stirring "liberty or death" speech. Reenactment of the Second Virginia Convention late May-early September: Sunday. Guided tours. Daily.

City Hall Observation Deck
901 E. Broad St.,
Richmond,
804-646-5990
Eighteenth-floor observation deck offers a panoramic view of the city, including

VIRGINIA

the Capitol grounds, James River and Revolutionary and Civil War-era buildings contrasted with modern skyscrapers. Monday-Friday.

Civil War Visitor Center
470 Tredegar St.,
Richmond,
804-771-2145;
www.nps.gov/rich
Begin your exploration of Richmond's Civil War heritage at the National Park Service Center at the restored Tredegar Iron Works near the James River. On the bottom floor, a continuously running film orients you to the 12 battlefields in the area. Park Service guides explain to kids how to fire the kind of cannon that Tredgar Iron Works made for the war. Daily.

The Fan District and Monument Avenue
Main and Belvidere Streets,
Richmond
Named for the layout of streets that fan out from Monroe Park toward the western part of town. Historic neighborhood has restored antebellum and turn-of-the-century houses, museums, shops, restaurants and famed Monument Avenue. The fashionable Boulevard, between Lombard and Belmont streets, is dotted with imposing statues of Generals Lee, Stuart and Jackson.

Children's Museum of Richmond
2626 W. Broad St.,
Richmond,
804-474-2667, 877-295-2667;
www.c-mor.org
A nice range of hands-on exhibits including the interactive James River Waterplay, which explores the hydrology and history of the James River. Memorial Day-Labor Day: daily; rest of year: Tuesday-Sunday.

Science Museum of Virginia
2500 W. Broad St.,
Richmond,
804-864-1400;
www.smv.org

Located in the historic Broad Street Station (train tracks are still on the ground floor), this is an engaging museum that will appeal to children with exhibits about space, flight, electricity, physics and the atom. Be sure to check out the laboratories and animal exhibits on the second floor. Daily 9:30 a.m.-7 p.m.

Virginia Historical Society
428 N. Blvd. St.,
Richmond,
804-358-4901;
www.vahistorical.org
The society has a comprehensive collection of Virginia history housed in its museum with permanent and changing exhibits, and the Library of Virginia History with historical and genealogical research facilities. It is well worth an afternoon to explore the city's changing place in history. Daily.

Virginia Museum of Fine Arts
200 N. Blvd.,
Richmond,
804-340-1400;
www.vmfa.state.va.us
America's first state-supported museum of art. Collections of paintings, prints and sculpture from major world cultures; Russian Imperial Easter eggs and jewels by Faberge; decorative arts of the Art Nouveau and Art deco movements; sculpture garden. Cafeteria. Wednesday-Sunday.

Federal Reserve Money Museum
701 E. Byrd St.,
Richmond,
804-697-8108;
www.richmondfed.org
Exhibits of currency include rare bills, gold and silver bars and other; money-related artifacts. Monday-Friday 9:30 a.m.-3:30 p.m.

Historic Richmond Tours
707 E. Franklin St.,
Richmond,
804-649-0711

372

VIRGINIA

★
★
★
★
★

Offers guided van tours with pickup at Visitor Center and major hotels (daily); reservations required. Also guided walking tours (April-October: daily; fee).

Hollywood Cemetery
412 S. Cherry St.,
Richmond,
804-648-8501;
www.hollywoodcemetery.org
(1847) James Monroe, John Tyler, Jefferson Davis, other notables and 18,000 Confederate soldiers are buried here; audiovisual program. Daily.

Jackson Ward
Broad and Belvidere Streets,
Richmond
Historic downtown neighborhood that was home to many famous black Richmonders, including Bill "Bojangles" Robinson. The area has numerous 19th-century, Greek Revival and Victorian buildings with ornamental ironwork that rivals the wrought iron of New Orleans.

Bill "Bojangles" Robinson Statue
Leigh and Adams Streets, Richmond
Memorial to the famous dancer who was born at 915 N. 3rd St.

Black History Museum and Cultural Center
3 E. Clay St., Richmond,
804-780-9093;
www.blackhistorymuseum.org
Limited editions, prints, art, photographs; African memorabilia; Sam Gilliam collection. Tuesday-Sunday 10 a.m.-5 p.m.

Maggie Walker National Historic Site
110 1/2 E. Leigh St.,
Richmond,
804-771-2017
Commemorates the life and career of Maggie L. Walker, daughter of former slaves, who overcame great hardships to become successful in banking and insurance; early advocate for women's rights and racial equality. Two-story, red brick house was home to her family from 1904 to 1934. Monday-Saturday.

John Marshall House
818 E. Marshall St., Richmond,
804-648-7998;
www.apva.org/marshall
(1790) Restored house of famous Supreme Court justice features original woodwork and paneling, family furnishings and mementos. Tuesday-Sunday. Combination ticket available for Marshall House, Valentine Museum, Museum of the Confederacy, and White House of the Confederacy.

Kanawha Canal Locks
12th and Byrd Streets, Richmond,
804-649-2800
Impressive stone locks were part of the nation's first canal system, planned by George Washington. Narrated audiovisual presentation explains the workings of the locks and canal. Picnic grounds. Monday-Saturday.

Meadow Farm Museum
General Sheppard Crump Memorial Park,
3400 Mountain Rd.,
Glen Allen,
804-501-5520;
www.co.henrico.va.us/rec/
current_programs/meadow_farm.html
Living history farm museum depicting rural life in the 1860s. Orientation center, farmhouse, barn, outbuildings, crop demonstration fields and 1860s doctor's office. Also a 150-acre park with picnic shelters, playground. March-November: Tuesday-Sunday; December-February: weekends.

Monumental Church
1224 E. Broad St.,
Richmond
(1812) Located on the Medical College of Virginia campus of Virginia Commonwealth University. Octagonal domed building designed by Robert Mills, architect of the Washington Monument. Commemorative structure was built on the site where many prominent people, including the governor, perished in a theater fire in 1811. Interior closed. Behind the church is the distinctive Egyptian Building (1845).

373

VIRGINIA

Museum of the Confederacy
1201 E. Clay St., Richmond,
804-649-1861;
www.moc.org

The museum features the world's largest collection of Confederate artifacts: uniforms, weapons, tattered flags and daguerreotypes. Many of the exhibits feature artifacts from Confederate officers with descriptions of their demise. While it is comprehensive, the museum hasn't taken advantage of technology. You'll find yourself reading one typed description after another. Daily.

Paddlewheeler *Annabel Lee*
Richmond,
804-377-2020, 800-752-7093;
www.spiritcitycruises.com/Richmond/onboard

Departs from Intermediate Terminal. Triple-decked, 350-passenger, 19th-century-style riverboat cruises the James River. Narrated tour; entertainment. Lunch, brunch, dinner and plantation cruises. April-December, at least one cruise Tuesday-Sunday.

Parks
Richmond,
804-646-5733

For general information, contact the Department of Parks and Recreation.

Joseph Bryan Park
Bellevue Ave. and Hermitage Rd., Richmond

A 279-acre park, 20 acres of which are an azalea garden with more than 55,000 plants (best viewed late April-mid-May). Picnic facilities, tennis courts.

James River Park
W. 22nd St. and Riverside Dr., Richmond,
804-646-8911;
www.jamesriverpark.org

The James River drops 105 feet over a 7-mile stretch that passes through downtown Richmond and produces Class IV whitewater rapids. When the river is high enough—generally April through October—you can whitewater raft practically in the shadows of the city's skyline. Check with Richmond Raft Co., 800-540-7238; www.richmondraft.com; or Adventure Challenge, 804-276-7600; www.adventurechallenge.com/james.htm

Maymont
1700 Hampton St., Richmond,
804-358-7166;
www.maymont.org

Dooley mansion, late Victorian in style, houses an art collection and decorative arts exhibits (Tuesday-Sunday; fee). Also here are formal Japanese and Italian gardens, an arboretum, a nature center with wildlife habitat for native species, an aviary, a children's farm and a working carriage collection. Daily.

William Byrd
Blvd. St. and Idlewood Ave., Richmond,
www.wbch.org

Includes 287 acres of groves, artificial lakes, picnic areas. Tennis courts, softball fields and a fitness course. Amphitheater (June-August). Virginia's World War I memorial, a 240-foot, pink brick carillon tower.

Plantation Tours
401 E. Marshall St., Richmond,
804-783-7450

The Richmond-Petersburg-Williamsburg area has many fine old mansions and estates. Some are open most of the year; others only during Historic Garden Week. The Metro Richmond Visitors Center has maps, information folders and suggestions.

Regency Square
1420 Parham Rd., Richmond,
804-740-7467;
www.shopregencysqmall.com

The largest department stores in the area, including JCPenney, Macy's and Sears, are located in this mall off exit 181A on Interstate 64. Among the specialty shops are American Eagle Outfitters, Champs Sports and Spencer Gifts. Monday-Saturday 10 a.m.-9 p.m., Sunday noon-6 p.m.

374

VIRGINIA

Richmond Braves
The Diamond, 3001 N. Blvd.,
Richmond,
804-359-4444, 800-849-4627;
www.rbraves.com
The Richmond Braves are the AAA affiliate of the Atlanta Braves, playing their home games in a 12,134-seat stadium just off Interstate 95.

Shockoe Slip
11 S. 12th St., Richmond
Restored area of historic buildings and gaslit cobblestone streets; shopping, restaurants and galleries.

St. Paul's Church
815 E. Grace St., Richmond,
804-643-3589;
www.stpauls-episcopal.org
(Episcopal) Established in 1843, the church survived the Civil War intact. It was here that Jefferson Davis received news of Robert E. Lee's retreat from Petersburg to Appomattox. Beginning in 1890, the church added many fine stained-glass windows, including eight from the Tiffany studios. Sanctuary ceiling features decorative plasterwork interweaving Greek, Hebrew and Christian motifs around a central panel. A Tiffany mosaic of da Vinci's "Last Supper" surmounts the altar. Daily.

Valentine Museum
1015 E. Clay St., Richmond,
804-649-0711;
www.valentinemuseum.com
Traces the history of Richmond. Exhibits focus on city life, decorative arts, costumes and textiles and industrial and social history; tour of restored 1812 Wickham House. Lunch is served in a walled garden. Closed Mondays.

Virginia Aviation Museum
5701 Huntsman Rd., Richmond,
804-236-3622;
www.vam.smv.org
Exhibits and artifacts on the history of aviation, with an emphasis on Virginia pioneers. Daily.

Virginia War Memorial
621 S. Belvidere St., Richmond,
804-786-2060;
www.vawarmemorial.org
Honors Virginians who died in World War II and the Korean and Vietnam wars. Mementos of battles; eternal flame; more than 12,000 names engraved on glass and marble walls. Daily.

White House of the Confederacy
12th and Clay Streets, Richmond,
804-649-1861;
www.moc.org
Next door to the Museum of the Confederacy downtown, this Classical Revival house (1818) was used by Jefferson Davis as his official residence during the period when Richmond was the capital of the Confederacy. Abraham Lincoln met with troops here during the Union occupation of the city. It has been restored to its pre-wartime appearance with many of its original furnishings. Daily.

Wilton House Museum
215 S. Wilton Rd.,
Richmond,
804-282-5936;
www.wiltonhousemuseum.org
(1753) Georgian mansion built by William Randolph III. Fully paneled, authentic 18th-century furnishings. Headquarters of the National Society of Colonial Dames in Virginia. Tuesday-Sunday. Open during Historic Garden Week.

SPECIAL EVENTS
Historic Garden Week in Virginia
12 E. Franklin St., Richmond,
804-644-7776;
www.vagardenweek.org
Many private houses and gardens of historic or artistic interest are opened for this event, which includes more than 200 houses and gardens throughout the state. Tours. Mid-late April.

June Jubilee
Performing and visual arts festival with ethnic foods, folk dances, music and crafts. First weekend in June.

Richmond Newspapers Marathon
Last Sunday in October.

Virginia State Fair
600 E. Laburnum Ave., Richmond,
804-228-3200;
www.statefairva.org
Animal and 4-H contests, music, horse show
and carnival. Late September-early October.

HOTELS

★★★The Berkeley Hotel
1200 E. Cary St., Richmond,
804-780-1300, 888-780-4422;
www.berkeleyhotel.com
This hotel opened in 1988 but its stylish look seems much more historic. The
Berkeley Hotel is located at the crossroads
of the business district and Historic Shockoe
Slip. Dark wood paneling adorns the lobby
and dining room. Dramatic windows to the
ceiling give the hotel a European appearance. And diners at the hotel's restaurant
get a view of the Slip's cobblestones and
lamplights.
55 rooms. **$$**

★★Courtyard by Marriott
6400 W. Broad St., Richmond,
804-282-1881, 800-321-2211;
www.courtyard.com
145 rooms. **$**

★★★Crowne Plaza
555 E. Canal St.,
Richmond,
804-788-0900, 877-424-4225;
www.crowneplaza.com
Just nine miles from Richmond Interna-
tional Airport, this hotel is situated in the
heart of the historic district on the Canal
Walk. Its higher floors have a spectacu-
lar view of the James River. The hotel is
located minutes from area attractions such
as Shockoe Slip, Sixth Street Market Place,
museums, theaters and fine dining. Brown's
Island, a concert and special events venue,
is located behind the hotel. Richmond Bal-
let is adjacent to the hotel, and ballet pack-
ages are available.
299 rooms. **$**

★Days Inn
6910 Midlothian Turnpike, Richmond,
804-745-7100, 800-329-7466;
www.daysinnrichmond.com
115 rooms. Complimentary continental
breakfast. **$**

★★Doubletree Hotel
5501 Eubank Rd., Sandston,
804-226-6400, 800-222-8733;
www.doubletree.com
160 rooms. Airport transportation avail-
able. Airport. **$**

★★Embassy Suites
2925 Emerywood Pkwy., Richmond,
804-672-8585, 800-362-2779;
www.embassysuites.com
226 rooms, all suites. Complimentary full
breakfast. Airport transportation available.
$$

★★★★★The Jefferson Hotel
101 W. Franklin St., Richmond,
804-788-8000, 800-424-8014;
www.jeffersonhotel.com
The Jefferson Hotel is an institution in the
heart of Richmond. A historic Beaux Arts
landmark dating to 1895, the hotel offers
elegant guest rooms furnished in a traditional style with antique reproductions and
fine art. Pedigreed residents take afternoon
tea here. TJ's provides a casual setting for
fine dining with local dishes like oyster
chowder and peanut soup, while the hotel's
star restaurant, Lemaire, offers a sparkling
ambience and a refined menu. Near the
city's financial district, museums, shopping
and the state capitol. Complimentary car
service transports guests to these and other
destinations within a three-mile radius.
264 rooms. Airport transportation available.
$$

★★Linden Row Inn
100 E. Franklin St., Richmond,
804-783-7000, 800-348-7424;
www.lindenrowinn.com
70 rooms. Complimentary continental
breakfast. Restaurant (public by reserva-
tion). **$**

★★★Marriott Richmond
500 E. Broad St., Richmond,
804-643-3400, 800-228-9290;
www.marriott.com/ricdt

Attached to the Convention Center via skybridge, this high-rise hotel in the heart of the city is close to the Coliseum and both the historic and river districts. Business travelers will appreciate high-speed Internet access in their rooms, while families will love the spacious rooms, indoor pool and downtown location. The hotel offers complimentary shuttle service to Shockoe Slip, as well as to all major businesses within 3 miles.
401 rooms. $$

★★★Omni Richmond Hotel
100 S. 12th St., Richmond,
804-344-7000, 888-444-6664;
www.omnihotels.com

This contemporary hotel is conveniently located in the center of the financial and historic districts in the James Center and features scenic river views. It's across the street from the famous Tobacco Company restaurant, and a great place to stay if you intend to explore Shockoe Slip and Shockoe Bottom.
361 rooms. $

★Quality Inn
8008 W. Broad St., Richmond,
804-346-0000, 877-424-6423;
www.qualityinn.com
191 rooms. Complimentary continental breakfast. $

★★★Sheraton Richmond West Hotel
6624 W. Broad St., Richmond,
804-285-2000, 800-325-3535;
www.sheraton.com

With luxurious furnishings, such as plush pillows and duvets on Sweet Sleeper beds, this upscale hotel offers its guests comfortable accommodations set in a richly landscaped business park just off the highway. With oversize writing desks and in-room WiFi, the hotel is geared toward the business traveler, but tourists and families will be just as comfortable here.
372 rooms. $

RESTAURANTS

★★Acacia
3325 W. Cary St., Richmond,
804-354-6060;
www.acaciarestaurant.com
American menu. Lunch, dinner. Closed Sunday. Bar. Casual attire. Reservations recommended. Outdoor seating. $$$

★★Amici
3343 W. Cary St., Richmond,
804-353-4700;
www.amiciristorante.net
Italian menu. Lunch, dinner. Bar. Casual attire. Reservations recommended. Outdoor seating. $$$

★★Byram's Lobster House
3215 W. Broad St., Richmond,
804-355-9193;
www.byrams.com
American, seafood menu. Lunch, dinner. Bar. Children's menu. Casual attire. $$

★★Cabo's Corner Bistro
2053 W. Broad St., Richmond,
804-355-1144;
www.cabosbistro.com
American menu. Dinner. Closed Sunday-Monday. Bar. Business casual attire. Reservations recommended. $$$

★★★The Dining Room at the Berkeley Hotel
1200 E. Cary St., Richmond,
804-225-5105, 888-780-4422;
www.berkleyhotel.com
Located in a European-style hotel, this handsomely decorated dining room serves elegant, impeccably prepared meals in a sophisticated and tranquil atmosphere. Entrée selections include seared rockfish with fried okra, sautéed spinach, Virginia spoon bread and lobster demi glace; and grilled black angus bistro steak with a sautéed zucchini medley and horseradish butter.
American menu. Breakfast, lunch, dinner, Sunday brunch. Bar. Children's menu. Business casual attire. Reservations recommended. Valet parking. $$$

★★Half Way House
10301 Jefferson Davis Hwy., Richmond,
804-275-1760, 800-897-0848;
www.halfwayhouserestaurant.com
American menu. Lunch, dinner. Business casual attire. Reservations recommended. $$$

★★Helen's
2527 W. Main St., Richmond,
804-358-4370
International menu. Dinner. Closed Monday. Bar. Casual attire. Reservations recommended. $$

★★Kabuto Japanese House of Steak
8052 W. Broad St., Richmond,
804-747-9573
Japanese menu. Lunch, dinner. Bar. Business casual attire. Reservations recommended. $$

★★La Petite France
2108 Maywill St.,
Richmond,
804-353-8729;
www.lapetitefrance.net
French menu. Lunch, dinner. Closed Sunday-Monday; also the last two weeks in August. Jacket required (dinner). Reservations recommended. $$$

★★★Lemaire
101 W. Franklin,
Richmond,
804-788-8000, 800-424-8014;
www.jeffersonhotel.com
Old-world fine dining comes to life at Lemaire, located in the historic Jefferson Hotel. The restaurant is named for Etienne Lemaire, who served as maitre d' to President Jefferson and was widely credited for introducing the fine art of cooking with wines to America. His love of food and wine is continued at Lemaire, where contemporary Southern cooking goes upscale with French accents, homegrown herbs, featherweight sauces and seasonal ingredients.
American menu. Breakfast, lunch, dinner. Bar. Children's menu. Business casual attire. Valet parking. $$$

★★★The Old Original Bookbinder's
2306 E. Cary St.,
Richmond,
804-643-6900;
www.bookbindersrichmond.com
The first Bookbinder's to open outside of Philadelphia, this restaurant is located in a historic building that was once a Philip Morris manufacturing plant. Menu selections include high-quality seafood and homemade desserts. There is an outdoor courtyard area for alfresco dining.
Seafood menu. Dinner. Bar. Children's menu. Business casual attire. Reservations recommended. Valet parking. Outdoor seating. $$$

★O'Tooles
4800 Forest Hill Ave.,
Richmond,
804-233-1781;
www.otoolesrestaurant.com
American menu. Lunch, dinner, brunch. Bar. Children's menu. Casual attire. $$

★★Sam Miller's Ocean Grill & Oyster Bar
1210 E. Cary St.,
Richmond,
804-644-5465;
www.sammillers.com
Seafood menu. Lunch, dinner, late-night. Bar. Business casual attire. Reservations recommended. $$$

★★Skilligalee
5416 Glenside Dr.,
Richmond,
804-672-6200
Seafood menu. Lunch, dinner. Bar. Children's menu. Business casual attire. Reservations recommended. $$

★Strawberry Street Cafe
421 N. Strawberry St.,
Richmond,
804-353-6860;
www.strawberrystreetcafe.com
American menu. Lunch, dinner, brunch. Bar. Children's menu. Casual attire. Reservations recommended. $$

378

VIRGINIA

★★★The Tobacco Company
1201 E. Cary St.,
Richmond,
804-782-9555;
www.thetobaccocompany.com

The Tobacco Company, the restaurant that helped pioneer the renaissance of Richmond's Shockoe Slip neighborhood, is carved from a former tobacco warehouse. Its centerpiece is a dramatic, skylit atrium with an antique cage elevator servicing three floors of dining. The menu is extensive if not inventive: steaks, prime rib, lobster, veal, shrimp, scallops, salmon, rainbow trout, chicken, crab, Virginia ham and pasta. Enjoy live music, a free buffet during happy hours (5-7 p.m., Wednesday through Friday) and cigars in the bar.

American menu. Lunch, dinner, late-night, Sunday brunch. Bar. Business casual attire. Reservations recommended. **$$$**

★Trak's
9115 Quioccasin Rd., Richmond,
804-740-1700

Greek, Italian menu. Lunch, dinner. Closed Sunday. Children's menu. Casual attire. Reservations recommended. **$$**

★Yen Ching
6601 Midlothian Turnpike,
Richmond,
804-276-7430;
www.yenchingdining.com

Chinese menu. Lunch, dinner. Business casual attire. Reservations recommended. **$$**

RICHMOND NATIONAL BATTLEFIELD PARK

The Union made a total of seven drives on Richmond, the symbol of secession, during the Civil War. Richmond National Battlefield Park, 770 acres in 10 different units, preserves sites of the two efforts that came close to success: McClellan's Peninsula Campaign of 1862 and Grant's attack in 1864.

Of McClellan's campaign, the park includes sites of the Seven Days' Battles at Chickahominy Bluffs, Beaver Dam Creek, Gaines' Mill (Watt House) and Malvern Hill. Grant's campaign is represented by the battlefield at Cold Harbor, where on June 3, 1864, Grant hurled his army at fortified Confederate positions, resulting in 7,000 casualties in less than one hour. Confederate Fort Harrison, Parker's Battery, Drewry's Bluff (Fort Darling) and Union-built Fort Brady are also included. Park (daily).
Information: 3215 E. Broad St., Richmond, 23223,
804-226-1981; www.nps.gov/rich

379

VIRGINIA

★
★
★
★
★

WHAT TO SEE AND DO
Main Visitor Center
3215 E. Broad St.,
Richmond,
804-226-1981
Information, exhibits, film, slide program. Daily.
From here start:

Self-guided Tour
Richmond National Battlefield Park

Auto drive (60 miles) with markers, maps, recorded messages providing background, detailed information for specific places. Visitors may select own route, including all or part of the drive.

Other Visitor Centers
Cold Harbor, Hwy. 156 (daily, unstaffed) and Fort Harrison, Hwy. 5 and Battlefield Park Road June-August: daily.

ROANOKE

The view from the top of Mill Mountain standing under the famous Roanoke Star (the world's largest man-made star) reveals the spectacular beauty and vastness of the Roanoke Valley, which seems to go on forever in every direction.

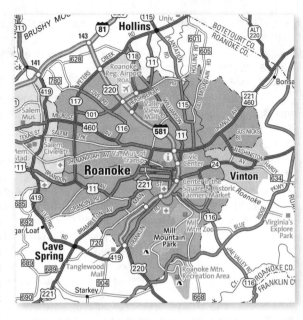

Tucked in the valley's center, the city itself evolved from a thriving, industrial railroading nexus in the late 1800s to a state-of-the-art destination where electrons are now the currency of choice. Over the years, Roanoke has become a sophisticated place, with a thriving arts community, a wealth of museums, and varied entertainment and theater offerings, which now share the stage with several world-class educational institutions. The hustle and bustle of the Norfolk and Southern Railroad has given way to health care, education, travel, conventions, industry and trade.

Information: Roanoke Valley Convention & Visitors Bureau, 101 N.E. Shenandoah Ave., Roanoke, 540-342-6025, 800-635-5535; www.visitroanokeva.com

VIRGINIA

WHAT TO SEE AND DO

Center in the Square
1 Market Square,
Roanoke,
540-342-5700;
www.centerinthesquare.org
Restored 20th-century furniture warehouse housing five independent cultural organizations: three museums, including Art Museum of Western Virginia, and two professional theater companies. Tuesday-Sunday.

Also here:

History Museum of Western Virginia
1 Market Square S.E.,
Roanoke,
540-342-5770;
www.artmuseumroanoke.org
Permanent exhibits deal with Roanoke history from days of Native Americans to present. Archives, library (by appt). Tuesday-Sunday.

Science Museum of Western Virginia & Hopkins Planetarium
1 Market Square, Roanoke,
540-342-5710;
www.smwv.org
Museum contains hands-on exhibits in the natural and physical sciences: animals of land and ocean, computers, TV weather station. Workshops, programs and classes for children and adults; special exhibits. Hopkins Planetarium shows films. Tuesday-Sunday.

George Washington and Jefferson National Forests
5162 Valleypointe Pkwy., Roanoke,
540-265-5100;
www.southernregion.fs.fed.us/gwj
Consist of approximately nearly two million acres. Swimming; fishing for trout, bluegill, and bass; hunting for deer, bear, wild turkey and small game; riding trails, camping, picnicking. Scenic drives past Crabtree Falls,

hardwood forests and unusual geologic features. Overlooks of the Shenandoah Valley. Part of the Appalachian Trail crosses through the forest. Fees are charged at some recreation sites. Trails for the visually impaired.

Mill Mountain Zoological Park
Hwy. 220/I-581 and Blue Ridge Pkwy.,
Roanoke,
540-343-3241;
www.mmzoo.org
Zoo sits atop Mill Mountain; offers picnic areas with magnificent views of city and valley. Daily.

Virginia Museum of Transportation
303 Norfolk Ave., Roanoke,
540-342-5670;
www.vmt.org
Vehicles from the past and present. Large steam, diesel and electric locomotive collection. Aviation exhibits; model of miniature traveling circus. Hands-on exhibits. March-December: daily; rest of year, Wednesday-Sunday.

Virginia's Explore Park
3900 Rutrough Rd. S.E., Roanoke,
540-427-1800, 800-842-9163;
www.explorepark.org
This 1,300-acre living history museum and nature center features re-created frontier settlement that depicts life in western Virginia in 1671, 1740 and 1850. Six miles of hiking trails. Picnic areas. May-mid-November: Wednesday-Sunday.

SPECIAL EVENTS
Mill Mountain Theatre
1 Market Square S.E., Roanoke,
540-342-5740;
www.millmountain.org
Center in the Square. Musicals, comedies, dramas. Nightly Tuesday-Sunday; Saturday-Sunday matinees. Regular season, October-August.

Virginia State Championship Chili Cookoff
City Market, Roanoke,
540-342-4716

Teams compete to represent Virginia in World Cook-off. Samples, entertainment. First Saturday in May.

HOTELS
★★Holiday Inn
3315 Ordway Dr. N.W.,
Roanoke,
540-362-4500, 800-282-0244;
www.holidayinn.com
154 rooms. Airport transportation available.
$

★★Holiday Inn
4468 Starkey Rd.,
Roanoke,
540-774-4400, 800-282-0244;
www.holidayinn.com
196 rooms. Airport transportation available. $

★★Doubletree Hotel
110 Shenandoah Ave.,
Roanoke,
540-985-5900, 800-222-8733;
www.hotelroanoke.com
332 rooms. Airport transportation available. $

RESTAURANTS
★★Kabuki Japanese Steak House
3503 Franklin Rd. S.W.,
Roanoke,
540-981-0222;
www.kabukiva.com
Japanese menu. Dinner. Bar. Children's menu. Casual attire. Reservations recommended. $$

★★★Library
3117 Franklin Rd.,
Roanoke,
540-985-0811
Not only is this 1785 New England-style mansion a historic landmark, but it has served the likes of George Washington and a host of other presidents.
French, American menu. Dinner. Closed Sunday. Business casual attire. Reservations recommended. $$$

SALEM

Salem, part of the industrial complex of the Roanoke Valley, sits with Roanoke between the Blue Ridge and Allegheny mountains. Historic markers throughout Salem indicate the city's colonial heritage.

Information: Salem/Roanoke County Chamber of Commerce, 9 N. College Ave., Salem, 540-387-0267; www.s-rcchamber.org

WHAT TO SEE AND DO

Dixie Caverns
5753 W. Main St., Salem,
540-380-2085;
www.dixiecaverns.com
Stalactites in lofty chambers; modern lighting system makes 45-minute tour comfortable as well as interesting. Pottery shop and mineral shop (all year). Camping facilities (fee). Daily.

HOTELS

★Days Inn
1535 E. Main St., Salem,
540-986-1000, 800-329-7466;
www.daysinn.com
70 rooms. Complimentary continental breakfast. $

SHENANDOAH NATIONAL PARK

About 450 million years ago, the Blue Ridge was at the bottom of a sea. Today, it averages 2,000 feet above sea level, and some 300 square miles of the loveliest Blue Ridge area are included in Shenandoah National Park.

The park is 80 miles long and two to 13 miles wide. Running its full length is the 105-mile Skyline Drive. Main entrances are the North Entrance (Front Royal), from I-66, Hwys 340, 522 and 55; Thornton Gap Entrance (31.5 miles south), from Hwy. 211; Swift Run Gap Entrance (65.7 miles south), from Hwy. 33; and the South Entrance (Rockfish Gap), from I-64, Hwy. 250, and the Blue Ridge Parkway. The drive, twisting and turning along the crest of the Blue Ridge, is one of the finest scenic trips in the East. Approximately 70 overlooks give views of the Blue Ridge, the Piedmont and to the west, the Shenandoah Valley and the Alleghenies.

The drive offers much, but the park offers more. Exploration on foot or on horseback attracts thousands of visitors. Most of the area is wooded, predominantly in white, red and chestnut oak, with hickory, birch, maple, hemlock, tulip poplar and nearly 100 other species. At the head of Whiteoak Canyon are 300-year-old hemlocks. The park, a sanctuary for deer, bears, foxes and bobcats, along with more than 200 varieties of birds, bursts with color in the fall, which makes this season particularly popular with visitors.

Accommodations are available in the park, with lodges, motel-type units and cabins at Big Meadows and Skyland, and housekeeping cabins at Lewis Mountain. For reservations and rates (which vary), contact ARA-MARK Virginia Sky-Line Company, Inc., P.O. Box 727, Luray, 22835-9051; 800-999-4714. Nearby communities provide a variety of accommodations. In the park, there are restaurants at Panorama, Skyland and Big Meadows; light lunches and groceries are available at Elkwallow, Big Meadows, Lewis Mountain and Loft Mountain waysides.

The park is open all year; lodge and cabin accommodations, usually March-December; phone ahead for the schedule. Skyline Drive is occasionally closed for short periods during November-March. As in all national parks, pets must be on a leash. The speed limit is 35 miles per hour. $15 per car per week, annual permit $30; Golden Age, Golden Access and Golden Eagle Passports are accepted.

Park Headquarters is five miles east of Luray on Hwy. 211. Detailed information and pamphlets may be obtained by contacting the Superintendent, Shenandoah National Park, 3655 Hwy. 211 E, Luray, 22835; 540-999-3500; www.nps.gov/shen

WHAT TO SEE AND DO

Big Meadows
Mile 51.1, Shenandoah
(3,500 feet) Accommodations, restaurant; store, gas; tent and trailer sites; picnic grounds; nature trail. Usually April-November.

Byrd Visitor Center
Mile 51, Shenandoah
Exhibits, information, book sales, orientation programs, maps. Usually April-November: daily.

Dickey Ridge Visitor Center
Mile 4.6, Shenandoah
Exhibits, programs, information, book sales; picnic grounds. Usually April-November: daily.

Elkwallow
Mile 24.1, Shenandoah
(2,445 feet) Picnic grounds; food, store. May-October: daily.

Lewis Mountain
Mile 57.5, Shenandoah
(3,390 feet) One- and two-bedroom cabins with heat; tent and trailer sites; picnic grounds, store. Usually May-October.

Loft Mountain
Mile 79.5, Shenandoah
(3,380 feet) Picnicking, camping; wayside facility; gas, store. May-October.

Loft Mountain Information Center
Mile 79.5, Shenandoah
Exhibits, information; programs, nature trail. Usually May-November.

Mary's Rock Tunnel
Mile 32.4, Shenandoah
(2,545 feet) Drive goes through 600 feet of rock (clearance 13 feet).

Panorama
Mile 31.5, at junction Hwy.,
211, Shenandoah
(2,300 feet) Dining room, gift shop. Trail to Mary's Rock. Closed in winter.

Pinnacles
Mile 36.7, Shenandoah
(3,500 feet) Picnic grounds.

Skyland
Mile 41.7, Shenandoah
(3,680 feet) Accommodations, restaurant, gift shop; guided trail rides; Stony Man Nature Trail.

South River
Mile 62.8, Shenandoah
(2,940 feet) Picnic grounds, 2 1/2-mile round-trip trail to falls.

SPRINGFIELD

HOTELS

★Hampton Inn
6550 Loisdale Court, Springfield,
703-924-9444, 800-426-7866;
www.hamptoninn.com
153 rooms. Complimentary continental breakfast. **$**

★★★Hilton Springfield
6550 Loisdale Rd., Springfield,
703-971-8900, 800-445-8667;
www.hilton.com
The Hilton Springfield is located just 15 minutes from Washington, D.C., and offers complimentary shuttle service to the Springfield/Franconia Metro station. This modern, welcoming hotel puts every comfort at your fingertips. Accommodations are streamlined and stylish. Guest rooms feature complimentary wireless Internet access. The hotel's restaurant, Houlihan's, serves dishes such as grilled rosemary chicken and blackened, center-cut pork medallions. 244 rooms. **$**

RESTAURANTS

★★Mike's American Grill
6210 Backlick Rd., Springfield,
703-644-7100
Steak menu. Lunch, dinner. Bar. **$$**

VIRGINIA

STANLEY

HOTELS

★★★Jordan Hollow Farm Inn
326 Hawksbill Park Rd., Stanley,
540-778-2285, 888-418-7000;
www.jordanhollow.com
Find serene relaxation at this restored colonial horse farm. Some guest rooms feature beautiful vistas of the Blue Ridge Mountains. The Shenandoah Valley location offers many outdoor recreations, not the least of which is simply taking in the scenery.
15 rooms. Complimentary full breakfast. **$$**

STAUNTON

To historians, Staunton (STAN-ton) is known as the birthplace of Woodrow Wilson, and to students of government, as the place where the city manager plan was first conceived and adopted. Set in fertile Shenandoah Valley fields and orchards between the Blue Ridge and Allegheny mountain ranges, the area around Staunton produces poultry, livestock and wool. Manufacturing firms in the city make air conditioners, razors, candy and clothing.

A Ranger District office of the George Washington and Jefferson national forests is located here.

Information: Travel Information Center, 1250 Richmond Rd., Staunton, 540-332-3972, 800-332-5219

WHAT TO SEE AND DO

Frontier Culture Museum
1290 Richmond Rd., Staunton,
540-332-7850;
www.frontiermuseum.org
Living history museum consists of working farms brought together from England, Germany, Northern Ireland and an American farm. The European farms represent what America's early settlers left; the American farm, from the Valley of Virginia, reflects the blend of the various European influences. Visitors are able to see and take part in life as it was lived on these 17th-, 18th- and 19th-century farmsteads. Costumed interpreters demonstrate daily life at all four sites. Visitor center. Daily; closed first week in January.

Gypsy Hill Park
Chruchville and Thornrose avenues,
Staunton,
540-332-3945
Lake stocked with fish, swimming (late May-Labor Day, fee); lighted softball field with concession stand, outdoor basketball courts, tennis, 18-hole golf, picnicking, miniature train ride, playgrounds, fairgrounds. Daily.

Trinity Episcopal Church
120 W. Beverley St.,
Staunton,
540-886-9132;
www.trinitystaunton.org
(1855) Founded as Augusta Parish Church (1746), original building on this site served as Revolutionary capital of state for 16 days in 1781. Open on request Monday-Friday.

Woodrow Wilson Birthplace and Presidential Museum
24 N. Coalter St., Staunton,
540-885-0897;
www.woodrowwilson.org
Restored Greek Revival manse with period furnishings and Wilson family mementos from 1850s; museum building on grounds houses seven-gallery presidential exhibit, "The Life and Times of Woodrow Wilson," and his 1919 Pierce-Arrow limousine. Victorian gardens. Daily.

SPECIAL EVENTS

Jazz in the Park
Gypsy Hill Park,
1000 Montgomery Ave., Staunton,
540-332-3945
Thursday nights. July-August.

HOTELS

★★★Belle Grae Inn
515 W. Frederick St., Staunton,
540-886-5151, 888-541-5151;
www.bellegrae.com
This century-old bed and breakfast offers carefully restored Victorian accommodations in four buildings.
14 rooms. Children over 12 years only. Complimentary full breakfast. 1870s restored Victorian mansion. **$$**

★Best Western Staunton Inn
92 Rowe Rd., Staunton,
540-885-1112, 800-752-9471;
www.dominionlodging.com
80 rooms. Complimentary continental breakfast. Airport transportation available. **$**

★Comfort Inn
1302 Richmond Ave., Staunton,
540-886-5000, 877-424-6423;
www.comfortinn.com
98 rooms. Complimentary continental breakfast. High-speed Internet access. Airport transportation available. **$**

★★★Frederick House
28 N. New St., Staunton,
540-885-4220, 800-334-5575;
www.frederickhouse.com
Built in 1809, the Frederick House's five restored buildings offer spacious rooms furnished with antiques and period furniture.
24 rooms. Complimentary full breakfast. **$**

STEPHENS CITY

HOTELS

★Comfort Inn
167 Town Run Lane, Stephens City,
540-869-6500, 877-424-6423;
www.comfortinn.com
60 rooms. Complimentary continental breakfast. **$**

★★★The Inn at Vaucluse Spring
231 Vaucluse Spring Lane,
Stephens City,
540-869-0200, 800-869-0525;
www.vauclusespring.com

★★Holiday Inn
I-81, Hwy. 275,
Staunton,
540-248-6020, 800-932-9061;
www.histaunton.com
114 rooms. Airport transportation available. **$**

SPECIALTY LODGINGS

Thornrose House
531 Thornrose Ave.,
Staunton,
540-885-7026, 800-861-4338
Georgian Revival house (1912); wraparound veranda.
5 rooms. Children over 5 years only. Complimentary full breakfast. **$**

RESTAURANTS

★Mrs. Rowe's Restaurant & Bakery
74 Rowe Rd., Staunton,
540-886-1833;
www.mrsrowes.com
American menu. Breakfast, lunch, dinner. Children's menu. Casual attire. **$**

★★Pullman Restaurant
36 Middlebrook Ave.,
Staunton,
540-885-6612;
www.thepullman.com
American menu. Lunch, dinner, Sunday brunch. Bar. Children's menu. Casual attire. Reservations recommended. Outdoor seating. **$$**

Located on 100 acres, this inn consists of four buildings: the Manor House, Chumley Homeplace, Gallery and Millhouse Studio. Visitors will enjoy the nearby wineries and scenic location.
15 rooms. Complimentary full breakfast. Restaurant. **$$**

385

VIRGINIA

★
★
★
★
★

STRASBURG

Lying at the base of Massanutten Mountain and on the north fork of the Shenandoah River, Strasburg was founded in 1761 by German settlers. Prospering in the early 19th century as a center of trade and flour milling, the village later became identified with the manufacture of high-quality pottery, earning the nickname "Pottown" after the Civil War. Strasburg played a pivotal role in Stonewall Jackson's Campaign of 1862 because of its location on the Manassas Gap Railroad and the Shenandoah Valley Turnpike. The first western Virginia town to be served by two railroads, Strasburg became a prominent railroad town, manufacturing center, and home of printing and publishing businesses after 1890.

Today Strasburg is located near the entrance to the Skyline Drive, attracting visitors with its antebellum and Victorian architecture and its burgeoning art community. The town calls itself the "antique capital of Virginia."

Information: Chamber of Commerce, Strasburg, 540-465-3187; www.strasburgva.com

WHAT TO SEE AND DO

Belle Grove
336 Belle Grove Rd., Strasburg,
540-869-2028;
www.bellegrove.org
(1794) This limestone mansion's design reflects Thomas Jefferson's influence. Used as Union headquarters during the Battle of Cedar Creek, October 19, 1864. Unusual interior woodwork; herb garden in rear. Guided tours. April-October: daily.

Hupp's Hill Battlefield Park and Study Center
33229 Old Valley Pike, Strasburg,
540-465-5884
Former campsite for six different Civil War generals' troops, now a museum and hands-on interpretive center. Artifacts, documents, exhibits. Guided battlefield tours (by appointment; fee). Daily.

Strasburg Museum
440 E. King St., Strasburg,
540-465-3175
Blacksmith, cooper and potter shop collections; displays from colonial homes; relics from Civil War and railroad eras; Native American artifacts. Housed in Southern Railway Depot. May-October: daily.

SPECIAL EVENTS

Mayfest
Celebration of town's German heritage with parade, entertainment and arts, crafts, antiques and foods fairs. Third weekend in May.

HOTELS

★★**Hotel Strasburg**
213 S. Holliday St.,
Strasburg,
540-465-9191, 800-348-8327;
www.hotelstrasburg.com
29 rooms. Complimentary continental breakfast. Victorian building. **$**

RESTAURANTS

★★★**Hotel Strasburg**
213 S. Holliday St.,
Strasburg,
540-465-9191, 800-348-8327;
www.hotelstrasburg.com
The inn's ornate Victorian lobby gives way to an invitingly cozy country restaurant, where locals and travelers alike dine on fine wines and elegant cuisine, including seasonal seafood dishes.
Mediterranean menu. Lunch, dinner. Bar. Children's menu. Reservations recommended. **$$**

VIRGINIA

★
★
★
★
★

STUART

WHAT TO SEE AND DO

Fairy Stone State Park
Hwy. 346 N., Stuart,
276-930-2424;
www.dcrvirginia.gov/state_parks/fai.shtml
Located in the foothills of the Blue Ridge Mountains, the park features a number of cabins and campsites as well as swimming, a boathouse, boating (launch, rentals, electric motors only), hiking and biking trails, picnic facilities, and a concession stand. Fishing is allowed (license required), and a dump station and electrical hook-ups are available. The legendary fairy stones found in the park come from staurolite stones, a combination of silica, iron and aluminum.

TAPPAHANNOCK

Bartholemew Hoskins patented the first land here in 1645. Following his lead, others came, and a small village soon sprang up, known at that time as Hobbes His Hole. Formally chartered in 1682 as New Plymouth, the town was to experience yet another name change. Built around the Rappahannock River, which means "running water," the town port became known as Tappahannock or "on the running water." Four hundred men gathered here in 1765 to protest the Stamp Act.

Today the area around Prince and Duke streets and Water Lane of Tappahannock has been declared a historic district. Highlights include the beautifully renovated Ritchie House, the Anderton House, once used for the prizing of tobacco into hogsheads, and Scot's Arms Tavern.

Information: Chamber of Commerce, Tappahannock, 804-443-5241

HOTELS

★**Days Inn**
Route 17 Tappahannock Blvd.,
Tappahannock,
804-443-9200;
www.daysinn.com
60 rooms. Complimentary continental breakfast. **$**

RESTAURANTS

★★**Lowery's Seafood Restaurant**
Route 17 and 360,
Tappahannock,
804-443-4314;
www.lowerysrestaurant.com
Seafood menu. Lunch, dinner. **$$**

TREVILIANS

HOTELS

★★★**Prospect Hill Plantation Inn**
2887 Poindexter Rd.,
Trevilians,
540-967-0844, 800-277-0844;
www.prospecthill.com

This romantic 1732 manor house is set on 50 acres of lawn.
13 rooms. **$$$$**

TRIANGLE

Quantico Marine Corps Base is three miles east of town.
Information: Prince William County/Manassas Conference & Visitors Bureau,
8609 Sudley Rd.,
703-396-7130; www.visitpwc.com

★
★
★
★
★

WHAT TO SEE AND DO
National Museum of the Marine Corps
18900 Jefferson Davis Hwy.,
Triangle,
703-640-7965, 800-397-7585;
www.usmcmuseum.org
Chronological presentation of the Marine Corps Air-Ground Team's role in American history; artifacts on exhibit include aircraft, engines, armor, tracked and wheeled vehicles, artillery, small arms, uniforms, dioramas and photographs in pre-World War II aviation hangars. Daily.

Prince William Forest Park
18100 Park Headquarters Rd.,
Triangle,
703-221-7181;
www.nps.gov/prwi
Consists of 18,000 acres. Hiking, bicycling, picnicking, camping (14-day limit; no hookups; fee; group cabins by reservations only), trailer campground off Hwy. 234 (fee; hookups, showers, laundry). Naturalist programs. Daily.

VIENNA
Information: Vienna-Tysons Regional Chamber of Commerce, 513 Maple Ave. W., Vienna, 703-281-1333; www.vtrcc.org

WHAT TO SEE AND DO
Barns of Wolf Trap
1624 Trap Rd.,
Vienna,
703-938-2404;
www.wolf-trap.org
A 350-seat theater with chamber music, recitals, mime, jazz, folk, theater and children's programs. For schedule contact the Barns. Late September-early May.

Wolf Trap Farm Park for the Performing Arts
1624 Trap Rd.,
Vienna,
703-255-1900
Varied programs include ballet, musicals, opera, classical, jazz and folk music. Filene Center open theater seats 3,800 under cover and 3,000 on lawn. Picnicking on grounds, all year. Also free interpretive children's programs, July-August. Late May-September.

Meadowlark Botanical Gardens
9750 Meadowlark Gardens Court,
Vienna,
703-255-3631;
www.nvrpa.org/parks/meadowlark
Lilac, wildflower, herb, native plants, and landscaped gardens on 95 acres. Includes three ponds; water garden, gazebos, trails. Visitor center. Daily. Children under 7 free.

HOTELS
★★★Marriott Tysons Corner
8028 Leesburg Pike,
Vienna,
703-734-3200, 800-228-9790;
www.marriott.com
390 rooms. Airport transportation available. $$

RESTAURANTS
★★Aarathi
409 Maple Ave. E.,
Vienna,
703-938-0100
Indian menu. Lunch, dinner. Reservations recommended. $$

★★Bistro 123
1961 Chain Bridge Rd.,
McLean,
703-288-1369;
www.bistro123.com
French menu. Lunch, dinner. Closed Sunday. Bar. Outdoor seating. $$

388

VIRGINIA

★★Bonaroti
428 Maple Ave. E.,
Vienna,
703-281-7550
Italian menu. Lunch, dinner. Closed Sunday.
Bar. Children's menu. **$$**

★★Clyde's
8332 Leesburg Pike,
Vienna,
703-734-1901;
www.clydes.com
American menu. Lunch, dinner, Sunday brunch. Bar. Business casual attire. Reservations recommended. **$$**

★★Hunan Lion
2070 Chain Bridge Rd.,
Vienna,
703-734-9828;
www.hunanlion.com
Chinese menu. Lunch, dinner. Bar. **$**

★★La Provence
144 W. Maple Ave.,
Vienna,
703-242-3777
French menu. Lunch, dinner. Closed Sunday. Bar. Reservations recommended. **$$**

★★★Le Canard
132 Branch Rd.,
Vienna,
703-281-0070;
www.le-canard.com
The formal interior of dark red fabrics and mahogany wood sets the tone for an elegantly traditional dining experience. Rich, sumptuous dishes are followed by unique flaming specialty coffees.
French menu. Lunch, dinner. Bar. Reservations recommended. **$$**

★★Marco Polo
245 Maple Ave. W.,
Vienna,
703-281-3922;
www.marcopolorestaurant.com
Italian, seafood menu. Lunch, dinner. Sunday brunch. Closed Monday-Tuesday. **$$**

★★★Morton's, The Steakhouse
8075 Leesburg Pike,
Vienna,
703-883-0800;
www.mortons.com
Consistent with expectations, this outlet serves the same famed entrees as its sister restaurants. The tableside menu presentation reveals generous portions and high-quality ingredients in the restaurant's warm, club-like atmosphere.
Steak menu. Lunch, dinner. Bar. Jacket required. Reservations recommended. Valet parking. **$$$**

★★★Nizam's
523 Maple Ave. W.,
Vienna,
703-938-8948
Doner kebob, otherwise known as gyros, is the legendary mainstay of this refined Turkish restaurant. Thin, tender slices of marinated, spit-roasted lamb nestle inside soft pita bread in a dish that rivals anything Istanbul could turn out. Service is polished and attentive.
Lunch, dinner. Closed Monday. Bar. Reservations recommended. **$$**

★★Panjshir II
224 W. Maple Ave.,
Vienna,
703-281-4183
Vegetarian menu. Lunch, dinner. Closed Monday. Bar. **$$**

★★Tara Thai
226 Maple Ave. W.,
Vienna,
703-255-2467
Thai menu. Lunch, dinner. Bar. Reservations recommended. **$$**

★★That's Amore
150 Branch Road S.E.,
Vienna,
703-281-7777;
www.thatsamore.com
Italian menu. Lunch, dinner. Closed Labor Day. Bar. **$$$**

389

VIRGINIA

★
★
★
★
★

VIRGINIA BEACH

Strolling down the newly expanded boardwalk, you can relive the pleasures of your youth and enjoy the buzz of entertainment, good food and people-watching at its finest.

The area's historical sites tie Virginia Beach to the first permanent English settlement over 400 years ago. In fact, First Landing State Park is where John Smith alighted before he went on to Jamestown. There are museums too, including the Virginia Marine Science Museum, voted one of the top ten marine science aquariums/museums in the United States.

Virginia Beach is also home to more than 106 square miles of wetlands and water, a 3,000-acre state park and two wildlife refuges. Amazingly, being this close to Virginia's largest city, the natural ecological areas surrounding Virginia Beach are among the most pristine and undiscovered areas along the mid-Atlantic. Even on a rainy day, the wildlife— native birds, whales and dolphins—are close enough for you to get a good look.

Information: Visitor Information Center, 2100 Parks Ave., Virginia Beach, 757-437-4882, 800-822-3224; www.vbfun.com

WHAT TO SEE AND DO

Adam Thoroughgood House
1636 Parish Rd., Virginia Beach, 757-460-7588
(Circa 1680) One of the oldest remaining brick houses in U.S.; restored, furnished; restored gardens. Closed Mondays.

Association for Research and Enlightenment
67th St. and Atlantic Ave., Virginia Beach, 757-428-3588;
www.are-cayce.com
Headquarters for study and research of work of psychic Edgar Cayce. Visitor Center has bookstore, library, displays, ESP-testing machine, movie and daily lecture. Daily.

Contemporary Art Center of Virginia
2200 Parks Ave., Virginia Beach, 757-425-0000;
www.cacv.org
This 32,000-square-foot facility is devoted to the presentation of 20th-century art through exhibitions, education, performing arts and special events. Daily.

First Landing/Seashore State Park
2500 Shore,
Virginia Beach,
757-412-2300;
www.dcr.virginia.gov/state_parks/fir.shtml
More than 2,700 acres with lagoons, cypress trees and sand dunes. Swimming at own risk, fishing, boating (ramp); hiking, bicycle and self-guided nature trails; picnicking, tent and trailer sites (March-November; fee), 20 cabins (open all year round). Visitor center, interpretive programs. Access for disabled to nature trail. Daily. Standard fees.

Fishing
Linkhorn Bay and Rudee Inlet,
Virginia Beach
In the Lynnhaven and Rudee Inlets for channel bass, speckled trout, spots, croakers, flounder and whiting in season; in the Back Bay area, 18 miles S on Hwy. 615, for largemouth black bass, pickerel and perch. Pier fishing and surf casting from piers jutting into the Atlantic and piers in the Chesapeake Bay. Reef, deep-sea and Gulf Stream fishing from charter boats for sea bass, weakfish, flounder, cobia, bonito, tuna, marlin, false albacore, blue and dolphin. Lake and stream fishing at Lake Smith, Lake Christine, and the inland waterways of the Chesapeake and Albemarle Canal. Crabbing for blue crabs in Lynnhaven waters, Linkhorn Bay and Rudee Inlet. No license or closed season for saltwater fishing.

Francis Land House Historic Site and Gardens
3131 Virginia Beach Blvd., Virginia Beach, 757-431-4000
Late 18th-century plantation home features period rooms, special exhibits, gardens and museum gift shop. Tuesday-Saturday, also Sunday afternoons.

VIRGINIA

Lynnhaven House
4405 Wishart Rd., Virginia Beach,
757-460-1688;
www.apva.org/lynnhaven
(Circa 1725). This stately story-and-a-half masonry structure is a well-preserved example of 18th-century architecture and decorative arts. May and October: weekends only; June-September: Tuesday-Sunday.

Motor World
700 S. Birdneck Rd., Virginia Beach,
757-422-6419;
www.vbmotorworld.com
Park includes go-carts, arcade. Also a 36-hole miniature Shipwreck Golf Course, batting cages and large Children's Zone. May-early September: daily.

Norwegian Lady Statue
25th St. and Boardwalk, Virginia Beach
A gift to Virginia Beach from the people of Moss, Norway. The statue commemorates the tragic wreck of the Norwegian bark *Dictator* off the shores of Virginia Beach in 1891.

Ocean Breeze Water Park
849 General Booth Blvd.,
Virginia Beach,
757-422-4444, 800-678-9453;
www.oceanbreezewaterpark.com
"Get wet, get wild" at this Caribbean paradise with slides, wave pool, rapids and children's water amusements. Mid-May-early September: daily.

Old Cape Henry Lighthouse and Memorial Park
www.apva.org/capehenry
On Fort Story, an active army base. First U.S.-government-built lighthouse (circa 1791). Daily.

Old Coast Guard Station
24th St. and Atlantic Ave.,
Virginia Beach,
757-422-1587;
www.oldcoastguardstation.com

Former Coast Guard Station (1903); visual exhibits of numerous shipwrecks along the Virginia coastline tell of past bravery and disaster. "The War Years" exhibit relates United States Coast Guard efforts during World War I and World War II. Photographs, ship models, artifacts. Gift shop. Closed Mondays.

Virginia Marine Science Museum
717 General Booth Blvd.,
Virginia Beach,
757-385-3474;
www.vmsm.com
Live animals, interactive exhibits, six-story screen, 300-seat IMAX 3-D theater. Exhibits include ocean aquarium with sharks, large fish; sea turtle aquarium; seal and other habitats; aviary; salt marsh preserve; touch tank; river room; garden. Daily.

SPECIAL EVENTS
Boardwalk Art Show
Works by more than 350 artists from U.S. and abroad. Mid-June.

Neptune Festival
265 Kings Grant Rd.,
Virginia Beach,
757-498-0215, 866-637-3378;
www.neptunefestival.com
Last two weeks in September.

Pungo Strawberry Festival
916 Princess Anne Rd., Virginia Beach,
Saturday and Sunday of Memorial Day weekend.

Virginia Saltwater Fishing Tournament
968 S. Oriole Dr., Virginia Beach,
757-491-5160
The Commonwealth of Virginia sponsors this annual program. No entry fee or registration requirements; open to everyone who fishes in tournament waters and complies with tournament rules. March-December.

Winter whale-watching boat trips
Virginia Beach,
757-385-4700, 800-822-3224

January-March: Monday, Wednesday, Friday-Sunday.

HOTELS

★★★Crowne Plaza Hotel Virginia Beach
4453 Bonney Rd.,
Virginia Beach,
757-473-1700, 877-424-4225;
www.cpvabeach.com
Just off Interstate 264, this traditional hotel is conveniently located in the Town Center Business District with easy access to downtown Virginia Beach, Norfolk, Chesapeake and many corporate offices. Guests are treated to comfortable rooms, a 24-hour fitness center, indoor pool and whirlpool; and saunas. Golf courses and tennis courts are nearby.
149 rooms. Airport transportation available. $$

★★Doubletree Hotel
1900 Pavilion Dr.,
Virginia Beach,
757-422-8900, 800-222-8733;
www.doubletree.com
292 rooms. $$

★★★Founders Inn
5641 Indian River Rd., Virginia Beach,
757-424-5511, 800-926-4466;
www.foundersinn.com
Sitting on 26 manicured acres, this Georgian-style inn has a southern-colonial decor and a unique combination of intimate charm and extensive meeting space.
240 rooms. Children's activity center. Airport transportation available. $

★★Holiday Inn
2607 Atlantic Ave., Virginia Beach,
757-491-6900, 800-282-0244;
www.holidayinn.com
143 rooms. $$

★La Quinto Inn and Suites
2800 Pacific Ave., Virginia Beach,
757-428-2203;
www.laquinta.com
137 rooms. Complimentary full breakfast. $

★★Wyndham Virginia Beach Oceanfront
5700 Atlantic Ave., Virginia Beach,
757-428-7025, 877-999-3223;
www.wyndham.com
216 rooms. Children's activity center. $$

RESTAURANTS

★★Aldo's
1860 Laskin Rd., Virginia Beach,
757-491-1111;
www.aldosvb.com
Italian menu. Lunch, dinner. Bar. Outdoor seating. $$

★★Blue Pete's Seafood and Steak
1400 N. Muddy Creek Rd., Virginia Beach,
757-426-2005
Seafood, steak menu. Dinner. Closed Sunday. Bar. Children's menu. Casual attire. Reservations recommended. Outdoor seating. $$

★★Coastal Grill
1427 N. Great Neck Rd., Virginia Beach,
757-496-3348;
www.coastalgrill.com
American menu. Dinner, late-night. Bar. Business casual attire. Reservations recommended. Outdoor seating. $$

★Cuisine and Company
3004 Pacific Ave., Virginia Beach,
757-428-6700;
www.cuisineandcompany.com
California menu. Breakfast, lunch, dinner. $

★★Il Giardino
910 Atlantic Ave., Virginia Beach,
757-422-6464;
www.ilgiardino.com
Italian menu. Dinner. Bar. Children's menu. Valet parking. Outdoor seating. $$

★★Lucky Star
1608 Pleasure House Rd., Virginia Beach,
757-363-8410
American menu. Dinner. Closed Sunday. Bar. Business casual attire. Reservations recommended. $$

392

VIRGINIA

★
★
★
★
★

★★Lynnhaven Fish House
2350 Starfish Rd., Virginia Beach,
757-481-0003;
www.lynnhavenfishhouse.net
Seafood menu. Lunch, dinner, brunch. Bar. Children's menu. Casual attire. Reservations recommended. Valet parking. **$$**

★Pungo Grill
1785 Princess Anne Rd.,
Virginia Beach,
757-426-6655
American menu. Lunch, dinner. Closed Monday; also winter. Bar. Children's menu. Casual attire. Reservations recommended. Outdoor seating. **$$**

★★Rudee's on the Inlet
227 Mediterranean Ave.,
Virginia Beach,
757-425-1777, 800-883-0850;
www.rudees.com
Seafood, steak menu. Lunch, dinner, Sunday brunch. Bar. Children's menu. Casual attire. Valet parking (dinner). Outdoor seating. **$$**

WALLOPS ISLAND

WHAT TO SEE AND DO
NASA Visitor Center
Wallops Island,
757-824-1344
Showcases world of past, present and future flight. Features moon rock brought from *Apollo 17* mission; scale models of space probes, satellites and aircraft; displays of current and future NASA projects; full-scale aircraft and rockets; films on space and aeronautics. Model rocket demonstrations (March-November: first Saturday; June-August also third Saturday, weather permitting). Picnic facilities. Gift shop. Thursday-Monday.

WARM SPRINGS
Nestled at the foot of Little Mountain (3,100 feet), the spring wildflowers and groves of fall foliage make Warm Springs a very scenic spot for sightseeing, hiking and water activities. There are also walking tours to view the many historic buildings.

HOTELS
★★★Inn at Gristmill Square
Hwy. 619, Warm Springs,
540-839-2231;
www.gristmillsquare.com
Wake up to the smell of fresh-baked muffins every morning at the Inn at Gristmill Square, a village-like collection of restored 19th-century buildings. Tucked into picturesque Warm Springs, the inn offers 17 guest rooms with a comfortable, country décor. After exploring the area, end your day with a dinner of fresh local trout at the inn's restaurant in a converted mill.
17 rooms. Complimentary continental breakfast. **$**

RESTAURANTS
★★Waterwheel
Route 619, Warm Springs,
540-839-2231;
www.gristmillsquare.com
American menu. Dinner, brunch. Bar. Reservations recommended. Outdoor seating. **$$**

VIRGINIA

★
★
★
★
★

WARRENTON

Warrenton was named for General Joseph Warren, who fought at Bunker Hill in the Revolutionary War. The town is situated in the Piedmont Valley near the foothills of the Blue Ridge Mountains and is known for its cattle and thoroughbred horse farms. Many old buildings and houses provide for an interesting walking tour of the town.

Information: Warrenton-Fauquier County Visitor Center, 33 N. Calhoun St., Warrenton, 540-341-0988, 800-820-1021; www.fauquierchamber.org

SPECIAL EVENTS

Flying Circus
Morrisville Rd. and Brookes Store Dr., Warrenton,
540-439-8661;
www.flyingcircusairshow.com
Flying shows of the barnstorming era, from comedy acts to precision and stunt flying. Rides, picnic area. 7 miles S on Hwy 15/29, then 7 miles SE on Hwy 17 near Bealeton. Sunday. May-October.

HOTELS

★Comfort Inn
7379 Comfort Inn Dr., Warrenton,
540-349-8900, 877-424-6423;
www.comfortinn.com
97 rooms. Complimentary continental breakfast. High-speed Internet access. $

RESTAURANTS

★★Napoleon's
67 Waterloo St.,
Warrenton,
540-347-1200;
www.napoleonsrestaurant.com
International menu. Lunch, dinner, brunch. Bar. Children's menu. Casual attire. Reservations recommended. Outdoor seating. $$$

★

★

☆

☆

☆

WASHINGTON

The oldest of more than 25 American towns to be named after the first president, this town was surveyed in 1749 by none other than George Washington himself. The streets remain laid out exactly as surveyed and still bear the names of families who owned the land on which the town was founded. It is rumored that Gay Street was named by the 17-year-old Washington after the lovely Gay Fairfax. The town is situated in the foothills of the Blue Ridge Mountains, which dominate the western horizon.

HOTELS

★★★Blue Rock Inn
12567 Lee Hwy., Washington,
540-987-3190;
www.thebluerockinn.com
The Blue Rock Inn, a turn-of-the-century farmhouse that now holds a dining room, a pub and five guest rooms, sits on 80 rolling acres, which guests can enjoy from their private balconies.
5 rooms. Complimentary full breakfast. Restored farmhouse (1899) on lake; rustic setting; vineyard. $$

★★★★★The Inn at Little Washington
309 Main St., Washington,
540-675-3800;
www.theinnatlittlewashington.com
Savvy epicureans book a room—and a table—at the Inn at Little Washington. Tucked away in the foothills of the Blue Ridge Mountains, the inn offers visitors a taste of the good life, complete with afternoon tea with scones and tartlets. Tempting as it may be to indulge, guests save their appetites for the evening's cuisine. Many make special trips just for the talented chef's award-winning meals, though lucky guests recount their memorable feasts

while ensconcing themselves in one of the inn's lovely guest rooms. The surrounding area provides opportunities for hiking, fly-fishing, hot air ballooning, antiquing and wine tasting.

15 rooms. Closed Tuesday in January-March and July. Complimentary continental breakfast. $$$$

Middleton Inn
176 Main St.,
Washington,
540-675-2020, 800-816-8157;
www.middletoninn.com
This historic country estate was built in 1850 by Middleton Miller, who designed and manufactured the Confederate uniform of the Civil War. The inn faces the Blue Ridge Mountains, and the original slaves' quarters have been converted into a two-story guest cottage.

5 rooms. Children over 12 years only. Complimentary full breakfast. $$$

RESTAURANTS
★★★Blue Rock Inn
12567 Lee Hwy., Washington,
540-987-3190;
www.thebluerockinn.com
This country-inn farmhouse is located on 80 acres of rolling hillside overlooking the Blue Ridge Mountains and adjoining

vineyards. It is a great place to stop between Harrisonburg and Washington, D.C.
French menu. Dinner. Closed Monday-Tuesday. Bar. Business casual attire. Reservations recommended. Outdoor seating. $$$

★★★★★The Inn at Little Washington
309 Main St., Washington,
540-675-3800;
www.theinnatlittlewashington.com
Chef Patrick O'Connell has amassed almost every culinary award in existence. Seasonal dishes include a crab cake "sandwich" with fried green tomatoes and tomato vinaigrette; sesame-crusted Chilean sea bass with baby shrimp, artichokes and grape tomatoes; rabbit braised in apple cider with wild mushrooms and garlic mashed potatoes; and for dessert, pistachio and white chocolate ice cream terrine with blackberry sauce.
American menu. Dinner. Closed Tuesday (except in May and October). Bar. Business casual attire. Reservations recommended. Valet parking. $$$$

★
★
★
★
★

WAYNESBORO
Waynesboro is at the southern end of the Skyline Drive and the northern end of the Blue Ridge Parkway.
Information: Waynesboro Augusta County Chamber of Commerce,
301 W. Main St., Waynesboro,
540-942-6644, 866-253-1957; www.waynesboro.va.us

WHAT TO SEE AND DO
P. Buckley Moss Museum
150 P. Buckley Moss Dr.,
Waynesboro,
540-949-6473, 800-343-8643;
www.pbuckleymoss.com
Museum's exhibits and programs examine the symbolism and aesthetic ideas of one of America's most notable living artists. Daily.

Shenandoah Valley Art Center
126 S. Wayne Ave., Waynesboro,
540-949-7662;
www.svacart.com
Art galleries, studios. Working artists; performing arts. Tuesday-Sunday.

Sherando Lake Recreation Area
Waynesboro,
540-942-5965

Facilities include 21-acre lake with sand beach and bathhouses, swimming, fishing; picnicking, camping (April-October, fee). Amphitheater, campfire programs. April-November: daily.

SPECIAL EVENTS
Fall Foliage Festival
540-942-6644
First and second weekends in October.

HOTELS
★Days Inn
2060 Rosser Ave., Waynesboro,
540-943-1101, 800-329-7466;
www.daysinn.com

WHITE POST

HOTELS
★★★L'Auberge Provencal French Country Inn
Route 340 S., White Post,
540-837-1375, 800-638-1702;
www.laubergeprovencale.com

97 rooms. Complimentary continental breakfast. $

Iris Inn
191 Chinquapin Dr.,
Waynesboro,
540-943-1991, 888-585-9018;
www.irisinn.com
Overlooking the Shenandoah Valley, the Great Room at the Iris Inn features a 28-foot stone fireplace and a large mural of the wildlife in the mountains. A full and hearty breakfast is included, as is a "bottomless" cookie jar.
9 rooms. Complimentary full breakfast. Whirlpool. $$

This French-style inn, decorated with Victorian and European antiques, is located in the heart of Virginia hunt country.
11 rooms. Children over 10 years only. Complimentary full breakfast. Restaurant. $$

WILLIAMSBURG
After the Native American massacre of 1622, this Virginia colony built a palisade across the peninsula between the James and York rivers. The settlement that grew up around the palisade was called Middle Plantation, now the site of Colonial Williamsburg.

Middle Plantation figured prominently in Bacon's Rebellion against Governor Berkeley. Renamed in honor of William III of England, the new capital gradually became a town of about 200 houses and 1,500 residents. For 81 years, Williamsburg was the political, social and cultural capital of Virginia.

The colony's first successful printing press was established here by William Parks, and in 1736 he published Virginia's first newspaper. Williamsburg's capitol was the scene of stirring colonial events such as Patrick Henry's Stamp Act speech (1765).

The First Continental Congress was called from here by the dissolved House of Burgesses in 1774. Two years later, the Second Continental Congress was boldly led by delegates from Virginia to declare independence; George Mason's Declaration of Rights, which became the basis for the Bill of Rights, was adopted here.

Williamsburg's exciting days came to an end in 1780 when the capital was moved to Richmond for greater safety and convenience during the Revolutionary War. For a century and a half it continued as a quiet college town, its tranquility interrupted briefly by the Civil War. In 1917, when a munitions factory was built near the town and cheap housing for the factory's 15,000 workers was hastily erected, Williamsburg seemed destined to blandly live out its days.

In 1926, however, John D. Rockefeller, Jr., and Dr. W. A. R. Goodwin, rector of Bruton Parish Church, who saw the town as a potential treasure-house of colonial history, joined forces for Williamsburg's restoration. For more than 30 years, Rockefeller devoted personal attention to the project and contributed funds to accomplish this nonprofit undertaking.

Today, after many years of archaeological and historical research, the project is near completion. The Historic Area, approximately a mile long and a half-mile wide, encompasses most of the 18th-century capital. Eighty-eight of the original buildings have been restored; 50 major buildings, houses and shops and many smaller outbuildings have been reconstructed on their original sites; 45 of the more historically significant buildings contain more than 200 exhibition rooms, furnished either with original pieces or reproductions, and open to the public on regular seasonal schedules.

Visitors stroll Duke of Gloucester Street and mingle with people in 18th-century attire. Craftsmen at shops ply trades such as wig-making and blacksmithing, using materials, tools and techniques of pre-Revolutionary times. The Historic Area is closed to private motor vehicles 8 a.m.-10 p.m.

Information: Chamber of Commerce, 421 N. Boundary Ave., Williamsburg, 757-229-6511, 800-211-7165; www.williamsburgcc.com

WHAT TO SEE AND DO

Abby Aldrich Rockefeller Folk Art Center

307 S. England St.,
Williamsburg,
757-229-1000

An outstanding collection of American folk art. Items in this collection were created by artists not trained in studio techniques, but who faithfully recorded aspects of every-day life in paintings, sculpture, needlework, ceramics, toys and other media. Daily.

America's Railroads on Parade

1915 Pocahontas Trail,
Williamsburg,
757-220-8725

More than 4,000 square feet of model train layouts, hands-on exhibits and a gift shop. Daily.

Brush-Everard House

Home of an early mayor, with programs on slave life.

Bruton Parish Church

331 Duke of Gloucester St., Williamsburg,
757-229-2891;
www.brutonparish.org

One of America's oldest Episcopal churches, in continuous use since 1715. Organ recitals (March-December: Tuesday and Saturday). Daily; no tours during services.

Busch Gardens Williamsburg

1 Busch Gardens Blvd., Williamsburg,
757-253-3000, 800-343-7946;
www.buschgardens.com

This European-style theme park on 360 acres features re-created 17th-century German, English, French, Italian, Scottish and Canadian villages. Attractions include more than 30 thrill rides, including the Drachen Fire roller coaster, one of the nation's largest; the 3-D movie "Haunts of the Olde Country," with in-theater special effects; live shows, an antique carousel, celebrity concerts, miniature of Le Mans racetrack, and rides for small children. Theme restaurants; shops. Transportation around the grounds by sky ride or steam train. A computer-operated monorail links the park with the Anheuser-Busch Hospitality Center, where visitors can take a brewery tour. Mid-April-August: daily; late March-mid-April and September-October: weekends.

Carriage and Wagon Rides

Take a ride through the Historic Area in a carriage or wagon driven by a costumed coachman. General admission ticket holders can make reservations on the day of the ride at the Lumber House ticket office. Daily, weather permitting.

Children's Tours

Special programs, tours and experiences exclusively for children and families are offered in the summer.

VIRGINIA

★
★
★
★
★

College of William and Mary

Richmond Rd., Williamsburg,
757-221-4000;
www.wm.edu
(1693) With a student body of 7,000, William and Mary is America's second-oldest college (only Harvard is older). It initiated an honor system, an elective system of studies, and schools of law and modern languages; it was the second to have a school of medicine (all in 1779). The prestigious Phi Beta Kappa Society was founded here as well (1776).

On campus:

Muscarelle Museum of Art

Jamestown Rd. and Phi Beta Kappa Circle, Williamsburg,
757-221-2700;
www.wm.edu/muscarelle
Traveling displays and exhibitions from an extensive collection. Closed Monday.

Wren Building

Richmond Rd. and Duke of Gloucester St., Williamsburg
Oldest (1695-1699, restored 1928) academic building in America; designed by the great English architect Sir Christopher Wren. Tours. Daily.

Colonial Williamsburg Visitor Center

102 Information Center Dr., Williamsburg,
757-220-7645, 800-246-2099;
www.colonialwilliamsburg.com
An admission ticket is necessary to enjoy the full scope of Colonial Williamsburg. Daily.

Courthouse

Duke of Gloucester St., Williamsburg
County and city business was conducted here from 1770 until 1932. The interior has been carefully restored to its original appearance. Visitors often participate in scheduled reenactments of court sessions.

DeWitt Wallace Decorative Arts Gallery

Henry and Francis Streets, Williamsburg,
757-220-7724, 800-447-8679
Modern museum adjoining Public Hospital, features exhibits, lectures, films and related programs centering on British and American decorative arts of the 17th to early 19th centuries. Daily.

Disabled Visitor Information

Williamsburg,
800-246-2099
Efforts are made to accommodate the disabled while still retaining the authenticity of colonial life. Many buildings have wheelchair access once inside, but it should be noted that most buildings are reached by steps. The Visitor Center has a list detailing accessibility of each building; wheelchair ramps may be made available at some buildings. In addition, there are wheelchair rentals and parking. A hands-on tour of several historic trades may be arranged for the visually impaired and sign language tours are available with advance notice.

Evening Entertainment

Colonial Williamsburg presents "rollicking 18th-century plays" throughout the year; wide variety of cultural events, concerts and historical reenactments (fees vary). Chowning's Tavern offers colonial "gambols" (games), music, entertainment and light food and drink (evenings).

Ford's Colony Williamsburg

240 Ford's Colony Dr., Williamsburg,
800-334-6033;
www.fordscolony.com
This Dan Maples-designed course features 54 holes, comprising the par-72 Marsh Hawk Course, the par-71 Blackheath Course, and the par-72 Blue Heron Course. Ford's Colony was chosen as one of America's best golf courses by "Golf Week" Magazine. The course touts itself as a "player's course" that appeals to golfers of all levels.

Go-Karts Plus

6910 Richmond Rd., Hwy. 60 W., Williamsburg,

757-564-7600;
www.gokartsplus.com

This eight-acre park has four go-kart tracks that appeal to various ages and driving skills, as well as bumper cars and boats, a miniature golf course and an arcade. Admission is free; tickets must be purchased for activities. March-May: daily; September-October: limited hours.

Governor's Palace and Gardens

Residence of Royal Governor, one of the most elegant mansions in colonial America; set in 10-acre restored gardens.

Haunted Dinner Theater

5363 Richmond Rd.,
Williamsburg,
757-258-2500, 888-426-3746;
www.wmbgdinnertheatre.com

Help unravel a murder mystery tame enough for little ones while feasting on a 71-item, all-you-can-eat dinner buffet at Capt. George's World Famous Restaurant. Performances are held Wednesday-Sunday evenings at 7 p.m.

Historic Trades

Craftsmen in 18th-century costume pursue old trades of apothecary, printer, bookbinder, silversmith, wigmaker, shoemaker, blacksmith, harnessmaker, cabinetmaker, miller, milliner, gunsmith, wheelwright, basketmaker, cook, cooper and carpenter.

James Geddy House

Once home of a prominent silversmith with working brass, bronze, silver and pewter foundry.

James River State Park

Rte. 1, Williamsburg,
434-933-4355, 800-933-7275;
www.dcr.state.va.us/parks/jamesriv.htm

This 1,500-acre park has three fishing ponds and three miles of river frontage. The park offers pond and river fishing. An excellent spot is Pony Pasture, located on the south bank two miles downstream from the Huguenot Bridge on Riverside Dr. The area is also considered one of Richmond's

best locations for bird-watching and inner-tubing.

There are two boat launches at the park. Canoeing is also popular here. There is a canoe launch at the Canoe Landing Campground at Dixon Landing. Belle Isle is directly under the Lee Bridge and may be reached on foot from the north side of the river via the pedestrian bridge suspended under the Lee Bridge. Excellent whitewater rapids are found at Belle Isle, with kayaking and canoeing being popular sports here for skilled paddlers. Ancarrows Landing is a boat landing and fishing spot that is one of the areas most valuable historic sites. It is the place where William Byrd is believed to have established Richmond when he set up his trading post. Later, slave ships docked there in the 1700s and 1800s. It became known as Ancarrows Landing because it also was the home of Newton Ancarrows speedboat manufacturing company.

Jamestown Settlement

Route 31 S. Jamestown Rd., Williamsburg,
757-253-4838, 888-593-4682;
www.historyisfun.org

Living history museum re-creates the first permanent English settlement in the New World. Recalls early-17th-century Jamestown with full-scale reproductions of ships which arrived in 1607 and the triangular James Fort. The Powhatan Indian Village depicts Native American culture encountered by English colonists. Museum complex features an orientation film, changing gallery and three exhibit galleries focusing on the history of Jamestown and the Powhatan. Food service available. Combination ticket with Yorktown Victory Center available. Daily.

Lanthorn Tour

Williamsburg,
800-246-2099

A costumed interpreter conducts evening walking tour of selected shops that are illuminated by candlelight. March-December: daily.

★
★
★
★
★

Music Theatre of Williamsburg
7575 Richmond Rd., Williamsburg,
757-564-0200, 888-687-4220
This 752-seat theater, which opened in 1998, features ever-changing shows that appeal to and are appropriate for all ages. Call for the performance schedule.

Peyton Randolph House
(1716) Home of president of First Continental Congress. Rochambeau's headquarters prior to Yorktown campaign.

Play Booth Theater
Scenes from 18th-century plays in open-air theater. Open to all Colonial Williamsburg ticket holders. Spring-fall: daily.

Public Gaol
Where debtors, criminals and pirates (including Blackbeard's crew) were imprisoned.

Public Hospital
Reconstruction of first public institution in the English colonies devoted exclusively to treatment of mental illness.

Raleigh Tavern
Frequent meeting place for Jefferson, Henry, and other Revolutionary patriots; a social center of the Virginia Colony.

"Ride with Me to Williamsburg"
Williamsburg,
301-299-7817, 800-840-7433
Informative and entertaining 90-minute audiocassette describes events from Williamsburg's colorful colonial, revolutionary and Civil War past. The town's famous restoration is summarized by one of the architects who worked on the project.

Shirley Pewter Shop
417 Duke of Gloucester St., Williamsburg,
757-229-5356, 800-550-5356;
www.shirleypewter.com
This shop features Williamsburg's own brand of pewter, Shirley Pewter. Items available include dinnerware, oil lamps and tableware. Many items can be engraved. Daily.

1700s Shopping
Superior wares typical of the 18th century are offered in nine restored or reconstructed stores and shops; items include silver, jewelery, herbs, candles, hats and books. Two craft houses sell approved reproductions of the antiques on display in the houses and museums.

Skate Park
5301 Longhill Rd., Williamsburg,
757-259-3200;
www.james-city.va.us/recreation/
skatepark.html
A great, safe place for inline skating, skateboarding and biking. The park is open to ages nine and up, and all skaters and bikers must wear protective gear. November-March: closed Monday, Tuesday, Thursday; rest of year: daily.

Special Focus and Orientation Tours
Orientation tours (30 minutes) for first-time visitors; special tours (90 minutes), called history walks, include African-American life, gardens, religion and women of Williamsburg. Reservations are available at any ticket sales location.

The Capitol
Duke of Gloucester St., Williamsburg
The House of Burgesses met here (1704-1779); it was also the scene of Patrick Henry's speech against the Stamp Act.

The Magazine
Duke of Gloucester St.,
Williamsburg
Arsenal and military storehouse of Virginia Colony; authentic arms exhibited.

Water Country USA
176 Water Country Pkwy.,
Williamsburg,
757-253-3350, 800-343-7946;
www.watercountryusa.com
This park, the mid-Atlantic's largest water park, features water slides, thrill rides and

400

VIRGINIA

live entertainment. If you're interested in visiting Busch Gardens as well, which is just three miles from Water Country USA, you can save money by purchasing a Bounce Pass, which gives admission to both parks. May, early-mid-September: weekends from 10 a.m.; June-August: daily from 10 a.m.

Wetherburn's Tavern

One of the most popular inns of the period.

Williamsburg National Golf Course

3700 Centerville,
Williamsburg,
757-258-9738, 800-859-9182;
www.wngc.com

This 18-hole, par-72 public course is the only Jack Nicklaus-designed course in Virginia. Call for tee times.

Williamsburg Winery

5800 Wessex Hundred,
Williamsburg,
757-229-0999;
www.williamsburgwinery.com

Founded in 1985, the winery carries on a Virginia tradition that began with the Jamestown settlers in 1607. Located two miles from the Historic Area, it has 50 acres of vineyards. Visitors can take 30-45 minute guided walking tours and tastings are available after the tour. Daily.

Wythe House

Home of George Wythe, America's first law professor, teacher of Jefferson, Clay and Marshall. This was Washington's headquarters before siege of Yorktown.

York River State Park

5526 Riverview Rd., Williamsburg,
757-566-3036;
www.dcr.virginia.gov/state_parks/
yor.shtml

A 2,500-acre park along the York River and its related marshes. Includes the Taskinas Creek National Estuarine Research Reserve. Fishing, boating (launch), canoe trips; hiking and bridle trails, picnicking, interpretive center, programs, nature walks. Daily.

SPECIAL EVENTS

18th-Century Comedy

Williamsburg Lodge Auditorium,
5363 Richmond Rd., Williamsburg,
800-447-8679
Saturday nights, March-December.

Antiques Forum

102 Information Center Dr., Williamsburg,
800-447-8679
Colonial Williamsburg. Mid-February.

Colonial Weekends

Williamsburg,
800-246-2099
Package weekends on 18th-century theme, features introductory lecture, guided tours, banquet at Colonial Williamsburg. January-early March.

Fife and Drum Corps

Carter's Grove and S. England St.,
Williamsburg,
757-220-7453
Colonial Williamsburg. Performances in the Historic Area. April-October: Saturday.

Garden Symposium

102 Information Center Dr., Williamsburg,
800-447-8679
Colonial Williamsburg. Lectures and clinics. Mid-late April.

Living History Programs

1340 S. Pleasant Valley Rd., Williamsburg
Colonial Williamsburg. Includes "An Assembly, Cross or Crown," and "Cry Witch!" Varying schedule weekly. Spring, summer and fall.

Military Drill

Market Square Green, Duke of Gloucester and Colonial Streets, Williamsburg,
757-229-6511
Costumed weekly drill by Williamsburg Independent Company. Mid-March-October.

Prelude to Independence

102 Information Center Dr., Williamsburg,
800-447-8679
Colonial Williamsburg. Mid-May.

401

VIRGINIA

★
★
★
★
★

Publick Times

102 Information Center Dr., Williamsburg,
800-447-8679
Colonial Williamsburg. Re-creation of colonial market days; contests, crafts, auctions, military encampment. Labor Day weekend.

Traditional Christmas Activities

102 Information Center Dr., Williamsburg,
800-447-8679
Colonial Williamsburg. Featuring grand illumination of city; fireworks. December.

HOTELS

★★Crowne Plaza

6945 Pocahontas Trail, Williamsburg,
757-220-2250, 877-424-4225
303 rooms. $

★★★Kingsmill Resort

1010 Kingsmill Rd., Williamsburg,
757-253-1703, 800-832-2665;
www.kingsmill.com
This playground for adults attracts golfers, tennis players and those seeking rest and relaxation to its 2,900 manicured acres along the James River. Three 18-hole golf courses and a nine-hole par-three course challenge players while the Golf Academy provides clinics and individual instruction. Tennis players take their pick from fast-drying clay, Deco-Turf and hydro courts at the state-of-the-art facility, while other racquet sports and a fitness center are available at the Sports Club. After a day filled with activities, hearty appetites are always satisfied at the resorts six restaurants and lounges.
425 rooms. Complimentary continental breakfast. Children's activity center. Beach. Airport transportation available. $$$

★★★Marriott Williamsburg

50 Kingsmill Rd., Williamsburg,
757-220-2500, 800-228-9290;
www.williamsburgmarriott.com
The closest hotel to Busch Gardens, the Marriott Williamsburg is also conveniently located near Colonial Williamsburg, Jamestown and Yorktown, as well as shopping and outlet centers. After a busy day spent

sightseeing, relax in the Marriott's well-appointed guest rooms.
295 rooms. Children's activity center. $

★Waller Mill Inn

201 Bypass Rd., Williamsburg,
757-220-0880, 800-289-0880;
www.williamsburgaccommodations.com
121 rooms. Complimentary full breakfast. $

★★★★Williamsburg Inn

136 E. Francis St., Williamsburg,
757-229-1000, 800-447-8679
Furnished in English Regency style, the guest rooms have just the right amount of sophistication to appeal to adults while keeping children comfortable and satisfied. Blessed with a central location in the heart of this re-created 18th-century village, the inn is within a leisurely stroll of the blacksmith's shop, candlemaker and cobbler. After reliving history, guests reap the rewards of the inn's plentiful activities and play a round of golf, dive into the spring-fed pool, rally on the clay tennis courts, head to the fitness center to keep in shape, or spoil themselves at the spa or gourmet restaurant.
110 rooms. Complimentary full breakfast. $$$$

★★Williamsburg Lodge

310 S. England St., Williamsburg,
757-220-7976, 800-447-8679;
www.colonialwilliamsburg.com
261 rooms. Complimentary continental breakfast. Children's activity center. $$

★★★Woodlands Hotel And Suites

105 Visitor Center Dr., Williamsburg,
757-220-7960, 800-447-8679;
www.colonialwilliamsburg.org
One of Colonial Williamsburg's five resorts and inns, Woodlands Hotel and Suites is located on the grounds of the visitor center at the edge of a 40-acre pine forest.
300 rooms. Complimentary continental breakfast. $

★
★
★
★
★

SPECIALTY LODGINGS

Colonial Capital Bed and Breakfast
501 Richmond Rd., Williamsburg,
757-229-0233, 800-776-0570;
www.ccbb.com
5 rooms. Children over 8 years only. Complimentary full breakfast. Built in 1926; antiques. **$$**

Colonial Gardens Inn
1109 Jamestown Rd., Williamsburg,
757-220-8087, 800-886-9715;
www.colonial-gardens.com
4 rooms. Children over 14 permitted. Complimentary full breakfast. Built in 1960. **$$**

Colonial Houses-Historic Lodging
305 S. England St., Williamsburg,
757-220-7978, 800-447-8679;
www.colonialwilliamsburg.com
These 18th-century historic buildings are very secluded, located on the 173 acres of Colonial Williamsburg. Guests can choose from a small house or a larger one with up to 16 rooms, each furnished with period reproductions. All are within walking distance of shops, museums and horse-drawn carriages.
74 rooms. **$$**

Liberty Rose Bed and Breakfast
1022 Jamestown Rd.,
Williamsburg,
757-253-1260, 800-545-1825;
www.libertyrose.com
This restored house is decorated in a Victorian-style with European antiques and is located just one mile from Colonial Williamsburg's historic village.
4 rooms. No children allowed. Complimentary full breakfast. **$$**

Williamsburg Sampler Bed and Breakfast
922 Jamestown Rd., Williamsburg,
757-253-0398, 800-722-1169;
www.williamsburgsampler.com
This 18th-century, plantation-style colonial home is located in the City of Williamsburg's Architectural Corridor Protection District.
4 rooms. Complimentary full breakfast. **$$**

RESTAURANTS

★★Berret's Seafood Restaurant and Taphouse Grill
199 S. Boundary St., Williamsburg,
757-253-1847;
www.berrets.com
American menu. Lunch, dinner, late-night. Closed Monday in January and February. Bar. Children's menu. Casual attire. Reservations recommended. Outdoor seating. **$$**

★★★The Dining Room at Ford's Colony
240 Ford's Colony Dr.,
Williamsburg,
757-258-4107;
www.fordscolony.com
Rich, imaginative American and European dishes are served in a quiet, elegant dining room.
American menu. Dinner, Sunday brunch. Closed Sunday-Monday. Bar. Jacket required. Reservations recommended. Outdoor seating. **$$$**

★★Giuseppe's
5601 Richmond Rd., Williamsburg,
757-565-1977;
www.giuseppes.com
Italian menu. Lunch, dinner. Closed Sunday. Children's menu. Casual attire. Reservations recommended. Outdoor seating. **$$**

★★King's Arms Tavern
416 E. Duke of Glouchester St.,
Williamsburg,
757-229-2141, 800-828-3767;
www.colonialwilliamsburg.com

403

VIRGINIA

American menu. Lunch, dinner. Bar. Children's menu. Casual attire. Reservations recommended. Outdoor seating. **$$$**

★★Le Yaca
1915 Pocahontas Trail #C10,
Williamsburg,
757-220-3616;
www.leyacawilliamsburg.com
French menu. Lunch, dinner. Closed Sunday. Bar. Children's menu. Business casual attire. Reservations recommended. **$$$**

★Old Chickahominy House
1211 Jamestown Rd.,
Williamsburg,
757-229-4689;
www.visitwilliamsburg.com
American menu. Breakfast, lunch. Casual attire. 18th-century stagecoach stop atmosphere. **$**

★★Peking
122 Waller Mill Rd.,
Williamsburg,
757-229-2288
Chinese, Japanese menu. Lunch, dinner, brunch. Casual attire. Reservations recommended. **$**

★Pierce's Pitt Bar-B-Que
447 E. Rochambeau Dr.,
Williamsburg,
757-565-2955;
www.pierces.com
American menu. Breakfast, lunch, dinner. **$**

★★★Regency Dining Room
136 E. Francis St., Williamsburg,
757-229-2141, 800-828-3767;
www.colonialwilliamsburg.com
Set in the charming Williamsburg Inn, the Regency Dining Room offers diners a graceful setting in which to enjoy a leisurely dinner of contemporary Southern fare. The menu runs the gamut from modern dishes like tomato-rosemary ravioli with smoked duck and oxtail rillettes to tried-and-true classics like Chateaubriand and the signature Williamsburg Inn crab

cake. Live music and dancing are offered on Friday and Saturday nights. American menu. Breakfast, lunch, dinner. Bar. Children's menu. Jacket required. Outdoor seating. **$$$**

★★River's Inn Restaurant & Crab Deck
8109 Yacht Haven Dr., Gloucester Point,
804-642-9942, 888-780-2722;
www.riversinnrestaurant.com
Seafood menu. Lunch, dinner. Closed Monday September-March. Bar. Children's menu. Casual attire. Outdoor seating. **$$**

★★Seasons Cafe
110 S. Henry, Williamsburg,
757-259-0018;
www.seasonsofwilliamsburg.com
International menu. Lunch, dinner, brunch. Bar. Children's menu. Casual attire. **$$**

★★★The Trellis
403 Duke of Gloucester St.,
Williamsburg,
757-229-8610;
www.thetrellis.com
Entrees include deep-dried catfish with vegetable slaw, screaming peanuts, watercress and cucumber mayonnaise; and grilled pork tenderloin with string beans and bourbon-and honey-glazed sweet potatoes. American menu. Lunch, dinner, brunch. Bar. Casual attire. Outdoor seating. **$$$**

★★Whaling Company
494 McLaw Cir.,
Williamsburg,
757-229-0275;
www.thewhalingcompany.com
Seafood menu. Dinner. Bar. Children's menu. Casual attire. **$$**

★★Yorkshire Steak and Seafood House
700 York St.,
Williamsburg,
757-229-9790;
www.yorkshire-wmbg.com
American menu. Dinner. Children's menu. Casual attire. Reservations recommended. In colonial-style building. **$$**

VIRGINIA

WINCHESTER

Winchester is the oldest colonial city west of the Blue Ridge, a Civil War prize that changed hands 72 times (including 13 times in one day). Sometimes called the "apple capital of the world," it is located at the northern approach to the Shenandoah Valley.

George Washington, a red-haired 16-year-old, headed for Winchester and his first surveying job in 1748, and began a decade of apprenticeship for the military and political responsibilities he would later assume as a national leader. During the French and Indian Wars, Colonel Washington made the city his defense headquarters while he built Fort Loudoun in Winchester. Washington was elected to his first political office as a representative from Frederick County to the House of Burgesses.

At the intersection of travel routes, both east-west and north-south, Winchester grew and prospered. By the time of the Civil War it was a major transportation and supply center, strategically located to control both Union approaches to Washington and Confederate supply lines through the Shenandoah Valley. More than 100 minor engagements and six battles took place in the vicinity. General Stonewall Jackson had his headquarters here during the winter of 1861-1862. From his headquarters in Winchester, Union General Philip Sheridan started his famous ride to rally his troops at Cedar Creek, 11 miles away, and turn a Confederate victory into a Union rout.

Approximately 3.5 million bushels of apples are harvested annually in Frederick County and are one of Winchester's economic mainstays. The world's largest apple cold storage plant and one of the world's largest apple processing plants are here.

Information: Winchester-Frederick County Visitor Center, 1360 S. Pleasant Valley Rd., Winchester, 540-662-4135, 800-662-1360; www.visitwinchesterva.com

WHAT TO SEE AND DO

Abram's Delight and Log Cabin
1340 S. Pleasant Valley Ave., Winchester, 540-662-6519
(1754) Oldest house in city, restored, furnished in 18th-century style; boxwood garden; log cabin, basement kitchen. (April-October: daily; rest of year, by appointment, weather permitting). Inquire about combination ticket.

First Presbyterian Church of Winchester
116 S. Loudoun St., Winchester, 540-662-3824;
www.firstchurch-winchester.org
(1788) Building has been used as a church, a stable by Union troops in Civil War, a public school, and an armory; restored in 1941. Daily.

Handley Library and Archives
100 W. Piccadilly St., Winchester, 540-662-9041;
www/hrl.lib.state.va.us/handley
Completed in 1913, the public library was designed in Beaux Arts style. Rotunda is crowned on the outside with a copper-covered dome and on the inside by a dome of stained glass. Interesting interior features include wrought-iron staircases and glass floors. Historical archives are housed on lower level (nonresident fee). Monday-Saturday, Sunday also January-April, October, November.

Stonewall Jackson's Headquarters
415 N. Braddock St., Winchester, 540-667-3242
Jackson's headquarters November 1861-March 1862; now a museum housing Jackson memorabilia and other Confederate items of the war years. (April-October: daily; rest of year, by appointment, weather permitting). Inquire about combination ticket.

Washington's Office-Museum
Cork and Braddock Streets, Winchester, 540-662-4412
Building used by George Washington in 1755-1756 during construction of Fort Loudoun. Housed in this museum are French and Indian, Revolutionary and Civil War relics. April-October: daily; rest of year, by appointment, weather permitting.

★
★
★
★
☆

SPECIAL EVENTS

Apple Harvest Arts & Crafts
Jim Barnett Park, Winchester
Pie contests, apple-butter making, music, arts and crafts. Third weekend in September.

Historic Garden Tour
1340 S. Pleasant Valley Rd., Winchester, 540-542-1326, 877-871-1326
Open house and gardens in historic Winchester. Mid-late April.

Shenandoah Apple Blossom Festival
135 N. Cameron St., Winchester, 540-662-3863
Apple Blossom Queen, parades, arts and crafts, band contests, music, food and attractions. Late-April-early May.

HOTELS

★Hampton Inn
1655 Apple Blossom Dr., Winchester, 540-667-8011, 800-426-7866; www.hamptoninn.com
103 rooms. Complimentary continental breakfast. **$**

★★Holiday Inn
1017 Millwood Pike, Winchester, 540-667-3300, 800-282-0244; www.holidayinn.com
173 rooms. **$**

WINTERGREEN

WHAT TO SEE AND DO

Wintergreen Resort
Hwy. 664, Wintergreen, 434-325-2200; www.wintergreenresort.com
Quad, three triple, double chairlifts; patrol, school, rentals, snow making; lodge, nursery. Twenty runs; longest run 1 1/2 miles; vertical drop 1,003 feet. December-March: daily. Night skiing. Summer activities include fishing, boating; golf, tennis, horseback riding.

HOTELS

★★★Wintergreen Resort
Route 664, Wintergreen, 434-325-2200, 800-266-2444; www.wintergreenresort.com
300 rooms. Children's activity center. Ski in/ ski out. Airport transportation available. **$$**

WOODSTOCK

A German immigrant, Jacob Mller, received a land grant from Lord Fairfax and came here in 1752 with his wife and six children. A few years later, he set aside 1,200 acres for a town, first called Mllerstadt, later Woodstock. In January 1776 in a small log church here, John Peter Gabriel Mhlenberg preached his famous sermon based on Ecclesiastes 3:1-8: "There is a time to every purpose . . . a time to war and a time to peace," at the end of which he flung back his vestments to reveal the uniform of a Continental colonel and began to enroll his parishioners in the army that was to overthrow British rule. The Shenandoah Valley-Herald, a weekly newspaper established in 1817, is still published here.
Information: Chamber of Commerce, 143 N. Main St., Woodstock, 540-459-2542

WHAT TO SEE AND DO

Shenandoah County Court House
Main St., Woodstock
(1792) Oldest courthouse still in use west of the Blue Ridge Mountains; interior restored to original design. Monday-Friday.

Shenandoah Vineyards
3659 S. Ox Rd., Woodstock, 540-984-8699; www.shentel.net/shenvine
Valley's first winery. Premium wines; hand-picked and processed in the European

style. Picnic area. Tours, free tastings available. Daily.

Woodstock Tower
Panoramic view of seven horseshoe bends of the Shenandoah River.

SPECIAL EVENTS
Shenandoah County Fair
300 Fairgrounds Rd.,
Woodstock,
540-459-3867;
www.shencofair.com
One of the oldest county fairs in the state. Harness racing last four days. Late August-early September.

Shenandoah Valley Music Festival
102 N. Main St., Woodstock,
540-459-3396;
www.musicfest.org
Symphony pops, classical, folk, jazz, country and big band concerts. Pavilion and lawn seating. Outdoor pavilion on grounds of historic Orkney Springs Hotel in Orkney Springs. Four weekends, mid-July-Labor Day weekend.

HOTELS
★★Holiday Inn Express
1130 Motel Dr., Woodstock,
540-459-5000, 800-282-0244;
www.holidayinn.com
124 rooms. Airport transportation available.
$

Inn at Narrow Passage
Route 11,
30 Chapman Landing Rd., Woodstock,
540-459-8000, 800-459-8002;
www.narrowpassage.com
This restored colonial wagon stop along the Old Valley Pike is located on the Shenandoah River. The guest rooms are decorated with Early American reproductions and antiques are available. The inn offers views of both the river and the Massanutten Mountains.
12 rooms. Complimentary full breakfast. Check-in 2-9:30 p.m. $

WYTHEVILLE
With lead mines and the only salt mine in the South nearby, Wytheville was a Union target during the Civil War. One story states that a detachment of Union cavalry attempted to take the town in July 1863, only to be thwarted by Molly Tynes, who rode 40 miles over the mountains from Rocky Dell to tell the countryside that the Yankees were coming. The alerted home guard turned them away. A transportation center today, Wytheville is also a vacationland nestled between the Blue Ridge and Allegheny mountains. Rural Retreat Lake is nearby. Wythe Ranger District office for the George Washington and Jefferson national forests is located here.
Information: Wytheville-Wythe-Bland Chamber of Commerce, 150 E. Monroe St., Wytheville, 276-223-3365; chamber.wytheville.com

WHAT TO SEE AND DO
Big Walker Lookout
US 52 N., Wytheville,
276-228-4401
A 120-foot observation tower at 3,405-foot elevation; swinging bridge. Gift shop; snack bar. April-late May: Thursday-Sunday; Memorial Day-mid-November: Tuesday-Sunday.

Shot Tower Historical Park
176 Orphanage Dr., Wytheville,
540-699-6778
(1807) On bluff overlooking New River. One of three shot towers still standing in the U.S.; fortress-like stone shaft has 2 1/2 foot thick walls rising 75 feet above ground and boring 75 feet below to a water tank. Molten lead was poured through sheet iron colanders from the tower top; during the 150-foot descent it became globular before hitting the water. Pellets were then sorted by rolling them down an incline; well-formed shot rolled into a receptacle; faulty ones zig-zagged off and were remelted. Visitor

center, programs; hiking trails, picnicking. Memorial Day-Labor Day: daily. Standard fees.

Wytheville State Fish Hatchery
1260 Red Hollow Road, Wytheville, 276-637-3212

Approximately 150,000 pounds of rainbow trout produced annually. Five-tank aquarium; displays. Self-guided tours. Daily.

SPECIAL EVENTS
Chautauqua Festival
276-228-6855

Held over a nine-day period. Includes parade, educational events, performing arts, art shows, children's activities, music, food, entertainment. Third week in June.

HOTELS
★Best Western Wytheville Inn
355 Nye Rd., Wytheville, 276-228-7300, 800-224-9172; www.bestwestern.com

100 rooms. Complimentary continental breakfast. **$**

★★Red Roof Inn
1900 E. Main St., Wytheville, 276-228-5483, 800-733-7663; www.redroof.com
199 rooms. **$**

RESTAURANTS
★★Log House
520 E. Main St., Wytheville, 540-228-4139

American menu. Lunch, dinner. Closed Sunday. Bar. Children's menu. Colonial motif; built 1776. Casual attire. Reservations recommended. Outdoor seating. **$$**

YORKTOWN

Free land offered in 1630 to those adventurous enough "to seate and inhabit" the 50-foot bluffs on the south side of the York River brought about the beginning of settlement. When the Assembly authorized a port, started in 1691, the town slowly expanded and in the following years became a busy shipping center, its prosperity peaking around 1750. From then on the port declined along with the Tidewater Virginia tobacco trade.

Yorktown's moment in history came in 1781. After raiding up and down Virginia with minimal resistance from the Marquis de Lafayette, British commander Cornwallis was sent here to establish a naval base in which supplies and reinforcements could be shipped to him. The Comte de Grasse's French fleet effectively blockaded the British, however, by controlling the mouth of the Chesapeake Bay. At the Battle of the Capes on September 5, 1781, a British fleet sent to investigate the French presence was defeated by the French. Cornwallis found himself bottled up in Yorktown by combined American and French forces under Washington, which arrived on September 28.

Shelling began October 9. The siege of Yorktown ended on October 17 with Cornwallis requesting terms of capitulation. On October 19, Cornwallis' troops marched out with flags and arms cased, their bands playing. Then they laid down their arms, bringing the last major battle of the Revolutionary War to a close.

Yorktown Battlefield, part of Colonial National Historical Park, surrounds the village. Though Yorktown itself is still an active community, many surviving and reconstructed colonial structures supply an 18th-century atmosphere.

Information: Colonial National Historical Park, Yorktown, 757-898-3400; www.nps.gov/colo

WHAT TO SEE AND DO

Grace Episcopal Church
111 Church St., Yorktown,
757-898-3261;
www.gracechurchyorktown.com
(1697) Walls of local marl (a mixture of clay, sand and limestone); damaged in 1781, gutted by fire in 1814. A 1649 communion service is still in use. Daily.

Yorktown Battlefield in Colonial National Historic Park
Yorktown,
757-898-2410;
www.nps.gov/yonb
Surrounds and includes part of town. Remains of 1781 British fortifications, modified and strengthened by Confederate forces in Civil War. Reconstructed American and French lines lie beyond. Roads lead to headquarters, encampment areas of Americans, French. Admission fee includes access to Visitor Center, battlefield tour, Moore House and Nelson House. Golden Access, Age and Eagle passports honored. Daily.

Moore House
224 Ballard St., Yorktown,
757-898-3400
In this 18th-century house the "Articles of Capitulation" were drafted. These were signed by General Washington in the captured British Redoubt #10 on October 19. Mid-June-mid-August: daily; spring and fall: weekends.

Nelson House
Nelson and Main Streets, Yorktown,
757-898-2410
Original restored mansion built by "Scotch Tom" Nelson in the early 1700s. Home of his grandson, Thomas Nelson, Jr., a signer of the Declaration of Independence. Impressive example of Georgian architecture. April-October: daily.

Self-guided Battlefield Tour
Markers, displays aid in visualizing siege. Highlights include headquarters sites of Lafayette, von Steuben, Rochambeau, Washington; a key point is Surrender Field where British forces laid down their arms.

Visitor Center
Colonial Pkwy. and Yorktown Visitor Center, Yorktown,
757-898-3400
Information, special exhibits, General Washington's field tents. Daily.

Yorktown National Civil War Cemetery
2,183 interments (1,436 unknown). Yorktown Victory Monument Elaborately ornamented 95-foot granite column memorializes American-French alliance in Revolutionary War.

Yorktown Victory Center
Route 1020, Williamsburg,
757-253-4838, 888-593-4682
Museum of the Revolutionary War chronicles the struggle for independence from the beginning of colonial unrest to the new nation's formation. Exhibit galleries, living history Continental Army encampment and late-18th-century farm. Daily. Combination ticket with Jamestown Settlement available.

SPECIAL EVENTS

Yorktown Day
Observance of America's Revolutionary War victory at Yorktown in 1781. October 19.

HOTELS

★Duke of York Motor Hotel
508 Water St., Yorktown,
757-898-3232;
www.dukeofyorkmotel.com
57 rooms. $

★
★
★
★
★

WASHINGTON, D.C.

WHEREVER YOU'RE STANDING IN DOWNTOWN D.C., CHANCES ARE THE WASHINGTON Monument is within sight. By law, no building may be taller than the 12-story monument—but regardless of their physical stature, the rest of D.C.'s buildings cannot be overshadowed. World-renowned museums and monuments, first-rate restaurants and shops situated within quaint neighborhoods, grassy parks and tree-lined streets. And all are just a short ride away on the city's efficient mass-transit system.

Washington was not the first capital of the United States. The city didn't even exist at the time the nation gained its independence in 1789. For a year, the nation's new government met in New York City before relocating to Philadelphia. In 1790, President Washington selected a site for the nation's capital at the junction of the Potomac and Anacostia rivers, 14 miles north of his home in Mount Vernon. Andrew Ellicott surveyed the area, aided by Benjamin Banneker, a free black from Maryland. Using celestial calculations, Banneker, a self-taught astronomer and mathematician, laid out 40 boundary stones at one-mile intervals to mark the city's borders.

President Washington chose Pierre-Charles L'Enfant to plan the new capital. L'Enfant, a French-born architect and urban designer who served in the American Revolutionary Army, created a bold and original plan, one that called for a grid pattern of streets intersected by wide, diagonal avenues. The diagonal avenues would meet at circles, which would anchor the residential neighborhoods. Today, Logan Circle is a clear example, where four different thoroughfares converge, including Rhode Island and Vermont avenues. The large open circle sits at the core of a beautiful neighborhood, with many of the residences built soon after the Civil War.

L'Enfant envisioned the Congress House (now the Capitol) situated atop Jenkins Hill, which offered sweeping views of the Potomac River. To the west of Jenkins Hill, L'Enfant planned a 400-foot-wide avenue (now the National Mall) bordered by embassies and cultural institutions. Not everyone was pleased with his plan. Though he had the president's support, L'Enfant faced opposition from some of the district commissioners who had been appointed to oversee the capital city's development. Secretary of State Thomas Jefferson, a noted architect in his own right, disapproved of the plan, but L'Enfant refused to compromise his vision. In 1792, Washington dismissed the genius planner whom he had appointed only a year earlier. In L'Enfant's place, Washington appointed Andrew Ellicott to prepare a map of the city. Along with Benjamin Banneker, Ellicott produced a map of the city that adhered closely to L'Enfant's plan.

L'Enfant sought $95,500 for his services but received less than $4,000. He died in 1825, financially destitute and never having received acclaim for his work in planning Washington. He was buried in Maryland, then disinterred and reburied at Arlington National Cemetery in 1909. A marble monument marks the site of his grave.

L'Enfant's visionary plan fostered the growth of the city's eclectic mix of neighborhoods: Capitol Hill, with its 19th-century row houses and brick-lined streets; the National Mall's massive stone monuments, museums and government buildings; Georgetown's quaint shops and restaurants; cosmopolitan Dupont Circle; Adams Morgan, with its bustling nightlife; and Woodley Park's leaf-shaded residential streets.

Thanks to L'Enfant's plan, which identified parks and open spaces as essential elements in urban design, D.C. possesses the sorts of places, as L'Enfant wrote, that may be attractive to the learned and afford diversion to the idle. Pulitzer Prize-winning historian David McCullough has expressed his appreciation of the capital's natural beauty. "In many ways it is our most civilized city," McCullough wrote of Washington. "It accommodates its river, accommodates trees and grass, makes room for nature as other cities don't."

All three branches of the U.S. federal government are based in Washington, D.C., and the number of federal employees commuting downtown has grown significantly over the years. In 1800, there were 130 federal workers; at the end of the Civil War, there were 7,000; now there are well over half a million. From politicians on the Hill to lobbyists on K Street to visiting dignitaries, D.C. hosts some of the nation's busiest movers and shakers.

Tourists, too, flock to the nation's capital, visiting their senators and representatives on Capitol Hill, touring the Smithsonian museums along the National Mall, and posing for pictures in front of the Washington Monument and the Lincoln and Jefferson memorials. Sightseeing opportunities abound in this picturesque city. Dining and nightlife options are just as plentiful in neighborhoods such as Georgetown, DuPont Circle, Adams Morgan and the U Street Corridor.

Information: www.washington.org

★ SPOTLIGHT

★ During World War II, to protect the city from possible enemy invasion, anti-aircraft guns were placed on top of several government office buildings. One of those guns accidentally went off and the projectile hit the roof of the Lincoln Monument.

WHAT TO SEE AND DO

African American Civil War Memorial
1200 U St. N.W.,
Washington, DC,
202-667-2667;
www.afroamcivilwar.org
Sculpture pays tribute to the more than 200,000 African American soldiers who fought in the Civil War.

American Red Cross Museum
430 17th St.,
Washington, DC,
202-303-7066;
www.redcross.org/museum/history/
visitorinfo.asp
National headquarters includes three buildings bounded by 17th, 18th, D and E streets N.W. The 17th St. building includes marble busts Faith, Hope and Charity by sculptor Hiram Powers and three original Tiffany stained-glass windows. Tours must be scheduled 72 hours in advance. Wednesday and Fridays 10:00 a.m. and 2:00 p.m., Saturdays noon and 2:00 p.m.

Arena Stage
1101 Sixth St. S.W.,
Washington, DC,
202-488-3300;
www.arena-stage.org

Art Museum of the Americas, OAS
201 18th St. N.W.,
Washington, DC,
202-458-6016;
www.museum.oas.org
Dedicated to Latin American and Caribbean contemporary art; paintings, graphics, sculpture. Tuesday-Sunday 10 a.m.-5 p.m.

B'nai B'rith Klutznick Museum
B'nai B'rith International Center,
2020 K St. N.W.,
Washington, DC,
202-857-6583;
http://bnaibrith.org/museum/index.cfm
Permanent exhibition of Jewish ceremonial and folk art. Changing exhibits. Reservations only. Not open to the public.

Basilica of the National Shrine of the Immaculate Conception
400 Michigan Ave. N.E.,
Washington, DC,
202-526-8300;
www.nationalshrine.com
Largest Roman Catholic church in the U.S. and one of the largest in the world. Byzantine and Romanesque architecture; extensive and elaborate collection of mosaics and artwork. Guided tours. Daily. Carillon concerts. November-March 7 a.m.-6 p.m.; April-October 7 a.m.-7 p.m.

Black History Recreation Trail
1100 Ohio Dr. S.W.,
Washington, DC,
202-619-7222;
http://americantrails.org/
nationalrecreationtrails/stateNRT/
DCnrt.html
Trail through Washington neighborhoods highlights important sites in African-American history.

Blair-Lee House
1651 Pennsylvania Ave. N.W.,
Washington, DC,
www.blairhouse.org
(1824) Guest house for heads of government and state visiting the U.S. as guests of the president. Not open to the public.

Blues Alley
1073 Wisconsin Ave. N.W.,
Washington, DC,
202-337-4141;
www.bluesalley.com
For nearly 40 years, serious jazz lovers have flocked to this intimate club to hear Dizzy Gillespie, Sarah Vaughan and Maynard Ferguson, among others. Nightly shows run the gamut from vocal and instrumental sounds to solo performers and larger ensembles. Located in an 18th-century brick carriage house in Georgetown, the club has a sophisticated ambience and a Creole-themed dinner menu.

Bureau of Engraving and Printing

14th and C Streets S.W.,
Washington, DC,
202-874-2330, 866-874-2330;
www.bep.treas.gov

The tour allows visitors to watch currency being printed. Learn about the latest high-tech steps the Bureau has taken to thwart counterfeiting. You can buy uncut sheets of bills in different denominations as well as shredded cash at the BEP store. Guided tours 9 a.m.-2 p.m. Closed weekends, federal holidays and December 24-January 3.

The Capitol

Capitol Hill, Washington, DC,
202-225-6827;
www.aoc.gov

The Capitol has been home to the legislative branch of the U.S. government for more than 200 years. Visitors can take guided tours of several sections, including the beautifully restored Old Supreme Court Chamber and Old Senate Chamber. The Rotunda, a ceremonial space beneath the soaring dome, is a gallery for paintings and sculptures of historic significance. Below it is the Crypt, built for the remains of George Washington (who asked to be buried at Mount Vernon instead), now used for exhibits. Don't miss the National Statuary Hall, where statues of prominent citizens have been donated by all 50 states, and the ornate Brumidi Corridors, named for the Italian artist who designed their murals and many other decorative elements in the Capitol. A state-of-the-art visitor center is currently under construction. Monday-Saturday 9 a.m.-4.30 p.m. Tickets for tours are available at the Capitol Guide Service kiosk near the intersection of First St. S.W. and Independence Ave.

Old Senate Chamber

First and Constitution Avenues N.E.,
Washington, DC,
202-225-6827;
www.aoc.gov/cc/capitol/old_sen_ch.cfm

Original Senate chamber has been restored to its 1850s appearance.

West Front

Capitol Hill, Washington, DC,
202-225-6827

Along the Capitol's west front are terraces, gardens and lawns designed by Frederick Law Olmstead. Halfway down the hill are the Peace Monument (on the north) and the Garfield Monument (on the south). At the foot of Capitol Hill is Union Square with a reflecting pool and the Grant Monument.

Capitol City Brewing Company

2 Massachusetts Ave. N.E.,
Washington, DC,
202-842-2337;
www.capcitybrew.com

Shiny copper vats and a large, oval copper bar are the centerpieces of this huge—and hugely popular—brewpub in the beautifully restored 1911 Postal Square Building. Hill staffers and tourists crowd in for made-on-the-premises ales, lagers and pilsners that go down well with warm pretzels and mustard or with whole meals. Monday-Saturday 11 a.m.-midnight, Sunday from noon.

Catholic University of America

620 Michigan Ave. N.E.,
Washington, DC,
202-319-5000;
www.cua.edu

(1887) (5,510 students.) Open to all faiths. Performances at Hartke Theatre (year-round).

Chesapeake & Ohio Canal Boat Rides

1057 Thomas Jefferson St. N.W.,
Washington, DC,
202-653-5190;
www.nps.gpv/archive/choh/boatrides/
publicboatrides.html

Narrated, one-hour, round-trip canal tours by park rangers in period clothing aboard mule-drawn boats. The ticket office is adjacent. April-October: Wednesday-Sunday.

Chesapeake & Ohio Canal Towpath

1057 Thomas Jefferson St.
N.W. (Georgetown Visitor Center),
Washington, DC,
202-653-5190

413

WASHINGTON, D.C.

Biking (or strolling) along the Chesapeake & Ohio Canal towpath is a great way to immerse yourself in history and nature. The canal, which runs 184.5 miles between Georgetown and Cumberland, Md., was completed in 1850. Locks, lock houses, aqueducts and other original structures remain. Expect spectacular scenery and all manner of wildlife along the way, including deer, fox and woodpeckers. Fee per cyclist at Great Falls. Georgetown Visitor Center Saturday-Sunday.

Chinatown

700 19th St. N.W.,
Washington, DC,

Marked by the Chinatown Friendship Archway at 7th and H streets, which is decorated in Chinese architectural styles of Qing and Ming dynasties and is topped with nearly 300 painted dragons.

Constitution Gardens

Constitution Ave. and 18th St.,
Washington, DC,
202-426-6841;
www.nps.gov/coga

This 50-acre park, with a man-made lake, is also the site of the Signers of the Declaration of Independence Memorial.

Corcoran Gallery of Art

500 17th St. N.W.,
Washington, DC,
202-639-1700;
www.corcoran.org

★
★
★
★
★

The city's oldest art museum and its largest non-federal one. Known for its strong collection of 19th-century American art (don't miss John Singer Sargent's luminous Oyster Gatherers of Cancale) and its support for local artists, the museum also shows important European pieces and contemporary works, including photography, performance art and new media. A glamorous, Frank Gehry-designed addition to the landmark beaux arts building is in the works. Wednesday, Friday-Monday 10 a m.-5 p.m., Thursday to 9 p.m.

DAR Headquarters

1776 D St. N.W., Washington, DC,
202-628-1776;
www.dar.org

Includes Memorial Continental Hall (1904) and Constitution Hall (1920); DAR Museum Gallery, located in the administration building, has 33 state period rooms; outstanding genealogical research library (fee for nonmembers). Guided tours Monday-Saturday.

DC, United (MLS)

RFK Memorial Stadium, 2400 E. Capitol St., S.E., Washington, DC,
202-587-5000;
www.dcunited.com

Professional soccer team.

Department of Commerce Building

1401 Constitution Ave. N.W.,
Washington, DC, 20230,
202-482-2000;
www.commerce.gov

(1932)

Department of Energy

1000 Independence Ave. S.W.,
Washington, DC,
202-586-5575, 800-342-5363;
www.energy.gov

Includes the Interstate Commerce Commission (1934), Constitution Ave. between 12th and 13th streets N.W; Customs Department, Constitution Ave. between 13th and 14th streets N.W; and the District Building, Pennsylvania Ave. between 13th and 14th streets N.W., Washington's ornate 1908 city hall.

Department of Justice Building

950 Pennsylvania Ave.,
Washington, DC

(1934) Not open to the public.

Department of State Building

2201 C St. N.W., Washington, DC,
202-647-4000;
www.dos.gov

The State Department's diplomatic reception rooms, furnished with 18th-century American furniture and decorative art, are used by the Secretary of State and cabinet members for formal entertaining. Tours (Monday-Friday; closed federal holidays and special events; three- to four-weeks advance reservations; children over 12 years only preferred).

Department of the Interior
1849 C St. N.W., Washington, DC,
202-208-3100;
www.doi.gov
(1938) Inside is a museum including exhibits and dioramas depicting the history and activities of the department and its various bureaus. A photo ID is required for admission. (Monday-Friday) Reference library is open to the public.

Department of the Treasury
1500 Pennsylvania Ave. N.W.,
Washington, DC,
202-622-0896;
www.treasury.gov
According to legend, this Greek Revival building, one of the oldest (1836-1869) in the city, was built in the middle of Pennsylvania Ave. because Andrew Jackson was tired of endless wrangling over the location and walked out of the White House, planted his cane in the mud and said, "Here." The building has been extensively restored. Saturday mornings.

Dumbarton Oaks
1703 32nd St. N.W.,
Washington, DC,
202-339-6401;
www.doaks.org
(1800) Famous gardens spanning 16 acres, both formal and Romantic. Mansion has antiques and European art, including El Greco's "The Visitation," galleries of Byzantine art, and a library of rare books on gardening and horticulture. Museum of pre-Columbian artifacts housed in structure by Philip Johnson. Gardens (closed Mondays). The house & museum are currently closed and will reopen once renovation & reinstallation of collections are complete. Tuesday-Sunday afternoons.

Dupont-Kalorama Museum Walk
Washington, DC;
www.dkmuseums.com
Seven museums joined forces to create an awareness of the area. Information and brochures available.

Anderson House Museum
2118 Massachusetts Ave. N.W.,
Washington, DC,
202-785-2040
Revolutionary War museum and national headquarters of the Society of the Cincinnati has portraits by early American artists; 18th-century paintings; 17th-century tapestries; decorative arts of Europe and Asia; and displays of books, medals, swords, silver, glass and china. Tuesday-Saturday afternoons.

Fondo del Sol Visual Arts Center
2112 R St. N.W., Washington, DC,
202-483-2777
Dedicated to presenting, promoting and preserving cultures of the Americas, the museum presents exhibitions of contemporary artists and crafters, holds special events and hosts traveling exhibits for museums and other institutions. Tuesday-Saturday 12:30-5:30 p.m.

Meridian International Center
1624 Crescent Pl. N.W., Washington, DC,
202-939-5568
Housed in two historic mansions designed by John Russell Pope, the center hosts international exhibits, concerts, lectures and symposia promoting international understanding. Period furnishings, Mortlake tapestry; gardens with linden grove. Wednesday-Sunday 2-5 p.m.

Phillips Collection
1600 21st St. N.W., Washington, DC,
202-387-2151
First museum of modern art in the nation. Founded in 1918, the museum continues to emphasize the work of emerging as well as established international artists. Permanent collection of 19th- and 20th-century Impressionist, Post-Impressionist and modern painting and sculpture. Tuesday-Saturday

415

WASHINGTON, D.C.

★
★
★
★
★

10 a.m.-5 p.m., Thursday to 8:30 p.m., Sunday 11 a.m.-6 p.m. Concerts October-May: Sunday.

Textile Museum
2320 S St. N.W., Washington, DC, 202-667-0441
Founded in 1925 with the collection of George Hewitt Myers, the museum features changing exhibits of non-Western textiles, Oriental rugs and other handmade textile art. Guided tours daily. Monday-Saturday 10 a.m.-5 p.m., Sunday from 1 p.m.

Woodrow Wilson House
2340 S St. N.W., Washington, DC, 202-387-4062
(1915) Red brick Georgian Revival townhouse to which President Wilson retired after leaving office; family furnishings and gifts-of-state. Tuesday-Sunday 10 a.m.-4 p.m.

Eastern Market
225 Seventh St. S.E., Washington, DC
Meat, fish and produce are sold. Also antiques, crafts and farmers market on weekends. Tuesday-Sunday.

Emancipation Statue
Lincoln Park, 11th and E. Capitol St. N.E., Washington, DC
This bronze work of Thomas Ball, depicting Lincoln presenting the Emancipation Proclamation, was paid for by voluntary subscriptions from emancipated slaves. It was dedicated on April 14, 1876, the 11th anniversary of Lincoln's assassination. Fredrick Douglass was in attendance.
Also here is:

Mary McLeod Bethune Memorial
E. Capitol St. S.E., Washington, DC
Honors the noted educator and advisor to President Lincoln and founder of the National Council of Negro Women.

Embassy Row
Massachusetts Ave. and 23rd St. N.W., Washington, DC

This neighborhood within the city's northwest quadrant is centered around Sheridan Circle and is home to dozens of foreign legations.

Explorers Hall
1145 17th St. N.W., Washington, DC, 202-857-7588
National Geographic Society headquarters. Several traveling exhibits, call for information. Daily.

Federal Reserve Building
C and 21st streets N.W., Washington, DC, 202-452-3149
(1937) Primarily an office building but noteworthy for its architecture; rotating art exhibits; film (20 minutes).

Federal Trade Commission Building
600 Pennsylvania Ave. N.W., Washington, DC, 202-326-2222; www.ftc.gov
(1938) Monday-Friday.

Federal Triangle
Pennsylvania Ave. and 13th St. N.W., Washington, DC
The Triangle holds a group of government buildings, nine of which were built for $78 million in the 1930s in modern classic design. The "crown jewel" of the triangle is the Ronald Reagan International Trade Center, located on Pennsylvania Ave. at 13th St. N.W.

Ford's Theatre
511 10th St. N.W., Washington, DC, 202-426-6924; www.fordstheatre.org
The site of Abraham Lincoln's assassination. Ford's became a working theater again in 1968; recent productions have included the play "Inherit the Wind" and a one-man show about George Gershwin. The theatre & the museum (below) are now closed to the public as of 8/27/07 except for performances (by ticket sale). The Petersen House is still open to the public.
In basement is:

Lincoln Museum

511 10th St. N.W., Washington, DC, 20004,
202-347-4833

Petersen House

516 10th St. N.W., Washington, DC, 20004.
The house where President Lincoln was
taken after the shooting at Ford's Theatre;
he died here the following morning. The
house has been restored to its appearance at
that time. Daily 9 a.m.-5 p.m.

Fort Dupont Park

Randle Cir. and Minnesota Ave. S.E.,
Washington, DC,
202-426-7723;
www.nps.gov/fodu
Picnicking, hiking and bicycling in hilly terrain; cultural arts performances in summer.
Also films, slides and activities involving
natural science; environmental education
programs, nature discovery room, Junior
Ranger program; garden workshops and pro-
grammed activities by reservation.

Fort Dupont Sports Complex

3779 Ely Pl. S.E., Washington, DC,
202-584-5007
Skating, ice hockey (fee); tennis courts,
basketball courts, ball fields (daily; free),
jogging.

Fort Stevens Park

13th and Quackenbos St. N.W.,
Washington, DC,
202-895-6000
General Jubal Early and his Confederate
troops tried to invade Washington at this
spot on July 11-12, 1864. President Lincoln
risked his life at the fort during the fighting.
Daily.

Franciscan Monastery

1400 Quincy St. N.E.,
Washington, DC,
202-526-6800;
www.myfranciscan.org
Within the church and grounds is the
"Holy Land of America;" replicas of sacred
Holy Land shrines including the Manger

at Bethlehem, the Garden of Gethsemane
and the Holy Sepulchre. Also the Grotto
at Lourdes and Roman catacombs. Guided
tours by the friars. Daily.

Franklin Delano Roosevelt Memorial

West Basin Dr.,
Washington, DC,
202-426-6841;
www.nps.gov/fdrm
This newer memorial, dedicated in 1997,
features a series of sculptures depicting the
32nd U.S. President and his wife, Eleanor.
Four outdoor rooms represent each of
FDR's four presidential terms, which began
in the Great Depression and ended at the
close of World War II. His "fireside chats"
are broadcast throughout the exhibits. Daily
24 hours; interpretive ranger staff on site
8 a.m.-11:45 p.m.

Frederick Douglass National Historic Site

1411 W St. S.E.,
Washington, DC,
202-426-5961, 800-967-2283;
www.nps.gov/frdo
This 21-room house on nine acres is where
Douglass, a former slave who became minister to Haiti and a leading black spokes-
man, lived from 1877 until his death in
1895; visitor center with film, memorabilia.
Mid-April-mid-October 9 a.m.-5 p.m., mid-
October-mid-April 9 a.m.-4 p.m.

Fresh Farm Market

20th St. N.W.,
Washington, DC,
202-331-7300;
www.freshfarmmarket.org
More than 25 local farmers bring in-season
fruits, vegetables, artisanal cheeses and
organic offerings to this weekly market.
Daily 9 a.m.-1 p.m.

General Services Administration Building

18th and F streets N.W.,
Washington, DC
(1917) Was originally the Department of
Interior.

WASHINGTON, D.C.

George Washington University

2121 I St. N.W., Washington, DC,
202-994-1000;
www.gwu.edu
(1821) (20,000 students.) Theater; art exhibits in Dimock Gallery (Monday-Friday) and University Library.

Georgetown Flea Market

Wisconsin Ave. N.W.,
Washington, DC,
202-775-3532;
www.georgetownfleamarket.com
Offering antique furniture, jewelry, books, rugs, toys, linens and other vintage treasures on Sundays since 1973. (Actress Diane Keaton has been a frequent patron.) About 70 dealers set up booths year-round; come early for the biggest selection or late for the best bargains. Saturday & Sunday.

Georgetown University

37th and O streets N.W.,
Washington, DC,
202-687-0100;
www.georgetown.edu
(1789) (12,000 students.) Oldest Catholic college in the U.S. Campus tours Monday-Saturday, by reservation.

Government Printing Office

732 N. Capitol St. N.W.,
Washington, DC,
202-512-0000
Four buildings with 35 acres of floor space where most of the material issued by U.S. government is printed, including production and distribution of the Congressional Record, Federal Register and U.S. passports. (No public tours; for information on the agency, call 202-512-1991.) Office includes the Main Government Bookstore. Nearly 20,000 publications available Monday-Friday.

Gray Line bus tours

50 Massachusetts Ave. N.E.,
Washington, DC,
301-386-8300, 800-862-1400
Tours of city and area attractions depart from Union Station.

House Office Buildings

Independence and New Jersey avenues,
Washington, DC,
202-224-3121
Pedestrian tunnel connects two of the oldest House office buildings with the Capitol.

Howard University

2400 Sixth St. N.W., Washington, DC,
202-806-6100;
www.howard.edu
Main campus: 2400 6th St. N.W. between W and Harvard streets N.W., West campus: 2900 Van Ness St. N.W., 20008. Three other campuses in the area. (1867) (12,000 students.) Main campus has a Gallery of Fine Art with a permanent Alain Locke African Collection; changing exhibits September-July: Monday-Friday.

HR-57

1610 14th St. N.W., Washington, DC,
202-667-3700;
www.hr57.org
This ultra-friendly, bare-bones spot is the performance arm of the Center for the Preservation of Jazz and Blues, a not-for-profit cultural center that named its club after a 1987 House Resolution designating jazz as a rare and valuable national American treasure. Expect to hear well-known and lesser-known artists at the top of their game. Wednesday-Saturday 11 a.m.-5 p.m.

The Improv

1140 Connecticut Ave. N.W.,
Washington, DC,
202-296-7008;
www.dcimprov.com
The crowd is youngish and the comedy free-flowing here. Onstage talent includes established stars as well as hilarious, original newcomers you may have caught on Comedy Central. Appetizers, sandwiches, beer and wine are available. Daily.

International Spy Museum

800 F St. N.W., Washington, DC,
202-393-7798, 866-779-6873;
www.spymuseum.org

418

WASHINGTON, D.C.

Opened in 2002, this museum sheds light on the world of international espionage with artifacts including invisible ink, high-tech eavesdropping devices, a through-the-wall camera and a KGB lipstick pistol. Find out how codes were made and broken throughout history, how successful disguises are created and what real-life James Bonds think of the high-stakes game of spying. Daily 10 a.m.-8 p.m.

Islamic Center
2551 Massachusetts Ave. N.W.,
Washington, DC,
202-332-8343;
www.islamiccenterdc.com
Leading mosque in the U.S. has landscaped courtyard, intricate interior mosaics. Daily; no tours during Friday prayer service.

Iwo Jima Statue
Meade St., Washington, DC
Across Theodore Roosevelt Bridge on Arlington Boulevard.

John F. Kennedy Center for the Performing Arts
2700 F St. N.W.,
Washington, DC,
202-416-8340, 800-444-1324;
www.kennedy-center.org
The home of the National Symphony Orchestra and Washington Opera hosts an impressive array of internationally known artists in dance, theater and music. Opened in 1971 as a memorial to John F. Kennedy, a large bronze bust of the former president graces the Grand Foyer, and paintings, sculptures and other artwork presented by foreign governments are also displayed. Daily.

Judiciary Square
D and Fourth streets N.W.,
Washington, DC
Two square blocks of judiciary buildings, including five federal and district courts, the U.S. District Court (1820), and the U.S. Court of Appeals (1910). At D St. halfway between 4th and 5th streets is the first completed statue of Abraham Lincoln (1868).

Kenilworth Aquatic Gardens
1550 Anacostia Ave. S.E.,
Washington, DC,
202-426-6905
Water lilies, lotuses and other water plants bloom from mid-May until the frost. Gardens (daily). Guided walks Memorial Day-Labor Day: Saturday-Sunday and holidays, also by appointment.

Korean War Memorial
French Dr. S.W. and Independence Ave.,
Washington, DC,
202-426-6841;
www.nps.gov/kwvm
This massive sculpture honors the Americans who served in the Korean War, showing 19 soldiers dressed and armed for battle heading toward the American flag, their symbolic goal. The adjacent wall features etched photographs that pay tribute to military support personnel. Daily 8 a.m.-11:45 p.m.

Labor Department
Francis H. Perkins Building,
200 Constitution Ave. N.W.,
Washington, DC,
202-693-6613, 866-487-2365;
www.dol.gov
Lobby contains the Labor Hall of Fame, an exhibit depicting labor in the U.S.; the library on the second floor is open to the public. Monday-Friday.

Lafayette Square
Pennsylvania Ave. N.W.,
Washington, DC
Statue of Andrew Jackson on horseback in the center was the first equestrian figure in Washington (1853). One of the park benches was known as Bernard Baruch's office in 1930s and is dedicated to him.
On the square is:

Decatur House Museum
1610 H St. N.W., Washington, DC
202-842-0920;
www.decaturhouse.org
(1818) Federal townhouse built for naval hero Commodore Stephen Decatur by

419

Benjamin H. Latrobe, second architect of the Capitol. After Decatur's death in 1820, the house was occupied by a succession of American and foreign statesmen, and was a center of political and social life in the city. The ground floor family rooms reflect Decatur's Federal-period lifestyle. Operated by the National Trust for Historic Preservation. Tuesday-Saturday 10 a.m.-5 p.m., Sunday noon-4 p.m.

Library of Congress
101 Independence Ave. S.E.,
Washington, DC,
202-707-6400;
www.loc.gov
(1800) Treasures include a Gutenberg Bible, the first great book printed with movable metal type, and the Giant Bible of Mainz, a 500-year-old illuminated manuscript. Collection includes manuscripts, newspapers, maps, recordings, prints, photographs, posters and more than 30 million books and pamphlets in 60 languages. In the elaborate Jefferson Building is the Great Hall, decorated with murals, mosaics and marble carvings; exhibition halls. In the Madison Building, a 22-minute audiovisual presentation, America's Library, provides a good introduction to the library and its facilities. Monday-Saturday 10 a.m.-5:30 p.m.

Folger Shakespeare Library
201 E. Capitol St. S.E.,
Washington, DC,
202-544-4600;
www.folger.edu
(1932) Houses the finest collection of Shakespeare materials in the world, including the 1623 First Folio edition and large holdings of rare books and manuscripts of the English and continental Renaissance. The Great Hall offers year-round exhibits from the Folgers' extensive collection. The Elizabethan Theatre, which was designed to resemble an theater of Shakespeare's day, is the site of the Folger Shakespeare Library's series of museum and performing arts programs, which include literary readings, drama, lectures and education and family

programs. Self-guided tours. Guided tours. Monday-Saturday 10 a.m.-5 p.m. Reading room Monday-Friday 8:45 a.m.-4:45 p.m., Saturday 9 a.m.-4:30 p.m.

Lincoln Memorial
23rd St. N.W., Washington, DC,
202-426-6841;
www.nps.gov/linc
Dedicated in 1922, Daniel Chester French's Abraham Lincoln looks across a reflecting pool to the Washington Monument and the Capitol. Lincoln's Gettysburg Address and Second Inaugural Address are inscribed on the walls of the temple-like structure, which is particularly impressive at night. The 36 columns represent the 36 states in the Union in existence at the time of Lincoln's death.

Martin Luther King, Jr. Memorial Library
901 G St. N.W., Washington, DC,
www.dclibrary.org/mlk
(1972) Main branch of the DC public library was designed by architect Mies van der Rohe. Martin Luther King mural. Books, periodicals, photographs, films, videocassettes, recordings, microfilms, Washingtoniana and the "Washington Star" collection. Library for the visually impaired; librarian for the hearing impaired; black studies division; AP wire service machine; community information service. Underground parking. Monday-Saturday.

National Academy of Sciences
2100 C St. N.W., Washington, DC,
202-337-8566;
www.nationalacademies.org
(1924) Established in 1863 to stimulate research and communication among scientists and to advise the federal government in science and technology. A famous 21-foot bronze statue of Albert Einstein by Robert Berks is on the front lawn. Art exhibits, concerts. Schedule varies.

National Aquarium
Department of Commerce Building,
14th St. and Constitution Ave. N.W.,
Washington, DC,
202-482-2825;
www.nationalaquarium.com

★
★
★
★
★

The nation's oldest public aquarium was established in 1873. It now exhibits more than 1,700 specimens representing approximately 260 species, both freshwater and saltwater. Touch tank; theater. Shark feedings (Monday, Wednesday, Saturday); piranha feedings (Tuesday, Thursday, Sunday). Daily 9 a.m.-5 p.m.

National Archives
Constitution Ave, Washington, DC,
202-501-5205;
www.archives.gov
(1934) Original copies of the Declaration of Independence, the Bill of Rights and the Constitution; a 1297 version of the Magna Carta and other historic documents, maps and photographs. Guided tours by appointment only. Archives are also available to the public for genealogical and historical research Monday-Saturday. mid-March-Labor Day 10 a.m.-7 p.m., Labor Day-Mid-March 10 a.m.-5:30 p.m.

National Building Museum
401 F St. N.W.,
Washington, DC,
202-272-2448;
www.nbm.org
Deals with architecture, design, engineering and construction. Permanent exhibits include drawings, blueprints, models, photographs, artifacts and the architectural evolution of Washington's buildings and monuments. The museum's enormous Great Hall is supported by eight of the world's largest Corinthian columns. Group and open tours daily. Monday-Saturday 10 a.m.-5 p.m., Sunday 11 a.m.-5 p.m.

National Gallery of Art
Fourth and Constitution avenues N.W.,
Washington, DC,
202-737-4215;
www.nga.gov
The West Building (1941), designed by John Russell Pope, contains Western European and American art spanning periods between the 13th and 20th centuries: highlights include the only Leonardo da Vinci painting on display outside of Europe, "Ginevra de' Benci;" a comprehensive collection of Italian paintings and sculpture; major French Impressionists; numerous Rembrandts and examples of the Dutch school; masterpieces from the Mellon, Widener, Kress, Dale and Rosenwald collections; special exhibitions. The East Building (1978), designed by architect I. M. Pei, houses the gallery's growing collection of 20th-century art, including Picasso's "Family of Saltimbanques" and Jackson Pollock's "Lavender Mist." Daily.

National Museum of Health and Medicine
Walter Reed Army Medical Center,
Building #54, 6900 Georgia Ave.
and Elder St., Washington, DC,
202-782-2200;
http://nmhm.washingtondc.museum
One of the most important medical collections in America. Interprets the link between history and technology; AIDS education exhibit; an interactive exhibit on human anatomy and lifestyle choices; and a collection of microscopes, medical teaching aids, tools and instruments (1862-1965) and famous historical icons exhibits. Daily 10 a.m.-5:30 p.m.

National Museum of Women in the Arts
1250 New York Ave. N.W.,
Washington, DC,
202-783-5000, 800-222-7270;
www.nmwa.org
More than 1,200 works by female artists from the Renaissance to the present. Paintings, drawings, sculpture, pottery, prints. Library, research center by appointment. Performances. Guided tours (by appointment). Monday-Saturday 10 a.m.-5 p.m., Sunday noon-5 p.m.

National Presbyterian Church and Center
4101 Nebraska Ave. N.W.,
Washington, DC,
202-537-0800;
www.natpresch.org
Chapel of the President contains memorabilia of past U.S. presidents; faceted glass windows depict the history of man and church. Self-guided tours (daily). Guided tours (Sunday following service).

421

WASHINGTON, D.C.

★
★
★
★

★
★
★
★
★

National Theatre

1321 Pennsylvania Ave. N.W.,
Washington, DC,
202-628-6161, 800-447-7400;
www.nationaltheatre.org

Theatrical luminaries such as Sarah Bernhardt, Laurence Olivier and the Barrymores have performed at this historic playhouse, which is said to be haunted by the ghost of a murdered actor. These days, you'll see touring productions of shows including "The Tale of the Allergist's Wife" and "42nd Street." On Mondays, there are films in summer and performances drawing on local talent the rest of the year. Saturday mornings feature children's shows. Tours (Monday-Friday 11 a.m.-3 p.m. 202-783-6854). Fees vary by performance.

Navy Yard

901 M St. S.E., Washington, DC,
202-433-4882

Founded in 1799 along the Anacostia River at a location chosen by George Washington, the yard was nearly destroyed during the War of 1812. Outside the yard at 636 G St. SE is the John Philip Sousa house, where the "March King" wrote many of his famous compositions. The house is private.

One block east is:

Marine Barracks

Eighth St. and I St. S.E., Washington, DC,
202-433-6060;
www.mbw.usmc.mil

The parade ground, more than two centuries old, is surrounded by handsome and historic structures, including the Commandant's House facing G St., which is said to be the oldest continuously occupied public building in the city. The parade is open to the public on Friday evenings in summer.

Navy Museum

805 Kidder Breese S.E.,
Washington, DC,
202-433-6897

History of the US Navy from the Revolutionary War to the space age. Dioramas depict achievements of early naval heroes; displays development of naval weapons; fully rigged foremast fighting top and gun deck from frigate Constitution on display; World War II guns that can be trained and elevated; submarine room has operating periscopes. Approximately 5,000 objects on display including paintings, ship models, flags, uniforms, naval decorations and the bathyscaphe "Trieste." Two-acre outdoor park displays 19th- and 20th-century guns, cannon, other naval artifacts; US Navy destroyer "Barry" located on the waterfront. Monday-Friday 9 a.m.-5 p.m., weekends and holidays 10 a.m.-5 p.m.

New York Avenue Presbyterian Church

1313 New York Ave. N.W.,
Washington, DC,
202-393-3700;
www.nyapc.org

The church where Lincoln worshipped. It was rebuilt 1950-1951, with Lincoln's pew. Dr. Peter Marshall was pastor from 1937 to 1949. Mementos on display include the first draft of the Emancipation Proclamation. Tuesday-Friday, services Sunday morning.

The Octagon Museum

1799 New York Ave. N.W.,
Washington, DC,
202-638-3221;
www.archfoundation.org/octagon

(1799-1801) Federal townhouse built for Colonel John Taylor III based on designs by Dr. William Thornton. It served as temporary quarters for President and Mrs. James Madison after the White House burned in the War of 1812; it also was the site of the ratification of the Treaty of Ghent. Restored with period furnishings (1800-1828). Changing exhibits on architecture and allied arts. By appointment only.

Old Stone House

3051 M St. N.W.,
Washington, DC,
202-426-6851;
www.nps.gov/archive/rocr/oldstonehouse

(1765) Believed to be the oldest pre-Revolutionary building in Washington. Constructed on parcel No. 3 of the original tract of land that was then Georgetown, the house was used as both a residence and a place of business; five rooms are furnished with household items that reflect a middle-class residence of the late 18th century. The grounds are lush with fruit trees and seasonal blooms. Wednesday-Sunday noon-5 p.m.

Organization of American States (OAS)
17th St. N.W. and Constitution Ave.,
Washington, DC,
202-458-3000;
www.oas.org
Headquarters of OAS, set up to maintain international peace and security and to promote integral development in the Americas. Monday-Friday.

Pavilion at the Old Post Office
1100 Pennsylvania Ave. N.W.,
Washington, DC,
202-289-4224;
www.oldpostofficedc.com
(1899) Romanesque structure, which for years was headquarters of the U.S. Postal Service. The building has been remodeled into a marketplace with 100 shops and restaurants and daily entertainment. In the 315-foot tower are replicas of the bells of Westminster Abbey, a Bicentennial gift from Great Britain; and the tower, which is the second-highest point in D.C., offers spectacular views from an open-air observation deck. Above the Pavilion shops are headquarters for the National Endowment for the Arts. Daily.

Potomac Park (East and West)
1100 Ohio St. S.W., Washington, DC,
202-619-7222;
www.nps.gov/nacc
Features 720 riverfront acres, divided by Washington's famous Tidal Basin into East and West Potomac Parks. East Potomac Park has three golf courses, a large swimming pool, picnic grounds, tennis courts and biking and hiking paths. Pedal boats can be rented at the Tidal Basin. At West Potomac Park, you'll find the Vietnam, Korean, Lincoln, Jefferson and FDR memorials; Constitution Gardens; and the Reflecting Pool. Also the site of the famous D.C. cherry trees; enjoy the two-week burst of pink and white cherry blossoms from more than 3,000 trees, a 1912 gift of friendship from Japan, in late

March/early April. The Cherry Blossom Festival begins each year with the lighting of the 300-year-old Japanese Stone Lantern, presented by the governor of Tokyo in 1954.

President Kennedy's Gravesite
South Gate, Arlington National Cemetery,
Washington, DC

Rock Creek Park
3545 Williamsburg Lane N.W.,
Washington, DC,
202-895-6070;
www.nps.gov/rocr
Just five miles from the White House are dozens of miles of clearly marked, well-maintained, easy and moderately hard hiking trails through the park's 1,754 acres of meadows and woodlands. There's also a gentle walk along Beach Drive that takes you through dramatic Rock Creek Gorge; on weekends and holidays, cars are prohibited, making it even more peaceful. Daily, dawn-dusk.

Carter Barron Amphitheatre
16 St. and Colorado Ave. N.W.,
Washington, DC,
202-426-0486;
www.nps.gov/rocr/cbarron
This 4,200-seat outdoor theater in a wooded area is the setting for summer performances of symphonic, folk, pop and jazz music and Shakespearean theater.

Senate Office Buildings
114 Constitution Ave. N.E.,
Washington, DC
Linked by private subway to the Capitol.

Sewall-Belmont House
144 Constitution Ave. N.E.,
Washington, DC,
202-546-1210;
www.sewallbelmont.org
(1680, 1800) The Sewall-Belmont House is a monument to Alice Paul, the author of the Equal Rights Amendment. From this house, she spearheaded the fight for the passage of the amendment. Now a national landmark, the house contains portraits and sculptures of women from the beginning of

423

WASHINGTON, D.C.

★
★
★
★
★

the suffrage movement; extensive collection of artifacts of the suffrage and equal rights movements; historic headquarters of the National Woman's Party. Tuesday-Friday 11 a.m.-3 p.m., Saturday noon-4 p.m.

Shakespeare Theatre at the Lansburgh
450 Seventh St. N.W., Washington, DC, 202-547-1122, 877-487-8849; www.shakespearedc.org

Shops at Georgetown Park
3222 M St. N.W., Washington, DC, 202-298-5577; www.shopsatgeorgetownpark.com
This stylish urban mall has four levels of upscale shops and restaurants to explore and is especially strong in apparel. Concierge Center. Monday-Saturday 10 a.m.-9 p.m., Sunday noon-6 p.m.

Shops at National Place
1331 Pennsylvania Ave. N.W., Washington, DC, 202-662-1250
Trilevel marketplace featuring more than 100 specialty shops and restaurants. Monday-Friday 11 a.m.-7 p.m., Saturday noon-6 p.m.

Smithsonian Institution
1000 Jefferson Dr. S.W., Washington, DC, 20560, 202-633-1000; www.si.edu
The majority of Smithsonian museums are located on the National Mall. All buildings open daily 10 a.m.-5:30 p.m.; Anacostia Museum and National Zoo hours vary.
   Smithsonian museums on the Mall include:

Anacostia Museum
1901 Fort Pl. S.E., Washington, DC, 202-633-4820; www.anacosta.si.edu
An exhibition and research center for black heritage in the historic Anacostia section of southeast Washington. Changing exhibits. Daily 10 a.m.-5 p.m.

Arthur M. Sackler Gallery
1050 Independence Ave. S.W., Washington, DC, 202-357-2700; www.asia.si.edu
Changing exhibitions of Asian art, both Near- and Far-Eastern, from major national and international collections. Permanent collection includes Chinese and South and Southeast Asian art objects presented by Arthur Sackler.

Freer Gallery
Jefferson Dr. at 12th St. S.W., Washington, DC, 202-633-4880; www.asia.si.edu
Asian art with objects dating from Neolithic period to the early 20th century. Also works by late 19th- and early 20th-century American artists, including a major collection of James McNeill Whistler's work, highlighted by the famous Peacock Room. Next to the Freer is the Smithsonian Institution Building, or "the Castle."

Hirshhorn Museum and Sculpture Garden
Independence Ave. and Seventh St. S.W., Washington, DC, 202-633-4674; http://hirshhorn.si.edu
The modernity of the paintings and sculptures here—and of the curvy building itself—are a respite for history-sated visitors. Inside is some of the most interesting art produced in the last 100 years: everything from Constantin Brancusi's egglike "Sleeping Muse I" to Nam June Paik's "Video Flag" made with 70 video monitors. The lush plaza (7:30 a.m.-5:30 p.m.) and sculpture garden (7:30 a.m.-dusk) also make this an inviting spot.

National Air and Space Museum
600 Independence Ave. S.W., Washington, DC, 202-633-2563
View the Wright brothers' 1903 Kitty Hawk Flyer, Charles Lindbergh's Spirit of St. Louis and the command module Columbia, which carried the first men to walk on the moon.

In the Apollo to the Moon exhibit, you'll see lunar rocks, spacesuits and John Glenn's squeeze-tube beef stew, among other artifacts. An IMAX theater enables you to view on a huge, five-story-high screen Earth as seen from the space shuttle. And don't miss the high-tech shows at the Albert Einstein Planetarium. Daily 10 a.m.-5:30 p.m.

National Museum of African Art
950 Independence Ave. S.W.,
Washington, DC,
202-633-4600;
www.nmafa.si.edu

Permanent exhibits display masks, musical instruments, sacred objects, ceramics, textiles, household tools and the visual arts of the sub-Sahara. Traveling shows cover even more ground; recent ones have featured colonial-era photography and Ethiopian religious icons. A full schedule of films, musical presentations, lectures and children's events keeps things lively. Daily 10 a.m.-5:30 p.m.

National Museum of American History
14th St. and Constitution Ave. N.W.,
Washington, DC,
202-633-1000

More than 17 million artifacts cover aspects of American cultural heritage. Check out Julia Child's cheerfully comfortable kitchen from the famous chef's longtime home in Cambridge, Mass., reassembled here in 2001. Or watch textile conservators take painstaking steps to restore the fragile "Star-Spangled Banner," the actual flag that inspired Francis Scott Key in 1814 to write the poem that became America's national anthem. The museum's collections include the lap desk at which Thomas Jefferson drafted the Declaration of Independence, Henry Ford's 1913 Model-T, first ladies' inaugural gowns and Dorothy's ruby slippers from The Wizard of Oz. This museum closed 9/6/06 for renovations and is due to reopen by the summer of 2008. Children will especially enjoy the Hands On History Room, where they can harness a life-size

model of a mule or tap out a telegraph message in Morse code.

National Museum of Natural History
Constitution Ave. and 10th St. N.W.,
Washington, DC,
202-633-1000;
www.mnh.si.edu

Before you enter this museum, stop on the Ninth Street side of the building to see the mesmerizing Butterfly Garden. The National Museum of Natural History holds more than 124 million artifacts and specimens dating back to the Ice Age. Museum exhibits include an insect zoo with thousands of live specimens, a section on gems (including the 45.52-carat, billion-year-old Hope Diamond), dinosaur skeletons, a live coral reef, and botanical, zoological and geological materials. Daily 10 a.m.-5:30 p.m.

National Zoo
3001 Connecticut Ave. N.W.,
Washington, DC,
202-633-4800;
http://nationalzoo.si.edu

A branch of the Smithsonian Institution, the National Zoo features 5,000 animals of 500 species. Come when the zoo first opens or after 2 p.m. if you want to see giant pandas Tian Tian and Mei Xiang without waiting in long lines. The zoo is set amid the urban greenery of Rock Creek Park. Daily from 10 a.m.

Renwick Gallery at the American Art Museum
Pennsylvania Ave. at 17th St. N.W.,
Washington, DC,
202-633-2850;
http://americanart.si.edu/renwick

The American Art Museum's Renwick Gallery, housed in an elegant Second Empire-style building, displays American crafts and decorative arts. The permanent collection features superb, one-of-a-kind pieces in clay, fiber, glass, metal and wood. Make sure to see the sculptural furniture by

★
★
★
★
★

Sam Maloof and the playful Game Fish by Larry Fuente. Daily 10 a.m.-5:30 p.m.

St. John's Church Georgetown Parish
3240 O St. N.W.,
Washington, DC,
202-338-1796;
www.stjohnsgeorgetown.org
Oldest Episcopal congregation in Georgetown, established 1796; original design of church by William Thornton, architect of the Capitol. Many presidents since Madison have worshiped here. Francis Scott Key was a founding member. Tours (by appointment).

Supreme Court of the United States
First St. N.E. and Maryland Ave.,
Washington, DC,
202-479-3211;
www.supremecourtus.gov
Designed by Cass Gilbert in Neoclassical style. Court is in session October-April (Monday-Wednesday, at two-week intervals from the first Monday in October) and on the first workday of each week in May and June; court sessions are open to the public (10 a.m. and 1 p.m.), on a first-come, first-served basis; lectures are offered in the courtroom (Monday-Friday except when court is in session; 20-minute lectures hourly on half hour); on the ground floor are exhibits and a film (23 minutes), cafeteria, snack bar and gift shop. Monday-Friday 9 a.m.-4:30 p.m.

Thomas Jefferson Memorial
East Basin Dr. S.W., Washington, DC,
202-426-6841;
www.nps.gov/thje
This memorial, dedicated in 1943, honors the third President and author of both the Declaration of Independence and the Bill of Rights. The white marble dome surrounded by columns, representing the classic style that Jefferson introduced to the U.S., is quite beautiful when lit up at night. In the basement, you'll find a museum and the plaster statue from which the 19-foot bronze one in the center of the monument was created.

Tourmobile Sightseeing
1000 Ohio Dr. S.W.,
Washington, DC,
202-554-5100;
www.tourmobile.com
Narrated shuttle tours to 18 historic sites on the National Mall and in Arlington National Cemetery. Unlimited reboarding throughout day (daily). Additional tours separately or in combinations: Arlington National Cemetery; Mount Vernon (seasonal) and Frederick Douglass Home (seasonal).

Tudor Place
1644 31st St. N.W., Washington, DC,
202-965-0400;
www.tudorplace.org
(1805) This 12-room Federal-style mansion was designed by Dr. William Thornton, architect of the Capitol, for Martha Custis Peter, granddaughter of Martha Washington. The Peter family lived in the house for 180 years. All furnishings and objets d'art are original. More than five acres of gardens (Monday-Saturday). Guided tours Tuesday-Sunday.

Union Station
50 Massachusetts Ave. N.E.,
Washington, DC,
202-289-1908;
www.unionstationdc.com
Architect Daniel Burnham designed Union Station in 1907, and it was restored to its former glory and reopened in 1988. The white granite Beaux Arts masterpiece is still a functioning train station and is now home to more than 130 upscale restaurants and shops, many of them catering to the special needs of travelers. But many locals patronize the shops, too (including President Bill Clinton, who regularly bought holiday presents here). Also located within the station are the Amtrak depot and Gray Line and Tourmobile Sightseeing operators. Daily.

U.S. Botanic Garden

100 Maryland Ave. S.W.,
Washington, DC,
202-225-8333;
www.usbg.gov

The Botanic Garden, one of the oldest in the country, was established by Congress in 1820 for public education and exhibition. It features plants collected by the famous Wilkes Expedition of the South Seas. Conservatory has tropical, subtropical and desert plants; seasonal displays. Exterior gardens are planted for seasonal blooming; also here is Bartholdi Fountain, designed by the sculptor of the Statue of Liberty. Daily 10 a.m.-5 p.m.

U.S. Holocaust Memorial Museum

100 Raoul Wallenberg Plaza S.W.,
Washington, DC,
202-488-0400;
www.ushmm.org

Opened in 1993, this privately funded museum hosts temporary exhibits that cover everything from the diary of Anne Frank to the role of Oskar Schindler in saving the lives of hundreds of Jews. At the heart of the museum is its self-guided Permanent Exhibition, which includes powerful photos, film footage, eyewitness testimonies, clothing, children's drawings and other victims' belongings, as well as reconstructions of concentration camp buildings. Especially stirring is the Hall of Faces, a narrow, three-story-high space crammed with framed photographs of the Jewish residents of a single Lithuanian town, more than 3,000 of whom were murdered in September 1941. Daily 10 a.m.-5:30 p.m. April-mid-June: 10 a.m.-6:30 p.m.; closed Yom Kippur. Timed daily-use passes are necessary for visiting the museum's permanent exhibition and can be obtained each day at the museum starting at 10 a.m. or in advance by calling 800-400-9373.

U.S. National Arboretum

3501 New York Ave. N.E.,
Washington, DC,
202-245-2726;
www.usna.usda.gov

Floral displays in spring, summer, fall and winter on 446 acres; Japanese garden, National Bonsai and Penjing Museum (daily); National Herb Garden, major collections of azaleas (15,000), wildflowers, ferns, magnolias, crabapples, cherries and dogwoods; aquatic plantings; dwarf conifers (the world's largest evergreen collection). Daily 8 a.m.-5 p.m. Under 16 years admitted only with adult.

U.S. Navy Memorial

701 Pennsylvania Ave. N.W.,
Washington, DC,
202-737-2300;
www.lonesailor.org

Dedicated to those who have served in the Navy in war and in peacetime. A 100-foot-diameter granite world map dominates the Plaza, where the Lone Sailor, a 7-foot bronze sculpture, stands and the US Navy Band stages performances (Memorial Day-Labor Day: Tuesday evenings). Visitor Center features electronic kiosks with interactive video displays on naval history; also Navy Memorial Log Room and U.S. Presidents' Room. Tuesday-Saturday.

Verizon Center

601 F St. N.W., Washington, DC,
202-628-3200;
www.verizoncenter.com

This 20,000-seat, state-of-the-art arena, home to the NBA's Washington Wizards, the WNBA's Washington Mystics, the NHL's Washington Capitals and Georgetown Hoyas basketball, is also a popular venue for concerts and other events, from Liza Minnelli to the Harlem Globetrotters. Even when nothing is scheduled, you can check out Nick and Stef's Steakhouse (open for dinner every day, lunch Monday-Friday), the F Street Sports Bar, or Modell's Sporting Goods for team-themed athletic wear. Monday-Saturday; days and fees for events vary.

Vietnam Veterans Memorial

900 Ohio Drive S.W.,
Washington, DC,
202-426-6841;
www.nps.gov/vive

Designed by Maya Ying Lin and funded by private citizens' contributions, this memorial's polished black granite walls are inscribed with the names of the 58,175 U.S. servicemen who died in or remain missing from the Vietnam War (a large directory helps visitors locate specific names). Deliberately apolitical, the memorial aims to foster reconciliation and healing given the divisiveness the war caused in American society. Also on site are the Three Servicemen Statue and Flagpole and the Vietnam Women's Memorial. Daily.

Warner Theatre
13th and E streets N.W.,
Washington, DC,
202-783-4000;
www.warnertheatre.com
This theater, with over 1,800 seats, has been restored to its 1924 glory, with a sparkling chandelier, stained-glass lamps and Portuguese draperies. The Warner is host to many performances, including comedies, musicals, an annual Nutcracker performance and from time to time movie premieres.

Washington Capitals (NHL)
Verizon Center,
601 F St. N.W., Washington, DC,
202-661-5050;
www.washingtoncapitals.com
Professional hockey team.

Washington Convention Center
801 Mount Vernon Place N.W.,
Washington, DC,
202-249-3000, 800-368-9000;
www.dcconvention.com
Washington's biggest building is also one of its newest. Opened in 2003, the Washington Convention Center occupies six city blocks, housing 700,000 square feet of exhibit space and 125,000 square feet of meeting space. The roof of the structure alone covers 17 acres. The Washington Convention Center is located immediately north of Mount Vernon Square, offering convenient access to some of the city's finest hotels and restaurants. Many other attractions can be found nearby, including Chinatown, the

National Portrait Gallery, Ford's Theatre and the Verizon Center.

Washington Harbour
3000 K St. N.W., Washington, DC
Dining and shopping complex that features lavish fountains, life-size statuary and a boardwalk with a view of the Potomac River.

Washington Monument
15th St. S.W., Washington, DC,
202-426-6841;
www.nps.gov/wamo
This obelisk, the tallest masonry structure in the world, at 555 feet, was dedicated in 1885 to the memory of the first U.S. president. Before its dedication, it had been under construction for almost 40 years, as a lack of funds and the Civil War interrupted its progress. You can see where construction resumed after a 28-year delay about a quarter of the way up the monument, where two different shades of marble meet. Views of the majestic structure can be enjoyed anytime, but to enter, you must have a ticket. You can try your luck at getting one of the free tickets distributed at the kiosk at 15th and Madison starting at 8 a.m. for same-day tours, or you can reserve tickets by calling 800-967-2283. There is an elevator to the observation room at the 500-foot level. To take the 898 steps up or down, arrangements must be made in advance. Daily 9 a.m.-5 p.m.

Washington Mystics (WNBA)
Verizon Center, 601 F St. N.W.,
Washington, DC,
202-661-5050;
www.wnba.com/mystics
Professional women's basketball team.

Washington National Cathedral
3000 Wisconsin Ave. N.W.,
Washington, DC,
202-537-6207;
www.cathedral.org/cathedral
This inspiring edifice, 83 years in the making, was completed in 1990, its $65 million cost covered by private donations. It was built largely of Indiana limestone using

traditional methods, with flying buttresses rather than steel providing support. Graced with intricate carvings inside and out, it has a 30-story central tower and 215 stained-glass windows, including one that contains a piece of lunar rock presented by the astronauts of Apollo XI. Bring binoculars if you want to see close up the more than 100 gargoyles, which depict not just dragons but also a child with his hand in a cookie jar and "Star Wars" villain Darth Vader. Worshippers of all faiths are welcome at services held daily. There are also frequent musical events, including recitals given on the magnificent pipe organ most Sundays at 5 p.m. Famous Americans interred at the cathedral include Woodrow Wilson and Helen Keller. Monday-Friday 10 a.m.-5:30 p.m., Saturday 10 a.m.-4:30 p.m., Sunday 8 a.m.-6:30 p.m.

Washington Walks
Washington, DC,
202-484-1565;
www.washingtonwalks.com
Guided tours sponsored by Washington Walks are a great way to see the city up close. The group (along with Children's Concierge) runs two tours that kids will especially enjoy: for Goodnight Mr. Lincoln, children can show up in pajamas at the Lincoln Memorial for stories, games and music about Honest Abe. The White House Un-Tour offers role-playing (you might be asked to impersonate the president who loved bowling) and fun facts about the executive mansion. April-October, days vary; rest of year by appointment.

Washington Wizards (NBA)
Verizon Center,
601 F St. N.W., Washington, DC,
202-661-5050;
www.nba.com/wizards
Professional men's basketball team.

The White House
1600 Pennsylvania Ave. N.W.,
Washington, DC,
202-456-7041;
www.whitehouse.gov

Constructed in 1800 under George Washington's supervision, the house has hosted every U.S. president since John Adams. The British burned it during the War of 1812, and it was reconstructed under the guidance of James Monroe (1817-1825). The West Wing, which includes the Oval Office, was built during Theodore Roosevelt's administration (1901-1909); before its construction, executive offices shared the second floor with the president's private quarters. The interior of the White House was gutted and rebuilt, using modern construction techniques, during the Truman administration. The Library and the Vermeil Room (on the Ground Floor); the East, Green, Blue and Red Rooms, and the State Dining Room (on the State Floor) are accessible to groups of 10 for tours. In this era of heightened security, you'll find Secret Service agents in every room, doubling as tour guides. Obtain tickets through your congressperson or senator. Tuesday-Saturday 7:30 a.m.-12:30 p.m.; closed for presidential functions.

World War II Memorial
National Mall, 17th St.,
Washington, DC,
202-426-6841;
www.nps.gov/nwwm
The World War II Memorial honors America's Greatest Generation, the men and women who emerged from the Depression to serve in a hard-fought war that took the lives of 50 million people worldwide. Situated on the National Mall between the Lincoln Memorial and the Washington Monument, this memorial opened to visitors in the spring of 2004. Twin Atlantic and Pacific pavilions are divided by an oval-shaped pool, symbolizing a war fought across two oceans. Fifty-six wreath-adorned stone pillars—each representing a U.S. state or territory—form semicircles on the memorial's north and south sides. To the west, the Reflecting Pool cascades over twin waterfalls that bookend the Freedom Wall, which glitters with 4,000 gold stars (one-tenth the number of Americans who lost their lives in the war). National park

★
★
★
★
★

rangers staff an information station south of the memorial, answering questions and providing brochures.

Yellow House
1430 33rd St. N.W.,
Washington, DC
(1733) One of Georgetown's oldest homes (a private residence), typical of the area's mansions.

SPECIAL EVENTS

Cherry Blossom Festival
Tidal Basin and Ohio Drive N.W.,
Washington, DC,
202-789-7000;
www.nationalcherryblossomfestival.org
About 150 trees remain from the original 1912 gift of 3,000 from the city of Tokyo, but thousands of others have been planted in parks along the Tidal Basin, and for two weeks each year their lush pink and white blooms transform the cityscape. The festival celebrates this annual event with activities that appeal to visitors of all ages: the Smithsonian's Kite Festival on the National Mall, the rousing parade or Sakura Matsuri, a day-long Japanese street festival. Visitors can enjoy drummers, traditional dancers and musical performances; demonstrations of flower arranging, calligraphy and martial arts; a Taste of Japan food fair; and the bustling Ginza Arcade, with shops selling everything from origami paper to antique kimonos. Late March-early April.

Concerts
Independence and 15th St. N.W.,
Washington, DC,
202-619-7222
Sylvan Theater, Washington Monument grounds, June-August, days vary, 202-619-7222. U.S. Capitol, west terrace, June-late August, Monday-Wednesday, Friday, Sunday, 202-619-7222. National Gallery of Art, west garden court, October-June, Sunday evenings; first-come basis, 202-842-6941. Phillips Collection, at Dupont-Kalorama Museum, September-May, Sunday, 202-387-2151.

Easter Egg Roll
White House Lawn, 1600 Pennsylvania
Ave. N.W., Washington, DC,
202-456-2200;
www.whitehouse.gov/easter
First introduced to Washington by Dolly Madison. Monday after Easter.

Evening Parade
Eighth and I streets S.E., Washington, DC,
202-433-6060;
www.mbw.usmc.mil/parade_
eveningdefault.asp
Spectacular parade with Marine Band, U.S. Marine Drum and Bugle Corps, Color Guard, Silent Drill Team and marching companies. Submitting a written request for reservations at least three weeks in advance is recommended. Friday evenings, early May-late August.

Festival of American Folklife
National Mall, Constitution Ave.,
Washington, DC, 20004,
202-357-2700;
www.folklife.si.edu/center/festival.html
Festival of folklife traditions from America and abroad. Sponsored by the Smithsonian Institution and National Park Service. Late June-early July.

Fort Dupont Summer Theatre
Fort Dupont Park, Minnesota Ave. and
Randle Circle, Washington, DC
Musicals, concerts, plays and dancing. Early July-late August: Saturday evenings.

Georgetown House Tour
3240 O St. N.W., Washington, DC,
202-338-2287;
www.georgetownhousetour.com
Held since 1927, participants view 8-10 houses in Georgetown. St. John's Episcopal Church members serve as hosts and guides, and serve tea in the Parish Hall in the afternoon. Late April.

July 4th Fireworks on the Mall
National Mall, Washington, DC,
202-426-6841;
www.nps.gov/nama/events/july4/july4.htm

Fireworks over the monuments on the National Mall. One of the best viewing spots is the Capitol, where the National Symphony Orchestra gives a rousing concert before the fireworks begin. Arrive early (the crowds get quite large) and picnic while you wait. July 4.

Musical programs

Carter Barron Amphitheater, Rock Creek Park, 16th & Colorado avenues N.W., Washington, DC, 20015, 202-426-0486; www.nps.gov/rocr/planyourvisit/cbarron.htm Mid-June-August.

Pageant of Peace

Ellipse, south of White House, 15th and E streets N.W., Washington, DC, 202-619-7222 Seasonal music, caroling; the president lights a giant Christmas tree near the White House. December.

HOTELS

★★★The Fairmont Washington, DC

2401 M St. N.W., Washington, DC, 202-429-2400, 800-257-7544; www.fairmont.com Located in the West End, this hotel is an ideal base for corporate travelers or vacationers. The well-appointed rooms and suites are comfortable and spacious, and guests on the Gold Floor level are treated to additional perks, such as private check-in and dedicated concierge service. Hotel guests and local denizens celebrate the weekend at the Colonnade's special brunch, while the Juniper is an informal spot for contemporary American fare. 415 rooms. $$$

★★★★★Four Seasons Hotel, Washington, DC

2800 Pennsylvania Ave. N.W., Washington, DC, 202-342-0444, 800-332-3442; www.fourseasons.com

This Four Seasons, located in Washington's historic Georgetown neighborhood, delivers a refined, residential experience that extends from your first step in the modern, sophisticated lobby to lights out in one of the luxuriously appointed guest rooms. Yoga classes, a lap pool and cutting-edge equipment are found in the well-equipped fitness center, while the seven spa treatment rooms are a quiet spot for indulging in signature services, like the cherry blossom Champagne body wrap. The hotel's restaurant, Seasons, offers a menu with a focus on fresh, regional ingredients, while the Garden Terrace lounge is the capital's top spot for afternoon tea. 211 rooms. Pets accepted, some restrictions. High-speed wireless Internet access. Restaurant, bar. Fitness room, fitness classes available, spa. Indoor pool, whirlpool. Airport transportation available. $$$$

★★★Grand Hyatt Washington

1000 H St. N.W., Washington, DC, 202-582-1234, 800-633-7313; www.grandwashington.hyatt.com The Grand Hyatt Washington, D.C., is situated in Penn Quarter, a newly revitalized shopping and dining district, and is close to attractions such as the Verizon Center, the Spy Museum, Ford's Theater and the U.S. Capitol. 888 rooms. $$$$

★★★Georgetown Inn

1310 Wisconsin Ave. N.W., Washington, DC, 202-333-8900, 800-368-5922; www.georgetowncollection.com This hotel, located in the heart of historic Georgetown, puts travelers close to the eclectic and charming shops and restaurants for which this neighborhood is known. Rooms come equipped with marble bathrooms, fluffy terry-cloth robes and complimentary turn-down service. The inn's restaurant, the Daily Grill, serves classic American fare. 96 rooms. $$

★
★
★
★
★

★★The Hamilton Crowne Plaza

14th and K streets N.W.,
Washington, DC,
202-682-0111, 800-263-9802;
www.hamiltonhoteldc.com
318 rooms. **$$**

★★★The Hay-Adams

1800 16th St. N.W.,
Washington, DC,
202-638-6600, 800-424-5054;
www.hayadams.com
Set on Lafayette Square across from the White House, this hotel has welcomed notables since the 1920s. The guest rooms are a happy marriage of historic preservation and 21st-century conveniences—intricately carved plaster ceilings and ornamental fireplaces reside alongside high-speed Internet access and CD players. Windows frame views of the White House, St. John's Church, and Lafayette Square. All-day dining is available at Lafayette, while the Off the Record bar is a popular watering hole for politicians and hotel guests.
145 rooms. **$$$$**

★★★Hilton Washington Embassy Row

2015 Massachusetts Ave. N.W.,
Washington, DC,
202-265-1600, 800-445-8661;
www.hilton.com
This elegant hotel is in the heart of D.C.'s international business community and is conveniently located a half a block from the Metro transit system. In the evening, you can relax with drinks and hors d'oeuvres in the lobby lounge or take in the fabulous view of D.C. from the seasonal rooftop pool. As its name suggests, the International Marketplace restaurant features cuisine from around the world.
193 rooms. Children's activity center. **$$**

★★Holiday Inn Georgetown

2101 Wisconsin Ave. N.W.,
Washington, DC,
202-338-2120, 800-465-4329;
www.higeorgetown.com
296 rooms. **$**

★★Holiday Inn On The Hill

415 New Jersey Ave. N.W.,
Washington, DC,
202-638-1616, 800-282-0244;
www.holidayinn.com
343 rooms. **$**

★★★The Hotel George

15 E St. N.W.,
Washington, DC,
202-347-4200, 800-576-8331;
www.hotelgeorge.com
Travelers book this boutique hotel for its dynamic interiors and central Capitol Hill location. The rooms offer bold artwork, monochromatic tones, clean lines and high-tech amenities. The hotel's restaurant, Bistro Bis, is often considered one of the top tables in town and its French bistro fare is a favorite of politicos and celebrities. Those traveling with pets will appreciate the hotel's "Pet Amenity Program," which includes water and food dish, dog mat and special treats. Lonely guests who left their pet at home can take part in the "Guppy Love" program, where the hotel lends a goldfish for guests to keep in their room throughout their stay.
142 rooms. **$$$**

★★Hotel Washington

515 15th St. N.W., Washington, DC,
202-638-5900, 800-424-9540;
www.hotelwashington.com
374 rooms. **$$$**

★★★The Jefferson

1200 16th St. N.W.,
Washington, DC,
202-347-2200;
www.thejeffersonwashingtondc.com
Built in 1923 just four blocks from the White House, this Beaux Arts hotel is a stylish and centrally located retreat, with antique-filled public rooms and a museum-quality collection of artwork and original documents signed by Thomas Jefferson. A fitness center is available, as are privileges at the University Club, with its Olympic-size pool.

★
★
★
★
★

The restaurant feels like old Washington with faux tortoiseshell walls and leather chairs, yet it serves New American cuisine. 100 rooms. **$$**

★★★J. W. Marriott Hotel On Pennsylvania Avenue
1331 Pennsylvania Ave. N.W.,
Washington, DC,
202-393-2000;
www.marriotthotels.com/wasjw
Just two blocks from the White House, the J.W. Marriott Hotel offers well-appointed guest rooms with flat-screen TVs and unique black-and-white art.
738 rooms. **$$$**

★Jury's Normandy Inn
2118 Wyoming Ave. N.W.,
Washington, DC,
202-483-1350;
www.jurys.com/usa/normandy.htm
75 rooms. **$**

★★★Latham Hotel
3000 M St. N.W., Washington, DC,
202-339-6318, 888-587-2377;
www.georgetowncollection.com
This European-style boutique hotel is located in the heart of Georgetown, where shopping and dining options abound. But when your stomach growls, you might not want to leave the Latham. Michele Richard, a high-profile local chef with an international reputation, owns and operates the on-site Michele Richard Citronelle, where diners savor award-winning French and American cuisine. Well-appointed guest rooms offer marble showers and high-speed Internet access. In summer, cool off in the rooftop swimming pool.
146 rooms. Airport transportation available. **$$**

★★★L'Enfant Plaza Hotel
480 L' Enfant Plaza S.W.,
Washington, DC,
202-484-1000, 800-636-5065;
www.lenfantplazahotel.com
The L'Enfant Plaza Hotel offers special packages for kids and pets and in fact caters

to all guests. Its rooms are stocked with feather-top mattresses, and its roof comes equipped with a pool and sunday deck. The hotel is only steps away from the Air and Space museum and Holocaust museum.
370 rooms. **$$**

★★★The Madison
1177 15th St. N.W.,
Washington, DC,
202-862-1600, 800-424-8577;
www.loewshotels.com
This hotel's Georgian architecture and clock tower cupola stand in pleasant contrast with its fitness center and indoor pool. High-speed Internet access.
353 rooms. Airport transportation available. **$$$**

★★★★Mandarin Oriental, Washington DC
1330 Maryland Ave. S.W.,
Washington, DC,
202-554-8588, 888-888-1778;
www.mandarinoriental.com
Overlooking the Tidal Basin with views of the Jefferson Memorial, this Washington outpost of the Asian hotel brand delivers a scenic and central location on the Potomac River. Guest rooms mix an Eastern sensibility with East Coast style (think preppy plaids and toiles alongside clean-lined furniture and fresh-clipped orchids). Contemporary Asian-influenced cuisine pleases palates in the two restaurants, while the Lounge offers a casual alternative with cocktails and small plates like the lobster salad BLT. A more than 10,000 square foot spa, fitness center and indoor pool offer water front views, a full spa menu and on-call personal trainers.
400 rooms. Pets accepted, some restrictions; fee. High-speed wireless Internet access. Two restaurants, two bars. Fitness room, fitness classes available, spa. Indoor pool, whirlpool. Airport transportation available. **$$$$**

★★★Marriott Wardman Park Hotel
2660 Woodley Rd. N.W.,
Washington, DC,
202-328-2000, 888-733-3222;
www.marriotthotels.com/wasdt

★

★

★

★

★

This hotel gracefully combines historic charm, beauty and convenience. Its Wardman Tower, built in 1928, is listed on the National Historic Register. The award-winning gardens have been featured on the "NBC Nightly News" and boast nearly 100,000 seasonal flowers. With an in-house gourmet market, full-service Starbucks and jewelry store, you can easily make this your home away from home.
1,334 rooms. **$$**

★★★Omni Shoreham Hotel
2500 Calvert St. N.W.,
Washington, DC,
202-234-0700, 800-444-6664;
www.omnihotels.com
The Omni Shoreham Hotel is an urban resort. Its full-service spa and fitness center are state-of-the-art. If you prefer the outdoors, hike, bike, jog or horseback ride through the scenic trails of nearby Rock Creek Park, or just relax on a hammock on the hotel's beautiful grounds. The hotel's Woodley Park location puts you close to attractions and restaurants, and the eclectic Adams-Morgan neighborhood is only minutes away.
832 rooms. **$$$**

★★One Washington Circle Hotel
1 Washington Circle N.W.,
Washington, DC,
202-872-1680, 800-424-9671;
www.onewashcirclehotel.com
151 rooms. **$$**

★★★Renaissance Mayflower Hotel
1127 Connecticut Ave. N.W.,
Washington, DC,
202-347-3000;
www.renaissancehotels.com
Built in 1925 for Calvin Coolidge's inauguration, this hotel has played host to the likes of Franklin Delano Roosevelt and J. Edgar Hoover. The block-long lobby features gilded trim, crystal chandeliers and Oriental rugs, but the guest rooms are quite homey. For groups, the Mayflower offers state-of-the-art meeting facilities.
657 rooms. **$**

★★★★The Ritz-Carlton, Georgetown
3100 South St. N.W.,
Washington, DC,
202-912-4100, 800-241-3333;
www.ritzcarlton.com
Embassy delegations often stay at the Ritz-Carlton, Georgetown, with its contemporary décor and historic setting. Many of the hotel's guest rooms offer views of the Potomac River, along with feather duvets, goose-down pillows and marble baths. Sip one of the fire-red martinis in the Degrees Bar and Lounge, and then dine on American/Italian cuisine in Fahrenheit.
86 rooms. Airport transportation available. **$$$$**

★★★★The Ritz-Carlton, Washington
1150 22nd St. N.W.,
Washington, DC,
202-835-0500, 800-241-3333;
www.ritzcarlton.com
The Ritz-Carlton offers noteworthy attention to detail along with innovative amenities. On-call technology butlers assist with computer woes, while the Luggage-less Travel program allows frequent visitors to leave items behind for their next stay. Guests staying in the Club Level rooms are treated to five food and beverage presentations each day. And all guests are granted access to the Sports Club/LA fitness complex next door.
300 rooms. Airport transportation available. **$$$$**

★★River Inn
924 25th St. N.W.,
Washington, DC,
202-337-7600, 888-874-0100;
www.theriverinn.com
126 rooms, all suites. **$$**

★★★Sofitel Lafayette Square Washington DC
806 15th St. N.W.,
Washington, DC,
202-730-8800;
www.sofitelwashingtondc.com
Just a short walk from the White House, the National Mall and the Metro, this historic

hotel is located in a downtown business area. Its décor is 1930s Art Deco with a contemporary edge. With gold leaf crown molding, marble and velvet furniture, the Sofitel Lafayette Square has earned a spot on the National Register of Historic Places. Pets receive a welcome bag, silver bowls and a small version of Sofitel's guest bed with goose down bedding.
237 rooms. $$$

★★Topaz Hotel
1733 North St. N.W.,
Washington, DC,
202-393-3000, 800-775-1202;
www.topazhotel.com
99 rooms. Complimentary continental breakfast. $$

★★★Washington DC, City Center Hotel
1400 M St. N.W., Washington, DC,
202-429-1700;
www.starwoodhotels.com/westin
Conveniently located near both Georgetown and Dupont Circle, this hotel offers comfortable rooms that feature Herman Miller Aeron ergonomic desk chairs and flat-screen TVs. Enjoy a meal at the hotel's restaurant, 1400 North, overlooking the main lobby.
352 rooms. $$

★★★The Westin Embassy Row
2100 Massachusetts Ave. N.W.,
Washington, DC,
202-293-2100, 800-434-9990;
www.westin.com
Since 1927, this Embassy Row property has welcomed guests with turn-of-the-century style. All rooms and suites are decorated with Federal and Empire furnishings, including rich fabrics and antique reproductions, and boast beautiful views of Washington National Cathedral and historic Georgetown. Join the distinguished political and social crowd at the Jockey Club for innovative American cuisine.
206 rooms. $$$

★★★The Westin Grand
2350 M St. N.W.,
Washington, DC,
202-429-0100, 888-627-8406;
www.westin.com
Not as glitzy as many of the other top D.C. hotels, the Westin offers attentive service and a more low-key environment. The stylish rooms offer ultra-comfortable beds, sizable bathrooms, leather furniture and CD players. Westin Doggie Beds offer the same plush sleep experience to our four-legged friends. The hotel's location is within walking distance of Georgetown and many waterfront restaurants along the Potomac.
263 rooms. Airport transportation available. $$$

★★★Willard InterContinental Washington
1401 Pennsylvania Ave. N.W.,
Washington, DC,
202-628-9100, 877-424-4225;
www.washington.interconti.com
Only two blocks from the White House, this legendary Beaux Arts hotel has been at the center of Washington's political scene since 1850. In the Willard's lobby, Lincoln held fireside staff meetings, Grant escaped the rigors of the White House to enjoy brandy and cigars, and the term "lobbyist" was coined. The guest rooms and suites are a traditional blend of Edwardian and Victorian styles furnished in deep jewel tones. The Jenny Lind suite is perfect for honeymooners with its mansard roof and canopy bed, while the Oval suite, inspired by the Oval Office, makes guests feel like masters of the universe.
334 rooms. bar. Airport transportation available. $$$$

★Windsor Park Hotel
2116 Kalorama Rd. N.W.,
Washington, DC,
202-483-7700, 800-247-3064;
www.windsorparkhotel.com
43 rooms. Complimentary continental breakfast. $

★
★
★
★
★

The St. Regis Washington, D.C.
923 16th St. N.W.,
Washington, DC,
202-638-2626, 888-627-8087;
www.starwoodhotels.com/stregis/
index.html
Since 1926, the St. Regis Hotel has hosted presidents and dignitaries in the heart of Washington. Closed for renovations until 2008; the hotel return refreshed with its gilded lobby and well-appointed guest rooms. English-style butlers and formal afternoon tea add to the luxurious experience.
193 rooms. **$$$$**

SPECIALTY LODGINGS
The Dupont at The Circle
1604-06 19th St. N.W.,
Washington, DC,
202-332-5251, 888-412-0100;
www.dupontatthecircle.com
Built in 1885, this property consists of two connected Victorian townhouses located on a residential street in DuPont Circle. Authentic Victorian dècor is mixed with eclectic art, and many rooms come with working fireplaces and whirlpool tubs.
9 rooms. Children over 13 years only. Complimentary continental breakfast. Airport transportation available. **$$**

SPAS
★★★**The I Spa at the Willard**
Intercontinental Washington
1401 Pennsylvania Ave. N.W.,
Washington, DC,
202-628-9100;
www.ispawillard.com
The 5,000-square-foot spa in the Willard InterContinental offers innovative treatments in a warm, clean-lined space. The spa menu lists 11 massage therapies—including 60- and 90-minute Swedish, deep-tissue, sports, hot stone and shiatsu massages—and an assortment of skin-renewing facials and aromatherapy baths. In the spa's signature treatment, the Body Champagne by Algotherm, the guest is wrapped in seaweed and champagne grape yeast, doused with champagne and given a marine body scrub. **$$**

★★★★**The Spa at the Mandarin Oriental,**
Washington, D.C.
1330 Maryland Ave. S.W.,
Washington, DC,
202-787-6100
The staff at the Spa promotes the time ritual concept, a customized two- or three-hour experience during which clients receive a one-on-one consultation with a therapist to determine which treatments are best suited to the clients' needs. Clients can also book specific treatments such as facials, massages and body therapies, each enhanced with Eastern philosophies and techniques. In the Spa's signature Cherry Blossom Scrub, the staff uses cherry tea leaves, sugar and nourishing oils to strengthen the immune system and remove dead skin cells. **$$**

RESTAURANTS
★★★**1789 Restaurant**
1226 36th St. N.W., Washington, DC,
202-965-1789;
www.1789restaurant.com
Located in a restored Federal mansion just on the edge of Georgetown University's campus, this restaurant is a top destination for students with visiting relatives or diners celebrating a special occasion. The restaurant features Victorian decor with fine china, Civil War pictures and artifacts, antiques and a gas fireplace. The menu changes seasonally, but the popular rack of lamb is always available. A chef's tasting menu is offered, as well as a pre/post-theater menu.
American menu. Dinner. Bar. Children's menu. Jacket required. Reservations recommended. Valet parking. **$$$**

★★★**701 Restaurant**
701 Pennsylvania Ave. N.W.,
Washington, DC,
202-393-0701;
www.701restaurant.com
Overlooking the Navy Memorial fountains and just steps from the Washington National Mall, this fine-dining restaurant features a diverse menu and a caviar bar. The roomy tables, comfortable chairs and live piano music provide a nice atmosphere. And the lounge, which features a sunken bar, is the

perfect place to meet friends for a drink. The Navy Band performs on Tuesday evenings, so try to grab a table on the exterior patio for a great view.

American menu. Lunch, dinner. Bar. Business casual attire. Reservations recommended. Valet parking. Outdoor seating. $$$

★★Aditi
3299 M St. N.W.,
Washington, DC,
202-625-6825
Indian menu. Lunch, dinner. Bar. $

★Afterwords
1517 Connecticut Ave. N.W.,
Washington, DC,
202-387-1462
American menu. Breakfast, lunch, dinner, Saturday-Sunday brunch. Bar. Outdoor seating. In two-story greenhouse and terrace behind Kramer Books bookshop. $

★★Anna Maria's
1737 Connecticut Ave. N.W.,
Washington, DC,
202-667-1444
Italian menu. Lunch, dinner, late-night. Bar. Casual attire. $$

★Austin Grill
750 E St. N.W.,
Washington, DC,
202-393-3776;
www.austingrill.com
Southwestern menu. Lunch, dinner, Sunday brunch. Bar. $$

★★Bacchus
1827 Jefferson Place N.W.,
Washington, DC,
202-785-0734
Middle Eastern menu. Lunch, dinner. Closed Sunday. Casual attire. $$

★Billy Martin's Tavern
1264 Wisconsin Ave. N.W.,
Washington, DC,
202-333-7370;
www.billymartinstavern.com

American menu. Breakfast, lunch, dinner, late-night, Saturday-Sunday brunch. Bar. Casual attire. Established 1933. $$

★★★Bistro Bis
15 E St. N.W., Washington, DC,
202-661-2700;
www.bistrobis.com
This popular French restaurant is located in the contemporary Hotel George on Capitol Hill. Its sleek, modern interior features a zinc bar, cherry wood accents, an open kitchen, leather banquettes, pendant lamps and high ceilings. The menu offers extensive wine pairings.
French menu. Breakfast, lunch, dinner, brunch. Bar. Business casual attire. Reservations recommended. Outdoor seating. $$$

★★Bistro Francais
3128 M St. N.W., Washington, DC,
202-338-3830
French menu. Lunch, Saturday-Sunday brunch. $$

★★Bistrot Lepic & Wine Bar
1736 Wisconsin Ave. N.W.,
Washington, DC,
202-333-0111;
www.bistrotlepic.com
French menu. Lunch, dinner. Bar. Casual attire. Reservations recommended. $$

★★★Bombay Club
815 Connecticut Ave. N.W.,
Washington, DC,
202-659-3727
One of the most respected Indian restaurants in the area, the Bombay Club has an extensive menu that is divided into sections including house, vegetarian, Goan, Moghlai and Northwest Frontier specialties.
Indian menu. Lunch, dinner, Sunday brunch. Bar. Outdoor seating. $$

★★Bombay Palace
2020 K St. N.W.,
Washington, DC,
202-331-4200;
www.bombay-palace.com
Indian menu. Lunch, dinner. Bar. $$

★The Bread Line
1751 Pennsylvania Ave. N.W.,
Washington, DC,
202-822-8900
Breakfast, lunch. Closed Saturday-Sunday.
Outdoor seating. **$**

★Burma
740 Sixth St. N.W.,
Washington, DC,
202-638-1280
Pacific-Rim/Pan-Asian menu. Lunch, dinner. **$**

★★Busara
2340 Wisconsin Ave. N.W.,
Washington, DC,
202-337-2340;
www.busara.com
Thai menu. Lunch, dinner. Bar. Casual attire.
Outdoor seating. **$$**

★C. F. Folks
1225 19th St. N.W.,
Washington, DC,
202-293-0162;
www.cffolksrestaurant.com
American menu. Lunch. Closed Saturday-
Sunday. Outdoor seating. **$**

★★★Cafe 15
806 15th St. N.W., Washington, DC,
202-730-8700;
www.sofitelwashingtondc.com
Cafe 15, the Sofitel's fine-dining room,
serves Michelin-starred French chef Antoine
Westermann's lauded cuisine. Though the
menus change seasonally, entrees include
sauteed frog legs with ravioli, duck foie
gras terrine, roast squab salad and beef filet
tips in a red pepper sauce. With only 50
seats in an art-filled room, Cafe 15 keeps
the experience intimate and elegant.
American, French menu. Breakfast, lunch,
dinner. Bar. Business casual attire. Reserva-
tions recommended. Valet parking. Outdoor
seating. **$$$**

★★★Cafe Atlantico
405 Eighth St. N.W., Washington, DC,
202-393-0812;
www.cafeatlantico.com

One of celebrity chef Jose Andres' restaurants, Cafè Atlantico is known for having
one of the best cocktail lists in D.C. The
caiprinhas and mojitos are delicious, as are
the agua frescas. The menu offers a mix of
everything, from strip loin with a plantain
puree to a daily fish served Veracruz-style
and guacamole made tableside. For brunch,
the restaurant offers Latino Dim Sum.
Latin American menu. Lunch, dinner. Bar.
Casual attire. Reservations recommended.
Valet parking. Outdoor seating. **$$$**

★★Cafe Milano
3251 Prospect St. N.W.,
Washington, DC,
202-333-6183;
www.cafemilano.net
Italian menu. Lunch, dinner, late-night. Bar.
Casual attire. Reservations recommended.
Outdoor seating. **$$$**

★Cafe Mozart
1331 H St. N.W., Washington, DC,
202-347-5732;
www.cafemozartgermandeli.com
Continental, German menu. Breakfast, lunch,
dinner. Bar. Children's menu. German deli
on premises. **$$**

★★★The Capital Grille
601 Pennsylvania Ave. N.W.,
Washington, DC,
202-737-6200;
www.thecapitalgrille.com
Dark, polished wood accents and dark
leather chairs and booths may be remi-
niscent of a "boys' club" steakhouse, but
everyone flocks for the fresh seafood and
signature dry-aged steaks. The restaurant
offers an impressive wine list with more
than 400 labels.
Steak menu. Lunch, dinner. Bar. Business
casual attire. Reservations recommended.
Valet parking. **$$$**

★★Cashion's Eat Place
1819 Columbia Rd. N.W.,
Washington, DC,
202-797-1819;
www.cashionseatplace.com

International menu. Dinner, Sunday brunch. Closed Monday; hours vary. Bar. Casual attire. Reservations recommended. Valet parking. Outdoor seating. **$$$**

★★★★CityZen
1330 Maryland Ave. S.W., Washington, DC, 202-787-6006; www.mandarinoriental.com
Under Chef Eric Ziebold, CityZen serves modern American-French cuisine. Ziebold offers a new three-course prix-fixe menu monthly including appetizers such as purèe of Savoy cabbage soup with a lobster custard, globe artichoke ravioli, sashimi of Japanese hamachi and broiled Boston mackerel. Desserts include crispy brioche bread pudding, a CityZen peanut butter cup or a chocolate mint julep. Ziebold also offers a multi-course tasting menu, available as a vegetarian option. The restaurant and the lounge, designed by the acclaimed Tony Chi, feel intimate despite the large space and vaulted ceilings.
American, French menu. Dinner. Closed Sunday-Monday. Bar. Business casual attire. Reservations recommended. Valet parking. **$$$$**

★★Clyde's of Georgetown
3236 M St. N.W., Washington, DC, 202-333-9180; www.clydes.com
American. Lunch, dinner, Saturday-Sunday brunch. Bar. Children's menu. Atrium dining. **$$**

★★★DC Coast
1401 K St. N.W., Washington, DC, 202-216-5988; www.dccoast.com
Seafood menu. Lunch, dinner. Closed Sunday. Bar. Casual attire. **$$$**

★★District Chophouse & Brewery
509 Seventh St. N.W., Washington, DC, 202-347-3434; www.districtchophouse.com
American menu. Lunch, dinner, late-night. Bar. Children's menu. Casual attire. **$$$**

★Felix Restaurant & Spy Lounge
2406 18th St. N.W., Washington, DC, 202-483-3549
Mediterranean menu. Dinner. Bar. Casual attire. **$$**

★★★Galileo
1110 21st St. N.W., Washington, DC, 202-293-7191; www.robertodonna.com/restaurants/
This is the flagship enterprise of Roberto Donna, the celebrity chef behind Il Radicchio, I Matti and many others. In keeping with the cutting-edge trends, there's a much-sought-after kitchen table. The European country decor features terra-cotta floors, small alcoves in the dining room and a mural of Galileo.
Italian menu. Lunch, dinner. Bar. Reservations recommended. Valet parking. Outdoor seating. **$$$**

★★★Georgia Brown's
950 15th St. N.W., Washington, DC, 202-393-4499; www.gbrowns.com
At this popular McPherson Square spot, diners have trouble choosing from among the many creative, modern dishes, such as fried green tomatoes stuffed with herbed cream cheese and served on a bed of green tomato relish with lemon-cayenne mayonnaise and watercress. The dining room features blonde wood and a bronzed ceiling scroll.
American menu. Lunch, dinner, Sunday brunch. Bar. Casual attire. Reservations recommended. **$$**

★★★Gerard's Place
915 15th St. N.W., Washington, DC, 202-737-4445; www.gerardsplacedc.net
Gerard's Place is an intimate hideaway near the White House with high-back chairs, sheaths draped overhead, vibrant colors and a large glass chandelier with amber-colored tones. Two menus are offered nightly: a five-course chef's tasting menu as well as a three-course prix fixe menu. Expect classic

★
★
★
★
★

French dishes with refined twists, such as sautèed scallops with garlic flan and parsley mousse, braised short ribs with potato galette, and coconut dacquoise with roasted pineapple and lime sorbet.
French menu. Lunch, dinner. Closed Sunday. Business casual attire. Outdoor seating. **$$$**

★★★The Grill at Ritz-Carlton, Washington, DC
1150 22nd St. N.W.,
Washington, DC,
202-974-5556;
www.ritzcarlton.com
The Grill, located in the Ritz-Carlton, Washington, D.C., reinforces the Washingtonian charm with dark wood paneling accented by brass fixtures and a large, inviting fireplace. Chef de Cuisine Quang Duong, honed his skills throughout the Mid-Atlantic area, applying artistic touches to fresh, regional ingredients. Signature dishes include lobster bisque, pan-seared foie gras with brioche French toast and lady apples, and the crème brulee trio.
American menu. Breakfast, lunch, dinner, Sunday brunch. Bar. Children's menu. Business casual attire. Reservations recommended. Valet parking. **$$$**

★★Grill from Ipanema
1858 Columbia Rd. N.W.,
Washington, DC,
202-986-0757;
www.thegrillfromipanema.com
Brazilian menu. Lunch, dinner. Bar. Casual attire. Outdoor seating. **$$**

★Guapo's
4515 Wisconsin Ave. N.W.,
Washington, DC,
202-686-3588;
www.guaposrestaurant.com
Latin American, Mexican menu. Lunch, dinner. Bar. Outdoor seating. **$$**

★Guards
2915 M St. N.W., Washington, DC,
202-965-2350
Seafood, Steak menu. Lunch, dinner, Sunday brunch. Bar. **$$**

★Haad Thai
1100 New York Ave. N.W.,
Washington, DC,
202-682-1111
Thai menu. Lunch, dinner. Bar.

★J. Paul's
3218 M St. N.W., Washington, DC,
202-333-3450;
www.j-pauls.com
American menu. Lunch, dinner, Saturday-Sunday brunch. Bar. Children's menu. **$$**

★★Jaleo
480 Seventh St. N.W., Washington, DC,
202-628-7949;
www.jaleo.com
Spanish menu. Lunch, dinner. Bar. Casual attire. Valet parking. Outdoor seating. **$$**

★★★The Jefferson
1200 16th St. N.W., Washington, DC,
202-833-6206
Located inside the Jefferson hotel, this 60-seat restaurant has served politicians, celebrities and dignitaries for years. Nineteenth century historical prints and portraits from the White House and Blair House are displayed throughout the restaurant.
American menu. Breakfast, lunch, dinner, Sunday brunch. Bar. Children's menu. Casual attire. Valet parking. **$$$**

★★★Kinkead's
2000 Pennsylvania Ave. N.W.,
Washington, DC,
202-296-7700;
www.kinkead.com
Senators, journalists, models, financiers and media moguls rub elbows at chef/owner Bob Kinkead's spot for distinctive global fare. The deep, cherry wood-paneled dining room has an intimate, clubby feel to it, with warm, low lighting, vintage wrought-iron staircases and elegant table settings. The menu, which changes daily and draws influences from Spain, France, Italy, Morocco and Asia, offers a terrific selection of appetizers, soups, salads, chops and seafood. To complement the menu, the user-friendly wine list is color-coded from

light to dark according to nose, weight, body and flavor. Kinkead's hosts live jazz in the evenings.

Seafood menu. Lunch, dinner. Bar. Business casual attire. Reservations recommended. Valet parking. Outdoor seating. **$$$**

★Krupin's
4620 Wisconsin Ave. N.W.,
Washington, DC,
202-686-1989

American menu. Breakfast, lunch, dinner. Children's menu. Casual attire. **$$**

★★La Chaumiere
2813 M St. N.W.,
Washington, DC,
202-338-1784

French menu. Lunch, dinner. Closed Sunday. **$$**

★★Lauriol Plaza
1835 18th St. N.W.,
Washington, DC,
202-387-0035

Latin American, Mexican menu. Lunch, dinner, Sunday brunch. Bar. Casual attire. Outdoor seating. **$$**

★★Lavandou
3321 Connecticut Ave. N.W.,
Washington, DC,
202-966-3002

French menu. Lunch, dinner. Closed August. Bar. Casual attire. **$$**

★Les Halles
1201 Pennsylvania Ave. N.W.,
Washington, DC,
202-347-6848;
www.leshalles.net

American, French menu. Lunch, dinner, Saturday-Sunday brunch. Bar. Children's menu. Outdoor seating. Three-level dining area. **$$$**

★★Luigino
1100 New York Ave. N.W.,
Washington, DC,
202-371-0595;
www.luigino.com

Italian menu. Lunch, dinner. Closed Labor Day. Bar. Casual attire. Reservations recommended. Outdoor seating. **$$**

★Market Inn
200 E St. S.W., Washington, DC,
202-554-2100;
www.marketinndc.com

American menu. Lunch, dinner, Sunday brunch. Bar. Children's menu. Outdoor seating. English pub ambience. **$$**

★★★Mendocino Grill and Wine Bar
2917 M St. N.W., Washington, DC,
202-333-2912;
www.mendocinodc.com

The most impressive feature of this restaurant is of course its excellent, all-American wine list. The food is designed to complement the wine. Wood and slate dominate the dècor, accented with wall mirrors.

American menu. Lunch, dinner. Bar. Business casual attire. Reservations recommended. **$$$**

★★★★Michel Richard Citronelle
3000 M St. N.W., Washington, DC,
202-625-2150;
www.citronelledc.com

Like Chef Michel Richard's food, the restaurant is stylish and elegant. Filled with fresh flowers and lit with a creamy, golden glow, the room has a chic vibe and a glass-enclosed open kitchen for a bird's-eye view of the cooks. Ingredients are the stars here; the chef manages to wow diners by highlighting the simple flavors of each dish's main component. Nabbing a seat at one of his coveted tables is like winning the lottery.

French menu. Dinner. Bar. Business casual attire. Reservations recommended. Valet parking. Outdoor seating. **$$$$**

★★Monocle
107 D St. N.E., Washington, DC,
202-546-4488

American menu. Lunch, dinner. Closed Saturday-Sunday. Bar. Children's menu. Valet parking. Close to the Capitol; frequented by members of Congress and other politicians. **$$**

WASHINGTON, D.C.

★★Morrison-Clark
1015 L St. N.W.,
Washington, DC, 20001
202-898-1200;
www.morrisonclark.com
American menu. Dinner. Closed Monday. Bar. Outdoor seating. **$$$**

★Mr. Smith's
3104 M St. N.W., Washington, DC,
202-333-3104;
www.mrsmiths.com
American menu. Lunch, dinner, Saturday-Sunday brunch. Bar. Outdoor seating. **$$**

★Murphy's of DC
2609 24th St. N.W., Washington, DC,
202-462-7171
American, Irish menu. Lunch, dinner. Children's menu. Outdoor seating. **$$**

★Nathan's
3150 M St. N.W., Washington, DC,
202-338-2000;
www.nathanslunch.com
American menu. Lunch, dinner, brunch. Bar. Casual attire. **$$**

★★New Heights
2317 Calvert St. N.W.,
Washington, DC,
202-234-4110;
www.butterfield9.com
American menu. Dinner. Closed Sunday. Bar. Business casual attire. Reservations recommended. Outdoor seating. **$$$**

★★★Obelisk
2029 P St. N.W., Washington, DC,
202-872-1180
This intimate restaurant in DuPont Circle serves simple and authentic Italian food made from scratch. Homemade breads, pastas, butter and desserts are offered along with artisan cheeses in an unpretentious—and somewhat romantic—setting.
Italian menu. Dinner. Closed Sunday-Monday. Bar. Business casual attire. Reservations recommended. **$$$**

★★Occidental Grill
1475 Pennsylvania Ave. N.W.,
Washington, DC,
202-783-1475;
www.occidentaldc.com
American menu. Lunch, dinner. Bar. **$$$**

★★Old Ebbitt Grill
675 15th St. N.W., Washington, DC,
202-347-4800;
www.ebbitt.com
American menu. Breakfast, lunch, dinner, late-night, Saturday-Sunday brunch. Bar. Children's menu. Casual attire. **$$**

★★Old Europe
2434 Wisconsin Ave. N.W.,
Washington, DC,
202-333-7600;
www.old-europe.com
German menu. Lunch, dinner. Closed Monday. Bar. Children's menu. Casual attire. **$$**

★★Oval Room
800 Connecticut Ave. N.W.,
Washington, DC,
202-463-8700;
www.ovalroom.com
American, Mediterranean menu. Lunch, dinner. Closed Sunday. Bar. Outdoor seating. **$$$**

★★★★Palena
3529 Connecticut Ave. N.W.,
Washington, DC,
202-537-9250;
www.palenarestaurnat.com
Executive Chef Frank Ruta and Pastry Chef Ann Amernick met while working in the White House kitchen in the 1980s and decided to open a restaurant together in 2000. They now offer a seasonal menu of French- and Italian-influenced fare—such as sea scallops with chestnut puree or gnocchi with roasted endive, turnips, black truffle and shaved pecorino—complemented by comforting desserts including a chocolate-toffee torte and a lime tartlet.

American menu. Dinner. Closed Sunday. Bar. Business casual attire. Reservations recommended. **$$$**

★★The Palm
1225 19th St. N.W.,
Washington, DC,
202-293-9091;
www.thepalm.com
Steak menu. Lunch, dinner. Bar. Casual attire. Valet parking. **$$$**

★★Paolo's
1303 Wisconsin Ave. N.W.,
Washington, DC,
202-333-7353;
www.capitalrestaurants.com
Italian menu. Lunch, dinner, late-night, Saturday-Sunday brunch. Bar. Children's menu. Casual attire. Outdoor seating. Wood-burning pizza oven. **$$**

★★Pesce
2016 P St. N.W.,
Washington, DC,
202-466-3474;
www.pescebistro.com
Seafood menu. Lunch, dinner. Casual attire. Valet parking. **$$**

★Pizzeria Paradiso
2029 P St. N.W.,
Washington, DC,
202-223-1245;
www.eatyourpizza.com
Pizza, sandwich menu. Lunch, dinner. Casual attire. **$$**

★★★Prime Rib
2020 K St. N.W.,
Washington, DC,
202-466-8811;
www.theprimerib.com
This K Street business spot features the decor of a 1930s New York supper club. It remains one of the best steakhouses inside the Beltway.
Steak menu. Lunch, dinner. Closed Sunday. Bar. Jacket required. Reservations recommended. Valet parking. **$$$**

★Raku-An
1900 Q St. N.W.,
Washington, DC,
202-265-7258
Pan-Asian menu. Lunch, dinner. Bar. Casual attire. Outdoor seating. **$$**

★★★Restaurant Nora
2132 Florida Ave. N.W.,
Washington, DC,
202-462-5143;
www.noras.com
In this 19th-century grocery store turned organic American eatery, seasonal ingredients are the stars. Chef/owner Nora Pouillon is a pioneer in the organic movement; Restaurant Nora was the first certified organic restaurant in the country (95 percent of the products used are organic). Pouillon integrates flavors from the American South to Spain and from Latin America to Asia and India, and the menu changes daily. The rustic dining room is decorated with dried flowers and museum-quality antique Mennonite and Amish quilts.
American, Mediterranean menu. Dinner. Closed Sunday; also late August-early September. Bar. Business casual attire. Reservations recommended. Valet parking. **$$$**

★★★Sam and Harry's
1200 19th St. N.W.,
Washington, DC,
202-296-4333;
www.samandharrys.com
This upscale steak house in downtown D.C. is decorated with jazz-themed artwork, green leather booths and dark wood accents. Along with prime aged center New York strip steak, center cut filet mignon and rack of lamb, a number of fresh seafood options are available, from whole Maine lobster to jumbo lump crab cakes. A full bar features a wide selection of liquors and spirits, and the extensive wine list features 25 selections available by the glass.
Steak menu. Lunch, dinner. Closed Sunday. Bar. Casual attire. Reservations recommended. Valet parking. **$$$**

★★Sea Catch

1054 31st St. N.W., Washington, DC,
202-337-8855;
www.seacatchrestaurant.com
Seafood menu. Lunch, dinner. Closed Sunday. Bar. Valet parking. Outdoor seating on a deck overlooking the historic Chesapeake and Ohio Canal. **$$$**

★★★Seasons

2800 Pennsylvania Ave. N.W.,
Washington, DC,
202-944-2026;
www.fourseasons.com
With deep upholstered armchairs, dark wood and fresh flowers, Seasons is the flagship restaurant of the Four Seasons Hotel. The sophisticated American-French menu offers simple, elegant fare and an extensive wine list. For an afternoon delight, stop by the Garden Terrace for tea service with all the trimmings—scones with clotted cream, cucumber and watercress sandwiches with the crusts cut off, petit fours, chocolate-dipped strawberries and assorted butter cookies. The Sunday brunch should not be missed.
American, French menu. Breakfast, lunch, dinner, Sunday brunch. Bar. Children's menu. Business casual attire. Reservations recommended. Valet parking. Outdoor seating. **$$$**

★★Sequoia

3000 K St. N.W., Washington, DC,
202-944-4200;
www.arkrestaurants.com
American menu. Lunch, dinner, Saturday-Sunday brunch. Bar. Casual attire. Outdoor seating. **$$**

★Sesto Senso

1214 18th St., Washington, DC,
202-785-9525;
www.sesto.com
Italian menu. Lunch, dinner. Closed Sunday. Bar. Casual attire. **$$**

★Sushi-Ko

2309 Wisconsin Ave. N.W.,
Washington, DC,
202-333-4187;
www.sushiko.us
Japanese menu. Lunch, dinner. Casual attire. **$$$**

★★★Taberna del Alabardero

1776 I St. N.W.,
Washington, DC,
202-429-2200;
www.alabardero.com
For 16 years, Taberna del Alabardero has served classic Spanish cuisine such as chorizo paella with chicken or gazpacho andaluz to D.C. diners. Executive Chef Santi Zabaleta also uses locally grown produce to enhance seasonal menu selections.
Spanish. Lunch, dinner. Closed Sunday. Bar. Casual attire. Outdoor seating. **$$$**

★★★Teatro Goldoni

1909 K St. N.W., Washington, DC,
202-955-9494;
www.teatrogoldoni.com
Named after a famous Venetian playwright from the 1800s, this downtown restaurant is decorated like a Venetian theater during the carnival, with a wall of masks, velvet curtains, blown-glass pendant lights and harlequin and striped patterns. Innovative but simple Venetian dishes are served, and a pianist performs on weekends. The restaurant also serves a pre-fixe theater menu and offers wine dinners and cooking classes.
Italian menu. Lunch, dinner. Closed Sunday. Bar. Business casual attire. Reservations recommended. Valet parking. **$$$**

★Thai Kingdom

2021 K St. N.W., Washington, DC,
202-835-1700;
www.thaikingdom.org
Thai menu. Lunch, dinner. Bar. **$$**

444

WASHINGTON, D.C.

★The Tombs
1226 36th St. N.W., Washington, DC,
202-337-6668;
www.clydes.com
American menu. Lunch, dinner, Sunday
brunch. Bar. **$$**

★Tony and Joe's Seafood Place
3000 K St. N.W., Washington, DC,
202-944-4545;
www.tonyandjoes.com
Seafood menu. Lunch, dinner, late-night,
Sunday brunch. Bar. Casual attire. Outdoor
seating. **$$$**

★★Two Quail
320 Massachusetts Ave. N.E.,
Washington, DC,
202-543-8030, 800-543-8030;
www.twoquail.com
American, French menu. Lunch, dinner.
Casual attire. Reservations recommended.
Outdoor seating. **$$**

★★★Vidalia
1990 M St. N.W., Washington, DC,
202-659-1990;
www.vidaliadc.com
Taking his lead from the South and the
Chesapeake Bay area, Chef/owner Jeffrey
Buben serves up inventive appetizers such
as warm crayfish and sweet corn ragout
with crispy plantain, piquillo pepper purèe,

catfish boudin blanc and rich crayfish con-
sommè. Entrèes include wild gulf shrimp
and creamy anson mill grits with kale, sweet
onion ragout and tasso ham ravigote.
American menu. Lunch, dinner. Bar. Chil-
dren's menu. Casual attire. **$$$**

★★★Willard Room
1401 Pennsylvania Ave. N.W.,
Washington, DC,
202-637-7440;
www.washington.intercontinental.com
Located in the Willard InterContinental
Washington hotel, this Victorian-style
dining room serves a seasonal, eclectic
American-French menu, which includes
innovative takes on fish, shellfish, game,
lamb, beef and poultry. The also restaurant
offers desserts such as the tableside bananas
Foster and cherries jubilee, an extensive
wine list and a classic cocktail list.
American, French menu. Breakfast, lunch,
dinner. Closed Columbus Day. Bar. Business casual attire. Reservations recom-
mended. Valet parking. **$$$**

★Zed's Ethiopian Cuisine
1201 28th St. N.W., Washington, DC,
202-333-4710;
www.zeds.net
Middle Eastern menu. Lunch, dinner.
Communal dining from trays. Silverware
provided at customer's request. **$$**

WEST VIRGINIA

JOHN DENVER SAID IT BEST: WEST VIRGINIA IS ALMOST HEAVEN. FOR NATURE LOVERS AND outdoor sports enthusiasts, the Mountain State is a natural paradise of rugged mountains and lush, lyric-inspiring countryside.

With the highest total altitude of any state east of the Mississippi River, West Virginia's ski industry has opened several Alpine and Nordic ski areas. Outfitters offer excellent whitewater rafting on the state's many turbulent rivers. Rock climbing, caving and hiking are popular in the Monongahela National Forest. And West Virginia's state parks and areas for hunting and fishing are plentiful.

West Virginia is also a land of proud traditions, with many festivals held throughout the year as tributes to the state's rich heritage. These events include celebrations honoring the state's sternwheel riverboat legacy, its spectacular autumn foliage, and even its strawberries, apples and black walnuts.

Archaeological evidence indicates that some of the area's very first settlers were the Mound Builders, a prehistoric Ohio Valley culture that left behind at least 300 conical earth mounds. Many have been worn away by erosion, but excavations in some have revealed elaborately adorned human skeletons and artifacts of amazing beauty and utility.

Centuries later, pioneers who ventured into western Virginia in the 18th century (West Virginia did not break away from Virginia until the Civil War) found fine vistas and forests, curative springs and beautiful rivers. George Washington and his family frequented the soothing mineral waters of Berkeley Springs, and White Sulphur Springs later became a popular resort among the colonists. But much of this area was still considered "the wild West" in those days, and life here was not easy.

The Commonwealth of Virginia largely ignored its western citizens—only one governor was elected from the western counties before 1860. When the western counties formed their own state during the Civil War, it was the result of many years of strained relations with the parent state. The war finally provided the opportunity the counties needed to break away. Although many sentiments in the new state remained pro-South, West Virginia's interests were best served by staying with the Union.

The war left West Virginia a new state, but like other war-ravaged areas, it had suffered heavy losses of life and property, and the recovery took many years. West Virginians eventually rebuilt their state. New industry was developed, railroads were built, and resources like coal, oil and natural gas brought relative prosperity.

★ SPOTLIGHT

★ West Virginia was the first state to have sales tax. It became effective July 1, 1921.

West Virginia continues to be an important source of bituminous coal and a major producer of building stone, timber, glass and chemicals. The state is also home to technological wonders such as the National Radio Astronomy Observatory, where scientists study the universe via radio telescopes, and the New River Gorge Bridge, the world's longest steel span bridge.

Information: www.state.wv.us

ANSTED

WHAT TO SEE AND DO

Contentment Museum Complex
WV. Route 60, Ansted,
304-658-5212, 800-255-5982
(Circa 1830) Former residence of Confederate Colonel George W. Imboden contains original woodwork, period furniture, toy collection. Adjacent Fayette County Historical Society Museum features displays of Native American relics, local artifacts, Civil War items; restored one-room schoolhouse. June-August: Monday-Saturday; rest of year, by appointment.

Hawk's Nest State Park
177 W. Main St., P.O. Box 857, Ansted,
304-658-5212, 800-225-5982;
www.hawksnestsp.com

Approximately 280 acres on Gauley Mountain with fine views of New River Gorge from rocks 585 feet above the river. A 600-foot aerial tramway carries passengers to canyon floor. Swimming pool, fishing; hiking trails, tennis, picnic area, playground, concession, restaurant, lodge. Log museum with early West Virginia artifacts. May-November: daily.

HOTELS

★★Hawks Nest State Park Lodge
Rte. 60, Ansted,
304-658-5212, 800-225-5982;
www.hawksnestsp.com
31 rooms. Children's activity center. $

AURORA

Located at the summit of Cheat Mountain, Aurora offers visitors clean air and high altitude.

WHAT TO SEE AND DO

Cathedral State Park
Rte. 50, Aurora,
304-735-3771, 800-225-5982;
www.cathedralstatepark.com

Hiking trails through 132 acres of deep, virgin hemlock forest; cross-country skiing, picnicking.

BECKLEY

The "smokeless coal capital of the world" is a center for more than 200 small mining and farming towns. Beckley is situated on a high plateau surrounded by fertile valleys. During the Civil War, the village was held at various times by both armies; Union troops shelled it in 1863. Coal was found here in 1774 but was not mined until 1890. Smokeless coal became the standard bunker fuel during World War I, and the demand continued for years thereafter. Beckley now serves as a commercial, medical and tourist center.

Information: Southern West Virginia Convention & Visitors Bureau,
1406 Harper Rd., Beckley, 304-252-2244, 800-847-4898; www.visitwv.org

WHAT TO SEE AND DO

Babcock State Park
HC 35, Box 150, Clifftop,
304-438-3003, 800-225-5982;
www.babcocksp.com
More than 4,100 acres of rugged mountain scenery with trout stream and waterfalls, views of New River Canyon, rhododendrons (May-July); restored operating gristmill. Swimming pool, lake and stream fishing, boating (rowboat, paddleboat rentals); hiking trails, horseback riding, game courts (equipment rentals), cross-country skiing, camping, 26 cabins (rentals, spring and fall). Nature and recreation programs (summer). Mid-April-October.

Beckley Exhibition Coal Mine
513 Ewart Ave., Beckley,
304-256-1747;
www.beckleymine.com
Riding tours in coal cars through 1,500 feet of underground passageways, constant 56 F temperature; museum, coal company house, superintendent of coal mines' house, church, campground. April-October: daily.

Lake Stephens
350 Lake Stephens Rd., Beckley,
304-934-5323;
www.lakestephenswv.com
A 303-acre lake with swimming, fishing and boating, plus trailer camping.

Plum Orchard Lake Wildlife Management Area
Rt. 1 Box 186, Scarbro,
304-469-9905;
www.plumorchardlakewma.com
More than 3,200 acres with rabbit, grouse, squirrel hunting. Also a 202-acre lake with more than six miles of shoreline; boating, fishing for bass, channel catfish, crappie and bluegill; picnicking, playground, camping.

Whitewater Rafting
New River Park, Beckley,
304-252-2244, 800-847-4898
Many outfitters offer guided trips on the New and Gauley rivers.

Youth Museum of Southern West Virginia
106 Adair St., Beckley, 25801,
304-252-3730, 800-718-1474
Hands-on exhibits, planetarium, log house. May-Labor Day: daily; rest of year, Tuesday-Saturday.

SPECIAL EVENTS

Appalachian Festival
245 N. Kanewha St., Beckley,
304-252-7328, 800-718-1474
Exhibitions and demonstrations of native crafts; entertainment, food. August.

HOTELS

★Hampton Inn
110 Harper Park Dr., Beckley,
304-252-2121;
www.hamptoninn.com
108 rooms. Complimentary continental breakfast. Swim. $

RESTAURANTS

★★Macado
3815 Robert C. Byrd Drive, Beckley,
304-256-3882;
www.macados.com
American menu, Italian menu. Lunch, dinner, late-night. Bar. Children's menu. Casual attire. $$

BERKELEY SPRINGS

Popularized by George Washington, who surveyed the area for Lord Fairfax in 1748, Berkeley Springs is the oldest spa in the nation. Fairfax later granted the land around the springs to Virginia. The town is officially named Bath, for the famous watering place in England, but the post office is Berkeley Springs. The waters, which are piped throughout the town, are fresh and slightly sweet, without the medicinal flavor of most mineral springs. Washington and his family returned again and again.

The resort's popularity peaked after the Revolutionary War, becoming something of a summer capital for Washingtonians in the 1830s. But like all resort towns, Berkeley Springs declined as newer, more fashionable spas came into vogue. The Civil War completely destroyed the town's economy. Today, the town is again visited for its healthful waters, spas and charming downtown.

Information: Berkeley Springs-Morgan County Chamber of Commerce, 127 Fairfax St., Berkeley Springs, 304-258-3738, 800-447-8797; www.berkeleyspringschamber.com

GEORGE WASHINGTON'S SPA AND BERKELEY SPRINGS

Tucked in a narrow, rock-shadowed valley along the Cacapon River, the little mountain community of Berkeley Springs has transformed itself into "Spa Town USA." A total of five separate spas employ more than 40 massage therapists—three times the number of practicing lawyers, town officials claim.

The town's clustering of so many spas is relatively new, but Berkeley Springs has a long heritage as a spa destination. Well before white settlers arrived, Native Americans sought out the warm, 74.3 degree mineral springs. Still bubbling forth from the base of Warm Springs Ridge at 2,000 gallons per minute, the water was believed to have curative powers. George Washington, who first visited the springs in 1748 as a 16-year-old surveyor, returned nearly a dozen times in later years seeking health benefits. In 1776, he and prominent friends and family established the Town of Bath, intent on making it a popular spa, and the first bathhouses were built. Thus, Berkeley Springs claims to be "the country's first spa."

You can explore the town's spa heritage in a 30-minute, half-mile stroll in Berkeley Springs State Park, which doubles as the community's town square. One of America's most curious public parklands, the seven-acre Berkeley Springs State Park operates year-round as a very affordable, government-run spa. Begin a loop around the park at the large public swimming pool, fed by spring waters. Heading clockwise, take a peek inside the Main Bath House, where you can enjoy a private hot-tub soak and Swedish-style massage. Continue on to a stone-lined natural pool of flowing spring water, dubbed "George Washington's Bath Tub" in his honor. Move on to the Gentlemen's Spring House, where you are welcome to draw jugs of the famed drinking water for free. Conclude this plunge into historic bathing with a look into the Roman Bath House, where you can indulge in a private hot-tub soak without an accompanying massage.

★
★
★
★
★
★

WHAT TO SEE AND DO

Berkeley Springs State Park
121 S. Washington St., Berkeley Springs, 304-258-2711

Famous resort with health baths of all types (fees); five warm springs. Main bathhouse (daily). Roman bathhouse with second-floor museum (Memorial Day-mid-October: daily). Swimming pool (Memorial Day-Labor Day: daily; fee).

Cacapon Resort State Park
2 S. Washington St., Berkeley Springs, 304-258-2711, 800-225-5328; www.berkeleyspringssp.com

More than 6,100 acres with swimming, sand beach, fishing, boating (rowboat and paddleboat rentals); hiking and bridle trails, horseback riding, 18-hole golf course, tennis, game courts, cross-country skiing, picnicking, playground, concession, restaurant, lodge. No camping; 30 cabins. Nature, recreation programs. Nature center.

Sleepy Creek Wildlife Management Area
1910 Sleepy Creek Road,
Berkeley Springs,
304-754-3855
Approximately 23,000 acres of rugged forest offer wild turkey, deer, grouse and squirrel hunting; boating and bass fishing on 205-acre lake; primitive camping. Skiing. Also 70 miles of hiking trails crossing two mountains, several valleys.

View from Prospect Peak
Berkeley Springs
Potomac River winds through what the National Geographic Society has called one of the nation's outstanding vistas.

SPECIAL EVENTS
Apple Butter Festival
304 Fairfax St.,
Berkeley Springs,
800-447-8797
www.berkeleysprings.com/apple
Crafts demonstrations, music, contests. Columbus Day weekend.

HOTELS
★★Cacapon Resort State Park
818 Cacapon Dr., Berkeley Springs,
304-258-1022, 800-225-5982;
www.cacaponresort.com
52 rooms. Children's activity center. Beach. $

★★Coolfont Resort
3621 Cold Run Valley Rd.,
Berkeley Springs,
304-258-4500, 800-888-8768;
www.coolfont.com
19 rooms. Complimentary full breakfast. Children's activity center. $$

★★The Country Inn At Berkeley Springs
110 S. Washington St.,
Berkeley Springs,
304-258-2210, 866-458-2210;
www.theinnandspa.com
68 rooms. Complimentary continental breakfast. Spa. Airport transportation available. $

SPECIALTY LODGINGS
Highlawn Inn
171 Market St.,
Berkeley Springs,
304-258-5700, 888-290-4163;
www.highlawninn.com
This Victorian-style manor, built in the late 1890s, has authentic furnishings and ornate fireplaces. The mineral bath waters of the area are an added feature.
12 rooms. Children over 14 years only. Complimentary full breakfast. $

BETHANY

WHAT TO SEE AND DO
Bethany College
1 Main St., Bethany,
304-829-7000;
www.bethanywv.edu
(1840) (800 students.) Founded by Alexander Campbell, the leading influence in the 19th-century religious movement that gave rise to the Disciples of Christ, Churches of Christ and Christian churches. Historic buildings on the 300-acre campus include Old Main, styled after the University of Glasgow in Scotland; Pendleton Heights, a 19th-century house used as the college president's residence;

Old Bethany Meeting House (1852); and Delta Tau Delta Founder's House (1854).
   Also here is:

Campbell Mansion
Bethany,
304-829-4258
A 24-room house where Campbell lived; antique furnishings. On property are hexagonal brick study, one-room schoolhouse and smokehouse. The Campbell family cemetery, "God's Acre," is across from the mansion. April-October: Tuesday-Sunday; rest of year, by appointment.

BLUEFIELD

Named for the bluish chicory covering the nearby hills, Bluefield owes its existence to the Pocahontas Coal Field. The town came to life in the 1880s when the railroad came through to transport coal.

This commercial and industrial center of southern West Virginia is known as nature's "air-conditioned city" because of its altitude—one-half mile above sea level. Bluefield has a sister city by the same name in Virginia, directly across the state line.

Information: Convention & Visitors Bureau, 500 Bland St., Bluefield, 304-325-8438, 800-221-3206; www.mccvb.com

WHAT TO SEE AND DO

Eastern Regional Coal Archives
Craft Memorial Library, 600 Commerce St., Bluefield, 304-325-3943
Center highlights the history of West Virginia coal fields; exhibits, photographs, mining implements; films, research material. Monday-Friday afternoons.

Panther State Forest
Bluefield,
304-938-2252;
www.pantherstateforest.com
More than 7,800 acres of rugged hills. Swimming pool (Memorial Day-Labor Day), fishing; hunting, hiking trails, picnicking, playground, concession, camping.

Pinnacle Rock State Park
P.O. Box 1, Bluefield,
304-248-8565;
www.pinnaclerockstatepark.com
Approximately 250-acre park contains a 15-acre lake and interesting sandstone formations, which resemble a giant cockscomb. Hiking, picnicking.

HOTELS

★★Holiday Inn
3350 Big Laurel Hwy.,
Bluefield,
304-325-6170, 800-465-4329;
www.holidayinn.com/bluefieldwv
120 rooms. $

BUCKHANNON

Information: Buckhannon-Upshur Chamber of Commerce, 16 S. Kanawha St., Buckhannon, 304-472-1722; www.buchamber.com

WHAT TO SEE AND DO

Audra State Park
Rte. 4 Box 564,
Buckhannon,
304-457-1162, 800-225-5982;
www.audrastatepark.com
Approximately 360 acres offer swimming in a natural mountain stream surrounded by tall timber; bathhouse. Hiking trails, picnicking, playground, concession, tent and trailer camping.

West Virginia Wesleyan College
59 College Ave.,
Buckhannon,
304-473-8000;
www.wvwc.edu

(1890) (1,600 students.) An 80-acre campus featuring Georgian architecture. Wesley Chapel, the largest place of worship in the state, contains a Casavant organ with 1,474 pipes.

SPECIAL EVENTS

West Virginia Strawberry Festival
Buckhannon,
304-472-9036;
www.wvstrawberryfestival.com
Parades, dances, exhibits, air show, arts and crafts, other activities. Usually the week before Memorial Day.

★
★
★
★
★

HOTELS

★Bicentennial Motel
90 E. Main St.,
Buckhannon,
304-472-5000, 800-762-5137
45 rooms. $

★Hampton Inn Buckhannon
1 Commerce Blvd., Buckhannon,
304-473-0900
62 rooms. Complimentary continental breakfast. $

CHARLES TOWN

Charles Town is serene, aristocratic and full of tradition, with orderly, tree-shaded streets
and 18th-century houses. It was named for George Washington's youngest brother,
Charles, who laid out the town and named most of the streets after members of his family.
Charles Washington's family lived here for many years. Charles Town is also known as the
place where John Brown was jailed, tried and hanged in 1859 after his antislavery raid on
Harpers Ferry.
Information: Jefferson County Chamber of Commerce, 201 Frontage Road,
Charles Town, 304-725-2055, 800-624-0577;
www.jeffersoncounty.com

WHAT TO SEE AND DO

Charles Town Races and Gaming
Flowing Springs Rd., Rte. 340 N.,
Charles Town,
304-725-7001, 800-795-7001;
www.ctownraces.com
Thoroughbred racing; clubhouse, video
machines, dining room. Daily.

Jefferson County Courthouse
100 E. Washington, Charles Town,
304-728-3240
(1836) This red brick, Georgian colonial
structure was the scene of John Brown's
trial, one of three treason trials held in the
U.S. before World War II. The courthouse
was shelled during the Civil War but was
later rebuilt; the original courtroom survived both the shelling and fires and is open
to the public. In 1922, leaders of the miners' armed march on Logan City were tried
here; one, Walter Allen, was convicted and
sentenced to 10 years. Monday-Friday.

Jefferson County Museum
200 E. Washington, Charles Town,
304-725-8628;
www.jeffctywvmuseum.org
Houses John Brown memorabilia, old
guns, Civil War artifacts. April-November:
Monday-Saturday.

Site of John Brown Gallows
S. Samuel and Hunter streets,
Charles Town
Marked by a pyramid of three stones sup-
posedly taken from Brown's cell in Charles
Town jail. At the execution, 1,500 troops
were massed around the scaffold. Some
were commanded by Thomas "Stonewall"
Jackson; among them was John Wilkes
Booth, Virginia militiaman.

Tours of Charles Town
Charles Town, 304-728-7713
Historical walking tours; candlelit tours of
Jefferson County Courthouse (evenings);
carriage rides. All tours by appointment.

Zion Episcopal Church
300 E. Congress St., Charles Town,
304-725-5312; www.zionepiscopal.net
(1852) Buried in the cemetery around
the church are about 75 members of the
Washington family, as well as many Revolutionary War and Confederate soldiers.
Interior, by appointment.

SPECIAL EVENTS

Founders Day-Washington Heritage
Charles Town, 800-733-5469
Exhibits, performances, tours. First week-
end in May.

Fairgrounds, Charles Town,
304-728-7415
Livestock show, entertainment, amusement rides, exhibits. Late August.

CHARLESTON

Charleston, the state capital, is the trading hub for the Great Kanawha Valley, where deposits of coal, oil, natural gas and brine have greatly contributed to this region's national importance as a production center for chemicals and glass. Two institutions of higher learning, West Virginia State College and the University of Charleston, are located in the metropolitan area. Charleston is also the northern terminus of the spectacular West Virginia Turnpike.

Daniel Boone lived around Charleston until 1795. In 1789, during his residence in Charleston, he was appointed a lieutenant colonel in the county militia and was elected to the Virginia assembly. The area became important as a center of salt production in 1824, when steam engines were used to operate brine pumps. After Charleston became the capital of West Virginia in 1885 following a dispute with Wheeling, the town came into its own. During World War I, an increased demand for plate and bottle glass, as well as for high explosives, made Charleston and the nearby town of Nitro boom.

Information: Convention & Visitors Bureau, Charleston Civic Center, 200 Civic Center Drive, Charleston, 304-344-5075, 800-733-5469; www.charlestonwv.com

WHAT TO SEE AND DO

Coonskin Park
2000 Coonskin Dr., Charleston,
304-341-8000
Recreation area includes swimming, fishing for bass and catfish, pedal boating; hiking trails, 18-hole golf, miniature golf, tennis. Picnicking, playground, concession. (daily; some activities seasonal) Fees for activities.

Cultural Center
1900 E. Kanawha Blvd., Charleston,
304-558-0220

The Center houses the Division of Culture and History and Library Commission; archives library (Monday-Saturday); state museum; special events, changing exhibits. Daily.

Also here is:

Mountain Stage
1900 Kanawha Blvd. E.,
Charleston,
304-342-5757
Live public radio show heard on stations nationwide; features jazz, folk, blues and

HOTELS
★★Turf Motel
741 E. Washington St., Charles Town,
304-725-2081, 800-422-8873;
www.turfmotel.com
45 rooms. $

453

WEST VIRGINIA

CANYON COUNTRY-AROUND NEW RIVER GORGE

The New River has cut a deep and narrow gorge for more than 50 miles through the rugged mountains of southeastern West Virginia. Rafting enthusiasts consider this to be one of the best whitewater rivers in the nation. It's also very pretty to look at while standing on dry ground—albeit on a cliff's edge high above.

This two-day, 300-mile scenic drive out of Charleston, which circles the gorge, provides plenty of scenic viewing opportunities. At the same time, the tour offers a look at the state's coal-mining heritage. At the turn of the century King Coal ruled the gorge, and at one time two dozen coal-mining towns prospered on the banks of the New River. Now, much of the gorge is protected as the New River Gorge National River.

From Charleston, head east on Highway 60, following the old Midland Trail up the Kanawha River. In the first few miles, the highway winds past industrial plants. The mountain scenery begins after about 30 miles at Gauley Bridge, where the New River flows into the Kanawha. Here, as the New River begins to display whitewater turbulence, the road climbs steeply and you spot the first of many waterfalls. One of finest gorge views is just ahead at Hawk's Nest State Park, which has a 31-room lodge at cliff's edge. A steep hiking trail down to the river provides a chance to stretch your legs.

About 25 minutes on, detour south on Highway 19 to the Canyon rim Visitor Center, which provides information about the park and the region. You also get a good look at the New River Gorge Bridge, one of the highest bridges in the country. Linking the north and south rims of the gorge, it has become famous for its once-a-year parachute jumps in October. Dozens of parachutists leap from its concrete safety barriers and float 876 feet to the river sandbar below. A stairway takes you partway down the cliff for more river and bridge views.

Continue east on Highway 60 to Route 41, where you again detour south (right) to Babcock State Park to see its old stone gristmill and to try its hiking trails. Back on Highway 60, head east to Route 20 south to Hinton, a picturesque riverfront town. A river-level road leads to view of Sandstone Falls on the New River. You can stay in Hinton or continue south on Route 20 to Pipestem Resort State Park, a 4,000-acre preserve with a 113-room lodge and an 18-hole golf course.

From Pipestem, double back on Route 20 to Route 3 west to Highway 19 north to Beckley. Here you can ride a coal car deep into the Beckley Exhibition Coal Mine. From Beckley, take Route 61 north to Glen Jean and then head east on Route 25 to Thurmond, a former riverside mining boomtown. The still-active train tracks run down the main street next to the sidewalk. An Amtrak station doubles as a railroad museum. Return to Route 61 north to I-64/I-77 and back to Charleston. Approximately 300 miles.

WEST VIRGINIA

rock. Visitors may watch show; afternoon performances (Sunday).

Elk River Scenic Drive
Charleston
Beautiful drive along the Elk River from Charleston northeast to Sutton (approximately 60 miles). Begins just north of town; take Highway 119 NE to Clendenin, then Highway 4 NE to Highway 19 in Sutton.

Information Center
Shenandoah and High streets, Charleston, 304-535-6029
Restored Federalist house built in 1859 by U.S. government as residence for the master armorer of the U.S. Armory. During the Civil War, it was used as headquarters by various commanding officers. Also on this street is the site of the U.S. Armory that John Brown attempted to seize; it was destroyed during the Civil War.

Kanawha State Forest
Loudendale Rd., Rte. 2 Box 285, Charleston, 304-558-3500, 800-225-5982; www.kanawhastateforest.com
Approximately 9,300 acres with a swimming pool, bathhouse (Memorial Day-Labor Day); hunting, hiking, interpretive trail for the disabled, horseback riding, cross-country skiing, picnicking, playground, concession and camping.

State Capitol
1900 E. Kanawha Blvd., Charleston, 304-558-4839, 800-225-5982
(1932) One of America's most beautiful state capitols, the building was designed by Cass Gilbert in Italian Renaissance style. Within the gold-leaf dome, which rises 300 feet above the street, hangs a 10,080-piece, hand-cut imported chandelier weighing more than two tons. Guided tours available. Monday-Friday, Saturday afternoons.

Across the grounds is the:

Governor's Mansion
1716 Kanawha Blvd. E., Charleston, 304-558-3809
(1925) Beautiful Georgian structure of red Harvard brick with white Corinthian columns. Tours Thursday and Friday; also by appointment.

Sunrise Museum
746 Myrtle Rd., Charleston, 304-344-8035
On 16 acres of wooded grounds with gardens and trails, this art and science museum is housed in two historic mansions built by William MacCorkle, ninth governor of West Virginia. Guided tours by appointment. Wednesday-Sunday.

Located here are:

Ackland Art Museum
746 Myrtle Rd., Charleston, 304-344-8035, 800-344-8035
American paintings, graphics and sculpture from the 19th and 20th centuries; rotating exhibits; films and lectures.

Science Museum
746 Myrtle Rd., Charleston, 304-344-8035, 800-344-8035
Exhibits in natural sciences and technology; planetarium, programs, lectures. Interactive exhibits, demonstrations.

Whitewater Rafting
90 Mac Corkle Ave. S.W., Charleston, 304-558-2200, 800-225-5982; www.wvriversports.com
Many outfitters offer guided rafting, canoeing and fishing trips on the New and Gauley rivers.

SPECIAL EVENTS
Sternwheel Regatta Festival
P. O. Box 20185, Charleston, 304-348-6419; www.sternwheelregatta.com
Sternwheeler and towboat races, parades, contests, hot-air balloon race, fireworks; nationally known entertainers nightly; arts and crafts. Late August-early September.

Vandalia Gathering
1900 Kanawha Blvd. E., Charleston,
304-558-0220;
www.wvculture.org/vandalia
A festival of traditional arts; craft demonstrations, clogging, gospel music, fiddling, banjo picking, special exhibits. Memorial Day weekend.

HOTELS

★**Comfort Suites Charleston**
107 Alex Lane, Charleston,
304-925-1171, 800-424-6423;
www.choicehotels.com
67 rooms, all suites. Complimentary full breakfast. $

★**Country Inn & Suites-Charleston**
105 Alex Lane, Charleston,
304-925-4300, 800-456-4000;
www.countryinns.com
64 rooms. Complimentary continental breakfast. $

★★**Embassy Suites Hotel Charleston**
300 Court St., Charleston,
304-347-8700, 800-362-2779;
www.embassysuites.com
253 rooms, all suites. Complimentary full breakfast. Airport transportation available. $

★**Fairfield Inn by Marriott Charleston**
1000 Washington St. E., Charleston,
304-343-4661, 800-228-2800;
www.marriott.com
136 rooms. Complimentary continental breakfast. $

★**Hampton Inn**
1 Preferred Place, Charleston,
304-746-4646, 800-426-7866;
www.hamptoninn.com
104 rooms. Complimentary continental breakfast. Airport transportation available. $

★★**Holiday Inn**
600 Kanawha Blvd. E.,
Charleston,
304-344-4092, 888-465-4329;
www.holidayinn.com

256 rooms. Airport transportation available. $

★**Holiday Inn Express**
100 Civic Center Dr., Charleston,
304-345-0600, 800-315-2621;
www.hiexpress.com
196 rooms. Complimentary continental breakfast. Airport transportation available. $

★★★**Marriott Charleston Town Center**
200 Lee St. E., Charleston,
304-345-6500, 800-228-9290;
www.charlestonmarriott.com
This hotel, which is conveniently located just off the I-77 and I-64 interchange, sits adjacent to the Charleston Town Center and Civic Center in the heart of downtown. Many services and amenities are offered here, and there are plenty of recreational activities, restaurants and shops in the immediate area. Guest rooms are attractively decorated in hues of green and terra-cotta.
352 rooms. Airport transportation available. $

RESTAURANTS

★★**Blossom Deli**
904 Quarrier St., Charleston,
304-345-2233;
www.blossomdeli.com
American menu. Breakfast, lunch, dinner. Closed Sunday. $$

★★**Joe Fazio's Spaghetti House**
1008 Bullitt St., Charleston,
304-344-3071
Italian menu. Dinner. Closed Monday. Children's menu. $$

★★★**Laury's**
350 MacCorkle Ave. S.E.,
Charleston,
304-343-0055
Located downtown near the Kanawha River in the old C&O Railroad Depot, this French-American Continental restaurant has welcomed diners since 1979. The dining room is an elegant space with dramatic high ceilings, floor-to-ceiling windows, oil paintings, mirrors in ornate gold frames,

★

★

★

★

★

crystal chandeliers and fresh flowers. If you get the right table, you will be rewarded with an amazing view.

American, French menu. Dinner. Closed Sunday; week of July 4. Bar. Business casual attire. Reservations recommended. Credit cards accepted. $$

CLARKSBURG

In the heart of the West Virginia hills, Clarksburg is the trading center for an area of grading lands, coal mines, and oil and gas fields. The Criminal Justice Information Services Division of the FBI is located here. During the Civil War, Clarksburg was an important supply base for Union troops. Famous Civil War general "Stonewall" Jackson was born in Clarksburg in 1824. His statue stands before the courthouse.

Information: Greater Bridgeport Conference & Visitors Center, 164 W. Main St., Bridgeport, 304-842-7272, 800-368-4324; www.bridgeportwv.com

WHAT TO SEE AND DO

Stealey-Goff-Vance House
123 W. Main St.,
Clarksburg,
304-622-2157
House restored by Harrison County Historical Society as a museum with period rooms, antique furniture, tools and Native American artifacts. May-September: Friday, limited hours.

SPECIAL EVENTS

West Virginia Italian Heritage Festival
340 W. Main St.,
Clarksburg,
304-622-7314;
www.wvihf.com
Italian arts, music, contests, entertainment. Labor Day weekend.

HOTELS

★Sutton Inn
250 Emily Dr.,
Clarksburg,
304-623-2600, 866-726-2322;
www.suttoninn.com
112 rooms. Complimentary continental breakfast. $

RESTAURANTS

★★Minard's Spaghetti Inn
813 E. Pike St.,
Clarksburg,
304-623-1711
Italian menu. Lunch, dinner. Bar. Children's menu. Casual attire. $$

CROSS LANES

WHAT TO SEE AND DO

Tri-State Greyhound Park
1 Greyhound Dr.,
Cross Lanes,
304-776-1000, 800-224-9683;
www.tristateracetrack.com
Indoor grandstand, clubhouse, concessions. Monday-Saturday evenings; matinees Saturday-Sunday. Must be 18 to wager.

HOTELS

★Comfort Inn
102 Racer Dr.,
Cross Lanes,
304-776-8070, 800-798-7886;
www.choicehotels.com
112 rooms. Complimentary continental breakfast. Airport transportation available. $

DAVIS

Davis, the highest town in the state, was founded by Henry Gassaway Davis, U.S. senator from 1871 to 1883. Senator Davis established the first night train in America (1848). He and his son-in-law, Senator Stephen B. Elkins, became wealthy from coal, lumber and railroading.

Information: West Virginia Mountain Highlands, Elkins, 304-636-8400, 800-982-6867; www.mountainhighlands.com

WHAT TO SEE AND DO

Blackwater Falls State Park
County Rte. 29, Davis,
304-259-5216, 800-225-5892;
www.blackwaterfalls.com

This 1,688-acre park includes a deep river gorge with 66-foot falls of dark, amber-colored water. Swimming in lake (fee), bath houses (Memorial Day-Labor Day), fishing, boating (rowboat, paddleboat rentals); nature trails, horseback riding; cross-country ski trails, center (rentals, school); sledding, picnicking, playground, concession, lodge, cabins, tent and trailer campground. Nature, recreation programs and tours. Paved falls viewing area for the disabled.

Canaan Valley Resort State Park
Davis,
304-866-4121, 800-662-4121;
www.canaanresort.com

Approximately 6,000 acres, including a valley 3,200 feet above sea level, which is surrounded by spectacular mountain peaks. Swimming pool, bathhouse, fishing, boating; hiking trails, 18-hole golf course, tennis courts, skiing, ice rink, playground, lodge, cabins, camping. Nature, recreation programs. Standard hours, fees.

Also here is:

Canaan Valley Resort State Park Ski Area
Hwy. 32, Davis,
304-866-4121, 800-622-4121

Quad, two triple chairlifts, Pomalift; patrol, school, SKIwee program, rentals, snowmaking; restaurant, cafeteria, lodging, nursery; night skiing (Friday-Sunday). Twenty-two trails, 34 slopes; vertical drop 850 feet. December-March: daily. Eighteen miles of cross-country trails. Chairlift rides (early May-October: daily). Special programs for the disabled.

Timberline Four Seasons Resort
Hwy. 32, Davis,
304-866-4801, 800-766-9464;
www.timberlineresort.com

Triple, two double chairlifts; patrol, school, SKIwee program, rentals, snowmaking; restaurant, bar, nursery, lodging, night skiing and special events. Thirty-five slopes and trails; longest run two miles, vertical drop 1,000 feet. (December-April: daily). Cross-country skiing. Chairlift rides (July-October: Saturday-Sunday, also Monday).

White Grass Touring Center
Freeland Rd., Davis,
304-866-4114;
www.whitegrass.com

Thirty-six miles of cross-country trails, some machine-groomed; patrol, school, rentals, snowfarming, telemark slopes; restaurant; guided tours. Late November-March: daily.

Whitewater Rafting
200 Sycamore St., Davis,
800-225-5982;
www.wvriversports.com

Many outfitters offer guided trips on the Cheat River.

SPECIAL EVENTS

Tucker County Alpine Winter Festival
William Ave. and Fourth St., Davis,
304-866-4121

Governor's Cup ski races. First weekend in March.

HOTELS

★★Alpine Lodge
Williams Ave.,
Davis,
304-259-5245
46 rooms. $

★
★
★
★
★

★★Blackwater Lodge
County Rte. 29, Davis,
304-259-5216, 800-225-5982
80 rooms. Children's activity center. All state park facilities available. **$**

★★Canaan Valley Resort and Conference Center
Hwy. 32, Davis,
304-866-4121, 800-622-4121;
www.canaanresort.com
256 rooms. Children's activity center. Naturalist program. **$**

DROOP

WHAT TO SEE AND DO
Beartown State Park
Hwy. 219, Droop, 304-653-4254;
www.beartownstatepark.com
Approximately 110 acres of dense forest with unique rock formations created by erosion; a boardwalk with interpretive signs winds through the park.

Droop Mountain Battlefield State Park
Hwy. 219, Droop,
304-653-4254, 800-255-5982;
www.droopmountainbattlefield.com

Encompasses approximately 285 acres on site where on November 6, 1863, Union forces under General William W. Averell defeated Confederates under General John Echols, destroying the last major rebel resistance in the state. Park features graves, breastworks and monuments. Hiking, picnic areas, playground. Museum. Battle reenactments (second week of October, every even year).

ELKINS
Elkins was named for U.S. Senator Stephen B. Elkins, an aggressive politician and powerful industrial magnate who was secretary of war under Benjamin Harrison (1888-1892). This town is in a coal and timber region and is also a railroad terminus and trade center. Some of the finest scenery in the state can be seen in and around Elkins.
Information: Randolph County Convention & Visitors Bureau, 1035 N. Randolph Ave., Elkins, 304-636-2780, 800-422-3304; www.randolphcountywv.com

WHAT TO SEE AND DO
Bowden National Fish Hatchery
Rte. 33 (SR-55), Elkins,
304-637-0245
Produces brook, brown and rainbow trout for stocking in state and national forest streams; also striped bass for Chesapeake Bay restoration project. Hatchery (daily). Visitor center. Memorial Day-mid-October: daily.

SPECIAL EVENTS
Augusta Festival
100 Campus Dr., Elkins,
304-637-1209
Celebration of traditional folk life and arts, featuring local and national performers,

dances, juried craft fair, storytelling sessions, children's activities and homemade foods. Mid-August.

Mountain State Forest Festival
101 Lough St., Elkins,
304-636-1824;
www.forestfestival.com
Queen Silvia is crowned; carnival, parades, entertainment, tilting at rings on horseback, sawing and wood-chopping contests, championship fiddle and banjo contest, juried craft fair and art exhibit. Late September-early October.

WEST VIRGINIA

★
★
★
★
★

SENECA ROCKS

Serious rock climbers rate West Virginia's massive Seneca Rocks as one of the top East Coast destinations for their sport. More than 375 major mapped climbing routes ascend the sheer, slender rocks that thrust 900 feet above the North Fork River. On any nice day, you're apt to see a half-dozen or more climbers laboriously pulling themselves, hand over hand, slowly up the wall. It might take them hours to get to the top. You can enjoy the same view from the summit, but without the effort.

A 1 1/2-mile foot trail—rated only moderately difficult—zig-zags to the top. Heavily traveled and well-marked, it is a non-climber's introduction to West Virginia's panoramic vistas. A notable West Virginia landmark, the dramatic rock formation is worth a visit simply as a scenic attraction. From the edge of the river, which tumbles in a fury of white water, a thickly forested ridge forms an imposing pedestal for the rocks. From this base, the twin towers form a rough, craggy wall with a knife's-edge point barely 15 feet wide.

Begin your ascent near the foot of the rocks at Seneca Rocks Discovery Center, a beautiful structure of stone and glass. Inside, exhibits detail the natural history of the rocks; outside, the deck is positioned for great views of the climbers. The hiker's trail to the top begins just across the river from the Discovery Center. It climbs steadily through shady woods. Sturdy benches are placed along the way if you need to rest. At several especially steep points, stone steps seem to stretch endlessly above, but that's only your imagination. From the summit overlooks, the view of the river-traced valley below is a generous reward for your pains. Give yourself an hour to reach the top, 30 minutes to enjoy your lofty perch, and another 30 minutes for the much easier descent. Afterward, cross the road for refreshments in the village of Seneca Rocks at Harper's Old Country Store, which looks much as it must have on its opening day in 1902.

HOTELS

★★**Elkins Motor Lodge**
Harrison Ave., Elkins,
304-636-1400, 877-636-1863
55 rooms. Airport transportation available. **$**

★**Super 8**
350 Beverly Pike, Rte. 219 S., Elkins,
304-636-6500, 800-800-8000;
www.super8.com
44 rooms. Complimentary continental breakfast. **$**

RESTAURANTS

★★**Cheat River Inn**
Hwy. 33 E., Elkins,
304-636-2301;
www.cheatriverlodge.com
Dinner. Closed Monday. Bar. Children's menu. Outdoor seating. Mounted fish on display. **$$**

SPRUCE KNOB/MONONGAHELA HIGH COUNTRY

In the big cities of the Mid-Atlantic, it's sometimes hard to believe that there is a vast and rugged mountain wilderness just to the west. You can find plenty of this unspoiled nature in West Virginia, where soaring mountain ridges stretch into the distance, interspersed with countless streams.

This one-day, 150-mile loop out of the pretty college town of Elkins takes you through some of the Mid-Atlantic's most scenic mountain terrain. The route crisscrosses 100,000-acre Spruce Knob-Seneca Rocks National Recreation Area in the Monongahela National Forest. From Elkins, take Highway 250 south through the national forest to Thornwood. Mile after mile, the road climbs and dips alongside splashing streams. At Thornwood, head north on Route 28 toward Riverton. Two miles south of Riverton, turn west (left) onto Forest Service Road 112 and follow the signs to Spruce Knob, about 15 miles. At an altitude of 4,861 feet, Spruce Knob is the state's loftiest mountain peak—although peak isn't really an apt description. The summit is a broad plateau scattered with piles of age-smoothed rocks. A thin forest of red spruce, stunted by the strong and near-constant westerly winds, struggles for a foothold. This is one of the most remote and rugged areas of the Mid-Atlantic that can be reached in a passenger sedan. A rock-lined trail leads to the Observation Tower, a three-story stone structure that boosts sightseers above the trees for a majestic 360-degree panorama.

Return to Route 28 and continue north to Seneca Rocks, a slender 900-foot-high forested ridge favored by rock climbers. You can watch them from the Discovery Center or take the easier 1 1/2-mile trail to the summit. Pause for snacks or lunch at Harper's Old Country Store. To continue, head west on Route 55 to Harmon and pick up Route 32 north to Davis. The road passes alongside 6,000-acre Canaan Valley Resort State Park, where you can stop to hike, bicycle or go for a swim in the outdoor pool. A year-round resort, the park operates a downhill skiing complex. In summer, the chairlift will carry you to the top for grand views. About 15 miles long and three miles wide, the valley is situated at an altitude of 3,200 feet, which all but guarantees moderate summer temperatures.

Just to the north, the town of Davis has become a major center for mountain biking, mostly on abandoned U.S. Forest Service roads. Outfitters offer rentals and maps. On the edge of Davis, turn left into Blackwater Falls State Park, a rumpled expanse of woodland ridges and valleys cut by the Blackwater River's impressively deep canyon. Motorists approach the park's 55-room lodge on a long, winding road that carries them deeper and deeper into the forest. Suddenly a clearing appears, revealing the lodge on the edge of the canyon. Visitors can view Blackwater Falls' 65-foot plunge from the canyon rim just upriver from the lodge or descend 214 steps to its base. In summer, the beach at little Pendleton Lake makes a refreshing rest stop. Continue north two miles to Thomas, an old mining town built in a double tier on a mountainside, and then return to Elkins on Highway 219 south. Approximately 150 miles.

WEST VIRGINIA

FAIRMONT

Fairmont was a Union supply depot plundered by Confederate cavalry in April 1863. General William Ezra Jones's division swept through town, took 260 prisoners, destroyed the $500,000 bridge across the Monongahela River, and raided the governor's residence. After the war, resources in the region were developed and coal became the mainstay. Today, Fairmont manufactures aluminum, mine machinery and other products.
Information: Convention & Visitors Bureau of Marion County, 110 Adams St., Fairmont, 304-368-1123, 800-834-7365; www.marioncvb.com

WHAT TO SEE AND DO

Fairmont State College
1201 Locust Ave.,
Fairmont,
304-367-4892, 800-641-5678;
www.fairmontstate.edu
(1867) (7,000 students.) On campus is a one-room schoolhouse with original desks, books and other artifacts related to the early era of education. April-October, schedule varies.

Marion County Museum
200 Jackson St.
Fairmont,
304-367-5398
Displays of B & O china; five furnished rooms covering 1776-1920s; doll, train and toy collection. Monday-Friday 10 a.m.-2 p.m.; also Saturday from Memorial Day-Labor Day.

Prickett's Fort State Park
Rte. 3 Fairmont,
304-363-3030, 800-225-5982;
www.prickettsforststatepark.com
Approximately 200 acres with reconstructed 18th-century log fort, colonial trade and lifestyle demonstrations by costumed interpreters, outdoor historical drama (July: Wednesday-Saturday). Boating (ramps);

picnicking. Visitor center. Fort and museum (mid-April-October: daily). Museum (fee).

SPECIAL EVENTS

Three Rivers Festival
Fairmont, 304-363-2625
Entertainment, parade, Civil War re-enactment, carnival, games. Third weekend in May.

HOTELS

★Comfort Inn
1185 Airport Rd., Fairmont,
304-367-1370, 877-424-6423;
www.choicehotels.com
82 rooms. Complimentary continental breakfast. $

★★Holiday Inn
930 E. Grafton, Fairmont,
304-366-5500, 800-315-2621;
www.holidayinn.com/fairmontwv
106 rooms. $

RESTAURANTS

★★Muriale's
1742 Fairmont Ave., Fairmont,
304-363-3190;
www.murialesrestaurant.com
Italian menu. Lunch, dinner. Bar. Children's menu. Casual attire. Outdoor seating. $$

FRANKLIN
Information: Franklin Chamber of Commerce, Franklin, 304-358-7068; www.visitpendleton.com

SPECIAL EVENTS

Treasure Mountain Festival
Franklin,
304-249-5117
Square dancing, clogging; parade, gospel and mountain music, drama; rifle

demonstration, cross-cut sawing contest; children's contests, games; trail rides craft exhibits, country food. Third weekend in September.

462

WEST VIRGINIA

GAULEY BRIDGE

This town, at the junction of the New and Gauley rivers, was the key to the Kanawha Valley during the Civil War. In November 1861, Union General W.S. Rosecrans defeated Confederate General John B. Floyd, a victory that assured Union control of western Virginia. Stone piers of the old bridge, which was destroyed by retreating Confederates in 1861, can be seen near the present bridge.
Information: Upper Kanawha Valley Chamber of Commerce, Montgomery, 304-442-5756

WHAT TO SEE AND DO
Whitewater Rafting
Gauley Bridge,
800-225-5982
Many outfitters offer guided trips on the New and Gauley rivers.

SPECIAL EVENTS
Bridge Day
Gauley Bridge,
304-465-5617, 800-928-0263;
www.officialbridgeday.com

Bridge is open to pedestrians; parachutists test their skills by jumping off the bridge and floating to the bottom of the gorge. Third Saturday in October.

GLEN JEAN

WHAT TO SEE AND DO
Gauley River National Recreation Area
104 Main St., Glen Jean,
304-465-0508;
www.nps.gov/gari/index.htm
Designated a federally protected area in October 1988, the 25-mile stretch of the Gauley from the Summersville Dam west to just above the town of Swiss is famous for whitewater rafting. There are no developed sites. Large tracts of land along the river are privately owned.

Grandview Unit of New River Gorge National River
Glen Jean,
304-763-3715
Nearly 900 wooded acres at the northern end of the New River Gorge National River area; offers spectacular overlooks of New River Gorge and Horseshoe Bend; rhododendron gardens. Hiking trails, game courts (some fees), cross-country skiing, picnicking, playgrounds and concession. Outdoor dramas June-Labor Day: Tuesday-Sunday.

New River Gorge National River
104 Main St.,
Glen Jean,
304-465-0508;
www.nps.gov/neri
One of the oldest rivers on the continent, the New River rushes northward through a deep canyon with spectacular scenery. The 52-mile section from Hinton to Fayetteville is popular among outdoor enthusiasts, especially whitewater rafters and hikers. The Hinton Visitor Center is located along the river at Highway 3 Bypass (Memorial Day-Labor Day: daily); 304-466-0417. A year-round visitor center is located on Highway 19 near the New River Gorge Bridge.

★
★
★
★
★

GRAFTON

Mother's Day originated in Grafton in 1908 when Anna Jarvis observed the anniversary of her mother's death during a religious service. The idea caught on nationally, and in 1914 President Woodrow Wilson issued a proclamation urging nationwide observance. The International Shrine to Motherhood in the original Mother's Day church is located at 11 East Main Sreet.

During the Civil War, Grafton was an important railroad center and 4,000 Union troops camped here before the Battle of Philippi in 1861. General McClellan also had his headquarters in the town. The first land soldier killed in the war, T. Bailey Brown, fell at Grafton and is buried in the Grafton National Cemetery.

Information: Grafton-Taylor County Convention and Visitors Bureau, 214 W. Main St., Grafton, 304-265-1589, 800-225-5982

WHAT TO SEE AND DO

Tygart Lake State Park

Grafton,
304-265-3383, 800-225-5982;
www.tygertlake.com

This scenic 2,100-acre park contains one of the largest concrete dams east of the Mississippi (1,900 feet by 209 feet). Swimming, waterskiing, fishing, boating (ramp, rentals, marina); hiking, game courts, picnic area, playground, concession, lodge, tent and trailer camping, ten cabins. Nature and recreation programs, dam tours (summer; 304-265-1760).

SPECIAL EVENTS

Taylor County Fair

Fairgrounds, Hwy. 50, Grafton, 304-265-3303

Horse racing, livestock shows, auctions, carnival, crafts. Last week of July.

HOTELS

★★Tygart Lake State Park Lodge

Hwy. 1, Grafton,
304-265-6144, 800-225-5982;
www.tygartlake.com
20 rooms. Closed January-mid April. Beach. $

WEST VIRGINIA

HARPERS FERRY

Scene of abolitionist John Brown's raid in 1859, Harpers Ferry is at the junction of the Shenandoah and Potomac rivers, where West Virginia, Virginia and Maryland meet. A U.S. armory and rifle factory made this an important town in early Virginia, and John Brown had this in mind when he began his insurrection. He and 16 other men seized the armory and arsenal the night of October 16 and took refuge in the engine house when attacked by local militia. On the morning of the 18th, the engine house was stormed, and Brown was captured by 90 marines from Washington under Brevet Colonel Robert E. Lee and Lt. J.E.B. Stuart. Ten of Brown's men were killed, including two of his sons. He was hanged in nearby Charles Town for treason, murder and inciting slaves to rebellion.

When war broke out, Harpers Ferry was a strategic objective for the Confederacy, which considered it the key to Washington. The town changed hands many times in the war, during which many buildings were damaged. In 1944, Congress authorized a national monument here, setting aside 1,500 acres for that purpose. In 1963, the same area was designated a National Historical Park, now occupying more than 2,200 acres. Information Jefferson County Chamber of Commerce, 201 Frontage Road, Charles Town, 304-725-2055, 800-624-0577; www.jeffersoncounty.com/index.html

WHAT TO SEE AND DO

Harpers Ferry National Historical Park

Shenandoah and High streets,
Harpers Ferry, 304-535-6029;
www.nps.gov/hafe

The old town has been restored to its 19th-century appearance; exhibits and interpretive presentations explore the park's relation to the water-power industry, the Civil War, abolitionist John Brown, and Storer College, a school established for freed slaves after the war. A visitor center is located just off Highway 340. Visitors should park there; a bus will take them to Lower Town. Daily.

Located in the park are:

Camp Hill

Shenandoah and High streets,
Harpers Ferry

Four restored, private houses built 1832-1850.

Harper House

Shenandoah and High streets,
Harpers Ferry

Three-story stone house built between 1775 and 1782 by the founder of the town; both George Washington and Thomas Jefferson were entertained as overnight guests. Restored and furnished with period pieces.

Jefferson's Rock

Harpers Ferry

From here Thomas Jefferson, in 1783, pronounced the view "one of the most stupendous scenes in nature."

John Brown Wax Museum

168 High St., Harpers Ferry,
304-535-6342;
www.johnbrownwaxmuseum.com

Contains an exhibit and film on John Brown, and a 10-minute slide presentation on the history of the park. To the right of the museum is High St., which has two Civil War museums and two black history museums. Daily.

John Brown's Fort

Shenandoah and High streets,
Harpers Ferry

Where John Brown made his last stand; rebuilt and moved near original site.

Lockwood House

Harpers Ferry

(1848) Greek Revival house used as headquarters, barracks and stable during Civil War; later used as a classroom building by Storer College (1867), which was founded to educate freed men after the war.

Ruins of St. John's Episcopal Church

Harpers Ferry

Used as a guardhouse and hospital during the Civil War.

The Point

Shenandoah and High streets,
Harpers Ferry

Three states—West Virginia, Virginia and Maryland—and two rivers, the Shenandoah and Potomac, meet at the Blue Ridge Mountains.

Whitewater Rafting

Harpers Ferry,
800-225-5982

Many outfitters offer guided trips on the Shenandoah and Potomac rivers.

SPECIAL EVENTS

Election Day 1860

Shenandoah St.,
Harpers Ferry,
304-535-6298

More than 100 people in 19th-century attire reenact the 1860 presidential election. Second Saturday in October.

465

WEST VIRGINIA

★
★
★
★

Mountain Heritage Arts and Crafts Festival
102 Frontage Rd.,
Harpers Ferry,
304-725-2055, 800-624-0577
More than 190 craftspeople and artisans demonstrate quilting, wool spinning, pottery throwing, vegetable dyeing and other crafts; concerts. Second full weekend in June and last full weekend in September.

Old Tyme Christmas
Harpers Ferry,
304-925-8019

Caroling, musical programs, children's programs, taffy pull, candlelight walk. First two weekends of December.

HOTELS
★Comfort Inn
Rte. 340 and Union St.,
Harpers Ferry,
304-535-6391, 877-424-6423;
www.choicehotels.com
50 rooms. Complimentary continental breakfast. **$**

HILLSBORO
Civil War troops marched through Hillsboro, and Confederates camped in town before the decisive Battle of Droop Mountain. Novelist Pearl S. Buck was born in her grandparents' house here while her parents, missionaries on leave from China, were visiting.
Information: West Virginia Mountain Highlands,
Elkins, 304-636-8400; www.mountainhighlands.com

WHAT TO SEE AND DO
Pearl S. Buck Birthplace Museum
Rte. 219, Box 126, Hillsboro,
304-653-4430;
www.pearlsbuckbirthplace.com
(Stulting House) Birthplace of the Pulitzer and Nobel Prize-winning novelist, restored to its 1892 appearance; original and period furniture; memorabilia. Sydenstricker House, home of Buck's father and his ancestors, was moved 40 miles from its original site and restored here. Guided tours. May-November: Monday-Saturday.

Watoga State Park
Hwy. 39 and Beaver's Creek Rd., Hillsboro,
304-799-4087, 800-225-5982;
www.watoga.com
More than 10,100 acres make this West Virginia's largest state park. Watoga, derived from the Cherokee term "watauga," means "river of islands." It aptly describes the Greenbrier River, which forms several miles of the park's boundary. Swimming pool, bathhouses, fishing, boating on 11-acre Watoga Lake (rentals); hiking and bridle trails, horseback riding, tennis, game courts, cross-country skiing, picnicking, playground, concession, restaurant (seasonal), tent and trailer camping, 33 cabins. Brooks Memorial Arboretum; nature, recreation programs (summer).

Adjacent to the park is:

Calvin Price State Forest
Hwy. 39 and Beaver's Creek Rd., Hillsboro,
304-799-4087
This vast, undeveloped forest has more than 9,400 acres for fishing; deer and small-game hunting, hiking and primitive camping (fee).

HINTON
This railroad town on the banks of the New River is the seat of Summers County, where the Bluestone and Greenbrier rivers join the scenic and protected New River.
Information: Summers County Chamber of Commerce, 200 Ballangee St.,
Hinton, 304-466-5332;
www.summerscounty.net

WHAT TO SEE AND DO

Bluestone State Park
Hwy. 20, HC 78 Box 3, Hinton,
304-466-2805;
www.bluestonesp.com

More than 2,100 acres on Bluestone Lake, which was created by the Bluestone Dam. Swimming pool (Memorial Day-Labor Day), wading pool, bathhouses, water-skiing, fishing, boating (ramps, marina nearby; canoe, rowboat and motorboat rentals); hiking trails, game courts, picnicking, playground, tent and trailer camping (dump station), 25 cabins. Nature, recreation programs (summer). Gift shop. Standard hours, fees.

Pipestem Resort State Park
Hinton,
304-466-1800, 800-225-5982

More than 4,000 acres with 3,600-foot aerial tramway to Bluestone River complex. Swimming, bathhouses, fishing, canoeing, paddle-boating; hiking trails, horseback riding, 9- and 18-hole golf courses, miniature golf, tennis, archery, lighted game courts, cross-country skiing, sledding, playground, two lodges, four restaurants, tent and trailer camping (dump station), 25 cabins. Visitor center; nature, recreation programs. Aerial tramway, arboretum, observation tower. Amphitheater; dances.

RESTAURANTS

★Kirk's
RR 3, 215 Main St., Hinton,
304-466-4600

American menu. Breakfast, lunch, dinner. Casual attire. Outdoor seating. **$**

HUNTINGTON

The millionaire president of the Chesapeake & Ohio Railroad, Collis P. Huntington, founded this city and named it for himself. Originally a rail and river terminus, commerce and industry have made it the second-largest city in the state. Thoroughly planned and meticulously laid out, Huntington is protected from the Ohio River by an 11-mile floodwall equipped with 17 pumping stations and 45 gates. Glass, railroad products and metals are important city industries.

Information: Cabell-Huntington Convention & Visitors Bureau, Huntington, 304-525-7333, 800-635-6329; www.wvvisit.org

WHAT TO SEE AND DO

Beech Fork State Park
5601 Longbranch Rd.,
Huntington,
304-528-5794, 800-225-5982;
www.beechforksp.com

Nearly 4,000 acres on 720-acre Beech Fork Lake. Fishing, boating (ramp, marina); hiking trails, physical fitness trail, tennis, game courts, picnicking, camping. Store. Visitor center; nature, recreation programs (summer). Meeting rooms.

Camden Park
Hwy. 60 E.,
Huntington,
304-429-4231, 866-822-6336;
www.camdenpark.com
Amusement park with 27 rides, games, concession; boat and train rides, log flume, miniature golf, roller rink, picnicking. Rides individually priced; also unlimited ride plan. Mid-April-Memorial Day: Saturday-Sunday; Memorial Day-Labor Day: Tuesday-Sunday.

Heritage Farm Museum & Village
3300 Harvey Rd.,
Huntington,
304-522-1244;
www.heritagefarmmuseum.com
Tours of Museum of Progress, Museum of Transportation and Country Store Museum.Restored Victorian B & O Railroad yard surrounding brick courtyard. Restaurant in original passenger station (1887), restored Pullman car, shops in renovated freight and box cars, warehouses. Monday-Saturday.

Huntington Museum of Art
2033 McCoy Rd., Huntington,
304-529-2701; www.hmoa.org

Museum with American and European paintings, prints and sculpture; Herman P. Dean Firearms Collection; Georgian silver; Asian prayer rugs; pre-Columbian art; Appalachian folk art; Ohio Valley historical and contemporary glass. Complex includes exhibition galleries, library, studio workshops, amphitheater, auditorium, sculpture garden, observatory, art gallery for young people, nature trails. Tuesday-Saturday, also Sunday afternoons.

HOTELS
★Days Inn
5196 Rte. 60 E.,
Huntington,
304-733-4477;
www.daysinn.com
153 rooms. Complimentary continental breakfast. $

RESTAURANTS
★★Rebels & Redcoats Tavern
412 W. 7th Ave.,
Huntington,
304-523-8829
American menu. Lunch, dinner. Closed Sunday, Monday; also the week of July 4. Bar. Children's menu. Casual attire. $$$

LEWISBURG
At the junction of two important Native American trails, the Seneca (now Hwy. 219) and the Kanawha (now Hwy. 60), Lewisburg was the site of colonial forts as well as a Civil War battle. The town's 236-acre historic district has more than 60 buildings from the 18th and 19th centuries in a variety of architectural styles.
Information: Greenbrier County Convention & Visitors Center, 540 N. Jefferson St., Lewisburg, 304-645-1000, 800-833-2068; www.greenbrierwv.com

WHAT TO SEE AND DO
Lost World Caverns
Fairview Rd.,
Lewisburg,
304-645-6677, 866-228-3778;
www.lostworldcaverns.com
Scenic trail over subterranean rock mountain; prehistoric ocean floor; stalagmites, stalactites; flow stone, ribbons, hex stones. Self-guided tours (daily).

North House Museum
301 W. Washington St., Lewisburg,
304-645-3398
Colonial and 19th-century objects and artifacts. Monday-Saturday.

Old Stone Presbyterian Church
200 Church St., Lewisburg,
304-645-2676;
www.oldstone.us

Original log church (1783) was replaced by present native limestone structure (1796). Daily.

HOTELS

★★Brier Inn & Conference Center
540 N. Jefferson St., Lewisburg,
304-645-7722;
www.brierinn.com
162 rooms. Airport transportation available. $

★★★General Lewis Inn
301 E. Washington St., Lewisburg,
304-645-2600, 800-628-4454;
www.generallewisinn.com

Operating as a guest house since 1928, this bed-and-breakfast was built in the early 1800s. It is surrounded by flower gardens and lawns with a lily pond. Every room is furnished with antiques and crafts made by early settlers.
25 rooms. No children allowed. Restaurant. $

MARLINTON

Marlinton is the seat of Pocahontas County, an area known for its wide variety of outdoor recreational opportunities. A Ranger District office of the Monongahela National Forest is located in the town.
Information: West Virginia Mountain Highlands, Elkins,
304-636-8400; www.mountainhighlands.com

WHAT TO SEE AND DO

Cranberry Mountain Visitor Center-Monongahela National Forest
Hwy. 150 and Hwy. 39/55, Marlinton,
304-653-4826, 800-336-7009
Exhibits, videos and publications on conservation and forest management. April-November: daily.

Cranberry Glades
Hwy. 150 and Hwy. 39-55, Marlinton,
304-653-4826
A USDA Forest Service botanical area. Approximately 750 acres featuring open bog fringed by forest and alder thicket. Boardwalk with interpretive signs. Guided tours leave from visitor center (June-Labor Day: weekends). Glades (year-round, weather permitting).

Greenbrier River Trail
Hwy. 39 and Beaver's Creek Rd.,
Marlinton,
304-799-4087;
www.greenbrierrivertrail.com

Part of the state park system, this 76-mile trail runs along the Greenbrier River from the town of Cass, on the north, through Marlinton to North Caldwell on the south; passes through small towns, over 35 bridges, and through two tunnels. Originally the trail was part of the Chesapeake & Ohio Railroad. Activities include backpacking, bicycling and cross-country skiing; trail also provides access for fishing and canoeing. No developed sites.

Pocahontas County Historical Museum
810 2nd Ave., Marlinton,
304-799-6659
Displays on history of the county from its beginning to present. Extensive photo collection. Early June-Labor Day: daily.

Seneca State Forest
Rte. 1, Marlinton,
304-799-6213, 800-255-5982;
www.senecastateforest.com
Approximately 12,000 acres with fishing and boating on a 4-acre lake; hunting, hiking trails, picnicking, playground. Camping, eight rustic cabins.

Pioneer Days

900 9th St., Marlinton,

304-799-4315, 800-336-7009

Craft exhibits and demonstrations; horse-pulling contests, frog and turtle races; blue-grass and mountain music shows; 4x4 truck pulling; parade; antique car show. Early-mid-July.

MARTINSBURG

Martinsburg is located in the center of an apple- and peach-producing region in the state's eastern panhandle. Because of its strategic location at the entrance to the Shenandoah Valley, the town was the site of several battles during the Civil War. The famous Confederate spy Belle Boyd was a resident. Officially chartered in 1778, Martinsburg is recognized for the preservation of its many 18th- and 19th-century houses, along with its mercantile and industrial buildings.

Information: Martinsburg-Berkeley County Chamber of Commerce,

198 Viking Way, Martinsburg,

304-267-4841, 800-332-9007;

www.berkeleycounty.org

WHAT TO SEE AND DO

General Adam Stephen House

309 E. John St.,

Martinsburg,

304-267-4434

(1789) Restored residence of Revolutionary War soldier and surgeon Adam Stephen, founder of Martinsburg. Period furnishings; restored smokehouse and log building. May-October: Saturday-Sunday, limited hours; also by appointment.

Adjacent is:

Triple Brick Building

309 E. John St., Martinsburg,

304-267-4434

Completed in three sections just after the Civil War, the structure was used to house railroad employees. A museum of local history is located on the top two floors. May-October: Saturday-Sunday, limited hours; also by appointment.

SPECIAL EVENTS

Mountain State Apple Harvest Festival

Martinsburg,

304-263-2500;

www.msahf.com

Parade, celebrity breakfast, contests, entertainment, Apple Queen coronation, square dancing, grand ball, arts and crafts show. Third weekend in October.

HOTELS

★**Comfort Inn Aikens Center**

1872 Edwin Miller Blvd.,

Martinsburg,

304-263-6200, 877-424-6423;

www.choicehotels.com

109 rooms. Complimentary continental breakfast. Airport transportation available. **$**

★★**Holiday Inn**

301 Foxcroft Ave.,

Martinsburg,

304-267-5500, 800-315-2621;

www.holidayinn.com/martinsburgwv

120 rooms. **$**

470

WEST VIRGINIA

MATEWAN

This tiny hamlet was the site of the famous feud between the West Virginia Hatfields and the Kentucky McCoys. On Election Day, August 7, 1882, three McCoy sons stabbed and shot Ellison Hatfield. Devil Anse Hatfield avenged his brother by executing the three McCoys. Soon Kentucky bounty hunters made raids into West Virginia to capture the Hatfieds, who retaliated in 1888 by attacking a McCoy homestead. By 1890 the killings had ended but the feud continued to be sensationalized. In 1920, Matewan was the scene of a shootout between union organizers and coal company operators that left 10 dead, including the mayor.

Tug Valley Chamber of Commerce, 304-235-5240;
www.tugvalleychamberofcommerce.com

MORGANTOWN

Morgantown is both an educational and an industrial center. West Virginia University was founded here in 1867, and the Morgantown Female Collegiate Institute in 1839. Known internationally for its glass, Morgantown is home to a number of glass plants, which produce wares ranging from lamp parts to decorative paper weights and crystal tableware. The town is also home to a number of research laboratories maintained by the federal government.

Information: Greater Morgantown Convention & Visitors Bureau,

68 Donley St., Morgantown, 800-458-7373; www.visitmorgantown.com

WHAT TO SEE AND DO

Coopers Rock State Forest
Rte. 1, Morgantown,
304-594-1561;
www.coopersrockstateforest.com
More than 12,700 acres. Trout fishing; hunting, hiking trails to historical sites; Henry Clay iron furnace (1834-1836). Cross-country ski trails, picnicking, playground, concession, tent and trailer camping.
   Adjacent is:

Chestnut Ridge Regional Park
Sand Springs Rd., Bruceton Mills,
304-594-1773

Swimming beach, fishing; tent and trailer camping, rustic cabins, lodge (fees), hiking, picnicking, cross-country ski trails (December-February). Nature center. Park (daily).

West Virginia University
Visitors Resource Center,
One Waterfront Place, Morgantown,
304-293-0111;
www.wvu.edu
(1867) (22,712 students.) University has 15 colleges. Tours (Monday-Saturday; for reservations 304-293-3489). The Visitors Center in the Communications Building on Patterson Drive has touch-screen

monitors and video presentations about the university and upcoming special events (304-293-6692 for 24-hour event information). Of special interest on the downtown campus are Stewart Hall and the university's original buildings, located on Woodburn Circle. In the Evansdale area of Morgantown are the Creative Arts Center, the 75-acre Core Arboretum, and the 63,500-seat Coliseum.

Also in the Evansdale area are:

Cook-Hayman Pharmacy Museum
1 Medical Dr., Morgantown,
304-293-5101
Re-creates pharmacy of yesteryear with old patent medicines. Monday-Friday; weekends by request.

Personal Rapid Transit System (PRT)
88 Beechhurst Ave.,
Morgantown,
304-293-5011
A pioneering transit system, the PRT is the world's first totally automated system. Operating without conductors or ticket takers, computer-directed cars travel between university campuses and downtown Morgantown. Monday-Saturday; may not operate holidays and university breaks.

Whitewater Rafting
Morgantown,
800-458-7373
Many outfitters offer guided trips on the Cheat and Tygart rivers.

SPECIAL EVENTS
Mason-Dixon Festival
Morgantown Riverfront Park,
Morgantown,
304-599-1104;
www.masondixonfestival.org
River parade, boat races, arts and crafts, concessions. Mid-September.

Mountaineer Balloon Festival
Morgantown Municipal Airport,
100 Hart Field Rd., Morgantown,
304-296-8356;
www.mountaineerballoonfestival.com

Hot air balloon races, carnival, music, food. Mid-October.

HOTELS
★Clarion Hotel
127 High St.,
Morgantown,
304-292-8200, 877-424-6423;
www.clarionhotelmorgan.com
76 rooms. Complimentary continental breakfast. **$**

★Comfort Inn
225 Comfort Inn Dr.,
Morgantown,
304-296-9364, 877-424-6423;
www.choicehotels.com
80 rooms. Complimentary continental breakfast. **$**

★Hampton Inn
1053 Van Voorhis Rd.,
Morgantown,
304-599-1200, 800-486-7866;
www.hamptoninn.com
107 rooms. Complimentary continental breakfast. **$**

★★★Lakeview Golf Resort & Spa
1 Lakeview Dr.,
Morgantown,
304-594-1111, 800-624-8300;
www.lakeviewresort.com
The Lakeview Golf Resort & Spa offers more than just driving ranges and putting greens. In the foothills of the Allegheny Mountains, the resort offers comfortable guest rooms, conference and meeting space, event space, a fitness center, a spa and several dining and recreation options.
187 rooms. Children's activity center. Airport transportation available. Tennis. **$**

★★Quality Inn
1400 Saratoga Ave.,
Morgantown,
304-599-1680, 877-424-6423;
www.choicehotels.com
147 rooms. **$**

RESTAURANTS

★★Back Bay
1869 Mileground, Morgantown,
304-296-3027
Seafood menu. Lunch, dinner. Bar. Children's
menu. Casual attire. Outdoor seating. **$$**

★Puglioni's
1137 Van Voorhis Rd., Morgantown,
304-599-7521
Italian menu. Lunch, dinner. Bar. Children's
menu. Casual attire. **$$**

PARKERSBURG

After the Revolutionary War, Blennerhassett Island, in the Ohio River west of Parkersburg, was the scene of the alleged Burr-Blennerhassett plot. Harman Blennerhassett, a wealthy Irishman, built a lavish mansion on this island. After killing Alexander Hamilton in a duel, Aaron Burr came to the island, allegedly to seize the Southwest and set up an empire; Blennerhassett may have agreed to join him. On December 10, 1806, the plot was uncovered. Both men were acquitted of treason but ruined financially in the process. The Blennerhassett mansion burned in 1811 but was later rebuilt.

Today, Parkersburg is the center for many industries, including glass, chemicals, petrochemicals, and ferrous and other metals. Fishing is popular in the area, especially below the Belleville and Willow Island locks and dams on the Ohio River.

Information: Parkersburg/Wood Co. Convention & Visitor's Bureau, 350 7th St., Parkersburg, 304-428-1130, 800-752-4982; www.parkersburgcvb.org

WHAT TO SEE AND DO

Actors Guild Playhouse
724 Market St., Parkersburg,
304-485-1300;
www.actorsguildonline.com
Musical, comedic and dramatic performances. Friday-Sunday.

Blennerhassett Island Historical State Park
137 Juliana St., Parkersburg,
304-420-4800, 800-225-5982;
www.blennerhassettislandpark.com
A 500-acre island accessible only by sternwheeler. There are self-guided walking tours of the island, horse-drawn wagon rides and tours of the Blennerhassett mansion. Bicycle rentals, picnicking, concessions. Tickets are available for the boat ride at the Blennerhassett Museum. May-Labor Day: Tuesday-Sunday; September-October: Thursday-Sunday.

Blennerhassett Museum
2nd and Juliana streets,
Parkersburg,
304-420-4840
Features archaeological and other exhibits relating to history of Blennerhassett Island and Parkersburg area; includes artifacts dating back 12,000 years. Theater with video presentation. May-October: Tuesday-Sunday; rest of year, Saturday-Sunday.

City Park
Park Ave. and 23rd St., Parkersburg,
304-424-8400
A 55-acre wooded area with the Cooper Log Cabin Museum, which dates from 1804. Swimming pool, fishing, paddleboats; miniature golf, tennis, shelters and picnic facilities.

North Bend State Park
Rte. 1, Parkersburg,
304-643-2931, 800-225-5982;
www.northbendsp.com
Approximately 1,400 acres in the wide valley of the North Fork of the Hughes River; scenic overlooks of famous horseshoe bend. Swimming pool, bathhouse, fishing; miniature golf, tennis, game courts; hiking, bicycle and bridle trail; 71-mile North Bend Rail Trail. Picnicking, playground, concession, restaurant, lodge, tent and trailer camping, skiing, eight cabins. Nature, recreation programs. Nature trail for disabled.

473

WEST VIRGINIA

Parkersburg Art Center
725 Market St., Parkersburg,
304-485-3859;
www.parkersburgartcenter.com
Changing exhibits. Tuesday-Sunday 10 a.m.-
5 p.m., Sunday 1-5 p.m.

Rubles Sternwheelers Riverboat Cruises
2nd and Ann streets, Parkersburg,
740-423-7268
Public and private riverboat cruises. May-
October: daily.

SPECIAL EVENTS
Parkersburg Homecoming
Point Park, 2nd and Avery streets,
Parkersburg, 304-422-9970;
www.parkersburg-homecoming.com
Riverfront celebration features entertainment, parade, sternwheeler races, waterskiing show, miniature car races, fireworks.
Third weekend in August.

West Virginia Honey Festival
4-H Grounds, Parkersburg,
304-424-1960
Honey-related exhibits, baking, food, arts
and crafts. Mid-September.

HOTELS
★★★Blennerhassett Hotel
320 Market St., Parkersburg,
304-422-3131, 800-262-2536;
www.theblennerhassett.com
This landmark hotel was built before the
turn of the century in the "gaslight era"
and was fully restored in 1986. The hotel's
Victorian style is evident in the rich crown
molding, authentic English doors, brass and
leaded-glass chandeliers, and antiques.
94 rooms. $

★Econo Lodge Parkersburg
1954 E. 7th St., Parkersburg,
304-428-7500, 800-424-6423;

www.econolodge.com
63 rooms. Complimentary continental breakfast. $

★Hampton Inn
64 Elizabeth Drive Parkersburg,
304-489-2900, 800-426-7866;
www.hamptoninn.com
68 rooms. Complimentary continental
breakfast. $

★★Holiday Inn
225 Holiday Hills Dr., Parkersburg,
304-485-6200;
www.holidayinn.com
149 rooms. $

RESTAURANTS
★Mountaineer Family Restaurant
4006 E. 7th St., Parkersburg,
304-422-0101
American menu. Breakfast, lunch, dinner,
late-night. Children's menu. Casual attire. $

★★★Spats at the Lennerhassett
320 Market St., Parkersburg,
304-422-3131, 800-262-2536;
www.theblennerhassett.com
Its downtown location makes Blennerhassett a great place to stop for a lunch break,
and its continental menu makes it easy for
everyone to find something to eat. The restaurant features dark wood ceilings, crown
molding, wainscoting and leather armchairs.
A charming garden patio area includes a
bar, a dining area, a music stage and a large
screen for sporting events. The restaurant
also features a martini night, wine tastings
and live music.
Continental menu. Breakfast, lunch, dinner.
Brunch bar. Children's menu. Business
casual attire. Reservations recommended.
Valet parking. Outdoor seating. $$$

PETERSBURG
A Ranger District office of the Monongahela National Forest is located in Petersburg.
Information: West Virginia Mountain Highlands,
1200 Harrison Ave., Elkins, 304-636-8400; www.mountainhighlands.com

★

★

★

★

★

WHAT TO SEE AND DO

Monongahela National Forest
USDA Forest Service,
Petersburg,
304-257-4488
Recreation area is popular for canoeing, hiking and other outdoor sports. Camping (fee).

PHILIPPI

The first land battle of the Civil War, a running rout of the Confederates known locally as the Philippi Races, was fought here on June 3, 1861. A historical marker on the campus of Alderson-Broaddus College marks the site. The Union attacked to protect the Baltimore & Ohio Railroad, whose main line between Washington and the West ran near the town.
Information: Barbour County Chamber of Commerce, Philippi, 304-457-1958; www.barbourchamber.com

WHAT TO SEE AND DO

Barbour County Historical Society Museum
146 N. Main St., Philippi,
304-457-4846
This B & O Railroad station (1911), used until 1956, is now restored as a museum; also local arts and crafts. May-October: daily; rest of year, by appointment.

Covered Bridge
200 N. Main St.,
Philippi
Spanning the Tygart River since 1852; restored in recent years; believed to be the only two-lane bridge of its type still in daily use on a federal highway (Hwy. 250).

SPECIAL EVENTS

Barbour County Fair
Fairgrounds, Hwy. 250 between Phillipi and Belington, Philippi,
304-823-1328;
www.barbourcountyfair.com
Horse and antique car shows, quilt and livestock exhibits, carnival rides, nightly entertainment, parade and more. Week before Labor Day.

Blue & Gray Reunion
Philippi,
304-457-1958

HOTELS

★★Hermitage Motor Inn
203 Virginia Ave.,
Petersburg,
304-257-1711, 800-437-6482;
www.hermitageinn.net
38 rooms. Complimentary continental breakfast. Craft shop, bookstore in 1840s inn. **$**

Commemorates the first land battle of the Civil War; reenactment, parade, crafts. First weekend in June.

HOTELS

★Philippi Lodging
Hwy. 250 S. Route 4, Philippi,
304-457-5888
39 rooms. **$**

RESTAURANTS

★★Bluestone Dining Room
Pipestem Resort, Pipestem,
304-466-1800
American menu. Breakfast, lunch, dinner. Children's menu. Casual attire. **$$**

★★Mountain Creek
Pipestem Resort, Pipestem,
304-466-1800
French, American menu. Dinner. Closed November-April. Bar. Children's menu. Casual attire. Dining room at 1,000-foot-deep gorge; accessible by tram only; park in Pipestem Resort State Park. **$$$**

★★Oak Supper Club
Just N.of Pipestem State Park entrance, Pipestem,
304-466-4800
American menu. Dinner. Closed Sunday, Monday; also January-mid-February. Bar. Children's menu. Casual attire. **$$**

475

WEST VIRGINIA

★
★
★
★

POINT PLEASANT

On October 10, 1774, British-incited Shawnees under Chief Cornstalk fought a battle here against 1,100 frontiersmen. The colonists won and broke the Native American power in the Ohio Valley. Historians later argued that this, rather than the battle at Lexington, Massachusetts, was the first battle of the Revolutionary War. In 1908, the U.S. Senate rewrote history by recognizing this claim.

Information: Mason County Area Chamber of Commerce, 305 Main St., Point Pleasant, 304-675-3844

WHAT TO SEE AND DO

East Lynn Wildlife Management Area
McClintic Rd.,
Point Pleasant,
304-675-0871
Almost 23,000 acres used primarily by sportsmen; trails, primitive camping. Skiing.

Krodel Park and Lake
Hwy. 2 and Hwy. 62,
Point Pleasant,
304-675-1068
A 44-acre park with a replica of Fort Randolph (circa 1775). Fishing (license required), paddle boats (fee); miniature golf (fee), playground, camping. April-November; fee.

McClintic Wildlife Management Area
McClintic Rd.,
Point Pleasant,
304-675-0871
Approximately 2,800 acres with primitive camping (fee). Also fishing and hunting (licenses required).

Tu-Endie-Wei State Park
1 Main St.,
Point Pleasant,
304-675-0869, 800-225-5982;
www.wvparks.com/pointpleasant
An 84-foot granite shaft was erected here in 1909, after the U.S. Senate agreed to a claim made by historians that the first battle of the Revolutionary War was fought here. The park also contains a marker where Joseph Celeron de Bienville buried a leaden plate in 1749, claiming the land for France, and the graves of Chief Cornstalk and "Mad Anne" Bailey, a noted pioneer scout.
Also here is:

Mansion House
1 Main St.,
Point Pleasant,
304-675-0869
(1796) Oldest log building in Kanawha Valley, restored as a museum. May-October: daily.

West Virginia State Farm Museum
Hwy. 1,
Point Pleasant,
304-675-5737
Contains more than 30 farm buildings depicting early rural life, including a log church, one-room schoolhouse, kitchen, scale house and four-unit building. Barn contains mount of one of the largest horses in the world; also animals. April-November: Tuesday-Sunday.

SPECIAL EVENTS

Mason County Fair
County Fairgrounds,
Point Pleasant,
304-675-5463
Livestock show, arts and crafts, contests, Nashville entertainers. Mid-August.

HOTELS

★Lowe Hotel
401 Main St.,
Point Pleasant,
304-675-2260
42 rooms. $

WEST VIRGINIA

ROANOKE

HOTELS

★★★**Stonewall Resort**
940 Resort Dr., Roanoke,
304-269-7400, 888-278-8150;
www.stonewallresort.com
On the shore of Stonewall Jackson Lake, this resort offers accommodations in a lodge, private villa or waterfront home. The comfortable rooms come equipped with wireless Internet access, and the resort features a signature Arnold Palmer golf course.
198 rooms. Children's activity center. **$**

SENECA ROCKS

WHAT TO SEE AND DO

Smoke Hole Caverns
Hwy. 28 S., Seneca Rocks,
304-257-4442, 800-828-8478;
www.smokehole.com
These caverns were used centuries ago by the Seneca both for shelter and the smoking of meat. During the Civil War, they were used by troops on both sides for storing ammunition. Later, they hid "moonshiners," illegal distillers of corn whiskey. It is claimed that the caverns contain the longest ribbon stalactite and the second highest cave room in the world. Guided tours. Large gift shop with wildlife exhibits; concessions. Tours. Daily 9 a.m.-5 p.m.

HOTELS

★**Smoke Hole Hotel & Log Cabins**
Hwy. 28 S., Seneca Rocks,
304-257-4442, 800-828-8478;
www.smokehole.com
10 rooms. Adjacent to Smoke Hole Caverns.
$

WEST VIRGINIA

SHEPHERDSTOWN

In 1787, Shepherdstown was the site of the first successful public launching of a steamboat. However, James Rumsey, inventor of the craft, died before he could exploit his success. Rival claims by John Fitch, and Robert Fulton's commercial success with the "Clermont" 20 years later, have clouded Rumsey's achievement.

The state's first newspaper was published here in 1790, and Shepherdstown almost became the national capital. (George Washington considered it as a possible site, according to letters in the Library of Congress.) Shepherdstown is also the location of one of the early gristmills, which was most likely constructed around 1739. It finally ceased production in 1939. This is the oldest continuously settled town in the state.
Information: Jefferson County Chamber of Commerce, 201 Frontage Rd., Charles Town, 304-725-2055, 800-624-0577; www.jeffersoncounty.com/chamber

WHAT TO SEE AND DO

Historic Shepherdstown Museum
129 E. German St., Shepherdstown,
304-876-0910;
www.historicshepherdstown.com/museum.htm
Artifacts dating to the 1700s, including many items concerning the founding of the town. Guided tours (by appointment). April-October: daily.
Also available:

Guided Walking Tours
129 E. German St., Shepherdstown,
304-876-0910
Historic sites in Shepherdstown.

HOTELS

★★★**Bavarian Inn & Lodge**
164 Shepherd Grade Rd., Hwy. 34,
Shepherdstown,
304-876-2551;
www.bavarianinnwv.com

This inn is decorated with Federal period reproductions and provides European-style hospitality. Four-poster mahogany beds, brass chandeliers and bathrooms with imported marble grace each room. 72 rooms. **$$**

★★★Yellow Brick Bank & Little Inn

201 German at Princess St., Shepherdstown, 304-876-2208

Housed in a 19th-century bank building in a rural town near the upper Potomac, this surprisingly inventive restaurant serves creative cuisine in an airy, high-ceilinged dining room.

Lunch, dinner, Sunday. brunch. Bar. Overnight stays available. **$$**

SPECIALTY LODGINGS

Thomas Shepherd Inn

300 W. German St., Shepherdstown, 304-876-3715, 888-889-8952; www.thomasshepherdinn.com

This cozy inn was built in 1868 in the Federal style of architecture. The guest rooms have been lovingly restored and feature the original floors and Oriental rugs.

6 rooms. Complimentary full breakfast. **$**

RESTAURANTS

★★★Bavarian Inn and Lodge

164 Shepherd Grade Rd., Hwy. 34, Shepherdstown, 304-876-2551; www.bavarianinnwv.com

Few places serve such authentic traditional German fare. Seasonal entrees include pork tenderloin picatta on sautéed spatzle, wilted spinach and a Dijon mustard sauce; and seared grouper filet over rainbow couscous, fresh cilantro, tomato and red sauce. Stone fireplaces and dark woods create a rustic yet elegant ambience.

German menu. Breakfast, lunch, dinner. Bar. Children's menu. **$$$**

SUMMERSVILLE

Twenty-year-old Nancy Hart led a surprise Confederate attack on Summersville in July 1861, captured a Union force and burned the town. She was captured, but her jail guard succumbed to her charms. The guard was then disarmed and killed by the young woman. She escaped to Lee's lines. After the war she returned to Summersville.

Information: Chamber of Commerce, 411 Old Main Dr., Summersville, 304-872-1588, 800-760-6158; www.summersvillechamber.com

WHAT TO SEE AND DO

Carnifex Ferry Battlefield State Park

1194 Carnifex Ferry Rd., Summersville, 304-872-0825; www.carnifexbattlefieldstatepark.com

Here on September 10, 1861, 7,000 Union troops under General William S. Rosecrans fought and defeated a lesser number of Confederates under General John B. Floyd. The 156-acre park includes Patterson House Museum (Memorial Day-weekend after Labor Day: Saturday, Sunday, holidays), which displays Civil War relics. Hiking trails, picnicking, game courts, playgrounds, concession. Civil War reenactment (weekend after Labor Day). Park (May-early September: daily).

Summersville Lake

Summersville, 304-872-3459

A 2,700-acre lake. Swimming, waterskiing, fishing, boating; hiking, picnicking. Battle Run Campground is three miles W on Highway 129 (fee). May-October: daily. Fee for some activities.

SPECIAL EVENTS

Nicholas County Fair

616 Church St., Summersville, 304-872-1454

Midway, flower show, agricultural and crafts exhibits. July.

Nicholas County Potato Festival
411 Old Main Dr., Summersville,
304-872-1211
Includes parades, entertainment, volleyball tournament, arts and crafts show, bed races. First full week in September.

HOTELS
★**Best Western Summersville Lake Motor Lodge**
1203 Broad St., Summersville,
304-872-6900, 800-214-9551;
www.bestwestern.com

57 rooms. Complimentary continental breakfast. **$**

★**Comfort Inn**
903 Industrial Dr. N., Summersville,
304-872-6500, 877-424-6423;
www.choicehotels.com
99 rooms. Complimentary continental breakfast. **$**

SUTTON

WHAT TO SEE AND DO
Sutton Lake
S. Stonewall St., Sutton,
304-765-2816
Swimming in designated areas, boat launch (fee); camping (May-December; some electric hookups; fees) at Gerald R. Freeman Campground.

HOTELS
★★**Days Inn**
2000 Sutton Lane, Sutton,
304-765-5055, 800-329-7466;
www.daysinn.com
201 rooms. **$**

VIENNA

SPECIALTY LODGINGS
Williams' House Bed-and-Breakfast
5406 Grand Central Ave., Vienna,
304-295-7212
Built in 1920, this red brick home is a romantic getaway near the Ohio state line. Many antiques and family memorabilia, along with canopy and four-poster beds, add warmth and charm to this country home. Nearby attractions include the Grand Central Shopping Mall, Blennerhassett Island Historical Park, historical Marietta, Ohio, and plenty of dining.

5 rooms. Children over 12 years only. Complimentary full breakfast. **$**

WEBSTER SPRINGS
Once a resort famed for its medicinal "lick," or spring, the town is now a trading center and meeting place for sportsmen.
Information: Mayor's Office, 146 McGraw Ave., Webster Springs, 304-847-5411

WHAT TO SEE AND DO
Holly River State Park
Webster Springs,
304-493-6353;
www.hollyriver.com
More than 8,100 acres and the second largest state park in the state. Camping, cabins, picnicking, hiking. Standard fees.

Kumbrabow State Forest
Webster Springs,
304-335-2219;
www.kumbrabow.com
More than 9,400 acres of wild, rugged country with trout fishing; deer, turkey and grouse hunting; hiking trails, cross-country

WEST VIRGINIA

★
★
★
★
★

skiing, picnicking, playground, tent and trailer camping, five rustic cabins.

SPECIAL EVENTS
Webster County Fair
Webster Springs,
304-226-3888
Rides, agricultural exhibits, entertainers, horse show. Labor Day week.

Webster Springs Woodchopping Festival
Webster Springs,
304-847-7666;
www.woodchoppingfestival.com
Southeastern World Woodchopping Championships; state championship turkey calling contest, draft horse pull, horse show, fireman's rodeo; arts and crafts, music, parades, concessions. Memorial Day weekend.

WEIRTON
Weirton has been a steel-producing town since its founding in 1910 by Ernest T. Weir, who also founded the Weirton Steel Company. In 1984, Weirton Steel became the largest employee-owned steel company in the world. Modern plants produce tin plate and hot-rolled, cold-rolled, and galvanized steels for containers, automobiles, appliances and other products.
Information: Chamber of Commerce, 3200 Maine St., Weirton, 304-748-7212; www.weirtonchamber.com

WHAT TO SEE AND DO
Tomlinson Run State Park
Weirton,
304-564-3651;
www.tomlinsonrunsp.com
Approximately 1,400 acres. Swimming pool, bathhouse, fishing, boating on 27-acre lake (rowboat and paddleboat rentals); hiking trails, miniature golf, tennis, picnicking, playground, tent and trailer camping (dump station). Nature, recreation programs (summer).

Weirton Steel Corp and Half Moon Industrial Park
400 Three Springs Dr.,
Weirton,
304-797-2828
Tours of Alpo and others. Contact Chamber of Commerce for details.

WESTON
Surveyed originally by "Stonewall" Jackson's grandfather, Weston is a center for coal, oil and gas production, as well as the manufacture of glass products. The Weston State Hospital, completed in 1880 and said to be the largest hand-cut stone building in the nation, is located in town.
Information: Lewis County Convention & Visitors Bureau, 499 U.S. Hwy. 33 E., Weston, 304-269-7328; www.stonewallcountry.com

WHAT TO SEE AND DO
Cedar Creek State Park
2947 Cedar Creek Rd., Weston,
304-462-7158;
www.cedarcreeksp.com
More than 2,400 acres. Swimming pool, bathhouse, fishing, boating (rentals); hiking trails, miniature golf, tennis, game courts, picnicking, playground, concession, tent and trailer camping (dump station). Park office in restored log cabin.

Jackson's Mill State 4-H Conference Center
160 WVU Jackson Mill, Weston,
304-269-5100, 800-287-8206
First camp of its kind in U.S.; 43 buildings, gardens, swimming pool, amphitheater, interfaith chapel. Picnicking.
Also here is:

Jackson's Mill Historic Area
Weston, 304-269-5100
Includes Blaker's Mill, an operating water-powered gristmill; blacksmith shop;

480

WEST VIRGINIA

McWharten cabin (circa 1700s); Mary Conrad's cabin (circa 1800s); and Jackson's Mill Museum, where "Stonewall" Jackson lived and worked as a boy. Museum represents grist and saw milling agriculture and home arts of the area as practiced 100 years ago. Memorial Day-Labor Day: Tuesday-Sunday; May and after Labor Day-mid-October: weekends only.

Stonewall Jackson Lake and Dam
Rte. 33 W., Weston,
304-269-4588
Approximately 2,500-acre lake with over 82 miles of shoreline created by impounding the waters of the West Fork River. Swimming, scuba diving, waterskiing, fishing, boating (ramps, rentals, marinas); picnicking, camping. Visitor center.

Stonewall Jackson Lake State Park
Rte. 19, Weston,
304-269-0523, 888-278-8150;
www.stonewallresort.com

Approximately 3,000 acres. Fishing, boating (launch, marina); nature and fitness trails, picnicking, playground, camping (hookups). Visitor center. Standard hours, fees.

SPECIAL EVENTS
Horse Show
Trefz Farm, Rte. 88 and National Rd., Weston, 304-269-3257
Saddle, walking, harness, pony, western and Arabian riding. Usually July.

Stonewall Jackson Heritage Arts & Crafts Jubilee
Weston, 304-269-1863
Mountain crafts, music, dance and food. Labor Day weekend.

HOTELS
★Comfort Inn
Rte. 33 E. and I-79, Weston,
304-269-7000, 877-424-6423;
www.choicehotels.com
70 rooms. Complimentary continental breakfast. $

WHEELING
Wheeling stands on the site of Fort Henry, built in 1774 by Colonel Ebenezer Zane and his two brothers, who named the fort for Virginia's Governor Patrick Henry. In 1782 the fort was the scene of the Revolutionary War's final battle, a battle in which the valiant young pioneer Betty Zane was a heroine. The fort had withstood several Native American and British sieges during the war. However, during the last siege (after the war had officially ended), the fort's defenders ran out of powder. Betty Zane, sister of the colonel, volunteered to run through the gunfire to the out-

★
★
★
★

lying Zane cabin for more. With the powder gathered in her apron, she made the 150-yard trek back to the fort and saved the garrison. Zane Grey, a descendant of the Zanes, wrote a novel about Betty and her exploit.

Today, Wheeling is home to many industries, including producers of steel, iron, tin, chemical products, pottery, glass, paper, tobacco, plastics and coal.

Information: Convention & Visitors Bureau, 1401 Main St., Wheeling, 304-233-7709, 800-828-3097; www.wheelingcvb.com

WHAT TO SEE AND DO

Artisan Center
1400 Main St., Wheeling,
304-232-1810;
www.artisancenter.com
Restored 1860s Victorian warehouse houses River City Ale Works, West Virginia's largest brew pub. "Made in Wheeling crafts and exhibits; artisan demonstrations. Daily.

Jamboree USA
Capitol Music Hall, 1015 Main St., Wheeling,
304-234-0050, 800-624-5456
Live country music shows presented by WWVA Radio since 1933. Saturday.

Kruger Street Toy & Train Museum
144 Kruger St., Wheeling,
304-242-8133, 877-242-8133;
www.toyandtrain.com
Collection of antique toys, games and playthings in a restored Victorian-era schoolhouse. Daily 10 a.m.-6 p.m.

Oglebay Resort Park
Rte. 88 N., Wheeling,
304-243-4000, 800-624-6988;
www.oglebay-resort.com
A 1,650-acre municipal park. Indoor and outdoor swimming pools, fishing, paddle boating on three-acre Schenk Lake; three 18-hole golf courses, miniature golf, tennis courts, picnicking, restaurant, snack shop, cabins, lodge. Train ride; 65-acre Good Children's Zoo (fee) with animals in natural habitat. Benedum Natural Science Theater; garden center; arboretum with four miles of walking paths; greenhouses; observatory. Fee for most activities.
    Also in the park is:

Mansion and Glass Museum
The Burton Center, Wheeling,
304-242-7272

Period rooms, exhibits trace history from 1835-present. Daily.

Site of Fort Henry
11th and Main streets, Wheeling,
304-233-7709
Bronze plaque marks the location of the fort that Betty Zane saved.

West Virginia Independence Hall
1528 Market St., Wheeling,
304-238-1300
(1859) Site of the meeting at which Virginia's secession from the Union was declared unlawful, and the independent state of West Virginia was created. The building, used as a post office, custom office and federal court until 1912, has been restored. It now houses exhibits and events relating to the state's cultural heritage, including an interpretive film and rooms with period furniture. March-December: daily; rest of year, Monday-Saturday.

Wheeling Park
1801 National Rd., Wheeling,
304-242-3770
Approximately 400 acres. Swimming pool, water slide, boating on Good Lake; golf, miniature golf, indoor/outdoor tennis, ice skating (rentals), picnicking, playground, refreshment area with video screen and lighted dance floor. Aviary. Fees for activities. Daily; some facilities seasonal.

SPECIAL EVENTS

Winter Festival of Lights
Oglebay Resort Park, Rte. 88 N., Wheeling,
304-243-4000, 800-624-6988
A 350-acre holiday lighting display featuring lighted buildings and more than 500,000 lights, including 28-foot candy canes and giant swans on Schenk Lake. Winter Fantasy in Good Zoo. November-January.

Jamboree in the Hills
1015 Main St., Wheeling,
800-624-5456;
www.jamboreeinthehills.com
A four-day country music festival featuring more than 30 hours of music; top country stars. Camping available. Third weekend in July.

Oglebayfest
Oglebay Resort Park, Route 88 N., Wheeling,
304-243-4000, 800-624-6988
Country fair, artists' market, fireworks, parade, ethnic foods, contests, square and round dancing, entertainment. First weekend in October.

HOTELS
★Hampton Inn
795 National Rd., Wheeling,
304-233-0440, 800-426-7866;
www.hamptoninn.com
104 rooms. Complimentary continental breakfast. $

★★Oglebay Family Resort
Oglebay Park, Rte. 88 N., Wheeling,
304-243-4000, 800-624-6988;
www.oglebay-resort.com

212 rooms. Children's activity center. Airport transportation available. $$

SPECIALTY LODGINGS
Wheeling Island
1 S. Stone St.,
Wheeling,
877-943-3546;
www.wheelingisland.com
Greyhound racing has been a tradition in Wheeling since before the Civil War, and continues at Wheeling Island, where the downs have been augmented with casino action, three restaurants, a bar and a full-service hotel.
151 Rooms. Casino. $$

RESTAURANTS
★★★Ernie's Esquire
1015 E. Bethlehem Blvd.,
Wheeling,
304-242-2800
A local landmark for nearly 50 years, this fine dining restaurant serves a wide variety of options to suit any palate.
Lunch, dinner, late-night, Sunday brunch. Bar. Children's menu. Casual attire. Valet parking. $$$

483

WHITE SULPHUR SPRINGS
In the 18th century, White Sulphur Springs became a fashionable destination for rich and famous colonists who came for the "curative" powers of the mineral waters. It has, for the most part, remained a popular resort ever since. A number of U.S. presidents summered in the town in the days before air-conditioning made Washington habitable in hot weather. The Tylers spent their honeymoon at the famous "Old White" Hotel. In 1913, the Old White Hotel gave way to the present Greenbrier Hotel, where President Wilson honeymooned with the second Mrs. Wilson. During World War II the hotel served as an internment camp for German and Japanese diplomats and later, as a hospital.

The first golf course in America was laid out near the town in 1884, but the first game was delayed when golf clubs, imported from Scotland, were held for three weeks by customs men who were suspicious of a game played with "such elongated blackjacks or implements of murder."
Information: Chamber of Commerce,
White Sulphur Springs, 304-536-2500

WHAT TO SEE AND DO

Fishing, Swimming, Boating, Camping, Hiking
White Sulphur Springs,
304-536-2144
In Monongahela National Forest: Blue Bend Recreation Area, 6 miles N. on WV 92, then 4 miles W. on WV 16/21; Lake Sherwood Recreation Area, 23 miles N. via WV 92, then 11 miles N.E. on WV 14.

Memorial Park
Greenbrier Ave.,
White Sulphur Springs
Swimming pool (Memorial Day-Labor Day; fee); tennis courts, ball fields, track, horseshoe pits, playground. Daily.

National Fish Hatchery
400 E. Main St.,
White Sulphur Springs,
304-536-1361
Rainbow trout in raceways and ponds. Visitor center has display pool, aquariums and exhibits. Memorial Day-Labor Day: daily.

SPECIAL EVENTS

Dandelion Festival
White Sulphur Springs,
304-536-2323
Entertainment, exhibits; arts and crafts. Memorial Day weekend.

HOTELS

★★★★The Greenbrier
300 W. Main St.,
White Sulphur Springs,
304-536-1110, 800-453-4858;
www.greenbrier.com
Resting on a 6,500-acre estate in the picturesque Allegheny Mountains, The Greenbrier is one of America's oldest and finest resorts. The resort offers more than 50 recreational activities on its sprawling grounds. In addition to three championship golf courses, the highly acclaimed Golf Digest Academy, tennis courts and fitness and spa facilities, guests are invited to partake in unique adventures like falconry, sporting clays and trap and skeet shooting.

Consisting of rooms, suites, guest and estate houses, the accommodations reflect the resort's renowned tradition. The new Hemispheres restaurant serves up creative cuisine in a relaxed setting.
721 rooms. Children's activity center. Airport transportation available. **$$$**

RESTAURANTS

★★★The Greenbrier Main Dining Room
300 W. Main St. (Hwy. 60),
White Sulphur Springs, 24986,
304-536-1110;
www.greenbrier.com
Breakfast adapts with the seasons and the dinner menu changes daily at this elegant yet family-friendly resort, where diners can expect contemporary riffs on classic dishes along with a Southern-influenced continental style. The dinner menu offers lighter meals for those watching their intake, as well as a tempting dessert menu for those who are not.
American, French menu. Breakfast, dinner. Children's menu. Jacket required. Reservations recommended. Valet parking. **$$$**

SPAS

★★★★The Greenbrier Spa
300 W. Main St.,
White Sulphur Springs,
800-453-4858
White Sulphur Springs has long drawn visitors to its waters for their purported healing powers. Modern-day wellness seekers visit the Greenbrier for its state-of-the-art spa facility. The spa's treatment menu draws on the history of the mineral springs, and guests are encouraged to enjoy one of the spa's famous hydrotherapy treatments, from mountain rain showers and sulphur soaks to detoxifying marine baths and mineral mountain baths. Mud, rose petal, mineral and marine wraps release toxins and revitalize skin, while black walnut and aromatherapy salt glows exfoliate and polish skin. Treatments designed for male guests, pregnant clients and teenagers round out this spa's comprehensive approach to well-being.

484

WEST VIRGINIA

WILLIAMSON

The center of the "billion-dollar coal field," Williamson is truly a coal town; the walls of the local Chamber of Commerce building, at the west corner of Courthouse Square, are made of coal.

Information: Tug Valley Chamber of Commerce, 45 E. 2nd Ave., Williamson, 304-235-5240; www.tugvalleychamberofcommerce.com

WHAT TO SEE AND DO

Cabwaylingo State Forest

Rte. 1, Williamson, 304-385-4255

Approximately 8,100 acres. Swimming pool (Memorial Day-Labor Day), fishing; hunting, hiking trails, game courts, picnicking, playground, concession, tent and trailer camping (dump station), 13 cabins.

SPECIAL EVENTS

King Coal Festival

28 Oak St., Williamson, 304-235-5560

Entertainment, exhibits; theatrical presentation; country music, square dancing. Mid-September.

485

WEST VIRGINIA

INDEX

487

INDEX

★
★
★
★
★

489

INDEX

★

★

★

☆

☆

491

INDEX

493

INDEX

★ ★ ★ ★ ☆ ☆

494

INDEX

495

INDEX

★
★
★
★
★

497

INDEX

★

★

★

★

★

★
★
★
★
★

499

INDEX

502

INDEX

503

INDEX

505

INDEX

★

★

★

★

★

507

INDEX

★
★
★
★
★

508

INDEX

★

★

★

★

509

INDEX

★

★

★

★

★

★

511

INDEX

★
★
★
★

512

INDEX

513

INDEX

★
★
★
★

515

INDEX

516

INDEX

517

INDEX

★
★
★
☆
☆

519

INDEX

★

★

★

★

521

INDEX

522

INDEX

V

Vagabond Players (Baltimore, MD), *38*

Valentine Museum (Richmond, VA), *375*

Van Riper-Hopper (Wayne) Museum (Wayne, NJ), *141*

Van Saun County Park (Paramus, NJ), *126*

Vandalia Gathering (Charleston, WV), *456*

Vandiver Inn (Havre de Grace, MD), *64*

Venango County Court House (Franklin, PA), *179*

Verizon Center (Washington, DC), *427*

Vetri (Philadelphia, PA), *245*

Vicino (Silver Spring, MD), *73*

Victorian Christmas Week (Lancaster, PA), *203*

Victorian Houses (Cape May Court House, NJ), *99*

Victorian Ice Cream Festival (Wilmington, DE), *18*

Victorian Inn Bed and Breakfast (Lock Haven, PA), *208*

Victorian Lace Inn (Cape May, NJ), *97*

Victorian Sunday (Williamsport, PA), *278*

Victorian Week (Cape May, NJ), *96*

Vidalia (Washington, DC), *445*

Vietnam Veterans Memorial (Washington, DC), *427*

View from Prospect Peak (Berkeley Springs, WV), *450*

Villa d'Este (Alexandria, VA), *290*

Village Bistro (Arlington, VA), *296*

Village Inn (Bird-in-Hand, PA), *157*

Village Inn (Little Creek, DE), *9*

Village Inn Restaurant (Harrisonburg, VA), *332*

Vine Cottage Inn (Hot Springs, VA), *334*

Vineyard and Winery Tours (Leesburg, VA), *338*

Virginia Air and Space Center and Hampton Roads History Center (Hampton, VA), *330*

Virginia Aviation Museum (Richmond, VA), *375*

Virginia Children's Festival (Norfolk, VA), *360*

Virginia Creeper National Recreation Trail (Abingdon, VA), *283*

Virginia Highlands Festival (Abingdon, VA), *284*

Virginia Historical Society (Richmond, VA), *372*

Virginia Horse Center (Lexington, VA), *340*

Virginia Hotel (Cape May, NJ), *97*

Virginia Institute of Marine Science, College of William and Mary (Gloucester Point, VA), *327*

Virginia Lake Festival (Clarksville, VA), *310*

Virginia Living Museum (Newport News, VA), *357*

Virginia Marine Science Museum (Virginia Beach, VA), *391*

Virginia Military Institute (Lexington, VA), *340*

Virginia Museum of Fine Arts (Richmond, VA), *372*

Virginia Museum of Natural History (Martinsville, VA), *349*

Virginia Museum of Transportation (Roanoke, VA), *381*

Virginia Mushroom and Wine Festival (Front Royal, VA), *325*

Virginia Opera (Norfolk, VA), *361*

Virginia Quilt Museum (Harrisonburg, VA), *331*

Virginia Saltwater Fishing Tournament (Virginia Beach, VA), *391*

Virginia Scottish Games (Alexandria, VA), *287*

Virginia State Championship Chili Cookoff (Roanoke, VA), *381*

Virginia State Fair (Richmond, VA), *376*

Virginia State Library and Archives (Richmond, VA), *371*

Virginia Symphony (Norfolk, VA), *361*

Virginia War Memorial (Richmond, VA), *375*

Virginia War Museum (Newport News, VA), *357*

Virginia Waterfront International Arts Festival (Norfolk, VA), *361*

Virginia Zoological Park (Norfolk, VA), *360*

Virginia's Explore Park (Roanoke, VA), *381*

Visitor Center (George Washington Birthplace National Monument, VA), *326*

Visitor Center (Jamestown, VA), *335*

Visitor Center (Manassas (Bull Run) National Battlefield Park, VA), *348*

Visitor Center (Petersburg National Battlefield, VA), *366*

Visitor Center (Uniontown, PA), *269*

Visitor Center (Valley Forge, PA), *271*

Visitor Center (Yorktown, VA), *409*

Visitor Center-Electric Map-Gettysburg Museum of the Civil War (Gettysburg, PA), *184*

Visitor Centers (Blue Ridge Parkway, VA), *299*

W

Wade's Point Inn (St. Michaels, MD), *76*

Wagner Free Institute of Science (Philadelphia, PA), *232*

Waldameer Park & Water World (Erie, PA), *175*

Walking tour (Charlottesville, VA), *305*

Walking Tour of Historic Sites (Alexandria, VA), *287*

Walking Tours of the Historic District (Cape May, NJ), *96*

Wallace House State Historic Site (Somerville, NJ), *135*

Waller Mill Inn (Williamsburg, VA), *402*

Walnut Street Theatre (Philadelphia, PA), *233*

Walt Whitman Arts Center (Camden, NJ), *94*

Walt Whitman House State Historic Site (Camden, NJ), *94*

Walters Art Museum (Baltimore, MD), *38*

Wanamaker, Kempton & Southern, Inc (Kempton, PA), *197*

★
★
★
★
★

525

INDEX

526

INDEX

NOTES

NOTES

★

★ ★

★ ★ ★

★ ★ ★ ★

★ ★ ★ ★ ★

NOTES

★
★
★
★
★

NOTES

★
★
★
★
★

NOTES

531

INDEX

★
★
★
★
★

NOTES

★

★

★

★

★

NOTES

★
★
★
★
★

NOTES

★

★

★

★

★

NOTES

NOTES

★

★

★

★

★

NOTES

★
★
★
★
★

NOTES

538

★
★
★
★
★

NOTES

NOTES

★
★
★
★
★

NOTES

NOTES

542

★
★
★
★
★

NOTES

★
★
★
★
★

NOTES

544

INDEX

★
★
★
★
★

NOTES

★
★
★
★
★

NOTES

★

★

★

★

★

NOTES

NOTES

INDEX

★
★
★
★
★

NOTES

NOTES

★
★
★
★
★

NOTES

★
★
★
★
★

NOTES

552

INDEX

★
★
★
★
★

NOTES

★
★
★
★
★

NOTES

★
★
★
★
★